Marriages of

ORANGE COUNTY NORTH CAROLINA

1779-1868

Marriages of

ORANGE COUNTY
NORTH CAROLINA

1779-1868

Compiled by
BRENT H. HOLCOMB

With an Index by Robert & Catherine Barnes

CLEARFIELD

Reprinted for
Clearfield Company, Inc. by
Genealogical Publishing Co., Inc.
Baltimore, Maryland
2001

INTRODUCTION

THIS VOLUME contains abstracts of all marriage bonds issued in Orange County, North Carolina, from 1779 until 1868, when marriage bonds—as prerequisites for marriage—were discontinued. (Although Orange Couny was formed in 1752, bonds issued prior to 1779 are no longer extant.) The abstracts were made from a microfilm copy of the bonds and are arranged throughout in alphabetical order by the name of the groom, each entry further providing the name of the bride, the date of the bond, and the names of bondsmen and witnesses. To facilitate research, brides and bondsmen are also listed in the index.

Marriage bonds are the only public records of marriage prior to 1851. Although the marriage bond law was enacted in 1741 and remained in force until 1868, the clerk of the county court was required from 1851 to keep a register of all marriages performed by license (issued with the bond).

The researcher should bear in mind that bonds alone are not proof that a marriage took place, only that a marriage was intended. Also, not everyone who married in Orange County between 1779 and 1868 is identified in this work, for some marriages were performed after publication of banns and no bond, license, or other public record of marriage was required.

BRENT H. HOLCOMB, C.A.L.S.
Columbia, South Carolina

Abbet, Richd & Mary Hufman, 17 Sep 1782; James Johnson, bm.

Abbott, Andrew & Polley Elmore, 4 Nov 1807; John Elmore, bm.

Abbott, James & Jemimah Minson, 6 July 1792; John Rippey, Wm McKerall, bm.

Abbott, John & Susannah Flenthan, 7 Oct 1798; William Jinkins, bm.

Acock, Jesse & Barbery Hoofman, 16 Aug 1788; John Hutson, Wm Gwinn, bm.

Adams, James & Elizabeth Baldwin, 4 Dec 1819; M. Adams, bm.

Adams, James & Mary Baldwin, 16 Oct 1834; Joel C. Yancy, bm.

Adams, James & Lucretia Collier, 7 Sept 1845; Thos Adams, bm.

Adams, John & Marg. Young, 13 Nov 1788.

Adams, John & Margret Rumley, __ 179-; James Linch, bm.

Adams, John & Phobe Lynch, 20 Aug 1800; Ross Hutcheson, bm.

Adams, John & Mary A. Stanford, 26 Jan 1855; Wm. H. Stanford, J. L. Turner, bm.

Adams, John Y. & Eliza M. Fuller, 18 Nov 1852; James Parks, E. G. Gray, bm; m 18 Nov 1852 by John J. Freeland, J. P.

Adams, Meredeth & Fanny Hughs, 27 April 1815; James Adams, bm.

Adams, Merridith & Jane Clancy, 5 Dec 1826; Wm. Nelson, bm.

Adams, Nicholas & Elizabeth Coureton, 29 Aug 1834; Richard Coureton, bm.

Adams, Peter & Susannah McFarland, 31 Dec 1804; Moses Jones, bm.

Adams, Thomas & Harriett Hunt, 25 May 1820; John R. Cumming, bm.

Adams, Thomas & Susan Fuller, 17 Nov 1852; R. M. Jones, bm; m 17 Nov 1852 by Thos. C. Hayes, minister.

Adams, William & Salley Hughs, 23 June 1808; John Young, James Clancy, bm.

Adams, William H. & Mary A. Cheek, 8 Nov 1866; W. R. Faucett, bm; m 8 Nov 1866.

Adcock, Alexandria & Sabrinah Ellis, 23 Oct 1858; Robert Adcock, bm; m 24 Oct 1858 by Wm. J. Roberts, J. P.

Adcock, Henry C. & Lisy Ann Vaughan, 19 Jan 1866; Benjn. Ellis, bm.

Adcock, John & Lucretia Wheeler, 11 Oct 1848; Thomas Woods, bm.

Adcock, Jonathan & Patsy Johnston, 8 Sept 1812; Thomas Rheu, bm.

Adcock, Robert & Furnetta Ellis, 2 April 1858; G. W. Dixon, bm.

Adcock, Thomas & Adaline Wheeler, 27 June 1858; Walter Edwards, bm.

Addison, Pomphery & Hawkins Ross, 24 Aug 1855; William Stanley, bm; m 1 Sept 1855 by Gabriel Barbee.

Adkinson, Thomas & Margaritt Kennady, 24 July 1795; James Clindenin, bm.

Aivey, Andey & Elizabeth Fann, 14 July 1835; Matthew McCauley, bm.

Akers, Leeroy & Rebecca Nealey, 29 Oct 180-; Samuel Faucett, bm.

Albea, Wm. W. & Eugenia E. Hooker, 27 Oct 1851; S. D. Schoolfield, bm.

Albert, John & Martha McCaddams, 7 June 1832; James Murrey, bm.

Albert, Sidney & Julia Rippey, 24 Nov 1846; J. D. MCadam, bm.

Albert, Yancey & Mary E. Scott, 5 Feb 1867; John W. Strowd, bm; m 7 Feb 1867 by Wm. W. Pickett, J. P.

Albright, Andrew & Sally Shofner, 2 Dec 1817; James Green, bm.

Albright, Daniel & Milla Holt, 10 May 1824; Jesse Cain, bm.

Albright, Elias & Elizabeth Hobbs, 24 Oct 1822; Jn. Boon, bm.

Albright, George & Patsey Albright, 11 Jan 1819; Daniel Albright, bm.

Albright, George & Molley May, 8 Nov 1813; Michl Holt, bm; Rachel Holt, wit.

Albright, George & Barbara K. Holt, 10 Feb 1842; Edwin M. Holt Junr, bm.

Albright, Gideon & Mary Fortner, 10 Feb 1846; John P. Albright, bm.

Albright, Henry & Letty Foust, 21 July 1824; Daniel Albright, bm.

Albright, Henry & Hanah J. Kirkpatrick, 12 April 1848; William P. Albright, bm.

Albright, Isaac & Philpina Rich, 1 Oct 1818; Wm. Holt, bm.

Albright, Jacob & Nelley Holt, 29 April 1784; Wm. Oneal, bm.

Albright, Jacob & Salley Niece, 29 July 1807; Joseph Cledenen, bm.

Albright, Jacob & Sally Albright, 18 Oct 1819; Daniel Rankin, bm.

Albright, Jacob & Ann Dailey, 10 Aug 1848; Liman Lumley, bm.

Albright, James & Sally Albright, 10 March 1835; Wm. M. Rogers, Michl Holt, bm.

Albright, Joel & Sally Ingle, 11 Aug 1813; George Albright, bm.

Albright, Joel & Catharin A. Holt, 15 July 1832; Austin Whitsitt, bm.

Albright, John & Caty Albright, 13 Sept 1810; David Troxlar, bm.

Albright, John Sr. & Margaret Busick, 16 Sept 1823; Daniel Albright, bm.

Albright, Jonas & Susannah Strator, 17 Oct 1815; Barnabe Troxler, bm.

Albright, Joseph & Nancey Whitsitte, 5 May 1818; Ja. Whitsitt, bm.

Albright, Joshua & Jane Patton, 19 Jan 1836; William Patton, bm.

Albright, Levi & Caty Sharp, 18 July 1833; Frederick Sharp, bm.

Albright, Ludwick & Betsy Sharp, 2 Oct 1787; John Albright, bm.

Albright, Ludwick & Mary Troxler, 1 April 1784; Thos Mulhollay, bm.

Albright, Luis & Anna Freeland, 2 March 1805; Thomas Freeland, bm.

Albright, Solomon & Sally Fogleman, 12 May 1818; Daniel Coble, bm.

Albright, William & Polly Wood, 17 Sept 1817; Sabret Hood, bm.

Albright, Wm. & Louisa Wood, 5 Feb 1816; George Foust, bm.

Aldridge, John & Dicey Taylor, 10 Nov 1830; Jacob Horner, bm.

Aldridge, Joseph & Susannah Ashley, 3 Jan 1788; Robert Fergerson, bm.

Aldridge, Peter & Judith Waggenor, 4 Feb 1786; Robert Berry, bm.

Alexander, George & Elizabeth McCulloh, 11 March 1809; Andrew Gibson, bm.

Alexander, J. M. & Sue F. Watson, 2 March 1865; Jas. Y. Watson, bm; m 2 March 1865 by Solomon Pool.

Alexander, Thomas & Mary Hornady, 21 March 1803; Joshua Snipes, bm.

Alexander, Thomas & Elizabeth Kimbro, 4 May 1820; Jacob Kimbro, bm.

Allbright, Alexander & Rachel Thompson, 1 Mar 1819; Anderson Thompson, bm.

Allbright, William & Nelly Stockard, 28 Feb 1822; John Stockard, bm.

Allen, Abram & Jane Allen, 15 Oct 1834; Low Whitsitt, bm.

Allen, Alexander & Jane Scott, 12 Dec 1820; David Nelson, bm.

Allen, Alexander & Polley Freshwater, 13 Feb 1841; Alexander Potts, John Thompson, bm.

Allen, Bartlit & Mary Downs, 9 Sept 1785; Thomas Holloway, bm.

Allen, Benjamin & Macons Murphey, 19 Nov 1831; Aaron Fletcher, bm.

Allen, Christopher & Elizabeth Moore, 11 March 1823; Lewis Moore, bm.

Allen, David & Polly Tyrrell, 23 Jan 1827; Alex Mebane, bm.

Allen, Edmund & Peggy Caldwell, 9 April 1807; J. Henderson, bm.

Allen, George & Margaret Tate, __ June 1795; George Tate, bm.

Allen, George & Elizabeth Blackwood, 27 Dec 1795; Wm. Craige Jr., bm.

Allen, George & Patsy Dunn, 30 Sept 1807; Alexander Allen, bm.

Allen, George & Anne White, 30 Sept 1819; Alexr. Allen, bm.

Allen, George A. & Keziah Elizabeth Roberson, 18 Feb 1851; Johnston Patton, bm.

Allen, George N. & Martha S. Whitbey, 2 Jan 1837; Abram Tarpley, bm.

Allen, Hermon & Rebecca Hornaday, 21 Dec 1841; John Mabery, bm.

Allen, Jesse & Betsy Spears, 20 Dec 1816; Perry Dockery, Perkin Thompson, bm.

Allen, Joel & Charity Wells, 23 Sept 1813; John Wells, bm.

Allen, John & Elizabeth Russel, 31 Dec 1796; John Forrest, bm.

Allen, John & Christina Wrightsman, 30 Aug 1805; John Whithed, bm.

Allen, John & Sally Crawford, 18 Dec 1827; Samuel Nelson, bm.

Allen, John & Martha Ann Whithed, 24 Nov 1830; A. Parks, bm.

Allen, John & Sarah Hutchison, 1 May 1834; Presley Nelson, bm.

Allen, John & Elizabeth Kirkpatrick, 13 Nov 1844; Joseph Allen, bm.

Allen, Joseph & Elizabeth Smith, 26 Dec 1846; Enoch Smith, bm.

Allen, Nathan & Lydia Stout, 8 Feb 1837; Samuel McDaniel, bm.

Allen, Nathan F. 7 Sally Ammons, 3 April 1848; Manleff J. Staley, bm.

Allen, Nathan M. & Martha Haithcock, 5 Dec 1866; Robert Allen, bm.

Allen, Robert & Selah Brownen, 26 July 1792; Jesse Allin, bm.

Allen, Ruffin & Martha Jane Suit, 25 Aug 1857; C. C. Linning, bm; m 30 Aug 1857 by O. Churchill.

Allen, Samuel & Isber Nelson, 13 Dec 1807; David Nelson, bm.

Allen, Samuel & Celia Douglas, 21 Feb 1826; George Hutchison, bm.

Allen, Samuel & Abi Steward, 21 Oct 1856; Samuel F. Martin, bm; m 23 Oct 1856 by John Stadler, Caswell County.

Allen, Sharod & Rachel Lytle, 12 Nov 1794; Robert Lytle, bm.

Allen, Simon & Hannah Woody, 27 July 1833; George Counsilman, bm.

Allen, Thomas & Elizabeth Terrell, 18 July 1818; Jas. Roney, bm.

Allen, Thomas & Nancy Roberts, 22 Mar 1821; Wright Stanley, bm.

Allen, Thomas & Anne Murray, 19 Nov 1840; Jas Roney, James M. Gilbert, bm.

Allen, Thomas & Patsey Jane Pugh, 4 July 1848; John Mosely, bm.

Allen, Thos. F. & Sinthia E. Lashley, 15 July 1866; Johnston Lashley, Franken Lashley, bm.

Allen, William & Lettice Tate, 3 Jan 1792; Andw. Murdock, bm.

Allen, William & R. H. Caneday, 15 Nov 1851; Gideon Canedy, bm; m 15 Nov 1857 by J. S. Floyd, J. P.

Allen, William & Ann Mitchell, 23 Feb 1854; Millon Taylor, bm; m 23 Feb 1854 by S. S. Burkhead, Pastor of M. E. Church South, in Chapel Hill, Orange Co.

Alley, Samuel & Sarah Ferrell, 13 Jan 1802; Major Downs, bm.

Allen, Wm. & Anne Jones, 12 Nov 1830; Wm. James, bm.

Allin, Samuel & Nancey Hester, 27 Aug 1782 Henry Burch, bm.

Allin, Samuel & Elizabeth Barbee, 3 Sept 1791; Christo Barbee, bm.

Allin, William & Rachel S. Corn, 27 April 1860; Thad Jes Wilson, bm.

Allison, Adam & Mary Slade, 20 April 1796; no bm.

Allison, Alvis & Jane Faucett, 3 April 1849; Saml P. Moore, E. G. Gray, bm.

Allison, David & Jeane Gwin, 18 Dec 1789; Robert Furgueson, bm.

Allison, David & Frances Ward, 23 Sept 1860; Jas. R. Hester, bm.

Allison, David R. & Susan F. Woods, 18 Feb 1831; James Allison, S. R. Woods, bm.

Allison, David S. & Martha E. Montgomery, 2 June 1859; Joseph W. Allison, bm; m 5 June 1859 by Thos. U. Faucette, M. G.

Allison, Elbridge & Rebecca Thompson, 27 April 1838; Elkines Pettigrewe, Allen P. Elliss, bm.

Allison, Giles J. & Eliza D. Hughes, 23 Dec 1850; E. G. Gray, bm; m 24 Dec 1850 by Archibald Currie.

Allison, Hamilton & Betsey Steward, 30 Sept 1794; Joshua Berry, bm.

Allison, James & Grizzel Porterfield, 20 Feb 1782; John Wood, bm.

Allison, James & Elizabeth Jane Jordan, 7 April 1846; E. G. Gray, bm.

Allison, John & Sarah Tolar, 13 April 1789; John Porterfield, bm.

Allison, John J. & Jane M. Hughes, 23 Dec 1844; Wm. W. Taylor, bm.

Allison, John J. & Martha Madden, 24 Nov 1856; Henry J. Murfree, bm.

Allison, Joseph & Polly Barlow, 15 Oct 1817; D. Woods Jun, bm.

Allison, Joseph B. & Margaret A. Hughs, 19 April 1858; J. F. Allison, R. M. Jones, bm.

Allison, Joseph W. & Susan Murdock, 31 Aug 1827; David R. Allison, bm.

Allison, Mathew & Mary Cocklerease, 9 March 1796; John Stalcup, Edard King, bm.

Allison, William A. L., son of Sack and Hannah Allison, & Bettie A. Bain, m 17 Jan 1868 by D. W. Thompson, minister.

Allison, William H. & Martha Christopher, 29 Sept 1841; Jno. M. Faucett, bm.

Allison, Zillman & Celia Clarke, 6 Nov 1816; John Ray, bm.

Allred, Alphonso & Martha A. Halden, 2 Jan 1846; Luis Maleble, bm.

Allsbrook, Edward & Dolly Hunter, 27 Aug 1817; John Taylor, bm.

Almond, Edward & Jenney Dutton, ___ 1784; Danl Stephens, bm.

Alsbrook, David B. & Mary Neal, 16 June 1825; John W. McGee, bm.

Alsobrook, Samuel & Salley Clancy, 24 Dec 1822; Thos Thompson, bm.

Alston, Alexander M. & Frances D. Yarbrough, 13 July 1831; Wm. L. Strudwick, Thos. S. Ashe, bm.

Alston, George W. & Martha Lewis, 22 July 1820; F. J. Kearny, bm.

Alston, John Jr. & Elizabeth Kennon, 28 Jan 1797; Solomon Jones, Charles Alston, bm.

Alston, Philip & Sally Gear, 29 Dec 1811; James Alston, bm.

Alves, Walter & Emlia Johnston, 11 May 1787; John Hogg, bm.

Amick, Henry & Caty Lang, 17 June 1827; Elias Green, bm.

Amick, Joseph & Caty Glass, 2 Nov 1814; Amos Swinney, bm.

Amick, Nicholas (Nicklaus Emig) & Sally Foust, 30 March 1805; Peter Faust, bm.

Amick, Nicholas & Durania Wingate, 23 July 1809; Robert Harrison, Asa Foster, bm.

Amis, Jas. S. & Mary W. Scott, 4 Dec 1849; Jos. J. Davis, bm.

Ammons, John & Sally Croker, 25 Jan 1852; Aron Burnett, bm.

Amy, Matthew, son of Charles & Rhoda Amy, & Polly Cameron, dau. of Grace & Lemuel Cameron, m 16 April 1868 by Saml. H. Turrentine, J. P.

Anders, David & Joanna Edwards, 11 Oct 1816; Jesse Bowers, bm.

Anderson, Abraham & Elizabeth Veasey, 9 Oct 1801; Henry Lewis, bm.

Anderson, Alexander & Phebe Hall, 19 May 1787; Samuel Allen, Jr., bm.

Anderson, Alexdr. & Susannah Thompson, 7 June 1818; Hunter McCulloch, bm.

Anderson, Amos & Chaney Battle, 2 Feb 1867; John Weaver, bm.

Anderson, Carnes T. & Nancy Faucette, 4 Nov 1847; E. G. Gray, bm.

Anderson, Charles & Edy Rigsbee, 19 Oct 1820; Moses Hutchins, bm.

Anderson, David & Elizabeth Newman, 16 June 1839; Laire Carmichal, bm.

Anderson, James & Martha Murray, 23 Aug 1795; David Lasslie, bm.

Anderson, James & Margret Ector, 29 Aug 1810; D. Bradford, bm.

Anderson, James & Barbara Whitsal, 24 July 1822; W. Montgomery, bm.

Anderson, John & Jeany Clark, 30 Dec 1807; Jas. Lasslie, bm.

Anderson, John & Nancy House, 24 Feb 1823; Daniel Holder, bm.

Anderson, John & Martha Carlton, 22 June 1842; Mark Rigsby, Thomas Cope, bm.

Anderson, John H. & Mary A. Vickers, 10 Jan 1863; m 11 Jan 1863 by John Burroughs, J. P.

Anderson, Joseph & Margaret Tinnin, 1 Oct 1800; Peter Biley, Jno Taylor, bm.

Anderson, Joseph J. & Mary A. Reeves, 17 May 1848; E. G. Gray, bm.

Anderson, Josiah C. & Mary Herndon, 5 Dec 1848; Jesse Rigsby, bm.

Anderson, Kennith & Nancy Thompson, 12 June 1801; R. Huntington, Thomas Fosett, bm.

Anderson, Lewis & Laura Ann George, 31 May 1866; William Anderson, Burows C. Cheek, bm; m 1 June 1866 by A. B. Gunter, J. P.

Anderson, Quinton & Susannah Bird, 20 Feb 1810; Jehu Bird, W. A. Whitted, bm.

Anderson, Robert & Anne McKee, 7 Jan 1783; Alexander McKee, bm.

Anderson, Robert & Margret Turner, 31 Aug 1832; John Faucett, bm.

Anderson, Robert & Elizabeth Peeler, 14 Dec 1835; James Allison, J. Taylor, bm.

Anderson, Robt Jr. & Elizabeth Hicks, 2 Dec 1816; J. H. Taylor, bm.

Anderson, R. Walker & R. B. Cameron, 28 April 1863; George P. Collins, bm; m 28 April 1863 by M. A. Curtis, D. D., Rector of St. Matthew's Church, Hillsboro.

Anderson, Sidney & Polley Hurdle, 14 Feb 1839; Henderson Scott, Wm. Holt, bm.

Anderson, Thomas & Mary Williams, 15 July 1810; Paul Kinnion, bm.

Anderson, Thornsbury & Sarah Meacum, 11 Dec 1794; Wm Maynord, bm.

Anderson, William & Mille Cyntam, 22 Dec 1797; Abraham Anderson, bm.

Anderson, William & Nancy Freeman, 20 March 1809; Demsey Douglass, bm.

Anderson, William & Elizabeth Allison, 1 June 1811; James Taylor, bm.

Anderson, William & Sally Rider, 10 Dec 1815; H. D. Pratt, bm.

Anderson, William & Patsy Fossett, 25 Sept 1825; Hugh Crawford, bm.

Anderson, William & Matilda Terrell, 14 Nov 1826; Jas Roney, bm.

Anderson, Wm. & Jenney Williams, 6 Jan 1794; Thomas Scott, bm.

Andres, George & Delilah Loyd, 1 June 1820; Levi Andrus, bm.

Andres, Haywood & Espran Smith, 2 Sept 1848; Manley Brewer, bm.

Andres, Isaac & Unity Calisles, 17 Aug 1848; Charles Smith, bm.

Andres, John & Candis Carrel, 4 Nov 1812; Lacy Lloyd, bm.

Andres, John & Hannah Williams, 29 Aug 1849; Boroughs Cheek, bm.

Andres, William & Abi Cheek, 29 Aug 1810; Jas Cheek, bm.

Andress, John & Polley Cheek, 30 Nov 1801; Jesse Cate, bm.

Andreus, Willie P. & Wady C. Ivey, 30 Nov 1864; Wm. H. Andreus, bm.

Andrew, James & Elizabeth Glosson, 20 March 1817; Ensley Glosson, Hynes Drake, bm.

Andrew, Mark & Elisabeth Bailey, 5 Sept 1796; Will Andrus, bm.

Andrew, Samuel & Delilah Baker, 12 Oct 1805; Jno. Rickard, bm.

Andrews, Adlai & Eliza Hunter, 17 Aug 1832; William Smith, John Andrews, bm.

Andrews, Archibald & Polley Reeves, 8 Jan 1811; Lacy Lloyd, bm.

Andrews, Archibald & Susannah Reaves, 20 Oct 1831; Green Andress, bm.

Andrews, Berry & Polly Beavers, 8 Sept 1826; William Andrews, bm.

Andrews, Chesley & Martha Ann Ivey, 24 Oct 1864; Calvin Andrews, Thomas Long, bm; m 25 Oct 1864 by Alvis Durham, J. P.

Andrews, Henry & Candis Caurather, 13 Jan 1808; Thos. Brewer, bm.

Andrews, Henry & Mary Durham, 15 March 1841; John Andrews, William Turner, bm.

Andrews, Henry C. & Mary E. Faucett, 11 Jan 1848; Manly M. Brewer, bm.

Andrews, Henry C. & Susan A. Faucett, 12 Feb 1856; Rufus Andreus, bm; m 13 Feb 1856 by N. C. Cate, J. P.

Andrews, James J. & Frances A. Barbee, 4 Sept 1855; Calvin Andreus, bm; m 6 Sept 1855 by Jas. N. Patterson, J. P.

Andrews, James M. & Hetty A. Thompson, 3 Sept 1849; Porter Thompson, bm.

Andrews, John & Roxanna Pendergrass, 26 Aug 1863; Alvis Daniel, bm; m 26 Aug 1863 by N. W. Wilson.

Andrews, Laban & Sarah King, 23 Sept 1841; Adley Andres, George Nevill, bm.

Andrews, Levi & Susannah Durham, 24 June 1832; Ruffin Andrews, bm.

Andrews, Manley & Martha J. Cheek, 23 Aug 1853; Alexr Hunter, Geo. W. Bruce, bm; m 25 Aug 1853 by N. C. Cate, J. P.

Andrews, Mitchell & Cornelia A. Griffin, 23 Nov 1848; James M. Watson, Haywood Andrews, wit.

Andrews, Ruffin & Martha Strayhorn, 22 Jan 1861; Manly D. Stroud, bm; m 22 Jan 1861 by Manly Andrews.

Andrews, Rufus & Isabella Crabtree, 3 Dec 1857; Stephen A. Andrus, bm; m 3 Dec 1857 by N. C. Cate, J. P.

Andrews, Thomas I. & Frances Coplin, 18 Dec 1858; Franklin McPherson, bm; m 19 Dec 1858 by A. Edwards, J. P.

Andrews, Turner & Cynthia Caruthers, 15 May 1841; Green Andress, John Richardson, bm.

Andrews, Wesley & Frances Blackwood, 14 May 1859; John Creel, bm.

Andrews, William & Patsey Carroll, 12 March 1818; John Loyd, bm.

Andrews, William & Salley Cheek, 23 Aug 1823; John Tedder, Nathaniel Roberson, bm.

Andrews, William & Sarah Ashley, 1 March 1851; Manly Andrews, bm.

Andrews, William & Louisa Harris, 31 Oct 1857; m 31 Oct 1858 by Wm. Cheek, J. P.

Andrews, William & Secelina Lloyd, 7 July 1863; John Q. Loyd, bm; m 16 July 1863 by J. W. Strowd, J. P.

Andrews, Wm. & Sarah Ann Strayhorn, 6 Feb 1866; J. A. Andrews, bm.

Andrus, Granville & Louisia Medows, 15 May 1854; S. S. Lloyd, bm; m 8 June 1854 by Nelson P. Hall, J. P.

Andrus, John & Harriet A. E. Hopson, 20 July 1847; Calvin Andrus, bm.

Andrus, Lindsy & Charity Andrews, 28 Oct 1835; Adley Andrus, bm.

Andrus, Wm. H. & Mary Jane Montgomery, 4 May 1860; B. M. Andrus, bm; m 4 May 1860 by John Cheek.

Angier, M. A. & Jane Pearson, 8 Feb 1853; J. W. Markham, bm; m 10 Feb 1853 by Jas. N. Patterson, J. P.

Angier, Matthew B. & Rhoda Rhodes, 14 Aug 1817; George Rhodes, bm.

Angier, Matthew B. & Sally Dollar, 25 Sept 1817; Wesley Rhodes, bm.

Ansley, Gilbert & Airey Dunnagan, 2 Dec 1797; John Faddis, bm.

Anthony, Adam & Sally Sharp, 24 April 1819; Daniel Garrett, bm.

Anthony, Daniel & Barbara Albright, 11 Dec 1837; Wm. Anthony, bm.

Anthony, Wm. & Deborah Sharp, 7 March 1838; Daniel Anthony, bm.

Anthony, Young & Polly Fogleman, 7 Oct 1823; William Fogleman, bm.

Apple, Daniel & Barbara Garrett, 2 Nov 1809; Martin Isley, bm.

Apple, Eli & Frances Rich, 13 June 1829; E. M. Holt, bm.

Apple, Lewis J. & Celia J. Tinne, 8 Oct 1855; Robt. G. Rinnon, Geo. Laws, bm.

Archer, Moses & Polley Roberts, 23 April 1813; Mathias Milton, Moses Bass, bm.

Archey, Jessee & Pattie Heathcock, 24 Oct 1807; Holiday Heathcock, bm.

Archey, Robert & Caty Ann Chavis, 2 Nov 1840; John Archey, bm.

Archie, John & Rebeccah Stephens, 1 Oct 1834; Lewis Tinnen, bm.

Archie, Samuel & Sarah Caroline Mitchel, 29 Dec 1841; Reuben Day, bm.

Archy, Larkin & Tempy Croker, 17 Dec 1844; John Thompson, bm.

Argo, T. M. & Mattie H. Hubbard, 24 May 1864; D. C. McDade, bm; m 25 May 1864 by Francis W. Hilliard, Rector Chapel of the Cross (Episcopal), Chapel Hill.

Armfield, Isaac & Hannah Hoskins, 8 Jan 1807; James Peel, Wm. Horton, bm.

Armstrong, James & Mary Stubbins, 14 Dec 1821; S. Clark, bm.

Armstrong, Jas. & Polley Allen, 7 Jan 1803; Thos. Armstrong, bm.

Armstrong, Jesse & Ellen Bowls, 24 Dec 1826; Alex Robinson, bm.

Armstrong, John & Jenney Sinkler, 21 Jan 1783; John Shanklin, bm.

Armstrong, John & Kitty Shaw, 1 Feb 1817; David Tinnin, bm.

Armstrong, Joseph & Frances Tinnen, 15 May 1786; Joseph Tede, bm.

Armstrong, Joseph & Peggy Watson, 21 Aug 1802; Willis Benefield, bm.

Armstrong, Thos & Susannah Pratt, 22 Jan 1793; James Lasslie, bm.

Armstrong, Thomas & Fanny Anderson, ___ 1794; James Christmas, bm.

Armstrong, Thomas & Elizabeth Anderson, 26 April 1819.

Armstrong, Thomas D. & Jency Tuitt, 23 Sept 1822; John Tate, bm.

Armstrong, Wm. & Mary Robenson, 14 Aug 1800; James Bryan, bm.

Arnold, Ira E. & Elizabeth Cottrell, 8 Jan 1818; John Arnold, bm.

Arnold, John & Sarah Murray, 26 Dec 1812; Walter Muray, bm.

Artz, Rev. Wm. & Sally Troxlar, 20 Oct 1829; Michl. Holt, bm.

Ashe, Paoli P. & Elizabeth Strudwick, 23 Aug 1811; J. Taylor, bm.

Ashe, Richard J. & Mary P. Mitchell, 27 Oct 1845; G. H. Mitchell, bm.

Ashe, Sam. & Elizabeth Shepperd, 10 Oct 1806; Ed. Jones, bm.

Ashe, Sam. P. & Mary Shepperd, 31 Aug 1813; J. Taylor, bm.

Ashe, Samuel T. & Caroline Burgwinne, 13 June 1837; Martin J. Pickett, J. Taylor, bm.

Ashe, Thos. & Eliza S. Bell, 22 Aug 1817; J. Taylor, bm.

Ashford, Demcey & Nelly Stalcup, 20 Feb 1809; John Pleasant, bm.

Ashford, Willm. & Judah Roberts, 17 Dec 1815; Roland Roberts, bm.

Ashley, Clarence & Rebecca Baxter, 12 July 1828; Gilbird Hopkins, bm.

Ashley, Edward & Jamimah Fitch, 11 Dec 1793; William Ritch, bm.

Ashley, Harrison & Jane James, 17 June 1853; H. Parker, bm.

Ashley, James & Charity Cates, 15 Dec 1815; Robert Hall, bm.

Ashley, Jeremiah & Morrah Gates, 5 Sept 1849; Wm. L. Moore, bm.

Ashley, Jeremiah, son of Elizabeth Ashley, & Rebecca Paschael, dau. of M. and M. Paschael, m 31 March 1868 by R. H. J. Blount, J. P.

Ashley, John & Catherine King, 31 Dec 1816; Lond King, bm.

Ashley, John H. & Sarah Ann Hunley, 6 Dec 1852; Wm. H. Smith, m 12 Dec 1852 by Hezekiah Terry, J. P.

Ashley, Parson & Jane Mack, 3 Oct 1845; Jeremiah Ashley, bm.

Ashley, Robert & Sarah Rue, 5 Nov 1797; Thomas Fitch, bm.

Ashley, Robert & Polley Sanders, 10 Nov 1822; Young Duke, bm.

Ashley, Robert & Amanda Ashley, 27 Sept 1854; James Ashley, bm.

Ashley, William & Elizabeth Roberts, 9 Sept 1826; John Mattison, bm.

Atkerson, ___ & Polly Price, 21 Sept 1818; James Atkison, George Isley Jr., bm.

Atkins, Daniel & Polley Moore, 9 March 1808; John Moore, bm.

Atkins, James & Mary Carson, 8 Feb 1790; Jehu Whitted, bm.

Atkins, Josiah Jun. & Mary Couch, 23 Oct 1860; Josiah Atkins Sr., bm; m 5 Oct 1860 by Jas. N. Patterson, J. P.

Atkins, Leslie & Lidia A. Carlton, 16 Feb 1861; James Atkins, bm; m 21 Feb 1861 by B. C. Hopkins, J. P.

Atkins, Lesley & Mattie A. Piper, 28 Nov 1863; Thomas Hogan, bm; m 3 Dec 1863 by S. Pool.

Atkins, Rufus & Harriet Atkins, freedmen, 22 Feb 1867; William J. Blalock, bm; m 18 March 1867 by C. G. Markham, J. P.

Atkins, Smith D. (Genl.) & Ella H. Swain, 21 Aug 1865; H. B. Gurthrie, bm; m 23 Aug 1865 by F. M. Hubbard, Chapel Hill.

Atkins, W. H. & Demaris M. Leigh, 7 July 1855; P. T. Hogans, bm; m 23 July 1855 by John J. Allison, J. P.

Atkins, William & Jane D. Ballard, 25 May 1835; John Boroughs, Allin Petty, bm.

Atkinson, Reding & Margaret Anderson, 23 May 1808; William Anderson, bm.

12

Atterson, John H. & Elizabeth Crabtree, 1 Feb 1862; Wm. Mangum, bm; m 2 Feb 1862 by Thomas Ferrell, J. P.

Atterson, James & Nancy Glenn, 7 April 1835; James C. Turrentine, bm.

Attison, Pomphrey & Annis Glenn, 10 Feb 1849; Duncan C. Glenn, bm.

Attwater, Wilson & Eleanor McCauley, 17 Dec 1819; Charles McCauley, bm.

Atwater, Matthew & Martha Snipes, 7 July 1865; Wm. F. Strowd, bm; m 9 July 1865 by A. D. Betts, minister.

Atwater, Moses & Amy Wilson, 17 Jan 1797; Job Pendergast, bm.

Atwood, Stanford & Nancy Andrews, 24 Jan 1829; James Caruthers, Wm. Caruthers, bm.

Atwood, Thomas & Nancy Redding, 1 Feb 1810; Sterling Anders, bm.

Austin, Charles & Silvia Workman, 21 Jan 1812; David Cate, bm.

Austin, Moses & Mary Williams, 23 March 1790; no bm.

Austin, Samuel & Mary Conner, 28 June 1783; William Austin, bm.

Avrey, Henry & Fanay Ferrill, 3 June 1811; Ellis Arnold, bm.

Bachelor, Reuben & Peggy Couch, 30 June 1817; Jarratt Yeargin, bm.

Bachelor, Thomas & Margaret Craig, 29 Aug 1833; William Self, Jas. Blackwood, bm.

Bachelor, William & Sally Craig, 25 March 1840; Thomas Bachelor, M. H. Turner, bm.

Backus, John & Mary Allison, 25 June 1792; Henry White, bm.

Bacon, William H., son of Joseph G. & Rebecca Bacon, & Mahala Crabtree, dau. of William and Cyntha Crabtree, m 5 Jan 1868 by C. J. Freeland, J. P.

Bacon, Wm. T. & Frances Monk, 19 Dec 1866; Charles M. Latimer, bm; m 20 Dec 1866 by J. W. McKee, J. P.

Bacum, Simon & Mary Ray, 8 Feb 1798; Henry Ray, bm.

Bagley, Henry & Mary Jane Evens, 28 Sept 1846; Jas. M. Palmer, bm.

Bagley, William & Nelley Dear, 29 March 1799; David Hicks, bm.

Bailey, Daniel & Mary Norwood, 4 March 1831; Daniel Baliff, Thos Thompson, bm.

Bailey, Henry & Polley Price, 21 Aug 1804; James Bailey, bm.

Bailey, James & Tabitha Durham, 23 Jan 1817; Simon Holaday, Nathaniel Durham, bm.

Bailey, John & Mary Thompson, 17 July 1800; Alexander Finley, bm.

Bailey, Wm. & Anne Forsyth, 24 June 1798; Jones Bailey Sen., bm.

Bailey, William H. & Anna C. Howerton, 4 Oct 1852; Samuel S. Kirkland, bm; m 20 Oct 1852 by J. B. Donnelly, minister, St. Matthews Parish, Hillsboro.

Bailiff, John & Tellitha Cate, 7 April 1803; Thos. Cate, bm.

Bailiff, Thos. & Elizabeth Baker, 24 June 1790; Will Bailey, bm.

Baily, Nathaniel & Polly Bailey, 15 March 1821; John Morris, bm.

Bain, James M. & Mary P. Paul, 31 Jan 1854; Wm. D. Faucett, Saml. P. Merre___, bm.

Bain, Lorenzo D. & Nancy Shofner, 25 May 1833; Allen Robberson, bm.

Bain, N. D. & Catharine Patterson, 21 Sept 1864; Jno Laws, bm.

Bain, Thomas & Kissiah Walton, 1 Dec 1784; Brice Collins, bm.

Baines, George & Nancy Cook, 5 Jan 1820; John Lackey, bm.

Bains, Samuel & Elizabeth Jones, 25 Jan 1814; Crosley Brinkley, bm.

Bains, Theophilus F. & Leonora C. Adams, 1 Nov 1855; Thomas Scarlett, R. M. Jones, bm; m 1 Nov 1855 by H. T. Hudson, M.G.

Baird, George & Ida Cameron, m 19 May 1866 by Mayer Green, J. P.

Baker, Albert & Eliza Couch, 2 Feb 1842; Henry D. Turner, bm.

Baker, James & Mary Scoby, 2 Jan 1792; John Scoby, bm.

Baker, James & Elizabeth Logan, 12 March 1792; Georg Long, bm.

Baker, John & Jennet Long, 10 Jan 1784; George Long, bm.

Baker, John & Jane Scoby, 20 Aug 1794; James McCauley, A. B. Bruce, bm.

Baker, John & Elizabeth Hargens, 22 July 1795; Samuel Shaw, bm.

Baker, Joseph & Elizabeth Patterson, 28 March 1785; Jno. Sturgess, bm.

Baker, Joseph & Elizabeth Greeman, 9 Oct 1818; A. Roney, bm.

Baker, Robert & Ferabee Fossett, 6 Jan 1800; Burris Estridge, John Pitman, bm.

Baldridge, Andrew & Peggy Gourley, 1 Jan 1805; Thos. Woods, bm.

Baldridge, Danl. & Rebecca Douglass, 6 March 1805; Stephen Baldridge, bm.

Baldridge, John & Sarah Clark, 24 Dec 1801; Wm. McCanless, bm.

Baldridge, Robert & Betsey Dickey, 1 March 1803; David Woods, bm.

Baldridge, Stephen & Nelly Thompson, 10 Feb 1804; Thos. Woods, bm.

Baldridge, William & Elizabeth Kulin, 10 Aug 1798; William McCanless, bm.

Baldwin, C. Nelson & Mary James, 11 Oct 1832; Jno. A. McAnannen, bm.

Baldwin, Henry & Margaret E. Stroud, 6 Feb 1867; J. J. Baldwin, bm.

Baldwin, Henry, son of Jesse Baldwin & Patsey McDaniel, & Lucy McGuire, dau. of John and Sarah McGuire, colored, m 30 April 1868 by Charles Phillips, M. G.

Baldwin, John & Peggy Horn, 16 Jan 1802; William Horn, bm.

Baldwin, John & Lettice Newton, 29 Aug 1802; James Newton, bm.

Baldwin, John & Rutha C. Lloyd, 13 Sept 1865; Henry C. McCauley, bm.

Baldwin, John R. & Mary Craig, 9 Oct 1838; Wm. F. Strayhorn, bm.

Baldwin, N. William & Nancy Reeves, 4 Oct 1802; George Reeves, bm.

Baldwin, Robert & Nelly Rumley, 19 Aug 1800; Henry Rumbly, Joseph Rumbly, bm.

Baldwin, Samuel & Matilda Winningham, 15 Nov 1847; A. J. Baldwin, bm.

Baldwin, Wm. & Rebecca Cole, 5 Oct 1817; James B. Cole, bm.

Baldwin, William & Elizabeth Carroll, 10 July 1846; Thos. J. Freeland, bm.

Baldwin, William & Oma Andrews, 21 Jan 1854; William Baldwin, Minnick Miller, bm; m 23 Jan 1854 by Thos. Long, J. P.

Balkham, Henderson G. & Edney Harward, 17 Dec 1860; James M. Herndon, bm; m 17 Dec 1860 by A. B. Gunter, J. P.

Balkham, James M. & Casanda Hawrard, 11 Feb 1861; James M. Herndon, bm; m 14 Feb 1861 by A. B. Gunter, J. P.

Ball, Crutcher & Jemima Brinkley, 4 Aug 1821; Robert Cazort, bm.

Ball, James & Amelia Harris, 14 Sept 1822; Thomas Lattle, bm.

Ball, James S. & Emily H. Jackson, 23 Dec 1863; Robert J. Walker, bm; m 24 Dec 1863 by C. J. Freeland, J. P.

Ball, Marcus & Edney Ray, 19 Dec 1848; James Riggs, bm.

Ball, Marcus & Nancy Tilly, 10 April 1852; James C. Turrentine, bm.

Ball, Richard & Susanna Cate, 27 Aug 1798; Richard Cate, bm.

Ball, William & Rhody Edwards, 30 March 1793; Silvanus Brewer, Robert Gee, bm.

Ball, William H. & M. P. Woodrough, 19 Sept 1860; G. W. Morton, bm; m 30 Sept 1860 by John Mitchell.

Ballard, John W. & Sarah A. Tinny, 14 June 1861; Thomas Scarlett, Thomas Webb, bm; m 17 June 1861 by B. F. Guthrie.

Ballard, William M. & Elizabeth Bragg, 2 Dec 1803; James Johnson, bm.

Balyff, Freric & Sally Moon, 15 April 1848; Charles A. Brewer, bm.

Bane, Jno & Louisa Benton, 7 Jan 1836; Giles Mebane, bm.

Bane, John & Jane Wilson, 8 April 1841; Eli Sharp, bm.

Bane, Nathanl & Polley McKee, 28 Aug 1824; Stephen Moore, bm.

Barbe, John Planter & Mary Hester, 24 May 1793; Abner B. Bruce, C. C., wit.

Barbe, Thomas C. & Rebecca Trice, 9 March 1867; H. P. Smith, bm; m 14 March 1867 by C. G. Markham, J. P.

Barbee, Abemelech & Hannah Whitteker, 10 Nov 1789; Abraham Whitteker, bm.

Barbee, Allen & Elizabeth Carson, 17 Dec 1797; Wm. Horton, Jno Taylor, bm.

Barbee, Alston A. & Rowan Edwards, 27 June 1860; James Hester, bm; m 26 Aug 1860 by D. Tilley, J. P.

Barbee, Christopher & Jeany Shepperd, 6 Jan 1814; Thos Bilbo, bm.

Barbee, Christopher & Sarah Patterson, 4 Jan 1820; William Barbee, bm.

Barbee, Fletcher & Eliza Harrod, 4 Dec 1847; Ezekiel George, E. G. Gray, bm.

Barbee, Frances & Caroline Cook, 26 Dec 1846; Simeon R. Hailey, bm.

Barbee, Francis & Elizabeth Nevils, 8 Feb 1794; David Craig, bm.

Barbee, Gabriel A. & Carolina Freeman, 20 Oct 1860; F. M. Barbee, bm; m 23 Oct 1860 by H. J. Pearson.

Barbee, George & Martha Moring, 16 Feb 1832; William J. O'Kelly, bm.

Barbee, George W. & Phebe Ann Barbee, 23 Nov 1846; Gray Barbee, bm.

Barbee, Gray & Hawkins Scoggins, 17 Sept 1836; W. N. Pratt, J. Taylor, bm.

Barbee, Gray & Drucilla Barbee, 25 May 1861; M. A. Angier, bm; m 26 May 1861 by M. A. Angier, J. P.

Barbee, H. T. & Ann Eliza Rigsbee, 2 Jan 1861; A. J. Rhodes, bm; m 5 Jan 1861 by M. A. Angier, J. P.

Barbee, Henry H. & Sarah Ann Davis, 30 March 1861; W. W. Davis, bm; m 31 March 1861 by Benja. D. Rogers, J. P.

Barbee, James R. & Mary Holder, 10 Nov 1844; Riley Neal, bm.

Barbee, James R. & Mary Ann Cape, 25 Aug 1851; Thomas J. Anderson, bm.

Barbee, Jesse, son of Handy and Fanny Barbee, & Milly Jenkins, dau. of Betsy and Sandy Jenkins, m 10 Oct 1867 by C. G. Markham, J. P.

Barbee, Jno & Sally Roberts, 27 Nov 1827; Wm. R. Herndon, bm.

Barbee, John & Esther Herndon, 20 March 1790; Benjamin Barbee, bm.

Barbee, John & Mary Hester, 24 May 1793; Henry Burch, bm.

Barbee, John & Elizabeth Pickett, 9 Feb 1832; W. N. Pratt, bm.

Barbee, John, son of Ceaser & Aggy Barbee, & Amey Mickle, dau. of Henry & Lucy Mickle, colored, m 17 Aug 1868 by S. S. Clayton, J. P., at the residence of John Barker, Chapel Hill.

Barbee, Jones & Frances Lloyd, 25 Oct 1831; John Freeland, bm.

Barbee, King & Nancy Herndon, 27 May 1812; James Herndon, bm.

Barbee, M. B. & Mary A. E. Gorman, 20 Aug 1849; Thos. J. Freeland, bm.

Barbee, Mark & Elizabeth Mulhollan, 24 Oct 1804; James Rainey, bm.

Barbee, Mark & Nancy Alsobrook, 8 June 1811; Geo. Johnston, bm.

Barbee, Mathew & Christiana Arkins, 27 Nov 1799; Samuel Carson, bm.

Barbee, Matthew & Louisa Atkins, 8 Dec 1853; Bartley Barbee, bm; m 20 Dec 1853 by A. B. Gunter, J. P.

Barbee, Nevill & Sally Hopson, 16 March 1821; Christopher Barbee, bm.

Barbee, Pleasent G. & Mary A. Boroughs, 22 Dec 1854; Cornelius T. Boroughs, bm; m 24 Dec 1854 by B. J. Hackney.

Barbee, Samuel & Ceila Cotton, 18 Oct 1866; P. H. McDade, bm; m 18 Oct 1866 by Jones Watson, J. P.

Barbee, Walter A. & Elizabeth J. Leathers, 4 Feb 1854; Geo Laws, bm.

Barbee, William & Salley Scarlett, 24 Dec 1810; James Rainey, bm.

Barbee, William, son of Mark & Fanny Barbee, & Isabella Patterson, dau. of Hardy & Amey Patterson, colored, m 26 Dec 1867 by C. G. Markham, J. P.

Barbee, William Jr. & ____, 26 Sept 1833; Alexr Strain, bm.

Barbee, Young & Elize Doller, 27 Nov 1849; Thomas Houghinton, bm.

Barbee, Zachariah & Melinda Dilliard, 8 May 1819; O. B. Rogers, bm.

Barbee, Zachariah & Tabitha Trice, 23 Dec 1819; Reuben Barbee, bm.

Barber, David & Margaret Tate, 12 May 1821; James Moore, bm.

Barber, James C. & Catharine Campbell, 7 March 1809; Wilhelm Mador(?), bm.

Barber, James D. & Hephzibah Molessa Kernodle, 24 Nov 1846; A. B. Tarpley, bm.

Barber, William & Elizabeth Dunlap, 29 April 1798; Andrew McCulley, bm.

Barham, Benjamin & Eliza Judkins, 15 Nov 1819; John Morris, bm.

Barix, John & Celia Shanklin, 20 Sept 1840; Harris J. Smith, bm.

Barker, George & Barbary Fitch, 8 Feb 1812; Freeman Leath, bm.

Barker, John & Polley Mason, 22 Feb 1815; Wm. Clifton, bm.

Barker, William & Marget Jeffres, 4 Dec 1815; James Vickers, bm.

Barkins, William & Mary Harris, 26 April 1796; Francis Dunn, bm.

Barlow, John & Betsey Nichols, 7 June 1792; James Comb, bm.

Barlow, Joseph & Lucinda Crossett, 12 Dec 1838; John H. Barlow, bm.

Barlow, Thomas & Leucy Hargus, 26 Dec 1796; John Turrentine, bm.

Barlow, William & Dona Dorotha Eubank, 31 Dec 1832; William Ray, bm.

Barnet, Daniel & Milley Foster, 15 Dec 1812; J. Taylor, bm.

Barnhart, Henry & Polly Lynn, 24 Jan 1821; Joel Low, bm.

Barnhill, William & Elizabeth Harper, 23 Aug 1804; Samuel Barnhill, bm.

Barnwell, Edward & Mary McCord, 1 Oct 1800; James Breeze, bm.

Barnwell, John & Elizabeth Eccles, 26 Nov 1822; Andw. Murray, bm.

Barnwell, William & Nancy Martin, 23 March 1824; John Barnwell, bm.

Barracks, Wm. & Winney Tate, 26 Nov 1806; David McCrorey, bm.

Barrick, Charles & Clarey Moss, 13 March 1813; John Kenorey, bm.

Barrix, John & Marinda Brown, 13 June 1829; James M. Pearson, Zion Pearson, bm.

Barry, John & Rhody Richards, 29 June 1796; Roswald Huntington, bm.

Bartley, Samuel & Mary Whinnery, 9 Sept 1809; Robert Graham, bm.

Barton, Henry L. & Elizabeth McFarthing, 17 March 1860; A. S. Glenn, bm; m 19 March 1860 by Wm. J. Duke.

Barton, James & Elizabeth Crabtree, 5 July 1792; James McCauley, bm.

Barton, John & Nelly Thompson, 29 April 1793; John Faddis, bm.

Barton, Josiah & Elizabeth Easton, 23 Aug 1825; John Woods, bm.

Barton, Samuel & Nancy Barton, 10 Nov 1824; D. B. Alsobrook, bm.

Barton, Sym & Suzaney Bowles, 8 Sept 1842; John Bowles, bm.

Barton, Thomas & Elizabeth Campbell, 22 Dec 1798; James Campbell, bm.

Barton, Thomas & Fanny Davis, __ July 1826; John J. Freeland, bm.

Barton, William & Mary Wilkey, 10 Feb 1821; Jos. Stubbins, bm.

Barton, William & Sarah Carroll, 16 Jan 1822; Wm. Brown, bm.

Barton, William & Nancy Dockery, 12 Dec 1825; Wm. Barton, bm.

Barton, Wiseley & Eliza Clark, 10 Feb 1852; Eaton Walker, bm; m 12 Feb 1852 by Richd. Nichols, J. P.

Basket, Thomas & Susa ODananel, 2 March 1793; John Faucett, bm.

Bason, Calvin & Martha Woods, 3 Jan 1840; William H. Holden, A. W. Parker, bm.

Baxon, Frederick & Margaret McBane, 6 March 1812; William Lasley, bm.

Bason, Frederick & Mary Pye, 20 Oct 1807; William Anderson, bm.

Bason, Henry & Mary Trolinger, 3 April 1832; Benjamin Trolinger, bm.

Bason, Jacob & Elizabeth McAdams, 23 Oct 1806; Stephen Thompson, bm.

Bason, Jeremiah & Celia Dickey, 27 Nov 1834; Henry Foust, bm.

Bason, John & Catey Whitesides, 25 Nov 1800; John Collins, bm.

Bason, Joseph & Barbary Foust, 9 Nov 1805; Fredrick Bason, bm.

Bason, Joseph G. & Rebecca Carrington, 31 Jan 1825; J. Reynolds, bm.

Bass, Carrington & Mary Bass, 14 March 1865; Nelson Rhue, bm.

Bass, Cullen & Anne Elizabeth Mayho, 14 Dec 1835; Jefferson Roberson, Tho. Anderson, bm.

Bass, Cullin & Elizabeth Curtis, 22 Nov 1859; Bennaham Bass, bm.

Bass, Dred & Ibby Gilston, 19 March 1813; W. Thompson, bm.

Bass, James & Polly Carter, 1 Dec 1847; John Burnes, bm.

Bass, John & Catharine Whiteker, 29 Dec 1860; J. P. Brasfield, bm; m 29 Dec 1860 by Solomon Shepherd.

Bass, Roland & Lyda Whitehead, 12 Nov 1782; Patrick St. Lawrence, bm.

Bass, Stephen & Susanna Carter, 6 Feb 1833; Edward Philips, bm.

Bass, Young & Martha J. Peterson, 7 June 1855; James C. Turrentine, bm.

Batchelor, Elias & Netty Perry, 13 Feb 1833; James Mebane, bm.

Batchelor, Reuben & Martha Brazill, 18 Dec 1850; J. B. McDade, bm.

Batchler, Elderd & Jane Parrish, ___ 1845; Elias Batcheler, bm.

Batie, William J. & Tebitha J. Thompson, 24 Dec 1853; Thos Thompson, Geo. W. Bruce, bm.

Baugh, Josiah T. & Sarah Dannel, 27 Feb 1797; Frances Moreland, bm.

Bawlar, Shaderick & Susan Mason, 22 Aug 1855; Wm. McCauly, bm; m 22 Aug 1865 by J. P. Greeland, J. P.

Baxter, Samuel & Mary Witte, 27 Dec 1781; Jas Russell, bm.

Bean, Thomas & Kissiah Walton, 1 Dec 1784; Brice Collins, bm.

Bean, Thos. & Keziah Kelly, 26 May 1812; Thos Armstrong, T. Ferguson, bm.

Bean, Nethal. & Elizabeth Faucett, 6 Jan 1813; William Fausett, bm.

Beard, George & Ida Cameron, 19 May 1866; Wm. Hamlen, bm.

Beard, Lewis & Philpane Murray, 12 Oct 1838; John Craig, bm.

Beasley, Carey & Polley Self, 22 Dec 1809; John OKelly, Younger Hopson, bm.

Beasley, Merril & ___, 1 Aug 1807; William O. M. Ballard, bm.

Beasley, Robert B. & Sarah T. Holeman, 22 Jan 1859; S. J. Hester, bm; m 25 Jan 1859 by T. W. Moore.

Beasley, Samuel & Milley Hurdle, 28 April 1798; Joseph Ming, bm.

Beasley, William & Lucretia Tilley, 24 Feb 1840; Silus M. Link, Jno. M. Faucett, bm.

Beaver, Jehu & Delia Cheek, 13 March 1850; George A. Oldham, bm.

Beaver, John & Polley Wilkey, 13 Feb 1820; Page Carroll, bm.

Beaver, William & Lucy Edwards, 27 Nov 1807; John Edwards, bm.

Beavers, Charles E., son of George & Mary Beavers, & Margaret E. Carlton, dau. of A. M. and D. J. Carlton, 9 Oct 1867; m 15 Oct 1867 by J. P. Mason, minister.

Beckham, Joseph & Sindy Giford, 21 Dec 1820; Green Beckham, bm.

Beckum, David & Salley Woody, 18 May 1822; D. H. Ray, bm.

Beckum, Joshua & Polley Alexander, 28 Dec 1814; Green Beckum, Michl. Holt, bm.

Beckum, William & Nancey Freeman, 28 Oct 1816; George Courtner, bm.

Beckworth, Nedom & Ann Eliza Mason, 8 April 1850; Turner Mason, bm.

Belick, Saml. & Nancy Williams, 31 March 1798; Henry Holaday, bm.

Bell, Jordan & Sucky Minchew, 14 March 1822; George Glenn, bm.

Bell, Robert & Polley Haywood, ___ Oct 1785; Wm. Shepperd, bm.

Belvin, Doctor L. & Temessia S. Piper, 18 Sept 1865; Charles F. Crabtree, bm; m 19 Sept 1865 by James Stagg, J. P.

Benefield, Willis & Milley Forrest, 21 Aug 1802; Joseph Armstrong, bm.

Bennet, John & Roseanah Lainberry, 5 Sept 1807; Jacob Coble, bm.

Bennett, David & Sarah Coble, 3 Jan 1816; John Bennett, bm.

Bennett, Phillip & Nancy Forrester, 31 Oct 1806; Moses Dossett, bm.

Bennett, Richd. F. & Mary E. Ryder, 24 Feb 1851; Wm. J. Freeland, bm; m 24 Feb 1851 by W. H. Brown, J. P.

Bennitt, James & Nancy Pierson, 21 May 1831; Levin Carmichel, bm.

Benson, Beaufort P., & Julia Blanshard, 1 April 1830; Stephen Benson, bm.

Benson, Stephen & Sarah G. Fonville, 7 July 1831; Wm. Benson, bm.

Benson, Stephen & Emiley Picket, 17 May 1847; B. P. Benson, bm.

Benson, William & Catharine Hufman, 6 Dec 1831; Stephen Benson, bm.

Bering, David & Victory McKee, 24 Jan 1794; Wm. Lockhart, bm.

Berrick, Peter T. & Eliza Bingham, m 4 Nov 1857 by Thos. Lynch.

Berry, David & Mary Blealock, 21 Feb 1797; Henry Waggoner, bm.

Berry, Eli & Judy Betsey Taylor, 21 Dec 1846; Henderson Taylor, bm.

Berry, Henry & Lucy Weaver, 14 May 1835; James Shepard, bm.

Berry, James H. & Emley McCullock, 16 Jan 1856; James H. Berry, bm; m 24 Jan 1856 by C. Wilson, J. P.

Berry, John & Elizabeth Vincent, 6 March 1827; Jesse Hargrave, bm.

Berry, John R. & Bettie F. Bowling, 28 Nov 1865; James Allison, bm; m 30 Nov 1865 by Charles Wilson, J. P.

Berry, Joshua & Nancy Ellison, 28 Jan 1792; Henry Terryl, bm.

Berry, Lewis & Sally Toler, 13 Oct 1828; H. Terry, bm.

Berry, Thomas & Elizabeth Carter, 15 April 1791; George Maden, bm.

Berry, Thomas & Sarah Cate, 11 Aug 1800; John Cate, bm.

Berry, Thomas & Mary Berry, 7 March 1809; Henry Berry, bm.

Berry, Thomas Person & Sarah Lunsford, 28 Sept 1831; Henry Berry, bm.

Berry, William & Hannah Cates, 12 Aug 1799; Thomas Berry, bm.

Berry, William & Sally Bowles, 20 Nov 1826; Wm. Taylor, bm.

Berry, William H. & Sarah Francis King, 28 July 1857; C. S. Dunagan, bm; m 6 Aug 1857 by Charles Wilson, J. P.

Bets, William & Mary Manis, 11 Feb 1822; John Linn, bm.

Betts, Alexander D. & Mary E. Davis, 8 May 1855; Henry K. Nash, bm; m 12 May 1855 by Peter Doub, Pastor of M. E. Church, South, at Chapel Hill.

Bevelley, Elijah & Mary Freeman, 3 May 1787; Joel Ramsey, bm.

Bevil, Elisha & Sarah Davis, 2 Nov 1793; Chiles Davis, bm.

Bevil, Zachariah & Elizabeth Canada, 27 Sept 1826; John Lee, bm.

Bevill, Howel & Winney Davis, 2 Jan 1806; Elisha Bevill, bm.

Bevill, John & Franky Davis, 11 Nov 1799; Elisha Bevil, bm.

Bevings, Stepen & Sally Andrews, 18 Aug 1842; George Cobb, bm.

Bevins, James & Nina Williams, 17 Nov 1830; L. Albright, bm.

Bevins, Thomas & Elizabeth Carter, 24 July 1782.

Bevins, Thos. & Mary McPherson, 22 April 1814; Thomas Davis, bm.

Bigelow, Samuel & Mary Jane Montgomery, 19 May 1816; James Child, John R. Cumming, bm.

Biggelow, Norman & Rebeccah Whithead, 17 Jan 1787; Will Whithead, bm.

Bingham, Harrison & Amy Cotton, colored, 5 Aug 1866; John Morrow, bm; m 5 Aug 1866 by H. McDaniel, J. P.

Bingham, Will J. & Eliza A. Norwood, 22 Nov 1827; Will Norwood, bm.

Binum, Teply & Elizabeth Fann, 27 Feb 1810; John Pendergrass, bm.

Birch, Elijah & Nelly Mason, 20 Aug 1813; Mark Barbee, bm.

Birch, Harvy & Susanah Porterfield, 21 Jan 1850; John C. Crossett, bm.

Bird, Empson & Mary Jordan (no date); John Bird, bm.

Bird, Empson & Sarah Wyatt, 18 Jan 1831; John Wyatt, bm.

Bird, James & Rebeccah Thompson, 31 Oct 1797; S. Harris, bm.

Bird, Jehu & Patsy Moore, 31 Oct 1816; John McCawley, bm.

Bird, Jehu & Nancy Ann Brannock, 27 April 1838; William Murray, bm.

Bird, Joel & Nancy Wilson, 10 Sept 1797; Dennis Sampson, bm.

Bird, John Alvis & Frances Jones, 15 April 1851; John L. Faucett, bm; m 15 April 1851 by C. E. Smith, J. P.

Bird, Johnston & Deessy Hulet, 7 Feb 1846; Barenton Fullerton, Jackson Hulett, bm.

Bird, Joseph & Elizabeth Miller, 30 Dec 1781.

Bird, Samuel & Jinny Miller, 26 July 1822; Joseph Bird, bm.

Bird, Thomas & Sarah Vendrick, 10 Feb 1815; Zaccheus Paul, bm.

Bird, Thomas & Clara Crawford, 28 May 1839; Wiam Vincent, S. S. Clayton, bm.

Bird, William & Margret Murray, 28 Jan 1803; Samuel Craig, bm.

Bird, Wm. & Mary Thompson, 21 Sept 1798; Sir Harris, bm.

Bishop, Alves & Margret Kirkland, 28 Jan 1841; John C. Latta, Jno. M. Faucett, bm.

Bishop, Bartlett & Catharine McCauly, 30 Jan 1860; N. Cheek, bm; m 5 Feb 1860 by W. J. Hogan, J. P.

Bishop, Calvin & Margaret Pratt, 21 May 1842; W. McCauley, bm.

Bishop, James & Penine Williams, 10 Sept 1862; John Cheek, bm; m 10 Sept 1862 by John Cheek, J. P.

Bishop, James M. & Caroline Kirkland, 26 July 1862; M. B. Jones, bm.

Bishop, John & Nancy Ivey, 14 May 1841; W. McCauly, Connon Boney, bm.

Bishop, Lot & Elizabeth Patrun, 29 Jan 1828; John Patrun, bm.

Bishop, Macon & Susan Robison, 24 Oct 1840; Edmond Fields, bm.

Bishop, William & Elizabeth Cheek, 28 Dec 1814; John Johnston, bm.

Bivins, Daniel & Cornelia Ray, 29 Oct 1849; William Shaw, bm.

Bivins, James & Phebe Mitchell, 2 Oct 1825; James Moore, bm.

Bivins, Richard & Tempe Kimbrough, 5 Nov 1826; Wm. Ricketts, bm.

23

Blacknall, Willis B. & Sarah Blacknall, 12 Dec 1865; Wm. Mangum, bm.

Blackwell, John & Susan Bartlet, 27 Sept 1831; Henry Malone, bm.

Blackwell, Robert M. & Martha Malone, 9 Jan 1836; B. Cortell, bm.

Blackwood, Alexander & Susan Sparrow, 15 Dec 1836; John Hutchins, bm.

Blackwood, Anderson & Mary Barbee, 2 Nov 1833; Franklin L. Blackwood, bm.

Blackwood, Goodman & Mary McCarrall, 21 May 1854; Wilson Crabtree, bm; m 21 May 1854 by Alexr. Dickson, J. P.

Blackwood, James & Susan Brockwell, 1 June 1818; J. J. Freeland, bm.

Blackwood, John & Ellender Craig, 22 July 1800; James Craig, bm.

Blackwood, John & Mary McCawley, 13 April 1830; D. W. Craig, bm.

Blackwood, John M. & Virginia A. Fuller, 17 Dec 1860; D. D. Phillips, James Gill, bm; m 19 Dec 1860 by A. D. Blackwood, minister.

Blackwood, John T. & Martha E. King, 22 June 1866; William D. King, bm; m 26 June 1866 by C. W. Johnston, J. P.

Blackwood, Johnston & Sarah B. Craig, 25 Aug 1821; Jas. T. Boroughs, bm.

Blackwood, Philo & Martha A. Williams, 11 Oct 1863; J. Y. Watson, bm.

Blackwood, Samuel D. & Martha J. Craig, 9 Dec 1861; T. W. Laws, bm; m 12 Dec 1861 by James Phillips.

Blackwood, Samuel W. & Harriett A. McCauley, 8 March 1859; G. J. McCauley, bm; m 8 March 1859 by H. Whitted, J. P.

Blackwood, Washington & Nancy Pickett, 17 Nov 1860; Haywood Andreus, bm; m 18 Nov 1860 by D. Tilly, J. P.

Blackwood, William & Henly Hogan, 24 July 1813; David Craig, bm.

Blackwood, William J. & Mary E. Blackwood, 26 May 1863; Jos. Watson, bm; m 28 May 1863 by C. W. Johnston, J. P.

Blair, James & Mary Thompson, 29 Dec 1792; Samuel Woody, bm.

Blake, John & Nancy Burgess, 23 Aug 1832; Samuel Scarlett, Peter Kellom, bm.

Blalock, Andrew J. & Nancey Neal, 27 Nov 1840; Jas. N. Patterson, Levi McColluch, bm.

Blalock, Chesley & Eady Q. Trice, 22 Jan 1856; H. J. Rigsbee, William Herndon, bm; m 22 Jan 1856 by John Burroughs, J. P.

Blalock, David S. & Candass Durning, 28 Aug 1838; R. W. Dickson, bm.

Blalock, Egbert & Malinda Ware, 29 Dec 1837; Saml. Cole, bm.

Blalock, Giles & Dolley Justice, 28 March 1798; John Blalock, bm.

Blalock, Green M. & Jane Anderson, 24 Nov 1841; Ephraim Hawkins, Richd. Nichols, bm.

Blalock, Harberd & Eliza Tetterson, 4 Jan 1817; Hartwill Blalock, bm.

Blalock, Harrison & Anna Holloway, 13 Aug 1831; Thomas Hutchins, Henry B. Hutchins, bm.

Blalock, Harrison & Martha Johnston, 16 April 1840; D. S. Blalock, William George, bm.

Blalock, Hartwell & Cassey Sparks, 14 Aug 1817; Abraham Crabtree, bm.

Blalock, Hartwell & Patsy Herndon, 5 Nov 1822; John L. Woods, bm.

Blalock, Henderson & D. Hellen Evaline Hancock, 17 Feb 1852; Pleasant Pickett, bm; m 19 Feb 1852 by John Hancock, J. P.

Blalock, John & Polley Dormant, 6 Jan 1797; John Dorman, bm.

Blalock, Meredith & Tempe Riley, 3 Nov 1808; William Fauset, bm.

Blalock, Meredith & Burtess Hubbard, 7 Jan 1817; Andrew Meroney, bm.

Blalock, William & Sally Hargis, 11 Jan 1817; John W. McCracken, bm.

Blalock, William & Anguline Lunsford, 9 Dec 1835; Thos. P. Perry, James N. Lunsford, bm.

Blalock, William D. & Elizabeth F. Cole, 13 Dec 1865; William F. Cates, bm; m 21 Dec 1865 by B. C. Hopkins, J. P.

Blalock, William J. & Mary F. Thompson, 1 March 1867; Leslie F. Atkins, bm; m 18 April 1867 by John Burroughs, J. P.

Blalock, Wm. Green & Lucretie Tilly, 8 Nov 1845; D. Carrington, bm.

Blalock, Wilson Jarrett & Anne Williams, 9 June 1814; Samuel Bigelow, bm.

Blanchard, Fedrick & Polly Browning, 1 March 1822; George Hurdle, bm.

Blanchard, Frederick & Helen Truit, 9 Dec 1833; John Faucett, William ___, bm.

Blanchard, James & Molley McCullock, 13 Feb 1830; Jacob Hurdle, bm.

Bledsoe, Aaron & Betsy Hall, 6 July 1815; John Bledsoe, bm.

Bledsoe, David & Susanah Hall, 7 Feb 1823; John Hall Junr., bm.

Bledsoe, Giles & Mary Jane Waltun, 7 Jan 1854; Gray Barbee, Geo. W. Bruce, bm.

Bledsoe, Henry & Tempe Robbards, 19 May 1825; Jacob Bledsoe, br

Bledsoe, Isaac M. & Lucy Marshall, 28 May 1813; John Bledsoe, Woodson Daniel, bm.

Bledsoe, Jackson & Jane Copley, 27 Oct 1865; S. M. Ladd, bm; m 27 Oct 1865 by B. C. Hopkins, J. P.

Bledsoe, John T. & Nancy Martin, 18 Sept 1858; Allen Nance, bm m 18 Sept 1858 by Solomon Shepherd, J. P.

Bludso, Mecons & Margret Laws, 12 Aug 1824; John Horne, bm.

Boaz, Thomas & Francis Tait, 22 April 1822; G. A. Mebane, bm.

Bobbitt, Arthur & Elizabeth Woods, 10 Oct 1835; Duek Glenn, Wm. Nichols, bm.

Bobbitt, Willie & Drady Parker, 17 Nov 1849; P. Southerland, br

Bobit, Gren & Durina Wagoner, 1 July 1848; T. J. Latta, bm.

Boen, William E. W. & Louisa Brewer, 13 Oct 1866; William Strann, bm; m 14 Oct 1866 by Thos Long, J. P.

Boggs, Henry & Sally Councelman, 12 May 1818; Geo. Councelman, bm.

Boggs, Jacob & Sally Workman, 24 Nov 1838; Stanford Boggs, bm.

Boggs, Jerry & Emily Isley, 7 Oct 1846; Leonard Ray, bm.

Boggs, Jesse & Prissey Nease, 16 March 1825; Elias Nese, bm.

Boggs, Joel & Ebby Folkner, 6 Feb 1832; Jesse Boggs, bm.

Boggs, Lewis & Telitha Batie, 31 Jan 1867; W. H. Morris, bm.

Boggs, Peter & Polley Iseley, 3 Jan 1802; Jacob Nees, bm.

Boggs, Simpson & Mary O'Daniel, 18 Jan 1839; John B. Smith, bm

Boggs, Stanford & Mary Atkinson, 10 Jan 1837; Wm. McPherson, b

Boggs, William & Letty Thomas, 2 Aug 1827; Henry Boggs, bm.

Boggs, William Washington & Phebe Haliday, 30 May 1837; George Counselman, bm.

Boland, Benjamin & Farrabee Lynch, 28 Jan 1808; John Horner, b

Bolin, Baxter & Ann Bowling, 30 May 1816; Benjamin Bolings, bm

Bolin, Wm. & Eliza Neal, 19 Jan 1847; Geo. Crowder, bm.

Boling, Benjamin & Nancy Hall, 13 May 1836; William Link, Grie Lynch, bm.

Bollen, James L. & Catharin McCulloch, 2 March 1848; Dennis Woods, Kinchen Leather, bm.

Bond, Jno. W. & Mary F. Mebane, 4 Nov 1851; C. M. Latimer, bm; m 4 Nov 1851 by Alex Wilson, M. G. at the residence of Wm. Mebane.

Bond, Wm. & Fanny Doherty, 4 Oct 1804; C. Campbell, bm.

Bonner, Moses T. & Orrel Hopkins, 5 Jan 1839; Z. Hampton, bm.

Booker, Gaston & Martha M. Booth, 12 March 1849; H. B. Lloyd, bm.

Booker, Jas. & Elizabeth Trice, 3 July 1833; Jas. Huckabee, bm.

Booker, John & Susannah Thrift, 2 Nov 1803; Dixon Stroud, bm.

Booker, Joseph C. & Eugenia F. Lloyd, 28 June 1856; H. B. Loyd, bm; m 10 July 1856 by B. J. Hackney.

Booker, Paschal & Letha A. Strowd, 13 Feb 1866; W. F. Snipes, bm; m 13 Feb 1866 by Solomon Pool.

Boon, Charles A. & Mary Ann Pritchard, 13 Oct 1864; Wm. S. Petty, bm.

Boon, George & Sarah Brown, 30 Nov 1841; A. J. Picke, Lewis B. Bolt, bm.

Boon, Jacob & Milley Powel, 8 Feb 1798; Jesse Smith, bm.

Boon, Jesse & Jane Holt, 3 Aug 1841; Bedford Hurdle, bm.

Boon, Jessee & Sarah Keck, 13 Nov 1820; William Keck, bm.

Boon, John & Mary Coble, 24 Oct 1807; L. Cook, bm.

Booth, John & Elizabeth Harwood, 5 Aug 1782; Turner Harwood, bm.

Booth, Jno. W. & Anna J. Lynch, 12 Dec 1860; G. W. Ferrell, bm; m 12 Dec 1860 by G. W. Ferrill.

Booth, Mark & Dicey Castleberry, 22 Oct 1803; Wm. Jinkins, bm.

Booth, Ned, son of New Barbee and Anna Booth, & Nanna Evans, dau. of Mins and Agga Evans, colored, m 29 Dec 1867 by J. P. Mason.

Booth, Samuel, son of J. and Mary S. Booth, & M. B. Lynch, dau. of Thomas & Mary Lynch, m 11 Feb 1868 by Thos. Lynch.

Booth, Zachariah & Penelope Patterson, 10 July 1787; Turner Herod, bm.

Boothe, Alfred & Julia Long, 18 May 1864; J. P. Mason, bm; m 18 May 1864 by J. P. Mason, minister.

Boothe, Allen & Martha Hargrave, 11 May 1867; m 12 May 1867 by J. P. Mason.

Boothe, Jesse A. & Terminia L. Herndon, 14 Oct 1840; W. P. Vann, J. D. Boothe, bm.

Boothe, John & Patsy Castlebury, 14 Nov 1802; Jno. Davis, bm.

Boothe, Lemuel & Rosanna Jinkins, 19 Feb 1825; Wm. Stofle, bm.

Boothe, Tapley & Nancy Price, 8 Dec 1810; Mark Booth, bm.

Boothe, W. T. & Mary E. Hernden, 29 Aug 1850; Willie Herndon, bm.

Borland, A. J. & Lydia Reeves, 18 Sept 1850; Jno Laws, bm.

Borland, Alexr. & Letha Ann Strayhorn, 21 Oct 1844; J. M. Faucett, A. B. Cox, bm.

Borland, Andrew & Nancy Scarlet, 15 Dec 1846; J. Allison, bm.

Borland, Archibald & Mary Strayhorn, 4 Nov 1835; Card. Jones Jr., bm.

Borland, Edmund, son of Duke Patterson & Veance Boreland, & Mary A. Robertson, dau. of Robert Robertson, colored, m 23 April 1868 by M. A. Curtis, D. D.

Borland, Stephen & Dilcey Scarlett, 5 April 1866; Henry Crabtree, bm.

Borland, William & Mary Ann Scarlett, 28 Aug 1861; J. G. Strayhorn, bm; m 29 Aug 1861 by A. C. Hunter.

Borland, William G. & Susan H. Crabtree, 18 Jan 1866; Thos Dickson, Abram Hedgpeth, bm; m 18 Jan 1866 by Samuel Pearce.

Boshormer, Henry R. & Mary Clarke, 10 Jan 1838; Britton Boney, bm.

Boswell, James & Nancy Foster, 27 Jan 1829; William E. Foster, bm.

Boswell, Walter & Susannah Gardner, 16 March 1801; Peter Mankins, bm.

Boswell, William & Elizabeth Moore, 16 Aug 1803; David Underwood, bm.

Boulden, William & Delile Daniel, 27 Oct 1848; Daniel R. Huffham, bm.

Bourman, Peter & Recer Eccles, ___; Isaac Mayes(?), bm.

Bowers, Benjamin & Polly Cloud, 5 April 1815; Joseph H. Latta, bm.

Bowers, Cannon & Patsey Loyd, 22 Jan 1820; Alexander Cheek, William Andrus, bm.

Bowers, Henry & Sarah Wilson, 24 Dec 1845; A. W. Parker, bm.

Bowers, Henry & Nancy Brockwell, 18 Aug 1858; J. C. McCown, bm; m 18 Aug 1858 by Wm. McCown, J. P.

Bowers, James & Nancy Hicks, 16 Feb 1832; D. W. Hiecks, bm.

Bowers, Jesse & Sally Jones, 10 Oct 1816; David Anders, bm.

Bowers, John B. & Elizabeth Hinchy, 29 Dec 1812; John Leigh, bm.

Bowers, John B. & Rhodah Hinchy, 11 Nov 1813; Wm. Cumming, bm.

Bowers, Sampson & Caroline Jackson, 12 May 1847; Edmund Bowers, bm.

Bowers, William & Elizabeth Williams, 22 Jan 1823; Green O'Dan'l, bm.

Bowers, William G. & Mary Witherspoon, 24 Nov 1857; W. B. Faucett, Stephen L. Carll, bm; m 14 Nov 1857 by M. Baldwin, minister.

Bowles, John & Betsey Poulston, 30 Jan 1811; Vinson Roberts, bm.

Bowles, John & Caty Bass, 16 July 1843; Edmund Byrd, bm.

Bowles, John G. & Polley Boling, 8 Aug 1836; Anderson Monk, bm.

Bowles, William & Ruth Barlow, 19 Sept 1835; Robert Fitch, Wm. T. Shields, bm.

Bowlin, Henry C. & Adeline Hester, 8 June 1865; Leven Carmichael, bm; m 12 June 1865 by J. D. Unsted, L. Deacon.

Bowlin, John & Anna Wagoner, 19 Oct 1859; William Wagoner, bm; m 19 Oct 1859 by John L. Woods, J. P.

Bowling, John & Christiana Cozart, 28 March 1840; Williamson Parrish, bm.

Bowling, John Jun. & Elizabeth Cash, 26 Dec 1858; Ephraim Canough, James Ellis, bm; m 26 Dec 1858 by Williamson Parish, J. P.

Bowling, Joseph & Mary Kirkland, 6 Oct 1825; Willis Bowling, bm.

Bowling, William & Elizabeth W. Tapp, 29 Nov 1866; Nelson P. Hall, bm; m 13 Dec 1866 by T. N. Faucette, M. G.

Bowling, Wm. H. & Lucrecia Bowling, 9 May 1858; Prestley Bowling, bm; m 16 May 1858 by Williamson Parrish, J. P.

Bowling, Yancy & Polly Cozart, 15 May 1822; Willie Sweaney, bm.

Bowls, David & Mary Cates, 5 Aug 1853; Willis Mangum, J. Allison, bm.

Bowls, Thomas & Anne Davis, 16 May 1791; Robert Davis, bm.

Bowls, Thomas & Nancy Johnston, 18 July 1818; Joseph W. Allison, bm.

Bowls, Wm. & Anne Faucet, 13 Dec 1791; John Davis, bm.

Bowls, William & Nancy Rountree, 16 Sept 1818; Will Whittset, bm.

Bowman, Daniel & Elizabeth Fogleman, 7 Dec 1831; Peter Green, bm.

Bowman, Edward & Abigail Burnett, 20 Nov 1810; Wm. Marshill, bm.

Bowman, Jas. H. & Polley Campbell, 16 March 1799; Jno. Campbell, bm.

Bowman, Solomon & Nancy Laden, 8 March 1832; William Steel, bm.

Box, James & Barbary Griffin, 7 Nov 1812; Samuel Box(?), bm.

Box, Samuel & Mary Pannell, 25 Oct 1785; Jno. Pannell, bm.

Box, Thos. & Nelly Woods, 23 May 1808; James Crawford, bm.

Boxwell, William & Nancy Qualls, 14 Aug 1847; James Trolinger, bm.

Boyl, John & Elizabeth Boyl, 31 Dec 1781; James Boyle, bm.

Boyle, James & Lydia Bracken, 15 Sept 1792; no bm.

Boyle, James & Nancy Elen, 5 Aug 1841; Thos Anderson, bm.

Bracken, Isaac & Marjery Boyle, 20 Dec 1784; James Boyle, bm.

Bracken, Isaac & Susannah Street, 13 Dec 1813; Charlie Shanks, bm.

Bracken, John & Nancy Boswell, 6 July 1816; William Bracken, bm.

Bracken, William & Jeany Tate, 15 Dec 1799; John Tate, bm.

Brackin, Henry & Polly Gillam, 23 July 1794; John Donovan, Wm. Jackson, bm.

Brackin, Jesse & Jean Cantrel, 20 March 1790; Jacob Garrison, bm.

Bradbury, James F. & Margret Anne Hutchins, 18 Dec 1832; H. S. Hotchkiss, bm.

Bradford, David & Merryam Hamilton, 2 Aug 1783; William Bradford, bm.

Bradford, James & Nancy Bird, 15 Dec 1846; J. H. McCadams, bm.

Bradford, Samuel & Nancy Patterson, 6 Nov 1804; Jonathan Jones, bm.

Bradford, Thomas & Edith Ray, 24 Jan 1818; Robt. Morrow, bm.

Bradford, William & Sally King, 18 April 1815; Will J. Ray, bm.

Bradford, William & Betsy Jane Fossett, 18 Dec 1838; James Christopher, bm.

Bradley, James Darling & Priscilla Dennes, 25 July 1795; Porter Allen, bm.

Bradshaw, James & Betsey Allen, 16 Dec 1818; George Allen, bm.

Bradshaw, Robert & Mary J. Workman, 8 Jan 1861; John Cates, bm; m 10 Jan 1861 by R. R. Tapp, J. P.

Bradshaw, Samuel & Anne Tear, 2 Dec 1831; Wm. Holmes, bm.

Bradshaw, Thomas & Anne Turner, 15 Dec 1808; Jos. Clendenin, bm.

Bradhsaw, Thomas & Salley Sykes, 6 May 1820; Thomas Dodson, bm.

Bradshaw, Thomas & Eliza Baine, 24 Oct 1845; Thomas Allen, bm.

Bradshaw, Thomas P. & Sarah Jane Maner, 7 March 1860; m 8 March 1860 by C. H. Phillips.

Bradshaw, Thomas R. & Ann E. Anderson, 12 April 1860; J. W. Tripp, George A. Gaucett, bm; m 12 April 1860 by J. J. Allison, J. P.

Bradshaw, Wellington & Margaret Hill, 25 Sept 1865; Peter Trifford, bm; m 25 Sept 1865 by A. C. Murdoch, J. P.

Bradshaw, Wm. & Nelley Turner, 13 April 1823; Thos Cle___, bm.

Bradshaw, William & Mary Ann Brewer, 23 Jan 1827; Jos Stubbins, bm.

Bradshaw, William & Allice Faucett, colored, m 9 Jan 1868 by F. Walker, J. P.

Bradshaw, William L. & Margaret L. Stockard, 17 Feb 1849; Wm. Paris, bm.

Bradshaw, William T. & Sarah C. Stanford, 22 July 1854; Joseph S. Thompson, Geo. Laws, bm.

Bradsher, Augustus & Sarah A. Stewart, 19 March 1867; Joseph H. Hurdle, bm; m 19 March 1867 by F. Walker.

Branch, J. F. & Frances L. Waddell, 17 Oct 1848; H. M. Waddell, Thos. B. Bailey, bm.

Branick, William & Nancy Cook, 11 Oct 1805; Moses Thomas, bm.

Brannock, Henry & Delilah Brannock, 27 Feb 1821; William Brannock, bm.

Brannock, William & Patsy Shearman, 16 Dec 1811; Moses Thomas, bm.

Brasfield, Harvey & Nancy Bouland, 21 Jan 1823; Archd. Borland, Stephen Moore, bm.

Brasfield, Willie & Susan Hancock, 8 Oct 1823; Bazel Yates, bm.

Brashears, John & Salley Roberts, 8 Aug 1804; Stephens Robarts, bm.

Brasil, Benjamin & Mary Parrish, 3 Oct 1850; Thos. Boroughs, bm.

Bratchaw, Samuel N. & Nancy A. Edwards, 18 Jan 1862; m 19 Jan 1862 by Samuel Baldwin, ordained minister.

Bray, Mark & Peggy Patterson, 1 Nov 1850; David Coble, bm.

Breedlove, John & Bedy Fowler, 8 July 1824; Samuel Cole, bm.

Breedlove, Thomas & Hancy Bennet, 2 Oct 1826; David Coble, bm.

Breeze, John & Jean McMunn, 31 Dec 1792; William McMinn, bm.

Breeze, John H. & Ann Eliza Jordan, 3 March 1852; A. M. Breeze, bm; m 4 March 1852 by Hezekiah Terry, J. P.

Breeze, Richard & Nancy McEroom, 6 Jan 1811; John Ray, bm.

Breeze, Samuel H. & Mary Cabe, 26 Dec 1838; Samuel P. Merrit, Wm. Wilkinson, bm.

Brewer, Asbury & Elizabeth Mason, 2 Dec 1854; J. W. Carr, bm; m 3 Dec 1854 by J. W. Carr, J. P.

Brewer, Edmond & Susan Bolar, 13 Oct 1831; Benjamin Wheely, bm.

Brewer, Ezekiel & Biddy Morris, 7 June 1796; no bm.

Brewer, Manley M. & Martha A. Kirkland, 22 Dec 1866; Stephen A. Andrews, Geo. W. Bruce, bm; m 23 Dec 1866 by Manly Andrews.

31

Brewer, Newit & Caty Loyd, 28 April 1786; Owen Loyd, bm.

Brewer, Stephen W. & Cornelia King, 30 Aug 1864; James J. Allen, bm; m 30 Aug 1864 by N. W. Wilson.

Brewer, Silvanus & Mary Edwards, 30 March 1793; Silvanus Edwards, Robert Gee, bm.

Brewer, Silvanus & Mary Cates, 30 Nov 1797; Thomas Brewer, bm.

Brewer, Thomas & Nancy Loyd, 23 Jan 1789.

Brewer, Thos. & Nancy Grissam, 26 Aug 1811; R. Smith, bm.

Brewer, William & Beddy King, 27 Dec 1814; Jno Street, bm.

Brewer, William & Nancy Lloyd, 16 May 1818; Thos. Lloyd, bm.

Brewer, William & Sarah Lloyd, 22 Nov 1820; John H. Oneal, bm.

Brewer, William & Mary Ann Turner, 4 Dec 1849; A. J. Perry, bm.

Briant, Williamson & Nancy Picket, 29 Nov 1794; Henry Trice, bm.

Bridges, Benjamin & Winnefred Brown, 23 Jan 1810; Thomas Weaver, bm.

Bridges, Benjamin & Nancy Hunter, 9 Jan 1821; Joseph Brewer, bm.

Bridges, William & Winney Thorn, 29 Aug 179_; John Rhodes, bm.

Bridges, Young & Isabella Evans, 23 April 1840; William B. Sanders, bm.

Briggs, James & Nancy Hunter, 2 June 1822; John Johnston, bm.

Brinkley, Abner & Cynthia Medlin, 15 June 1821; William Hall, bm.

Brinkley, Alexander & Belza Mangum, 22 Nov 1836; Green A. Mangum, bm.

Brinkley, Alfred & Margret Ellis, 10 Feb 1831; Thomas Roberts, bm.

Brinkley, Bumpass & Elizabeth Jinkins, 13 Jan 1824; William Jinkins, bm.

Brinkley, Crasley & Rosanna Simpson, 18 March 1798; Wm. Banes, bm.

Brinkley, Isham & Nelly Duke, 13 Nov 1824; Dempsy Parrish, bm.

Brinkley, Jas. & Letha Adcocks, 18 Aug 1864; James C. Brinkley, bm; m 19 Aug 1864 by Wm. J. Roberts, J. P.

Brinkley, John & Polly Yoakley, 12 March 1835; Willie Wheeler, D. C. Parrish, bm.

Brinkley, Richard & Elizabeth Dollar, 26 July 1817; William Horton, bm.

Brinkley, Robert & Elizabeth Low, 29 Dec 1810; Jno Low, bm.

Brinkley, Robt. & Polley Mangum, 29 April 1805; Charles Parish, bm.

Brinkly, William & Margaret Cambell, 1 July 1813; Robt. Campbell, bm.

Bristow, Dolon & Elizabeth Haughton, 13 June 1835; Anthony Doherty, A. J. Davie, bm.

Bristow, John & Sarah Woods, 13 Nov 1802; Jesse Blalock, bm.

Bristow, William & Delilah Thomas, 25 Dec 1810; Moses Thomas, bm.

Briten, Benjamin & Cumfott Dunnagan, 30 July 1785; Sherid Dunnagan, bm.

Britt, William & Susan Glenn, 16 April 1833; Robert M. Graham, Sampson B. Glenn, bm.

Brittan, Joseph & Dolley Horner, 8 March 1786; James Hunter, bm.

Brockwell, Anderson & Polley Pickett, 30 Dec 1830; Thomas C. Davis, bm.

Brockwell, Andrew J. & Elizabeth Blalock, 19 April 1866; Joseph Reese, bm; m 19 April 1866 by A. C. Murdoch, J. P.

Brockwell, Archd. & Betsy Horn, 20 March 1815; John Scarlett, bm.

Brockwell, Archibald & Ellender Pond, 30 July 1801; Thomas Wynn, bm.

Brockwell, Benjamin & Sarah Brockwell, 17 Nov 1850; John H. McDade, bm.

Brockwell, Edmund & Lotty Rhodes, 25 June 1803; Mark Barbee, bm.

Brockwell, Hutson & Ann Proctor, 15 April 1857; J. A. Jenkins, bm; m 16 April 1857 by J. B. McDade, J. P., at Chapel Hill.

Brockwell, Jackson & Frances Warren, 19 Oct 1857; J. H. McDade, bm; m 20 Oct 1857 by W. H. Pratt, J. P.

Brockwell, Jas. W. & Elizabeth An Rhue, 23 Jan 1856; Willie G. Guess, bm.

Brockwell, John & Rachel Warren, 10 Jan 1832; Wm. Brockwell, Isaac Maden, bm.

Brockwell, John & Lucindy Carden, 27 Feb 1850; William W. Guess, bm.

Brockwell, John & Nancy Parrish, 13 Aug 1857; J. Y. Watson, bm; m 15 Aug 1857 by D. Tilley, J. P.

Brockwell, John & Harriet Hunt, 5 Nov 1860; Levi Pendergrass, bm.

Brockwell, Thos & Betsey Ann Brockwell, 25 Nov 1858; Wayne H. McDade, bm.

Brockwell, William & Polly Couch, 5 May 1828; Alfred Batchelor, bm.

Brockwell, William & Ellen Davis, 5 Dec 1849; Benjamin Brockwell, bm.

Brockwell, Wiot & Charlotte Deserne, 1 April 1819; Geo. Coplay, bm.

Brockwell, Wyatt & Nancy Woods, 20 April 1802; Burwell Henry, bm.

Brockwell, Wyatt & Nancy Desern, 30 March 1805; Thomas Christian, bm.

Brodnax, John W. & Susannah M. Ruffin, 9 Oct 1848; Pride Jones, bm.

Brogdon, William & Rebecca Ryecroft, 19 Feb 1820; John Young, bm.

Brookes, Iveson J. W. & Susan D. Roberts, 28 Jan 1850; John A. Watlington, bm.

Brooks, Albert G. & Sarah A. Blackwell, 29 Dec 1866; William A. Blalock, bm; m 3 Jan 1867 by R. G. Tinnin.

Brooks, Isaac & Burchess Beebe, 13 Nov 1834; Sam. Child, bm.

Brooks, William & Mary Moore, 4 Dec 1794; James Moore, bm.

Broome, Melus & Polley Harris, 21 Nov 1812; J. Taylor, bm.

Browder, William D., son of William & Sally Browder, & Anna Whitted, dau. of Martin Whitted & Margaret Estes, colored, m 12 March 1868 by W. R. Gaultney.

Brown, Absolem Y. & Mildred Dunegan, 7 Oct 1848; John E. Brown, bm.

Brown, Allen & Lettice Clark, 15 Jan 1840; Wm. Cabe, William Long, bm.

Brown, Asaph & Nancy Tart, 10 June 1828; Dowd Tart, bm.

Brown, Asaph & Martha Williams, 3 Jan 1860; Thomas V. White, bm; m 3 Jan 1860 by W. H. Brown, J. P.

Brown, Bennet & Lessy Maize, 1 March 1837; Ma. Co. Herndon, bm.

Brown, Brantley & Lucy A. Smith, 28 Nov 1854; E. D. Oakley, David B. McKee, bm; m 14 Dec 1854 by H. Terry, J. P.

Brown, Chesley O., son of Wilson & Eliza J. Brown, & Sarah Card, dau. of Martha Card, m 19 Dec 1867 by A. C. Hunter, J. P.

Brown, Conrod & Nelly Smith, 23 Aug 1827; Eli Staly, bm.

Brown, Daniel & Nancy Booth, 30 Oct 1851; Greer Stes(?), bm; m 30 Nov 1851 by W. J. Hogan, J. P.

Brown, Evans & Jane Smith, 20 March 1850; Henry Brown, bm.

Brown, George & Rebecca Stevens, 11 Dec 1811; Hugh Wilson, bm.

Brown, George & Polly Brinkley, 9 Nov 1825; John Lashly, bm.

Brown, Henry & Letta Ray, 2 Dec 1866; John M. Morris, bm; m 2 Dec 1866 by Alvis Durham, J. P.

Brown, Henry N. & Margaret Hooker, 24 July 1855; Thos. J. Strayhorn, bm; m 25 July 1855 by L. K. Willie.

Brown, James & Peggy Buckum, 8 Feb 1817; Joshua Bukum, bm.

Brown, James & Nancy Carden, 25 April 1825; Nathaniel Critcher, bm.

Brown, James & Nancy Ann Wix, 15 Jan 1848; Mark Fowler, John D. Williams, bm.

Brown, James & Louisey Smith, 1 March 1850; William Brown, bm.

Brown, James & Elizabeth Pickett, 7 Jan 1857; Wm. Barton, Wm. McLane, bm; m 8 Jan 1857 by Richison Nichols, J. P.

Brown, James P. & Muram Hart, 12 May 1834; Stephen Horn, bm.

Brown, Jas. R. & Rebecca Parker, 13 Aug 1824; Wm. Dunigan, bm.

Brown, Jefferson & Sally Lipscomb, 26 June 1866; John Lipscomb, bm; m 27 June 1866 by R. H. J. Blount, J. P.

Brown, Jehu & Jemima Burton, 30 Aug 1827; Moses McCown, bm.

Brown, Jesse & Pheobe R. Berry, 4 Jan 1856; W. H. Ross, bm; m 10 Jan 1856 by C. Wilson, J. P.

Brown, Jesse T. & Polly Proctor, 9 July 1828; Bennett Brown, bm.

Brown, Joel & Ann Barnes, 14 July 1792; Andrew Morrow, bm.

Brown, John & Anne Ivey, 30 Aug 1785; Alexander Moore, bm.

Brown, John & Salley Cabe, 9 Feb 1816; John Cabe, bm.

Brown, John & Charity Woods, 19 Jan 1822; James Leathers, bm.

Brown, John & Jane Hunter, 31 Aug 1839; Daniel Cable, bm.

Brown, John & Catharine Gates, 15 April 1848; Kinchen Leathers, David Brown, bm.

Brown, John M. & Mary A. Fowler, 22 Nov 1853; J. F. Hogan, bm.

Brown, Joseph & Martha E. Dunnagan, 14 March 1849; John L. Brown, bm.

Brown, Levi & Poly Linn, 7 May 1823; Abraham Kime, bm.

Brown, London & Winnefred Jinkins, 4 March 1799; William Jinkins, bm.

Brown, Mathw. & Elizabeth Cate, 16 Nov 1815; George Finley, bm.

Brown, Robert & Elizabeth Leathers, 27 April 1847; Burton Ray, bm.

Brown, Solomon & Hannah Cantol, 2 April 1791; William Brown, bm.

Brown, Thomas & Salley Morris, 15 Dec 1795; William Davis, bm.

Brown, Thos. & Ann Dannelly, 22 July 1805; James Danieley, bm.

Brown, William & Ruth Piper, 13 March 1783; John Piper, bm.

Brown, William & Lydia Garrison, 23 Jan 1793; Jacob Garrison, bm.

Brown, William & Martha Moore, 21 March 1800; James Moore, bm.

35

Brown, William & Elizabeth Craig, 18 May 1825; B. Cheek, bm.

Brown, William & Cythia Chizenhall, 25 Nov 1830; Bennet Brown, D. Booker, bm.

Brown, William & Marian Mitchel, 18 Sept 1835; John Hopkins, bm.

Brown, Wilson & Eliza Rainey, 26 Dec 1840; John L. Holloway, Norwood Latta, bm.

Brown, Wilson & Mary Gill, 19 April 1849; James Gill, Samuel Jones, bm.

Brownen, Thomas & Levinah Peelor, 14 June 1792; Benjamin Peelor, bm.

Browning, Alvin & Louisa Rhew, 4 March 1836; David Whitaker, bm.

Browning, Anderson & Leah Redmon, 30 Dec 1830; John Turner, Henry Wood, bm.

Browning, Andrew & Polley Scoggins, 2 Nov 1822; John Browning, bm.

Browning, Benjamin & Mary Ann Horn, 26 Jan 1833; Anthony Cole, bm.

Browning, Edmd. & Patsey Proctor, 22 Oct 1830; Joseph Dollar, bm.

Browning, Edmond & Jeany Martin, 9 March 1811; Simon Davis, bm.

Browning, Edmund & Milley Williams, 26 March 1802; Benjamin Peeler, bm.

Browning, George & Susannah Tatum, 13 May 1816; A. Clements, R. Penny, bm.

Browning, George & Rachael Couch, 8 Jan 1839; John Vickers, John Browning, bm.

Browning, Humphrey R. & Jane Hincye, 24 Dec 1836; ___ Cafe, bm.

Browning, Isaiah & Catherine Holt, 8 Aug 1795; Thomas Browning, bm.

Browning, James & Polley Hicks, 28 Sept 1820; R. Haughton, bm.

Browning, James & Elizabeth Redman, 15 Nov 1820; Francis H. Reeder, bm.

Browning, Jefferson & Hawkins Gilbert, 15 Jan 1855; Thomas O. Ferrel, bm.

Browning, John & Sally Grimes, 14 Feb 1808; William Rhodes, bm.

Browning, John & Betsy Grimes, 7 March 1822; Cader Peeler, bm.

Browning, Mark & Livina Woods, 7 Feb 1802; Wm. Turner, bm.

Browning, Simpson & Betsy Ann Jeffreys, 2 July 1859; David C. Warren, bm; m 3 July 1859 by B. C. Hopkins, J. P.

Browning, Thomas F. & Francis McCadams, 24 June 1847; G. M. Lea, bm.

Browning, Turner & Alsey Hutchins, 29 Aug 1837; John Browning, D. W. Hicks, bm.

Browning, William & Margret Rhodes, 13 May 1800; James Copley, Jno. Taylor, bm.

Browning, William & Delilah Shaw, 20 Sept 1815; Samuel Peelor, bm.

Browning, William & Nelly Carroll, 24 June 1832; James Browning, Wm. Warren, bm.

Browning, William & Elizabeth Extore, 20 Nov 1848; Benford F. Futch, bm.

Browning, William & Etney Scoggins, 14 April 1856; M. H. Turner, bm; m 16 April 1856 by Wm. McCown, J. P.

Browning, William A. & Elizabeth A. Cain, 11 Oct 1860; Thomas Webb, bm; m 12 Oct 1860 by John F. Lyon, J. P.

Bruce, George W. & Harriett Faucett, 14 May 1831; Thos. Clancy, bm.

Bruce, George W. & Elizabeth Davis, 21 June 1843; Jas. M. Pane, Leroy Johnston, bm.

Bruce, John & Louisa Tarbe, 18 Oct 1816; Francis Child, Henry Thomson, bm.

Bryan, James & Catharine Robinson, 12 June 1797; Michael Robinson, bm.

Bryan, James & Elizabeth Neely, 8 May 1798; Samuel Turrentine, bm.

Bryan, James & Martha Blanchet, 26 Feb 1828; Joseph Kirkpatrick, bm.

Bryan, Samuel & Margaret Steel, 11 Aug 1784; John Morrow, bm.

Bryan, William & Nancy Rider, 15 Sept 1821; Michael Ray, bm.

Bryant, Benjamin & Mary Cook, 17 Nov 1835; Alvis Cheek, bm.

Bryant, Mark & Salley Whittaker, 28 Jan 1823; Dempsy Pickett, bm.

Bryant, William & Nancy Shepperd, 5 Oct 1856; Willis Monk, Richd. Jones, bm.

Bryen, David & Nancy Roney, 4 Oct 1796; David McCanles, bm.

Bryen, John & Margaret Roney, 30 April 1796; David McCanles, bm.

Bryen, Thomas & Polly Baker, 20 Nov 1794; John Matthews, bm.

Buchannan, Thomas & Mary Murdoch, 17 June 1786; James Mordach, bm.

Buckingham, Joseph & Hailey Bukum, 29 June 1816; John Bukham, bm.

Bull, Richd. & Anne Anderson, 10 Sept 1788; Saml. Scott, bm.

Bullock, John & Elizabeth Wolf, 2 Feb 1789; John Bullock, bm.

Bullock, John & Cornelia Lewis, 6 Dec 1848; Thos. C. Davis, bm.

Bunch, Henry & Polley Cole, 19 March 1806; Stephen Pritchard, bm.

Bunch, Henry & Nelly Laycock, 12 Aug 1808; Thomas Holloway, bm.

Burch, Oliver L. & Cornelia R. Lewis, 28 Oct 1833; John Lewis, bm.

Burch, William & Elizabeth Hopkins, 23 Nov 1835; John Hopkins, Jas. J. Carrington, bm.

Burch, William & Martha Denson, 2 Oct 1839; Bisha Fossett, Tho. Anderson, bm.

Burch, Wm. H. & Margarett B. Long, 26 Jan 1856; Andrew J. King, bm; m 26 Jan 1856 by James Phillips, Presbyterian minister.

Burch, Zachariah & Mary Davis, 3 Feb 1826; Moss S. Pratt, bm.

Burgess, William & Nancy Carson, 12 March 1834; Thomas C. Davis, bm.

Burgis, William & Elizabeth Pendergrass, 2 March 1865; William A. Gattis, bm.

Burke, Archd. & Sally Johnston, 7 Dec 1830; Madison Burke, bm.

Burke, John & Catey Barlow, 1 Dec 1802; Thomas Barlow, bm.

Burkhead, Lingun & Sarah S. Utley, 31 Aug 1854; A. M. Shipp, T. A. Long, bm.

Burn, Thomas & Nancy Herenton, 25 May 1797; Jas Byrn, William Ray, bm.

Burnes, George W. & Elizabeth Leoy, 27 June 1846; Peter M. Montgomery, bm.

Burnes, Gideon & Anney Lashly, 12 June 1848; Alford G. Curnes, Zilphas G. Miller, bm.

Burnet, Wm. & Vicey Croker, 8 Feb 1837; John Hammond, bm.

Burnett, Alcey & Nancy Burnett, 26 Jan 1825; Samuel Jeffries, bm.

Burnett, Anderson & Catharine Swayne, colored, 16 March 1866; William Morrow, bm.

Burnett, Ellicksander & Elizabeth Herndon, 5 Jan 1793; Pomfrett Herndon, John Strowd, bm.

Burnett, Fearrington & Polly Herndon, 19 Dec 1814; Dan Burnett, bm.

Burnett, George, son of Cornelia Burnett, & Tempy Archey, dau. of Stephen & Lydia Archey, colored, m 6 Nov 1867 by Wiatt Cates, J. P.

Burnett, Henry & Cresie Husbands, 3 Feb 1817; Sam. Noe, bm.

Burnett, John & Mary Archey, 4 March 1859; William Mays, bm.

Burnett, William & Angeline Gowen, 21 Aug 1858; William Mays, John Rowland, bm.

Burnitt, Josiah & Jenney Herndon, 9 March 1799; Alex Burnett, bm.

Burns, Andw. & Martha Craig, 27 March 1798; Johnston Craig, bm.

Burns, Daniel & Polly Mallaby, 7 Sept 1826; James Allison, bm.

Burnside, James & Mary Elenor Odaniel, 12 Dec 1846; James Burnsides, bm.

Burnside, Robert & Elizabeth Durbin, 14 Aug 1793; Thos Bain, bm.

Burnside, Robert & Fanny Taylor, 27 Jan 1808; Jas. Lasslie, Wm. Woods, bm.

Burnside, Thomas & Anne Love, 18 July 1782; Isaac Geddiss, bm.

Burnsides, Benj. & Sarah Newman, 17 Nov 1799; H. Faucett, bm.

Burnwatts, James & Debby Weaver, 5 Jan 1809; John Weaver, bm.

Burridge, Edward & Mary Peeler, 30 March 1810; Benjn. Carroll, bm.

Burroughs, Thomas T. & Amelia H. Patterson, 22 Jan 1829; Geo. M. Johnston, bm.

Burrougs, James & Mary White, 18 March 1823; T. Long, bm.

Burrow, Ephraim & Marean Hirmon, ___ 1815; Leonard Harmon, bm.

Burrow, John & Margaret Piper, 3 May 1788; Alexander Piper, Wm. McCauley, bm.

Burrughs, John & Lucinda P. Atkins, 9 May 1835; Loften __, bm.

Burt, Maguire & Mary Ann Campbell, 17 July 1835; Daniel Cowan, bm.

Burt, Pascal & Mariah Panthea Johnston, 2 Aug 1853; Isaac Hudson, bm; m 2 Aug 1853 by James Phillips, minister of the Gospel.

Burton, Culbert & Christian Unter, 12 Dec 1795; William Wood, bm.

Burton, David & Fanny Wood, 28 Feb 1792; William Wood, Cutbud Burton, bm.

Burton, John & Jemima Cabe, 13 Feb 1825; James Cardin, bm.

Burton, John C. & Nancy Piper, 20 Dec 1848; John L. Brown, bm.

Burton, Laurence T. & Luniza Horton, 6 Jan 1836; Willie Norner, Nathl. Bain, bm.

Burton, Thos & Peggy Porterfield, 10 April 1827; Hugh Woods, bm.

Burton, Wilie & Mahala E. Miller, 11 Jan 1867; Thos C. Rountree, bm; m 17 Jan 1867 by Thos. Wilson, J. P.

Burton, William & Polley Cabe, 22 July 1822; Martin Murphey, bm.

Burton, William H. & Elizabeth Southerland, 5 March 1799; David Glenn, bm.

Burton, Willie & Nancy A. Cheek, m 24 June 1857 by Calvin E. Smith, J. P.

Bushop, William & Nancy Ray, 10 Dec 1807; John Roach, bm.

Busick, Caleb & Kesiah Busick, 8 Nov 1814; James Busick, bm.

Busick, Caleb & Sarah Morton, 23 Nov 1846.

Busick, Gabriel P. & Catey Sauls, 8 March 1806; John Busick, bm.

Butler, Absalom & Edy Pratt, 13 Dec 1810; Andrew Borland, bm.

Bynum, Augustus W. & Mary E. Winningham, 10 May 1840; Jehiel Atwater, bm.

Bynum, Kerney, son of Kerney & Margaret Bynum, & Mary C. Atwater, dau. of Jehial & Martha Atwater, m 19 Sept 1867 by W. H. Bobbitt.

Bynum, Luther B. & Saphronia J. Atwater, 2 March 1861; C. C. Atwater, bm; m 19 March 1861 by L. Burnett, minister.

Bynum & Charity, freedmen, 17 Nov 1865; Lewis, a freedman, bm.

Byrd, Edmund & Nancy Bass, 3 June 1838; Ezekiel Tinen, bm.

Byrd, Edmpson & Ellen Hart, 31 Aug 1835; William Heartt, bm.

Byrd, James & Polly Vincent, 21 Nov 1814; Will McCawley, bm.

Byrd, Thomas & Nancy Hamilton, 17 Dec 1824; Thos. Baner, bm.

Cabe, John & Nancy Moreland, 7 Dec 1802; Thos Reding, bm.

Cabe, John & Levina Brown, 5 April 1819; Wm. Brown, bm.

Cabe, John & Elizabeth Horner, 29 Aug 1822; Wm. Barton, Wm. McCauley, bm.

Cabe, John & Betsey Corethers, 27 Jan 1847; Solm. S. Faucett, bm.

Cabe, Jno. & Mary Streyhorn, 15 Feb 1786; Alexr. Borland, bm.

Cabe, William & Jane Link, 29 Jan 1841; Walter A. Norwood, Hiram Hansbrough, bm.

Cabe, William & Lueny Tilly, 9 Jan 1850; Samuel H. Breeze, John C. Burton, bm.

Cabe, Wm. & Jemima Piper, 23 Feb 1793; A. Tatom, bm.

Cabel, Maben & Elizabeth Huffman, 22 Nov 1848; Jacob Hufmon, bm.

Cable, Vallentine & Polly Summers, 6 Nov 1833; Jacob Huffman, bm.

Caffey, Charles & Nancy Lewis, 27 Nov 1811; John Hill, bm.

Cagen, William & Sally Ringstaff, 27 Feb 1851; Copeland Riley, bm.

Cain, Abel & Melinda Rhodes, 8 Dec 1831; Allen Cain, bm.

Cain, Allen & Mary Hester, 18 Feb 1792; Walter Alves, bm.

Cain, Allen & Susanna Carpenter, 24 Oct 1795; David Sloan, bm.

Cain, Allen & Elizabeth Scarlet, 29 Oct 1798; John Scarlett, bm.

Cain, Allen & Elizabeth Woods, 2 Jan 1829; Thomas Ward, bm.

Cain, Archibald & Parthenia Woods, 22 Dec 1827; W. Bradshaw, Levi McCollum, bm.

Cain, Archibald & Parthena Wood, 3 Oct 1828; Allen Cain, bm.

Cain, Hugh & Sarah Allen, 7 Dec 1809; Wm. Carrington, bm.

Cain, James & Elisabeth McKinly, 21 Dec 1781; William Cain Junr., bm.

Cain, Peter & Rebecca Jones, 8 Feb 1867; John A. Utley, bm; m 11 Feb 1867 by Thos. C. Hayes.

Cain, Willi & Elizabeth James, 23 Feb 1836; Jas. R. Carrington, bm.

Cain, William & Salley Dudley, 28 May 1783.

Cain, William & Mary Wilkins, 28 Dec 1839; Ellert Dosett, bm.

Cain, William & Mary Wilkins, 15 Oct 1842; Benton Ray, Archibald Nichols, bm.

Cain, William Jr. & Sarah J. Bailey, 21 July 1846; Henry Y. Webb, T. Ruffin Jr., bm.

Calder, Alexander & Margaret Lowry, 29 Feb 1792; Robert Scobey, bm.

Caldwell, Anthony & Nancy T. Walton, 29 Dec 1864; Thomas N. Williams, bm; m 29 Dec 1864 by A. C. Murdoch, J. P.

Caldwell, John & Martha Gattis, 1 June 1782; Charles Johnston, bm.

Caldwell, John & Hellen Hooper, 17 Aug 1809; Walter Alves, bm.

Caldwell, Joseph & Sarah Woody, 26 Jan 1823; Joseph Caldwell, bm.

Caldwell, Tod R. & Minerva Cain, 16 Dec 1840; R. B. Ruffin, James Webb Jr., bm.

Caldwell, Wilson & Susan Kirby, 27 Sept 1866; J. R. Clements, William Barham, bm; m 27 Sept 1866 by F. M. Hubbard, Rector of the Chapel of the Cross, Chapel Hill.

Cale, William & Jane Latta, 15 Jan 1863; Richard M. Jones, bm; m 22 Jan 1863 by W. S. Strayhorn, J. P.

Calisles, James & Nelly Fogleman, 2 Dec 1840; John Gurthrie, bm.

Callaway, Silas & Emeline Mebane, 18 Dec 1865; John W. Ray, bm; m 21 Dec 1865 by Wilson Brown, J. P.

Cameron, Archibald & Barbara Sharp, 6 May 1815; Jno Holt, bm.

Cameron, Archibald & Silvy Cameron, 21 Nov 1866; Plummer Tansel, bm.

Cameron, Dun. & Rebecca Benehan, 23 Nov 1802; Jno. Taylor, bm.

Cameron, Duncan & Nancey Winters, 5 May 1822; Frederic Kimry, bm.

Cameron, J. D. & Rebecca C. Waddell, 8 Nov 1848; H. M. Waddel, bm.

Cameron, Jno. A. & Lucy Martin, 20 March 1864; J. B. Hardy, bm; m 21 March 1864 by James Phillips, minister.

Cameron, Paul C. & Anne Ruffin, 20 Dec 1832; J. Taylor, bm.

Cameron, Stephen & Elisabeth Wells, 14 Feb 1805; Stephen Wells, bm.

Cameron, William & Emma Moore, 5 Dec 1837; J. M. Giles, bm.

Campbel, Jas. A. & Janee Prather, 26 Dec 1807; Alexdr. Russell, bm.

Campbell, Archd. & Rebeccah Kirk, 24 Feb 1784; Lewis Kirk, bm.

Campbell, Archd. & Martha Baldwin, 18 May 1864; James Parks, Alfred Baldwin, bm; m 18 May 1864 by Thos. Long, J. P.

Campbell, David & Betsey Flinthorn, 1 Oct 1817; Jacob Stout, bm.

Campbell, Dunkin & Letitia Ray, 27 April 1841; Chaplen Merritt, bm.

Campbell, Emanuel & Ruth Beavers, 24 Dec 1838; Hugh Edwards, Jehu M. Beever, bm.

Campbell, George & Susanah Mebane, 29 April 1802; Adam Sharp, bm.

Campbell, Henry & Charity Ray, 19 Oct 1842; William Ray, bm.

Campbell, James & Jeany King, 21 Feb 1803; Elijah Perry, bm.

Campbell, James & Jane Womble, 25 Jan 1841; James Watson, bm.

Campbell, James & Hulday Crabtree, 16 Feb 1843; Leroy Johnston, James Crabtree, bm.

Campbell, John & Jenny Pickard, 30 March 1810; Robert Woody, bm.

Campbell, Moses & Susan Baker, 21 July 1812; James Jones, bm.

Campbell, Richd. & Hannah Carter, 7 March 1809; William Johnson, bm.

Campbell, William & Sally Daniel, 2 Oct 1827; Saml. T. Tillinghast, bm.

Campbell, William & Ruth Ann Smith, 30 June 1833; Samuel Holemon, John J. Fredric, bm.

Canady, Ruffin & Mary Adams, 5 July 1855; J. Y. Watson, bm; m 5 July 1855 by Jones Watson, J. P.

Cannada, Ruffin & Margaret Adams, 5 Sept 1865; Thomas M. Faucett, William H. Adams, bm; m 10 Sept 1865 by N. C. Cate, J. P.

Cannady, Isaac G. & Margaret L. Coggin, 13 Dec 1860; J. B. Green, Tho. B. Lyon Jr., bm; m 18 Dec 1860 by Elder Andrew N. Hall.

Cannady, Nathaniel E., son of Wyatt and Elizabeth Cannady, & Salla A. Faucett, dau. of David & Mary A. Faucett, 28 Nov 1867; m 19 Dec 1867 by C. G. Markham, J. P.

Canter, Joseph & Milly Capps, 30 April 1827; James Capps, bm.

Cantral, Jones & Patsey Britt, 6 Feb 1828; Joseph Canter, James Capps, bm.

Cantral, Zeb. & Polley Morrow, 13 Feb 1792; John Dunavin, bm.

Cantril, Benjamin & Sophiah Robbs, 1 Jan 1795; William Cantril, bm.

Cantril, Thomas & Betsey Moring, 13 Feb 1795; William Fossett, bm.

Cape, Doctor & Rebecca Hinchey, 28 June 1836; William C. Christmas, bm.

Cape, Redding & Susan Cape, 12 March 1836; C. C. Smith, James Cheek, bm.

Capland, Abner & Frances Peniston, 15 Aug 1860; Samuel Couch, John Parker, bm; m 16 Aug 1860 by Samuel Couch, J. P.

Capps, Casin & Polly Rogers, 4 Dec 1792; Wm. Trousdall, bm.

Capps, James R. & Polley Tier, 24 Dec 1832; J. C. Turrentine, bm.

Capps, Robert & Mary Stout, 9 Nov 1825; Aaron Stout, bm.

Car, John Westly & Julian Armstrong, 1 Nov 1866; John C. Bingham, bm; m 1 Nov 1866 by Alvis Durham, J. P.

Card, John & Patsy Cheek, 14 Aug 1810; Paul Kinnion, bm.

Carddin, John & Mary Ann Stephens, 23 Oct 1827; George W. Brown, bm.

Cardel, Washington & Charlott Yeancy, 26 Dec 1861; Charles Davis, T. W. Laws, bm.

Carden, George & Lucretia Gilbert, 28 Oct 1848; John Brockwell, Jno. D. Carlton, bm.

Carden, Ishmael J. & Cornealia J. Cheek, 8 Feb 1854; George Brown, bm; m 9 Feb 1854 by Thos. Lynch, minister.

Carden, John & Patsy Carden, 6 Jan 1800; Campbell Sutton, bm.

Carden, John & Frances Marcom, 9 Feb 1866; Nathan Carlton, bm; m 11 Feb 1866 by John Burroughs, J. P.

Carden, Jones & Mary Crowder, 17 March 1805; Campbell Sutton, bm.

Carden, Pressly & Blatha C. Brown, 21 Feb 1840; William Brown, John Allison, bm.

Carden, Simpson & Julia A. Thompson, 16 Oct 1856; Silas Carden, bm; m 17 Oct 1856 by Wm. W. McCown, J. P.

Carden, Westley & Elizabeth Coply, 6 Sept 1837; James Williams, Thomas Anderson, bm.

Carden, Wiley & Mary Shaw, 14 March 1848; ___, bm.

Carden, William H. & Sarah C. Woods, 21 March 1862; W. S. Clinton, bm; m 23 March 1862 by Wm. F. Duke, J. P.

Carden, William N. & Mary A. F. Warren, 13 Dec 1854; m 21 Dec 1854 by Jno. Hancock, J. P.

Cardin, James & Arkridge Cardin, 10 May 1825; Jones Cardin, bm.

Cardin, James & Clare Shamley, 3 Feb 1831; Alfred Chamley, bm.

Cardin, John & Nancy Marlett, 9 July 1820; Matthew Crowder, bm.

Cardin, John & Polley Moore, 12 Feb 1825; John Cardin, bm.

Cardin, John W. & Ann Eliza Chamblee, 15 Feb 1859; W. G. Guess, bm; m 15 Feb 1859 by B. C. Hopkins, J. P.

Cardin, Paul & Frances Hailey, 23 March 1853; Jno. D. Lipscomb, bm; m 24 March 1853 by Wm. Lipscomb, J. P.

Cardin, Robert & Nancy Girldin Pettegrue, 15 Feb 1853; W. C. Cheek, William Cardin, bm.

Cardin, Silas & Elizabeth Bowersn, 5 Jan 1856; Giles Carden, R. M. Jones, bm; m 4 Jan 1856 by Wm. McCown, J. P.

Cardin, William & Elizabeth Jordan, 31 May 1848; John W. Cardin, bm.

Careathers, Jno. & Elizabeth Edwards, 17 Oct 1826; Haston Peo, bm.

Carethers, Wm. Gaston & Nancy Jane Durham, 21 Dec 1853; T. H. Robertson, bm.

Carey, Benjamin & Ester ODear, 4 Sept 1802; William Jenkins, bm.

Carey, Jordan & Salley Parker, 29 Aug 1831; William Horner, William Smith, bm.

Carey, Saml. & Sally Burgin, 5 Jan 1831; John Waggoner, bm.

Carleton, Lewis & Isabella Couch, 25 Dec 1866; Thomas Kerby, bm; m 27 Dec 1866 by John Borroughs, J. P.

Carlton, Daniel & Nancy Dannel, 29 June 1793; Thomas Christian, bm.

Carlton, Henry T. & Amelia Trice, 10 Oct 1835; Spencer Leigh, bm.

Carlton, John D. or William, & Jane Marcum, 7 Jan 1840; Thomas Anderson, Jno. D. Carlton, bm.

Carlton, John W. & Susan Gunter, 15 Dec 1866; Hiram Marcom, bm; m 20 Dec 1866 by B. C. Hopkins, J. P.

Carlton, Nathan & Nancy Davis, 11 April 1859; James Leech, bm; m 12 April 1859 by Jas. N. Patterson, J. P.

Carlton, Thomas Trice & Elizabeth Marcum, 25 Aug 1810; A. B. Bruce, bm.

Carlton, Wesley & Elizabeth Dixson, 20 Jan 1820; Willie Marcom, bm.

Carmichael, John H. & Nancy Stalcup, 9 Oct 1819; James Sutton, bm.

Carmichael, Levin & Susan Newman, 27 Jan 1842; John Dooly, John A. Cox, bm.

Carmikel, Archabel & Anne McClure, 24 Jan 1808; James Wilson, bm.

Carnal, Joshua & Sarah Dunn, 10 Sept 1830; John S. Moore, bm.

Carnal, Moses & Rebeckah Cozart, 18 Aug 1826; Riley Cozart, bm.

Caroll, Charles & Catharine Rainey, 8 April 1824; Archd. Carroll, bm.

Caroll, William & Nancy Medley, 1 Jan 1848; Ilai Copley, bm.

Carr, Alford & Martha E. Cate, 5 Oct 1866; Nathaniel King, bm; m 7 Oct 1866 by Thos. Long, J. P.

Carr, Henderson & Louisa Turrentine, colored, 22 Nov 1866; J. Henry Cates, bm; m 23 Dec 1866 by John C. Sykes, J. P.

Carr, John & Martha Baldwin, 17 March 1834; Michael Carroll, bm.

Carr, John W. & Elizabeth Bullock, 25 Dec 1839; James M. Palmer, James Sneed, bm.

Carr, Thomas & Elizabeth Tapp, 19 June 1866; George Mayo, bm; m 21 June 1866 by Wilson Brown, J. P.

Carragan, Edward & Margaret Paul, 29 Sept 1781; James Paul, bm.

Carragan, Hugh & Patsy Wood, 31 Oct 1835; James ___, David Cat, bm.

Carral, James & Nancy Barton, 10 Feb 1826; Willis Cheek, bm.

Carrall, Archibald Jr., & Eveline Rhodes, 5 Jan 1858; James Carrall, Thomas Webb, bm; m 5 Jan 1858 by Samuel Couch, J. P.

Carrall, Benjamin & Elizabeth Riley, 30 Jan 1856; John H. Dollar, Dudley Dollar, bm; m 1 Feb 1856 by John F. Lyon, J. P.

Carrall, Lemuel L. & Willey Ann Vaughan, 28 Sept 1864; John Laws, bm; m 2 Oct 1864 by Henry Gray, minister.

Carrall, Levi & Louisa Christian, 3 Nov 1860; Isreal Turner, bm; m 5 Nov 1860 by Solomon Shepherd, J. P.

Carrall, Stephen L. & Lydia Williams, 5 July 1854; Jno. M. Faucett, Henry J. Thompson, bm; m 6 July 1854 by Thos. Long, J. P.

45

Carrel, Alsey & Elizabeth Scarlett, 29 Dec 1825; W. Hudgins, bm.

Carrel, Benjamin & Nancey Peeler, 13 Jan 1786; Christian Peeler, bm.

Carrel, Charles & Edy Barbee, 27 Sept 1794; William Jenkens, bm.

Carrel, Wm. & Parthena Cain, 28 Nov 1856; J. R. Chamblee, bm; m 4 Dec 1856 by W. M. McCown, J. P.

Carrell, John & Patsy Cates, 26 May 1810; Isaiah Cate, bm.

Carrell, Moses & Elizabeth Workman, 10 Feb 1810; John Carroll, bm.

Carrell, Page & Mary Jane Jeffreys, 6 Dec 1862; Archd. Borland, bm.

Carrigan, see also Cagen

Carrigan, James & Jane Sample, 8 April 1786; John Carrigan, Jno. Mebane, bm.

Carrigan, John & Catey Sample, 16 Aug 1783.

Carrigan, Thomas W. & Ellen Jane Thomas, 7 Oct 1854; William W. Riley, bm.

Carrigan, William A. & Nancy M. Holt, 17 May 1827; Saml. L. Holt, bm.

Carrigan, William M. & Ann E. Moore, 15 June 1852; James C. Turrentine, bm; m 22 June 1852 by S. Milton Frost.

Carrigin, William & Aby Kirk, 12 June 1821; Berry Wesson, bm.

Carrigon, James & Margery Dobbs, 31 Jan 1791; Gining Gibson, bm.

Carrington, Alfred & Sarah Hall, 13 Sept 1820; Wms. D. Carrington, bm.

Carrington, Alfred & Drusilla Hopkins, 1 July 1826; Chuza Hopkins, bm.

Carrington, Archd. & Rachel Carrington, 13 Feb 1816; Isaac Rhew, bm.

Carrington, Ephraim & Priscilla Duke, 15 March 1811; Isaac Holden, bm.

Carrington, Ephraim & Rebecca Jones, 11 Dec 1852; Isham Parrish, bm.

Carrington, Ephraim & Manerva Ann Tilly, 2 Jan 1854; Thomas Adams, bm.

Carrington, Ephraim H. & Nancy Parrish, 2 Feb 1824; Green Davis, bm.

Carrington, James & Hanky Tilly, 28 Feb 1796; Robt. Horner, bm.

Carrington, James & Rachel Jones, 1 Oct 1808; Wm. Carrington Junr., bm.

Carrington, James & Catharine Carroll, 5 Jan 1841; Duke Glenn, Rchd. Horner, bm.

Carrington, James & Malindia A. Proctor, 18 April 1864; William Mangum, bm; m 18 April 1864 by Solomon Shepherd, J. P.

Carrington, Jas. H. & Areneah Carrington, 27 May 1800; George Carrington, bm.

Carrington, Jessey & Rebecca Chissenhall, 9 Aug 1816; John D. Carrington, bm.

Carrington, John & Fanny Carrington, 20 Jan 1810; Jehu Lee Jr., bm.

Carrington, John & Jeany Smith, 29 Jan 1816; Thomas Bradshaw, Robert Cates, bm.

Carrington, John & Polley Ashley, 29 April 1818; Benjn. Carrington, bm.

Carrington, John D. & Celia Jones, 5 Oct 1813; James Leathers, bm.

Carrington, Morgan & Elizabeth Latta, 23 Feb 1808; John Carrington, bm.

Carrington, Nathl. M. & Cynthia Mangum, 9 Feb 1826; N. H. Horton, bm.

Carrington, Thomas & Letha Parish, 20 Jan 1820; James Parrish, bm.

Carrington, William & Mary Garrard, 30 Dec 1797; Sharid Dunnagan, bm.

Carrington, William & Anne Jackson, 25 May 1822; William Lasley, bm.

Carrington, Wm. & Rachel Oneal, 6 Dec 1826; S. Hymer, bm.

Carrington, Wm. Junr & Salley May, 5 March 1804; Moses Dossett, bm.

Carrington, Wm. Junr. & Amelia Dunnagan, 28 May 1808; Isaac Rhew, bm.

Carrington, Wm. M. & Mary C. Southerland, 4 Nov 1865; Walter Edwards, bm; m 6 Nov 1865 by S. Umsted, L. Deacon.

Carrol, Charles & Nancy Cheek, 4 Jan 1796; John Williams, bm.

Carrol, Moses & Margaret Rhew, 3 Nov 1854; A. B. Pleasant, bm.

Carrol, Page & Vicey Riggins, 9 Aug 1819; George Stafford, William Glasson, bm.

Carroll, Archd. & Ester Warren, 22 Dec 1808; M. Guess, bm.

Carroll, Benja. & Pathenia Barbee, 18 Nov 1810; Samuel Cole, bm.

Carroll, Clemment & Ruth Thompson, 22 Dec 1829; Duke Glenn, bm.

Carroll, Eli & Sarah Turner, 6 June 1838; Wm. Browning, E. H. Carrington, bm.

Carroll, Eli Jr. & Ruthey Demaris Rhodes, 27 Feb 1861; A. J. Carroll, bm; m 27 Feb 1861 by Solomon Shepherd, J. P.

Carroll, James & Mary Lloyd, 25 June 1827; Moses Carroll, bm.

Carroll, John L. & Sarah G. Mitchell, 2 Nov 1865; John Cheek, bm; m 3 Nov 1865 by John Mitchell.

Carroll, Lemuel & Elizabeth Lloyd, 27 July 1804; Burres Estridge, bm.

Carroll, Stephen & Nancy Glenn, 24 Sept 1828; Payton C. Clin, Chas. Carroll, bm.

Carrolle, Nimrod & Rebecca Cole, 21 Dec 1807; Stephen Pritchard, bm.

Carson, Alexander & Elizabeth Clinton, 23 Feb 1819; Thos. W. Holden, bm.

Carson, John E. & Margaret Hunter, 25 Dec 1792; Matthew Hunter, bm.

Carson, John W. & Mary J. Batchelor, 4 July 1848; James P. Mason, bm.

Carson, Lemuel & Susan Edwards, 12 Dec 1855; T. E. Watson, bm; m 12 Dec 1855 by Durell Tilley, J. P.

Carson, Robert A. & Rebecca Clark, 20 Feb 1808; James Clancy, bm.

Carson, Solomon & Polley Scarlet, 6 Dec 1823; Stephen Scarlet, bm.

Carter, Brice & Anne Thompson, 17 March 1836; Albe J. Davie, bm.

Carter, Britian & Ruthe Bowdown, 19 July 1812; Jacob Johnston, bm.

Carter, Joseph & Mary Ann Carter, 17 Sept 1845; Jonathan Newlin, bm.

Carter, Nathaniel & Nancy Baker, 7 March 1801; Jno Taylor, Geo. Maden, bm.

Carter, Peterson & Polly Smith, 17 March 1862; Wesley Smith, bm.

Carter, Thomas & Ruth Edwards, 6 Nov 1795; Samuel Carter, bm.

Carter, Whitmel & Lucinda Albright, 8 Aug 1839; William P. Albright, Lewis Hobbs, bm.

Carter, William & Nelly Collins, 24 Feb 1806; Nathaniel Carter, bm.

Carter, William & Mary Bass, 26 Aug 1862; Nelson Rhew, bm.

Carter, William & Mary Hopkins, ___ Oct 1862.

Caruthers, William & Sally Edwards, 5 Nov 1816; Wm. Bailey, bm.

Cary, David & Theny Southerland, 4 Jan 1854; Minnick Mills, bm; m 8 Jan 1854 by Hezekiah Terry, J. P.

Cary, David & Nancy Faucett, 26 Feb 1861; Wilson Horner, Benton Ray, bm; m 3 March 1861 by Wm. J. Gray, J. P.

Cary, John & Anna G. Parker, 27 April 1864; A. M. Breeze, Thos. S. Jordan, bm; m 30 Apr 1860 by H. Terry, J. P.

Cary, William & Anzolett C. Cocke, 14 June 1860; Robert S. Anderson, bm; m 14 June 1860 by Hezekiah Terry, J. P.

Cash, Bryant & Elizabeth Adcock, 11 Sept 1819; Brewer King, bm.

Cash, James W. & Nancy Jane Teasley, 9 Jan 1865; D. T. Gordon, bm; m 15 Jan 1865 by B. C. Hopkins, J. P.

Cash, William & Samessinger Oakey, 15 Jan 1859; L. Meadows, bm.

Casle, John H. & Moriah Cane, 8 Dec 1847; Albert H. Casle, John Glenn, bm.

Castle, William & Jane Copeley, 7 Jan 1834; James Williams, John Glenn, bm.

Castlebeary, Joseph & Sarah Alman, 15 Dec 1827; Chesley M. Patterson, bm.

Castleberry, John & Catey Fennell, 2 Oct 1833; George Kelly, Francis Castleberry, bm.

Castleberry, Solomon & Delilah Hall, 22 May 1806; David Hall, bm.

Castlebery, Wm. C. & Rachel Pope, 23 Aug 1847; Joseph Boothe, bm.

Castlebury, Joseph & Nancy Hust, 1 Oct 1787; Thomas Hall, bm.

Cate, David & Mary Workman, 16 Aug 1809; Jesse Workman, bm.

Cate, David & Betsey Pender, 10 June 1824; John S. Cate, bm.

Cate, Ephram & Margaret Canady, 19 Oct 1793; James Kannedy, bm.

Cate, Ezra & Eleanor Thompson, 5 Nov 1819; Samuel Crawford, bm.

Cate, Harrison & Vina Teasley, 13 May 1835; William B. Williams, bm.

Cate, Henry A. & Delila Roberts, 11 Aug 1847; Henry Workman, bm.

Cate, Isaiah & Jane ODannel, 10 Feb 1794; John Faucett, bm.

Cate, James & Rebecca Cates, 1 Oct 1834; Wiatt Cate, bm.

Cate, James F. & Nancy M. Cate, 1 May 1855; James Gill, bm; m 2 May 1855 by Wiatt Cates, J. P.

Cate, Jehu & Susanah Deen, 20 April 1798; Robt Cate, bm.

Cate, Jehu M. & Margaret Rhue, 3 Oct 1849; James Holloway, Stephen Cate, bm.

Cate, Jeremiah & Susannah Cate, 26 March 1817; David Cate, bm.

Cate, Jesse & Sally Andrews, 15 Dec 1795; Henry Hastings, bm.

Cate, John & Nancy Beck, 27 Sept 1804; W. Fussell, bm.

Cate, John & Patsy Jackson, 8 April 1809; Richd Cate, bm.

Cate, Jno. & Hanny Smith, 27 Nov 1811; Andrew Collins, bm.

Cate, John & Polly Shears, 14 Aug 1820; John Carroll, Jacob Potts, bm.

Cate, Lazarus & Polley Nutt, 19 Nov 1826; Isaiah Cate, bm.

Cate, Mangum & Sally Conklin, 10 Oct 1849; John Crawford, bm.

Cate, Neverson C. & Sarah J. Hogan, 12 Oct 1858; Thomas J. Hogan, bm; m 12 Oct 1858 by Thos. Long, J. P.

Cate, Nevison & Salley Hunter, 5 June 1827; Tomas Cate, bm.

Cate, Peyton S. & Mary Ann Workman, 9 Sept 1834; Thos. C. Hayes, bm.

Cate, Ransom & Arena Andrews, 22 Sept 1835; Thomas A. Cate, bm.

Cate, Richard & Patsy Cooper, 15 Jan 1800; James Cate, bm.

Cate, Richard & Kesiah Cate, 5 May 1815; Burke Walker, bm.

Cate, Robert & Margret Carrigan, 13 Sept 1810; David Cate, bm.

Cate, Robert & Susannah Smith, 3 April 1824; John L. Cate, bm.

Cate, Solomon & Mary Cate, 22 March 1792; Stephen Cate, bm.

Cate, Solomon & Jane Nutt, 25 Jan 1823; William Caton, bm.

Cate, Solomon R. & Frances Roberts, 8 Aug 1849; William Sylls(?), James J. Cate, bm.

Cate, Stephen P. & Tillitha Garrett, 2 Nov 1859; Calvin Andrus, Thos Long, bm; m 3 Nov 1859 by Thos. Long, J. P.

Cate, Tho. & Martha Hastings, 12 Sept 1797; Elisha Cate, bm.

Cate, Thomas & Eastor Hastings, 30 July 1797; Henry Hastings, bm.

Cate, Thomas & Dicey Ledbetter, 2 Feb 1814; Bennett Ledbetter, bm.

Cate, Thomas & Nancy Cate, 11 June 1814; David Cate, bm.

Cate, Thomas & Patsey Mabrey, 24 April 1851; Abner Conklin, bm.

Cate, Thoms. & Nancy Sykes, 2 Jan 1839; Wm. Woodward, bm.

Cate, Thos. & Nancy Bailiff, 7 April 1803; John Bailiff, bm.

Cate, Thos. & Julie Morris, 27 Jan 1861; Hugh Edwards, bm; m 27 Jan 1861 by A. Edwards, J. P.

Cate, Thomas Junr. & Elizabeth Roach, 17 July 1805; Thomas Cate Sener, bm.

Cate, Thomas D. & Caroline Powell, 10 Dec 1841; Wiatt Cate, Moses Leathers Junr., bm.

Cate, Thomas J. & Jane Pickard, 23 Oct 1841; George Jackson, bm.

Cate, Thos. J. & Martha Cate, 29 Dec 1840; William Cate, bm.

Cate, Thomas S. & Martha Carrel, 9 Sept 1845; Nathaniel Jolly, bm.

Cate, Thomas S. & Sarah Ann Perry, 28 Dec 1848; Henry A. Sykes, bm.

Cate, William & Salley Berry, 26 July 1817; Thomas Berry, bm.

Cate, William & Polley Sykes, 7 Sept 1837; Eaton Walker, bm.

Cate, William D. & Jane Conklin, 30 July 1849; Thomas W. Pickard, bm.

Cate, Wm. Sanders & Susannah Cheek, 19 May 1838; Thos. C. Haynes, bm.

Cate, Willie N. & Elizabeth Pickard, 25 Aug 1857; Lafayette Pickard, Green Cate, bm.

Cates, Aaron & Nancy Andrews, 22 Sept 1821; Henry Andress, bm.

Cates, Abner & Stacey Turner, 18 Nov 1797; Ephraim Cates, bm.

Cates, Anderson & Rebecca Howard, 7 Nov 1836; John H. Crutch-field, Thos. C. Hayes, bm.

Cates, Anderson & Lucinda Sykes, 5 Dec 1848; John Kirk, bm.

Cates, Anderson P. & Mary E. Lloyd, 28 May 1861; T. W. Laws, bm; m 29 May 1861 by Wm. Cheek, J. P.

Cates, Barnnerd & Elenor Carrel, 2 July 1849; Thomas Cates, bm.

Cates, Benjamin & Elizabeth Cole, 23 Aug 1809; John Lynch, bm.

Cates, Bluford & Manurva Pope, 4 June 1854; John Thompson, bm; m 2 July 1854 by John F. Lyon, J. P.

Cates, E. J. & Dela J. Cates, 5 July 1856; W. N. Crowell, bm; m 6 July 1856 by A. B. Gunter, J. P.

Cates, Elisha & Huldah Cates, 3 July 1799; Thomas Cates, bm.

Cates, Ephraim & Rebecca Lindsey, 7 Oct 1803; John Bailiff, bm.

Cates, Ephraim & Rebecca Lindsey, 24 Aug 1804; Wm. Smith, bm.

Cates, Ephraim & Elizabeth J. Cates, 4 July 1850; E. S. Gray, bm.

Cates, Ephraim & Eliza Jane Copley, 31 July 1860; A. P. Cates, bm; m 1 Aug 1860 by Wiatt Cates, J. P.

Cates, Ezra & Polley Faucett, 2 Feb 1795; John Faucett, bm.

Cates, Green, son of Aaron & Nancy Cates, & Mary Webb, dau. of Wm. C. & Malinda Webb, m 22 Sept 1867 by Alvis Durham, J. P.

Cates, Henry A. & Elizabeth Ann Long, 24 Dec 1855; William P. Cate, bm.

Cates, Henry F., son of Thomas E. & Nancy E. Cates, & Mary E. Walker, dau. of John & Wady Walker, m 13 Oct 1867 by Wiatt Cates, J. P.

Cates, Isaac & Mary Miller, 7 Feb 1831; Jesse Miller, bm.

Cates, Isaiah & Rhoda Ray, m 22 Dec 1851 by Allen Edwards, J. P.

Cates, Isaiah & Jane Harris, 14 June 1855; Thomas Cates, John Dollar, bm; m 16 June 1855 by Charles Wilson, J. P.

Cates, Izra & Elcy Horn, 2 Feb 1804; William Horn, bm.

Cates, James & Martha Cates, 3 Aug 1860; Jno. Tilley, Jr., W. R. Tilley, bm; m 9 Aug 1860 by Jno. Hancock, J. P.

Cates, Jas. H. & Susan Miller, 9 Oct 1823; Richs. Nichols, bm.

Cates, James H. & Peggy D. Ray, 18 July 1819; H. W. Wilkins, bm.

Cates, Jim & Newdora Green, dau. of Edmund Green, m 2 Feb 1868 by D. W. Jordan, J. P.

Cates, Jno. & Iz. Cohorn, 31 Oct 1791; Tho. Hunt, bm.

Cates, John & Presilla Lloyd, 21 Nov 1797; William Roach, bm.

Cates, John & Lydia Rountree, 5 Nov 1799; Nathan Farmer, bm.

Cates, John & Nelly Laycock, 21 Dec 1813; William Leach, bm.

Cates, John & Holley Hawkins Hunt, 6 June 1840; James T. Terry, bm.

Cates, John E. & Eliza Jenet Reeves, 19 Jan 1861; H. N. Crabtree, bm; m 20 Jan 1861 by Thos. Long, J. P.

Cates, John J. & Louisa Gates, 30 March 1867; John Wagoner, H. B. Guthrie, bm; m 31 March 1867 by J. W. Mckee, J. P.

Cates, John M. & Martha Ann Clement, 10 Dec 1852; Jas. H. Cates, bm.

Cates, Joseph C. (Alvin) & Elizabeth Ann Carroll, 15 Oct 1850; A. Forrest, bm.

Cates, Joshua & Polly Hinchey, 2 Sept 1826; Nathl. Powell, bm.

Cates, Levi Franklin, son of Thomas & Margaret Cates, & Martha H. Pickett, dau. of Mark Rigsbee, m 17 June 1868 by B. C. Hopkins, J. P.

Cates, Moses & Hannah Bradford, 15 Oct 1795; Reuben Dixon, bm.

Cates, Norwood & Elizabeth Horn, 21 May 1841; David Whitaker, Moses Leathers Jr., bm.

Cates, Oliver & Elizabeth Webster, 1 Sept 1866; Buroghs Cheek, bm; m 2 Sept 1866 by Wm. Cheek, J. P.

Cates, Peter C. & Margaret E. Adams, 25 Feb 1846; D. D. Phillips, H. R. Boshormer, bm.

Cates, R. J. M. & Tempe C. Ferrell, 6 May 1856; E. L. Cates, bm.

Cates, Rial B. & Nancy Lynch, 31 Aug 1853; J. L. Turner, bm.

Cates, Richard & Margaret Crawford, 7 Feb 1866; Lafayett Pickard, bm; m 8 Feb 1866 by Alvis Durham, J. P.

Cates, Rob. & Sarah Coleman, 4 June 1785; John Riggs, bm.

Cates, Robert & Elizabeth Pugh, 11 July 1797; Solomon Cat, bm.

Cates, Robert & Mary J. Browning, 17 Feb 1857; John W. Rheu, James Gill, bm; m 19 Feb 1857 by Jno. Hancock, J. P.

Cates, Sollomon & Nancy Edwards, 17 Dec 1824; Alvis Parish, bm.

Cates, Thomas & Agnis Mangum, 15 Aug 1855; Isiah Cates, bm.

Cates, Thomas J. & Elizabeth Haward, 13 Sept 1864; T. W. Laws, bm.

Cates, Timothy & Betsey Pratt, 27 Nov 1806; H. Hunt, bm.

Cates, Vincent & Louisa Powell, 29 April 1837; Thomas Hasting, bm.

Cates, Westley & Salley Rhodes, 23 Dec 1840; Norwood Cates, bm.

Cates, William & Frances McGee, 12 June 1797; Henry Hunt, bm.

Cates, William & Elizabeth Wilson, 11 Nov 1799; Archelaud Wilson, bm.

Cates, William & Polley Bowers, 12 Sept 1822; Henry Andress, bm.

Cates, William & Penny Williams, 6 Feb 1856; Joseph Dunnagan, bm.

Cates, Wm. J. & Mariah D. Jackson, 30 March 1860; C. P. Warren, bm; m 8 April 1860 by Jno Hancock, J. P.

Cates, William P. & Mary Jane Long, 24 Nov 1853; H. A. Cate, bm.

Cates, Willie & Luena Piper, 12 Jan 1853; Thomas Crowder, James Turner, m 16 Jan 1853 by Wm. McCown, J. P.

Cates, Young & Susan Sanders, 30 Sept 1836; Chs. Jordan, bm.

Cats, Isaiah & Sally Manor, 19 Nov 1827; Levi Jackson, bm.

Cats, John Young & Sarah Hawkins Warrin, 8 March 1850; Rails Cats, bm.

Cats, Joshua & Nancy Minsey, 1 Aug 1807; Samuel Thomas, bm.

Cats, Presley M. & Mary Bollin, 30 Sept 1852; J. G. Strayhorn, bm; m 1 Oct 1852 by Alexr. Dickson, J. P.

Caudle, Columbus & Annie Harward, 23 March 1867; David Caudle, bm.

Caudle, David & Francis Elliot, 10 Oct 1835; James J. Cate, bm.

Caudle, Washington & Charlotte Yancey, m 26 Dec 1861 by D. Tilley, J. P.

Caudle, Wesley & Amelia Johnston, 5 Feb 1842; William Caudle, bm.

Caudle, Wm. H. & Martha Ellington, 18 Jan 1851; J. B. McDade, bm; m 18 Jan 1851 by J. B. McDade, J. P.

Causey, Thomas & Mary Birnley, 3 July 1819; Wm. Robson, bm.

Cave, Hudson M. & Delia M. Barbee, 19 Sept 1823; Richard Thompson, bm.

Cavin, William & Elizabeth Hogan, 15 Aug 1804; Robert Moore, bm.

Cazart, Gaston H. & Elizabeth Bowling, 30 Sept 1852; Zachariah Franklin, bm.

Centre, Brasil & Jane Stowers, 14 Sept 1830; Payton Clemments, Jos. A. Woods, bm.

Cerson, Samuel & Mary Spires, 4 May 1793; James Atkins, bm.

Chambers, James & Sary Weeks, 7 Dec 1795; Joseph Weekes, bm.

Chambers, James & Elizabeth Hobbs, 17 July 1805; James Clark, bm.

Chambers, William & Hannah King, 13 Oct 1808; John Thompson, John Young, bm.

Chambers, William & Nancy Thompson, 16 Feb 1833; W. H. Thompson, bm.

Chamblee, John R. & Alice Clinton, 21 April 1848; Norwood Warren, bm.

Chamless, Joseph & Hannah Pyke, 30 Aug 1819; William Shellton, bm.

Chamblee, Robert & Polley Warren, 31 Jan 1821; William Chamlee, bm.

Chamblee, William & Manervy Bowers, 6 Aug 1856; Jno Hancock, bm; m 6 Aug 1856 by Jno. Hancock, J. P.

Chamblee, William C. & Caroline Woods, 8 Jan 1852; John R. Chamblee, bm.

Chambless, Twitty & Ruth Horton, 13 Aug 1802; William Medison, bm.

Chambley, John R. & Elizabeth Hopkins, 9 Aug 1854; A. Proctor, J. L. Moore, bm; m 10 Aug 1854 by Wm. McCown, J. P.

Chambley, William & Elizabeth A. Pool, 16 Jan 1865; m 16 Jan 1854 by S. Shepherd, J. P.

Chamlee, Alfred & Sally Rhodes, 29 Oct 1823; David Warren, bm.

Chamlee, William & Mrs. Winifred Sutton, 23 Feb 1824; Wm. Warren, bm.

Chamley, Alfred & Nancy Link, 22 Feb 1827; John Guess, bm.

Chamley, Willie & Ann Johnston, 28 Nov 1853; W. W. Guess, Geo. W. Bruce, bm.

Chamlliss, John N. & Susan Miles, 30 Oct 1828; Seburn Sepreh, bm.

Chandler, Shadrack & Elizabeth Latta, 27 Feb 1810; Jas. Latta, bm.

Chandler, Shadreck & Elisabeth Sears, 19 Sept 1792; Henry Sears, bm.

Chapman, Benjamin & Anne Calep, 30 Aug 1786; James Young, bm.

Chapman, Benjamin & ____, 17 Nov 1794; John Dorris, bm.

Chapman, John & Elizabeth Jones, 19 Oct 1796; James Gordon, bm.

Chastle, Albert H. & Hawkins Copley, 17 Aug 1847; Hy. Nichols, bm.

Chatham, William & Rachael Polston, 21 July 1818; George Ward, bm.

Chavais, Mark & Derina Collins, 23 Dec 1854; Dennis Tilley, bm.

Chavers, Currie & Elizabeth Gowen, 21 July 1860; William Mays, bm; m 21 July 1860 by Thomas Hayes, minister.

Chavers, Willie & Silvey Hawley, 22 Feb 1840; W. R. Myers, J. P. Davis, bm.

Chaves, James & Prugant Hethpeth, 26 Feb 1859; James N. Brasfield, bm; m 27 Feb 1859 by S. Shepherd, J. P.

Chavis, Adam & Jane Mitchell, colored, 29 Aug 1855; Y. E. Watson, bm; m 30 Aug 1855 by L. S. Burkhead, minister.

Chavis, Henry & Eliza Ann Jones, 22 Dec 1859.

Chavis, Mark & Betsey Taborn, 5 July 1840; Christy Bass, bm.

Chavis, Richard & Mary Corn, 23 Nov 186_; G. W. Umsted, Urais Forsyth, bm.

Cheek, Adolphus W. & Cornelia Fowler, 19 July 1851; W. H. Thompson, bm; m 20 July 1851 by C. E. Smith, J. P.

Cheek, Alexander & Nancy Stroud, 22 Jan 1820; Frederick Loyd, William Andrews, bm.

Cheek, Alfred & Sarah C. Loyd, 5 Jan 1841; John Andrus, bm.

Cheek, Alfred & Malinda Smith, 26 Dec 1848; Henry Cheek, bm.

Cheek, Alfred & Martha Clark, 30 July 1859; Samuel Thompson, bm; m 31 July 1859 by Wiatt Cates, J. P.

Cheek, Alves & Nancy White, 17 Jan 1833; John Cheek, bm.

Cheek, Anderson & Tempe Williams, 30 Aug 1819; A. Green Williams, Stanford Cheek, bm.

Cheek, Burroughs & Sarah C. Benton, 22 Nov 1825; D. W. Craig, bm.

Cheek, Calvin & Carnelia Tinnen, 27 Nov 1854; Wm. M. Cheek, James M. Palmer, bm.

Cheek, Eli & Nancy Durham, 10 April 1820; Thos. Durham, bm.

Cheek, Eli & Polly Gean, 23 April 1822; Isaac Morris, bm.

Cheek, Green P. & Julia Pickard, 3 Oct 1866; John Laws, bm; m 4 Oct 1866 by Alvis Durham, J. P.

Cheek, Hartwell & Elizabeth Moulton, 19 Oct 1816; Wm. McClusky, Joseph Baker, bm.

Cheek, Henry & Silvay Williams, 2 Jan 1829; Laban Andrews, Daniel Clowd, bm.

Cheek, James & Pattey Estridge, 6 Sept 1783; Wm. McCauley, bm.

Cheek, James & Margaret Bailey, 1 May 1792; no bm.

Cheek, James & Janie Baker, 18 April 1807; Charles M'Cauley, bm.

Cheek, James & Polley Hobbs, 15 Feb 1809; Moses Carrell, bm.

Cheek, James & Deborah Wallis, 28 Nov 1822; B. Cheek, bm.

Cheek, James & Pathena Smith, 24 Sept 1828; John Cheek, bm.

Cheek, James A. & Mary L. Gaskill, 4 Dec 1845; J. H. McCadams, bm.

Cheek, James M. & Nancy Boothe, 25 Nov 1839; Robert Cheek, Henry Cheek, bm.

Cheek, James M., Jr., son of James M. & Nancy Cheek, & Julia Tilly, dau. of James & Tempy Tilly, m 25 July 1867 by J. P. Mason, minister.

Cheek, James W. & Rebecca H. Geer, 29 Oct 1861; T. W. Laws, bm; m 29 Oct 1861 by B. C. Hopkins, J. P.

Cheek, John & Susannah Estes, 1 April 1794; Jas. Cheek, bm.

Cheek, John & Polley Cox, 24 Aug 1814; Isaac Jones, bm.

Cheek, John & Jinney Williams, 31 Oct 1818; Anderson Cheek, bm.

Cheek, John & Patsey Stevens, 3 Oct 1822; James Partin, bm.

Cheek, John & Elizah Wynn, 8 May 1830; Alvis Cheek, B. Cheek, bm.

Cheek, John & Emeline Currie, 11 Aug 1846; James E. Howell, bm.

Cheek, John & Mary Jane Faucett, 12 July 1853; Wm. J. Freeland, bm.

Cheek, John & Margaret E. Shemwell, 20 Dec 1865; Charles M. Parks, bm; m 21 Dec 1865 by F. M. Jordan, minister.

Cheek, John A. & Mary Ann Strain, 22 Dec 1859; Ruffin Cheek, bm; m 24 Dec 1859 by W. J. Hogan, J. P.

Cheek, John M. & Malinda E. Proctor, 30 Oct 1865; E. W. Morris, bm.

Cheek, Lafayette & Rosannah Cheek, 21 Aug 1850; Wm. J. Freeland, bm.

Cheek, Laurin W. & Margret Jane Blackwood, 3 Nov 1842; B. M. Strowd, H. C. Strowd, bm.

Cheek, Mebane & Elizabeth Mallett, 5 May 1841; Alvis Crawford, J. H. Harden, bm.

Cheek, Mebane & Candace Allen, 15 Dec 1847; Thomas Burres, Saml. N. Tate, bm.

Cheek, Merritt & Fanny Hunter, 1 Jan 1832; Ruffin Anders, bm.

Cheek, Merritt & Elizabeth Weaver, 25 Jan 1848; Alvin Hunter, bm.

Cheek, Morton & Demaris Smith, 26 Sept 1839; W. R. Cheek, David Kirkland, bm.

Cheek, Nathaniel & Emeline Gattis, 2 Nov 1856; W. R. Franklin, bm; m 2 Nov 1856 by J. C. McDade, J. P.

Cheek, Newton & Julia Ann Andrews, 13 Oct 1854; Jno. M. Faucett, bm; m 15 Oct 1854 by Wiatt Cates, J. P.

Cheek, Richard & Jenney Andrews, 3 July 1805; Jesse Cate, bm.

Cheek, Robert & Patsey Andrus, 27 Nov 1798; Will Andrus, bm.

Cheek, Robert & Martha Ann Sykes, 24 Nov 1824; Burrhus Cheek, bm.

Cheek, Robert & Rebecca Whitlock, 28 May 1841; C. C. Smith, Alvis Cheek, bm.

Cheek, Stanford & Polly Williams, 20 Sept 1819; A. G. Williams, James Cheek, bm.

Cheek, William & Polley Craig, 1 Nov 1824; William Andrews, bm.

Cheek, William & Margaret Wilkins, 29 Nov 1853; David M. Cheek, Jones Watson, bm; m 8 Dec 1853 by William Green, J. P.

Cheek, Wm. & Nancy Jones, 27 Nov 1864; R. M. Jones, Jas. N. Patterson, bm; m 29 Nov 1864 by William F. Strayhorn, J. P.

Cheek, William M. & Eliza F. Lloyd, 31 March 1860; James Gill, bm; m 5 April 1860 by W. J. Hogan, J. P.

Cheek, William S. & Caroline B. Cox, 25 Dec 1849; L. Cheek, bm; m 26 Dec 1849 by Archibald Currie, minister.

Cheek, Willis & Martha Williams, 17 Nov 1827; Seton Cheek, bm.

Cheetham, William & Charlotte Wheeler, 24 Aug 1808; George Carey, bm.

Child, Fran & Frances McCarrel, 22 Jan 1784; Jno. Estes, bm.

Child, Sam & Christian Lewis, 19 Oct 1806; James Child, bm.

Chisenhall, Burwell & Mary Wood, 5 Nov 1798; Elisha Chizenhall, bm.

Chisenhall, Clements & Mary Woods, 6 Jan 1798; Elisha Chizenhall, bm.

Chisenhall, Delany & Polly Woods, 13 Aug 1816; Frederic Moize, bm.

Chisenhall, Elisha & Anna Woods, 26 Feb 1853; Little Chisenhall,
Jesse Lewis, bm.

Chisenhall, Elisha & Quintiney Hailey, 16 Feb 1863; William
Chisenhall, bm.

Chisenhall, James & Eliza M. Anderson, 1 Dec 1855; William Sim,
William Mangum, bm; m 13 Dec 1855 by M. A. Angier, J. P.

Chisenhall, James & Martha McKinny, 16 March 1867; Z. J. Lyon,
bm; m 16 March 1867 by R. F. Morris, J. P.

Chisenhall, John & Nancy Chizenhall, 6 Aug 1801; Elisha
Chizenhall, bm.

Chisenhall, John & Sarah J. Gates, 3 Oct 1855; Thos. J. Freeland Jr., bm; m 4 Oct 1855 by D. K. Blackwood, J. P.

Chisenhall, John & Edney Johnson, 4 Jan 1867; John A. Utley, bm.

Chisenhall, Litle & Candis Self, 15 April 1851; David Merret,
bm; m 20 April 1851 by H. Wilkerson, J. P.

Chisenhall, Person & Polley Carden, 11 March 1841; Benjamin
Johnson, bm.

Chisenhall, William & Mary Jane Woods, 23 Feb 1854; Thomas
OFerrell, bm; m 23 Feb 1854 by Harris Wilkerson, J. P.

Chism, John & Sarah Pound, 22 Sept 1781; Wm. Pound, bm.

Chissenhall, Saml. & Anne Primrose, 29 Sept 1824; Stephen
Larrote, bm.

Chissenhall, William & Mary Dollar, 14 Jan 1839; William Dollar,
John Taylor, bm.

Chizenhall, Alexander & Salley Watson, 29 Dec 1801; Walter Alves,
bm.

Chizenhall, Burwell & Sarah Barbee, 28 Jan 1834; Davis Chizenhall, Person Chisenhall, bm.

Chizenhall, David & Edy Rhodes, 14 Oct 1828; James Brockwell,
bm.

Chizenhall, Davis & Nancy Proctor, 19 April 1832; Duncan Glenn,
bm.

Chizenhall, Elisha & Elizabeth Woods, 4 Oct 1803; Solomon Wood,
bm.

Chizenhall, Parson & Eliza Moize, 12 Jan 1839; Bennett Brown,
And. Borland, bm.

Chizenhall, Reubin & Martha Woods, 22 June 1788; Tyree Glenn,
bm.

Chizenhall, William & Elizabeth Hancok, 26 Nov 1832; Person
Chisenhall, bm.

Christian, James N., son of Thomas & Martha Christian, & Nancy
J. Proctor, dau. of John & Mary Proctor, m 22 Jan 1868 by
R. F. Morris, J. P.

Christian, Robert & Nancy Lewis, 14 April 1829; John Pool, bm.

Christian, Thomas & Abitha Crombie, 24 Dec 1792; Daniel Carlton, bm.

Christian, Thomas & Martha Lynn, 2 Oct 1837; Wm. Marcum, bm.

Christian, W. J. & Louisa T. Gunter, 22 Nov 1866; E. W. Morris, V. C. Cheek, bm; m 22 Nov 1866 by B. C. Hopkins, J. P.

Christie, James H. & Susan Hart, 20 Dec 1834; J. C. Turrentine, bm.

Christmas, James & Betsey Courtney, 25 July 1793; Thos. Armstrong, bm.

Christmas, John C. B. & Mary Thompson, 25 April 1829; William Christmass, bm.

Christmas, Rd. & Anne Butler, 22 Dec 1788; James Christmas, bm.

Christmas, William & Elizabeth Kimbrough, 23 Sept 1809; John Newman, bm.

Christopher, George & Martha McCadams, 20 Dec 1859; William H. Ward, bm.

Christopher, James & Celia Bradford, 14 Dec 1830; John Compton, bm.

Christopher, John & Mary Hughs, 25 Jan 1802; Alexandder Fadis, Robert Morrow, bm.

Christopher, John & Cynthia Allison, 2 Jan 1841; Gabriel B. Smith, Wm. H. Allison, bm.

Christopher, Joseph & Anna Faucett, 6 May 1819; Thomas Bradford, bm.

Christopher, Wm. & Barbary Fitch, 19 July 1798; John Fitch, bm.

Claigs, Isac & Anna Thompson, 7 Oct 1822; Thomas Thompson, bm.

Clampit, Gary & Sarah Clifton, 20 March 1788; Jno. Hubanks, bm.

Clancy, George & Rebekah Clark, 17 Jan 1781; Thos. Clarke, bm.

Clancy, George & Sally Huntington, 19 Nov 1815; James Allison, bm.

Clancy, James & Phoebe Thompson, 16 Sept 1824; J. Taylor, bm.

Clancy, Thos. & Nancy Palmer, 24 Sept 1806; James Child, bm.

Clap, George, son of Jacob, & Elizabeth Graves, 19 Nov 1814; Jno. Bennet, bm.

Clap, John & Christina Shofner, 6 May 1808; John Hobs, bm.

Clap, John & Catherine Starr, 8 June 1806 or 1807; George Clap, bm.

Clap, John J. & Emaly Shofner, 15 Feb 1841; M. N. Robertson, bm.

Clap, Julius, son of Nelson & Judy Merritt, & Ann Kelly, dau. of Nelson & Candis Watson, colored; m 26 Dec 1867 by Jones Watson, J. P.

Clap, Wm. A. & Sally Wright, 30 Dec 1834; Jeremiah Clapp, bm.

Clapp, Augustine & Elizabeth Clapp, 22 Dec 1835; Wm. Shepherd, bm.

Clapp, Daniel & Barbara Fogleman, 6 Nov 1835; John Clapp, bm.

Clapp, Daniel & Temperance F. Roney, 1 Jan 1841; Em. Clapp, bm.

Clapp, Emanuel & Elizabeth Trolinger, 4 Sept 1837; Dan. Clapp, bm.

Clapp, Emanuel & Elizabeth Clapp, 4 April 1849; William Compton, bm.

Clapp, Henry & Polly Clapp, 17 Jan 1828; F. Clapp, bm.

Clapp, Isaac & Catherine Clapp, 16 Nov 1814; George Clapp, bm.

Clapp, Jacob & Mary Alexander, 7 March 1827; P. Eulys, bm.

Clapp, John & Ebbey Wagoner, 18 Aug 1837; David Clapp, bm.

Clapp, Stanley & Elizabeth Amick, 20 Jan 1849; John P. Byars, bm.

Clapp, Tobias & Marget Euless, 10 Oct 1819; W. B. Camp, bm.

Clapps, Alexdr. & Milly Robertson, 25 Jan 1836; M. S. Robertson, bm.

Clark, Archibald & Polley Lindsy, 7 March 1810; Joseph Smith, bm.

Clark, Calvin & Jane Allison, 5 March 1822; John Hunter, bm.

Clark, Calvin & Lucy Ann Riley, 6 Jan 1859; John R. Clark, bm; m 6 Jan 1859 by H. Terry, J. P.

Clark, David & Peggy Allison, 9 Sept 1825; J. W. Clark, bm.

Clark, David P. & Francis Goodloe, 13 Aug 1840; George W. Harrington, bm.

Clark, David T. & Carolina M. Anderson, 8 Sept 1849; William H. Ellis, Robert W. Anderson, bm; m 9 Sept 1849 by Archibald Currie, minister.

Clark, Ellis & Emaline Holder, 7 Oct 1834; Thomas Clark, bm.

Clark, Isaac & Sarah Glosson, 24 July 1822; M___ Glasson, bm.

Clark, James & Grace Thompson, 2 Nov 1788.

Clark, James & Anne Carr, 26 April 1796; Thos O'Neill, bm.

Clark, James & Jane Tinnin, 13 Jan 1807; Joseph Clark, bm.

Clark, James & Nancy Allison, 26 July 1836; James Clark, bm.

Clark, James M. & Winnifred L. Roundtree, 27 March 1851;
Laurenc N. Minnis(?), bm; m 27 March 1851 by Hezekiah Terry,
J. P.

Clark, James W. & Sally Lockhart, 2 Aug 1833; Joseph Smith, bm.

Clark, Jesse & Martha Lindsay, 27 Jan 1792; Jas. Lindsey, bm.

Clark, Jesse & Jenney Cearson, 7 Sept 1798; David Carson, bm.

Clark, Jesse & Mary Jane Miller, 28 July 1856; Jas. M. Clark,
bm; m 7 Aug 1856 by John F. Lyon, J. P.

Clark, John & Mahalah Ray, 28 July 1829; James Ray, bm.

Clark, John & Mary Ann Strain, 16 March 1853; Minnick Miller,
bm; m 16 March 1853 by James M. Palmer, J. P.

Clark, John N. & Nancy Tinnen, 1 March 1842; O. T. Long, bm.

Clark, John R. & Louisa Francis Allison, 30 March 1859; Abner J.
Tilly, bm; m 31 March 1859 by Hezekiah Terry, J. P.

Clark, Joseph & Nelly Tinnen, 8 Oct 1808; Thos. Clark, W. F.
Strudwick, bm.

Clark, Josiah & Elizabeth Elmore, 27 April 1805; James Stanford,
bm.

Clark, Josiah, son of John & Barsheba Clark, & Betty Shaw, dau.
of F. and Sally Shaw, m 13 Oct 1867 by Wiatt Cates, J. P.

Clark, Keling & Nancy Gooch, 29 June 1829; Thos. W. Gooch, bm.

Clark, Keling G. & Lydia Pearson, 23 April 1827; Green C.
Pearson, bm.

Clark, Peter S. & Susan Baker, 13 Jan 1826; Stephen White, bm.

Clark, Stephen & Martha Hastings, 26 March 1803; James Dixon,
George Tate, bm.

Clark, Stephen & Polly Roberts, 17 March 1823; Jos. A. Woods,
bm.

Clark, Thomas & Salley Thompson, 4 Oct 1813; John Ray, bm.

Clark, Thomas & Polly Nichols, 5 Dec 1818; Stephen Clark, bm.

Clark, Thomas A. & Nancy Pickard, 3 Aug 1861; Pleasant Cheek,
bm; m 4 Aug 1861 by Wiatt Cates, J. P.

Clark, William & Rachel Carson, daughter of James Carson, 19 Aug
1795; Robt. Carson, bm.

Clark, William & Letty Anderson, 31 Jan 1803; Thomas Bain, bm.

Clark, William & Catharine Ray, 30 Jan 1822; Michael Ray, bm.

Clark, William & Rozanah Caniday, 8 Nov 1856; James V. Clark,
bm; m 9 Nov 1856 by N. C. Cate, J. P.

Clark, William & Eliza Bowens, 17 March 1860; John Clark, bm.

Clark, William & Hawkins Halloway, 21 Aug 1865; Benjamin Carral, William Couch, bm.

Clark, Wm. & Mary Donalson, 24 Sept 1782; Wm. Clark, bm.

Clark, Wm. & Ellenor Love, 16 March 1782; Caleb Harvey, bm.

Clark, Wm. R. & Mariah L. Parker, 1 Aug 1864; John H. Pauld, bm.

Clark, William Y. & Nancy Lewis, 5 Jan 1849; R. F. Morris, bm.

Clarke, Joseph & Sophia Lewis, 30 Nov 1820; Abraham Lewis, bm.

Clayton, Alvin & Harriett Holden, 28 Jan 1828; Isaac Holden, bm.

Clayton, H. E. & Mary H. Breeze, 12 Oct 1864; P. H. Clayton, bm; m 13 Oct 1864 by Alexr. Dickson, J. P.

Clayton, Samuell S. & Rachel Cabe, 8 Nov 1824; Jno. Burton, bm.

Clayton, William C. & Margarett J. Lockhart, 6 Feb 1856; W. T. Hogan, bm; m 7 Feb 1856 by Alexr. Dickson, J. P.

Claytor, Jno. & Elizabeth G. Holden, 24 Nov 1819; Will. Whittset, bm.

Clegg, Henry C. & Mary E. Atwater, 1 March 1867; C. B. Clegg, bm; m 6 March 1867 by H. H. Gibbons, M. G.

Clegg, Luther & Jane Thompson, 1 Feb 1842; R. Stanford, Moses Leathers Jr., bm.

Clement, George G. & Martha Latta, 13 Feb 1850; E. W. Woods, bm.

Clement, Thos. P. & Martha Ann Herindon, 7 May 1840; Wmson. Parrish, bm.

Clement, William & Susanah Clement, 11 July 1853; Robert W. Clement, bm; m 11 July 1853 by Alexr. Dickson, J. P.

Clements, David A. & Mary E. Holloway, 15 Dec 1860; M. A. Angier, bm.

Clements, John R. & Nancy E. Hester, 16 Sept 1856; J. M. Reeves, bm.

Clements, Paton & Mary Chisenhall, 21 May 1866; E. W. Morris, bm.

Clements, Peyton & Patsey Pendergrass, 28 March 1840; Thomas Griffin, Thos. Adams, bm.

Clements, Thomas & Mary Collins, 8 April 1787; William Chisenhall, Richards Clements, bm.

Clements, William & Mary Jane Hall, 24 Aug 1848; Duncan C. Glenn, bm.

Clements, Wm. & Nancy Nichols, 16 Aug 1813; James Jackson, bm.

Clements, Willie G., son of Benjamin & Nancy Clements, & Annie E. Morring, dau. of James and Cynthia Moring, m 26 March 1868 by R. S. Webb, M. G.

Clemments, Daniel & Susannah Glenn, 1 Sept 1819; Tyree Glenn, John Clemments, bm.

Clemmons, David & Miram Hall, 15 April 1823; Gilbert Strayhorn, bm.

Clemmons, Leonard & Dilley Glenn, 24 Feb 1820; Williams Clemmons, bm.

Clemmons, Peyton C. & Elizabeth Ann Williams, 23 March 1853; William Clemmons, bm; m 24 March 1853 by Harris Wilkerson, J. P.

Clemmons, Ruffin & Elizabeth Umsted, dau. of Daniel Umsted, colored, m 5 Dec 1867 by Wm. D. Lunsford, J. P.

Clemons, John William & Frances Melvina Hicks, 27 June 1852; Alvin Rochell, bm; m 2 July 1852 by Harris Wilkerson, J. P.

Clendenin, Alexander & Polley Freshwater, 10 Sept 1811; Alexr. Allen, bm.

Clendenin, Charles & Frances Armstrong, 15 Sept 1827; Thos. Armstrong, bm.

Clendenin, Fisher & Rhodah Cook, 19 April 1836; Charles Clendenin, bm.

Clendenin, George & Mary Albright, 17 Jan 1829; Wm. Holmes, bm.

Clendenin, James & Mary Breadlove, 4 Jan 1827; John Clendenin, bm.

Clendenin, James & Emiline Weeks, 13 April 1832; Ch. Turner, bm.

Clendenin, John & Mary Dickson, 9 March 1818; David Turner, bm.

Clendenin, Joseph & Anne Webb, 20 Feb 1787; Walter Slaughter, bm.

Clendenin, Thaddeus & Elizabeth Stewart, 17 March 1836; R. M. Grimes, bm.

Clendenin, Thomas & Rachel Wood, 9 Oct 1817; James Bradshaw, bm.

Clendenin, William & Isabella Johnston, 23 June 1818; James Bradshaw, bm.

Clendenin, William & Jane Bradshaw, 25 Jan 1819; Wm. ____, bm.

Clendenin, Wm. & Jane Freeland, 4 Feb 1832; James Clendenin, bm.

Clendening, Fisher & Elizabeth Ann Freeland, 28 Jan 1839; John Gregson, bm.

Clendening, James & Mary Bradshaw, 20 Sept 1797; Bryson Dobbins, bm.

Clendennan, Fisher & Anna Bradshaw, 28 Jan 1797; Jonathan Thompson, bm.

Cleney, William & Alice Cearson, 26 Aug 1787; William Whitted Jr., bm.

Clenny, Saml. & Polley Thompson, 7 Sept 1793; Jehu Whitehead, bm.

Clifton, William & Rachel Mason, 21 March 1811; John Mason, bm.

Clindenin, William & Mary Ray, 30 Nov 1791; Charles Clindenin, bm.

Clindennen, John & ____ Clendenne, 27 Dec 1782.

Clindinnin, Jas. & Catey Bason, 18 March 1802; C. Cotton, bm.

Clindinnin, John & Elizabeth Anderson, 24 Oct 1798; Henry Thomson Jr., bm.

Clinton, Jesse & Rachel Vickers, 2 Aug 1825; John Vickers, bm.

Clinton, John & Nancy Grisham, 24 Dec 1800; Henry Dollar, bm.

Clinton, John & Rainy Duke, 27 March 1836; William Gray, bm.

Clinton, Robert & Polly Bobbitt, 17 June 1817; James Allison, bm.

Clinton, Saml & Eliza Allen, 26 Feb 1805; David Cozart, bm.

Cllindenin, Wm. & Polley Roney, 19 Dec 1814; William Mcaddams, bm.

Cloud, Daniel & Elizabeth Freeland, 23 Jan 1816; David Cloud, bm.

Cloud, Daniel & Susan Baker, 3 Dec 1840; Chs. Jordan, Ch. Cooley, bm.

Cloud, David & Elizabeth Murray, 9 Dec 1818; Joel Cloud, bm.

Cloud, Joel & Rebecca Thompson, 27 Aug 1812; Jacob Hubbard, bm.

Cloud, John D. & Mahala Strayhorn, 13 Oct 1852; J. J. Freeland, bm; m 13 Oct 1852 by Robert Burwell, minister.

Cloud, Samuel & Sarah Jackson, 3 April 1800; R. Thompson, bm.

Clower, Danl. & Nancy Wilson, 14 Oct 1785; John Wilson, bm.

Coal, Andrey & Elizabeth Evans, 25 Feb 1817; John Rhodes, bm.

Coapland, Samuel & Nancy Collins, 27 Jan 1837; Simon Coplen, Jas. Newlin, bm.

Cobb, David & Hannah Wagoner, 30 Nov 1829; Daniel Wagoner, bm.

Cobb, John & Rosannah Wagonner, 26 Nov 1827; Daniel Wagoner, bm.

Cobb, Robert & Mary Tate, 6 Oct 1818; Saml Tate, bm.

Cobb, Thom & Mindrel Hobbs, 29 Dec 1865; Elijah Jones, bm; m 30 Dec 1865 by T. C. Hayes.

Cobb, William & Frances Summers, 20 March 1849; Peter Thrift, bm.

Coble, Benjamin & Aggy Gerringer, 25 April 1838; John Coble, bm.

Coble, Christopher & Polly Boon, 29 March 1818; John Boon, bm.

Coble, Daniel & Eliza Preen(?), 9 Sept 1841; Isaac Patterson, Wm. McCauly, bm.

Coble, Henry & Nancy Coble, 1 Jan 1825; Anderton Brown, bm.

Coble, Jacob & Elisabeth Ware, 24 Aug 1807; Kinchen Pullum, bm.

Coble, John & Nancey Cook, 3 April 1819; D. C. Coble, bm.

Coble, John & Elizabeth Stockart, 17 Oct 1830; Alfred Whitsit, bm.

Coble, John & Sally Holt, 10 Oct 1835; Daniel Tickle, bm.

Coble, Martin & Surley Fogleman, 22 Dec 1827; Dl. Coble, bm.

Coble, Peter & Cathrine Kimbro, 24 March 1821; William Forgeson, bm.

Coble, Peter & Sally Holmes, 30 Aug 1829; Joseph Holmes, bm.

Coble, Samuel & Elizabeth Coble, 11 Nov 1818; Adam Ingold, bm.

Coble, Samuel & Burchet Jinkins, 16 Oct 1828.

Coble, William & Milly Clap, 1 July 1830; Wm. Cobb, bm.

Coble, William & Jane Loy, 4 March 1839; Willis Loy, bm.

Cocke, Erasmus & Jane Batchler, 25 Oct 1862; E. M. Holt, bm; m 26 Oct 1862 by Henry Gray, M. G.

Coe, John & Caty Sharp, 19 Feb 1814; Avery Coe, bm.

Coit, John C. & Ellen P. North, 10 June 1834; W. J. Bingham, bm.

Col, James & Mary Allen, 26 May 1818; Wm. B. Jamieson, bm.

Cole, Allen & Nancy Jane Wilkins, 9 Oct 1848; Saml. N. Tate, W. B. Holloway, bm.

Cole, Anderson & Polley Dollar, 14 Dec 1816; Merrimon Cole, bm.

Cole, Anderson & Betsy Doherty, 16 Dec 1836; Anthony Doherty, James Roberts, bm.

Cole, Anthony & Susannah Browning, 16 Sept 1822; James Cole, bm.

Cole, Carleton B. & Susan U. Taylor, 6 Sept 1827; J. Taylor, bm.

Cole, Elijah & Mary Jane Riggsbee, 6 March 1851; Chesley H. Dollar, bm; m 6 March 1851 by W. J. Hogan, J. P.

Cole, Furguson & Mary A. Daniel, 20 Sept 1856; J. Shuler, bm; m 2 Oct 1856 by John F. Lyon, J. P.

Cole, Henry & Elizabeth Pritchett, 16 Sept 1841; James F. Bradshaw, bm.

Cole, Henry & Sarah Cirtenton, 29 Sept 1864; D. C. McDade, bm; m 17 Sept 1865 by James Phillips, D. D.

Cole, Isaiah & Lois Wilson, 9 Sept 1805; William Pritchet, bm.

Cole, James A. & Jane Latta, 11 Dec 1846; Thos ___, bm.

Cole, James R. & Frances Wilbourne, 17 July 1826; Thos. Deadmon, bm.

Cole, Jesse & Sarah Proctor, 10 March 1835; William Link, bm.

Cole, Jesse M. & Penny Howington, 9 Sept 1833; John Piper, bm.

Cole, John & Gilley Fowler, 7 Feb 1825; John Kimbrow, bm.

Cole, John & Frances Christian, 5 Dec 1827; A. Parks, bm.

Cole, John & Dicey Warren, 19 Aug 1831; Allen Parks, bm.

Cole, John & Salley Holloway, 2 March 1836; William Proctor, bm.

Cole, John & Polly Daugharty, 12 Dec 1845; James A. Cole, bm.

Cole, John & Elizabeth Freeman, 20 Nov 1846; Richd. Nichols, bm.

Cole, John, son of William & Catherine Cole, & Martha Pool, dau. of Riley & Patsy Etheridge, m 7 July 1868 by R. F. Morris, J. P.

Cole, John A. & Cynthia Warren, 21 Dec 1840; Stephen Cole, bm.

Cole, John P. & Janetta Gooch, 24 Jan 1831; K. G. Clapp, bm.

Cole, Levi & Susan Scarlett, 18 Sept 1816; Samuel Cole, bm.

Cole, Martin & Susan Glenn, 7 Sept 1825; also 15 Sept 1825; Eli N. Woods, bm. (two bonds)

Cole, Martin & Susanah M. Glenn, 8 Jan 1826; H. Parks, bm.

Cole, Merrimon & Ester Doherty, 25 Dec 1812; James Daugharty, bm.

Cole, Pendleton & Nancy White, 8 Jan 1831; Charles McCauley, bm.

Cole, Saml. & Peggy Rainey, 3 Nov 1810; Edward McDade, bm.

Cole, Samuel & Polley Doherty, 17 Oct 1795; Matthew McCauley, bm.

Cole, Samuel & Sarah Laws, 13 July 1811; John Nichols, bm.

Cole, Samuel A., son of Anthony & Susan Cole, & Bettie Montgomery, dau. of James & Jane Montgomery, m 24 Dec 1867 by R. S. Webb, M. G.

Cole, Samuel F. & Olive H. Walker, 4 Nov 1851; Matthew Clinton, bm.

Cole, Stephen & Amanda Jackson, 6 Jan 1852; Wm. Jackson, bm; m 8 Jan 1852 by Alexr. Dickson, J. P.

Cole, Stephen & Anna Sutton, 21 Sept 1819; Matthew Crowder, bm.

Cole, Thomas & Elizabeth Phillips, 3 April 1802; David Phillips, bm.

Cole, Vetus & Elizabeth F. Chamley, 4 March 1862; Martin Cole, bm.

Cole, Wesley & Margret Craig, 1 April 1839; Georg Freeland, bm.

Cole, Will & Nelly Carroll, 18 Sept 1810; Joel Low(?), bm.

Cole, William & Mary Rhodes, 13 Nov 1792; John Cole, bm.

Cole, William & Nancy White, 6 March 1820; William Dollar, bm.

Cole, William & Margaret Lewis, 28 Jan 1856; Thomas Cole, bm; m 31 Jan 1856 by John F. Lyon, J. P.

Cole, Wm. & Elizabeth Faddis, 12 Jan 1802; James Williams, bm.

Cole, Wm. & Mary Steward, 16 July 1859; S. P. Cole, bm; m 17 July 1859 by Benjamin L. Kennion, J. P.

Cole, William T. & Martha Ann Strayhorn, 7 June 1847; Williamson B. Holloway, bm.

Coleman, John A., son of Joseph & Melena B. Coleman & Martha E. Ray, dau. of George C. & Martha Ray, m 21 Nov 1867 by J. E. Montague, R. M.

Coleman, John & Mary Riley, 17 Jan 1785; Robt. Cates, bm.

Coleman, John & Rebecca Allen, 12 Nov 1803; David Cozart, bm.

Coleman, Levy & Jean Reddick, 16 Nov 1782; Saml. Coleman, bm.

Coleman, Thos. & Hetty McClary, 24 Sept 1806; William Barnhill, bm.

Collens, Eli & Mary Durbin, 30 Aug 1781; Jas. Gray, bm.

Collens, Samuel & Elmiry Husky, 28 Oct 1852; John Cheek, bm.

Collier, Charles & Patty Gains, 17 April 1794; Jno. Casey, bm.

Collier, Edward & Amey Gilmore, 23 Dec 1829; Thomas C. Davis, bm.

Collier, Federick & Lucretia Hunt, 18 Feb 1824; Moses S. Pratt, bm.

Collier, Frederick & Rebecca Watson, 9 May 1798; Bennitt Watson, John Thompson, bm.

Collier, Isaac J. & ____, 6 Jan 1832; John Blake, Samuel Scarlett, bm.

Collier, John G. & Lucy Jenkins, 23 March 1818; Presley Rottenbery, bm.

Collier, Lewis & Susanna Dudley, 24 May 1792; David Ray, bm.

Collins, Alfred & Elizabeth Ashley, 26 May 1862; James M. Bain, bm; m 27 May 1862 by Nathl. Bain, J. P.

Collins, Allen & Betsey Jordan, 13 Sept 1817; Henry Ringstep, bm.

Collins, Andrew & Izbell Hastins, 26 Feb 1784; James Hastings, bm.

Collins, Andrew & Nelly Weeks, 25 Sept 1810; J. Turner, John Young, bm.

Collins, Bradley & Jane Ray, 22 Feb 1817; Dana B. Alsobrook, bm.

Collins, Brassfield & Elizabeth Cook, 15 May 1835; James Rippy, bm.

Collins, Brice & Clarissa Vincent, 25 Feb 1807; Rt. Glenn, bm.

Collins, Brice A. & Priscilla W. Faucett, 8 Sept 1842; Robert W. Glenn, bm.

Collins, Daniel & Nelly Baker, 28 April 1803; Willie Mangum, bm.

Collins, Eli & Mary Durbin, 30 Aug 1781; James Gray, bm.

Collins, Enoch & Peggy Carson, 31 Aug 1805; James Reeves, bm.

Collins, Enoch R. & Susan Clark, 28 April 1847; William J. Clark, bm.

Collins, George & Polley McKee, 14 April 1810; Solomon Jacobs, bm.

Collins, George & Mary Biley, 2 April 1838; Ralph Faucett, bm.

Collins, George P. & Annie R. Cameron, 18 Dec 1860; Josiah Collins Jr., bm; m 20 Dec 1860 by M. A. Curtis, rector of St. Matthews Church.

Collins, James & Elizabeth King, 7 March 1809; John Young, bm.

Collins, James & Barbara Brinkley, 1 June 1825; Wm. Van Hook, bm.

Collins, James & Elizabeth Britt, 8 Sept 1835; J. Blackwood, bm.

Collins, John & Polly Jackson, 21 July 1797; Isaac Jackson, bm.

Collins, John & Holly Brown, 28 Oct 1822; A. Parker, Allen Parrish, bm.

Collins, Josiah Jr. & Sarah R. Jones, 12 Dec 1859; Robin A. Jones, bm; m 13 Dec 1859 by M. A. Curtis, Rector of St. Matthews Church, Hillsborough, N. C.

Collins, Labon & Elizabeth Beason, 9 Nov 1805; James Wilkins, bm.

Collins, Osbern & Mary Cain, 21 Nov 1866; J. W. Latta, C. H. Lyon, bm; m 21 Nov 1866 by J. W. Latta, J. P.

Collins, Samuel P. & Susan F. Taylor, 22 Jan 1853; Carnes T. Anderson, bm; m 26 Jan 1853 by D. D. Phillips, J. P.

Collins, William & Vicey Hudlar, 20 March 1815; James Adams, bm.

Collins, William & Rebeckah Griffin, 26 Nov 1826; Jos. B. Johnson, bm.

Collins, William & Lucy Anna Rhew, 15 Jan 1848; Thomas Crowder, bm.

Collins, Willie & Margert Davis, 2 Sept 1850; James Long, Thomas OFarhell, bm.

Colly, Drury & Catherine Burchett, 5 Dec 1809; John Hobs, bm.

Colter, Hanson & Tabitha Partin, 7 March 1785; Wm. Partin, bm.

Colter, Henson & Eliza Dawson, 26 May 1815; J. Taylor, bm.

Comb, James & Elizabeth Barton, 2 Nov 1811; Asyl Barton, bm.

Comb, John & Eliza Watson, (no date); John McKerall, bm.

Combs, Aron & Betsy Justice, 25 Aug 1791; John Johnston, bm.

Combs, David W. & Martha Price, 1 Feb 1831; James Long, Thomas
Griffin, bm.

Compton, Aaron, son of Aaron Warren & Manerva Compton &
Elizabeth Murphey, dau. of Jacob & Silvey Murphey, colored,
m 12 Dec 1867 by F. Walker, J. P.

Compton, Alfred & Sally Lea, 23 Jan 1818; Jno. Campbell, bm.

Compton, Aquila & Pheebe Marsh, 23 Jan 1798; Norris Compton, bm.

Compton, B. B. & Euphrasien Hester, 12 Sept 1866; H. L. McDade,
bm; m 16 Sept 1866 by Thos. H. Hughes, J. P.

Compton, Erasmus & Peggy Smith, 21 Dec 1801; Norris Compton, bm.

Compton, James F. & Nancy Ray, 20 Dec 1857; William H. Riley,
bm; m 25 Dec 1851 by Freeman Walker, J. P.

Compton, Jeremiah & Tamson Kemp, 31 March 1819; Wm. Ward, bm.

Compton, John & Jeany Faddis, 11 March 1824; John Compton, bm.

Compton, John & Elizabeth Christopher, 4 Oct 1827; Aquilla
Compton, bm.

Compton, John & Lucinda Fuller, 29 Dec 1866; Cornelius Fuller,
bm; m 3 Jan 1867 by F. Walker, J. P.

Compton, John F. & Nancy Lorson Blackwell, 29 Sept 1858;
Wesley S. Compton, bm.

Compton, Lemuel & Lucy Scott, 24 May 1838; James Ward, Tho.
Anderson, bm.

Compton, Levy & Hannah Compton, 19 Feb 1815; J. A. Benton, bm.

Compton, Solomon & Hannah Ward, 30 Jan 1811; Alfred Compton, bm.

Compton, Thomas & Polley McCaddams, 4 Jan 1833; Sieria G.
Compton, bm.

Compton, William & Eliza Debruler, 16 Nov 1847; Lemuel Compton,
bm.

Compton, Wm. & Elizabeth A. Boswell, 24 Dec 1847; N. A. Williams,
bm.

Compton, William C. & Susanah Massey, 19 Dec 1850; J. Allison,
bm.

Conklin, Abner & Margret Pickard, 3 Jan 1826; Sam. Child, bm.

Conklin, Abner H., son of Abner & Margaret Conklin, & Matilda
Smith, dau. of Thomas & Fanny Smith, m 25 June 1867 by Wiatt
Cates, J. P.

Conklin, John & Sally Sykes, 16 May 1854; John T. Crawford, bm;
m 23 May 1854 by Wiatt Cates, J. P.

Conklin, John & Jane Crawford, 16 Dec 1859; John B. Guthre, bm; m 28 Dec 1859 by Wiatt Cates, J. P.

Conklin, William H. & Fanney Pugh, 12 June 1855; William Moore, bm; m 12 June 1855 by Wiatt Cates, J. P.

Connally, Thomas & Tempy Partin, 25 Sept 1792; John Connally, bm.

Cook, Anderson & Barbara Hufphines, 18 Sept 1846; John P. Albright, bm.

Cook, Doncan & En. A. Stanford, 15 Nov 1859; S. Stanford, bm; m 15 Nov 1859 by C. H. Phillips.

Cook, Edward & Anne Thomas, 4 Feb 1786; Jesse Thomas, bm.

Cook, Edward & Anne Tippy, 26 Aug 1808; Thomas Rippy, bm.

Cook, Edward & Nancy Rippy, 27 Feb 1823; Stephen Rippy, bm.

Cook, Edward & Elizabeth Williams, 11 July 1835; Wiley Malone, bm.

Cook, George & Hannah Thomas, 12 Nov 1817; Barnabas Perry, bm.

Cook, Henry C. & Mary Bryan, 18 April 1836; Bengni Blany, bm.

Cook, Isaac & Mary Smith, 12 Nov 1835; John Guffy, bm.

Cook, James & Sally Melone(?), 20 Aug 1808; B. Giles, bm.

Cook, James & Dicey McFarland, 23 July 1819; Francis Roberts, bm.

Cook, James W. & Sarah J. Holloway, 27 Feb 1866; Benjamin Carroll, bm; m 3 March 1866 by A. B. Gunter, J. P.

Cook, John & Hannah Kelton, 17 Dec 1796; Martin Shoftner, bm.

Cook, John & Elizabeth McCauley, 4 Jan 1820; Richard Thompson, bm.

Cook, Jonathan & Rachel Piles, 21 Oct 1809; Nehemiah Cook, bm.

Cook, Joseph & Franky Dodd, 10 April 1802; David Holden, bm.

Cook, Paschal & Elizabeth Scarlett, 6 Oct 1866; Andrew McFarlin, John M. Blackwood, bm.

Cook, Thomas & Milley Marchum, 18 Nov 1796; William Horn, bm.

Cook, William & Margaret Crabtree, 19 March 1796; Wm. Crabtree, bm.

Cooley, Charles L. & Eliza A. Chapman, 25 Jan 1826; Nathaniel J. Palmer, bm.

Cooly, John & Elizabeth Adams, 14 Aug 1827; Stephen Moore, bm.

Cooper, Absolem & Catharine Armstrong, 1 Oct 1799; Thos. Armstrong, bm.

Cooper, Kennon & Milley Cate, 7 May 1803; Richard Cate, bm.

Cooper, Michl. & Mary Clifton, 12 Jan 1784; James Green, bm.

Cooper, Robert E. & Annie E. Davis, 29 June 1863; D. C. McDade, bm; m 29 June 1863 by James Phillips, D. D.

Cope, George & Hannah Boyd, 25 Aug 1795; Richd. Cope, bm.

Cope, James & Holley Merritt, 2 Feb 1809; Vincent Falkner, bm.

Cope, Richd. & Sarah Whitsitt, 17 Sept 1795; Morgan Hart, bm.

Copeland, Andrew J. & Nancy Lamb, 8 Oct 1847; John S. Albright, bm.

Copeland, John & Delilah Evans, 13 Aug 1831; Dirk Lindeman, bm.

Copeland, Lord & Barbara May, 9 June 1821; Daniel McPherson, bm.

Copland, Abner & Eliza McCall, 27 Sept 1827; Daniel Boothe, bm.

Copland, Simon & Sienea Grissom, 4 Jan 1824; Joseph Miarrey, bm.

Coplay, John W. & Polly Rials, 7 Aug 1822; John Boling, bm.

Copley, Allen & Caroline Proctor, 16 April 1847; James Horn, bm.

Copley, George Jr. & Mary Roan, 18 Aug 1842; William Case, Step. Moore, bm.

Copley, James & Mary McFarland, 15 May 1800; James Ramey, bm.

Copley, Jesse & Susannah Marcum, 5 Jan 1815; Moses Guess, bm.

Copley, John & Esther Peelor, 1 Aug 1805; James Rainey, bm.

Copley, John & Mary Bryant, 27 Feb 1838; Robert Johnston, D. H. Cate, bm.

Copley, Walter & Demaris Riggsbee, 12 Oct 1848; Hurlys J. Glenn, bm.

Copley, William & Eliza Turner, 16 July 1841; Moses Leather Jr., James Browning, bm.

Copley, William & Penisey Copley, 4 Oct 1851; J. A. Mabrie, bm; m 12 Oct 1851 by King Barbee, J. P.

Coplin, James M. & Susanah Andrews, 6 Dec 1852; Wiley P. M. Andrews, bm; m 16 Dec 1852 by Alvis Durham, J. P.

Coplin, Jerry & Harriett Jones, colored, 5 Aug 1860; Job Bery, bm; m 17 Aug 1860 by M. A. Curtis, D. D.

Coply, George & Susannah Desern, 21 Sept 1812; Samuel Peelor, bm.

Coply, Ilai & Polly Bradley, 1 June 1814; Ds. Bradley, bm.

Coply, Potter & Avy Pitman, 17 June 1861; Simeon Ferrell, bm; m 17 June 1861 by Solomon Shepherd, J. P.

Corall, James & Margret Rhew, 18 June 1859; William Gilbert, bm; m 24 June 1859 by S. Shepherd, J. P.

Corbit, James & Jeany Lynch, 19 Dec 1805; James Elmore, bm.

Corbitt, John W. & Sarah C. Walker, 15 Oct 1866; B. B. Warren, bm.

71

Cordel, Lewis & Lotty Desern, 17 June 1822; William Trice, bm.

Corder, Lewis & Marey Garner, 4 Nov 1785; William Parks, bm.

Corn, Dixon & Tempe Jeffers, 5 Feb 1821; Lewis Jeffers, bm.

Corn, Thomas & Francis Jones, 14 Feb 1861; Cisarow Anderson, bm.

Cornick, Samuel & Betsey Moore, 29 Jan 1793; Joseph Shaw, bm.

Cortner, Peter & Jeany McGrigory, 5 June 1811; David Renny, St. Wells, bm.

Cosens, Richard & Mary A. Ellick, 22 Sept 1848; Henry Ellick, bm.

Cothrane, Alex. & Jenny Robinson, 9 Aug 1811; John Jimeson, bm.

Cothron, James & Salley Bowles, 31 Dec 1808; Henry Shult, bm.

Couch, Anderson & Peggy Browning, 9 Oct 1841; George Browning, John Browning, bm.

Couch, Asa & Milinda Patterson, 26 March 1827; Chesley M. Patterson, bm.

Couch, Chesley P., son of Elijah & Mary Couch, & Mary A. Garrard, dau. of Wm. B. Garrard, m 3 Dec 1867 by C. P. Warren, J. P.

Couch, Eligey & Saly Tucker, 22 Oct 1792; John Couch, bm.

Couch, Elijah & Mary Warren, 30 April 1835; John Warren, bm.

Couch, Harden & Sally Warren, 18 Feb 1820; James Warren, bm.

Couch, Isaac & Susannah Burch, 19 Jan 1808; James Horne, bm.

Couch, James & Polley Rainey, 8 Jan 1831; Jesse Hargraves, bm.

Couch, James M. & Emaline Carden, 29 July 1852; John W. Chamblee, bm; m 29 July 1852 by King Barbee, J. P.

Couch, Jesse & Alee Lee, 23 Jan 1789; Jacob Lemmon, bm.

Couch, John & Elizabeth Campbell, 2 Dec 1783.

Couch, John & Susannah Carlton, 19 Jan 1823; James Dancy, bm.

Couch, John & Rhodah Wilson, 16 Jan 1832; Sampson Couch, bm.

Couch, John & Julia A. Shields, 12 Sept 1865; Wm. T. Shields, bm.

Couch, Loften K. & Nancy Cain, 16 Jan 1856; Sherwood H. Garrard, T. Webb, bm.

Couch, Sampson & Charlotte Yeargin, 16 March 1824; Asa Couch, bm.

Couch, Sampson, son of John & Emeline Couch, & Emily Nunn, dau. of Ruffin & Rachel Nunn, colored, m 15 Feb 1868 by J. P. Mason.

Couch, Simon & Lucretia Stewart, 9 April 1836; James Kimbrough, Levi McCallum, bm.

Couch, Thomas & Genney Nelson, 13 Sept 1793; John Couch, bm.

Couch, Thomas & Delilah Browning, 12 Feb 1835; George Browning, bm.

Couch, Wesley & Frances Snipes, 17 Jan 1849; Jno. D. Carlton, bm.

Couch, William & Peggy Riley, 15 Oct 1806; Isaac Lint, bm.

Couch, William & Dicey White, 8 Jan 1823; William White, bm.

Couch, William & Margaret Pickett, 17 Dec 1860; Redding Cape, bm; m 19 Dec 1860 by John Borroughs, J. P.

Couch, William, son of Nancy Couch, & Mary Cates, dau. of Mary Cates, m 23 Oct 1867 by C. P. Warren, J. P.

Couch, Wm. & Sarah Fowler, m 2 July 1857 by David Tilley, J. P.

Couch, Willie G. & Ema Crabtree, 7 July 1860; Thomas Couch, bm; m 7 Aug 1860 by Samuel Couch, J. P.

Couertner, George & Elizabeth Albright, 27 Mar 1821; Jonas Albright, bm.

Coulter, Andisan & Jenny Rigsby, 14 May 1810; William Pendergrass, bm.

Councelman, George & Nancey Boggs, 13 Oct 1818; Jacob Isley, bm.

Coupland, Wm. & Sarah Trice, 10 Dec 1782.

Courtner, Aron & Charity Wells, 4 Feb 1830; Simon Hornaday, bm.

Courtner, Danl. & Elizabeth Linn, 6 Aug 1810.

Courtner, Jacob & Milly Nease, 27 Feb 1814; Peter Courtner, bm.

Courtner, Ludwk. & Polly Smith, 20 May 1813; Stephen Wells, bm.

Courtner, Saml. & Jenny Huphines, 12 March 1808; Jacob Huphines, bm.

Courtney, Wm. & Mary Thomas, 28 July 1785; Thos. M. Davis, bm.

Couton, Nevel & Creasey Williams, 15 Dec 1822; Samuel L. Adams, bm.

Couton, William & Hannah Gent, 13 Jan 1833; Richard Coureton, Joshua R. Gant, bm.

Covington, William & Nancy Williams, 31 May 1806; Samuel Clenny, bm.

Cowden, Green & Mary Ann Vaughan, 24 Nov 1835; James Vaughan, bm.

Cowell, James B. & Laney Rogers, 6 May 1804; John Galbraith, bm.

Cox, Bolling & Polley Hughs, 26 May 1808; James Clancy, bm.

Cox, Charles & Elizabeth Adams, 28 July 1813; George Clancy Junr., bm.

Cox, John A. & Bettie S. Morris, 9 Dec 1852; E. W. Woods, Alexr. Dickson, bm; m 9 Dec 1852 by Robert Burwell, M. G.

Cox, John H. & Nancy Pugh, 19 Oct 1830; Isaac Jones, Isaac Holt, bm.

Cox, Moses & Margaret Morrow, 8 Oct 1788; Robt. Hodg, bm.

Cozart, Brodie & Mary Ann Johnston, 24 Oct 1834; Oxford Moise, bm.

Cozart, David & Polley Carrington, 14 April 1820; Wms. D. Carrington, bm.

Cozart, David B. & Rebecca Watson, 17 Oct 1836; D. C. Parrish, J. B. Geer, bm.

Cozart, James & Sarah Brinkley, 23 Aug 1796; Thomas Langhorn, bm.

Cozart, James & Polly Murdock, 25 Oct 1821; Jos. A. Woods, bm.

Cozart, Riley & Halley Carrington, 6 Nov 1829; ___ Parrish, bm.

Cozart, Robert & Charlotte Carrington, 5 Jan 1815; John Walters, bm.

Cozart, Simeon & Parthinia Armstrong, 9 Jan 1838; Thomas Anderson, bm.

Cozart, William & Dicey Carrington, 29 May 1810; Josiah Carrington, bm.

Cozart, William & Holley Mangum, 8 March 1792; Wm. Mangum, bm.

Crabtree, Abraham & Isabella Barton, 12 May 1824; D. B. Alsobrook, bm.

Crabtree, Abram. & Polley Horne, 22 Nov 1800; Samuel Crabtree, bm.

Crabtree, Abram & Peggy Riley, 19 April 1820; Saml Hancock, bm.

Crabtree, Anderson & Mahala Rhodes, 24 Dec 1829; James Crabtree, James M. Pearson, bm.

Crabtree, Andw. & Tempe Horn, 26 Dec 1810; Wm. Crabtree, bm.

Crabtree, Archey & Bitsey Neal, 24 Jan 1818; Archable Horn, bm.

Crabtree, Archibald & Polley Hastings, 22 May 1813; James Hastings, bm.

Crabtree, Asa, son of James & Nancy Crabtree, & Nancy Barton, dau. of Betsy Barton, m 22 Aug 1867 by W. S. Strayhorn, J. P.

Crabtree, Calvin & Jane Crabtree, 26 Nov 1863; Archd. C. Hunter, bm.

Crabtree, Charles F. & Frances J. Newman, 30 Jan 1850; William J. Freeland, bm.

Crabtree, Clement & Charity Pritchet, 19 Nov 1836; Wilson Jackson, John Holden, bm.

Crabtree, Clemuel & Mary Crabtree, 22 Dec 1859; J. T. Holloway, bm; m 22 Dec 1859 by William F. Strayhorn, J. P.

Crabtree, Clemuel & Anniah Jenkins, 2 Sept 1859; D. McDaniel(?), bm.

Crabtree, Edward & Susannah Holsenback, 2 April 1832.

Crabtree, George W. & Sally Dollar, 9 March 1830; James R. Cole, bm.

Crabtree, Henary & Sally Hastings, 4 Dec 1861; Thos. W. Laws, bm; m 4 Dec 1861 by John Cheek, J. P.

Crabtree, Henry & Louisa Crabtree, 6 Jan 1840; Hugh L. Reeves, James Hastings, bm.

Crabtree, Henry & Margaret F. Cole, 28 Oct 1866; Wm. L. Rhew, bm; m 28 Oct 1866 by John F. Lyon, J. P.

Crabtree, Henry M. & Eda Baldwin, 14 Aug 1859; Thos. Long, bm; m 14 Aug 1859 by Thos. Long, J. P.

Crabtree, J. W. & Elizabeth Laycock, 26 Dec 1866; Henry A. Murrell, bm; m 27 Feb 1866 by Geo. W. Purfrey, minister.

Crabtree, Jackson & Caroline Jackson, 22 Dec 1860; Henry Murdoch, bm; m 31 Dec 1860 by Benjamin J. Kinnion, J. P.

Crabtree, Jacob & Susan Brown, 8 Jan 1848; James Crabtree, bm.

Crabtree, James & Elizabeth Sparrow, 22 Feb 1822; Lewis Partin, Richard Blackwood, bm.

Crabtree, James & Fanny Crabtree, 25 Aug 1827; Saml. Crabtree, bm.

Crabtree, James, son of James & Rachel Hunter, 12 Feb 1851; Green Strayhorn, bm; m 12 Feb 1851 by Alexr. Dickson, J. P.

Crabtree, James, son of Abe & Eliza Crabtree, 13 June 1856; Clemul Jackson, James Gill, bm; m 14 June 1856 by John F. Lyon, J. P.

Crabtree, James Monroe & Mary Ann Crabtree, 26 Sept 1854; John Crabtree, James Gill, bm.

Crabtree, James W. & S. C. Whittaker, 21 Sept 1853; Wm. J. Freeland, bm; m 27 Oct 1853 by Alexr. Dickson, J. P.

Crabtree, John & Phebe Campbell, 1 Feb 1819; Jno. R. Cummins, bm.

Crabtree, John & Hannah Mary Jackson, 28 June 1840; Charles J. Freeland, bm.

Crabtree, John & Jane Atterson, 13 Feb 1856; S. Shepherd, bm; m 14 Feb 1856 by Wm. Nelson, J. P.

Crabtree, John & Margaret J. Halsonback, 29 Nov 1859; S. J. Hester, bm; m 4 Feb 1860 by Wm-son Parrish, J. P.

Crabtree, John, son of Anderson & Mahala Crabtree, & Eliza Wright Riley, dau. of Saml. & Patsy Pool, m 4 Sept 1867 by W. B. Holloway, J. P.

Crabtree, John J. & Elizabeth Willett, 7 July 1866; John R. Riley, bm; m 8 July 1866 by Daniel W. Thompson, bm.

Crabtree, John M. & Louisa McCauley, 25 Aug 1849; Abram
Crabtree, bm.

Crabtree, Johnson & Patsey Price, 28 Oct 1817; James Crabtree,
bm.

Crabtree, Monroe & Caroline Horne, 17 Oct 1850; Page Scarlett,
bm.

Crabtree, Munroe & Sarah Crabtree, 29 Jan 1861; Jno. Dison,
Israel Turner, bm; m 29 Jan 1861 by John Borroughs, J. P.

Crabtree, Norwood & Nancy Whittaker, 19 Jan 1843; Robert
Blackwood, Thos. Adams, bm.

Crabtree, Poter A. & Emeline Riley, 28 Dec 1861; Thomas A.
Williams, bm; m 2 Jan 1862 by Lambert N. Hall, J. P.

Crabtree, Richard & Polley Latta, 4 April 1809; Thomas Latta, bm.

Crabtree, Richard & Kenah Bommit, 25 May 1834; Willie Wheeler,
Saml. B. Taylor, bm.

Crabtree, Richard W. & Martha Rhew, 31 Aug 1866; H. B. Guthrie,
bm.

Crabtree, Robert H. & Lucy Whitaker, 27 Dec 1866; David Mays,
Saml. H. Breeze, bm; m 27 Dec 1866 by Wm. B. Holloway, J. P.

Crabtree, Saml. & Mary Newcum, 27 March 1802; Abram Crabtree,
bm.

Crabtree, Samuel & Edith Neal, 31 Oct 1823; Stephen Scarlet, bm.

Crabtree, Samuel & Barsheba Glenn, 3 Nov 1826; Isaac Pool,
Elisha Glenn, bm.

Crabtree, Samuel H. & Elizabeth Ann Strayhorn, 5 June 1860;
Alex Pleasants, bm; m 17 June 1860 by Samuel Couch, J. P.

Crabtree, Sterling & Letha Hicks, 24 May 1853; Alexr. Borland,
bm; m 26 May 1863 by J. J. Freeland, J. P.

Crabtree, Tho. & Catey Horn, 5 March 1807; Jas. Crabtree, Henry
Stutt, bm.

Crabtree, Thomas & Elisabeth Campbell, 18 May 1792; James
Crabtree, bm.

Crabtree, Thomas & Sally ODaniel, 9 Dec 1806; John Young, James
Pratt, bm.

Crabtree, Thomas & Minerva Faucett, 24 Feb 1838; Leo. E. Heartt,
Saml. Hughes, bm.

Crabtree, Thomas & Mary F. Barton, 21 Jan 1855; William McCauly,
bm; m 21 Jan 1855 by Richison Nichols, J. P.

Crabtree, Thomas & Susan Thompson, 14 Sept 1811; William
Crabtree, bm.

Crabtree, Thomas H. & Sally Ray, 22 Dec 1857; James R. Clark,
bm; m 22 Feb 1857 by Wiatt Cates, bm.

Crabtree, Thomas W. & Ellinder Rhew, 21 Nov 1832; Harrison Srote,
bm.

Crabtree, Uriah & Iby Collins, 30 Dec 1816; Lewis Phillips, bm.

Crabtree, Walter & Elizabeth Price, 17 June 1831; Pleasant Haithcock, bm.

Crabtree, Walter & Susan Strayhorn, 23 Feb 1858; Wm. Barton, R. T. Thompson, bm; m 24 Feb 1858 by Samuel Couch, J. P.

Crabtree, William & Elizabeth McCauley, 29 March 1819; James Crabtree, bm.

Crabtree, William & Cynthia Latta, 27 Sept 1833; Edward Crabtree, bm.

Crabtree, William & Melisey Dickey, 26 Nov 1849; W. Wh. Latta, bm.

Crabtree, William E. & Nancy J. Brown, 23 Dec 1858; Oren W. Williams, bm; m 23 Dec 1858 by Thomas Ferrell, J. P.

Crabtree, William F. & Mary Crabtree, 11 Feb 1861; John M. Crabtree, Moses Redding, bm; m 14 Feb 1861 by Wilson Brown, J. P.

Crabtree, William G. & Eliza McCauley, 6 Jan 1852; M. H. Sharp, bm; m 8 Jan 1852 by J. J. Freeland, J. P.

Crabtree, William P. & Elizabeth Redden, 3 Feb 1854; Abram Crabtree, Jno Laws, bm; m 5 Feb 1854 by Alexr. Dickson, J. P.

Crabtree, William R. & Elizabeth Watson, 24 Jan 1855; William H. Redding, J. Turner, bm; m 25 Jan 1855 by William W. Guess, J. P.

Craft, John Charles & Sarah Loyd, 4 May 1796; John Andus, bm.

Craig, Abram & Jane Murdock, 16 Dec 1805; Samuel Craig, bm.

Craig, Alexander & Jane Strayhorn, 6 June 1801; James Yarbrough, bm.

Craig, Cameron & Harriett L. Jacobs, 12 Nov 1841; Jas. N. Craig, Moses Leathers Jur., bm.

Craig, Charles & Rose Craig, 23 Dec 1865; Lea Allison, bm; m 23 Dec 1865 by Jas. N. Craig, J. P.

Craig, David & Betsey Durroughs, 8 Feb 1794; Samuel Craig, bm.

Craig, David & Nancy Stockard, 30 May 1803; Abram Craig, bm.

Craig, David & Nancy Strayhorn, 2 Feb 1835; A. C. Murdock, bm.

Craig, David W. & Iby Nelson, 23 April 1814; David Tate, bm.

Craig, Gilbert & Margaret A. Strayhorn, 2 Jan 1849; Jno. W. Strayhorn, bm.

Craig, Gilbert & Heneretta D. Strayhorn, 18 June 1866; John M. Blackwood, bm; m 18 June 1866 by H. G. Hill, minister.

Craig, Isaac & Elizabeth Murray, 22 Jan 1803; David Craig, bm.

Craig, Isaac & Nancy Jacobs, 3 Dec 1838; Wm. F. Strayhorn, John R. Baldwin, bm.

Craig, James & Ellinor Turner, 2 Oct 1787.

Craig, James & Sally Burns, 9 Jan 1801; Jas. Burns, Jno. Craig, bm.

Craig, James F. & Elizabeth McCauley, 11 Feb 1867; Fadis Lloyd, Thomas Griffin, bm; m 14 Feb 1867 by N. W. Wilson.

Craig, John & Susan White, 29 Nov 1832; James B. Bowen, bm.

Craig, John M. & Elizabeth Barbee, 6 March 1834; Samuel D. Strain, bm.

Craig, Johnston & Martha Blackwood, 30 April 1798; William Craig, bm.

Craig, Samuel & Patsy Kirkland, 15 April 1809; James Kirkland, bm.

Craig, Samuel & Patsey Eastridge, 24 April 1820; John Long, bm.

Craig, Soloman & Catherine Crabtree, 5 Sept 1866; Dick Webb, bm; m 5 Sept 1866 by A. C. Murdoch, J. P.

Craig, William & Mary McBride, 28 Jan 1783; Andrew McBride, bm.

Craig, Wm. & Sarah Woods, 10 Jan 1795; Matthew Wood, bm.

Craige, Anderson, son of Charles & Martha Craige, & Adeline Emerson, dau. of Tim. & Mariah Emerson, colored, m 23 Jan 1868 by Jones Watson, J. P.

Craige, William, son of Charles & Martha Craige, & Edy Thompson, dau. of Lewis & Phillis Thompson, m 4 July 1867 by Solomon Pool.

Crawford, Alvis W. & Mary Thompson, 23 July 1838; Levi N. Morrow, bm.

Crawford, Elijah & Margaret Turner, 27 Aug 1846; James Clendenin, bm.

Crawford, Henderson & Jane Holt, 6 Jan 1836; Joab Walker, bm.

Crawford, Hugh & Clarissa W. Shaw, 6 Nov 1828; J. McDade, bm.

Crawford, James & Sarah Tate, 3 Sept 1831; Joseph Crawford, bm.

Crawford, James A. & Sally J. ODaniel, 12 Sept 1866 by H. McDaniel, J. P.

Crawford, John & Ruth Woods, 10 Oct 1801.

Crawford, John & Celia Ann Rogers, 21 Jan 1833; Henderson Crawford, bm.

Crawford, John & Salley Pickard, 6 Dec 1833; Alvis Crawford, Allen J. Davie, bm.

Crawford, John S. & Nancy Smith, 4 Aug 1858; James Phillips, bm; m 8 Aug 1858 by Ruffin R. Tapp, J. P.

Crawford, Joseph & Letty Thompson, 13 Jan 1832; John R. Minnis, Sidney Whitted, bm.

Crawford, Phillip & Harriet Walker, 11 April 1828; Hugh Crawford, bm.

Crawford, Robert A. & Sarah Jane Pickard, 5 Oct 1866; Henry A. Edwards, bm; m 7 Oct 1866 by Alvis Durham, J. P.

Crawford, Samuel & Mary Walker, 26 March 1800; George Fossett, bm.

Crawford, Samuel & Elizabeth Pickard, 4 Dec 1819; Hynes Drake, bm.

Crawford, Samuel & Rebecca Minnis, 9 Aug 1839; James C. Paton, bm.

Crawford, William & Jane Morrow, 2 Oct 1810; John Wood, bm.

Crawford, William & Elizabeth Howard, 1 Oct 1841; Julia Howard, bm.

Crawford, William & Margarett Conklin, 21 Aug 1866; R. A. Crawford, bm; m 26 Aug 1866 by H. McDaniel, J. P.

Creal, John W. & Elizabeth Andrews, 30 Jan 1853; Granville Andrues, bm; m 30 Jan 1853 by Stephen S. Lloyd, J. P.

Creedle, David S. & Elizabeth L. White, 7 Feb 1848; R. M. Jones, Jonathan H. Jones, bm.

Creedle, Thomas & Cloe Freshwater, 26 Dec 1814; B. A. Rainey, bm.

Creekmore, John A. & Malinda Linnings, 9 Jan 1840; Brantley Lennings, bm.

Creel, Nathan & Betsy Pendergrass, 10 March 1827; George Thomas, bm.

Crene, George & Nancey Nichols, 2 April 1806; John Dickie, bm.

Creswell, Wm. & Jane Baker, 21 April 1823; A. W. Horton, bm.

Crisco, Danl. & Sopha Ingle, 22 May 1811; Jacob Huffman, bm.

Crisp, Clabourn & Elizabeth Hardie, 3 Dec 1821; Jesse Crisp, bm.

Crisp, David & Margaret Bryant, 4 June 1866; John M. Blackwood, bm.

Crittenton, Jimes & Polley Ritch, 9 July 1831; Michae Peary, bm.

Croker, Francis & Levice Pettiford, 5 Sept 1812; William Croker, bm.

Croker, Francis & Betsey Harris, 21 Dec 1816; Dempsey Roberts, bm.

Croker, Robert C. & Mandy Archey, 14 April 1867; m by Wiatt Cates, J. P.

Croker, William & Lucy Pettiford, 27 Nov 1813; Robert Moore, bm.

Crompton, David & Polley Elmore, 14 Nov 1807; Joseph Baker, bm.

Crompton, William & Sarah Davis, 12 Dec 1804; Allsee Morray, bm.

Crossett, William & Polley Wood, 24 Feb 1806; James Crosett, bm.

Crous, Jesse & Patsey Pendergrass, 24 Feb 1807; Wm. Pendergrass, bm.

Crover, George & Jenny Scott, 17 Nov 1810; John Scott, bm.

Crowder, George & Susan Johnston, 3 March 1834; Green Crowder, bm.

Crowder, Matthew & Nancy Carden, 4 Dec 1808; Jones Cardin, bm.

Crumpton, William & Mary Freeland, 9 Feb 1792; Jesse Rippey, bm.

Crumton, Wm. & Rebeccah Ward, 7 May 1789; John Ward, Thomas Barton, bm.

Crutcher, Mastin & Mary Hancock, 3 July 1816; John Reavis, bm.

Crutcher, Nathl. & Cynthia Clark, 21 April 1825; John W. Handcock, bm.

Crutchfield, Benjamin & Mate Cate, 9 Nov 1804; John Crutchfield, bm.

Crutchfield, Benjamin & Sally Stubbins, 4 Feb 1825; John Crutchfield, bm.

Crutchfield, Calvin & Hannah Lashley, 5 March 1840; James W. Crutchfield, Thos. C. Hayes, bm.

Crutchfield, Elijah F. & Catherine Gill, 19 Dec 1866; James H. Crutchfield, bm.

Crutchfield, Enoch & Tama Albright, 5 Dec 1826; James Cheek, bm.

Crutchfield, George P., son of John & Jane Crutchfield, & Mary J. Thompson, dau. of George & Jane Morraw, m 12 Aug 1868 by A. M. Love, minister, in Hillsboro.

Crutchfield, Henry & Elizabeth Morrow, 21 Aug 1818; William Crutchfield, bm.

Crutchfield, Henry & Polly ODaniel, 30 Oct 1823; Henry ODaniel, bm.

Crutchfield, Henry & Hannah Walker, 16 Feb 1851; William Daniel, bm; m 16 Feb 1851 by Henry McDaniel, J. P.

Crutchfield, James, of Chatham Co., & Mary Steel, 15 Dec 1794; Joseph Short, of Orange Co., bm.

Crutchfield, James & Sarah Moore, 18 July 1828; Walter A. Parrish, bm.

Crutchfield, James & Lavinia Lashley, 15 March 1836; Thos. Jones, bm.

Crutchfield, James H. & Bettie Gill, 18 Feb 1867; Jas. Jones, Thomas W. Laws, bm.

Crutchfield, James M. & Jane Criswell, 26 April 1850; P. H. Jones, bm.

Crutchfield, John & Jinney ODaniel, 21 Oct 1820; John Pickard, bm.

Crutchfield, John & Mary Tripp, 2 Oct 1852; Charles Cates, bm; m 3 Oct 1852 by Wiatt Cates, J. P.

Crutchfield, John H. & Elizabeth Workman, 5 Nov 1835; Samel. Smith, Pinckney Sykes, bm.

Crutchfield, John H. & Mary Ann Young, 28 Jan 1862; Daniel R. Efland, Wm. Cheek, bm.

Crutchfield, William & Frances Pickard, 19 Dec 1795; Elisha Pickard, bm.

Crutchfield, William & Elizabeth Chambers, 3 May 1822; Harbert Hobbs, bm.

Cumins, Jno. & Elizabeth Woods, 12 Nov 1819; Wesley Hanks, bm.

Cummens, John & Jane Freeland, 1 July 1835; J. P. Gibson, bm.

Cummins, Alexander & Grizzel Woods, 2 Feb 1824; David Cummins, bm.

Cummins, David & Margaret Woods, 19 April 1823; Jos. A. Woods, bm.

Cummins, Jacob & Mary Ana Alexander, 27 Dec 1840; Joseph Evans, bm.

Cumpton, Norris & Mary Marsh, 3 Feb 1795; Thos. Compton, bm.

Cunningham, Jeremiah M. & Polley Lynch, 31 Jan 1824; Thos. Lynch, bm.

Cunningham, Matthew & Betsey Galbreath, 16 Jan 1793; Francis McCamey, bm.

Curl, George & Margery Pickett, 22 Jan 1803; Isaac Richardson, bm.

Curl, William & Mary Allen, 24 Dec 1796; Samuel Chambers, bm.

Currey, John & Alesy Riley, 1 Sept 1795; James Riley, bm.

Currie, Ezekiel & Elizabeth Allen, 11 Oct 1800; Jno. Campbell, bm.

Currie, Hugh & Elizth. Nunn, 22 Nov 1790; Wm. Muzzale, bm.

Currie, James & Sarah Forrester, 19 Oct 1793; John Currey, bm.

Currie, John & Dulceneah Armstrong, 11 Dec 1827; A. Armstrong, bm.

Currie, William N. & Martha Thompson, 17 Nov 1822; T. Long, bm.

Curry, Hugh & Martha A. Strain, 25 Jan 1853; J. M. Watson, bm; m 26 Jan 1853 by Stephen S. Lloyd, J. P.

Curtis, Christopher C. & Temperance C. Graves, 11 April 1838; Peter L. Boon, bm.

Curtis, Clement C. & Polly Shofner, 28 Oct 1845; J. R. Boswell, bm.

Curtis, John & Dolley Honeycut, 17 Nov 1803; Pomfrett Herndon, bm.

Curtis, Paul, son of Peter & Elizabeth Curtis, & Delila Smith, dau. of Anderson & Martha Smith, colored, m 18 Dec 1867.

Dailey, John G. & Sarah E. Compton, 12 Aug 1865; Bedford Compton, bm; m 17 Aug 1865 by Thomas H. Hughes, J. P.

Dalley, James W. A. & Lucindah Catharine Kimbrough, 22 May 1859; William A. Birl, bm.

Dally, John & Rebecca Ray, 27 Dec 1823; Junius Hall, bm.

Dameron, James S. & Keate E. Roberts, 14 July 1860; Azariah Dameron, bm.

Danely, Jas. & Jeaney Thomas, 2 Sept 1800; Caleb Pyle, bm.

Daniel, Alvis L. & Louisa Couch, 12 Nov 1855; Alvis Cheek, bm; m 12 Nov 1855 by Durell Tilley, J. P.

Daniel, Christopher & Nancy Massey, 23 Aug 1803; Enoch Massey, bm.

Daniel, Isiah & Charlotte King, 3 Nov 1834; John Lewis, bm.

Daniel, Isiah & Mary Whiteker, 4 Sept 1850; Simpson Crabtree, bm.

Daniel, James & Sarah J. Anderson, 4 Jan 1867; John A. Utley, bm; m 6 Jan 1867 by Thos. Wilson, J. P.

Daniel, John & Mary Walton, 7 Sept 1805; Edwd. Walton, bm.

Daniel, Moore & Elizabeth Reeves, 8 June 1832; W. F. C. Smith, Saml. Smith, bm.

Daniel, Moore & Jane Murdock, 6 Aug 1841; Dowd Hayes, bm.

Daniel, Robert & Kitty Pritchett, 19 Nov 1831; John Cheek, Alvis Cheek, bm.

Daniel, William & Mary A. Killian, 20 Nov 1848; Isaac Killian, bm.

Danly, John & Patsy Mason, 2 Dec 1813; Aaron Rumbly, bm.

Danly, William & Margaret Ireland, 27 Dec 1846; Jesse T. Dannly, bm.

Dannel, Christopher & Tilley Shepperd, 7 Nov 1786; Roger Dannel, bm.

Danniel, John & Catey Couch, 28 Dec 1814; Henry Trice, bm.

Dark, Willis & Mary McPherson, 6 Jan 1821; Stephen McPherson, bm.

Daugherty, Anthony & Mary McCool, 30 July 1788; James Daugherty, bm.

Daugherty, James & Hesther Cohern, 13 April 1790; Anthony Daugherty, bm.

Daugherty, Thomas & Unus Monroe, 28 Oct 1802; Samuel Scarlett, bm.

Daughorty, James & Phebe Cole, 15 Dec 1818; Merriman Cole, bm.

Daughrity, James M. & Sally Smith, 28 Jan 1852; George Jackson, bm; m 28 Jan 1852 by William Dickson, J. P.

Daves, Graham & Allice L. DeRossett, 27 Nov 1862; Geo. Patterson, bm; m 27 Nov 1862 by M. A. Curtis, Rector St. Matthew's Church, Hillsborough, N. C.

Davey, Ashbourne & Jane Borland, 8 July 1820; Moses S. Pratt, bm.

Davies, Baxter & Margaret E. Long, 1 March 1862; Wm. J. Long, bm; m 3 March 1862 by Charles W. Johnston, J. P.

Davies, Wm. W. & Emily J. Stevenson, 10 Oct 1866; Jno. A. Owen, bm; m 10 Oct 1866 by N. W. Wilson.

Davis, Abner & Caty Jinkins, 29 Nov (1799-1802); John Bragg, bm.

Davis, Asa N. & Mary Warren, 19 Nov 1850; Lucian Price, bm.

Davis, Baxter & Betsey Strain, 30 Nov 1811; James Cain, bm.

Davis, Benjamin & Amelia Brockwell, 27 Feb 1838; W. Chambers, Orrin Lewis, bm.

Davis, Charles & Ann E. Caudle, 22 Dec 1856; Jn. Closs, bm.

Davis, Christopher & Salley Rich, 22 Dec 1831; James Davis, bm.

Davis, Christopher & Mary Pritchett, 26 May 1857; S. S. Clayton, bm.

Davis, Daniel & Josephine Kelly, 4 Sept 1867; m 5 Sept 1867 by J. J. W. McCauley.

Davis, Demarcrus & Nancy Pendergrass, 25 Aug 1860; Jas. J. Brockwell, bm; m 26 Aug 1860 by James Phillips, minister.

Davis, Duncan C. & Mariah Strain, 17 Feb 1862; D. McCauley, bm.

Davis, F. A. & Ann R. Wilson, 27 Sept 1855; L. H. Newton, bm; m 27 Sept 1866 by Peter Doub, Pastor.

Davis, George, son of Jesse & Lucy Davis, & Susan McKee, colored, m 12 June 1868 by C. P. Warren, J. P.

Davis, Green & Jenny Hall, 2 Feb 1824; E. H. Carrington, bm.

Davis, Henry & Charity Patterson, 13 April 1867; m 13 April 1867 by J. P. Mason, min.

Davis, James & Sarah Wood, 15 April 1784; John Davis, bm.

Davis, James & Sarah Scoggins, 30 Jan 1810; John Edwards, bm.

Davis, James & Sarah Couch, 28 Aug 1815; John Bevill, bm.

Davis, James & Elizabeth Marlett, 7 March 1820; Benja. A. Yeargin, bm.

Davis, James & Nancy Blackwood, 18 Sept 1833; William Gattis, bm.

Davis, James & Lydia Bishop, 6 Sept 1851; James Fowler, bm; m 11 Sept 1851 by Elder Littlejohn Utley, bm.

Davis, James G. & Margaret Garner, 10 Dec 1827; John Albright, bm.

Davis, James G. & Elizabeth A. Leigh, 21 Jan 1856; Sampson Davis, Edward R. Davis, bm; m 22 Jan 1856 by John Burroughs, J. P.

Davis, James T., son of Miles W. & Fanny Davis, & Jenny C. Reeves, dau. of Azariah & Betsey Reeves, m 11 Dec 1867 by Charles Phillips, minister.

Davis, John & Sarah Wheeler, 13 April 1809; Jas. Nicholson, bm.

Davis, John & Nancy McFerson, 15 Nov 1828; Jesse Crutchfield, bm.

Davis, John F. & Mary Brown, 12 Aug 1847; P. H. Mangum, bm.

Davis, Jno. W. & Euphrasia P. Allison, 10 Nov 1846; E. Murray, Jr., bm.

Davis, Miles & Susannah Bevill, 27 May 1814; M. Yeargin, bm.

Davis, Miles W. & Frances King, 20 May 1848; J. W. Carr, bm.

Davis, Nicholas & Frances Austin, 26 Sept 1785; Henry Davis, bm.

Davis, Pleasant & Margret Ivey, 15 Sept 1837; F. Moize, bm.

Davis, Pleasant & Mary Allbert, 27 Feb 1865; Adley Andres, bm; m 28 Feb 1865 by D. Tilley, J. P.

Davis, Ransom & Susanna Bragg, 9 Sept 1797; Joseph Fennel, bm.

Davis, Robert & Elizabeth Latta, 16 April 1810; John Latta, bm.

Davis, Roling & Sally Herndon, 28 Aug 1829; Pleasant Rhodes, bm.

Davis, Saml. & Nancy Townsey, 15 May 1801; Phillip Roberts, bm.

Davis, Saml. & Cornelia Mangum, 21 Feb 1854; E. A. Heartt, bm.

Davis, Silas & Nancy Davis, 28 March 1836; Wm. H. Hall, bm.

Davis, Simon & Rebecca Wilkinson, 19 Aug 1816; David Davis, bm.

Davis, Thomas & Deborah Hall, 5 April 1786; John Latta, bm.

Davis, Thomas & Barsena Proctor, 21 April 1857; R. H. Proctor, bm; m 23 April 1857 by S. Shepherd, J. P.

Davis, Tho. C. & Elizabeth Davis, 8 Jan 1849; John Bullock, bm.

Davis, Thos. H. Jr. & Elizabeth Clemming, 14 Nov 1826; Wm. H. Hardin, bm.

Davis, Wiett & Catharine Daniel, 28 July 1810; Anderson Davis, bm.

Davis, Wm. & Lydia Dugger, 4 Dec 1794; Richard Davis, bm.

Davison, David & Elizabeth King, 25 Feb 1800; Samuel King, bm.

Davison, Joseph & Ester Craig, 20 March 1787; Robert Fauset, bm.

Davison, Samuel & Margaret Pike, 10 Sept 1797; Thomas King, bm.

Dawson, Joseph & Nancy King, 25 Feb 1817; Jon Pendergrass, bm.

Dawson, Westley & Nancy Hathcock, 25 July 1860; Joseph Dawson, bm; m 25 July 1860 by Allen Edwards, J. P.

Day, Adolphus & Jane Day, 10 July 1858; Wmson Parrish, bm.

Day, Anderson & Sophia Jones, 11 Jan 1860; W. B. Murray, bm.

Day, Archabald & Ruthy Woody, 8 April 1820; John Woody, bm.

Day, Benjamin & Fanny Reves, 15 April 1823; William Day, bm.

Day, Haywood & Caroline Evans, 11 Oct 1860; Alvis K. Umsted, bm.

Day, Jeremiah & Nicey Mitchell, 28 Jan 1823; William Day, bm.

Day, Jesse & Love Pettiford, 27 Jan 1819; William Day, bm.

Day, Reuben & Mary Brooks, 21 Jan 1841; Thomas Anderson, bm.

Day, Robert & Rebecca Ann Taburn, colored, m 11 Feb 1861 by A. W. Gray, J. P.

Day, Saml. & Polly Ann McGhee, 27 May 1848; Wm. Day, bm.

Day, Washington & Mary Harris, colored, 26 Dec 1863; John H. Paul, bm.

Day, Wesley Richeson & Sally M. Stewart, 10 April 1849; Albert Stewart, bm.

Day, William & Jinsey Pettiford, 6 Oct 1818; James Hopkins, Edward Harris, bm.

Day, William & Betsey Revels, 24 Nov 1840; Ga. Hurdle, C. Stroud, bm.

Day, William & Jane Bird, 16 Jan 1858; Jno. Turner, bm.

Day, William & Rowan Johnson, 20 May 1858; Wmson Parrish, bm.

Day, William H. & Polly Ann Mayho, 9 Nov 1848; Jno. Laws, bm.

Day, Wm. H. & Matilda Day, 2 June 1840; H. Webb, R. F. Dupont, bm.

Dayvis, Edward R. & Elizabeth Herendon, 28 Aug 1848; Henderson B. Rochell, bm.

Dean, James A. & Mary Harris, 2 Aug 1854; H. N. Brown, bm.

Debow, Benjn. & Ellin Thompson, 14 June 1783; Abram Thompson, bm.

ORANGE COUNTY MARRIAGES, 1779-1868

Debruler, Greenfield & Salley Wilson, 8 Oct 1811; Jas. Lapslie, bm.

Debruler, William G. & Linney Crompten, 28 July 1824; Thomas Hicks, bm.

Deen, Thos. & Elizabeth Philips, 18 June 1798; Rob. Cate, bm.

DeGraffenreidt, Edwin L. & Martha S. Kirkland, 16 Nov 1820; John N. Kirkland, bm.

Degroot, Daniel & Elizabeth Murdock, 14 Nov 1846; Charles Jordan, bm.

Dennin, William & Abigail Baws, 6 July 1833; Ezekiel Tinen, bm.

Denning, William & Jeane Bowls, 22 June 1792; Peter Lemmons, bm.

Denny, Thomas & Martha Brown Williams, 7 May 1821; Saml. Webb, bm.

Denson, Samuel & Louisa Sykes, 19 April 1866; Thos S. Cates, bm; m 19 April 1866 by Alvis Durham, J. P.

Denton, William & Polly Shofner, 13 June 1807.

Derickson, James & Adawick Davis, 6 May 1794; James Davis, bm.

DeRossett, Wm. L. & Elizabeth S. Nash, 29 May 1863; Pride Jones, bm; m 10 June 1863 by M. A. Curtis.

Desarn, Edward & Cornelia Ann Scoggins, 20 April 1853; W. H. Turner, bm; m 20 April 1853 by John Hancock, J. P.

Desern, Edward & Rachel Copley, 18 March 1816; Samuel Peelor, bm.

Desern, Henderson & Eliza Jane Neal, 14 Aug 1843; H. Pratt, Geo Laws, bm.

Desern, John & Mary Carrell, 19 Nov 1847; Isreal Turner, bm.

Deshon, Nathl. & Jemima Matthews, 3 Jan 1814; Ed. King, bm.

Devenport, Isaac & Mary Campbell, 12 Jan 1805; Daniel Campbell, bm.

Devenport, John & Mary McMullan, 2 Oct 1804; James S. Turrentine, bm.

Dickerson, Bird & Celey Phillips, 3 Feb 1816; Henry Logan, bm.

Dickerson, John & Zilphia Burnes, 24 March 1810; Samuel Whitsitt, bm.

Dickey, Docton & Eliza Hughes, 13 March 1840; E. F. Watson, John Newlin, bm.

Dickey, James & Polley Garrison, 25 Jan 1801; Moses Lynch, bm.

Dickey, James & Phebe Faucett, 25 Sept 1816; John Plummer, bm.

Dickey, James B. & Elizabeth Shult, 3 Jan 1817; Chs. Bruce, bm.

86

Dickey, John, son of Munroe & Harriett Dickey, & Elizabeth Hopkins, dau. of Wm. W. & Susanah Hopkins, m 13 Oct 1867 by Joseph W. McKee, J. P.

Dickey, Robt. Johnston & Mary Lewis, 5 July 1805; John Rhodes, bm.

Dickey, Wm. & Margaret Brown, 8 Aug 1816; Hall Garrison, bm.

Dickey, Zachariah, son of Munroe & Harriett Dickey & Sarah E. Cates, dau. of Solomon & Jane Cates, m 11 June 1867 by Wm. D. Lunsford, J. P.

Dickie, James Jr. & Charity Fossett, 21 Nov 1833; Jacob Dickey, Elot. Watson, bm.

Dickie, John & Salley Robinson, 8 July 1808; William R. Robinson, bm.

Dickie, John W. & Sally E. Ray, 5 Feb 1866; John Malone, bm; m 13 Feb 1866 by Thos. Wilson, J. P.

Dickie, Zachariah & Polly Ellis, 31 Dec 1817; Hunter McCulloch, bm.

Dicks, James & Mary McFerson, 21 April 1826; Jonathan Parkes Sr., bm.

Dicks, Peter & Mary Lindley, 12 Aug 1790; James Woody, bm.

Dickson, Henry & M. E. Strayhorn, 22 Dec 1858; T. W. Laws, bm; m 23 Dec 1858 by Ro. Hooker, M. E. Church, South.

Dickson, Samuel & Betsey Stanford, 25 Sept 1827; Wilie Merrit, bm.

Dickson, Stewart & Salley Holmes, 16 April 1793; John McCallom, bm.

Dickson, Thomas & Nancy Dixon, 4 March 1837; Daniel Graves, bm.

Dickson, William & Thompson Whitley, 29 Dec 1795; James Dixon, bm.

Dickson, Wm. & Margaret Jane Walker, 10 Oct 1837; Robert Wilkins, bm.

Dicky, David & Harriet Clarke, 24 Oct 1832; L. W. Clark, bm.

Dicky, William & Eliza J. Barber, 23 Sept 1847; Ganrlle S. Holt, bm.

Diliard, Willie & Franky Campbell, 16 April 1809; Bolling Cox, bm.

Dilliard, Willis & Penelope Trice, 11 Aug 1835; James Trice, bm.

Dilworth, Junius & Elizabeth J. Lockhart, 28 June 1837; A. Parks, bm.

Dinning, John & Elizabeth Boyles, 2 Oct 1781; John Moody, bm.

Dishon, Augustine & Susanna Price, 18 April 1798; Augustine Dishon, bm.

Dishon, Jacob & Catharine McVey, 29 Oct 1797; Ghoston Dishon, bm.

Dishon, Jesse F. & Minerva Bowles, 21 July 1834; Geo. F. Dishough, James Faucet, bm.

Dishon, Luke & Sarah McClure, 15 Nov 1799; H. Faucett, bm.

Dishongs, Jacob & Nancy Tyrrell, 1 July 1848; Thomas Anderson, bm.

Dismukes, Alexander H. & Susan U. Mebane, 28 Oct 1835; Thos. T. Oldham, bm.

Dixon, Adam & Rachel Gray, 9 Jan 1805; George Clancy, bm.

Dixon, Alexander & Elizabeth Wilson, 15 April 1833; H. Terry, J. C. Turrentine, bm.

Dixon, Anderson & Louisa Tate, 20 July 1838; James Meband Jr., bm.

Dixon, Benj. & Maria Geer, 20 Oct 1865; F. C. Geer, bm; m 20 Oct 1865 by B. C. Hopkins, J. P.

Dixon, James & Jane Anderson, 23 Nov 1793; John McCallom, bm.

Dixon, James & Hannah Hill, 28 March 1801; S. Benton, bm.

Dixon, James & Jane Latta, 25 Feb 1860; A. S. Carrington, bm; m 26 Feb 1860 by Wm. J. Roberts, J. P.

Dixon, James C. & Salley Freshwaters, 30 April 1822; John Mulhollan, bm.

Dixon, James T., son of Abner A. & Jane Dixon, & Louisa Elizabeth Herndon, dau. of M. C. & Francis Herndon, m 14 May 1868 by B. C. Hopkins, J. P.

Dixon, John & Ruth Massey, 15 Aug 1799; H. McCollum, bm.

Dixon, John & Jeany Smith, 15 Dec 1800; Jonathan Workman, bm.

Dixon, John & Catharine Allen, 7 Feb 1832; James A. Craig, bm.

Dixon, John & Martha F. Scott, 18 Feb 1839; James Mebane Jr., bm.

Dixon, Maxwell & Elizabeth Herndon, 20 June 1812; Thos. Bilbo, bm.

Dixon, Reuben & Elizabeth Moore, 5 Nov 1796; Charles Cate, bm.

Dixon, Robert & Mary Galbreath, 6 April 1791; Benjamin Roney, bm.

Dixon, Robert & Frances Faucett, 18 Dec 1831; Robert J. White, bm.

Dixon, Robert W. & Lydia Holloway, 4 May 1846; M. C. Herndon, bm.

Dixon, Thomas & Anne Turner, 23 May 1793; James Dickson, bm.

Dixon, Thomas & Jane Grahams, 23 Dec 1840; William G. Stout, bm.

Dixon, William & Nancy Jane Moore, 27 Feb 1839; Thomas Dickson, bm.

Dixon, William Jur. & Delilah Albright, 18 Aug 1817; Simon Nease, bm.

Dixson, David & Sylvia Boothe, 30 Sept 1797; Ephraim Dixon, bm.

Doane, William & Mary Green, 13 Sept 1832; David Holt, bm.

Docary, Perry & Peggy Lamb, 13 Nov 1815; Thomas R. Cate, bm.

Dockery, John & Huldah Watson, 24 Jan 1816; Robert Watson, bm.

Dockery, Peyton & Elizabeth Watson, 7 Aug 1819; Thomas Griffin, James Clancy, bm.

Dockrey, Robert & Katy Jessup, 17 Oct 1820; Jos. Stubbins, bm.

Dodd, William & Milley Marcorm, 30 May 1793; Wm. Shepard, bm.

Dodson, Edmund G. & Catharine Sykes, 2 May 1842; Robert Sykes, bm.

Dodson, Edward & Elizabeth Cummings, ___ 1804; James Paull, bm.

Dodson, John & Martha Andrews, 6 May 1850; Ruffin Dodson, bm.

Dodson, Ruffin & Lucy Ann Lloyd, 20 Aug 1851; John Dodson, bm; m 21 Aug 1851 by Thomas Brewer, J. P.

Dodson, Thomas & Patsy Sykes, 7 Sept 1820; George Durem, Geo. Brown, bm.

Dodson, Thomas G. Jr. & Sarah Lloyd, 28 Sept 1857; Wm. Dodson, bm.

Dodson, Wm. & Sally Sikes, 3 June 1858; John H. Sykes, bm; m 3 June 1858 by Wilson Brown, J. P.

Dodson, Wm. James & Nancy Adams, 31 July 1848; Thos. R. Simpson, bm.

Dodson, Willie & Betsey Green, 16 Jan 1819; James Smith, bm.

Doherty, Geo. & Polley Burke, 23 April 1785; Absalom Tatom, bm.

Dollar, Guilford & Sophronian Hurdleson, 13 July 1857; John C. Reed, bm; m 16 July 1857 by Samuel Couch, J. P.

Dollar, Hapton & Mary Christian, 20 June 1831; Sterling Proctor, bm.

Dollar, Henry & Jeany Wair, 11 Jan 1799; Elijah Dollar, bm.

Dollar, Henry & Elizabeth James, 14 Sept 1820; Noah Rhodes, bm.

Dollar, Isaac D. & Polley Dollar, 19 Sept 1814; Moses Guess, bm.

Dollar, James & Betsey Tilly, 13 May 1819; Joshua Haughton, bm.

Dollar, James & Rebecca Guess, 4 March 1820; Noah Rhodes, bm.

Dollar, John & Haley Roberts, 17 April 1833; John Riley, bm.

Dollar, John & Jane Crabtree, 3 Jan 1835; Riley James, Richs. Nichols, bm.

Dollar, John & Lovina Cates, 18 Jan 1865; John Q. Lloyd, Wm. P. Cate, bm; m 26 Jan 1865 by John F. Lyon, J. P.

Dollar, John Jackson & Mary Jane Carrington, 5 May 1843; A. Parks, Alves Nichols, bm.

Dollar, Joseph & Cynthia Browning, 12 Feb 1825; Ilai Browning, bm.

Dollar, Madison & Malinda Clemons, 3 Jan 1856; William Mangum, bm; m 3 Jan 1856 by Harris Wilkerson, J. P.

Dollar, Mangum & Jane Smith, 30 July 1856; Willie Riley, bm; m 30 July 1856 by Charles Wilson, J. P.

Dollar, Milton & Elizabeth Rhodes, 18 Nov 1836; Stephen Dollar, John Holden, bm.

Dollar, Stephen & Frances Crabtree, 5 June 1835; Edward Crabtree, J. Taylor, bm.

Dollar, Thomas & Sarah Barbee, 12 Sept 1857; Young Barbee, bm; m 12 Sept 1857 by Solomon Shepherd, J. P.

Dollar, William & Mary Wilson, 25 Aug 1789; Stephen Wilson, bm.

Dollar, William & Salley Carroll, 21 May 1825; Noah Rhodes, bm.

Dollar, William & Jane Sparks, 22 May 1838; W. McCauley, George Browning, bm.

Dollar, William & Martha Bacon, 4 Jan 1859; Wm. R. Scautt, bm; m 6 Jan 1859 by Thomas G. Hayes, minister.

Dollar, Wm. & Selina G. Wilkerson, 3 Dec 1864; J. M. McDade, Thos. W. Laws, bm; m 4 Dec 1864 by D. W. Jordan, J. P.

Dollar, Wm. G. & Mary A. Shamlee, 1 Dec 1849; Jno. M. Faucett, bm.

Dollar, William S. & Mary E. Cheek, 23 Nov 1847; Elija Cole, bm.

Donaldson, James & Mary Riley, 28 May 1788; Charles Allison, bm.

Donnell, Robert & Salley Moore, 22 Oct 1802; James Moore, bm.

Donnell, Robert & Nancy Latta, 6 Nov 1820; Tho. N. S. Hargis, bm.

Doogan, Edmond & Anne Bradford, 25 Aug 1789; William McAdams, bm.

Dooley, Jno. & Susannah Hancock, 17 March 1843; Richs. Nichols, bm.

Dorhety, Leray & Milly Dollar, 14 Jan 1857; John Dollar, Thos. C. Hayes, bm; m 14 Jan 1857 by Thos. C. Hayes, minister.

Dorhety, Samuel & Caroline Cole, 22 Dec 1857; William Wilson, bm; m 24 Dec 1857 by John L. Woods, J. P.

Dorothy, Samuel & Polley Dickie, 30 July 1835; William Wilkison, bm.

Dorris, John & Phebe Culbertson, 12 Jan 1795; John Dorris, bm.

Dortch, David & Sarah Ryals, 17 Jan 1824; John E. Rial, bm.

Dortch, John & Ruth Carrington, 30 Dec 1830; Jos. A. Woods, William Porter, bm.

Dortch, John Y. & Sarah B. Bacon, 3 Aug 1843; Jno. McKerall, Ed. W. Bacon, bm.

Dortch, Young & Nancy Woods, 28 Aug 1799; William Carr, bm.

Dosset, Tho. & Nancy Cates, 10 Aug 1785; Benj. Brittain, bm.

Dossett, Elisha & Polly Self, 26 May 1820; Andrew Haley, bm.

Dossett, Elisha & Polley Self, 21 Oct 1822; John Self, bm.

Dossett, Newton & Elizabeth Woods, 16 Oct 1866; W. B. Clinton, bm; m 18 Oct 1866 by R. F. Morris, J. P.

Dossett, Phillip & Tempe Cole, 22 Aug 1806; Joseph Pyle, bm.

Dossett, Willis & Jeany Desern, 12 June 1806; Philip Bennett, bm.

Dossit, Wm. & Drucilla Forrister, 30 Dec 1783.

Dossitt, Elbert & Anne Cain, 11 Sept 1832; James Leathers, bm.

Dossitt, Willis & Sally Waer, 7 March 1805; Abner Cates, bm.

Dougherty, Samuel & Emeline Mitchell, 26 Aug 1851; Anthony Dortherty, bm; m 28 Aug 1851 by Nathaniel Bain, J. P.

Douglas, David & Elizabeth Pearson, 17 Jan 1832; John Thomas, J. Taylor, bm.

Douglas, Jno. & Polley Ray, 31 March 1813; Adam M. Douglas, bm.

Douglas, John & Lucy Clemens, 30 Oct 1856; Josep Harwood, bm.

Douglass, Adam & Nancy Cain, 28 Oct 1816; Hartwill S. Overbey, bm.

Douglass, Adam M. & Mary Ann Carington, 6 Nov 1850; Wm. L. Willis, bm.

Douglass, Ash & Dilley Pendergrass, 24 Dec 1837; Thomas Griffin, P. F. Plesant, bm.

Douglass, David & Margaret Watson, 25 Jan 1791; Peter Lemmon, bm.

Douglass, David & Rebecca Tudor, 23 May 1815; Thomas Crabtree, Conrod Ringstaff, bm.

Douglass, Henderson & Polley Bristo, 13 Feb 1810; Henry Dougles, William Bristow, bm.

Douglass, James & Elizabeth Bradford, 23 May 1796; Jno. Tate, bm.

Douglass, James F. & Catharine C. Tinnen, 19 Dec 1862; Abram Crabtree, bm; m 23 Dec 1862 by Archd. Currie.

91

Douglass, John C. & Rachel S. Lipscomb, 29 Jan 1838; Jas. Sneed, A. Mickle, bm.

Douglass, John & Margaret Hamilton, 14 July 1792; David Bradford, bm.

Douglass, John & Patsy Dishon, 20 Dec 1825; A. H. Leonard, Tho. W. Holden, bm.

Douglass, Pleasant & Martha Noble, 28 Feb 1842; Ga. B. Lea, James Clark, bm.

Douglass, William & Martha Hughs, 18 April 1789; James Hughs, bm.

Downs, William & Polley Tilley, 3 Feb 1794; George Tilley, bm.

Doyle, Gregory & Martha Gott, 19 Oct 1785; Thos. Farmer, bm.

Drake, George W. & Agnes Rhodes, 29 Sept 1865; J. C. McCown, bm; m 11 Oct 1865 by James Stagg, J. P.

Drake, Hynes & Nancy Crawford, 13 Nov 1817; John Crawford, bm.

Drew, Ben & Mason Griffiths, 10 May 1804; Charles Porter, bm.

Drew, Benjamin & Morning Jeffreys, 6 Oct 1821; Wm. Grifis, bm.

Drew, Buck & Betsey Griffeys, 16 June 1812; Mark Ammons, bm.

Driskel, David & Aggey Green, 26 Aug 1783; Archer Grissom, bm.

Dublin, Jacob & Susannah Lewis, 30 March 1805; Eps Hilliard, bm.

Dublin, James & Elizabeth Jackson, 13 Jan 1807; John Ray, bm.

Dugger, Leonard & Rhoda Castleberry, 11 Jan 1792; Wm. OKelly, bm.

Dugger, Shadrach & Salley Hogan, 16 Oct 1793; Benja. Yeargain, bm.

Duke, Green & Mary Hall, 23 Oct 1847; Benton Ray, bm.

Duke, Greif & Mary Cozort, 9 Feb 1821; John Erner, bm.

Duke, Henry & Ferabee Parker, 17 April 1802; Benjamin Peeler, bm.

Duke, Hiram & Cursey Forkner, 21 Dec 1815; Augt. Dickerson, bm.

Duke, James & Susan M. Proctor, 9 Sept 1852; Isreal Turner, Thomas Dollar, bm; m 9 Sept 1852 by Harris Wilkerson, J. P.

Duke, Jesse & Nancy Roberts, 1 Nov 1817; Shadrach Roberts, bm.

Duke, John & Elizabeth Duke, 20 June 1812; James Leathers, bm.

Duke, John & Lydia Lewis, 26 April 1817; Thos. Rhew, bm.

Duke, John & Susannah Brown, 13 Dec 1822; Nehemiah Thomas, bm.

Duke, Robert & Anne Rhew, 14 March 1794; George Horner, Robert Harris, bm.

Duke, Robert & Eliza A. Bennett, 18 Oct 1861; D. C. Parrish, bm; m 20 Oct 1861 by B. C. Hopkins.

Duke, Robert A. & Margarett Crawford, 19 May 1866; Alfred J. Pickard, bm; m 20 May 1866 by H. McDaniel, J. P.

Duke, Taylor & Dicey Jones, 14 Aug 1801; Moses Jones, bm.

Duke, Tyre & Elizabeth Rhew, 9 March 1813; Wm. Warren, bm.

Duke, Washington & Mary C. Clinton, 9 Aug 1842; Balay Nichols, Wm. J. Duke, bm.

Duke, William & Mary Carrington, 9 Aug 1783; Robert Ashley, bm.

Duke, William, son of Robt. & Peggy Cavuy, 19 Aug 1821; John Duke, bm.

Dunagan, William & Sally Peelor, 28 Jan 1793; George Carrington, bm.

Duncan, Nelson & Anne Carter, 10 May 1831; John Griffin, bm.

Dunn, Samuel & Peggy Nelson, 27 April 1811; Hugh Willson, bm.

Dunn, Samuel & Jane Scott, 8 Sept 1855; Eli J. Hester, bm.

Dunnagan, Charles & Jinney Scarlett, 13 Dec 1819; William Cates, bm.

Dunnagan, Charles & Catey Nutt, 4 Sept 1827; Robert Nutt, Jr., bm.

Dunnagan, Charles & Edny Umsted, 10 Oct 1865; Oved Umsted, bm.

Dunnagan, Charles L. & Edy C. Lunsford, 12 May 1847; Wm. H. Dunnagan, bm.

Dunnagan, James & Sibby Horner, 25 June 1795; Charles Dunnagan, bm.

Dunnagan, James & Nancy Waggoner, 8 Dec 1810; Timothy Dunnagan, bm.

Dunnagan, Norman & Catherine Link, 10 May 1854; Willie G. Guess, bm; m 11 May 1854 by Wm. McCown, J. P.

Dunnagin, Ashby & Polly May, 4 June 1795; Wm. Belvin, bm.

Dunnagon, Tho. & Nelley James, 25 Feb 1800; James Dunnagan, bm.

Dunnigan, Shareward & Cynthia Warren, 3 June 1823; Thomas Deadmon, bm.

Durham, Aaron & Sarah Cate, 23 May 1798; Charles Cate, bm.

Durham, Aaron & Rebecca Cates, 17 Feb 1855; Wm. McCauly, bm.

Durham, Alves & Catharine Strayhorn, 31 Oct 1838; Jno. M. Faucett, Wm. F. Strayhorn, bm.

Durham, Alvis & Susan Fossett, 1 Sept 1827; Thomas D. Faucett, bm.

Durham, Archebell & Peggy Stroud, 29 March 1803; John Jolley, bm.

Durham, David L. & Barbary Cheek, 2 Nov 1824; Green Lloyd, bm.

Durham, Dudley & Kesiah Durham, 22 Dec 1829; Isaac Durham, bm.

Durham, Elbert S. & Sarah Lloyd, 27 Dec 1841; Harrison O.
Durham, Silvanus W. Perry, bm.

Durham, Elisha & Mary Roach, 19 Oct 1847; James F. Cate, bm.

Durham, Ezra & Patsy Hunter, 18 April 1822; William Cates, bm.

Durham, Ferdinand & Susannah Carruthers, 8 Oct 1829; James
Caruthers, Alvis Durham, bm.

Durham, Harrison O. & Matilda Allen, 16 Jan 1846; John Pierce,
bm.

Durham, Ilai & Mourning Kirk, 11 May 1816; Thomas Durham, bm.

Durham, Isaac & Martha Carrothers, 31 March 1824; Thomas M.
Durham, bm.

Durham, James & Tempy Stewart, 7 March 1848; Jesse Jeffries, bm.

Durham, James G. & Mary E. Strawn, 19 July 1866; Thomas A.
Lasly, bm; m 22 July 1866 by Alvis Durham, J. P.

Durham, James S. & Harritt D. Stroud, 29 July 1865; James G.
Durham, bm; m 29 July 1865 by J. W. Strowd, J. P.

Durham, James W. & Mary E. Howard, 15 Sept 1849; John W. Latta,
bm.

Durham, Jason & Salley McCrackin, 14 June 1836; Jesse Durham,
G. B. Durham, bm.

Durham, Jesse & Susan Fossett, 7 March 1831; Alvis Durham, bm.

Durham, Jesse & Susannah Clark, 14 June 1836; G. B. Durham, bm.

Durham, John & Mary Robinson, 27 March 1798; John Taylor, bm.

Durham, John & Anne Latta, 13 May 1818; Jesse Daniel, bm.

Durham, John & Jane Hatch, 7 Sept 1819; John Durham Sr., bm.

Durham, John & Rebecca Whitted, 9 Oct 1834; James Howard, bm.

Durham, John & Mourning Ivey, 1 Jan 1841; Elbertes Durham, bm.

Durham, John & Sarah Ann Carathers, 31 Aug 1860; Q. G. Strayhorn, bm; m 8 Oct 1860 by John W. Strowd, J. P.

Durham, Lindsey & Salley Hatch, 1 Nov 1834; Jesse Durham, bm.

Durham, Lindsey & Sylvia Shaw, 2 Aug 1836; Wesley Edwards,
Geo. W. Morrow, bm.

Durham, Mark & Syllah Robertson, 10 Dec 1795; George Meacham,
bm.

Durham, Mark & Milly Coplin, 18 Nov 1853; D. M. Durham, bm;
m 18 Nov 1853 by Samuel Baldwin, M. G.

Durham, Mathew & Elizabeth Kirk, 22 July 1820; Samuel Faust, bm.

Durham, Matthew & Matilda M. Willett, 29 Sept 1847; Thomas Cate, James Cate, bm.

Durham, Mebane & Elizabeth Lloyd, 15 April 1835; Sam. Child, Jesse Durham, bm.

Durham, Nathaniel & Salley Hatch, 2 April 1811; Samuel Faucet, bm.

Durham, Robert & Salley Jones, 3 Jan 1826; Thomas Durham, bm.

Durham, Robert A., aged 24 & Elizabeth Manes, age 17, m 23 May 1867 by H. McC. Stroud, J. P.

Durham, Spencer & Delila Loyd, 26 Dec 1825; Thomas D. Faucitt, bm.

Durham, Tarlton & Catharine Cheek, 3 Sept 1839; David L. Durham, C. M. Latimer, bm.

Durham, Thomas & Nancy Hobbs, 10 Jan 1811; Samuel Faucett, bm.

Durham, Thos. & Jane Williams, 21 Jan 1836; D. H. Cate, bm.

Durham, Thomas M. & Louisa Caruthers, 15 Dec 1821; Wm. Durham, bm.

Durham, Thomas M. & Sarah F. Reeves, 26 Oct 1832; Jesse Durham, bm.

Durham, Thomas M. & Cornelia King, 30 March 1861; R. P. Poe, bm; m 31 March 1861 by Manly Andrews.

Durham, Warren & Mary Edwards, 25 Jan 1840; J. M. Beason, bm.

Durham, Westley & Hannah McCaddams, 14 Feb 1836; Jesse Durham, Jesse Miller, bm.

Durham, William B. & Permelia A. Roberson, 18 Oct 1856; Thos. S. Faucett, John Wilkinson, bm; m 23 Oct 1856 by Allen Edwards, J. P.

Durham, William J. H. & Ann B. Loyon, 23 June 1861; F. M. Proctor, bm; m 23 June 1861 by B. C. Hopkins, J. P.

Durham, Wm. P. & Nancy Stroud, 13 July 1865; Bryant Durham, bm.

Durnen, Lewis & Mary A. J. Vaughan, 5 March 1842; James ____, Ezekiel George, bm.

Durner, Nicholas & Betsy Lewis, 24 Dec 1784; John Flinthem, bm.

Durning, James & Sally Barby, 12 Jan 1813; Henry Hall, bm.

Durning, Lewis & Candess Barbee, 23 July 1814; Archibelle Carrington, bm.

Duskin, William & Mary Johnston, 17 March 1824; Geo. M. Johnston, bm.

Eapland, John & Sally Rich, 10 Oct 1810; John Ferrill, bm.

Eason, John & Peggy Bryan, 3 April 1800; James Mason, bm.

Eason, John & Peggy Trolinger, 23 Feb 1835; John Griffis, bm.

Eastridge, Ephraim & Mary Woody, 2 May 1788; Thomas Cate, bm.

Eaton, Robert & Jane Clark, 23 April 1795; Henry Thompson Junr., bm.

Eaton, Thos. Majr. & Elizabeth Willis, request for licence 27 March 1793, signed by John Willis, Thos. Eaton.

Eccles, John & Jean Anderson, 5 March 1792; William Eccles, bm.

Eccles, William & Margaret Hoovey, 24 March 1788; John Barnhill, bm.

Ector, Billy & Patsey Jones, 18 March 1812; Repps Steward, bm.

Ector, William & Elizabeth Gattis, 28 Oct 1824; Joseph Ector, bm.

Edmiston, Samuel & Jeany Gilston, 6 Feb 1805; Jon Tinen, bm.

Edmonds, William H. & Mary R. Cameron, 18 April 1839; Jno. Cameron, Benj. C. Edmunds, bm.

Edmondson, William & Delilah Desern, 22 Jan 1810; Wm. Martin, bm.

Edmunds, Benjamin C. & Rebecca T. Cameron, 18 Oct 1853; Wm. Cameron, bm; m 19 Oct 1853 by J. B. Donnelly, minister of St. Matthew's Parish, Hillsborough.

Edwards, Aaron & Susan Ann Durham, 15 March 1860; John Durham, bm; m 18 March 1860 by John W. Strowd, J. P.

Edwards, Allen & Nancy Coruthers, 12 May 1812; William Beaver, bm.

Edwards, Allen & Jane Boggs, 4 May 1839; Joel Boggs, bm.

Edwards, Allen & Lydia Quakenbush, m 5 Jan 1862 by J. W. Strowd, J. P.

Edwards, Allen Junr. & Polley Faucett, 12 Sept 1834; M. Durham, bm.

Edwards, Charles & Sarah Duggar, 6 Feb 1790; John Weems, bm.

Edwards, David & Elisabeth Andess, 28 Aug 1792; Ezekiel Brewer, bm.

Edwards, Frank, son of Phebe Snipes, & Lucinda Thompson, dau. of Britton Thompson, colored, m 12 Oct 1867 by Allen Edwards, J. P.

Edwards, Henderson, son of Jack & Dilla Edwards, & Cornelia Merritt, dau. of Sam. & Harriett Merritt, colored, m 21 Jan 1868 by J. P. Mason.

Edwards, Henry & Henretta R. Hardie, 12 Jan 1848; S. M. Barbee, bm.

Edwards, Irvin A. & Adaline Bennett, 28 May 1847; William Edwards, bm.

Edwards, Jeremiah & Milly Allen, 22 Sept 1833; Harman Lynch, bm.

Edwards, Joel & Rebecca Griffin, 8 May 1839; John Geer, bm.

Edwards, John & Peggy Grimes, 9 Nov 1800; Elisha Green, bm.

Edwards, John & Nancy Stevens, 3 Jan 1821; Charles Stevens, bm.

Edwards, John, son of Allen Edwards, & Sally Roberson, eldest dau. of David Roberson, m 19 June 1853 by John J. Roberson, J. P.

Edwards, Lewis & Nancy Mangum, 20 Sept 1830; Orford Moize, bm.

Edwards, Lynn & Mary Harris, 28 July 1823; James Woody, Duncan Newlin, bm.

Edwards, Nathan & Sally Brewer, 15 Dec 1806; Stephen Lloyd, bm.

Edwards, Presley H. & Jamima Mangum, 17 Sept 1852; H. McFarlin, bm.

Edwards, Pumphret & Sarah Oka, 12 July 1814; J. D. Carrington, bm.

Edwards, Richard & Celia Ward, 4 June 1817; Jones Fowler, bm.

Edwards, Silvanus & Mary Edwards, 30 March 1793; Robert Gee, bm.

Edwards, Thomas & Sarah Fulton, 28 Aug 1804; John Edwards, bm.

Edwards, Thomas H. & Christina Peck, 26 Sept 1839; Cannon Hopkins, bm.

Edwards, Wesley & Dorotha Justice, 2 Aug 1836; Geo. W. Morrow, bm.

Edwards, William & Betsey Williams, 31 March 1792; Benjm. Sharp, bm.

Edwards, William & Ruth Castlebury, 20 Jan 1798; Jno. Shepperd, bm.

Edwards, William & Nancy Carter, 15 Nov 1795-1798; John Anders, bm.

Edwards, William & Charity Allen, 5 July 1846; Saml. Jeffreys, bm.

Edwards, Wm. & Eliza Ann Collins, 27 Feb 1839; Thomas Edwards, bm.

Edwards, Wm. H. & Mary Doherty, 13 May 1847; R. F. Morris, bm.

Efland, see also Ephland

Efland, Daniel R. & Ruth Caroline Faustt, 6 May 1856; John A. Thompson, bm.

Efland, Daniel R. & Mary Jones, 11 Jan 1864; J. S. McDaniel, bm; m 14 Jan 1864 by Jas. R. Ball.

Efland, George & Anne Pain, 23 Sept 1815; Michael Pickard, bm.

Efland, Jacob & Catey Pickard, 9 July 1807; Thos. Pleasant, bm.

Efland, M. L. & Sally E. Bain, 4 April 1865; Wm. M. Albright, bm; m 4 April 1865 by Archd. Currie.

Efland, Peter & Elizabeth McDaniel, 18 Jan 1826; John Efland, Alfred A. Holt, bm.

Elkins, John & Elizabeth Strain, 6 Feb 1828; Geo. M. Johnston, bm.

Ellington, Marshal & Phebe Bevans, 12 Aug 1843; Green Moore, bm.

Ellington, Woodard H. & Jane Caudle, 15 May 1848; J. H. McDade, bm.

Elliott, John & Jean Collins, 9 Aug 1784; Humpy. Pasmore, bm.

Elliott, Joseph & Emaline Marcum, 13 Jan 1846; Henry J. Peason, Geo. W. Bruce, bm.

Ellis, Bartholomew & Elizabeth Faddis, 20 May 1816; John Weedon, bm.

Ellis, Benjamon & Rebecca Jane Wilkins, 29 March 1864; E. M. Holt, bm; m 3 April 1864 by Wm. J. Roberts, J. P.

Ellis, Daniel & Abigail Gifford, 12 Sept 1809; David Coble, bm.

Ellis, Elijah & Peggy Maddin, 17 Jan 1798; Andw. Madin, bm.

Ellis, George & Margret Ellis, 6 June 1832; Gilbert Hopkins, bm.

Ellis, George Jr. & Mary Mangum, 22 Aug 1859; Wm. J. Roberts, bm; m 28 Aug 1859 by Wm. J. Roberts, J. P.

Ellis, Geo. A. & Nancy Lynch, 7 Nov 1846; Stephen J. Ellis, bm.

Ellis, Henry & Margarett Davis, 13 March 1855; m 15 March 1855 by Litlejohn Utley, minister.

Ellis, James & Elizabeth Tadlocks, 9 March 1866; Rufus Mangum, bm; m 18 March 1866 by Wm. D. Lunsford, J. P.

Ellis, John H. & Jane Turner, 16 Jan 1841; P. F. Plesant, Wm. H. Hopkins, bm.

Ellis, Levin & Theresa Veazy, 23 Nov 1859; A. S. Carrington, bm.

Ellis, Nathan & Patsey Lee, 1 Jan 1817; George Browning, bm.

Ellis, Nathaniel & Cornelia Frances King, 5 Aug 1853; Charles Nevills, bm; m 6 Aug 1853 by W. Atwater, J. P.

Ellis, Nathaniel & Margarett Ryan, 3 July 1862; Charles Nevill, bm; m 3 July 1862 by Wilson Atwater, minister.

Ellis, William & Nancy Riley, 12 Feb 1831; John Reding, bm.

Ellis, William & Winnifred Ashley, 28 Jan 1835; William Vaughan, bm.

Ellis, William H. & Jane Clark, 26 Oct 1850; Wm. D. Faucett, Wm. Wilkinson, bm; m 30 Oct 1850 by Archibald Currie, minister.

Ellison, James & Jenny Scoby, 17 Dec 1808; Thomas Ellison, bm.

Ellison, John & Salley Stewart, 13 July 1801; Joseph Ellison, bm.

Ellison, Joseph & Elizabeth Maddin, 19 Aug 1809; J. Taylor, bm.

Ellison, Joseph & Patsy Woods, 6 Nov 1810; Richard Brag, bm.

Ellison, Thomas & Betsey H. Scoby, 5 Nov 1808; Joseph Ellison, bm.

Ellison, William & Margret Stewart, 13 June 1807; John Ellison, bm.

Ellit, Henry & Eliza Rabin, 23 Dec 1848; William Findley, bm.

Elmore, Athenatious & Susanah Pinix, 5 July 1788; Jno. Elmore, bm.

Elmore, James & Sarah Orrand, 19 Dec 1805; James Corbit, bm.

Elmore, James & Milley Gant, 20 Aug 1810; John Elmore, Luke Teer, bm.

Elmore, John & Anne Rippey, 3 Feb 1784; Edwd. Rippey, bm.

Elmore, John & Betsy Cocks, 8 Sept 1808; James Thomas, bm.

Elmore, John & Salley Lloyd, 18 Sept 1808; Thomas Lloyd, bm.

Elmore, Moses & Nancy Ray, 11 Sept 1834; William Ray, bm.

Elmore, William & Mary Rippey, 22 June 1782; James Elmore, bm.

Emanuel, James M. & Josephine Parks, 16 Nov 1863; A. Hedgepeth, bm; m 17 Nov 1863 by Alexr. R. Raven.

Emerson, Robert & Cornelia Hudson, 19 Aug 1857; Wm. H. Merritt, T. Webb, bm; m 19 Aug 1857 by B. J. Hackney.

Emery, Thomas R. & Julia R. Moore, 26 May 1856; Jonas Watson, bm.

Enoch, Rees & Susanna Stalcup, 19 Nov 1799; Benjamin Enoch, bm.

Ephland, David & Sally Pickard, 18 July 1820; John Crutchfield, bm.

Ervin, Archibald & Nancy Kerr, 18 July 1827; John McGrath, bm.

Erwin, George W. & Fanny I. Jones, 14 Oct 1856; Ja. J. Iredell, P. B. Ruffin, bm; m 14 Oct 1856 by M. A. Curtis, a minister of the Gospel, of Society Hill, South Carolina.

Espey, Jas. & Sarah Baker, 2 Jan 1786; James Baker, bm.

Estes, Aaron & Frances Hudson, 13 July 1790; Zachariah Bevil, bm.

Estes, Boroughs & Patty Loyd, 26 May 1792; James Cheek, bm.

Estes, James & Mary Weeks, 5 Nov 1785; Joseph Weeks, bm.

Estridge, Thomas & Milley Cato, 4 Nov 1820; Robert Cheek, bm.

Etherage, Lovett & Polley Glenn, 1 Oct 1813; James Glenn, bm.

Etheridge, Ryals & Patsey Glen, 27 April 1816; Elisha Glen, bm.

Eubank, Thomas & Caty Cook, 30 Jan 1800; John Wheley, bm.

Eubank, Warner & Elvira Kernell, 2 April 1831; Ast. Moore, bm.

Eucliss, Allen & Sally Spoon, 24 Jan 1830; John Spoon, bm.

Euless, Wm. & Nelly Allbright, 2 Oct 1826; Henry Webster, bm.

Euliss, George & Rebeca Patram, 27 Nov 1822; Potter Kimbro, bm.

Euliss, Hiram & Malinda Rightsell, 13 Nov 1841; Alfred Euless, bm.

Evans, Albert & Eveline Alston, 28 Dec 1865; Moses Evans, bm.

Evans, Andrews J. & Elizabeth Grinton, 14 April 1859; Henry Chavis, bm.

Evans, Charles N. B. & Elizabeth Clancy, 25 May 1836; Alfred E. Hanner, bm.

Evans, Elisha & Hally Walker, 7 Dec 1829; John W. Shaw, bm.

Evans, Henry & Elizabeth Hutchins, 5 July 1810; William Trice, bm.

Evans, James & Sally Weaver, 11 Jan 1861; William B. Williams, bm; m 13 Jan 1861 by H. J. Pearson, J. P.

Evans, Jeremiah & Martha Boreland, 9 April 1833; Willis Bowling, Jeremiah Boreland, bm.

Evans, John & Rebecca Hall, 22 Sept 1808; Wm. Smith, bm.

Evans, John & Elizabeth Evans, 4 Jan 1859; William Rawls, bm.

Evans, John & Eliza Phillips, colored, 25 Dec 1865; D. C. McDade, bm; m 28 Dec 1865 by James Phillips, D. D.

Evans, Reuben & Mary Pruit, 1 Aug 1809; Thomas Terry, bm.

Evans, Smith & Elizabeth Hill, 30 Dec 1857; James Ellis, Wmson Parrish, bm; m 30 Dec 1857 by W. M. Carrington, J. P.

Evans, Thomas & Lucy Jefferson, 26 Sept 1810; Henry Shult, bm.

Evans, Thomas & Elizabeth Coble, 15 Aug 1833; Eli Stailey, bm.

Evans, Thomas C. & Augustua F. Stevenson, 18 Dec 1863; Calvin E. Parish, bm; m 18 Dec 1863 by N. W. Wilson.

Evans, William & Nancy Parker, 13 Oct 1823; John Jackson, bm.

Evans, William & Cynthia Bryant, 27 April 1824; William Evans, bm.

Evans, William & Elizabeth Ann Johnson, 9 Dec 1864; Haywood Day, bm.

Evans, Young & Caroline Jones, colored, 19 Nov 1851; Wm. Maphis, bm; m 19 Nov 1851 by S. Milton Frost, of the N. C. Conference.

Everett, Lewis & Elizabeth Mitchell, 25 Nov 1865; Squire Bull, bm; m 1 Dec 1865 by Alex Wilson.

Evins, Brink & Malida Hethpeth, 18 Jan 1865; W. B. Williams, bm. (groom may be Winn, Brinkley).

Evins, Kerney & Polly Piles, 24 Jan 1847; Edmnd. Byrd, bm.

Ezell, James & Mary Pickard, 10 Aug 1804; Jessee Izzell, bm.

Ezzell, David J. & Maria F. Flintoff, 21 Dec 1859; A. W. Gattis, bm; m 22 Dec 1859 by A. W. Mangum, minister of the Gospel.

Facett, Chesly F. & Margret Shult, 7 July 1827; Wm. H. Adams, bm.

Faddis, Alexander & Sarah Lynch, 4 July 1794; James Hutcheson, bm.

Faddis, Andrew & Elizabeth Hicks, 8 Aug 1785; German Baxter, bm.

Faddis, Andrew & Margaret Hews, 13 April 1791; Andrew Walker, bm.

Faddis, James & Lotte Jacobs, 4 Aug 1819; A. Roney, bm.

Falkner, James & Julia Scott, 22 Sept 1866; Saml. H. Breeze, J. W. Sharp, bm; m 23 Sept 1866 by Robert G. Tinnin.

Falkner, John & Mary E. Mitchell, 19 March 1862; J. M. Bain, bm.

Falkner, Moses & Eliza Barton, 25 Jan 1826.

Falkner, Sanders & Mary S. Cape, 21 July 1860; A. C. Murdock, bm; m 22 July 1860 by Jas. N. Craig, J. P.

Falkner, Thomas & Betsy Bowers, 20 March 1838; William Mils, bm.

Falkner, Vincent & Lively Merritt, 14 Oct 1807; Robert Pender, bm.

Fann, Elijah & Jean Colter, 16 Oct 1809; Wm. Pendergrass, bm.

Fann, Raleigh & Anne Laurence, 6 Feb 1821; Henson Cautle, bm.

Farerest, William K. & Susan Guie, 3 Nov 1858; Andrew McFarlin, bm; m 7 Nov 1858 by Thomas Ferrell, J. P.

Fargeson, John & Mary Laws, 12 Feb 1811; Saml. Woods, bm.

Farmer, Jacob & Pency Shofner, 23 Oct 1816; George Shofner, bm.

Farmer, James & Rebecca Parker, 11 Jan 1801; Henry Duke, bm.

Farmer, Othneil & Jimimah Pruet, 6 Aug 1787; Daniel Green, bm.

Farrar, J. W. E. & Amelia B. Horn, 2 Jan 1828; H. Owen, bm.

Farrar, Stephen & Elizabeth Riggins, 28 July 1819; Mariott Roberson, bm.

Farrar, Warren & Rachel McCullock, 12 Aug 1839; James R. Miller, Wm. McCullohs, bm.

Farrel, John & Barbara Efland, 15 Sept 1804; John Wright, bm.

Farthing, Abner J. & Martha M. Cheek, 13 Sept 1847; Solomon Gooch, Stephen P. Holloway, bm.

Farthing, Hargis & Elizabeth Lewis, 20 Oct 1837; John C. Lewis, bm.

Farthing, John & Louiser Cheek, 7 July 1849; James F. Gattis, bm.

Farthing, Reuben & Anne Holloway, 12 Dec 1816; Thomas Holloway, bm.

Farthing, Thos. H. & Ermin B. Burton, 9 Jan 1841; W. A. Norwood, bm.

Farthing, William & Nancy Caroline Gooch, 30 Jan 1846; John C. Lewis, bm.

Faucet, Eli W. & Rebecca M. Patton, 12 Oct 1835; John R. Fausett, bm.

Faucet, James & Polley Moore, 3 May 1817; Wm. Busick, bm.

Faucett, Abishai & Mary Ann Faucett, 12 Oct 1820; Joseph Faucett, bm.

Faucett, Edmund, son of Green Faucett & Tamesia Patterson, & Detcy Nunn, dau. of David Nunn and Mary Barbee, m 5 Oct 1867 C. W. Johnston, J. P.

Faucett, George A. Jr. & Mary C. Hobbs, 15 Oct 1851; H. C. McCauley, bm; m 16 Oct 1851 by W. S. Strayhorn, J. P.

Faucett, Hugh & Nancy Christmas, 14 Dec 1836; Jno. Horner, bm.

Faucett, James & Elizabeth Bird, 13 June 1809; William Faucett, bm.

Faucett, James M. & Elmina Bowers, 1 Nov 1852; Henry C. Andrews, bm.

Faucett, John & Ferribee Pittman, 6 Feb 1797; Thomas Baker, Thomas ONeill, bm.

Faucett, John & Catey Hamilton, 12 Nov 1808; David Bradford, bm.

Faucett, John & Tempe Palmer, 29 March 1821; B. D. Alsobrook, bm.

Faucett, John & Betsey Beasley, 21 June 1828; Thomas Hurdle, bm.

Faucett, John L. & Polly Pettegrue, 18 Oct 1850; Joseph A. McCadams, bm.

Faucett, John A. & Susan Roberts, 14 Dec 1858; Albert F. Faucett, bm; m 15 Dec 1858 by F. M. Jordan, minister

Faucett, John R. & Catharine S. Freeland, 19 Dec 1835; John Freeland Jr., bm.

Faucett, John S. & Aurilla McCauley, 12 May 1848; James M. Faucett, bm.

Faucett, John W. & Martha Jane Crawford, 3 Jan 1854; Levi
Faucett, Geo. W. Bruce, bm.

Faucett, Joseph & Polley Tinnin, 25 Nov 1822; Robt. Tinnin, bm.

Faucett, Leonard H. & Harriet M. Faucett, 7 Sept 1841; James C.
Patten, bm.

Faucett, Ralph & Robina Riley, 27 Dec 1834; Jesse Miller, bm.

Faucett, Robert Jr. & Martha Jane Farra, 8 Jan 1862; John A.
Parker, bm; m 9 Jan 1862 by D. W. Jorden, J. P.

Faucett, Saml. H. & Martha Thompson, 9 Sept 1848; Robert Sykes,
bm.

Faucett, Samuel W. & Elizabeth Jane Gray, 18 Feb 1854; Alonzo
Gray, bm; m 23 Feb 1854 by John L. Woods, J. P.

Faucett, Thomas & Ruth Burnside, 27 March 1793; Joseph Collins,
bm.

Faucett, Thomas & Jeany Mitchel, 18 Dec 1810; Ge. Mitchell,
Samuel Faucett, bm.

Faucett, Thomas & Ann Durham, 13 Feb 1824; J. B. McDade, bm.

Faucett, Thomas & Catharine McCaddams, 15 Sept 1842; William
Pettigrew, bm.

Faucett, Thomas & Eliza Ellen McBroom, 2 May 1866; Isaac
McBroom, bm; m 2 May 1866 by John M. Kirkland, J. P.

Faucett, Thomas M., son of Thomas D. & Anna Faucett, & Laura B.
King, dau. Turner & Mary King, m 15 Sept 1867 by N. C. Cate,
J. P.

Faucett, William & Elizabeth Thompson, 16 May 1812; John
Thompson, bm.

Faucett, William & Peggy Carlisle, 7 Oct 1812; Nathaniel Bain,
bm.

Faucett, William & Catharine Cabe, 19 Dec 1822; Saml. S.
Claytor, bm.

Faucett, William & Edith McClure, 28 July 1834; George Dickey,
bm.

Faucett, Wm. A. & Mary Bradford, 5 July 1847; John L. Faucett,
bm.

Faucett, William D. & Josephine R. Wilkison, 24 Dec 1849;
J. P. Parker, bm.

Faucett, William D. & Margaret Jane Paul, 13 March 1855; J. A.
Faucett, Geo. W. Tate, bm; m 15 March 1855 by Archibald
Currie, minister.

Faucett, William M. & Ellen R. Patton, 21 Aug 1843; Randolph C.
Milrey, bm.

Faucette, Robert & Salley Thompson, 7 Oct 1820; D. B. Alsobrook,
bm.

Faucit, Samuel & Elizabeth Durham, 11 Jan 1796; Robert Faucit, bm.

Faucit, William & ____, 26 Feb 1795; Thomas Armstrong, bm.

Faucitt, Henry & Polley Findley, 15 Feb 1798; John Findley, bm.

Faucitt, David A. & Mary Ann Patterson, 2 Sept 1835; Wm. T. Shields, bm.

Fauset, William & Martha Hamilton, 18 June 1802; David Bradford, bm.

Fausett, Abel & Sobena Weeden, 23 Oct 1828; John Noble, bm.

Fausett, Abi H. W. & Rutha Brown, 17 July 1811; Absalom Harvey, bm.

Fausett, James & Elizabeth Jeffers, 29 March 1813; Absalom Harvey, bm.

Fausett, Ralph & Martha Bracken, 11 April 1803; William Brackin, bm.

Fausett, Richard & Mary McKee, 28 Jan 1792; David Faucett, bm.

Fausett, Robert & Phebe Hall, 14 Oct 1808; Jo. Moore, bm.

Fausett, Robert & Clara King, 26 Nov 1816; George Fausett, bm.

Fausett, Robert F. & Mary S. Holt, 11 March 1846; Alfred Wyatt, bm.

Fausett, Thomas S. & Carolina M. Pratt, 13 Jan 1846; Archibald Strayhorn, bm.

Fausett, William & Netia Bowers, 17 March 1856; Charles King, bm; m 16 March 1856 by N. C. Cate, J. P.

Fausett, Zepheniah & Mary Horn, 28 April 1829; William Mathise, bm.

Faust, Daniel & Patsey Stafford, 21 Feb 1842; Daniel Linebery, bm.

Faust, (Fossett) Edward & Anne McRory, 1 Jan 1799; Jas. Clindinin, bm.

Faustt, George & Elizabeth Kellon, 4 July 1807; David Harvey, bm.

Faustt, William & Elizabeth Wallace, 5 Oct 1825; Edward Fausett, bm.

Feagens, John & Sarah Underwood, 26 May 1849; Wm. R. Simpson, bm.

Fearington, James & Bythenia Fearington, 26 Jan 1867; Edward Mitchell, bm; m 26 Jan 1867 by Jones Watson, J. P.

Fedrick, Miles & Anne Watson, 24 Dec 1841; Moses Leathers Jun., bm.

Ferguson, John & Sarah Burton (no date, 1787-1789); Joseph Clindenin, bm.

Ferguson, Robt & Mary Leonard, 11 Aug 1787.

Ferrabo, Henderson & Margaret Jones, 2 Jan 1867; Primas Smith, bm.

Ferrell, Allen & Martha Lawes, 3 Jan 1825; T. W. Gooch, bm.

Ferrell, Anderson & Mary Ann Dixon, 20 Dec 1829; Allen Ferrell, bm.

Ferrell, Charles & Sarah Ackles, 19 April 1792; Isaac Hall, bm.

Ferrell, James T. & Francis F. Turner, 6 Oct 1860; P. T. Ferrell, P. J. Mangum, bm; m 6 Oct 1860 by Solomon Shepherd, J. P.

Ferrell, John H. & Rebecca O. Fowler, 10 Jan 1867; Thos. H. Hughes, bm; m 10 Jan 1867 by A. G. Anderson.

Ferrell, Lucoe & Nancy Jane Andrews, 25 Nov 1860; David Burch, bm; m 26 Nov by D. Tilley, J. P.

Ferrington, Wright & Wescot Cotton, 1 Aug 1865; Saml Morphis, bm.

Findley, Abisha T. & Mary C. Murray, 8 Dec 1858; H. M. Crabtree, bm.

Findley, Archibald & Ann Collins, 17 March 1827; D. W. Anderson, bm.

Findley, Hancy & Nancy Thompson, 9 Jan 1810; Thomas Finley, Anthy. Thompson, bm.

Findley, John & Clara Parish, 2 June 1826; Green Findley, bm.

Findley, Nathan & Celia Dickey, 1 Aug 1829; Jo. Hartt, bm.

Findly, Green & Nancy Faucett, 20 Jan 1821; William Newman, bm.

Finley, Alexander & Ellender Nucom, 27 Aug 1797; James Williams, bm.

Finley, Jacob & Catherine Raley, 15 Dec 1788; Willm. Raley, bm.

Finley, Josiah & Rachel Bowls, 6 Sept 1782; James Bowl, bm.

Finley, Josiah & Alicy Harvey, 8 April 1787; David Harvey, bm.

Finley, Josiah & Mary Harden, 22 Aug 1808; Joseph Harden, bm.

Finley, William & Margaret Nealy, 16 Feb 1795; Hugh Finly, bm.

Finney, Joseph Junr. & Rachel Barkley, 13 Dec 1783; John Hughbanks Jr., bm.

Fips, James & Julia King, 1 Dec 1856; Rufus Andieus, bm; 2 Dec 1856 by J. W. Carr, J. P.

Fitch, Abraham & Elizabeth Forest, 8 March 1792; John Fitch, A. Benton Bruce, bm.

Fitch, James & Isbelle Ray, 21 Sept 1804; Robt. Ray, bm.

Fitch, Peter & Jeane Hughs, 27 Sept 1796; Robt. Ray, bm.

Fitch, Robert & Lydia Watson, 4 Nov 1832; Thomas Saygle, bm.

Fitts, Henry Morgan & Orrill Southerland, 9 Jan 1819; Thos. W. Holden, bm.

Flack, Andrew & Nancy A. Tinnen, 20 July 1857; Joseph A. Tinnin, bm; m 6 Aug 1857 by Josiah McCully, minister.

Flint, Thomas & Alsey Lewis, 10 Dec 1836; M. Barton, J. C. Turrentine, bm.

Flinthem, John & Alse Ross, 24 Dec 1801; Thomas Browning, bm.

Flinthom, William & Nancy Baker, 15 July 1803; H. McCollum, bm.

Flintoff, William R. & Rebecca Hogan, 9 Aug 1842; Jno. Robeson, bm.

Flintom, Saml. G. & Nancy A. Walker, 19 Dec 1863; George C. Pickard, bm; m 21 Dec 1863 by Henry Gray, minister.

Florens, John P. & Patsey Cape, 18 Nov 1856; Jas. R. Hester, bm.

Flourence, Tolipher & Elizabeth Bird, 6 Jan 1812; Jehu Bird, bm.

Flowers, Jacob Junr & Mary Morgan, 28 Jan 1788; Benj. Yeargain, bm.

Floyd, Peter & Elizabeth Hawkins, 3 May 1826; Jno. Holstead, bm.

Fogerty, James & Elphany Thompson, 28 June 1787; Robert McIntire, bm.

Fogleman, John & Mary Albright, 3 Feb 1806; Malachi Hatmaker, bm.

Fogleman, Ludwick A. & Polley Garrot, 7 April 1840; William Fogleman, bm.

Fogleman, Peter & Hannah Boggs, 22 Nov 1803; Heinrich Fogleman, bm.

Fogleman, William & Sally Morris, 17 Nov 1824; Adam Ristell, bm.

Fogleman, William & Margaret Bane, 24 Dec 1827; Peter Greeson, bm.

Foglemon, William & Mary Isley, 31 March 1829; John Wason, bm.

Fonvielle, William & Rachel Blanshard, 2 Jan 1819; Chesley F. Faucett, bm.

Fonville, Asa G. & Susanah Hufmon, 5 Jan 1846; James Garrison, bm.

Fonville, Brice F. & Catharine Roney, 4 Dec 1845; John T. Roney, bm.

Fonville, Fredk. & Charity Graham, 30 May 1816; Jehu Hall, bm.

Fooshee, Adnah & Frances Roundtree, 31 March 1837; William Moore, bm.

Fooshee, Charles & Pressiee James, 9 Oct 1841; Anderson James, bm.

Fooshee, Charles & Ann E. Rike, 14 Aug 1848; Jabrel Fooshee, bm.

Forest, James & Elisabeth Gicie, 26 July 1862; Presley J. Mangum, bm.

Forest, Silas & Polley Lovins, 8 Oct 1799; James Curry, bm.

Formoy, Michael & Sally Burnett, 5 Nov 1804; James Daugharty, bm.

Forrest, Alexander & Elizabeth Thompson, 26 June 1838; A. Parks, D. H. Cate, bm.

Forrest, Alexander & Polley G. Taylor, 23 Aug 1820; J. P. Sneed, bm.

Forrest, Ila & Christy Chizenhall, 23 Nov 1804; James Watson, bm.

Forrest, James & Martha Jane Wolf, 27 May 1859; John M. Thompson, bm.

Forrest, John & Ellenor Russel, 18 Oct 1787; Richard Harper, bm.

Forrest, Jno. A. & Mary E. Goodloe, 23 Sept 1840; George W. Harrington, bm.

Forrest, John D. & Elizabeth Thompson, 7 Feb 1853; T. Webb, bm.

Forrest, Josiah & Rachel Dossett, 24 Feb 1809; Samuel Peelor, bm.

Forrest, Nathan & Nancy Baugh, 14 Jan 1799; Fras. Moreland, bm.

Forrest, Phillip & Lydia Cates, 26 Dec 1801; Major Downs, bm.

Forrest, Stephen Taylor & Margaret Thompson, 29 Sept 1840; J. W. Thompson, bm.

Forrest, William P. & Frances H. Tayloe, 1 Oct 1825; John M. Walker, bm.

Forrest or Forrester, Benjamin & Susannah Whitlow, 28 Feb 1799; John Rhodes, bm.

Forrist, Benjamin & Sarah Hill, __ Dec 1785; Edward Jarvais, bm.

Forrist, John & Mary Clark, 23 April 1784; John Griffin, bm.

Forsyth, Barnett & Sarah Glosson, 2 Feb 1816; H. Strowd, bm.

Forsyth, Urias & Ellonor Umsted, 28 Nov 1848; E. Hester, L. T. Burton, bm.

Forsythe, Phillip & Taylor Jones, 15 Oct 1842; Smith Forsythe, Jarrell Ashley, bm.

Fosset, John & Parthenia Armstrong, 17 Jan 1828; Wm. Fosset, bm.

Fossett, Chesly F. & Margret Hutcheson, 13 Dec 1824; William Faucett, Edward Fausett, bm.

Fossett, David & Elizabeth Davis, 9 Nov 1783; Richard Foset, bm.

Fossett, David & Jane Baker, 12 Nov 1794; Robt. Fossett, bm.

Fossett, George & Martha Ray, 21 Oct 1807; William Murray, bm.

Fossett, George & Nancy Cabe, 17 Dec 1835; Levi McCollum, bm.

Fossett, George A. & Nancy Fossett, 1 Dec 1840; Jas. Sneed, Jno. M. Faucett, bm.

Fossett, John & Mary Patterson, 28 Dec 1801; George Fossett, bm.

Fossett, Richard Junr. & Rebecca Durham, 19 April 1803; Richard Fossett Senr., bm.

Fossett, Thomas & Rosannah McCollum, 29 May 1829; Robert Pleasants, bm.

Fossett, Wm. & Mary Nichols, 17 Sept 1836; Mordand Jackson, bm.

Fossitt, Thos. & Martha Richards, 28 Aug 1787; Robt. Thompson, bm.

Foster, Asa & Salley Haley, 3 Oct 1800; Richard Jones, bm.

Foster, Asa & Sally Holt, 20 Nov 1841; Gabriel Holt, bm.

Foster, James & Eve Loinberry, 21 Feb 1816; John Coble, bm.

Foster, John & Polley Green, 29 Dec 1817; Henry Brannock Junr., bm.

Foster, William P. & Jane Jeffers, 7 March 1828; Isaac Jeffreys, bm.

Fouse, Peter & Polley Rogers, 18 Nov 1824; William Kirkpatrick, bm.

Foust, Daniel & Sally Coble, 22 Nov 1810; Daniell Staly, bm.

Foust, Daniel & Nelly Thompson, 8 Nov 1828; John McPherson, bm.

Foust, Daniel & Catharine Freeland, 20 May 1834; John Freeland, bm.

Foust, George & Maria Holt, 31 Dec 1816; Joseph Bason, bm.

Foust, Geo. & Barbara Ellen Foust, 31 July 1843; Calvin E. Graves, bm.

Foust, Jacob & Sopha Clapp, 18 Feb 1806; Anthony Thompson, bm.

Foust, John & Susannah Horniday, 14 June 1813; Daniel Foust, bm.

Foust, Wm. & Sarah C. Albright, 9 Feb 1847; Wm. Hornaday, bm.

Fowler, Green W. & Ruth Turner, 28 Nov 1837; W. N. Pratt, bm.

Fowler, Henderson & Harriett Falkner, 9 Sept 1830; Jo. Hartt, bm.

Fowler, James & Catey Johns, 26 July 1802; Henry Johns, bm.

Fowler, James & Nancy Thomas, 20 Dec 1805; Simeon Fowler, bm.

Fowler, James & Nancy Griffin, 31 May 1822; John Hastings, bm.

Fowler, James & Hannah Whittecar, 13 Aug 1822; Chessly Herndon, bm.

Fowler, James & Jane Hays, 1 April 1846; Simeon Fowler, bm.

Fowler, James W. & Martha M. Caudle, 28 Dec 1859; W. A. Gattis, James Turner, bm; m 28 Dec 1859 by D. Tilley, J. P.

Fowler, John & Minerva Proctor, 25 Jan 1851; M. A. Angier, bm.

Fowler, Leander & Julia A. Cheek, 26 April 1864; John W. Siler, bm; m 26 April 1864 by Wilson Brown, J. P.

Fowler, Mark & Rebeccah Smith, 8 April 1794; Reuben Smith, bm.

Fowler, Miles & Elizabeth Freemon, 2 May 1851; King Barbee, bm; m 28 April 1851 by King Barbee, J. P.

Fowler, Simeon & Candiss Morrow, 2 Aug 1825; John Thompson, bm.

Fowler, Simeon & Jeany Collins, 31 July 1830; James Griffin, bm.

Fowler, Thomas & Rebecca Pickard, 3 Dec 1864; John Isard, John W. Pickard, bm.

Fowler, Thomas J., son of Thomas & Phebe Fowler, & Margaret E. Davis, dau. of F. and Martha OKelly, m 28 Jan 1868 by A. G. Anderson.

Fowler, W. J. & Jane Burges, 6 Jan 1858; John M. Brown, bm; m 6 Jan 1858 by D. Tilley, J. P.

Fowler, William & Susan Bird, 3 Sept 1827; James Nelson, James Tate, bm.

Fowler, William C. & Hesther Davidson, 9 Sept 1841; William Gunn, bm.

Fowler, William O. & Mary A. Wait, 14 Oct 1861; Thomas Scarlett, bm; m 14 Oct 1861 by J. A. Cunninggim.

Fowler, William S. & Margret Roach, 6 June 1858; Samuel N. Crawford, bm; m 6 June 1858 by Allen Edwards, J. P.

Fox, Abram & Amelia Bristo, 13 March 1820; A. Hamilton, bm.

Fox, George & Elizabeth Moser, 3 Dec 1825; William Moser, bm.

Fox, Jacob & Nelle Moser, 29 Nov 1823; Tobias Moser, bm.

Franklin, Henry & Lucy Collins, 19 April 1851; Nelson Parrish, bm.

Franklin, Theodrick & Elizabeth Berry, 30 June 1832; Thos. P. Berry, William Bowls, bm.

Franklin, Thomas & Ann Teazley, 3 May 1853; Zachariah Franklin, E. G. Gray, bm.

Franklin, William & Fannie King, 5 Jan 1861; W. J. Hogans, bm; m 8 Jan 1861 by W. J. Hogan, J. P.

Franklin, Zachariha & Minerva Roberts, 10 April 1846; Henry Melchi, bm.

Free, John T. & Priscilla Ward, 27 July 1820; Isaiah Hornaday, bm.

Freeland, Charles J. & Rebecca Jacobs, 26 Sept 1854; T. Webb, bm.

Freeland, George & Polley Craig, 10 Feb 1834; Thos. J. Freeland, Joseph Freeland, bm.

Freeland, George S. & Sarah Craig, 15 Sept 1866; John S. Blackwood, bm; m 20 Sept 1866 by C. W. Johnston, J. P.

Freeland, James & Nancy Strayhorn, 6 Sept 1804; John F. Gibson, bm.

Freeland, James & Abby Thompson, 29 Aug 1815; Henry Y. Houze, bm.

Freeland, James & Jane Strain, 27 April 1817; W. N. Pratt, bm.

Freeland, Jno. & Catharine Johnston, 26 March 1787; Charles Johnston, bm.

Freeland, John & Polly Dixon, 3 Aug 1817; James Freeland, bm.

Freeland, John & Nancy Ray, 16 Jan 1827; John I. Freeland, bm.

Freeland, John D. & Deborah Fossett, 17 Sept 1836; Leonard Faucett, bm.

Freeland, Jno. J. & Mary Craig, 29 Nov 1819; Charles J. Freeland, bm.

Freeland, John T. & Lucinda McCauley, 16 Sept 1834; James McCauley, bm.

Freeland, Joseph & Anne Johnston, 4 March 1789; John Freeland, bm.

Freeland, Joseph & Polley Murray, 28 Feb 1822; Johnston Freeland, bm.

Freeland, Joseph & Lydia Miller, 23 Jan 1826; John S. Freeland, bm.

Freeland, Jos. M. & Mary Jane Tate, 15 Dec 1847; Wm. Zachary, bm.

Freeland, Thomas & Nancy Gant, 7 July 1804; John Freeland, bm.

Freeland, Thomas J. & Margaret F. Morrow, 30 Oct 1858; James R. Gattis, bm.

Freeland, Thomas J. & Josaphine N. McDade, 21 Oct 1863; L. G. Lynch, bm; m 21 Oct 186３ by Jess R. Ball.

Freeland, William J. & Harriett N. Holeman, 27 Feb 1859; James R. Gattis, bm; m 27 Feb 1859 by John Mitchell.

Freeland, Wm. Johnston & Frances M. Pratt, 10 April 1856; Thos. J. Freeland, bm; m 10 April 1856 by Thomas Lansdell, minister.

Freeman, B. B. & Mary E. Siler, 29 July 1858; J. F. Freeland, bm; m 29 July 1858 by J. B. McDade.

Freeman, John & Amey Hausey, 2 Feb 1801; Isaac Wells, bm.

Freeman, John & Charity Wells, 18 Feb 1805; William Williams, bm.

Freeman, Nathan & Mary Buckingham, 26 Dec 1813; Jno Bukinham, bm.

Freeman, Samuel & Polley Lunch, 17 Oct 1807; Jas. Lockhart, bm.

Freeman, Samuel & Jane Murray, 7 July 1810; Isaac Marshill, bm.

Freeman, Samuel & Rebecca Freeman, 24 Nov 1783; David Passmore, John Murray, bm.

Freeman, Thomas & Lutheniz Suit, 16 Feb 1856; Alvis Daniel, bm; m 16 Feb 1856 by J. B. McDade, J. P.

Freeman, William & Mary Edwards, 14 May 1811; John Murray, bm.

Freeman, Wm. & Elizabeth Marshall, 11 Oct 1805; James Morrow, bm.

Freeman, Willis & Alvira Godfrey, 7 March 1867; George Mayo, bm; m 8 March 1867 by Robert G. Tinnin.

Freshwater, David & Catharine Trolinger, 26 Nov 1821; W. F. Jones, bm.

Freshwater, William A. & Carnelia J. Wilkerson, 17 Dec 1859; James E. Wilkerson, Thomas Webb, bm.

Friddel, George & Winney Burns, 1 Nov 1841; F. A. Williams, bm.

Friddle, Henry & Polly May, 17 Nov 1826; David Clapp, bm.

Friddle, Jacob & Mary Sharpe, 11 May 1810; William Piles, bm.

Fridle, Jacob & Liddia Pyle, 9 June 1846; James R. Fonville, bm.

Fuller, Cornelius, son of Ben Dick and Judy Fuller & Rachel Fuller, m 1 Sept 1867 by Q. A. Ward, minister.

Fuller, Solomon W. & Elizabeth M. Phillips, 9 Oct 1833; A. Parks, bm.

Fulton, James Junr. & Elizabeth Briton, 28 May 1805; Wm. Carrington Junr., bm.

Fulton, Robert & Nancy Bason, 3 April 1815; W. Mebane, bm.

Fulton, Samuel & Mary Fulton, 26 Jan 1785; Jesse Fulton, bm.

Fulton, Thos. & Catharine Lynch, 2 Oct 1792; Saml. Fulton, bm.

Furgason, Presley, son of John & Orpah Furgason, & Martha ODaniel, dau. of Henry & Martha ODaniel, m 23 April 1868 by Samuel Baldwin, ord. minister.

Furguson, Daniel & Julia Evans, 24 Jan 1805; Samuel Freeman, bm.

Furlong, Wm. K. & Peteraugh N. Hopkins, 13 Dec 1848; Lewis Hutchins, bm.

Fussett, Wyatt & Delila Horner, 24 Feb 1795; Thomas Horner, bm.

Futral or Futel, Matt. & Rachel Chance, 6 Jan 1801; Reuben Smith, bm.

Gaddes, Thomas & Sophia Wilkins, 21 Feb 1842; S. D. Strain, Moses Leathers Junr., bm.

Gaine, Abram G. & Mary Chisenhall, 3 Jan 1853; M. A. Angier, bm.

Gamage, William & Charity Sexon, 19 Oct 1782; Jesse Benton, wit.

Gamble, John & Sally Boggs, 7 Feb 1821; John G. Coe, bm.

Gant, Benjamin & Polly Tarpley, 20 May 1833; Abram B. Tarply, bm.

Gant, Henry & Elizabeth Tapley, 5 Nov 1828; Henry Tarpley, Joshua R. Gant, bm.

Gant, Henry & Delilah May, 30 Sept 1837; Robert Pugh, bm.

Gant, Isham & Sally Rippy, 4 Feb 1798; Ed. Paston, bm.

Gant, Jacob & Doxey Isley, 26 March 1838; Joseph Trolinger, bm.

Gant, John & Nancy Judge, 28 April 1792; Thomas Gant, bm.

Gant, John & Ester Lovens, 9 Aug 1806; William Rainy, bm.

Gant, Joshua A. & Mary McCulley, 2 Dec 1847; James Trolinger, bm.

Gant, Joshua R. & Ann W. D. Reeves, 26 Aug 1833; Jesse Gant, bm.

Gant, Josiah & Nancy Faucett, 18 Aug 1830; J. Gant, bm.

Gant, Levi & Peggy Minnis, 29 Dec 1817; William Numan, J. P., bm.

Gant, Zachariah & Sarah McCracken, 24 Nov 1804; John McCracken, bm.

Gapins, James & Nancy Fowler, 19 Aug 1822; William McDaniel, bm.

Gappins, William & Ellender Whited, 7 Nov 1797; James Roberts, bm.

Garason, Henry & Lucy McCauly, 30 Oct 1836; John Garrison, bm.

Garison, George & Hannah Fonville, 15 Nov 1819; Henry Hurdle, bm.

Garniear, John & Elizabeth Waynick, 10 May 1847; S. G. Truit, bm.

Garrard, Hubard & Mackie Woods, 18 Oct 1833; James Montgomery, bm.

Garrard, James L. & Jane Cole, 17 Aug 1866; Jno. D. Lipscomb, bm.

Garrard, John & Sarah Glenn, 12 March 1782; Worham Glen, bm.

Garrard, John & Nancy Lea, 7 Jan 1817; Jno. J. Carrington, bm.

Garrard, John & Rachel Haley, 24 Feb 1846; Cannon Hopkins, bm.

Garrard, Joseph W., son of Wm. C. and Ann Garrard, & Susan E. Terry, dau. of James T. & Susan Terry, m 26 June 1867 by J. W. Latta, J. P.

Garrard, Sherwood H. & Elizabeth A. Warren, 16 Feb 1850; W. B. Garrard, bm.

Garrard, Skidmore, son of Wm. A. and Sarah Garrard & Tennesha C. Couch, dau. of Elijah & Mary Couch, m 1 April 1868 by C. P. Warren, J. P.

Garrard, Thomas & Elizabeth Chizenhall, 29 May 1841; Duke Glenn, Duncan Glenn, bm.

Garrard, Thomas & Malinda Vickers, m 18 April 1858 by Wm. J. Duke, J. P.

Garrard, Thompson & Martha T. Hall, 26 Nov 1855; Geo. Laws, bm.

Garrard, Tiree & Elizabeth Latta, 7 March 1809; John Latta, bm.

Garrard, Willie B. & Cozbi Ann Rhodes, 31 Jan 1854; J. W. Garrard, bm.

Garrard, Willson & Sylvia Brown, 22 June 1835; William H. Holden, bm.

Garrard, Woodson, son of Wilson & Silva Garrard, & Salina Smith, dau. of Reina Smith, m 12 Jan 1868 by Thos. Long, J. P.

Garrason, Farthing & Candess Latta, 2 April 1840; Caswill W. Durham, bm.

Garret, Henry H. & Moriah Tilly, 9 April 1847; Stephen Tilly, bm.

Garrett, Henry & Barbara Faust, 12 Jan 1810; Henry Anthony, bm.

Garrett, Jacob & Ann Albright, 9 March 1842; James Newlin, bm.

Garrett, James & Catharine Hutchins, 18 Dec 1847; Chesley P. Warren, bm.

Garrett, Jeremiah R. & Letitia A. Stockard, 24 March 1846; Eli Sharp, bm.

Garrett, John & Barbara Ingole, 1 Feb 1804; John Ingold, bm.

Garrett, John F. & ____, 20 Dec 1836; Lewis Albright, bm.

Garrett, Thomas & Melinda Rhodes, 17 April 1858; Washington Duke, bm.

Garrett, William & Sally Chisenhall, 19 Jan 1842; Wood Rigsbey, Moses Leathers Jr., bm.

Garrett, Youwain & Martha J. Bishop, 24 Aug 1859; Thos Long, Charles Jones, bm.

Garrison, Brice F. & Nancy Waggoner, 1 March 1849; James B. Fonville, bm.

Garrison, Charles G. & Margret Ellen Moore, 14 May 1839; Richard Maynard, bm.

Garrison, George & Nancy Hurdle, 10 March 1806; Charles Jordan, bm.

Garrison, Henry & Mary Moore, 14 Dec 1832; John M. Atkins, bm.

Garrison, John & Kitty Vickers, 23 Feb 1819; George Garrison, bm.

Garrison, John & Catharine Ector, 8 Dec 1834; Paton Brown, bm.

Garrison, Levi & Mary Graham, 30 Jan 1811; Jehu Hall, bm.

Garrison, William Howe & Polley Phillips, 16 March 1805; Thomas Philips, bm.

Garrott, Fielding & Nancy Horner, 5 Sept 1836; Wm. Fossett, Harrison Scott, bm.

Garton, Robert & Lidia White, 8 Nov 1796; William Stanford, bm.

Gaston, William & Sarah Johnson, 21 Feb 1860; Duncan Taylor, bm.

Gately, Thomas & Durinah Mangum, 12 Sept 1845; Addison Mangum, R. F. Morris, bm.

Gates, Elmore & Rebaca E. Hall, 26 Sept 1849; Ro. Britton, bm.

Gates, Frederick & Katharine Smith, 26 Nov 1793; John Waggoner, bm.

Gates, George T. & Mary Jane Rigan, 29 May 1866; John Gates, bm; m 7 June 1866 by L. W. Hall, J. P.

Gates, Henry & Mary Waggoner, 10 Aug 1832; John A. Faucett, bm.

Gates, Henry T. & Sophia Terry, 17 Sept 1852.

Gates, Jacob & Eliza Jorden, 15 Nov 1830; H. Terry, bm.

Gates, Jacob & Eliza Ray, 16 Dec 1851; John Turner, bm; m 18 Dec 1851 by Wm. Dickson, J. P.

Gates, James & Elizabeth Waggoner, 29 Aug 1824; John Waggoner, bm.

Gates, John & Rebecca Harris, 12 Feb 1817; Ephraim Harris, bm.

Gates, John, son of James & Elizabeth Gates, & Isabella Ragan, dau. of Thomas & Nancy Ragan, dau. of Thomas & Nancy Ragan, m 10 Nov 1867 by Lambert W. Hall, J. P.

Gates, John B. & Isabella Marcom, 15 Feb 1867; John P. Lockhart, bm.

Gates, Jno. W. & Nancy Latta, 7 Feb 1846; Robt. Webb, bm.

Gates, Leonard & Jenny Smith, 2 May 1826; Jacob Wagoner, bm.

Gates, Meridith & Mary Riley, 29 Dec 1852; J. J. Freeland, bm; m 5 Jan 1853 by Hezekiah Terry, J. P.

Gates, Stephen & Isbel Kelly, 27 Sept 1811; William Hill or Kelly, bm.

Gates, William & Frances Laws, 10 June 1831; Victor M. Murphey, John Waggoner, bm.

Gates, William F. & Mary Ann Gates, 15 Nov 1851; W. H. Jordan, bm; m 16 Nov 1851 by Hezekiah Terry, J. P.

Gates, Willie P. & Mary Monk, 27 Nov 1855; Henderson Monk, bm.

Gathirs, Jams & Eliza Durham, 27 April 1866; E. W. Morris, bm; m 27 April 1866 by R. F. Morris, J. P.

Gattis, Alexander & Rebecca King, 2 Aug 1800; Nathl. King, bm.

Gattis, Alexander & Rosannah Willson, 17 Sept 1806; Henry McCollum, bm.

Gattis, Anderson & Emma Murray, 18 Dec 1866; Louis Obrian, bm; m 20 Dec 1866 by F. Walker, J. P.

Gattis, Charles & Annis Tripp, 25 Sept 1823; N. Gattis, William King, bm.

Gattis, Isaac & Patty King, 28 Oct 1800; Nathl. King, bm.

Gattis, James & Anne King, 24 Oct 1783; John Caldwell, bm.

Gattis, James & Patsy Mason, 10 Jan 1821; Alexander Gattis, bm.

Gattis, James & Nancy Gattis, 16 Sept 1832; James Gattis, bm.

Gattis, James B. & Mary King, 23 Dec 1847; J. W. Carr, bm.

Gattis, John & Elizabeth Connelly, 19 Sept 1787; Thos Connaly, bm.

Gattis, John & Salley Blackwood, 11 Jan 1809; Andrew King, bm.

Gattis, John M. & Susan Gattis, 15 Aug 1834; James Gattis, bm.

Gattis, John R. & Nancy Gattis, 13 Dec 1845; Thos. W. Laws, bm.

Gattis, John T. & Bettie Jones, 9 Feb 1862; W. A. Maddry, bm; m 9 Feb 1862 by W. J. Hogan, J. P.

Gattis, John W. & Rachael D. Cale, 29 Jan 1863; James R. Gattis, bm; m 29 Jan 1863 by Solomon Pool.

Gattis, John Wesley & Lucinda A. Siler, 16 Nov 1853; J. B. McDade, bm; m 17 Nov 1863 by J. B. McDade, J. P.

Gattis, Nathaniel & Polley Cate, 9 Feb 1824; Charles Gattis, bm.

Gattis, Samuel & Margaret Allen, 25 Jan 1795; Abr. Allen, bm.

Gattis, Samuel & Nancy T. Gattis, 9 Sept 1846; Alex Gattis, bm.

Gattis, Sidney & Frances Gattis, 26 Feb 1866; Manly B. Jones, bm; m 27 Feb 1866 by R. S. Webb, M. G.

Gattis, Thomas & Polly Mason, 9 Feb 1808; Alexander Gattis, bm.

Gattis, Thomas W. & Bettie J. Burnett, 8 July 1856; Wesley Gattis, bm; m 8 July 1856 by J. B. McDade, J. P.

Gattis, William & Elizabeth Davis, 6 Oct 1808; James Gattis Jr., bm.

Gattis, William & Margret N. Gattis, 11 April 1835; John A. Gattis, bm.

Gattis, William M. & Sarah King, 12 March 1833; Thomas Gattis, bm.

Gaut, Richard & Mary Hines, 31 Sept 1795; Eli Nuland, bm.

Gawen, Henry & Salley Archey, 7 Dec 1861; Wm. Read, Freeman Howill, bm.

Gean, Burd & Mourning Cate, 2 Oct 1805; Robert Moore, bm.

Gean, William & Patsy Yarbrough, 1 Feb 1806; James Child, bm.

Geane, W. P. & Eliza Pickard, 30 Nov 1858; John Pickard, William T. Crawford, bm; m 1 Dec 1858 by Thos Lynch, minister.

Gee, Robert & Nancy Hatwood, 3 Aug 1793; Sillvanous Brewer, bm.

George, Brinkley & Milley Boothe, 6 March 1810; Joshua Horne, bm.

George, David & Betsey Trice, 18 Dec 1792; Edward Trice, bm.

George, David & Sylvina Herndon, 11 Dec 1837; Harmon Herndon, James C. Holland, bm.

George, Ezekiel & Martha Herndon, 8 Jan 1831; David George, bm.

George, Jno. & Dolly Barbee, 27 Nov 1866; Harday Massay, Jno. D. Wilbon, bm; m 15 Dec 1866 by H. J. Pearson, J. P.

George, Jonathan & Ferabee Locust, 27 Jan 1802; Lawrence Peteford, bm.

George, Solomon & Sarah Rich, 2 Oct 1784; Jesse George, bm.

George, Thomas & Cynthia Herndon, 24 March 1842; Harman Herndon, Moses Leathers, Jr., bm.

George, Redding & Sally Boothe, 1 Feb 1820; Chesley George, bm.

George, William & Matilda Herndon, 10 Jan 1826; Sampson Moore, Chesley George, bm.

Gerriner, Peter Junr. & Margaret Strader, 5 Aug 1847; Ic. W. Carden, bm.

Gibbs, John & Peggy Fitzgerald, 18 April 1815; J. Taylor, bm.

Gibson, David & Elizabeth Little, 13 Aug 1824; R. C. Mabray, bm.

Gibson, John & Jenney Pickard, 3 Feb 1803; John Carregan, bm.

Gibson, Thomas & Christiana Woody, 22 Nov 1819; Alexander Pickard, bm.

Gibson, William & Zilpha Shaw, 11 Aug 1841; Wesley Durham, Benton Ray, bm.

Gibson, Wm. & Rachel Ray, 11 Nov 1800; John Grimes, bm.

Gifferd, Levi & Margaret Wills, 12 May 1789; James McDaniel, bm.

Gifford, Jesse & Sarah Marshall, 30 April 1808; John Willis, Stephen Wells, bm.

Gifford, Joseph & Rosannah Courtner, 25 Aug 1819; D. Kimrey, bm.

Gilam, Wm. Henry & Betsey Baldwin, 28 Aug 1851; Nathaniel King, bm; m 28 Aug 1851 by Thos. Long, J. P.

Gilbert, Absalom & Frances Roberts, 6 Jan 1835; Wilie Gilbert, bm.

Gilbert, Absolem & Susannah Hawkins Roberts, 27 Oct 1842; Moses Leathers Jr., Wilie Gilbert, bm.

Gilbert, James M. & Mary Trice, 7 May 1841; Willis Vann, Moses Leathers Jr., bm.

Gilbert, Joel & Tabetha Barbee, 18 Feb 1837; Edmd. Herndon, James Rainey, bm.

Gilbert, Thadious & Louisa Lumly, 31 Oct 1866; M. A. Angier, bm; m 8 Nov 1866 by H. J. Pearson, J. P.

Gilbert, Wiles & America Herren, 8 April 1846; William Gilbert, bm.

Gilim, William H. & Jemima Dickerson, 21 July 1859; Jno. M. Faucett, Thos Long, bm; m 21 July 1859 by Jas. N. Craig, J. P.

Gill, E. E. & A. E. Caggin, 12 Nov 1858; James M. Pool, bm.

Gill, Thomas & Mary Jones, 4 April 1801; Richd. Gott, bm.

Gill, Thomas & Catherine Tate, 21 Aug 1826; Samuel Nelson, bm.

Gillam, Holal & Catey Pickard, 16 Nov 1833; John Crawford, bm.

Gillam, James & Polly Ray, 6 June 1827; James Ray, bm.

Gillam, John A. & Mary A. Sykes, 30 Nov 1861; m 1 Dec 1861 by Thos Long, J. P.

Gillispie, C. A. & Frances Sugg, 10 Oct 1850; Thos. Howerton, bm.

Gillom, Edmon & Nancy Holcup, 9 April 1805; Solomon Hulcup, bm.

Gilston, William & Mary McBroom, 6 June 1782; William McBroom, bm.

Gipson, Calvin & Emaline Sykes, 24 Dec 1866; James Maner, bm; m 25 Dec 1866 by Alvis Durham, J. P.

Girton, John & Susanah Suts, 12 Nov 1823; Adam Spoon, bm.

Gittings, Davis S. & V. S. Brandon, 15 June 1859; R. B. Saunders, bm.

Glason, Mason & Sarah Carter, 17 Oct 1821; William Moore, bm.

Glass, Eli & Tempey Isley, 25 Dec 1848; Jacob Neace, bm.

Glass, Richard C. & Margaret J. Kerr, 25 June 1841; Thos. Thompson, Robt. F. White, bm.

Glass, Stephen & Elizabeth Armstrong, 29 May 1809; John Lankston, bm.

Glasson, Jesper & Martha Moore, 28 Jan 1820; Joseph Glasson, bm.

Glasson, William & Rachel Marshell, 13 Sept 1819; George Stafford, bm.

Glaster, James & Acqullea Merick, 20 Dec 1793; Boling Jolley, bm.

Glen, Dunkn & Lucy Hall, 3 Nov 1832; J. Taylor, bm.

Glenn, David & Polley Southerland, 31 Dec 1798; William Southerland, bm.

Glenn, Duke & Rachel Carroll, 21 Oct 1822; Archd. Carroll, Allsy Carrol, bm.

Glenn, Duke or William & Delila Carrington, 5 March 1842; Moses Leathers Jr., bm.

Glenn, Duncan & Mary Jane Williams, 21 Sept 1852; Peyton Clements, bm; m 23 Sept 1852 by Harris Wilkerson, J. P.

Glenn, Elisha & Franky Etheridge, 2 Dec 1815; Ryals Etheridge, bm.

Glenn, George W. & Sarah E. Nichols, 28 Aug 1857; Leroy Daugherty, bm; m 3 Sept 1857 by Charles Wilson, J. P.

Glenn, Henry & Grissey Adeline Brown, 1 Feb 1838; Duke Glenn, William Adams, bm.

Glenn, Hilmon & Rendy McFarlin, 18 Dec 1858; James M. Wood, bm; m 19 Dec 1858 by Thomas Ferrell, J. P.

Glenn, Hinton Castley & Carolina Williams, 7 Aug 1860; Allison S. Glenn, bm; m 8 Aug 1860 by Thomas Ferrell, J. P.

Glenn, Irvan W. & Lucinda Batchler, 27 Feb 1861; H. C. McCauley, Richard B. Watson, bm.

Glenn, Isaac & Elizabeth Murphy, 12 Jan 1826; William Richardson, bm.

Glenn, James & Nancy Allenthorp, 8 Sept 1801; John Garard, bm.

Glenn, James S. & Mary Dollar, 27 Dec 1831; Jno. H. Ingram, bm.

Glenn, Jefferson & Mary J. Carrington, 7 May 1850; William Glenn, bm.

Glenn, John & Judah Roberts, 9 Oct 1800; Jeremiah Glenn, bm.

Glenn, Joseph & Margrit Hulbert, 5 Sept 1797; Chars. Wheeler, bm.

Glenn, Martin & Guilly Rigsby, 31 Dec 1816; Warren Rigsby, bm.

Glenn, Ransom & Lucinda Glenn, 21 May 1825; Thomas Riggsby, bm.

Glenn, Robert & Jeany Jackson, 29 April 1805; George Clancy, bm.

Glenn, Thomas & Anne Hall, 28 May 1843; Duncan C. Glenn, Thos. Sykes, of Allen, bm.

ORANGE COUNTY MARRIAGES, 1779-1868

Glenn, Tyre & Betsey Everydge, 14 March 1826; W. H. Woods, bm.

Glenn, Tyree & Susannah Sutherland, 22 June 1782; Reuben
Chishorn, bm.

Glenn, Vinard C. & Elisebeth N. Crabtree, 24 Sept 1859; Presley
J. Mangum, bm.

Glenn, Wiley & Tempy Boggs, 22 Dec 1838; Simpson Boggs, bm.

Glenn, William see Glenn, Duke

Glenn, Willis & Salley Glenn, 5 Dec 1824; William Hayes, bm.

Glenn, Wiseley R. & Mildredge A. Glenn, 2 Sept 1861; Washington
Hall, bm.

Glossen, Alfred A. & Juliann Lloyd, 19 Nov 1847; George
Thompson, bm.

Glosson, David & Tabetha Stroud, 15 Oct 1809; James Glosson, bm.

Gloster, Thos. Benn & Mary Hayes Willis, 23 May 1795; Wil.
Kirkland, bm.

Godfrey, James & Jane Thompson, 12 May 1784; Thomas Wilson, bm.

Gooch, James C. & Adline Horne, 6 Dec 1854; Jno. Turner, bm.

Gooch, John Alston & Eliza Jane Nutt, 31 Oct 1825; Arther Pool,
bm.

Gooch, Luico & Sally May, 26 June 1847; Andrew McFaling, bm.

Gooch, Pumphrett P. & Elizabeth Rust, 2 Feb 1822; Chesley D.
Rust, bm.

Gooch, Solomon & Charlotte Nancy, 10 Jan 1854; Robert Gooch,
John Laws, bm; m 12 Jan 1854 by Harris Wilkerson, J. P.

Gooch, Thomas & Jane Lewis, 13 Feb 1822; Dodson Dollar, bm.

Gooch, William & Susan May, 29 Nov 1838; John P. Cole, James
Browning, bm.

Goode, Miles & Celia Atkinson, 29 Nov 1814; Joshua Woody, bm.

Goodloe, William H. & Clara Thompson, 24 Nov 1836; William
Miles, bm.

Goodloe, Wm. Henry & Elizabeth Mebane, 26 Jan 1804; Henry
Thomson Jr., bm.

Goodrich, Henrey & Genny Tinnin, 1 July 1816; William Hannah,
bm.

Gorden, David C. & Mary E. Crabtree, 8 Dec 1855; Thomas A.
Faucet, bm; m 8 Feb 1855 by William H. Brown, J. P.

Gorden, William B. & Lucy R. Brown, 15 Dec 1861; Thomas
Scarlett, bm; m 16 Dec 1861 by B. F. Guthrie, bm.

Gorden, Yancy, son of Samuel & Lizzie Gorden, & Mariah Cobb,
colored, m 15 Sept 1867 by D. W. Jordan, J. P.

119

Gordon, Pompey, son of Junius & Rachel Gordon, & Grance
Thompson, dau. of Wm. & Evelina Thompson, colored, m 5 May
1868 by Charles Phillips, minister.

Gordon, Samuel J. & Caroline Hardie, 17 June 1831; Egbert H.
Shaw, bm.

Gorley, William & Polly Uless, 20 May 1819; Farmer Smith, bm.

Gossett, Leroy & Polley Ponds, 9 Dec 1805; Wm. Killon, bm.

Gott, Jno. & Gracey Stubbins, 2 Jan 1802; Jos. Stubbins Junr.,
bm.

Gott, Richard & Catey Gill, 1 Dec 1796; Thomas Gill, bm.

Gowan, Jesse & Salley Bass, 4 Jan 1815; Marvell J. Hays, bm.

Graff, William H. & H. A. E. Maddison, dau. of Mary J. Walker,
m 22 Jan 1868 by Henry Gray, minister.

Gragson, Baker & Rebecca Stevens, 18 Nov 1822; James Partin, bm.

Gragson, Eli & Salley Williams, 23 Sept 1824; George McCreey, bm.

Gragson, Robert & Patsey Sutton, 12 Oct 1819; John Cardin, bm.

Gragson, William & Fanny Williams, 26 May 1815; James Adams, bm.

Gragson, William J. & Mariah K. Walker, 17 Sept 1857; John Cheek,
bm.

Graham, Alexr. & Mary Picket, 6 March 1793; Kenneth Anderson, bm.

Graham, Charls & Christiana Dixon, 27 April 1866; Benj.
Cunaghm, bm; m 27 April 1866 by R. F. Morris.

Graham, George & Kitty Boswell, 21 Oct 1818; Edward Boswell, bm.

Graham, George W. & Avaline King, 22 Dec 1847; G. M. Lea, bm.

Graham, John & Mary Byrd, 11 Oct 1782.

Graham, John & Polley Hall, 17 Sept 1829; Sampson Glenn, bm.

Graham, John W., son of W. A. & S. W. Graham, & Rebecca B.
Anderson, dau. of P. C. and A. R. Cameron, m 9 Oct 1867 by
M. A. Curtis, Rector of St. Matthew's Church, Hillsborough

Graham, Joseph Dr. & Elizabeth Hill, 26 Oct 1859; John Kirkland
Jr., Joseph C. Webb, bm; m 26 Oct 1859 by M. A. Curtis,
Rector of St. Matthew's Church, Hillsborough.

Graham, Luke & Nancy Ricketts, 2 Jan 1792; Isaac Pickard, bm.

Graham, Thomas & Edney Fonville, 28 Aug 1824; Harrison Weedon,
Thomas Grahams, bm.

Grahams, Robert & Elizabeth Thompson, 31 Dec 1805; Thomas
Thompson, bm.

Grahams, William & Salley Hall, 8 May 1830; John Grahams, bm.

Grant, Richard S. & Eliza N. Mitchell, 16 Nov 1852; J. Thos Wheat Jr., bm; m at the home of Dr. Mitchell, Chapel Hill, 18 Nov 1852 by Alex Wilson, minister.

Graves, Alfred & Sally Rick, 18 Oct 1848; Wm. A. Carrigan, bm.

Graves, Daniel & Mary Noah, __ July 1814; George ___, bm.

Graves, Daniel & Sopha Fridell, 17 May 1814, Peter Graves, bm.

Graves, David & ___ Fogleman, 15 Aug 1818; Michael Shoffner, bm.

Graves, Eli & Delilah Shofner, 31 March 1820; ___, bm.

Graves, Frederik & Mary M. Wood, 19 Dec 1845; Levi R. Graves, bm.

Graves, Henry L. & Eliza H. Mebane, 12 Dec 1826; E. Graves, bm.

Graves, John L. & Julia A. Hill, 12 June 1836; Giles Mebane, Tho. Anderson, bm.

Graves, Ralph H. & Ema Taylor, 3 Dec 1849; J. S. Green, bm.

Graves, William & Caty Webster, 21 Sept 1833; William Webster, bm.

Gray, Adin & Elizabeth Pigg, 25 Jan 1787; Robert Smith, bm.

Gray, Alfred & Mary Lint, 15 Sept 1822; James Wilkerson, Isaac Lint, bm.

Gray, Alfred & Anne Jane Brown, 6 May 1843; Absalom Brown, bm.

Gray, Alonso Franklin & Astimisia Perlinea Bell, 15 Oct 1856; W. W. Allison, bm.

Gray, Andrew & Polley Jameison, 17 Nov 1807; John Brown, bm.

Gray, George & Elizabeth Suit (Lint?), 28 Oct 1824; Alfred Gray, bm.

Gray, J. A. & Emma E. Walker, 26 March 1861; W. J. Walker, bm.

Gray, Jas. & Mary Rayly, 31 Jan 1781; Thos. Gray, bm.

Gray, James & Hannah Allison, 12 June 1797; Wm. Fitch, bm.

Gray, John D. & Elizabeth P. Allison, 2 July 1857; J. R. Hester, bm.

Gray, John F., son of Grier & Parnithia Gray, & Margaret McCadams, dau. of James & Sarah J. McCadams, m 5 Jan 1868 by Alson Gray.

Gray, Thos. & Elizabeth Paul, 16 Jan 1781; Wm. Armstrong, Joshua Potts, bm.

Gray, Thos. & Polley Massey, 18 Nov 1796; Abner Massey, bm.

Gray, William & Elizabeth Finley, 8 Nov 1837; Robert Bell, A. T. Finley, bm.

Gray, William & Mary Jane Anderson, 15 Jan 1838; Carnes T. Anderson, bm.

Gray, William & Eliza Crabtree, 27 Aug 1841; William Trice, John Boroughs, bm.

Green, David & Nelly Daniel, 28 Oct 1800; Elisha Green, bm.

Green, Edward & Hannah Holmes, 8 March 1796; Edmund Green, bm.

Green, Edward & Bedy Anderson, 12 July 1851; Richard Mayo, bm; m 13 July 1851 by W. W. Albea, minister.

Green, Elisha & Nancy Edwards, 27 Nov 1798; John Edwards, bm.

Green, Green & Elizabeth Green, colored, 7 Dec 1866; L. M. Yearby, bm; m 8 Dec by James Stagg, J. P.

Green, James & Rosanna George, 3 Jan 1855; Thomas J. Turner, bm; m 6 Jan 1856 by A. B. Gunter, J. P.

Green, James S. & Kate S. Waddell, 28 Nov 1849; E. G. Gray, bm.

Green, John & Rebeccah Murray, 13 July 1811; Daniel Foust, bm.

Green, John & Elizabeth Chizenhall, 19 Jan 1830; Daniel Green, Richard Proctor, bm.

Green, John & Jane Holt, 19 Dec 1838; Daniel Cabe, bm.

Green, John H. & Jane Hust, 6 Aug 1860; A. B. Gunter, Henderson George, bm; m 6 Aug 1860 by A. B. Gunter, J. P.

Green, Joshay & Rachall Green, 23 Oct 1866; Mikel J. Green, bm; m 23 Oct 1866 by R. F. Morris, J. P.

Green, Mager A. & Martha M. Latta, 8 Jan 1866; Wm. Hamlen, bm; m 10 Jan 1866 by B. C. Hopkins, J. P.

Green, Michael & Polley Daniel, 18 Nov 1803; Roger Daniel, bm.

Green, Michael & Nancy Marcum, 31 Oct 1806; Jos. Marcom, bm.

Green, Nathan & Elizabeth Berry, 14 March 1811; Timothy Weaver, bm.

Green, Nicholas & Patsy Walker, 17 Dec 1797; Tredway(?), bm.

Green, Robert & Rebeckah Brackston, 7 Feb 1796; Jacob Lemmon, bm.

Green, Robert & Delilah Simpson, 26 May 1810; Saml. Chambers, bm.

Green, Robt. & Anne Johnson, 26 Dec 1815; John Hobbs, bm.

Green, Silas & Elizabeth Estis, 27 Dec 1810; George Reeves, bm.

Green, Thomas J. & Frances K. Burton, 5 Oct 1818; Geo. Allen, bm.

Green, William & Edney Leathers, 22 March 1841; Benton Ray, W. A. Norwood, bm.

Greer, Jacob & Polly Steele, 18 Sept 1804; Jno. Taylor, bm.

Greeson, Peter & Polly Fogleman, 29 Dec 1827; Ludwick Fogleman, bm.

Greeson, Peter & Patsey Jinkins, 24 Oct 1828; George Jynkins, bm.

Greeson, Solomon & Anna Adeline Freeland, 16 Feb 1833; John Freeland, bm.

Gregason, Wm. & Nancy Baker, 14 March 1796; Robert Baker, bm.

Gregory, E. S. & Allace J. Laws, 12 March 1867; Wm. H. Reeves, bm; m 12 March 1867 by H. B. Pratt.

Gregson, George & Martha Hunter, 28 July 1792; Kenneth Anderson, bm.

Gregston, Wm. & Hannah McCrory, 3 Nov 1832; Alfred King, bm.

Gresham, Thomas F. & Treasa Ann Rhods, 17 Oct 1846; Moses W. Guess, bm.

Griffin, Abner & Nancy Glosson, 26 Nov 1831; John R. Minnis, bm.

Griffin, Andw. & Nancy Rutherford, 15 June 1782; Jesse Benton, wit.

Griffin, Humphrey & Sarah Whittington, 28 Feb 1805; J. Taylor, bm.

Griffin, James & Sarah Moore, 10 Feb 1835; Henderson Griffin, J. Taylor, bm.

Griffin, James & Nancy Pickard, 6 Feb 1843; William Fouler, bm.

Griffin, John & Peggy Glosson, 22 Aug 1827; Franklin Kirk, bm.

Griffin, John & Rebecca Roach, 23 Oct 1861; R. A. Patterson, bm; m 27 Oct 1861 by Allen Edwards, J. P.

Griffin, Stanford & Delilah Dickerson, 28 March 1818; Felty Neace, bm.

Griffin, Thomas & ____, 8 March (no year, during admn. of Gov. Alexr. Martin, 1780's-1790's); John Tate, bm.

Griffin, Thomas & Patsey Watson, 1 Nov 1817; John Dockery, bm.

Griffin, Thomas G. & Liuizar Canody, 31 Aug 1865; Henry M. Crabtree, bm; m 31 Aug 1865 by Thos. Long, J. P.

Griffin, William & Polly Fowler, 15 March 1822; Thos Ravenscroft, bm.

Griffis, William & Salley Horn, 9 Aug 1804; Jo. Moore, bm.

Griffis, William & Tempey Jeffries, 6 Sept 1821; William Porter, Reuben Jeffries, bm.

Griffis, William & Polly Lyttle, 22 Sept 1821; Marks Ammonds, bm.

Grifyn, Isaac & Margaret Dulap, 1 Jan 1787; Joseph Tate, bm.

Grinton, Wm. J. & Elizabeth Jones, free colored, 2 Oct 1854; Jacob F. Harris, bm.

Grisham, David J. & Frances Crabtree, 27 Jan 1849; William G. Crabtree, bm.

Grisham, Harris & Franky Glenn, 27 Feb 1792; William Glen, bm.

Grisham, James & Elizabeth Weaks, 20 Feb 1796; Wm. Elliott, bm.

Grisham, John & Sally Flint, 22 June 1819; George Grisham, bm.

Grisham, Robert & Pegy Guess, 14 Oct 1833; John Mitchell, James Brockwell, bm.

Grisham, Thomas & Nancy Petty, 29 June 1802; Ambrose Petty, bm.

Grissum, John & Patsey Weaks, 5 April 1798; William Weeks, bm.

Grove, William Barry & Sarah Shepperd, 10 Aug 1801; A. Tatom, bm.

Guess, Harrison P. & Susan Strayhorn, 16 Dec 1851; P. M. Cates, bm; m 18 Dec 1851 by Alexr. Dickson, J. P.

Guess, Jas. H. & Helen Barbee, 21 July 1858; David C. Warren, bm; m 29 July 1858 by M. A. Angier, J. P.

Guess, John & Elizabeth Riggs, 18 Nov 1797; Sol. Turrentine, bm.

Guess, John & Nancy Warren, 27 Dec 1828; Wm. W. Guess, bm.

Guess, John R. & Nancy Jane Robinson, 22 Jan 1846; E. G. Gray, bm.

Guess, Joseph & Nancy Riggs, 26 Oct 1810; Alexr. G. Hall, bm.

Guess, Moses & Elizabeth Warren, 21 Feb 1800; Josiah Warren, bm.

Guess, Moses & Harriett M. Link, 23 Sept 1833; Anderson Rhodes, bm.

Guess, Thomas & Elizabeth Rhodes, 16 Aug 1830; James Horn, bm.

Guess, William & Margaret Oakley, 14 March 1848; W. Harris, bm.

Guess, Wm. & Anne Wilson, 9 Dec 1795; William Dollar, bm.

Guess, Wm. W. & Frances Laws, 29 May 1829; W. Hudgins, bm.

Guess, Wm. W. & Mary Jane Holemon, 13 Dec 1850; Minnick Miller, bm.

Guess, Willie G. & Adlaide M. Dixon, 7 Oct 1865; Bennett C. Hopkins, bm; m 11 Oct 1865 by B. C. Hopkins, J. P.

Guilliam, Mason & Sophia Moore, 13 March 1838; Jesse Durham, bm.

Guinn, Joseph & Elizabeth Smith, 5 Nov 1798; John Neves, bm.

Guion, Haywood & Caroline Moore, 29 Jan 1840; C. Battle, J. Taylor, bm.

Gun, John & Ruth Hinshawe, 18 Sept 1839; Joseph Green, bm.

Gunter, D. C. & Jane J. Trice, 2 Jan 1865; m 5 Jan 1865 by B. C. Hopkins, J. P.

Gunter, Landson & Emily Ferrill, 26 July 1841; Gilbert Strayhorn, bm.

Guthrie, Claburn & Nelly Newland, 9 Oct 1809; B. Guthrie, bm.

Guthrie, Hugh B. & Jane G. Cave, colored, 2 July 1866; Geo. Laws, bm; m 4 July 1866 by N. W. Wilson.

Guthrie, James & Jeane Smith, 25 Feb 1791; Andrew Smith, bm.

Guthrie, Thomas & Nancy Bevins, 23 Dec 1831; Green Britt, bm.

Guthrie, William A. & Mary E. Carr, 26 Nov 1866; John Laws, bm; m 29 Nov 1866 by James Phillips, D. D.

Guttry, Robert & Mary Smith, 29 Jan 1791; Andrew Smith, bm.

Guy, Buckner & Sylvia Jeffers, 16 July 1810; Merriday Chavis, bm.

Guy, Edmund & Tilley Wooten, 8 Sept 1813; Jesse Guy, Buckner Guy, bm.

Guy, Henry & Betsey Jeffers, 7 Dec 1821; Jesse Guy, bm.

Guy, Jesse & Betsey Merritt, 13 March 1821; John Jeffers, bm.

Guy, John & Aggy Whitmon, 21 Feb 1814; Merriday Chavis, bm.

Guy, Moore & Savina Jeffries, 22 Sept 1859; Jake Jeffres, bm.

Guy, Richard & Patsey Whitmore, 3 Sept 1819; Henry Guy, John Guy, bm.

Guy, Thomas & Harriet Adaline Burnett, 8 May 1848; John Ward, bm.

Guy, Vines & Elizabeth Jeffers, 8 Jan 1805; Jesse Blalock, bm.

Gwin, John & Sarah Harper, 26 Feb 1782; Henrey McClure, bm.

Gwin, William & Hannah McCombs, 4 May 1782; John Willey, John Gwin, bm.

Gwinn, Thomas & Milley Rhew, 17 April 1819; Thomas Christian, bm.

Gwyn, Robert & Rachael Moore, 24 Nov 1792; James Moore, bm.

Hadley, Jacob M. & Elizabeth E. Kirkpatrick, m 4 Sept 1860 by Edmund Strudwick, J. P.

Hagan, William & Nancy Huntington, 3 Nov 1831; W. A. Parish, bm.

Haggans, Jacob & Mary Acres, 25 Nov 1793; Stephen Hart, bm.

Hagwood, George & Elizabeth Brewer, 23 Jan 1821; Charles McCauley, bm.

Hailey, Alvan E. & Martha C. Roberts, 29 Sept 1834; Ezekiel Hailey, bm.

Hailey, Isaac & Betsey Monk, 16 May 1816; Solomon Wood, bm.

Hailey, James & Anney Ferrell, 30 Jan 1794; John Clemmons, bm.

Hailey, James & Winna Monk, 2 Nov 1816; Isaac Hailey, bm.

Hailey, James & Winna Monk, 2 Nov 1816; Isaac Hailey, bm.

Hailey, Richard & Martha Thompson, 24 Dec 1857; W. R. Hughes, bm; m 24 Dec 1857 by J. J. Allison, J. P.

Hailey, Simeon R. & Barrilla Jane Cook, 1 Dec 1841; Thomas L. Hailey, Moses Leathers Junr., bm.

Hailey, Thomas R. & Sarah Jane Bledsoe, 8 Dec 1866; Ezekiel C. Hailey, bm; m 9 Dec 1866 by R. F. Morris, J. P.

Haithcock, David & Peggy Mitchell, 19 April 1813; Thos. Colman, bm.

Haithcock, Merrit & Candacy Archer, 12 June 1828; James Hood, James Child, bm.

Haithcock, Solomon & Ritty Petteford, 5 May 1834; Vincent Falkner, bm.

Haithcock, Williamson & Minerva Stewart, 29 March 1834; Neverson Stewart, bm.

Haize, David & Jane Hasten, 21 May 1836; Thos. C. Hayes, James Hastings, bm.

Hale, Joseph & Dolly Herndon, 2 Oct 1792; William Whitted, Samuel Hale, bm.

Halen, Henry D. & Mary F. Addison, 25 Dec 1866; m 26 Dec 1866 by Mager Green, J. P.

Haley, Andrew & Carey Dossett, 24 May 1817; Willis Monk, bm.

Haley, Drudop & Beedy E. Turner, 27 Aug 1850; Francis Barbee, bm.

Haley, John & Eliza Madison, 26 Feb 1851; Urias Forsyth, bm.

Haley, Thomas & Milly Roan, 24 Jan 1805; Solomon Wood, bm.

Hall, Alex R. & Edney Wilson, 12 Dec 1853; Chs. P. Miller, bm; m 13 Dec 1853 by Hezekiah Terry, J. P.

Hall, Anderson & Ellen Barnwell, 24 Jan 1831; Junius Hall, bm.

Hall, Andrew & Caroline Crabtree, 17 Jan 1856; Willi H. Redding, Mich King, bm.

Hall, Gaston W. & Emeline Hicks, 19 Aug 1858; John H. Dollar, H. M. Crabtree, bm; m 19 Aug 1858 by John F. Lyon, J. P.

Hall, Henry & Betsy Rhodes, 28 April 1807; William Hall, bm.

Hall, Hickabud & Gatsey Trewit, 13 July 1822; John Roney, bm.

Hall, Isaac or Jehu & Ann Grimes, 8 April 1797; Isaac Hall, Jonathan Clenny, bm.

Hall, Isaac & Obedience Woods, 26 Aug 1866; Harry Hall, bm; m 26 Aug 1866 by Nelson P. Hall, J. P.

Hall, James & Lucy Stagg, 23 Nov 1865; Peyton Clements, bm; m 23 Nov 1865 by A. Nichols, J. P.

Hall, James T. & Elizabeth Rigsbee, 18 Aug 1860; Allison S. Glenn, bm; m 19 Aug 1860 by Thomas Ferrell, J. P.

Hall, Jehu see Hall, Isaac

Hall, Jehu & Elizabeth McCleure, 13 March 1828; Jo. Clendenen, bm.

Hall, John & Elizabeth Riggs, 24 May 1796; James Watson, bm.

Hall, John & Amey Bledsoe, 26 Nov 1816; John Garrard, bm.

Hall, John & Sally Whiteker, 19 March 1852; Allen Cole, bm; m 20 May 1852 by William McCown, J. P.

Hall, John W. & Martha B. Woods, 24 June 1854; L. W. Hall, bm; m 25 June 1854 by Archibald Currie, minister.

Hall, Jno. R. & Elizabeth Woods, 31 Jan 1824; Ezekiel Laws, bm.

Hall, Joseph & Manerva Riley, 8 March 1860; John Chisenhall, bm; m 8 March 1860 by Jno. Hancock, J. P.

Hall, Levi & Polly Burnsid, 29 Dec 1852; Bennett Hazell, bm; m 29 Dec 1852 by John J. Freeland.

Hall, Levi & Mary Ellen Quals, 7 May 1863; Robert Sykes, bm; m 10 May 1863 by Nathaniel Bain, J. P.

Hall, Nelson D. & Nancy R. Bowles, 10 Nov 1838; Nelson Nichols, bm.

Hall, Nelson P. & Martha C. Taylor, 3 Dec 1856; L. W. Hall, bm; m 10 Dec 1856 by Thomas H. Faucette.

Hall, Robbert & Milly Standiford, 29 Nov 1821; John Hall, bm.

Hall, Robert & Mary Erwin Riggs, 24 Aug 1795; Wm. Hall, bm.

Hall, Robert & Martha Walker, 24 March 1830; St. Terry, bm.

Hall, Robert & Mary A. Perry, 30 Dec 1865; Saml. W. Hughes, bm; m 30 Dec 1865 by Saml. M. Wilkinson, J. P.

Hall, Robert & Minerva Underwood, 26 Dec 1847; W. D. McC___, James Underwood, bm.

Hall, Robert N. & Aletha A. Nichols, 21 June 1856; Evans Turner, bm.

Hall, Samuel C. & Rebecca Brown, 18 Aug 1812; David Ewing, Perey Mitchel, bm.

Hall, Thomas & Nancey Haze, 16 Sept 1783; David Hall, bm.

Hall, Thomas & Sarah Wortham, 1 Sept 1796; Jno. Riggs, bm.

Hall, Thomas & Nancy Hicks, 7 Aug 1800; Isaac Hicks, bm.

Hall, Thomas B. & Maria T. Simpson, 15 Sept 1836; Allen C. Jones, Walter A. Norwood, bm.

Hall, Thomas J. & Sarah J. Wilson, 19 Oct 1865; Thomas H. Wilson, bm; m 19 Oct 1865 by Joseph W. McKee, J. P.

Hall, William & Frances Bruce, 27 June 1794; James Hays, bm.

Hall, William & Nancy Cate, 20 Nov 1804; Thomas Cates, John Cate, bm.

Hall, William & Polley Horner, 20 Sept 1809; John Edwards, bm.

Hall, William & Barsilla Hudgins, 11 April 1815; John Bledsoe, bm.

Hall, William & Annis Bird, 13 July 1822; Joseph Bird, bm.

Hall, William & Harriet Morton, 8 Oct 1834; Thos. Graham, bm.

Hall, Wm. & Polley Murduk, 9 Feb 1786; Robert Gray, bm.

Hall, William H. & Polly Woods, 30 May 1823; Richd. Nichols, bm.

Hall, Willis & Selvy Jeffreys, 15 Dec 1866; Lewis Cain, bm; m 15 Dec 1866 by Alex Bass, Elder A. M. E. Ch.

Hall, Willoughby & Elizabeth A. Whitaker, 6 May 1850; Wm. M. Whitaker, bm.

Halstead, Mathias & Nancy Rainy, 29 Jan 1828; Jesse Horlstead, bm.

Hamblton, Archibald & Fanny Bird, 7 Oct 1807; James Whitted, bm.

Hamilton, Daniel Heywood & Frances Gray Roulhac, 8 Dec 1859; A. B. Simmons, bm; m 8 Dec 1859 by M. A. Curtis, Rector of St. Matthew's Church, Hillsborough.

Hamilton, James & Jane Whitsitt, 6 Jan 1817; A. Hamilton, bm.

Hamilton, John & Talessa Thompson, 16 Dec 1835; Joseph Pickett, bm.

Hamilton, Joseph & Martha Whiteside, 18 Aug 1781; William Bradford, bm.

Hamilton, William & Sarah McCulley, 12 Aug 1817; Archd. Hamilton, bm.

Hamlen, James & Elizabeth VanHood, 10 June 1838; David Van Hook, bm.

Hamlen, William & Sarah M. Green, 13 Feb 1857; Jefferson Green, bm; m 15 Jan 1857 by Derham Hall, M. D.

Hamlett, Richd. R. & Margaret J. Lynch, 7 Sept 1864; Wm. F. Snipes, bm.

Hammond, Mark & Catey Jeffries, 10 May 1802; Richd. Hargreaves, John Reeves, bm.

Hamons, Thammas & Betsy Burnet, 8 Sept 1832; Zedekiah Husbands, bm.

Hmpton, Nolan & Dawsey Rust, 27 Nov 1821; Chesley Rust, bm.

Hampton, Nowlin & Winifred Cozart, 30 March 1793; James Cozart, bm.

Hampton, Thomas & Peggy Wall, 8 Aug 1817; Even Thomas, bm.

Hampton, Wilbourne L. & Polly Walker, 28 Aug 1834; Thomas Peed, bm.

Hampton, Zachariah H. & Lucie A. Monk, 19 May 1865; Zachariah T. Hampton, bm.

Hancock, Jacob & Jane Faucett, 21 Jan 1831; Loven Carmichl, J. Taylor, bm.

Hancock, John & Martha J. Chamblee, 13 Feb 1854; John C. McCown, bm; m 16 Feb 1854 by Wm. McCown, J. P.

Hancock, Samuel & Susannah Richards, 10 March 1803; William Newman Jr., bm.

Hanks, John & Mary Jane Armstrong, 8 Oct 1795; Joseph Armstrong, bm.

Hanks, William H., son of Benj. F. & Jane Hanks & Catherine R. Blunt, dau. of R. H. J. & Sarah Blunt, m 11 Dec 1867 by Jacob Doll, Pastor of the Presbyterian Churches of Yanceyville & Bethesda.

Hanley, William & Rebeccah Minstone, 27 July 1792; James Abbot, bm.

Hanner, John P. & Ceelia Murray, 27 Dec 1838; A. C. Murdock, bm.

Hanner, William & Nancy Dunnagan, 26 June 1815; Timothy Dunnagan, bm.

Harbert, Charles & Rebeccah Shinn, 30 Oct 1820; Dennis Heartt, bm.

Harden, Daniel C. & Mrs. Rebecca C. Foust, 4 Feb 1843; m 7 Feb 1843 by E. W. C.

Harden, Daniele & Kitty Garrison, 14 Nov 1835; G. Hurdle, bm.

Harden, James & Desdemona Brinckley, 22 Dec 1797; Solomon Stalkoop, bm.

Harden, Jeremiah & Sarah Wiley, 3 Dec 1789; Samuel Thompson, bm.

Harden, John & Rebeckah Holt, 26 Oct 1812; Thomas Sellars, bm.

Harden, Peter & Sarah E. Holt, 3 April 1848; George Hurdle, bm.

Harden, Thomas & Elisabeth Powell, 20 Dec 1791; John Powell, John Killion, bm.

Harder, Jacob & Elisabeth Server, 9 Oct 1805.

Harder, Joseph & Eliza. Sellers, 18 Nov 1796; Solomon Stalcup, bm.

Hardin, Edmund & Patty Davis, 2 Nov 1792; Benjamin Lacy, bm.

Hardin, John & Sarah Holt, 14 Dec 1783; Wm. Oneil, bm.

Hargis, Aaron & Elizabeth McKee, 18 Sept 1805; David Woods, bm.

Hargis, Dennis & Drucilla Shaw, 8 July 1808; Wm. McNeill, bm.

Hargis, Samuel & Nancy McMunn, 24 Jan 1794; Jno. Breeze, bm.

Hargis, Samuel, son of Thomas & Sarah Hargis, & Elmire Henry, dau. of Abner Bradshaw, m 15 March 1868 by D. W. Jordon, J. P.

Hargis, Tho. N. S. & Muriah B. Horton, 4 March 1815; John Scott, bm.

Hargiss, William R. & Sarah Allison, 12 Feb 1841; William Ray, Robert Graham, bm.

Hargrave, Jesse & Margret J. Barbee, 11 Feb 1843; Wm. F. Strayhorn, Duncan Nickols, bm.

Hargreaves, Richard & Mary Lynch, 21 March 1793; Edward Wilson, bm.

Hargrove, Monroe, son of Nelson & Phebe Hargrove & Harried Hill, dau. of Hannah Baker, m 12 Sept 1867 by O. S. Brent.

Hargroves, Henry & Pattey Harris, 4 Aug 1784; James Harris, bm.

Harill, Anderson & Jeany Barnhill, 6 Feb 1810; William Barnhill, bm.

Haris, Benton & Lucinda Piper, 13 July 1857; John C. Reed, bm; m 30 July 1857 by John F. Lyon, J. P.

Haris, Caleb & Matilda Keath, 27 Feb 1861; R. S. Ross, bm.

Harlough, Obediah & Rachael Jameson, 4 Jan 1797; George Hopkins, bm.

Harper, Braks & Patsey Carter, 1 Dec 1847; Emanuel Jones, bm.

Harper, Edmund & Rachel Smith, 27 Dec 1793; Reuben Smith, bm.

Harper, Richard & Anne Forrest, 11 Feb 1786; James Forrest, bm.

Harper, Willis & Rosannah Dolly, 19 Sept 1805; Reuben Smith, bm.

Harrell, William & Dicey Hern, 11 Feb 1808; Younger Hopson, bm.

Harrington, Elam J., son of W. D. & L. M. Harrington & Laura E. Boroughs, dau. of Thos. & L. Boroughs, m 19 Sept 1867 by Charles Phillips, minister.

Harris, Caleb & Matilda Keeth, m 27 Feb 1861 by Solomon Shepherd, J. P.

Harris, Charles & Eliza F. Laws, 14 Sept 1863; Henry C. McCauly, bm; m 14 Sept 1863 by C. Wilson, J. P.

Harris, Daniel & Frances Nichols, 4 Feb 1867; Samuel S. McBroom, George W. Glenn, bm; m 4 Feb 1867 by Lambert W. Hall, J. P.

Harris, Dudley & Rebeca Allon Murdock, 2 June 1849; Silas Wilson, bm.

Harris, Edward B. & Elizabeth Lynch, 7 March 1817; James Smith, bm.

Harris, Elsey & Sally Wilson, 14 Dec 1820; Ephraim Harris, bm.

Harris, Ephraim & Matilda Dunnagan, 6 Oct 1818; Sherwood Dunagan, bm.

Harris, Green & Rhodah Johnston, 22 Nov 1838; James Bullock, bm.

Harris, Jacob F. & Gusta Mitchell, colored, 22 Nov 1852; Mins Evans, bm; m 25 Nov 1852 by J. B. McDade, J. P.

Harris, James & Letitia Whitlow, 5 Oct 1792; Walter Alves, bm.

Harris, James R. & Nancy S. Rountree, 4 Nov 1862; William G. Mangum, Thomas W. Laws, bm; m 5 Nov 1862 by C. Wilson, J. P.

Harris, John & Nancy Dunning, 28 Jan 1825; William J. Glenn, And. Brown, bm.

Harris, Marcus & Louanna Parker, 6 Nov 1832; Jno. A. McMannen, bm.

Harris, Marcus & Parthena Ellis, 24 July 1852; G. G. Clement, D. C. Parish, bm; m 25 July 1852 by John A. McMannen, J. P.

Harris, Mark & Nancy Neiley, 17 Dec 1803; Samuel Turrentine, bm.

Harris, Nathaniel & Deborah Hopkins, 25 Feb 1801; Thomas Horner, bm.

Harris, Nathaniel & Elizabeth Garrard, 28 Aug 18, 1830; Wms. Harris, bm.

Harris, Richmond & Mary Jones, 27 March 1800; Benjamin Jones, bm.

Harris, Richmond & Leah Leigh, 31 Dec 1805; James Harris, bm.

Harris, Robert & Casiah Hopkins, 27 Jan 1795; Robert Ashley, bm.

Harris, Sterling & Hannah Shitehead, 5 June 1783; William Whitted Jr., bm.

Harris, Stirling & Lively Carrington, 4 Jan 1804; Samuel Turrentine, bm.

Harris, Thomas & Ellender Harris, 1 Jan 1807; Mack Harris, bm.

Harris, Thomas J. & Caroline Frances Hall, 9 Jan 1854; Geo. W. Bruce, bm; m 11 Jan 1854 by Nelson P. Hall, J. P.

Harris, Thomas J. & Lugenia C. Mangum, 21 Dec 1857; W. Harris, John H. Paul, bm; m 22 Dec 1857 by Charles Wilson, J. P.

Harris, William & Elizabeth Tate, 28 March 1811; Robert McCauley, bm.

Harris, William, son of Thos & Otly Harris, & Nancy Evans, dau. of Gidian & Betsy Haily, m 1 Sept 1867 by Joseph Woods, J. P.

Harris, Williams & Maria Briggs, 4 March 1822; J. S. Smith, bm.

Harris, Wms & Emaline B. Ward, 13 Nov 1849; James R. Willis, T. Webb, bm.

Harris, Wilson & Rebecca Tilly, 29 Sept 1863; Henry T. Gates, bm.

Harris, Yancey & Sarah Dolar, 16 Nov 1825; Jesse Harris, bm.

Harrison, James & Rachel Pendergrass, 2 Sept 1808; Geo. Pendergast, bm.

ORANGE COUNTY MARRIAGES, 1779-1868

Harrison, James & Jane Forrest, 24 May 1847; Thomas Lynch, bm.

Harrison, Robert & Izebel Ray, no date (during Gov. Alexander Martin's admn., 1780's, 1790's), James Hunter, bm.

Harrison, Samuel & Sarah Thomas, 24 Aug 1785; Philemon Thomas, bm.

Harriss, Edward & Nancey Carrington, 29 Sept 1807; Thos. H. Taylor, bm.

Harrod, Henry & Susan Sears, 13 Dec 1823; Bemmertuk Barbee, bm.

Hart, David & Elizabeth Petty, 12 June 1839; Jm. M. Faucett, John P. Faucett, bm.

Hart, Gilbert & Nancy Moore, 13 Nov 1816; John Strayhorn, bm.

Hart, James & Rachel Paul, 13 April 1790; William Clark, bm.

Hart, James & Salley Faucett, 22 May 1810; Jas. Taylor, bm.

Hart, James & Sally Strain, 24 May 1837; Stephen S. Floyd, Abel Maddry, bm.

Hart, James R. & Sally King, 8 June 1812; Ede. King, bm.

Hart, John & Fanny Moore, 9 Oct 1806; William Cook, bm.

Hart, John & Margret Nelson, 19 July 1836; P. Nelson, J. Taylor, bm.

Hart, John U. & Mary E. Tapp, 10 Feb 1853; G. M. Hobbs, bm; m 10 Feb 1853 by D. D. Phillips, J. P.

Hart, Joseph & Mary Cabe, 23 April 1788; Wm. McCauley, bm.

Hart, Joseph & Margaret Kelley, 2 April 1792; James Hart, bm.

Hart, Morgan & Margaret Woods, 11 Aug 1847; Samuel Thompson, bm.

Hart, Samuel & Nancy Qualls, 14 Sept 1819; William Wilson, bm.

Hart, Samuel & Elizabeth Tate, 7 Feb 1821; Thomas Tate, bm.

Hart, Thomas & Nancy Bain, 9 Jan 1812; Nathaniel Bain, bm.

Hart, William & Elizabeth Wyatt, 21 Dec 1829; Elbridge Morrow, James McAdams, bm.

Hartt, Thos. & Mary Thompson, 14 May 1829; Jo. Hartt, bm.

Harvey, Absalom & Elizabeth Hall, 14 Jan 1817; Junir Hall, bm.

Harvey, Charles & Julia Strowd, 24 May 1866; Geo. Laws, bm; m 24 May 1866 by T. C. Hayes.

Harvey, David & Margret Love, 25 Nov 1800; William Fussett, bm.

Harvey, John & Elizabeth Long, 18 March 1847; Cornelius Kelly, bm.

Harvy, Jonathan & Catharine Bird, 26 Jan 1787; James Muray, bm.

Harward, Henderson & Martha Carlton, 22 Jan 1861; Jas. M.
Herndon, bm; m 25 Jan 1861 by A. B. Gunter, J. P.

Harward, Rufus & Melvina Sears, 3 Jan 1857; Yancey Blalock,
Henry K. Nash, bm; m 13 Jan 1857 by Edward Mallett, J. P.

Harward, William & Caroline Kirkland, 26 May 1866; William
George, James Y. Whitted, bm; m 14 June 1866 by Solomon Pool.

Harward, Wyatt & Agness Holloway, 27 Nov 1809; Reuben Farthing,
bm.

Harwood, Henderson & Martha Carlton, 22 Jan 1861; Jas. M.
Herndon, bm; m 25 Jan 1861 by A. B. Gunter, J. P.

Harwood, Joseph & Mary Clemments, 12 March 1840; W. A. S.
Thompson, William Scarlet, bm.

Harwood, Wesley J. & Martha Ann Whiteker, 6 Jan 1862; Edward
Ivy, bm; m 9 Jan 1862 by D. Tilley, J. P.

Hastings, Eli & Jane Wilson, 12 June 1824; Charles Wilson,
Jos. A. Woods, bm.

Hastings, Henry & Martha Cates, 15 Feb 1790; William Hastings,
bm.

Hastings, Henry & Patsey McDaniel, 25 Nov 1806; John Young,
Bennett Partin, bm.

Hastings, James & Susannah Estridge, 8 April 1822; John
Hastings, bm.

Hastings, John & Anne Estridge, 3 Jan 1823; Thos. Hastings, bm.

Hastings, Robert & Mary Cate, 22 Dec 1798; Thomas Cate, bm.

Hastings, Robert & Jeany Pitman, 28 Aug 1804; Thomas Cate, bm.

Hastings, Thomas W. & Mary Ellen Williams, 4 Jan 1846; Jas. M.
Palmer, bm.

Hastings, William & Lydia Stubbens, 1 Feb 1793; Thos. O'Neill,
bm.

Hatch, Abijah & Frances Collier, 2 Feb 1831; Green(?) Carmichal,
bm.

Hatch, Alexr. & Rhody Snipes, 4 Dec 1793; Jno. Umstead, bm.

Hatch, John & Delila Andrews, 19 Sept 1860; Geo. Andrews, bm;
m 20 Sept 1860 by John W. Strowd, J. P.

Hatch, Thomas & Mary Bynum, 1 Aug 1818; Nathaniel Durham, bm.

Hatch, Thos. H. & Cinthia Brewer, 13 Nov 1802; Isham Brewer, bm.

Hatch, Thos J. & Anna E. Eackn, 15 June 1859; F. A. Davies, bm.

Hatch, William & Jinney Durham, 19 Oct 1820; William Durham, bm.

Hatch, William & Patsy Lindsey, 14 Aug 1825; Chesley Smith, bm.

Hatch, William & Kesiah Petty, 25 Dec 1830; George B. Hatch, bm.

Hatchel, Samuel & Metilda Stephens, 16 Feb 1851; J. J. Allison, bm.

Hatchell, David & Clary Burk, 17 March 1847; James R. Fonville, bm.

Hatchett, Edward & Aney Ross, 31 May 1804; Joseph Rumbley, bm.

Hatchett, Elisha & Nancy Taylor, 15 July 1804; Nemrod Philips, William Hatchett, bm.

Hatchett, Parish & Susannah Smothers, 16 Aug 1803; Edward Hatchett, bm.

Hatchett, William & Rhodah Powell, 11 Feb 1809; John Hervy, bm.

Hath, George B. & Susana Hesse, 23 May 1850; Robert M. Blackwell, bm.

Hathcock, Edward & Frances Stanford, 28 May 1812; Joshua Woody, bm.

Hathcock, Edward & Frankey Jeffries, 26 July 1813; James Upton, bm.

Hathcock, Jacob & Nancy Hathcock, 3 Sept 1836; Stanford Hathcock, bm.

Hathcock, John & Elizabeth Jeffires, 7 Feb 1835; John Hammons, bm.

Hathcock, Mebane & Dilly Phillips, 11 Jan 1838; John Chavis, bm.

Hathcock, Williamson & Frances Steward, 30 May 1854; John Guie, bm.

Hatwood, Alfred & Polly Berris, 20 Oct 1822; Richard Roberts, bm.

Hatwood, Sill & Elizabeth Hatwood, 2 May 1809; Andw. Collins, bm.

Haughton, John & Elizabeth Strain, 23 Feb 1843; John Richerson, H. C. Strowd, bm.

Haughton, Joshua & Elizabeth Dollar, 30 Jan 1819; K. Haughton, bm.

Haughton, Kenneday & Nancy Neal, 22 Sept 1822; James Neal, bm.

Haughton, Kenneday & Polley Crabtree, 27 Oct 1833; Riley Neal, bm.

Haughton, Kennedy & Betsy Hicks, 10 Aug 1816; John Horner, bm.

Haughawout, Jacob W. & Amanda Berry, 5 May 1847; Robert M. Shields, bm.

Haward, Benj., son of Benj. & Jane Haward, & Sally Wheaton, dau. of Stephen & Lavenia Wheaton, m 9 May 1867 by Harry F. Pope, M. G.

Hawkins, Calvin & Artelia F. J. Breeze, 12 Jan 1852; John H. Breeze, bm; m 15 Jan 1852 by Hezekiah Terry, J. P.

Hawkins, Hardress, & ___, 27 Feb 1794; Charles Christmas, bm.

Hay, David & Susan Shepperd, 3 Oct 1812; Thos. Evans, bm.

Hay, David & Ellen Crabtree, 11 Aug 1837; Thos. Sykes, bm.

Hayden, Leonard & Sarah McCracken, 17 Dec 1828; Stephen Moore, bm.

Hayes, Barnod & Elizabeth Sykes, 18 Dec 1831; David Hayes, bm.

Hayes, James & Rhody Shelton, 15 Dec 1803; William Cook, bm.

Hayes, John & Wiltha Anne Bryant, 15 Jan 1821; Edward Dodson, bm.

Hayes, Leonard & Rachel Harrel, 17 Feb 1789; Charles Johnston, bm.

Hayes, Richard & Sarah Cate, 22 Jan 1806; David Cate, bm.

Hayes, Robert T. & Mary Squires, 31 Oct 1863; John U. Hart, T. C. Hayes, bm.

Hayes, Thomas C. & Sarah Hobbs, 19 Nov 1840; George A. Faucett, bm.

Hayes, William & Sarah Tate, 3 Feb 1786; William Harper, bm.

Hayes, William J. & Mary A. Railey, 4 Oct 1855; Thomas S. Hayes, Thos. C. Hayes, bm; m 4 Oct 1855 by Thos. C. Hayes.

Haynes, Esaw & Annie Hopkins, 27 Dec 1866; Alexr. Long, bm; m 27 Dec 1866 by Thos. C. Hayes.

Haynes, Samuel & Violet Graves, 27 June 1866; Daniel Latta, bm.

Haynes, William Scott & Louisa C. Williams, 8 Feb 1837; Jesse Miller, bm.

Hays, Theophilus & Rebecca Taburn, 8 Feb 1809; Shadrack Volentine, Wm. Wall, bm.

Hays, Thomas S. & Mary E. Watson, 20 June 1861; Robert Faucett, bm; m 20 June 1861 by Thos. C. Hayes.

Haywood, Mumford & Emma Faucett, colored, 20 April 1866; Thos. J. Hancock, bm.

Headen, William & Francis Clendening, 28 Nov 1831; David S. Clendenin, bm.

Heald, Jacob & Martha Harvey, 13 Feb 1786; Joseph Heald, bm.

Heart, John U. & Maletha Ann Tapp, 25 July 1860; Thos. G. Pratt, Thomas Webb, bm; m 25 July 1860 by John Cheek.

Heartt, Edwin A. & Alice E. Wilson, 15 Dec 1847; John H. Webb, Thos. H. Turner, bm.

Heath, Freemon & Elizabeth Jones, 30 Dec 1858; Ellick Heath, bm.

Heath, Oliver P. & Jane Huskey, 17 April 1861; T. S. Cooley, bm; m 17 April 1861 by Samuel Pearce, minister.

Heath, O. P. & Mary E. Bennett, 20 Dec 1856; Saml. N. Collins, bm; m 21 Dec 1866 by William H. Brown, J. P.

Heathcock, Elijah & Sally Jeffers, 27 Jan 1842; William Heathcock, bm.

Heathcock, Henderson & Delila Day, 8 Feb 1860; John Heathcock, bm.

Hedgecock, William & Elizabeth White, 6 July 1791; Joseph Smith, bm.

Hedgpeth, Jesse A. & Emeline Warren, 2 Nov 1856; J. C. Payne, James Mansfield, bm.

Hedgpeth, Moses & Frances Evans, 11 Sept 1855; Reuben Day, bm.

Hedrick, Benjamin Sherwood & Mary Ellen Thompson, 2 June 1852; J. B. McDade, bm; m 3 June 1852 by James Phillips, minister.

Henderson, John & Frances Perry, 9 May 1831; James Crittenton, Joel Parish, bm.

Henderson, Joseph & Winney Husbands, 3 July 1811; James Bass, bm.

Henderson, Ludolphus & Elizabeth E. Parker, 15 April 1837; William H. Glass, bm.

Henderson, Richd. & Anne Alves, 25 March 1807; George Anderson, bm.

Henderson, Thomas & Elizabeth Cotton, 30 Oct 1826; Thos. Thompson, bm.

Henderson, Willie & Martha E. Boothe, 8 May 1850; J. B. McDade, bm.

Hendly, William & Lydia Wood, 22 Aug 1797; Sampson Wood, bm.

Hendon, E. D. & Sue Dusken, 1 March 1859; G. M. Duskin, bm.

Hendon, John A. & Margaret L. Johnston, 10 June 1858; Wm. Duskin, bm; m 15 June 1858 by James Phillips, minister.

Hendricks, James & Sophia Dishon, 23 Dec 1830; William Browning, bm.

Henry, George W. & Mary F. Crossett, 29 Nov 1866; Silas Hopkins, bm; m 2 Dec 1866 by Samuel B. Woods, J. P.

Henry, Glen & Leatha Crisp, 26 Nov 1867; m 30 March 1868 by Q. A. Ward, minister.

Hensley, Sprvy & Artelia F. Anderson, 5 Oct 1847; W. H. Jordan, bm.

Herman, Jno. & Martha Patten, 26 Dec 1792; William Trousdall, bm.

Hern, H. & Sarah Palmer, 13 Dec 1800; Jas. Palmer, James Child, bm.

Herndon, Anderson & Catharine Grisham, 1 Nov 1830; R. Eaton, bm.

Herndon, Bartlet & Termenia L. Booth, 27 April 1853; M. C. Herndon, bm.

Herndon, Bartlett H. & Martha Cook, 23 Dec 1858; A. B. Gunter, A. M. Herndon, bm; m 23 Dec 1858 by A. B. Gunter, J. P.

Herndon, Benjamin & Esther Smith, 15 May 1829; J. Taylor, bm.

Herndon, Cameron & Mary Bowers, 17 July 1854; Riley Niell, bm.

Herndon, Coslett & Margrett Guess, 29 Dec 1836; Samuel Merit, bm.

Herndon, Chesley & Tempe Rigsby, 19 Oct 1824; Charles Anderson, bm.

Herndon, Chesley & Sally Vickers, 19 April 1848; Marke Rigsbey, Josiah C. Anderson, bm.

Herndon, Chesley & Francis Warren, 13 Sept 1849; Josiah C. Anderson, bm.

Herndon, Chesley & Mary E. George, 3 Feb 1866; James M. Herndon, bm.

Herndon, Edmund & Rebeccah Rhodes, 14 Feb 1794; William Rhodes, bm.

Herndon, Edmund & Elizabeth Graham, 26 Nov 1810; John Graham, Miles Walles, bm.

Herndon, Elias & Polley Hopson, ___ 1795; Edward Wilson, bm.

Herndon, Gaston & Demaris Herndon, 10 March 1862; J. M. Herndon, bm; m 11 March 1862 by H. J. Pearson, J. P.

Herndon, Green E. & Mary Ann Barbee, 20 Dec 1842; P. B. Herndon, Moses Leathers Junr., bm.

Herndon, Harmon & Louisa Massey, 2 Nov 1858; John Hutchins, bm; m 4 Nov 1858 by A. B. Tuner, J. P.

Herndon, Harmon & Elizabeth George, 5 April 1837; David George, Peace McCullom, bm.

Herndon, James & Catherine G. Collier, 14 June 1802; King Barbee, bm.

Herndon, James & Polley Dixon, 3 May 1814; Rhodes Herndon, bm.

Herndon, James M. & Elizabeth Guess, 20 March 1858; Anderson W. Pope, bm.

Herndon, John & Emmeline Harward, 15 Dec 1840; Nathan Carlton, G. W. Trice, bm.

Herndon, Lewis & Polley Boothe, 22 Dec 1796; John Barbee, bm.

Herndon, Maturine C. & Frances A. E. Guess, 19 Aug 1835; Jos. Shaw, bm.

Herndon, M. C. Jr. & Merrise Vickers, 12 Feb 1861; Hardy Massay, bm; m 21 Feb 1861 by A. B. Gunter, J. P.

Herndon, Pomfrett & Polley King, 19 July 1805; John King, bm.

Herndon, Pomphrett & Anne Brasfield, 28 Oct 1812; James Herndon, bm.

Herndon, Ruben & Frances McCoy, 9 Aug 1784; Henry McCoy, bm.

Herndon, Tapley & Nelly Hutchins, 12 Nov 1798; William Herndon, bm.

Herndon, Thomas S. & Delila M. Rhodes, 4 Oct 1856; James G. Davis, bm; m 12 Oct 1856 by Jesse Howell, minister.

Herndon, Waller & Elizabeth Partin, 21 May 1798; William Partin, bm.

Herndon, Wesley & Jane Caudley, 12 Dec 1821; John Vickers, Gresham Horn, bm.

Herndon, Westley & America Roberts, 3 Dec 1828; Thos. Hutchins, bm.

Herndon, Will H. & Elizabeth George, 23 Jan 1866; Thos. S. Vickers, bm; m 27 Jan 1866 by A. B. Gunter, J. P.

Herndon, William & Hannah Hutchings, 11 Jan 1796; Charles Trice, bm.

Herndon, William & Caroline Dalehite, 27 Dec 1855; Thomas S. Herndon, bm; m 24 Jan 1856 by John Burroughs, J. P.

Herndon, Zachariah & Milley Rhodes, 28 June 1789; Wm. Rhodes, bm.

Herndon, Zachariah & Lydia Clifton, 18 March 1824; J. Taylor Jr., bm.

Herndon, Zachariah & Francis Dollerhit, 31 May 1860; C. P. Trice, bm; m 31 May 1860 by M. A. Angier, J. P.

Hesey, Marion & Izabella Scott, 13 Nov 1856; James S. Cameron, bm.

Hesse, John Henery & Rebecah Bowls, 20 Jan 1794; S. Benton, bm.

Hester, Egbert S. & Martha L. Walker, 13 Sept 1853; John Wood, bm.

Hester, Henderson & Susan Merritt, 24 March 1834; Thomas Atkins, James Crabtree, bm.

Hester, John & Mary E. Harwood, 30 June 1860; James K. Gattis, bm.

Hester, Wiley James & Mary Ann Burges, 21 Oct 1858; John R. Clements, bm.

Hester, Willis & Catharine Thompson, 20 April 1848; W. H. Thompson, bm.

Hester, Young & Salley Copley, 19 April 1839; Richd. Clemmons, bm.

Hester, Young & Nancy Paschael, 24 Sept 1866; Jno. M. Blackwood, bm; m 24 Sept 1866 by R. H. J. Blount, J. P.

Hestings, Joseph & Nancy Pittman, 9 April 1800; Joseph Hestings, bm.

Hethcock, Edward & Frankey Jeffires, 7 July 1814; John Artes, bm.

Hickman, Wyatt & Anna Anderson, 7 Nov 1819; Jas. Lapslie, bm.

Hicks, Daniel & Polley Cozort, 16 Aug 1798; P. Huntington, bm.

Hicks, George W. & Martha Ann Riley, 31 March 1849; A. W. Parker, E. G. Gray, bm.

Hicks, Gideon & Tabitha Puckett, 14 Feb 1838; Matthew Hicks, David Combes, bm.

Hicks, Harrison & Hawkins Williams, 23 June 1863; William Chisenhall, D. C. Parrish, bm; m 24 June 1863 by Wm. J. Duke, J. P.

Hicks, Howel T. & Sally Roberts, 19 Nov 1825; Willis Shaw, bm.

Hicks, James & Malinda Lynch, 24 July 1829; Nathaniel Hicks, bm.

Hicks, James & Malinda Ann Rigsbee, 24 March 1866; Wm. K. Duke, Wm. Chisenhall, bm; m 25 March 1866 by Wm. J. Duke, J. P.

Hicks, John & Sally Riley, 10 May 1824; John Hokins, bm.

Hicks, Nathan & Liddy Weaver, 6 Sept 1832; Stanford Cheek, Matthew Hicks, bm.

Hicks, Nathaniel & Anne Hailey, 7 Feb 1795; James Hailey, bm.

Hicks, Nathaniel & Lydia Beasling, 30 Oct 1826; James P. Laws, bm.

Hicks, Thomas & Mary C. Sawyer, 2 Nov 1820; Willie Shal, bm.

Hicks, William & Priscilla Hill, 27 May 1830; John Jinkins, bm.

Hicks, Williamson & Ann Clements, 13 Feb 1847; G. R. Herndon, bm.

High, William N. & Frances C. Herndon, 26 June 1831; John W. Shaw, Isaiah S. High, bm.

Hightower, Daniel & Jemima Ward, 21 Aug 1826; Thomas Ward, bm.

Hightower, John & Delilah Berry, 25 Sept 1827; Charles Holeman, bm.

Hildreth, William Henry & Elizabeth West Whitaker, both of Davenport, Iowa, m 29 June 1855 by Elisha Mitchell, V. D. M.

Hill, Calvin & Edney Jeffreys, 23 June 1855; Thomas Faucett, bm; m 25 June 1855 by John J. Freeland, J. P.

Hill, Clark & Harriot Staly, (no date, 1824-1827), S. Wynn, bm.

Hill, Eli & Elizabeth Dixon, 8 Aug 1799; Elihu Wood, bm.

Hill, Halbert G. & Annie R. Kirkland, 27 Nov 1865; Calvin E. Parish, bm; m 28 Nov 1865 by J. Henry Smith, V. D. M.

Hill, James & Elizabeth Fogleman, 5 May 1824; H. Fogleman, bm.

Hill, John & Polley Whitlock, 16 Dec 1797; John Faddis, bm.

Hill, John & Sarah Mason, 13 Nov 1812; George Horner, bm.

Hill, John & Martha E. Murdock, 7 March 1867; William N. Anderson, Wm. A. Hays, bm; m 7 March 1867 by H. B. Pratt.

Hill, Marell & Priscilla Jenkins, 18 June 1825; William Jenkins, bm.

Hill, Samuel & Hannah Anderson, 21 Aug 1793; Caleb Harvey, bm.

Hill, Whitmel & Mary Woods, 17 Sept 1828; Jacob Jackson, bm.

Hill, William & Anne Riggs, 11 Aug 1789; James Riggs, bm.

Hill, William & Elizabeth Pool, 29 Oct 1821; Isaac Pool, bm.

Hill, William Henry & Elizabeth Ashe, 29 Aug 1792; Alexander Duncan Moore, bm.

Hill, Willie & Peggy Dossett, 17 Sept 1799; John Hill, bm.

Hilton, Jesse & Elizabeth Helton, 26 Aug 1802; Isc. Holt, bm.

Hinchey, Bartlet & Vicey Horn, 3 Jan 1818; John C. Geer, bm.

Hinchey, Ezekel & Nancy Salter, 18 Nov 1783.

Hinchey, Gilbert & Fanny Mann, 22 June 1836; Elkines Petigruw, bm.

Hinchey, John & Elizabeth Collins, 15 April 1797; Thomas Wynn, John Selff, bm.

Hinchey, Levi & Celah Johnston, 1 April 1795; Michael Hinchey, bm.

Hinchey, Levi & Polly Williams, 19 Dec 1820; John Carroll, bm.

Hinchey, Levi & Elizabeth Bird, 22 April 1829; John Squires, bm.

Hinchey, Michael & Pheby Cole, 5 Jan 1793; Ezekial Hinchey, bm.

Hinchey, William & Charlotte Carroll, 13 Aug 1827; William Farr, bm.

Hinchy, David & Violet Salter, 11 April 1795; Ezekiel Hinchy, bm.

Hinchy, Jaconias & Nancy Durham, 13 Dec 1803; Levi Hinchy, bm.

Hinchy, Huriah & Ellendar Winn, 23 Nov 179_ (1796-1798); Thomas Wynn, bm.

Hines, Edward & Maria L. Pool, 16 Sept 1863; W. R. Kenan, bm; m 16 Sept 1863 by Jno. H. Wingfield, M. G.

Hines, John C. & Nannie F. Thompson, 16 Jan 1867; Henry J. Thompson, bm; m 17 Jan 1867 by Archibald Currie.

Hinshaw, Robt. & Abigail Chamness, 25 Jan 1846; Joshua Chamness, bm.

Hinshaw, William & Polly McVey, 27 July 1833; James Wilkerson, bm.

Hinton, Ned & Mary A. Stevens, 11 Dec 1866; m 11 Dec 1866 by Thos. H. Hughes, J. P.

Hinton, Robert D. & D. L. E. Taylor, 29 July 1859; J. J. Allison, bm.

Hix, David & Sally Woods, 26 Jan 1827; Wallen Chissenhall, bm.

Hix, Reaves & Patticar Evans, 2 Feb 1854; J. G. A. Mangum, bm; m 2 Feb 1854 by Nelson P. Hall, J. P.

Hobbs, David & Nancy Williams, 30 Sept 1815; Jonathan Hobbs, bm.

Hobbs, George M. & Rebecca J. Tapp, 9 Nov 1859; T. C. Hayes, bm; m 9 Nov 1859 by Thos. C. Hayes, minister.

Hobbs, James & Jane Fosset, 12 Dec 1797; Wm. Weeks, bm.

Hobbs, John & Catharine Clark, 13 April 1798; Elias Wihyt, bm.

Hobbs, John & Caty Coble, 25 May 1820; Philip Coble, bm.

Hobbs, Jonathan & Elizabeth Morrow, 13 Dec 1816; John Moore, bm.

Hobbs, William & Hetty Crabtree, 27 Oct 1810; Rt. Glenn, Wm. Jackson, bm.

Hobes, James & Harriet Thompson, 29 March 1847; Edmund P. Chambers, bm.

Hobs, John & Elizabeth Tool, 15 Jan 1806; Joseph Moore, bm.

Hobson, Chapman & Celia Marcum, 18 April 1805; Thomas Marcom, bm.

Hobson, William & Beckey Brewer, 10 Feb 1789; John G. Rencher, bm.

Hodge, George & Anne Lindsey, 25 Oct 1815; Jos. Hodge, bm.

Hodge, James & A. V. Thompson, 14 Dec 1865; m 14 Dec 1865 by N. W. Wilson.

Hodge, John & Marry Crawford, 27 Oct 1832; Henderson Crawford, bm.

Hodge, John H. & Mary M. Taylor, 18 Dec 1865; John H. Paul, bm; m 24 Dec 1865 by Samuel Pearce.

Hodge, Joseph & Sally Lindsey, 7 Sept 1812; James Rily, bm.

Hodge, Mason & Rachal Cook, 16 Jan 1838; Jas. Roney, D. H. Cate, bm.

Hodge, Robert & Mary Mebane, 4 Aug 1794; Jas. Mebane Junr., bm.

Hodge, Samuel & Nancy Allen, 6 March 1804; George Allen, bm.

Hogan, Alexander & Matilda Robson, 30 Oct 1854; J. C. Hogan, bm.

Hogan, Charles & Charlott Marcom, colored, 4 May 1866; Hugh B. Guthrie, bm; m 4 May 1866 by John H. Kirkland, J. P.

Hogan, Henry & Aggy Kirkland, 28 Nov 1865; Charles W. Johnston, bm; m 30 Nov 1865 by C. W. Johnston, J. P.

Hogan, James & Louiza Williams, 11 March 1847; Sidney Upchurch, bm.

Hogan, Jerry, son of Lucy Hogan & Margaret Mason, dau of Jesse & Candis Mason, colored, m 9 Jan 1868 by O. S. Brent.

Hogan, John T. & Julia Strayhorn, 20 Oct 1859; T. M. Kirkland, bm.

141

Hogan, John Jr. & Martha King, 10 Dec 1792; John Estes, bm.

Hogan, Joseph C. & Frances J. Boroughs, 25 Nov 1854; J. T. Hogans, bm; m 30 Nov 1854 by Brantley J. Hackney, M. G.

Hogan, Saml. & Lucy Smith, dau. of Mary Smith, m 4 June 1868 at the residence of Henry Hogans, by N. C. Cate, J. P.

Hogan, Thomas & Abi Stroud, 17 Feb 1795; Wm. Stroud, bm.

Hogan, Thomas & Elizabeth Freeland, 6 Nov 1807; Charles Freeland, bm.

Hogan, W. John & Mary Borrows, 25 Jan 1831; John Boroughs, bm.

Holaday, Simon & Delilah Durham, 4 Nov 1815; Simeon Durham, bm.

Holaday, Thomas & Lucinda Collins, 3 April 1835; Wm. Holmes, bm.

Holaway, James & Mary J. Horn, 1 Jan 1859; William Herndon, bm; m 6 Jan 1859 by Samuel Couch, J. P.

Holaway, John & Haner Herndon, m 15 March 1862 by S. Shepherd, J. P.

Holaway, Williamson B. & Caroline Martin, 14 April 1856; Wm. McCown, bm; m 14 April 1856 by Wm. McCown, J. P.

Holden, Addison L. & Loretta J. Lyon, 2 Jan 1865; John F. Lyon, bm; m 3 Jan 1865 by W. F. Strayhorn, J. P.

Holden, Isaac & Elisabeth Whitted, 15 June 1792; Wm. Jackson, bm.

Holden, Isaac & Mary Ann Faucett, 14 July 1851; Tho. W. Holden, bm; m 14 July 1851 by Wm. Dickson, J. P.

Holden, John & Catey Marley, 28 Dec 1805; George Douglas, bm.

Holden, Samuel Solomon & Peney Euless, 16 Oct 1837; Chartun Allen, bm.

Holden, Thomas W. & Sarah Nichols, 8 April 1823; Frs B. Phillips, bm.

Holden, William H. & Mary Walker, 17 June 1846; E. G. Gray, bm.

Holder, Daniel & Elizabeth Marcum, 20 Dec 1800; David Holder, bm.

Holder, Daniel & Nancy Standeford, 20 Sept 1816; Chesley Holder, bm.

Holder, David & Elizabeth Hatch, 15 Sept 1837; John Holder, Wm. Nevill, bm.

Holder, David & Matilda Scoggins, 21 March 1850; Solomon Gooch, bm.

Holder, Elijah & Elizabeth Lane, 16 Dec 1795; David Holder, bm.

Holder, Elijah & Susan Taylor, 16 July 1834; James Hendricks, bm.

Holder, Elisha & Eliza Clark, 18 Feb 1831; Thomas Clark, Elijah Holder, bm.

ORANGE COUNTY MARRIAGES, 1779-1868

Holder, James & Anne Withem, 9 March 1801; Sharwood Allin, bm.

Holder, John & Jane Durham, 28 April 1832; Nathaniel Durham, Thomas D. Faucet, bm.

Holder, William & Lucy Clement, 2 Dec 1851; Henry P. Williams, bm; m 12 Dec 1851 by King Barbee, J. P.

Holeman, Charles & Elisabeth Lipscomb, 18 April 1826; John N. Kirkland, bm.

Holeman, James Jr. & Emma B. Blacknall, 12 March 1826; J. J. Allen, bm; m 17 March 1863 by James Phillips, D. D.

Holeman, Richard & Lucretia Horner, 11 May 1831; David Lockhart, bm.

Holeman, Samuel & Jane Hall, 29 April 1818; James Woods, bm.

Holgan, Thomas & Fanney Ray, 8 May 1784; Robert Ray, John Wray, bm.

Holiday, Samuel & Dolly Meachum, 28 March 1814; John Young, bm.

Holland, Eason & Elizabeth Hicks, 8 April 1840; John Marshill, bm.

Holland, James C. & Rebecca T. Collier, 25 Sept 1833; J. J. Collier, bm.

Holland, Wm. & Caroline Caudle, 18 Dec 1849; Wesly Holland, bm.

Holloway, Bremilan & Sarah Proctor, 5 Feb 1798; Abram Whitaker, bm.

Holloway, James & Martha Leathers, 13 Feb 1838; W. A. Norwood, bm.

Holloway, John J. & Nancy J. Wilkerson, 3 Nov 1849; John D. Jones, bm.

Holloway, John J. & Nancy W. Farthing, 30 Dec 1862; William Farthing, bm; m 1 Jan 1863 by S. Shepherd, J. P.

Holloway, John T. & Ann Cooley, 9 May 1857; E. W. Woods, bm; m 13 May 1857 by John W. F. Pearson, minister.

Holloway, Samuel & Polley House, 7 April 1804; James Wood, bm.

Holloway, Stephen P. & Mary Ann Trice, 14 Feb 1849; Jno. D. Carlton, bm.

Holloway, Thomas & Johanna Caine, 5 Oct 1782; Robert Abercrombie, bm.

Holloway, Thomas & Jenney Latta, 15 Dec 1808; Thomas Holloway, bm.

Holloway, Thomas & Lydia Bryant, 25 Aug 1808; Mark Pickett, bm.

Holloway, William & Elizabeth Trice, 18 Feb 1805; Thomas Holloway, bm.

Holloway, William H., son of Nathl. & Nancy P. Holloway, & Mary J. Duke, dau. of Wm. J. & Sally Duke, m 1 Jan 1868 by R. S. Webb, M. G.

143

Holloway, Williamson B. & Martha Duke, 18 Oct 1851; John C. Lewis, bm.

Holloway, Wright & Ann Merritt, 7 Jan 1837; Marke Rigsbey, P. Stanford, bm.

Holman, Anderson & Ann Faucett, colored, 23 Sept 1865; Abel Pain, Walter Williams, bm; m 25 Sept 1865 by F. M. Jordan, minister.

Holmes, David H. & Martha A. F. Moore, 25 Sept 1866; M. W. Moore, bm; m 7 Oct 1866 by F. M. Jordan, minister.

Holmes, Haywood & Sarah Cooper, 17 Aug 1838; Anderson T. Glenn, bm.

Holmes, John & Frances Dukes, 29 July 1813; Thos. Christian, bm.

Holmes, John W. & Mary M. Sykes, 28 Aug 1866; David M. Sykes, bm; m 28 Aug 1866 by H. McDaniel, J. P.

Holmes, Lewallen & Mary Moffett, 2 Feb 1829; Tho. ____, bm.

Holmes, Lucian & Mary S. Mitchell, 2 Nov 1847; E. J. Mallett, bm.

Holmes, Moses & Geney Rogers, 8 Sept 1792; Joseph Holmes, bm.

Holmes, Nicholas G. & Nancey Moore, 4 March 1837; Wm. Holmes, John Stafford, bm.

Holmes, William & Jane A. Thompson, 8 Jan 1840; J. C. Patterson, bm.

Holms, John & Catharine Gibbs, 17 Oct 1791; Joseph Clendenin, bm.

Holns, Henry & Sally Wilkins, 16 Dec 1825; John Wason, bm.

Holsomback, Wm. & Nancy Duke, 1 Jan 1859; John Padlock, bm; m 2 Jan 1859 by Wm. J. Roberts, J. P.

Holstead, Arthur & Ann Hares, 12 Sept 1817; Benjamin Jackson, bm.

Holstead, John & Polley Freeland, 14 Dec 1824; Saymour Puryea, bm.

Holt, Alfred A. & Elizabeth A. T. Mebane, 28 Aug 1850; Josiah Turner Jr., bm.

Holt, Anthony & Phebe Pile, 9 Jan 1812; Luke Simpson, Jno. Cook, bm.

Holt, Cader & Sarah Cain, 31 Dec 1796; John Holt, bm.

Holt, Daniel & Phelpina Garrett, 31 Aug 1809; Henry Garrett, bm.

Holt, David & Barbara Anthony, 3 Aug 1817; Alexander Holt, bm.

Holt, E. M. & Nancy M. Parker, 3 June 1857; Geo. Laws, bm; m 9 June 1857 by H. Arnold, M. G.

Holt, Edwin M. & Mary L. Parker, 30 Sept 1858; J. B. Leathers, bm.

Holt, Edwin M. Jr. & Barbara Jane Forest, 27 Jan 1842; John H. Holt, bm.

Holt, Ezekiah & Jean Rodgers, 12 June 1809; Benjamin Whedbee, bm.

Holt, Henray & Anne Bowls, 20 Jan 1807; Daniel Hufman, bm.

Holt, Isaac & Letty Scott, 30 April 1795; Thomas Scott, bm.

Holt, Isaac B. & Francis B. Prier, 4 Sept 1838; Milton T. Holt, bm.

Holt, Jacob & Mary Stepney Wilkins, 28 Aug 1823; Philemon Holt, bm.

Holt, James & Ruth Holt, 11 Sept 1815; Nicholas Holt, bm.

Holt, Jeremiah & Catharine Albright, 14 April 1784.

Holt, Jeremiah & Sally Foust, 14 Jan 1818; Peter L. Ray, bm.

Holt, John & Izabel Purkins, 7 Dec 1788; Anthony Thompson, bm.

Holt, John & Nancy Hanks, 8 April 1828; E. M. Holt, bm.

Holt, John, of Henry, & Sally Stephens, no date (1834-1841); Joseph Garrison, bm.

Holt, John Jr. & Jane Holt, 6 Sept 1820; William R. Holt, bm.

Holt, Jno. R. & Catharine Trolinger, 21 Aug 1833; Michl. Holt, bm.

Holt, Joseph S. & Laura Ann Boon, 28 Aug 1827; Le. Sharp, bm.

Holt, Michael Junr. & Rachel Raney, 6 Oct 1797; S. Benton, wit.

Holt, Michael Wm. & Ann Webb, 11 Nov 1838; Wm. Holt, E. M. Holt, bm.

Holt, Milton & Martha Mebane, 16 Sept 1839; Michl. Wm. Holt, H. Webb, bm.

Holt, Nicholas & Anne Holt, 17 May 1820; Henry Cook, bm.

Holt, Peter & Martha Wood, 10 July 1847; Jeremiah Holt, bm.

Holt, Philemon & Sarah Elizabeth Wilkins, 26 Feb 1818; Robt. Dickie, bm.

Holt, Pleasant & Luvina Albright, colored, 8 Sept 1866; John Holt, Susan Laws, bm; m 24 March 1867 by C. W. Cheek.

Holt, Seymour P. & Nancy Ann Clendenning, 1 March 1849; Sabret M. Wood, bm.

Holt, William & Betsey B. Rainey, 14 May 1809; Wm. Holt Senr., bm.

Holt, William & Elizabeth Holt, 6 Feb 1822; John King, bm.

Holt, William & Martha Dixon, 23 Aug 1825; J. Taylor Jr., bm.

Holt, Wm. & Catherine Holt, 22 July 1790; Isaac Holt, bm.

Holt, William Junr. & Sarah Steel, 6 Jan 1805; Wm. Holt, Sr., bm.

Holt, Wm. A. & Julia A. Minnis, 1 Jan 1855; Jos. W. Steel, bm.

Holmes, Archd. D. & Caty Pickard, 31 Aug 1815; Henry Paris, bm.

Honeycut, Thomas & Cebe Coltur, 8 Aug 1787; Wm. McCauley, bm.

Honeycutt, David W. & Mary M. Umsted, 2 Feb 1857; Thos. Howerton, bm; m 3 Feb 1857 by L. C. Groseclose, Lutheran minister.

Hood, Charles & Patsey Johnston, 26 July 1805; James Douglass, bm.

Hood, David & Martha E. F. Turner, 12 Aug 1865; Ezekiel C. Hailey, David C. Warren, bm; m 13 Aug 1865 by A. B. Gunter, J. P.

Hood, James & Betsy Catron, 19 April 1828; Copeland Rily, bm.

Hood, James & Any Johnston, 1 May 1828; Thomas Anderson, bm.

Hood, Martin G. & Jane Wallis, 14 March 1861; Chesley Burch, bm; m 17 March 1861 by F. Walker, J. P.

Hooker, O. W. & Mary Turner, 9 July 1850; E. R. Hooker, bm.

Hooks, Jacob, son of Harry & Rhoda Hooks, 7 Margaret Justice, dau. of Thomas Morrow & Lucy Lloyd, m 21 May 1867 by Jones Watson, J. P.

Hooper, John D. & Mary Hooper, 19 Dec 1837; W. M. Green, bm.

Hooper, William & Helen Hogg, 26 June 1791; Henry Watters, bm.

Hopkins, Alexander & Susan Cothorn, 25 Jan 1832; Robert Burton, E. D. Moore, bm.

Hopkins, Bennett C., son of John & Mary Hopkins, & Louise E. Latta, dau. of Simpson & Hawkins Latta, m 2 Feb 1868 by J. W. Latta, J. P.

Hopkins, Chuze & Jane Latta, 11 Oct 1793; John Latta Junr., bm.

Hopkins, Chuza Jr. & Sally Ray, 26 Jan 1826; George Riggs, bm.

Hopkins, Cuza & Salley Ray, 7 Jan 1826; John Hopkins, Alfred Carrington, bm.

Hopkins, Elza & Sarah Ray, 1 March 1794; Wm. Ray Junr., bm.

Hopkins, Elzaphan & Sally Ray, 5 Feb 1826; John Hopkins, bm.

Hopkins, Gilberd & Jemima Barby, 25 Sept 1817; David Ray, bm.

Hopkins, James & Anne McAdams, 26 Aug 1789; Joseph Duncan, bm.

Hopkins, James & Peggy Woods, 28 Feb 1809; Frederic Moize, bm.

Hopkins, James & Elizabeth Hall, 15 Dec 1841; Benton Ray, Moses Leathers Jr., bm.

Hopkins, James P. & Margaret Roberts, 3 Aug 1860; R. N. Hall, bm.

Hopkins, Jas. P. & Rebecca A. Brooks, 29 Dec 1865; Lambert W. Hall, bm; m 31 Dec 1865 by Nelson P. Hall, J. P.

Hopkins, John & Polly Carrington, 3 July 1817; George Riggs, bm.

Hopkins, John M. & Tempe Woods, 1 March 1841; C. M. Latimer, F. A. Hill, bm.

Hopkins, Lorenzo & Sarah Thompson, 2 Dec 1864; Willie D. Garrard, bm.

Hopkins, Mathew & Nancy J. Minnis, 28 Dec 1865; William Pender, bm; m 28 Dec 1865 by Wilson Brown, J. P.

Hopkins, Ray & Fanny Benton, 28 June 1832; Wm. R. Hopkins, bm.

Hopkins, Thomas D., son of John Guess & Hally Hopkins, & Lucy Brown, dau. of Peter Brown, colored, m 28 Jan 1868 by B. C. Hopkins, J. P.

Hopkins, William & Susanna Crabtree, 8 June 1825; James Mangum, bm.

Hopper, John & Ally Harper, 14 Dec 1792; Edmond Harper, bm.

Hopson, Brinkley & Salley Wimberly, 27 Feb 1820; Merril Beasly, bm.

Hopson, Brinkley & Caroline Green, 30 Dec 1850; Ezekiel George, bm.

Hopson, Wiley & Rebecca Nevill, 30 Jan 1821; J. Taylor Jr., bm.

Hopson, William & Harriett Boothe, 4 Sept 1839; Th. D. Crain, Jorden Suit, bm.

Hopson, Zachariah & Ruthy George, 22 Dec 1789; John Bennet, bm.

Horn, Anderson & Eliza Patterson, 12 May 1820; Moses S. Pratt, bm.

Horn, Archibald & Tempe Horn, 23 Sept 1808; Stephen Pritchard, bm.

Horn, David & Jane Thomas, 26 Dec 1836; Low Whitsitt, Andrew Head, bm.

Horn, Hardy & Ally Patton, 31 July 1847; John Q. Pickett, bm.

Horn, James & Anny Stanford, 6 Jan 1804; William Horn, bm.

Horn, James & Elizabeth Redding, 4 April 1810; Stephen Reding, bm.

Horn, James F. & Elizabeth Whiteker, 14 Oct 1845; Lazerous Cates, bm.

Horn, John & Elizabeth White, 3 Jan 1812; John Scarlett, bm.

Horn, John & Nancy Hall, 24 Jan 1824; G. Jordan, bm.

Horn, John & Elizabeth Holloway, 18 Jan 1831; Anderson Rhodes, Ralph Thompson, bm.

Horn, John M. & Clarissa Warren, 7 Feb 1843; Elijah Couch, C. M. Latimer, bm.

Horn, Joshua & Mitchell Rhodes, 29 June 1785.

Horn, Joshua & Mary Rhodes, 1 Jan 1828; George Rhodes, Lem'l M. Morgan, bm.

Horn, Norflet A. & S. C. Jinkens, 4 Nov 1856; Raltt. J. Jeffrey, bm; m 11 Nov 1856 by Jas. N. Patterson, J. P.

Horn, Samuel J. & Elisabeth J. Hutchen, 15 April 1862; Sampson ____, bm; m 15 April 1862 by S. Shepherd, J. P.

Horn, Thos. A. & Mary Matthews, 20 Dec 1823; Tapley Horn, bm.

Horn, William & Jeany Faddis, 27 Nov 1804; James Finly, bm.

Horn, William W. & Letha Tapp, 27 Nov 1815; Thomas B. Cate, bm.

Hornaday, Alfred & Rachel Woody, 26 Dec 1840; John Crawford, bm.

Hornaday, Ezekiel & Mary Dicks, 18 Feb 1792; Richard Thompson, bm.

Hornaday, Ezekiel & Barbara Albright, 15 Dec 1846; Wm. Hornaday, bm.

Hornaday, John & Polly Hofner, 13 July 1814; Fredrick Shofner, bm.

Hornaday, William & Mary Hill, 22 Dec 1812; Jacob Moulden, bm.

Hornady, Balaam C. & Anna Johnston, 22 Feb 1843; William McPherson, bm.

Hornady, Nathan & Mariah Williams, 1 Nov 1827; Samuel Hill, bm.

Hornady, William & Nancy Stafford, 13 Nov 1848; Jesse Dixon, bm.

Hornbuckle, Richard & Sarah Foster, 22 Dec 1832; Eli F. Watson, bm.

Hornby, Nathan & Ruth Pike, 8 Dec 1792; Jacob Cloud, bm.

Horne, Anderson & Anne Stephens, 29 Dec 1831; Alfred K. King, Thomas McCrary, bm.

Horne, Chesley P. & Adaline Barbee, 22 Sept 1849; R. C. Jones, bm.

Horne, Henry & Polley Rhodes, 20 Dec 1800; John Cole, bm.

Horne, Joshua & Susannah Couch, 7 Sept 1804; John Cole, bm.

Horne, Tapley & Nancy McClusky, 11 Oct 1813; William Wasun, bm.

Horne, Thomas & Elizabeth Vickers, 6 May 1793; Henry Thompson, bm.

Horne, William & Nancy Flinthem, 1 July 1797; John Cole, bm.

Horner, David & Franky Watson, 2 July 1804; Stephen Pritchard, bm.

Horner, Frederick & Sally Smith, 25 Jan 1817; Jacob Wagoner, bm.

Horner, George & Elizabeth Fussel, 26 June 1793; Thomas Horner, bm.

Horner, Jacob & Betsy Murdock, 10 March 1826; Thomas Horner, bm.

Horner, James & Lucy Fuzzell, 18 Dec 1801; Jeremiah Holden, bm.

Horner, James & Elizabeth Parker, 6 Nov 1833; Jacob Horner, James F. Warren, bm.

Horner, James W. & Sarah Jane Burton, 9 Oct 1852; R. M. Jones, bm; m 28 Nov 1862 by Hezekiah Terry, J. P.

Horner, Jefferson & Holly Parker, 23 Oct 1832; Hiram B. Datchison, bm.

Horner, John & Oliff Linch, 23 Aug 1808; Jaspar Linch, bm.

Horner, John & Polly Leathers, 31 Oct 1815; Sampson Vaughan, bm.

Horner, John & Sarah Cozart, 1 Sept 1824; Wm. Horner, bm.

Horner, John & Eliza Thompson, 12 July 1849; Henry T. Gates, bm.

Horner, John & Elizabeth Cocke, 26 Dec 1855; James Parker, bm; m 27 Dec 1855 by Charles Wilson, J. P.

Horner, Jno. & Rebecca Hicks, 18 May 1847; Geo. C. Ray, bm.

Horner, Moses W. & Clementine Johnston, 16 Nov 1865; James D. Horner, bm; m 16 Nov 1865 by W. W. Guess, J. P.

Horner, Stephen & Franky Smith, 5 May 1838; James Horner, D. M. Cate, bm.

Horner, Thomas & Sarah Fuzzel, 7 Feb 1793; Thos. Reding, bm.

Horner, Thomas & Elizabeth Smith, 14 Jan 1804; Jacob Waggoner, bm.

Horner, Wilie & Clarissa Woods, 7 April 1834; Harrison Harris, bm.

Horner, William & Harriett Morgan, 24 Dec 1834; James Roberts, bm.

Horner, William & Salley Parker, 22 Nov 1819; Jno. J. Carrington, bm.

Horner, William E. & Luseta R. Ferrell, 23 Nov 1852; William Green, bm; m 25 Nov 1852 by William Green, J. P.

Horner, Wm. W. & Catharene Curry, 5 Aug 1853; John D. Wilbon, bm; m 21 Aug 1853 by Hezekiah Terry, J. P.

Horner, Wilson & Jane Maddin, 11 Oct 1839; Jacob Waggoner, bm.

Horniday, Soloman & Margret Low, 27 Oct 1809; Stephen Wells, bm.

Horton, Amos & Salley Brown, 12 March 1834; Bennett Brown, Thomas C. Davis, bm.

Horton, Haywood & Avelean Glenn, 5 Feb 1861; W. H. Glenn, bm; m 7 Feb 1861 by William Green, J. P.

Horton, Henry & Nancy Standeford, 24 Dec 1833; Bennett Brown, William Brown, bm.

Horton, James & Catharine Wallace, 4 Oct 1782; James Carrington, bm.

Horton, James & Elizabeth Carrington, 24 Aug 1796; John Carington, bm.

Horton, James & Nancy Scarlett, 5 Aug 1822; J. Taylor Jr., bm.

Horton, Levi & Polley Whitehead, 3 Jan 1828; Abel Johnston, bm.

Horton, William & McCillin Belvin, 3 Oct 1797; Jehu Whitehead, bm.

Horton, William & Lively Cozort, 17 July 1806; George Laws, bm.

Horton, William & Ellen Trice, 17 April 1849; J. B. McDade, bm.

Hosea, William & Rebecca Miles, 25 Jan 1823; Jas. Stubbins, bm.

Hostiter, Andrew J. & Coenlia Brockwell, 13 Aug 1865; James T. Watson, bm.

House, Daniel & Mary Kirk, 24 Dec 178_; Reuben Smith, bm.

House, Lewis & Clarissa Turner, 21 Dec 1819; Moses Guess, bm.

House, James & Melinda Marcom, 20 April 1853; M. H. Turner, bm; m 21 April 1853 by Harris Wilkerson, J. P.

House, John & Susan Crowder, 14 Aug 1849; Wm. Nelson, bm.

House, Peter & Nancy Trice, 2 Feb 1787; Thomas Trice, bm.

House, William & Mary A. Vickers, 27 Nov 1854; John W. Markham, Thos. J. Strayhorn, bm; m 30 Nov 1854 by Harris Wilkerson, J. P.

Houston, John B. & Harriot N. Barns, 21 Sept 1840; Isaac H. Foust, bm.

Houze, Jno. & Patsy Lee, 24 Aug 1813; Thos. Edwards, bm.

Houze, Wright & Polly Turner, 4 Jan 1817; Jesse Vikers, bm.

Howard, Anderson & Nancy C. Brigs, 27 Nov 1811; Thos. Reavis, bm.

Howard, Charles & Sarah Faucett, 26 March 1839; John W. Latta, Jno. M. Faucett, bm.

Howard, Geor W. & ____, 14 Sept 1865; A. S. Lewter, bm.

Howard, John & Elliner Bates, 16 Jan 1797; Jonathan Thompson, bm.

Howard, John & Frances Sykes, 17 Feb 1851; M. G. Sykes, bm.

Howard, Julis & Elizabeth E. Sikes, 19 Jan 1842; William Crawford, bm.

Howard, Larkin & Rachel Herndon, 21 Oct 1801; Richard Johnston, bm.

Howard, Richard & Peggy Wittie, 10 July 1813; David Tate, bm.

Howard, Richard & Ruth Whitted, 26 Dec 1821; Abel Smith, bm.

Howard, Richd. G. & Salin E. Workman, 12 March 1864; Thos. S. Cates, bm.

Howard, Thomas & Susannah Witty, 31 July 1811; William Goarly, bm.

Howard, Thomas & Jinney Pickard, 9 March 1819; Thomas Dodson, John L. Cate, bm.

Howard, Thomas & Sarah Sheeler, 10 May 1859; John P. Faucett, bm; m 12 May 1859 by Jas. N. Craig, J. P.

Howard, Thomas & Jensey Dickerson, 25 March 1826; Jesse ODaniel, bm.

Howard, Thomas W. & Elizabeth Riley, 10 Feb 1863; Thos. C. Hayes, bm.

Howard, William & Nancy Sanders, 25 March 1831; Robert Ashley, Richd. Howard, bm.

Howel, Alexander & Mary Jane Wallis, 1 Oct 1860; William Day, bm; m 4 Oct 1860 by F. Walker, J. P.

Howell, Freeman & Eliza Gowen, 16 Nov 1861; Currie Chavers, bm; m 17 Nov 1861 by W. F. Strayhorn, J. P.

Howington, Josiah & Edy Herndon, 3 Jan 1826; Tapley Herndon, bm.

Hubbard, James & Nancy Thomas, 24 March 1809; Edward Thomas, bm.

Hubbard, Thomas & ___, 9 Sept 1805; John Hues, bm.

Hubbart, John & Polley Thomas, 2 March 1803; Brice Collins, bm.

Hubberd, John & Mary Hull, 25 Nov 1801; Archibald Reaves, bm.

Huckeby, Gray & Patsey Johnston, 27 April 1817; Hugh Mulhollan, bm.

Huckeby, Green & Jeany Campbell, 20 Jan 1817; Jn. Bilbo, bm.

Huddleston, Samuel, son of Benj. Huddleston, & Annie Card, dau. of Saml Card, m 19 Dec 1867 by A. C. Hunter, J. P.

Hudgins, Willibough & Sarah Guess, 4 June 1823; James Trice, bm.

Hudson, Lemuel & Nancy Lewter, 28 Dec 1840; Ezekiel George, Joseph Woodrow, bm.

Hudson, William & ___, 19 Jan 1784; John Hughbanks Jr., bm.

Hueghs, Thos. H. & Susan Clark, 14 Aug 1834; John A. Clark, bm.

Hues, John & Nelly Lackey, 13 Dec 1802; Brice Collins, bm.

Huffhines, Daniel & Fanny Danely, 14 Feb 1849; Lewis Huffins, bm.

Huffhoines, Daniel & Bermilla A. Strader, 4 Jan 1847; Joshua Strader, bm.

Huffman, Andrew & Louisa May, 24 June 1847; Henderson May, bm.

Huffman, John & Nelly Wagoner, 30 Jan 1849; A. A. Holt, bm.

Hufheins, Gorg & Barbara Wagonnor, 1 Oct 1814; Peter Waggoner Juner., bm.

Hofheins, Jacob & Betsey Neace, 20 March 1816; Peter Summers, bm

Hufhines, John & Rachell Huffman, 11 Dec 1822; William Amick, bm.

Hufines, Peter & Rebeccah Boon, 10 March 1834; Joel Tickle, bm.

Hufman, Daniel & Elisabeth Stalcup, 3 Nov 1806; Henray Holt, bm.

Hufman, David & Polly Whitsett, 3 Nov 1818; Briscoe Warren, bm.

Hufman, George & Betsey Shofner, 15 Aug 1804; John Cook, bm.

Hufman, Jacob & Sally Cable, 9 Feb 1848; Jacob May, bm.

Hughes, Andrew & Sarah Hill, 8 April 1816; William Ireland, John H. Carmical, bm.

Hughes, James & Sarah Patton, 20 Oct 1789; John Hughes, bm.

Hughes, James F. & Martha Tinnin, 19 Dec 1851; Wm. P. Hughes, bm; m 25 Dec 1851 by Archibald Currie, minister.

Hughes, John K. & Mary A. Miller, 1 Oct 1860; John U. Hart, bm; m 3 Oct 1860 by Archibald Currie, minister.

Hughes, Samuel & Nancy Cook, 29 Dec 1809; David Cook, bm.

Hughes, William & Nancy Roney, 17 Jan 1809; John McCracken, bm.

Hughes, William & Anne Gattis, 16 Jan 1832; John H. Faucett, bm.

Hughes, Wmson Rice & Maria Louisa Link, 6 Dec 1859; Wm. K. Parrish, bm; m 7 Dec 1859 by Adolphus W. Mangum, minister.

Hughlet, Jesse & Nancy Christopher, 10 April 1843; Burley Smith, William H. Allison, bm.

Hughs, George & Sarah Pascal, 23 Oct 1839; Samuel Adams, Lewis B. Holt, bm.

Hughs, James & Fanny Simpson, 11 March 1833; Morgan Dickey, bm.

Hughs, John & Elizabeth Fulton, 25 Oct 1797; And. Faddis, bm.

Hughs, William R. & Sarah J. Minnis, 19 May 1855; Thos. Scarlett bm; m 22 May 1855 by Archibald Currie, minister.

Hulet, Samuel & Lydia Eubank, 21 Oct 1819; Jesse Crisp, bm.

Humphres, John Harwood & Nancy Halliburton, 20 Dec 1800; W. H. Burton, bm.

Humphrey, David & Elizabeth Busick, 1 Aug 1808; Wm. Busick, bm.

Hunneycut, Uriah & Nancy Bradford, 14 Aug 1796; William Wells, bm.

Hunt, Absalom & Patsey White, 25 June 1793; Mann Patterson, bm.

Hunt, Berry & Mary Starkey, 18 May 1792; Luke Prendergast, bm.

Hunt, Charles & Faithy Revill, 1 March 1800; Mark Carrigan, bm.

Hunt, Elijah & Mary Fowler, 16 Jan 1811; Thomas Horner, bm.

Hunt, Thomas & Mary Cate, 10 Dec 1783; Wm. Ray, bm.

Hunt, William & Emiley Riley, 8 Dec 1848; James R. Miller, bm.

Hunter, Aaron & Mary Curry, 10 Dec 1797; Jesse Hunter, bm.

Hunter, Aaron & Ruth Pipes, 21 July 1801; David Strayhorn, bm.

Hunter, Andrew & Susanna Hogan, 15 Aug 1800; John Adams, bm.

Hunter, James & Patsey Blackwood, 24 July 1820; M. Adams, bm.

Hunter, James T. & Cornelia A. Scott, 22 Aug 1848; William H. Thompson, bm.

Hunter, Jesse & Nancy Curry, 12 Sept 1793; James McCauley, bm.

Hunter, John & Anne Andrew, 22 Aug 1804; William Williams, bm.

Hunter, John & Betsey Thompson, 12 Dec 1818; John Thompson, bm.

Hunter, John & Elizabeth Crabtree, 15 Jan 1840; William Crabtree, bm.

Hunter, Pleasant & Rhodah Pearson, 6 Dec 1832; Richard Blackwood, bm.

Hunter, Robrt. Jr. & Peggy Rogers, 2 Feb 1802; A. B. Bruce, bm.

Hunter, Samuel & Elizabeth Maxedent, 7 Feb 1784; Wm. Burns, bm.

Hunter, Samuel & Dolley Tate, 18 Feb 1834; Archd. Borland, bm.

Hunter, Samuel & Ellen Perry, 30 Dec 1860; John R. Hancock, Gilford Dollar, bm; m 30 Dec 1860 by John F. Lyon, J. P.

Hunter, Samuel H. & Hannah Thompson, 8 Jan 1821; John Hunter, bm.

Hunter, Thomas H. & Cynthia Lloyd, 20 April 1829; Stephen Poe, bm.

Hunter, William & Rebecca Cook, 27 Dec 1824; Handy Wood, bm.

Huntington, Roswell & Mary Parmer or Palmer, 12 Oct 1789; Martin Palmer, bm.

Huntington, William & Frances House, 9 Dec 1819; J. Witherspoon, bm.

Hurdle, Bedford & Nancy Moore, 5 Jan 1847; Jacob Hurdle, bm.

Hurdle, George & Peggy Hardin, 28 Feb 1823; John Harden, bm.

Hurdle, Hardy & Sarah Moore, 6 Oct 1845; Jacob Hurdle, bm.

Hurdle, Henry C. & Mary E. Grahams, 17 Dec 1845; Benj. Hurdle, bm.

Hurdle, James & Susannah Dickey, 19 May 1810; Henry Hurdle, bm.

Hurdle, Josiah & Phoebe Beason, 1 Feb 1828; Benj. Hurdle, bm.

Hurdle, Obedier & Mary Blanshard, 22 April 1834; D. Dickey, bm.

Hurdle, Thomas & Polly Faucett, 13 March 1821; George Hurdle, bm.

Hurst, Leroy M. & Caroline L. Colton, 23 Feb 1867; Rufus Massey, bm; m 24 Feb 1867 by R. F. Morris, J. P.

Husbands, Zedekiah & Polley Burnett, 24 March 1832; Abram Burnett, bm.

Huse, Joseph & Mary Faddis, 28 March 1821; Hugh McCaddams, bm.

Husk, James & Mary Bletcher, 7 May 1828; Clemuel Carroll, bm.

Huske, Benjamin R. & Annabella Norwood, 4 Dec 1851; O. F. Long, bm; m at the residence of John Norwood, by Joseph C. Huske, minister.

Huske, Spencer & Lydia Ann Barber, 19 Dec 1829; H. Parrish, bm.

Huske, William & Carey Hall, 16 Jan 1823; John Huske, Andrew Cole, bm.

Huskey, Allen & Nelly Wall, 5 July 1808; Wms. Dods, bm.

Huskey, Isaac K. & Mary F. Bruce, 8 Aug 1849; John M. Griffin, bm.

Huskey, William & Charlotte Tate, 16 Aug 1833; M. Burton, Samuel Scarlett, bm.

Husky, William & Laney Brockwell, 2 April 1862; D. C. McDade, bm; m 2 April 1862 by D. Tilley, J. P.

Hust, Henry & Eliza Pope, 27 Oct 1845; Ezekiel George, bm.

Hust, John & Catharine Leigh, 23 Feb 1796; Leonard Carlton, bm.

Hust, Jno. & Sarah Willford, 23 Nov 1802; Jno. Shepperd, bm.

Hust, William & Anne Marcum, 23 Jan 1796; Jno. Marcom, bm.

Hutchen, Andrew J. & Elizabeth Blalock, 22 April 1858; W. G. Couch, bm; m 22 April 1858 by Samuel Couch, J. P.

Hutcheson, James & Sarah Jordan, 14 Dec 1796; M. Hart, bm.

Hutcheson, James & Nancy Tier, 24 Jan 1824; G. Jordan, bm.

Hutcheson, Ross & Elizabeth Jorden, 24 Feb 1803; James Hutcheson, bm.

Hutchins, Atlis & Isabela Ferrell, 12 Jan 1855; J. J. Allison, bm; m 16 Jan 1855 by John J. Allison, J. P.

Hutchins, James & Anne Terrill, 26 Jan 1781; Henry Meridith, bm.

Hutchins, James & Sally Carroll, 16 Nov 1829; John Hutchins, bm.

Hutchins, James & Julia Hogan, 4 Oct 1849; Saml. C. Kirkland, bm.

Hutchins, James G. & Sarah Lewis, 7 Oct 1829; Moses C. Hutchins, bm.

Hutchins, John & Betsey Rhodes, 18 Aug 1819; James Hutchins, bm.

Hutchins, John & Salley Rhodes, 5 Feb 1823; Thomas Hutchins, bm.

Hutchins, Moses & Mary Hogan, 15 April 1858; James Hutchins, bm.

Hutchins, Thomas & Phoebe Grimes, 9 Oct 1802; William Herndon, bm.

Hutchins, Thomas & Rebecca Acres, 2 Feb 1818; James Hutchins, bm.

Hutchins, William W. & Sarah A. Blake, 29 June 1849; Hardy Massey, bm.

Hutchinson, George & Amy Terrill, 4 Oct 1826; George McCrorey, bm.

Hutchinson, Jordan R. & Mary Willis, 29 July 1841; William Wolf, bm.

Hutson, Peter & Fanny Murray, 13 Sept 1812; James Moore, bm.

Hutson, Saml. & Mary Rogers, 24 July 1785; John Hutson, bm.

Hutton, William & Nelly Law, 11 Jan 1826; Eli Staly, bm.

Huzzah, Samuel & Sarah Jones, 26 Feb 1784; James Carrington, bm.

Iglehart, James Jr. & Sarah J. Waddell, 29 Oct 1855; J. D. Cameron, O. S. Inglehart, bm.

Ingle, David & Polly Tickle, 18 Nov 1824; David Lain, bm.

Ingold, Alfred & Priscilla Campbell, 23 Dec 1846.

Ingram, John H. & Elizabeth Boyle, 7 July 1828; Thomas Fausett, bm.

Inscore, James & Nancy Laycock, 5 Dec 1851; John C. McCown, bm; m 10 Dec 1851 by Wm. McCown, J. P.

Irby, John & Salley Clark, 26 Nov 1805; Thos. Clancy, bm.

Iseley, Austin & Polly Iseley, 26 Dec 1831; Miltn Isley, bm.

Iseley, Edwin & Elizabeth Spoon, 15 Nov 1839; Hiram Steel, bm.

Iseley, Henry & Milly Isley, 28 Aug 1830; William Foglemon, bm.

Iseley, Jacob & Rebeccah Isley, 31 Jan 1838; Christian Isley, bm.

Iseley, Jacob & Lucy Isley, 1 March 1847; Andy Isly, bm.

Isely, Lewis & Polly Rippey, 27 July 1839; Alford T. Rippy, bm.

Isley, Boston & Rachel Phillips, 21 July 1806; John James, bm.

Isley, Christian & Nancy Whitsell, 17 Aug 1822; Jn. Troxler, bm.

Isley, Eli & Delilah Jeffries, 8 April 1840; Edwin Iseley, bm.

Isley, Elias & Molly Moser, 25 Dec 1838; Jacob Iseley, bm.

Isley, George Jur. & Patsey Atkerson, 19 Sept 1814; Peter Boggs, bm.

Isley, Jacob & Elizabeth Councelman, 20 Jan 1809; Peter Boggs, bm.

Isley, Joel & Delilah Isley, 9 Feb 1839; Jacob Iseley, bm.

Isley, Lewis & Nancy Truant, 23 May 1846; Wm. H. Truehett, bm.

Isley, Malicah Jr. & Polly Loy, 16 Aug 1810; Henry Loy Jr., bm.

Isley, Peter & Mary Couton, 23 Aug 1836; Lewis Isley, bm.

Isley, Phillip & Polley Denbey, 20 March 1821; Archd. Cameron, bm.

Isley, Wm. & Sally Isley, 24 March 1823.

Isly, David & Sally Graves, 19 April 1820.

Isly, Philip & Mary Sharp, 2 Oct 1847; Martin Isly, bm.

Ivey, David & Rebecca Jinkins, 15 Oct 1782; Peter Johnston, wit.

Ivey, David & Betsey Gammage, 5 Sept 1794; John Edwards, bm.

Ivey, Edward & Sophia Clements, 12 Sept 1846; B. Utley, bm.

Ivey, John & Patsey Snipes, 8 Dec 1805; James Loyd, bm.

Ivey, Joseph & ____, 18 Jan 1832; John Andrews, bm.

Ivey, Patterson & Nancy Loyd, 28 Feb 1822; Wm. Coreathes, bm.

Ivy, James M. & Martha Freeland, 11 Dec 1858; W. T. Hogan, bm.

Ivy, William & Polley Couch, 13 June 1812; Wm. H. Adams, bm.

Izard, Benjamin & Polley ____, 17 July 1807; William Gean, John Young, bm.

Izard, Thomas Y. & Nancy Chambers, 14 Jan 1857; Jehu Izard, Redding Cope, bm.

Izzard, Anderson & Nancy Bryant, 12 June 1819; Green Jones, bm.

Izzard, Anderson & Polly Thomas, 26 Nov 1828; Stephen W. McPherson, bm.

Izzard, James & Hannah Honeycut, 18 May 1796; Richard Pickard, bm.

Izzell, George & Elizabeth Moore, 15 May 1813; Wm. Gean, bm.

Izzell, John & Polly Pearson, 25 Nov 1817; Richd. Jones, James Murdok, bm.

Izzle, Bird & Elizabeth Wright, 6 Sept 1804; William Pritchard, bm.

Jackson, Abel G. & Elizabeth D. Ellis, 7 June 1834; Richd. Nichols, bm.

Jackson, Brice & Polley Ray, 22 Oct 1823; Bradley Collins, bm.

Jackson, Clemuel & Jane Whitaker, 10 Oct 1846; Wilson Jackson, bm.

Jackson, Clemuel & Mary Ann Riley, 16 June 1860; C. J. Freeland, bm.

Jackson, George & Margret Nichols, 15 Dec 1832; James Jackson, bm.

Jackson, H. S. J. & Cornelia Jackson, 29 Aug 1866; J. W. McKerall, bm; m 29 Aug 1866 by John F. Lyon, J. P.

Jackson, Isaac & Elizabeth Armstrong, 25 Aug 1801; John Collins, bm.

Jackson, Jacob & Hannah Gragson, 26 May 1787; And. Brooks, bm.

Jackson, Jacob Jr. & Letey H. Ray, 15 Dec 1838; A. G. Jackson, Moreland Jackson, bm.

Jackson, James & Nancy Phillips, 17 Aug 1806; John Strader, bm.

Jackson, James & Charlotte Crabtree, 30 March 1811; James Jackson, bm.

Jackson, James & Salley Bateman, 11 July 1811; Joshua Walker, bm.

Jackson, Jasper & Louisa Crabtree, 18 Sept 1866; John Jackson, Joseph Reese, bm; m 18 Sept 1866 by C. J. Freeland, J. P.

Jackson, Jeremiah & Betsey Marcrom, 13 Aug 1794; Wm. Marcome, bm.

Jackson, John & Sarah Wallace, 10 Jan 1794; George Greshim, bm.

Jackson, John & Barbara Pile, 24 Sept 1806; Henry Snoterley, bm.

Jackson, John & Ruth Thomson, 28 Oct 1823; John Holstead, bm.

Jackson, John & Elizabeth Williams, 21 Dec 1835; T. Horner, Stephen Horner, bm.

Jackson, John & Mary A. Couch, 16 Dec 1859; Moses Redding, bm.

Jackson, John & Betty Riley, 22 June 1861; David Riley, William Thompson, bm.

Jackson, Martin & Mariah Cain, 19 Nov 1841; Samuel Thompson, Moses Leathers Jr., bm.

Jackson, Mebane & Sarah Dew, 24 Jan 1842; Wilson Jackson, Moses Leathers Jr., bm.

Jackson, Moreland & Mary Jane B. Ray, 10 Feb 1837; Bradley Collins, David G. Ray, bm.

Jackson, Nathan & Betsy Horner, 3 Jan 1797; Meryman Coleman, bm.

Jackson, Nathan & Elizabeth Rylie, 20 Dec 1797; John Riley, bm.

Jackson, Paskel & Mary S. Rhew, 9 May 1856; Thomas Cole, bm.

Jackson, Thomas & Susan Crabtree, 2 April 1857; T. Webb, bm.

Jackson, Thomas & Susan Crabtree, 20 June 1857; Sterling
Crabtree, bm; m 21 June 1857 by John F. Lyon, J. P.

Jackson, William & Susanah Brooks, 22 Dec 1787; And. Brooks,
Joseph Dickson, bm.

Jackson, William & Gilley Dennis, 22 Jan 1831; John Tapp, bm.

Jackson, William & Salley Thompson, 10 Nov 1836; Samuel
Thompson, James Thompson, bm.

Jackson, William & Elizabeth Rhew, 29 Nov 1866; Jesse Lewis,
bm; m 29 Nov 1866 by J. F. Lyon, J. P.

Jackson, Wm. & Anne Teasley, 11 Oct 1805; Joseph Renn, bm.

Jackson, Wm & Fanny Deblin, 22 Oct 1808; James Deblin, bm.

Jackson, Wm. & Susannah Pendar, 22 Feb 1809; John Pendar, bm.

Jackson, William G. & Martha Wilkerson, 20 Dec 1856; James
Moris, bm; m 21 Dec 1856 by Richeson Nicholes, J. P.

Jacob, Solomon & Patsy Leathers, 30 Nov 1810; Wm. B. Jameson,
bm.

Jacobs, Alford & Jeany Faddis, 5 Jan 1823; Jas. Roney, bm.

Jacobs, James 7 Aminda Roberts, 29 March 1819; Joseph McCraken,
bm.

Jacobs, John W. & Sarah Jane Gates, 21 May 1852; Minnick Miller,
James P. Hopkines, bm; m 23 May 1852 by Hezekiah Terry, J. P.

Jacobs, Josiah & Luena Rhew, 17 Nov 1851; Elmore Gates, bm.

James, George & Mary Hendricks, 6 Oct 1798; Thos. Scarlet, bm.

James, Henderson W. & Mary C. Rhoads, 21 Oct 1848; Moses W.
Guess, bm.

James, Jesse & Elizabeth Horne, 21 Jan 1791; Samuel Cleny, bm.

James, Jesse & Mary Tilley, 13 April 1826; John Piper, bm.

James, Jessie & Lucy Crabtree, 22 Dec 1857; Richard H___bank,
bm.

James, John & Hawkins Mangum, 26 Oct 1852; Duncan C. Glenn,
Zachariah Faussett, bm; m 2 Nov 1852 by Wm. Green, J. P.

James, Osborn & Polly Murray, 8 Jan 1835; Wiley Malone, Polly
Sullenger, bm.

James, Russell & Bedy Threw, 8 Oct 1829; John A. McMannen, bm.

James, Simeon & Caty Boon, 23 March 1837; Alford J. R___, bm.

James, Solomon & _____, 15 June 1785.

James, Thomas & Mariam Underwood, 4 July 1787; Samuel James, bm.

James, Thomas & Elizabeth Barbee, 26 Jan 1824; Reuben Barbee, bm.

James, Thomas N. & Annis Cates, 21 Feb 1860; Thomas Webb, bm; m 23 Feb 1860 by Jno. Hancock, J. P.

James, Willie & Nancy Jane Cole, 11 Jan 1854; W. B. Holloway, Geo. Laws, bm; m 12 Jan 1854 by Alexr. Dickson, J. P.

Jameson, Jno. & Tempe Howell, 24 July 1804; S. Turrentine, bm.

Jamison, Wm. B. & Mary E. W. Ray, 1 April 1817; James Clancy, bm.

Jarratt, Jno. & Rebecca Ulmstead, 23 Jan 1827; Jas. H. Carrington, bm.

Jean, John & Elizabeth Curl, 31 May 1806; William Richardson, bm.

Jeffers, Addison & Sophia Jeffers, 18 March 1840; Charles Jeffrs, Hugh Jeffrs, bm.

Jeffers, Andrew & Viney Jeffers, 18 Oct 1830; Eaton Jeffers, Addison Jeffers, bm.

Jeffers, Burton & Lucy Haithcock, 25 Feb 1839; Willson Jeffers, Henry Evans, bm.

Jeffers, Charles & Elizabeth Jeffers, 5 June 1841; Jacob Jeffers, Henry T. Moore, bm.

Jeffers, Elias & Polley Jones, 24 Nov 1815; Merreday Chavers, bm.

Jeffers, James & Betsy Jeffers, 19 Aug 1809; Aaron Boles, John Burnside, bm.

Jeffers, John & Dilley Ballard, 8 Dec 1824; Andrew Jeffers, Eaton Jeffers, bm.

Jeffers, Joshua & Polley Ball, 14 Dec 1809; Robt Scott, bm.

Jeffers, Littleton & Lucy Hathcock, 11 Jan 1809; Vins Guy, bm.

Jeffers, Peter & Lucy Jeffers, 18 Jan 1806; A. B. Bruce, bm.

Jeffers, Robert J. & Mary P. Jenkins, 1 July 1843; James Jeffrey, bm.

Jeffers, Willis & Dicey Jeffers, 23 Jan 1810; Armour King, bm.

Jeffers, Willson & Jane Evans, 29 Dec 1835; Joshua Jones, bm.

Jeffreys, Adkins & Harriet Corn, 3 Jan 1852; Green Mays, bm.

Jeffreys, Even & Rachl. Delap, 24 Nov 1792; John Lackey, bm.

Jeffres, Hutson & Milly Chavers, 26 Feb 1846; Wilson Jeffreys, bm.

Jeffreys, Ransom & Kizzey Heath, 6 June 1828; Allen Jeffreys, bm.

Jeffreys, Thomas W. & Rosanah J. McDade, 2 Dec 1850; Jno. N. Cox, bm.

Jeffreys, William & Rebecca Ann Hayes, 23 Dec 1851; Brody Hayes, bm.

ORANGE COUNTY MARRIAGES, 1779-1868

Jeffries, Jacob & Jane Moore, 5 Oct 1796; Josha. Witti, bm.

Jeffries, John & Winifred Whitmore, 21 April 1800; Charles Whitmore, bm.

Jeffries, Wm. & Penelope Evans, 21 Feb 1800; Rept Stewart, bm.

Jeffries, William & Polly Lyttle, 22 Sept 1821; Marks Ammonds, bm.

Jeffris, Zachariah & Jane Brinkly, 10 Feb 1856; D. Meadows, bm.

Jeffyes, Robt. & Pheebe Johnston, 2 June 1835; S. Piper, bm.

Jefreys, Samuel & Edith Burnet, 12 Aug 1841; Nathan Alben, bm.

Jenkins, Chesley P. & Mary Boothe, 28 May 1824; Albun Seears, bm.

Jenkins, Dennis & Milley Trice, 15 Nov 1830; Christopher Barbe, bm.

Jenkins, Jno. & Sarah Lynch, 25 Aug 1798; William Lewis, bm.

Jenkins, Man P. & Polly Davis, 11 Dec 1822; ____, bm.

Jenkins, William & Silvia Barby, 30 Dec 1789; Mark Barbe, bm.

Jenkins, William & Peggy Baxter, 24 Dec 1799; John Pettigrew, bm.

Jenkins, William & Milley Harper, 22 April 1800; T. Johnston, bm.

Jenkins, William & Elizabeth Pritchard, 22 July 1829; John Horner, bm.

Jennings, James R. & Sarah C. Cheek, 12 Aug 1854; John White, bm; m 12 Oct 1854 by L. S. Burkhead, minister.

Jepson, Leml. & Nancy Bowls, 20 Aug 1791; Isaac Brackin, bm.

Jerden, Will & Rachel Param, 12 Sept 1846.

Jesse, John & Polley Armstrong, 11 Jan 1800; Jno. Armstrong, bm.

Jinkins, Ephraim & Salley Lewis, 28 March 1807; William Cain, bm.

Jinkins, John & Nancy Blake, 18 Dec 1810; J. Taylor, bm.

Jinkins, Jonathan & Nancy Owens, 15 Sept 1802; Reuben Baxter, bm.

Jinkins, Joseph & Arena Herndon, 29 Nov 1823; Stanford Herndon, Willis Marcum, bm.

Jinkins, Thos. & Betsy Ballard, 29 Nov 1799; John Bragg, bm.

Joheson, Berry & Nancy Hatwood, 29 July 1813; David Andress, bm.

Johnson, Anderson & Mary Turner, 16 June 1866; Geo. Laws, bm; m 16 June 1866 by Thomas C. Hayes.

Johnson, Buck & Nancy Hendon, 2 March 1867; W. McCauly, bm; m 2 March 1867 by A. C. Murdock, J. P.

Johnson, Caleb, son of John & Peggy Johnson, & Celey Morehead, dau. of Jim & Jenny Morehead, colored, m 15 Aug 1867 by Thos. C. Hayes.

Johnson, Charles & Margaret Robson, 20 July 1814; John Robson, bm.

Johnson, Daniel, son of Coleman & Junny Farmer, & Jane Couch, dau. of Cinda Couch, colored, m 25 Dec 1867 by Willm. Hodge.

Johnson, Duke & Jane Allen, 30 Oct 1847; Henry Web, bm.

Johnson, Henry & Salena Hester, colored, m 23 Feb 1867 by A. M. Latta, J. P.

Johnson, Jeremiah & Nancy Forrest, 3 Nov 1800; Samuel Peelor, bm.

Johnson, John & Nancy A. Johnson, 21 Aug 1860; Zion Pearson, John M. Pearson, bm; m 21 Aug 1860 by Wilson Brown, J. P.

Johnson, John, son of Anthony Pratt & Polly Johnson, & Rachel Johnson, m 12 March 1868 by Samuel Couch, J. P.

Johnson, Robert & Nancy Patton, 5 Dec 1789; John Patton, bm.

Johnson, Sam, son of Abner & Jinny Johnson, & Mary F. Bumpass, dau. of Anderson & Jinny Bumpass, colored, m 15 Jan 1868 by William D. Lunsford, J. P.

Johnson, Samuel H. & Mary Jane Rhodes, 25 Aug 1863; Wesley Neeley, bm; m 30 Aug 1863 by John F. Lyon.

Johnson, Sanders & Mary Riggs, 11 Oct 1834; Clayton Jones, bm.

Johnson, Teppo & Sarah Isley, 3 Aug 1847; Allen Boggs, bm.

Johnson, Virgil, son of Luke Strayhorn & Hanah Johnson, & Louisa Blacknal, dau. of Hubbard Jackson & Charity Borland, m 24 May 1867 by C. W. Johnston, J. P.

Johnson, William & Debby Morrison, 24 Oct 1809; Thomas Carter, bm.

Johnson, Willis & Katharin Amick, 10 Jan 1828; Peter Brown, bm.

Johnston, Benjamin & Nancy Woods, 26 March 1810; A. Carrington, bm.

Johnston, Benjamin & Nancy Woods, 4 Nov 1810; Archibell Carrington, bm.

Johnston, Benjamin & Sally Cardin, 5 Dec 1832; John Holloway, bm.

Johnston, Charles W. & Lydia Cabe, 11 Sept 1819; J. S. Smith, bm.

Johnston, Daniel W. & Dulenia Barton, 9 Nov 1826; J. Taylor Jr., Carleton B. Cole, bm.

Johnston, David & Polley Gibson, 21 Jan 1811; Richd. Jones, bm.

Johnston, David & Mary Mebane, 17 May 1828; Eli Troxler, bm.

Johnston, David & Salley Jones, 14 May 1829; Thos. Jones, bm.

Johnston, David C. & Ellenor Rogers, 27 April 1822; Alex Patton, bm.

Johnston, Drury & Rody Cole, 7 May 1785; Thomas Brownen, bm.

Johnston, Durell & Lucretia Carrington, 7 Jan 1858; Jno. Laws, bm.

Johnston, Eli & Mary Lane, colored, 7 Dec 1854; J. R. Hutchins, bm; m 7 Dec 1854 by J. W. Carr, J. P.

Johnston, Fisher & Fanny Pearson, 20 May 1837; Zan(?) Pearson, bm.

Johnston, Geo & Mary Mulhollan, 5 June 1793; Thos. Mulhollan, bm.

Johnston, George & Jane Thompson, 11 March 1816; Geo. Clancy, bm.

Johnston, George & Elizabeth Lindsey, 17 May 1841; John T. Johnston, John Thompson, bm.

Johnston, George M. & Eliza M. Bond, 16 Sept 1831; J. Taylor, Will A. Graham, bm.

Johnston, Hargess & Betsy Cole, 12 Oct 1838; Benjamin Johnston, Stephen Dollar, bm.

Johnston, Henry & Barbara May, 25 July 1827; Matthias Johnston, bm.

Johnston, James & Margaret Craig, 4 March 1788; Baxter King, bm.

Johnston, James & Elizabeth Mason, 10 Oct 1800; James Mason, bm.

Johnston, James & Nancy Fossett, 25 Oct 1837; N. H. Blackwood, bm.

Johnston, John & Izabel Craig, 30 May 1795; James Johnston, bm.

Johnston, John & Sarah Clark, 16 Dec 1797; Wm. Bowls, bm.

Johnston, John & Nancy Roach, 18 Oct 1810; Richd. Jones, bm.

Johnston, John & Charity Tate, 26 July 1833; Robt. F. White, bm.

Johnston, John R. & Eliza E. Thompson, 17 Oct 1845; William H. Thompson, bm.

Johnston, John T. & Mary A. Thompson, 17 Oct 1845; William H. Thompson, bm.

Johnston, Leigh & Pattsy Collier, 4 July 1810; Harison Iving, M. Hart, bm.

Johnston, Major & Elizabeth Isley, 30 Nov 1838; Joel Isley, bm.

Johnston, Ransom & Ann Loinberry, 15 Sept 1830; John Wason, bm.

Johnston, Robert & Eliza Gibson, 26 Feb 1805; Ben Stevens, bm.

Johnston, Robert & Sarah Swain, 29 April 1867; m by Charles Phillips, minister.

Johnston, Robert M. & Anne McPherson, 15 May 1838; Thos. L. Carter, Jas. H. Christie, bm.

Johnston, Saml. & Margret Burgwinn, 23 Sept 1829; Ed. Strudwick, bm.

Johnston, Sanders & Beedy Mangum, 12 Dec 1827; Isham Brinkley, bm.

Johnston, Thomas & Nancy Fossett, 19 Nov 1798; Robert Fossett, bm.

Johnston, Thomas & Nancy Jones, 1 Jan 1791; Lewis Jones, bm.

Johnston, Thomas & Mary A. Thompson, 6 Nov 1857; Henr J. Thompson, bm; m 8 Nov 1857 by Ruffin R. Tapp, J. P.

Johnston, Thos. & Mary McCulloch, 21 May 1809; Henry Shutte, bm.

Johnston, Turner & Priscilla Ashley, 20 Aug 1828; Clarance Ashley, Jarrott Ashley, bm.

Johnston, William & Obedience Bobbitt, 27 April 1803; Willie Mangum, bm.

Johnston, William & Mary Fossett, 12 April 1837; Samuel Patton, bm.

Johnston, Willie & Franky Day, 19 Feb 1835; Chesley Bass, bm.

Jolley, Abel & Salley Hitchcock, 12 Jan 1824; Edward Caudle, bm.

Jolley, Boling & Hannah Pasmore, 1 Oct 1798; Stephen Jolly, bm.

Jolley, James & Kesiah Jolley, 19 July 1798; John Jolley, bm.

Jolley, Joseph & Tempey Gough, 4 Dec 1793; Alexr. Hatch, bm.

Jolley, Wm. & Rachel Davis, 1 Feb 1796; Davd. Lemmons, bm.

Jolly, Nathaniel & Nancy Williams, 31 Aug 1847; Henry A. Sykes, bm.

Jones, Abraham & Mary Rippey, 26 March 1839; Wm. P. Griffis, Wm. F. Strayhorn, bm.

Jones, Adolphus G. & Frances J. Hooker, 13 Dec 1851; James M. Palmer, bm.

Jones, Albert M. & Jane M. Cates, 23 July 1853; J. B. McDade, bm; m 24 July 1853 by Levi Andrews, minister.

Jones, Allen P. & Elizebeth Lasley, 5 Jan 1846; James Jones, Jas. H. Christie, bm.

Jones, Aquila & Hypsiga Hargis, 20 Feb 1794; John Smith, bm.

Jones, Aquilla & Ellender Thompson, 8 July 1800; Jonathan Jones, bm.

Jones, Aquilla & Ellen Webster, 2 Nov 1865; Alsun McDaniel, bm; m 2 Nov 1865 by H. McDaniel, J. P.

Jones, Barnet & Peggy Laurence, 9 Sept 1822; John Horne, bm.

Jones, Calvin & Mahala Pierce, 6 Oct 1842; Daniel Briggs, bm.

Jones, Charles & Elizabeth Cheek, 18 Jan 1806; Jas. Cheek, bm.

Jones, Charles & Mary C. Andrews, 25 Aug 1860; Jno. M. Faucett, bm; m 26 Aug 1860 by W. J. Hogan, J. P.

Jones, Charles W. & Mary Jane Gattis, 26 Nov 1860; James Jones, bm; m 27 Nov 1860 by W. J. Hogan, J. P.

Jones, Danill & Frances Harris, 1 May 1805; Richmond Harris, bm.

Jones, Edward & Anne Barbee, 6 Feb 1795; Chri Barbee, bm.

Jones, Elijah & Mary Haith, 22 Dec 1827; Allen Jeffers, bm.

Jones, Emanuel & Abigail Bowden, 9 Nov 1847; James Bass, bm.

Jones, Francis & Agness Thompson, 9 Jan 1789; James Allen, bm.

Jones, Geo. W. & Denesha C. Johnston, m 29 Sept 1854 by James Phillips.

Jones, Hamilton & Eliza Jane Henderson, 10 July 1820; M. H. Horton, bm.

Jones, Henry & Sally Bingham, colored, 30 Sept 1865; Amos Thompson, bm.

Jones, Isaac & Elizabeth Whitesitt, 5 Sept 1814; Moses Whitsitt, bm.

Jones, Isaac & Catey Whitsett, 20 Dec 1821; David Nelson, bm.

Jones, Jacob & Nelly Uless, 22 Sept 1808; Frederic Kimry, bm.

Jones, James & Betsy Nelson, 25 May 1822; Thomas Day, bm.

Jones, James & Catharine Cheek, 5 July 1822; John Cheek, bm.

Jones, James & Elizabeth Smith, 23 Nov 1831; Merit Cheek, bm.

Jones, James & Cornelia Sykes, 5 Nov 1857; James Gill, bm; m 5 Nov 1857 by Ruffin R. Tapp, J. P.

Jones, James H. & Margret Kirkland, 15 March 1866; M. B. Jones, bm; m 15 March 1866 by James F. Miner, J. P.

Jones, James V. & Cornelia J. Cates, 13 Nov 1866; David M. Syks, bm; m 15 Nov 1866 by John C. Sykes.

Jones, John & Mary Horneday, 9 Nov 1803; Archid. Holmes, bm.

Jones, John & Mary Woods, 26 June 1810; John Woods, bm.

Jones, John & Peggy Moore, 25 Feb 1823; Samuel Kirkpatrick, bm.

Jones, John & Elizabeth Sloan, 1 June 1831; Henry Yarborough, W. A. Parish, bm.

Jones, John & Rebecca Jones, 9 April 1835; Johnson Jones, bm.

Jones, John & Evelina Stewart, colored, 23 Dec 1845; Jesse Whitmore, bm.

Jones, John, son of William & Rilla Jones, & Jane Barbee, dau. of Joseph & Candis Barbee m 24 Dec 1867 by J. P. Mason, minister.

Jones, Johnston & Nancy Ball, 28 Aug 1790; Richard Thompson, bm.

Jones, Jonathan & Sarah Hargess, 22 Nov 1811; Valentine Moore, bm.

Jones, Jonathan & Rebecca Chance, 4 Feb 1812; Miles Jones, Samuel Wilson, bm.

Jones, Jonathan & Martha Moore, 5 Oct 1826; Thomas Jones, bm.

Jones, Joshua & Manerva Jeffires, 10 Sept 1855; Thomas S. Shelton, bm.

Jones, Lewis & Mary Wilson, 31 May 1787; Reuben Smith, bm.

Jones, Lewis & Ellenor White, 15 Oct 1795; Richard Moore, bm.

Jones, Lewis & Susannah Jones, 29 May 1824; Farmer Smith, bm.

Jones, Lewis & Elizabeth Alexander, 13 Jan 1828; Thomas Isler, bm.

Jones, Lewis K. & Caroline Jane Rhodes, 20 Dec 1837; Isai Davis, Thomas Anderson, bm.

Jones, Manly B. & Mary Jane Miner, 18 Feb 1864; A. C. McDaniel, bm; m 12 Feb 1864 by Thos. D. Oldham, J. P.

Jones, Miles & Catey Chance, 19 Aug 1805; Richard Pickard, bm.

Jones, Moore & Jane Corn, 9 April 1860; Marcom A. Lyon, bm.

Jones, Moses & Nancy Crabtree, 28 Dec 1835; Kirkland Duke, James Vaughan, bm.

Jones, Nathaniel & Mary J. Hester, 28 Nov 1855; Stephen Hamhill, bm.

Jones, Peter, son of Isaac & Susan Jones, & Lizza Archey, dau. of Saml. Archey & Sally Gawen, colored, m 10 Sept 1867 by H. B. Pratt.

Jones, Pride Dr. & Martha A. Cain, 20 May 1850; R. Ap. C. Jones, bm.

Jones, Richard & Patsey Chance, 16 Aug 1811; Samuel Wilson, Alexander Ray Jr., bm.

Jones, Richd. & Elizabeth Martin, 17 Oct 1807; Henry Paris, bm.

Jones, Richard A. & Angeline F. Jacobs, 11 Jan 1866; Charles R. Wilson, bm; m 11 Jan 1866 by C. Wilson, J. P.

Jones, Rile & Franky Rose, 12 Nov 1828; Spencer Cole, bm.

Jones, Robert & Nancy Thomas, 9 Nov 1793; Thomas Carrington, bm.

Jones, Robert & Mary A. Clemons, 11 July 1865; John Laws, bm; m 12 July 1865 by A. B. Gunter, J. P.

Jones, Roman, son of William & Rilla Jones, & Eliza Morphus, dau. of Saml. & Lizza Morphus, m 19 Feb 1868 by Charles Phillips, minister.

Jones, Samuel & Patsey Morris, 7 Oct 1806; John Morris, bm.

Jones, Samuel & Elizabeth Jones, 2 Aug 1849; Geo. W. Tate, Jas. Gill, bm.

Jones, Samuel S. & Elizabeth Pettigrew, 3 April 1850; R. M. Jones, bm.

Jones, Seabron R. & Martha Jeffires, 6 Jan 1858; P. B. Sharp, bm.

Jones, Stephen Jr., son of Stephen & Writta Jones, & Frances Anderson, dau. of Pinkney & Patsy Anderson, colored, m 2 Jan 1867 by H. F. Pope, minister.

Jones, Sugars & Rebecca Nicholson, 9 Jan 1798; Edmund Green, bm.

Jones, Sylvester & Jeany Ray, 7 May 1807; Fowler Jones, bm.

Jones, Thomas & Margaret Marshel, 13 Nov 1797; Benjamin Roney, bm.

Jones, Thomas & Ceney Moore, 13 Oct 1827; J. Taylor, bm.

Jones, Thomas & Jane Birch, 21 Dec 1866; George Mayo, bm; m 24 Dec 1866 by D. W. Jordan, J. P.

Jones, Thomas H. & Edna H. Moize, 6 May 1864; Zachariah T. Hampton, bm.

Jones, Thomas J. & Eliza A. Forrest, 11 Sept 1855; David Freshwater, bm.

Jones, Thos. J. & Fanny E. Moris, 8 Oct 1866; Charles M. Parks, bm; m 9 Oct 1866 by Samuel Pearce.

Jones, Thomas T. & Martha Ann Sykes, 10 Nov 1859; James Gill, bm; m 10 Nov 1859 by Ruffin R. Tapp, J. P.

Jones, William F. & Elizabeth Freshwater, 8 Oct 1818; Thads. Freshwater, bm.

Jones, William H. & Fanny R. Hall, 8 July 1833; M. Terry, bm.

Jones, William M. & Martha A. Parrish, 24 March 1860; m 25 March 1860 by F. M. Jordan, minister.

Jones, Willie & Dellah Jeffers, 10 Nov 1815; Saml. Crawford, Elias Jeffers, bm.

Jones, Willie P. & Nancy Horner, 10 Nov 1835; Willie Horner, bm.

Jonston, Hirum & Elizabeth Thompson, 9 Oct 1826; A. H. Leoned, bm.

Jordan, Andrew M. & Mary Wheeley, 15 May 1865; James Porterfield, bm; m 27 Aug 1865 by D. W. Jordan, J. P.

Jordan, Charles & Elizabeth Garrison, 7 Sept 1807; Ross Hutcheson, bm.

Jordan, Francis M. & Susan D. Holeman, 17 Oct 1853; Richd. Nichols, bm.

Jordan, John & Jeany Hammonds, 13 Nov 1812; William Wilkinson, bm.

Jordan, Lambert M. & Martha Taylor, 19 Dec 1855; Thomas J. Taylor, bm; m 23 Dec 1855 by John L. Woods, J. P.

Jordan, Nathan & Eliza Jane Miller, 4 Aug 1842; Nathan Ellis, Allen Collins, bm.

Jordan, Thomas & Prudence Harguiss, 5 June 1783; Jas. Baldridge, bm.

Jordan, Thos. R. & Salley Wilkinson, 18 March 1840; Alexr. Dickson, bm.

Jordan, William & Elizabeth Hannah, 12 Oct 1808; Saml. McB___, bm.

Jordan, William B. & Elvira E. Harrell, 31 May 1860; W. G. Lewis, bm; m 31 May 1860 by Jas. A. Harrold, minister.

Jorden, George & Delia Ann Love, 1 April 1830; Jacob Hurdle, Jordan R. Hutcheson, bm.

Jorden, Samuel & Nancy Oneal, 4 May 1838; Green Richard, Pevi McCollum, bm.

Jordern, William H. & Mary F. Faucett, 21 Dec 1847; W. H. Horner, Murphy Waggoner, bm.

Jordon, Robert & Anne Pinkerton, 17 March 1794; William McCanless, bm.

Jurden, David W. & Susan Dickson, 5 March 1836; Wm. Dickson, bm.

Jurden, John & Polly McBroom, 3 April 1817; Joseph W. Allison, bm.

Jurden, William & Rachel Farmer, 29 May 1806; James Wilkinson, bm.

Justus, David & Salley Payne, 12 Sept 1804; Aron Combs, bm.

Kater, John & Ann Stuart, 10 Feb 1813; Wm. Heram, bm.

Keates, Thos. & Martha Trice, 24 Feb 1784; Wm. Vickers, bm.

Keck, George & Polly A. Freddle, 25 Nov 1847; Laben Freddle, bm.

Keck, Henry & Julia Ann Freddle, 12 Aug 1842; Alfred Sharp, bm.

Keck, John & Milly Troxler, 14 Jan 1812; John Mason, bm.

Kee, Elijah & Sarah Babb, 27 July 1795; Samuel Hunter, bm.

Keelan, Wm. & Mary Cook, 15 Aug 1800; John Baldridge, bm.

Keelin, Woodley & Lucretia Tudor, 22 Feb 1843; James W. Keeler, bm.

Keeling, Thomas & Sarah Gains, 7 Nov 1798; John Cole, bm.

Keeling, William & Polley McKee, 1 April 1808; R. Smith, bm.

Keeling, William & Polley Perry, 13 Jan 1809; Saml. Thomas, bm.

Keeling, William & Alley Coleman, 7 April 1810; D. Dunn, bm.

Keeling, William & Polley Davis, 5 May 1810; Franck Davis Sen., bm.

Kell, Alen & Betsey Miller, 14 Dec 1847; Hardy Hurdle, bm.

Kellor, Linard & Polley Gains, 2 Oct 1811; Samuel Thomas, bm.

Kellow, Thomas & Sarah Ireland, 1 Oct 1807; James Moore, bm.

Kelly, Atkins & Mary Tate, dau. of Julia Tate, m 22 Feb 1868 by C. E. Smith, J. P.

Kelly, George, son of Austin & Harriett Kelly, & Harriett Carlton, dau. of Reuben & Mary Carlton, colored, m 11 Aug 1867 by C. G. Markham, J. P.

Kelly, George B. & Margret Lewter, 7 Dec 1833; Jarvis Lewter, Zachariah Trice, bm.

Kelly, John & Margaret Hutchinson, 26 May 1785; James Anderson, bm.

Kelly, Jones & Nancy Fennel, 27 Aug 1811; Edward Riggin, bm.

Kely, Henry & Josephine Masey, 22 Dec 1859; Hilary Sparrow, bm; m 22 Dec 1859 by J. W. Carr, J. P.

Kemrie, Paul & Elizabeth Euless, 22 July 1818; George Kemrie, bm.

Kemry, John & Elizabeth Rivers, 7 June 1814; Jeremiah Holt, bm.

Kenan, William R. & Mollie V. Hargrave, 25 March 1864; J. R. Shepard, bm; m 25 March 1864 by N. W. Wilson.

Kenion, Joseph & Sarah Smith, 18 Dec 1801; Thos Wynn, bm.

Kennedy, John & Elizabeth Sloss, 13 Aug 1793; Jos. Sloss, bm.

Kennedy, Jonathan & Delilah Lovine, 8 Dec 1805; John Rhodes, bm.

Kerkpatrik, Paisley & Elizabeth Allen, 12 March 1833; John N. Allen, bm.

Kernodle, Benjamin & Uzzy Starkes, 17 Nov 1817; Caleb Busick, bm.

Kernodle, George & Mary Waynach, 5 Dec 1848; Lewis J. Apple, bm.

Kerr, David W. & Martha J. Johnston, 14 Oct 1848; Wm. J. Long, bm.

Kerr, James & Nancy Ross, 27 Sept 1810; Andw. Mitchell, bm.

Kerr, Samuel & Mary White, 16 Sept 1818; Wm. Huntington, bm.

Kerr, William & Catey Ross, 10 Nov 1804; James Kerr, bm.

Kerr, William & Margarett Craig, 2 March 1827; James Mebane, bm.

Kerrell, Michael & Nancy Prichett, 6 Dec 1816; John Williams, bm.

Ketes, Hartwell & McKey Hicks, 15 Dec 1824; Dickerson Cain, bm.

Kilgrow, William & Catharine Grisham, 28 June 1841; W. H. Pratt, Moses Leathers Jr., bm.

Kilgrow, Wm. & Sarah Cole, 15 Sept 1860; Isaiah P. Markham, bm; m 16 Sept 1860 by Solomon Shepherd.

Killion, Levi & Alse Griffy, 26 Sept 1814; William Barbe, bm.

Kilpatrick, Alexander & Francis Clendennon, 1 Jan 1795; Moses Cox, bm.

Kimboro, George & Rachel Holt, 24 July 1801; Adam Long, bm.

Kimbre, George & Delilah Graves, 23 May 1840; Levi Greaves, bm.

Kimbro, Frederic & Turley Friddle, 19 Nov 1808; John Lue, bm.

Kimbro, Peter & Barbara Coble, 22 June 1818; George Kimbro, bm.

Kimbro, William & Milley Euliss, 15 Oct 1841; Hiram Euliss, bm.

Kimbrogh, Andrew & Catharine Bird, 24 July 1801; Robert Ray, bm.

Kimbrough, James & Elizabeth Ray, 18 Feb 1829; Thomas Sawyer, bm.

Kimbrough, James W. & Elemina Kimbrough, 10 Oct 1856; Thomas T. Warren, bm.

Kimbrough, Jeremiah & Eliza Burrow, 11 July 1795; Joshua Holt, bm.

Kimbrough, Stanford & Elizabeth Staley, 22 Feb 1841; William Kimery, bm.

Kimbrow, Federick & Elizabeth Iseley, 11 Dec 1813; Malicay Isley, bm.

Kimbul, Lewis & Margret Marcom, 17 Nov 1831; Henry S. Marcom, bm.

Kimery, Peter & Mary Chapel, 28 May 1822; George Curtner, bm.

Kimrey, John & Barbara Coble, 3 March 1829; E. Euliss, bm.

Kimrey, Roddy C. & Joanah Staly, 9 Jan 1848; Emsly Elliett, bm.

Kimrie, Jacob & Elizabeth Alexander, 3 Jan 1816; Paul Kemrie, bm.

Kimol, John & Peggy Hogon, 11 June 1794; Saml. Hopkins, bm.

Kincey, Wm. C. & Julia F. Cox, 12 March 1864; James E. Berry, bm; m 15 March 1864 by A. W. Mangum, minister.

Kinchen, John & Margaret Carver, 24 Sept 1788.

Kiney, Mebane & Mary Councilman, 22 March 1849; Jackson Beard, bm.

King, A. J. & Catherine Stroud, 7 June 1861; J. B. Adams, bm;
m 13 June 1861 by Charles W. Johnston, J. P.

King, Alves & Mary Ann Fossett, 29 May 1838; E. T. Watson, bm.

King, Alvis & Elizabeth J. McCulloch, 21 May 1853; Wm. Nelson,
bm.

King, Anderson & Kitty Barnhill, 13 Nov 1817; Wm. Turner,
Joseph Woods, bm.

King, Andrew & Hannah Gaddis, 16 July 1804; Isaac Gattis, bm.

King, Armour & Lucy Horner, 2 June 1809; Samuel King, bm.

King, Austin R. & Susan McCory, 26 Feb 1827; John S. Painey, bm.

King, Baxter & Lilah Davis, 7 Feb 1809; Nathl. King, bm.

King, Benjamin & Sarah Wallace, 18 March 1819; Robert Faust,
Decly Farley, bm.

King, Brewer & Rhodah Ashley, 27 Nov 1815; Leonard Laws, bm.

King, Charles & Milley Sparrow, 23 Oct 1830; Fieldin Strowd,
bm.

King, Charles & Tabitha Stroud, 5 Jan 1837; William Bowers, bm.

King, Charles & Tabitha Lloyd, 17 Dec 1837; B. Cheek, bm.

King, Dickson & Fanny Brewer, 13 Jan 1821; John Faddis Jr., bm.

King, Edward & Elizabeth Hart, 1 May 1815; Anderson King,
John Willis, bm.

King, Garrison & Sarah Cook, 16 May 1815; Henry King, bm.

King, Haywood & Catharine Bird, 27 Dec 1837; Joseph King, Alvis
King, bm.

King, Henry & Hannah Cook, 27 March 1810; Saml. King, bm.

King, Hilmon B. & Mary M. Miner, 29 Nov 1849; William J.
Feeland, bm.

King, James & Viney Garrison, 15 Nov 1810; David Davison, bm.

King, James & Winefred Collins, 12 Feb 1830; A. Blackwood, bm.

King, John & Patsy Herndon, 17 Dec 1800; Chas. King, bm.

King, John & Elizabeth Walker, 7 May 1803; Jno. Taylor, bm.

King, John & Rebbecca Mebane, 13 Aug 1805; David Davison, bm.

King, John & Patsey McCauley, 15 Jan 1809; John Watson, bm.

King, John & Mariah Sledge, 2 Jan 1832; Henry Sledge, bm.

King, John & Margarett Lloyed, 24 Aug 1848; Julian N. Price, bm.

King, Matthew & Nancy Lloyd, 8 May 1836; Edwin Blackwood, James
Culbertson, bm.

King, Moris & Cornelia Lloyd, 31 Aug 1850; Matthew McCauley, bm.

King, Morris, son of Charles & Tabitha King, & Emma Lloyd, dau. of Jackson & Mary A. Lloyd, m 9 Feb 1868 by Manly Andrews.

King, Nathanel & Alice Foster, 11 July 1807; James Moore, bm.

King, Nathaniel & Anne Kirkland, 4 May 1807; Joseph Kirkland, bm.

King, Nathaniel & Nancy Caroline Bolden, 21 Dec 1850; Josiah Danses, bm.

King, Nathl. & Sarah Gattis, 2 Aug 1800; Alexander Gattis, bm.

King, Nathaniel J. & Polley Heron, 23 May 1822; N. H. Horton, bm.

King, Samuel & Polley Bason, 6 March 1800; Samuel King, bm.

King, Samuel & Rebecca Davison, 20 March 1800; David Davison, bm.

King, Samuel & Jeaney Stanford, 15 June 1801; John King, bm.

King, Samuel & Sarah Harris, 6 May 1818; F. Nash, bm.

King, Smith & Ester Bodine, 28 Oct 1787; Patrick Duffey, bm.

King, Thomas & Betsey Brown, 26 Feb 1821; John Ashly, bm.

King, Thomas & Betsey Johnston, 16 May 1828; Nathaniel King, bm.

King, Turner & Mary Potts, 14 Oct 1842; John Richerson, bm.

King, Washington & Eliza Cates, 23 Nov 1841; Robert Hall Jr., bm.

King, William & Sopha Davis, 7 April 1800; Harwell Whitmore, bm.

King, William & Susannah Mason, 3 July 1813; Baxter King, bm.

King, William & Catharine McCauley, 8 Nov 1825; Matthew McCauley, bm.

King, William & Faney Fonville, 20 Jan 1847; Joseph Wyatt, bm.

King, William & Zilphey Shaw, 9 March 1847; Wesley Durham, bm.

King, William & Caroline Wilkerson, 31 Dec 1853; James A. Forrest, S. H. Breeze, bm; m 2 Jan 1856 by Thos. Lynch, minister.

King, William D. & Esspran Neville, 11 Aug 1865; Levan Carmikle, bm; m 17 Aug 1865 by Thos. Long, J. P.

King, William H. & Nancy Davis, 12 Nov 1861; Presley J. Mangum, bm; m 12 Nov 1861 by Ralph F. Morris, J. P.

King, Willis & Martha Whittaker, 24 Dec 1844; Robert Blackwood, N. D. Bain, bm.

Kinion, Joseph S. & Fanny V. C. Redding, 16 Jan 1866; John Cheek, bm; m 18 Jan 1866 by F. M. Jordan, minister.

Kinion, Lawrence & Eliza Reding, 26 Aug 1851; Harrell Hurdle, bm; m 28 Aug 1851 by Archibald Currie, minister.

Kinney, David & Susannah Cortner, 15 Sept 1802; Nathan Horneday, bm.

Kinnin, Larence & Ann Sharp, 28 July 1783; John Roberts, bm.

Kinnion, John C. & Sarah C. Freeland, 23 June 1850; Josiah Guess, bm.

Kinnion, Paul & Maria Shaw, 18 Feb 1813; Saml. Webb, bm.

Kirby, Edward, son of Thomas & Judith Kirby, & Annette Smith, dau. of Hariett Smith, colored, m 18 March 1868 by Charles Phillips, minister.

Kirby, Wiley & Celah Nevill, 29 Jan 1810; Jesse Nevill Jur., bm.

Kirby, William & Ellen Richmond, 28 April 1866; James Turner, bm; m 28 April 1866 by A. C. Murdock, J. P.

Kirk, Elisha & Elizabeth Dorman, 24 May 1802; Levi Jones, bm.

Kirk, Franklin & Elizabeth ODaniel, 5 Oct 1829; Green ODaniel, bm.

Kirk, James & Goodwin Nevils, 12 Dec 1785; Will Kirk, bm.

Kirk, John & Nancy Jones, 15 March 1850; Eaton Walker, bm.

Kirk, John & Martha Reeves, 30 July 1856; John E. Cates, J. Turner, bm.

Kirk, Thomas & Peggy Smith, 14 June 1813; _____, bm.

Kirk, Thomas & Tabitha Reeves, 28 Nov 1817; Ila. J. Durham, bm.

Kirkland, Alexander & Anne Cameron, 26 Feb 1835; Jno. Cameron, Pride Jones, bm.

Kirkland, David & Anne M. Carrell, 24 July 1832; Sidney Carrell, bm.

Kirkland, John & Nancy W. Prichard, 15 Nov 1841; Archy McCauly, Jno. M. Faucett, bm.

Kirkland, John & Mary Jane Strayhorn, 16 Dec 1851; Joseph Kirkland, bm; m 18 Dec 1851 by James Phillips, minister.

Kirkland, Joseph & Isbel Craig, 11 Jan 1808; Samuel Craig, bm.

Kirkland, Joseph & Julia A. Blackwood, 22 Dec 1860; Samuel Kirkland, bm; m 27 Dec 1860 by James Phillips, D. D.

Kirkland, Nelson, son of Benj. & Jane Kirkland, & Hellen Hogan, dau. of Alexr. & Eliza Hogan, m 18 July 1867 by W. F. Strayhorn, J. P.

Kirkland, Samuel & Mary Strain, 18 Aug 1832; John Strain, Matthew McCauly, bm.

Kirkland, Samuel & Myraw Davis, 11 Aug 1840; Samuel D. Strain, bm.

Kirkland, Samuel & Martha Craig, 17 March 1853; Joseph Kirkland, bm; m 24 March 1853 by James Phillips, Minister.

Kirkland, Samuel C. & Lucy Hogan, 3 March 1847; John W. Potts, bm.

Kirkland, Stephen & Eliza Ann Jane Day, 1 March 1866; J. A. Utley, bm; m 1 March 1866 by Alexander Bass, Elder A. M. E. Church.

Kirkland, Wil & Margaret B. Scott, 24 Dec 1792; John Allison, bm.

Kirkland, William & Elizabeth Craig, 28 Oct 1800; David Strain, bm.

Kirkland, William & Sarah Strayhorn, 5 March 1839; David Hart, bm.

Kirkland, William & Elizabeth Jane Craig, 19 Nov 1853; Samuel Kirkland, bm; m 24 Nov 1853 by James Phillips, V. D. M.

Kirkpatrick, Allexander & Fanny Dixon, 19 March 1824; Saml. Kirkpatrick, bm.

Kirkpatrick, David N. & Susan T. Bain, 21 Nov 1860; H. R. Forbis, bm; m 22 Nov 1860 by Archibald Currie, minister.

Kirkpatrick, Hinton & Synthia Ann Freeland, 9 March 1846; Henry Albright, bm.

Kirkpatrick, Hugh & Nancy Johnston, 20 Sept 1830; Joseph Kirkpatrick, bm.

Kirkpatrick, Hugh & Rosanna Jones, 18 Sept 1858; Nicholas G. Holmes, David Moore, bm; m 26 Sept 1858 by Wm. J. Ogburn.

Kirkpatrick, John & Ann Clendennen, 12 Jan 1793; Wm. Vastine, bm.

Kirkpatrick, John & Anne Clendenin, 5 Sept 1818; Joseph Clendenin, bm.

Kirkpatrick, Samuel & Hannah Woods, 25 Dec 1789; Samuel Allen Junr., bm.

Kirkpatrick, Samuel & Jane Currie, 6 Nov 1824; William Kirkpatrick, bm.

Kirkpatrick, Samuel S. & Rachel S. Miller, 25 Nov 1858; Wm. J. Freeland, bm; m 25 Nov by Ruffin R. Tapp, J. P.

Kirkpatrick, William & Nancy Jordon, 30 April 1828; Joseph Kirkpatrick, bm.

Knight, John & Mary Carrington, 17 Nov 1792; Jno. Whitehead, bm.

Knox, Reuben & Eliza Grist, 21 July 1840; Ed. Benson, Alex. C. Blount, bm.

Lacey, Philemon & Franky Durham, 3 March 1804; Ephraim Cates, bm.

Lack, John P. & Harriet Adams, 2 July 1855; M. Adams, Thos. J. Strayhorn, bm; m 2 July 1855 by H. T. Hudson.

Lackey, Alexander & Mary Dunlapp, 2 Feb 1795; John Dunavin, Samuel Thompson, bm.

Lackey, James & Hannah Wason, 14 Jan 1799; Daniel Wason, bm.

Lacock, Timothy & Polley Warren, 29 Aug 1811; M. Guess, bm.

Lacock, William & Salley Warren, 8 April 1806; Moses Guess, bm.

Ladd, Solomon & Caroline C. Wilkins, 13 Oct 1865; John Ladd, bm.

Lafferty, Vance & Elender Parck, 26 Nov 1804; Leonard Barroz, bm.

Lamb, Josiah & Priscillah Pyke, 27 Dec 1814; Isaac Marshall, bm.

Lamb, Richard & Jane Hatwood, 30 Sept 1794; Benjamin Lamb, bm.

Lamb, William & Andrine Eastridge, 14 March 1846; Andrew Eastridge, bm.

Lambeth, John & Sarah Burch, 20 Nov 1794; Thomas Hogan, bm.

Lambeth, Thos. & Mary Herndon, 24 Sept 1824; Edmd. Herndon, bm.

Lampkin, Charles & Hannah Greene, 11 Nov 1817; Richard Roberts, bm.

Lancaster, James W. & Julia M. Scott, 10 June 1847; Thos. Howerton, bm.

Landen, James & Patsey Ellis, 27 Feb 1804; Luke Dishon, bm.

Lane, Abner & Polly Sullenger, 11 Nov 1837; Wm. Artz, bm.

Laseter, James & Martha Auldredge, 23 Dec 1846; John Simpson, bm.

Lashley, Alexander & Anne Jones, 8 Dec 1812; Richard Pickall, bm.

Lashley, Alexander & Sidey Hicks, 16 Jan 1842; Thomas Thompson, bm.

Lashley, Alexander & Mary Fowler, 15 Jan 1848; Mark Fowler, John D. Willies, bm.

Lashley, Barney & Charlotte Jones, 5 July 1830; S. R. Woods, bm.

Lashley, David & Cinthy Crutchfield, 24 Nov 1846; John Odanel, bm.

Lashley, Franklin & Lydia C. Borland, 12 Jan 1866; Demetris C. Gunter, bm; m 14 Jan 1866 by Thos. Long, J. P.

Lashley, Isaac & Mary Toler, 29 May 1838; Eli Murray, M. H. Turner, bm.

Lashley, James & Ruth Holliday, 5 Aug 1817; James Smith, bm.

Lashley, Johnson & Mary Cate, 29 April 1848; A. Mickle, bm.

Lashley, Johnston & Sylvia Cate, 23 May 1854; Wiatt Cates, bm;
m 14 June 1854 by Wiatt Cate, J. P.

Lashley, Sidney M. & Martilia Durham, 13 Feb 1867; m 14 Feb
1867 by Alvis Durham, J. P.

Lashley, William & Martha Jones, 6 April 1831; Barney Lashley,
Wm. J. Duke, bm.

Lashley, William & Nancy Bason, 5 March 1836; Barnabas Lashley,
Levi McCollum, bm.

Lashley, William & Sarah Creedle, 31 March 1838; Barnard C.
Hayes, bm.

Lashley, William M. & Mary Pendergrass, 11 Oct 1838; Andrew J.
Pendergrass, James Lashley, bm.

Lasley, Henry & Cornelia Thompson, colored, 2 May 1866; John
Turner, bm.

Lasley, James H. & Sarah Edwards, 29 Dec 1848; Hugh Edwards, bm.

Lasley, John & Elizabeth Smith, 28 Aug 1847; Franklin Smith, bm.

Lasley, Sidney M. & Martilia Durham, 13 Feb 1867; John R.
Hancock; m 14 Feb 1867 by Alvis Durham, J. P.

Lasley, Thomas A. & Sarah Ann Durham, 8 Oct 1859; James Morris,
m 9 Oct 1859 by Allen Edwards, J. P.

Lasley, William & Celia Whiteheight, 12 Dec 1803; Willey
Whiteheight, bm.

Lasley, William H. & Sarah H. Moore, 23 April 1846; H. C.
Strowd, bm.

Lasly, Isaack & Mary Mebane, 4 Nov 1811; William Lasley, bm.

Laster, William & Parmelia Cooke, 31 Nov 1846; Wm. Thomas, bm.

Latham, Thos. J. & Cathleen Stevenson, 23 Jan 1865; Richd. N.
Taylor, M. A. Angier, bm; m 31 Jan 1865 by N. W. Wilson.

Latta, Duncan, son of James & Letty Latta, & Martha Phillips,
dau. of Rachail Johnson, m 25 May 1867 by Charles Phillips,
minister.

Latta, Henderson & Anne Rhew, 6 Nov 1834; Wm. Nelson, bm.

Latta, James & Nancy Allen, 24 Aug 1790; Jno. Cain, bm.

Latta, James & Elizabeth Dunlap, 21 April 1798; Alexander
Lackey, bm.

Latta, James & Patsy Moore, 27 June 1804; George Moore, bm.

Latta, James & Polly Scarlett, 18 Oct 1804; Jno. Piper, bm.

Latta, James & Hannah Holloway, 8 Oct 1806; John Latta, bm.

Latta, James & Winnie Veazey, 21 April 1865; William Latta, bm.

Latta, James C. & Sarah Thompson, 21 Sept 1845; James Hobbs, bm.

Latta, John & Sarah May, 10 June 1804; John Latta, bm.

Latta, John & Sarah Scarlett, 26 Aug 1806; James Latta, bm.

Latta, Jno. & Nancy Cabe, 8 Dec 1812; Joseph Latta, bm.

Latta, John & Maria Burton, 16 Dec 1835; Thomas Latta, bm.

Latta, Joseph & Sarah Cabe, 22 Jan 1810; John Latta, bm.

Latta, Joseph H. & Sarah Chambers, 25 Sept 1816; James Freeland, bm.

Latta, Joseph S. & Susan M. Turner, 9 Nov 1854; John W. Latta, bm; m 9 Nov 1854 by Daniel W. Thompson.

Latta, Priestly & Mary Ashley, 13 July 1859; William Ellis, bm; m 15 July 1859 by Wm. J. Roberts, J. P.

Latta, Richard & Allice Craig, 27 Jan 1866; Dick Webb, bm.

Latta, Robert & Nancy Rily, 29 June 1827; William Tilly, bm.

Latta, Simpson & Hawkins Malone, 2 Feb 1843; David Turner, bm.

Latta, Simpson & Hawkins Alston, 1 March 1852; Jno. A. McManus, bm; m 3 March 1852 by Wm. McCown, J. P.

Latta, Solomon & Elizabeth Wilson, 16 Aug 1814; Tyree Garrard, bm.

Latta, Thomas & Elizabeth Haisting, 25 Oct 1791; John Latta, bm.

Latta, Thos. & Polley Moore, 4 Oct 1803; John Moore, bm.

Latta, Thomas & Janey Scarlett, 28 Aug 1810; James Latta, bm.

Latta, Thomas & Nancy Roberts, 6 March 1822; A. Moore, bm.

Latta, Thomas J. & Elizabeth Crabtree, 20 Nov 1837; Solomon Latta, bm.

Latta, William & Margarett Hicks, 31 Jan 1856; William Warren, bm.

Latta, William G. & Sarah Jane Boroughs, 5 Feb 1861; Geo. M. Pratt, bm; m 7 Feb 1861 by John Mitchell.

Latta, William R., son of Thomas J. & Elizabeth Latta, & Rachel H. Jackson, dau. of Abel & Elizabeth Jackson, m 17 Nov 1867 by A. M. Latta, J. P.

Laughorn, Thomas & Nancy Brinkly, 23 Aug 1796; James Cozard, bm.

Laurence, John & Mary Lumley, 18 March 1848; John D. Ellis, bm.

Laws, Alexander E. & Mary A. McFarlin, 6 Nov 1866; Charles Harris, J. M. Blackwood, bm; m 11 Nov 1866 by J. W. McKee, J. P.

Laws, Ezekiel & Peggy Riggs, 2 March 1801; Jacob Pickle, bm.

Laws, George & Sarah Carpenter, 4 May 1801; Isaac Carpenter, A. B. Bruce, bm.

Laws, George & Peggy Horton, 5 Oct 1803; William Madison, bm.

Laws, George & Polly Pritchett, 6 Oct 1821; William P. Clancey, bm.

Laws, George R. & Durriney Waller, 14 Feb 1833; Charley Haris, bm.

Laws, Guilford & Nancy M. Mangum, 22 Nov 1865; Sampson M. Glenn, bm; m 23 Nov 1865 by Joseph W. McKee, J. P.

Laws, Harmon & Dicey Smith, 8 Oct 1836; Leonard Gates, Jesse Miller, bm.

Laws, Hiram & Jynsey Sims, 20 Feb 1827; Jas. P. Laws, bm.

Laws, Isaac & Louisa Neely, 12 Feb 1838; Jas. Sneed, bm.

Laws, James P. & Manerva A. Leathers, 25 April 1827; John Laws, bm.

Laws, John & Mary McCollum, 30 July 1846; Jno. D. Carlton, bm.

Laws, Leonard & Nancy Woods, 1 March 1804; Sterling Harris, bm.

Laws, Leonard & Elizabeth Leathers, 23 Feb 1805; John Waggoner, bm.

Laws, Leonard & Nancy Ray, 4 Dec 1854; Cyrus Laws, George W. Bruce, bm; m 5 Dec 1854 by Hezekiah H. Terry, J. P.

Laws, Robert & Mary Evens Brown, 21 Jan 1850; Leonard Laws, bm.

Laws, Robert & Mary Ann Ray, 18 Jan 1861; Leonard Laws, J. W. Norwood, bm; m 22 Jan 1861 by H. Terry, J. P.

Laws, Thomas & Jenney Riggs, 17 Aug 1799; George Laws, bm.

Laws, Thomas W. & Carolina Mangum, 19 Jan 1850; Wm. L. Moore, bm.

Lawson, James & Catharine Waggoner, 25 May 1793; John Waggoner, bm.

Lawson, James & Judah Parker, 24 Aug 1804; B. Burnside, bm.

Laycock, Britton & Mary Pearson, 24 Aug 1841; M. C. Herndon, bm.

Laycock, David W. & Sarah Chambley, 29 Jan 1829; Alfred Chamley, bm.

Laycock, James E. & Elizabeth Carden, 16 May 1854; William Carden, Thos. J. Strayhorn, bm.

Laycock, Joseph & Patsey Cardin, 25 Feb 1817; Joseph Proctor, Joseph A. Woods, bm.

Laycock, Joseph & Elizabeth Scarlett, 30 Dec 1820; John Scarlett, bm.

Laycock, Martin & Ester Laycock, 13 Jan 1826; Joseph Laycock, bm.

Laycock, Thomas & Elleanor Towsley, 15 April 1786; Lazarus Cate, bm.

Laycock, Thomas & Polly Carden, 7 March 1809; Jones Cardin, bm.

Lea, James & Peggy McCullock, 16 April 1842; Barney Lashley, Thomas Bradshaw, bm.

Lea, William A. Jr. & Nancy M. Terry, 20 Dec 1855; A. M. Breeze, bm; m 23 Dec 1855 by H. Terry, J. P.

Leach, Martin W. & Sallie A. Mangum, 17 Nov 1851; Thos. H. Turner, bm; m 18 Nov 1851 by J. B. Donnelly, minister.

Leak, James & Margaret Green, 3 Dec 1866; Allen A. Nancy, bm.

Leaman, David & Elizabeth Jolley, 28 May 1795; Jacob Leaman, bm.

Leath, Freeman Jr. & Martha Ann Ector, 9 Dec 1845; William S. Tate, bm.

Leath, James & Rachel Pond, 14 Oct 1813; Calvin M. Leth, bm.

Leathers, Alsey M. & Lucy L. Garrard, 9 Dec 1865; Thomas L. Cooley, bm; m 12 Dec 1865 by A. M. Mangum, bm.

Leathers, Daniel F., son of Henry & Betty Leathers, & Mary Webb, dau. of Jack Glen, colored, m 13 Sept 1867 by A. M. Latta, J. P.

Leathers, Fielding S. & Louisa M. Parish, 15 Dec 1866; Nathl. D. Harris, W. S. Guthrie, bm; m 18 Dec 1866 by A. W. Mangum, minister.

Leathers, James & Elizabeth Forrester, 12 Nov 1803; Willis Benfield, bm.

Leathers, John & Fanny Holloway, 9 Dec 1828; Js. H. Carrington, bm.

Leathers, John & Parthenia Armstrong, 20 Sept 1838; John Hancock, J. Taylor, bm.

Leathers, John & Ann Strowd, 6 Oct 1865; S. H. Johnson, bm; m 10 Dec 1865 by B. C. Hopkins, J. P.

Leathers, John & Frances Nichols, 31 March 1867; Major Hall, bm; m 31 March 1867 by Lambert W. Hall, J. P.

Leathers, Kenchen & Milley Holaway, 2 Dec 1848; Benton Ray, bm.

Leathers, Kinchen & Emiline Mangum, 3 Jan 1843; D. F. Parker, Benton Ray, bm.

Leathers, Moses & Polley Dunnagan, 20 Jan 1815; John Ray, bm.

Leathers, Moses & Polley Duke, 28 July 1820; S. Dunnagin, bm.

Leathers, Moses & Jeney Ray, 11 April 1848; Wm. McCown, James Holloway, bm.

Leathers, Moses & Margaret Sutton, 27 July 1866; Benton Ray, bm.

Leathers, Walker & Martha H. Mason, colored, m 20 Oct 1867 by Thos. J. Fowler, bm.

Leathers, William & Levinia Ray, 15 Feb 1837; William Link, James Holloway, bm.

Ledbetter, Benjamin & Nancy Incore, 8 Oct 1816; Owen Tudor, bm.

Lee, Gabriel B. & Mary McCauley, 10 June 1817; John Van Hook, bm.

Lee, John & Mary Bevill, 6 Dec 1824; Z. G. Burch, bm.

Lee, John T. & Louisa Mangum, 17 Jan 1860; Joseph Garard, James L. Garrard, bm.

Lee, Richd. H. & Anne Clark, 25 Oct 1838; A. Parks, bm.

Lee, Thomas W. & Hawkins Green, 13 March 1859; A. B. Gunter, Thoms B. Hopson, bm; m 13 March 1859 by A. B. Gunter, J. P.

Lee, William & Sarah Morrow, 6 June 1782; John Nichols, bm.

Lee, Willis & Ruth Lindsey, 19 May 1800; Henry Edwards, bm.

Leigh, Absalom & Francis Watkins, 9 June 1843; Hewel Whealy, James R. Brown, bm.

Leigh, Anderson N., son of R. S. & Nancy Leigh, & Leantine R. Pope, dua. of Erasmus & Frances Pope, m 4 Aug 1867 by R. F. Morris, J. P.

Leigh, Bird & Sarah Crompton, 6 Nov 1809; Henry Shutt, bm.

Leigh, Jack B. & Rachel Gray, 10 Dec 1798; Wm. Marcome, bm.

Leigh, John & Cata Watts, 14 Sept 1787; John Bryant, bm.

Leigh, John W. & Sarah A. E. Couch, 4 Jan 1866; Wm. H. Atkins, bm; m 18 Jan 1866 by John Burroughs, J. P.

Leigh, Reaves & Dolley Morgan, 11 Aug 1829; Benjamin Ludbetter, bm.

Leigh, Richard S. Ann Carlton, 10 July 1834; Spencer Leigh, bm.

Leigh, Richard S. & Leathy H. Hudgins, 4 May 1864; Daniel C. McDade, bm; m 5 May 1864 by J. P. Mason, minister.

Leigh, Samuel & Elizabeth Guilliam, 14 July 1801; James McMullin, bm.

Leigh, Spencer & Fanny Davis, 28 Aug 1828; Emel Leigh, bm.

Leigh, Spencer & Salley ___, 10 Oct 1833; R. S. Leigh, bm.

Leigh, Sulivan & Mary Lambeth, 1 Oct 1842; S. W. Fowler, Moses Leather Jur., bm.

Leigh, Sullivan & Nancy Shepperd, 27 March 1809; J. Taylor, bm.

Leigh, Sullivan & Catharine Clifton, 13 Nov 1828; J. Taylor, bm.

Leigh, Thomas J. & Hannah Herndon, 10 Jan 1838; S. Strayhorn, bm.

Leigh, Uel & Elizabeth Stubbins, 10 April 1828; Robert B. Pleasants, bm.

Leigh, Washington & Polley Trice, 30 Dec 1801; Wil Kirkland, bm.

Leigh, William & Sally Bevill, 28 July 1820; John Bevill, bm.

Leigh, William & ____, 7 June 1838; Chesley P. Grice, Tho. Anderson, bm.

Leigh, Wm. & Mary George, 26 Nov 1838; Fisher Clendenin, bm.

Lemley, Jesse & Salley Farthing, 20 Dec 1814; John Evans, bm.

Lemmon, Jacob & Anne Clark, 2 Feb 1786; Robt. Ferguson, bm.

Lemmon, Jacob & Eleanor Lockhart, 21 Sept 1816; James Clancy, bm.

Lemmon, Hardy & Mary Bailey, 8 Oct 1836; C. L. Cooley, bm.

Leonard, Micajah & Rachel Morgan, 7 Sept 1831; Isaac Holden, Samuel Scarlett, bm.

Lester, William & Patsy Fennell, 27 May 1806; John Bragg, bm.

Leuter, James C. & Nancy McCallum, 4 Oct 1866; Wm. R. Franklin, bm; m 4 Oct 1866 by J. P. Mason, minister.

Levins, Richard & Polly Greeson, 13 Feb 1838; Abram Long, bm.

Lewelling, Eligah & Anne M. L. Phillips, 22 Nov 1831; Allen Parks, bm.

Lewis, Abraham & Polly Simpson, 27 Aug 1821; Benjamin Simpson, bm.

Lewis, Fielding & Nancy Wood, 23 Feb 1798; Abner Veazey, bm.

Lewis, Henry & Alice Martin, 23 Sept 1800; John Rhodes, bm.

Lewis, Jas. & Molley Dudley, 27 April 1802; S. Benton, bm.

Lewis, James D. & Mary Dollar, 29 April 1858; Thomas Cole, F. Nash Jr., bm; m 1 May 1858 by John F. Lyon, J. P.

Lewis, Jesse & Hannah Cole, 13 Dec 1827; Levi Cole, bm.

Lewis, Jesse & Thena Garrard, 18 Aug 1831; Saml. Piper, bm.

Lewis, John & Elizabeth Manor, 20 Nov 1824; Archd. Crabtree, bm.

Lewis, John & Elizabeth Manor, 28 Nov 1824; Samuel Cloud, bm.

Lewis, John & Susan C. Roberson, m 5 April 1857; by John J. Roberson, J. P.

Lewis, John Comer & Nancy Forrest, 8 April 1802; John Rhodes, bm.

Lewis, Joseph & Susanah Durham, 20 Jan 1789; John McRae, bm.

Lewis, Owin & Elizabeth King, 17 Dec 1830; J. Lewis, bm.

Lewis, Robert & Patsey Griffin, 20 March 1817; Thomas Griffin, bm.

Lewis, Robert & Patsey Griffin, 25 March 1817; Ezra Cates, bm.

Lewis, William & Fanny Lynch, 16 Oct 1799; John Lynch, bm.

Lewis, William & Susanna Crutchfield, 4 Nov 1847; Irvin Lewis, bm.

Lewis, Zachariah & Rachel Bracken, 18 July 1796; Solomon Stalcup, bm.

Lewter, Charles M. (soldier) & Tulea H. Cheek, dau. of Ruffin Cheek, 25 June 1863; Manly B. Guess, bm; m 25 June 1863 by J. B. McDade, J. P.

Lewter, Hiram & Sally K. White, 23 Aug 1863; Foster Utley, bm.

Lewter, James & Salley Carlton, 10 Feb 1834; Patrick H. Moring, bm.

Lilley, Robert & Mary Denning, 19 March 1782; John Moody, bm.

Lils, William & Elizabeth Brister, 10 Dec 1821; William Brister, bm.

Linch, James & Jeane Hutcheson, 1 Nov 1791; James Hutcheson Jr., bm.

Linch, John & Ritta Bennett, 11 Sept 1808; Obadiah Harlow, bm.

Linch, Jonas & Anne Atkinson, 6 March 1799; Henry Holaday, bm.

Linch, Maridith & Lucretia Hailey, 24 Nov 1852; John W. Cardin, bm; m 24 Nov 1852 by Wm. Lipscomb, J. P.

Lindley, James & Susanah Stout, 12 Feb 1797; James Massy, bm.

Lindley, Joshua & Ritta Marshbourn, 19 Aug 1797; William Moore, bm.

Lindly, Thomas & Mariam Jones, 14 March 1795; John Workman, bm.

Lindly, Zachariah & Ann Braxton, 6 Jan 1798; Samuel Lindly, bm.

Lindsay, Atha & Sarah Loyd, 19 Nov 1792; Isaac Morris, bm.

Lindsay, Henry & Isabella Hannah, 11 Aug 1834; James M. Palmer, bm.

Lindsay, Stephen & Sally Snipes, 7 Jan 1826; John L. Woods, bm.

Lindsay, William R. D. & Lydia M. Hogg, 20 Oct 1830; Geo. C. Mendenhall, bm.

Lindsey, Adam P. & Elizabeth Edge, 13 March 1802; William Mearson, bm.

Lindsey, Alvis & Mary Loyed, 29 Oct 1846; Wm. A. Lindsey, Ephraim Cabe, bm.

Lindsey, Atha & Nancy Hogan, 15 Dec 1830; John Meacham, John Andrews, bm.

Lindsey, Caleb & Martha Brewer, 17 Dec 1807; Willis Lee, bm.

Lindsey, Hyder & Polley Barbee, 17 Dec 1833; David Roberson, bm.

Lindsey, James & Mary McMan, 28 Aug 1792; Joseph Ellison, bm.

Lindsey, James & Nancy Clark, 29 April 1809; James Clark, bm.

Lindsey, James C. & Alla C. Smith, 7 Aug 1863; Harvey Rountree, bm; m 8 Aug 1863 by John L. Woods, J. P.

Lindsey, James Clark & Nancy Jane Smith, 28 Dec 1846; Catlett C. Tinnin, bm; m 29 Dec 1846 by Archibald Currie, minister.

Lindsey, James J. & Polley W. Hall, 19 Dec 1815; Levi McCollum, bm.

Lindsey, John & Fanny Morris, 8 Feb 1800; Henry Lloyd, bm.

Lindsey, John & Elizabeth Hudson, 23 March 1803; James Milliken, bm.

Lindsey, John & Bethiah Clark, 25 Aug 1808; Wms. McNeill, bm.

Lindsey, John A. & Louisa Roberson, 26 Dec 1853; Wm. A. Lindsay, bm; m 29 Dec 1853 by Allen Edwards, J. P.

Lindsey, Merritt H. & Ephrasia Taylor, 15 Sept 1857; John H. Paul, bm.

Lindsey, Robert & Margret Ellison, 25 Oct 1804; Thomas Ellison, bm.

Lindsey, Sheffey & Elizabeth Nevill, 6 Oct 1834; Jesse Nevill, bm.

Lindsey, Wm. & Salley Fossett, 21 June 1806; Robert Glenn, bm.

Lindsy, Henry & Mary Green Hogan, 3 Oct 1822; J. Taylor Jr., bm.

Lineberry, Jacob B. & Edy Wilhoit, 28 July 1836; Edwin Miller, bm.

Linebery, Wm. & Sally Coble, 1 April 1824; James Foster, bm.

Linen, Thomas & Fanny Gibson, 1 Sept 1846; James S. Scott, bm.

Linens, Brantly & Nancy Beckum, 9 Jan 1839; John Linens, bm.

Linens, John & Polly Beckum, 15 Nov 1841; Thomas Linens, bm.

Lingo, Purnal & Elizabeth Glenn, 19 Sept 1825; John Weaver, bm.

Link, Henry C., son of Wm & Elizabeth Link, & Susan F. Cole, dau. of Thomas & Fanny Cole, m 8 Oct 1867 by R. S. Webb, minister.

Link, James A. & Fannie Martin, m 18 April 1864 by James Phillips, D. D.

Link, John A. & Elizabeth Wilkerson, 14 Sept 1858; William Josiah Turner Jr., bm; m 14 Sept 1858 by John F. Lyon, J. P.

Link, Silas M. & Bedy Harris, 24 Oct 1829; Jno. Lockhart, bm.

Link, William & Elizabeth Borland, 17 Dec 1837; James Holloway, bm.

Linley, James & Rachel Thompson, 14 Jan 1808; Andrew Faddis, George Clancy, bm.

Lint, Isaac & Mary Shanklin, 30 Sept 1783; Jno. Armstrong, bm.

Linte, Isaack & Nancy Shanklin, 10 Sept 1829; Elmore Fausette, bm.

Linzey, Elie & Jean Kerr, 15 Dec 1781; Mathew L___, bm.

Lipscomb, Charles & Ann Willard, 2 June 1866; William H. Willard, bm; m 3 June 1866 by R. H. J. Blount, J. P.

Lipscomb, L. D. & Eliza D. Paisley, 27 Feb 1847; Saml. Winstead, bm.

Lipscomb, William & Victory Rountree, 7 March 1823; John Van Hook, bm.

Lloyd, Albert & Lettie Bowers, 10 Feb 1861; William Loyd, bm; m 10 Feb 1861 by Manly Andrews.

Lloyd, Alvis C. & Margarett Jane King, 15 Dec 1855; m 15 Dec 1855 by J. W. Carr, J. P.

Lloyd, Andrew & Mary Jane Lloyd, 21 Jan 1861; C. F. Lloyd, bm; m 24 Jan 1861 by John W. Strowd, J. P.

Lloyd, Atlas J. & Mary Ann Stroud, 29 Sept 1846; Even Lloyd, Alvis Durham, bm.

Lloyd, Calvin W. & Haseltine Strowd, 3 Feb 1862; J. W. Siler, bm; m 6 Feb 1862 by A. Durham, J. P.

Lloyd, Campbell & Jenny Hunter, 1 Feb 1831; Wm. Lloyd, Alexander Hunter, bm.

Lloyd, Chesley P. & Winney Weaver, 4 March 1837; James Crabtree, H. B. Lloyd, bm.

Lloyd, Green & Delilah Durham, 26 Nov 1824; Thos. Lloyd, bm.

Lloyd, Harry, son of Harry & Nancy Taylor, & Lydia Stubbins, m 27 Dec 1867 by Wiatt Cates, J. P.

Lloyd, Henry & Nancy McCauley, 29 May 1854; Thomas Brewer, bm.

Lloyd, Henry & Frances Lloyd, 2 Jan 1866; Faddis Lloyd, W. D. King, bm; m 4 Jan 1866 by N. C. Cate, J. P.

Lloyd, Henry W., son of Thomas M. & Sarah Lloyd, & Mary E. Strowd, dau. of M. D. & Martha Strowd, m 5 Nov 1867 by Manly Andrews.

Lloyd, John & Salley Bishop, 21 Oct 1807; Henry Andrews, bm.

Lloyd, John L. & Mary R. Griffin, 10 June 1856; Urven Andrews, bm; m 13 June 1856 by Thos. Long, J. P.

Lloyd, Judson & Adeline Hunter, 2 Aug 1858; Ruffin Dodson, bm; m 2 Aug 1858 by Wm. Cheek, J. P.

Lloyd, Lucian J. & Permelia D. Strowd, 8 Jan 1867; Stephen A. Andres, James McAdams, bm; m 31 Jan 1867 by Manly Andrews.

Lloyd, Norris & Elizabeth Andrews, 31 Aug 1850; Manly Brewer, bm.

Lloyd, Orrin & Isperan Nevils, 18 Nov 1846; C. Bolling, bm.

Lloyd, Owen & Celia Andrews, 13 Oct 1836; Adley Andres, Isaac Craig, bm.

Lloyd, Owen & Esprann Nevils, 27 Sept 1847; E. G. Gray, bm.

Lloyd, Peasant & Margret Stroud, 14 Sept 1836; William Lloyd, H. Waddell, bm.

Lloyd, Richard, son of Franklin Lloyd & Louisa Durham, & Mary Perry, colored, m 22 Dec 1867 by J. W. Strowd, J. P.

Lloyd, Sidny S. & Susannah Barber, 23 Nov 1830; Stephen Pee, bm.

Lloyd, Stephen & ___ King, 31 Dec 1833; S. B. Durham, bm.

Lloyd, Stephen S. & Elizabeth Collins, 3 Aug 1856; Reiy E. P. Chambers, bm; m 3 Aug 1856 by N. C. Cate, J. P.

Lloyd, Stephen S. & Caroline Fossett, 18 Aug 1840; John H. Weaver, Jno. M. Faucett, bm.

Lloyd, Thomas & Martha Hubbard, 29 May 1785; Jesse Benton, bm.

Lloyd, Thomas & Sarah Durham, 9 Nov 1842; Hugh Edwards, Wm. Lloyd, bm.

Lloyd, Thomas & Caroline Cates, 3 Oct 1861; William Lloyd, bm; m 3 Oct 1861 by Manly Andrews.

Lloyd, Thomas A. & Susan Hunter, 22 Sept 1856; Thomas Brewer, bm.

Lloyd, William & Delilah Glosson, 6 Feb 1829; Wm. R. Durham, bm.

Lloyd, William & Frankey Davis, 29 June 1843; A. Hunter, Larkin Lloyd.

Lloyd, William M. & Harriett T. Cates, 17 Dec 1860; W. G. Bone, bm; m 18 Dec 1860 by Manly Andrews.

Locast, Martin & Molley Mitchel, 24 Jan 1800; Laurance Peteford, bm.

Lockhard, James & Nelly Sloan, 15 March 1807; Edward McDade, bm.

Lockhart, David & Emmeline Dortch, 26 Dec 1831; Tho. W. Holden, bm.

Lockhart, John P. & Caroline Riley, 16 Aug 1855; Isaac H. Ray, Francis Nichols, bm; m 19 Aug 1855 by Alexr. Dickson, J. P.

Lockhart, John S., son of John & Temperance Lockhart, & Emma A. Parish, dau. of D. C. & Rutha Parish, m 18 June 1867 by John Tillett.

Lockhart, Levi & Martha J. Breeze, 11 Sept 1866; Harvey E. Claytor, F. C. Geer, bm; m 13 Sept 1866 by Alexr. Dickson, J. P.

Lockhart, Saml. & Nelley Kelley, 3 Oct 1798; James Palmer, bm.

Lockhart, Wm. & Ann Moore, 27 Sept 1817; Thomas D. Walton, bm.

ORANGE COUNTY MARRIAGES, 1779-1868

Locklear, Major & Margret Hathcock, 1 Sept 1846; James S. Scott, bm.

Lockmon, Vincent & Anne Kirkland, 18 Dec 1783; Thos. Kirkland, bm.

Loder, Robert & Frances Watson, 8 Dec 1847; J. W. Carr, bm.

Loinberry, Adam & Catherine Linn, 6 Dec 1815; John Linn, bm.

Loinberry, Adam & Caty Johnston, 26 April 1832; Peter Lynn, bm.

Loinbery, Daniel & Charity Williams, 6 June 1819; John Linn, bm.

Long, Abram & Barbara Clap, 10 Dec 1837; James Nowlin, bm.

Long, Adam & Mary Greeson, 16 Nov 1825; Solly Shofner, bm.

Long, Albert & Elizabeth Ann Ray, 3 Feb 1860; John Clark, bm; m 5 Feb 1806 by Jas. N. Craig, J. P.

Long, Anderson & Fanny Blackwood, 28 Sept 1830; Jos. Kirkland, bm.

Long, Charles & Elizabeth Self, 19 Oct 1825; D. K. Blackwood, bm.

Long, Charles T., son of Charles & Elizabeth Long, & Dicy F. Sparrow, dau. of John & Elizabeth Sparrow, m 11 April 1868 by Geo. W. Purefoy, minister.

Long, David & Hannah Dixon, 11 March 1833; James A. Craig, bm.

Long, George & Isbel Craig, 20 June 1798; Samuel Craig, bm.

Long, George & Anne Bowles, 9 Nov 1801; Henry McCollum, bm.

Long, George & Mary Latta, 28 Oct 1829; Wm. H. Woods, bm.

Long, George Robert & Charter E. Boroughs, 6 Feb 1856; J. R. Hutchins, bm; m 14 Feb 1856 by B. J. Hackny, minister.

Long, Jacob & Jane Stockard, 31 Dec 1832; Austin Whitsitt, bm.

Long, James & Jane McCauly, 5 Sept 1838; Johnston McCauly, bm.

Long, James H. & Emeline Jenkins, 24 Sept 1851; Willis Smith, bm; m 25 Sept 1851 by Jno. R. Faucett, J. P.

Long, John & Letitia Jones, 2 June 1835; Jordan R. Hutcheson, bm.

Long, John C. & Rachel Holt, 5 Dec 1833; John Holt, P. H. Brown, bm.

Long, Osmond F. & Helen Webb, 2 Oct 1832; Henry Yarbrough, bm.

Long, Thos. & Margret Kirkland, 17 Feb 1830; Joseph Kirkling, bm.

Long, Thomas A. & Zora A. White, 31 Dec 1861; D. McCauley, bm; m 1 Jan 1862 by J. A. Cunninggim.

Long, William & Peggy Blackwood, 29 Aug 1806; Jas. Cheek, bm.

Long, William & Frances McAdams, 19 Jan 1818; Samson Nease, bm.

Long, William & Polly Murray, 27 Feb 1829; Jos. Freeland, bm.

Long, William & Mariah Jones, 26 Feb 1867; Nelson Long, bm; m 26 Feb 1867 by John Cheek, J. P.

Long, William H. & Emma Ellis, 9 Jan 1866; John D. Wilborn, bm.

Long, William J. & Mary Webb, 29 June 1843; John H. Webb, Walter A. Huske, bm.

Lough, David & Polly Keck, 31 Aug 1846; John Bain, bm.

Love, James & Jenny Brackin, 1 March 1793; William Fawssett, bm.

Love, Thomas & Mary Wilson, 18 Dec 1786; Jonathan Hawvey, William Fausett, bm.

Love, Thomas & Eleanor Faucett, 10 Oct 1816; David H. Hawes(?) or Harvey (?), bm.

Lovelace, Samuel & Charity Cross, 24 April 1805; Wm. Boswell, bm.

Lovins, Hugh & Elizabeth Forrest, 13 March 1798; Wm. Trousdale, bm.

Low, John & Drucilla Standiford, 17 July 1799; John Whitsitt, bm.

Low, Jno. B. & Nelly Clap, 29 March 1830; En. Clapp, bm.

Low, John C. & Sally Tickle, 8 Nov 1848; Lewis Huffhines, bm.

Low, Nathan & May Jane Boothe, 5 Oct 1841; Cannaday Low, P. F. Plesant, bm.

Low, Thomas & Jean Minniss, 23 Jan 1782.

Low, Wm. James & Leoise Ratlidge, 30 Sept 1817; Joseph Honeycutt, bm.

Lowdermilk, Emsley & Mary Ellen Clendening, 4 March 1846; James Clendenin, bm.

Lowe, Henry & Sarah Hufhines, 24 March 1818; Jacob Hufhines, bm.

Lowe, James & Ellissa York, 8 Dec 1845; Green Ferrell, James M. Palmer, bm.

Lowe, Weston & Ruth Horniday, 27 Oct 1830; Simon Hornaday, bm.

Lowry, James & Nancy Cearby, 24 June 1793; James McCauley, bm.

Loy, George & Nancy Ferguson, 22 April 1812; Henry Loy, bm.

Loy, George Jr. & Nancy Byrns, 29 Dec 1825; Alfred Byrns, bm.

Loy, Henry & Sophia Albright, 6 Sept 1796; John Allbright, bm.

Loy, Jacob & Elizabeth Pain, 22 March 1806; John Rogers, bm.

Loy, Jeremiah & Anna Holt, 14 Dec 1838; Henry McDaniel, bm.

Loy, John & Sally Williams, 16 March 1829; William Wolf, bm.

Loy, Marten & Polley Sellars, 18 Dec 1799; Cressley Brinkley, bm.

186

Loy, Yancy & Sally Essex, 2 May 1835; John Essex, bm.

Loyd, Frederick & Mary Thrift, 11 Dec 1821; Lemuel Carrell, bm.

Loyd, Green & Ellen King, 28 May 1840; Jonathan Tripp, bm.

Loyd, Green & Jane Ivy, 14 Oct 1845; H. C. Strowd, Atlas J. Lloyd, bm.

Loyd, Henry & Elizabeth Stourd, 1 Feb 1803; Thomas Brewer, bm.

Loyd, John & Nancy Hogan, 12 Oct 1819; Burres Coasts, bm.

Loyd, John Q. & Susanah Cate, 17 July 1847; Manley Andrews, bm.

Loyd, Joseph & Sarah Bacon, 1 April 1782; James Tate, bm.

Loyd, Lacy & Cynthia Grissum, 31 Dec 1819; Thomas Estridge, bm.

Loyd, Lafayette & Leathy Ann Strowd, 24 March 1806; T. J. Strowd, bm.

Loyd, Larkin & Sarah D. William, 25 Dec 1848; J. B. McDade, bm.

Loyd, Stephen & Polley Edwards, 20 Oct 1800; James Clendenin, bm.

Loyd, Thomas & Jane M. Culley, 4 March 1787; Isaac Bracken, bm.

Loyd, Thomas & Dilley Edwards, 18 Dec 1805; Stephen Lloyd, bm.

Loyd, Thomas & Charlotte Brewer, 18 Oct 1809; James Caruthers, bm.

Lue, John & Peny Clap, 20 Jan 1811; ___ (German signature), bm.

Lue, Michael & Mary Prior, 1824-1827; Jonathan Phifer, bm.

Lumley, John & Lethetna Hailey, 9 Oct 1852; Thomas L. Hailey, bm; m 13 Oct 1852 by Gabriel Barbee, minister.

Lunsford, James N. & Elizabeth Parish, 9 Dec 1835; Thos. P. Berry, bm.

Lunsford, Joseph & Edith Parrish, 29 Dec 1839; Wmson Parrish, bm.

Lunford, Samuel, son of Bob Satterfield & Winy Lunsford, & Adline Lockhart, dau. of Asa & Lucy Lockhart, colored, m 25 May 1868 by W. N. Patterson, J. P.

Lunsford, William & Edy Cozart, 4 May 1810; William Parrish, bm.

Lunsford, William D. & Salley B. Mangum, 13 Nov 1850; James N. Lunsford, bm.

Luter, Axim & Sally Fennel, 25 Jan 1825; Henry G. Kelly, bm.

Lynch, Ancyl & Adaline Horn, 15 Oct 1831; Wm. Cardin, bm; m 16 Oct 1851 by H. Wilkerson, J. P.

Lynch, Clayton & Polly Durnen, 28 Oct 1808; John Horner, bm.

Lynch, Daniel & Mary Ann Morgan, 14 Aug 1826; Wm. Morgan, bm.

Lynch, Edmond & Nancy Coling, 12 Oct 1808; John Lynch, bm.

Lynch, Grief & Sarah Barbee, 27 March 1827; Jesse Lewis, bm.

Lynch, Hiram & Jane Hopkins, 2 Oct 1845; Stephen Ascue, bm.

Lynch, Hugh & Jennett Moore, 31 Dec 1802; Thomas Moore, bm.

Lynch, James & Elizabeth M. Carden, 12 Sept 1853; T. M. Lynch, bm.

Lynch, Jesse & Mary Canady, 9 Jan 1792; Thos. Lynch, bm.

Lynch, John & Milley Horner, 7 Aug 1805; Enoch Collins, bm.

Lynch, John & Nancy Strayhorn, 19 Dec 1853; Egbert H. Strayhorn, Geo. W. Bruce, bm; m 22 Dec 1853 by Alexr. Dickson, J. P.

Lynch, Lemuel & Margaret W. Palmer, 25 Sept 1828; Geo. M. Johnston, bm.

Lynch, Lemuel G. & Julia F. Brown, 15 Jan 1866; Charles M. Parks, bm; m 16 Jan 1866 by Thos. Lynch, minister.

Lynch, Martin & Salley Hicks, 5 Sept 1816; Isaac Haley, bm.

Lynch, Moses & Susannah Dickey, 15 Feb 1793; Thos. Fulton, bm.

Lynch, Samuel & Jane Thompson, 22 Feb 1866; Calven E. Parish, Daniel Latta, bm; m 22 Feb 1866 by T. C. Hayes.

Lynch, Seburn & Mary Eliza Craig, 27 Sept 1828; James Lynch, bm.

Lynch, Thos. & Betsey Carden, 20 April 1826; Daniel Lynch, bm.

Lynch, Thomas & Nancy Vincent, 6 Nov 1822; Wm. Creswell, bm.

Lynch, Thos. & Mary S. Bingham, 30 April 1827; J. Witherspoon, bm.

Lynch, William & Racheal Scarlet, 28 May 1822; William James, bm.

Lyne, Francis & Nancy Faucet, 4 Feb 1792; Martin Armstrong, bm.

Lynn, Christopher & Candis Sparks, 12 Sept 1839; Thomas Christian, A. Cheek, bm.

Lynn, Mathew & Sally Trice, 6 Nov 1835; Nathl. D. Bain, Willis Marcom, bm.

Lynn, Peter & Nelly Jones, 8 June 1824; William Twiddle, bm.

Lynn, William & Sarah Proctor, 22 June 1842; Mark Rigsby, Thomas Cope, bm.

Lyon, Elkanah E. & Margaret J. Parker, 25 April 1849; John F. Lyon, R. M. Jones, bm.

Lyon, Flemming & Attelea Holden, 28 April 1842; Moses Leathers, Jr., Leo. E. Heartt, bm.

Lyon, Hugh & Caroline Herndon, 4 Feb 1840; William Nichols, W. N. Pratt, bm.

Lyon, John & Mary J. George, 29 Jan 1860; Chesley B. Herndon, A. B. Gunter, bm; m 30 Jan 1860 by A. B. Gunter, J. P.

Lyon, Thomas & Julia Williams, 5 Aug 1865; Job Berry, Abel Pain, bm; m 6 Aug 1865 by Thos. C. Hayes.

Lyon, Thos. & Hulda Tilley, 12 Jan 1867; Plummer Tansel, bm.

Lyon, Zachariah & Nancy Walker, 7 Oct 1837; Robert Hall Junr., bm.

Lyons, Philemon & Abigail Dickerson, 28 Dec 1826; Wm. H. Adams, bm.

McAdam, Hugh & Catey Beard, 3 Jan 1803; Henry Tyrrell, bm.

McAdam, Joseph & Sarah Bradford, 15 Nov 1789; Samuel McAddam, bm.

McAdams, Andrew F. & Elizabeth Christopher, 22 July 1856; Jas. F. McAdams, bm.

McAdams, Benjamin & E. C. Trolinger, 15 Jan 1849; Thos. E. Griffis, bm.

McAdams, James & Harriett Faddis, 2 Aug 1832; James McAdams, bm.

McAdams, James F. & Martha J. Carden, 29 April 1857; Robert J. Carden, bm; m 6 May 1857 by Thomas Lynch, J. P.

McAdams, John & Martha Faddis, 28 Jan 1830; James McAdams, bm.

McAdams, John T. & Mary Frances Scott, 16 May 1849; John Bradford, bm.

McAdams, Joseph & Laura Boon, 12 Aug 1848; W. J. Gragson, bm.

McAdams, Robert & Nancy Fonville, 22 May 1847; Benj. Clendenin, bm.

McAdams, William & Elizabeth Reeves, 7 April 1783.

McAdams, William & Fanny Whitesides, 31 Oct 1792; John Whitesides, bm.

McAdams, William & Perlina Durham, 16 Jan 1860; J. B. Snipes, bm; m 16 Jan 1860 by Alvis Durham, J. P.

McAdams, William R. & Sarah Patterson, 25 Sept 1810; John Smith, bm.

McAddam, James & Hannah Smith, 8 Jan 1793; William Smith, bm.

McAuley, Andrew & Polley McCauley, 26 Nov 1805; Charles McCauley, bm.

McAuley, John & Elizabeth McMullan, 23 Jan 1822; John W. Coplay, bm.

McBride, Samuel & Polley McClure, 17 June 1800; James Miles, bm.

McBroom, Andrew & Martha Baldridge, 2 Feb 1805; Jno. Taylor, bm.

McBroom, John W. & Mary Ellen Smith, 6 April 1854; Geo. W. Bruce, bm; m 6 April 1854 by Richison Nichols, J. P.

McBroom, Samuel S. & Sarah Harris, 23 Jan 1854; John W. McBroom, bm; m 24 Jan 1854 by Hezekiah Terry, J. P.

McBroom, William & Rebecca Chaffin, 2 Feb 1782; William Williams, bm.

McBroom, William Y. & Martha Jane Horn, 27 April 1850; John H. Breeze, bm.

McBroom, William Y. & Mary Harris, 26 Jan 1852; John W. McBroom, bm; m 27 Jan 1852 by Hezekiah Terry, J. P.

McCadam, John & Nancy Morrow, 6 Sept 1789; William McAdam, bm.

McCadam, Tinnin & Ann Armstrong, 28 March 1815; James Murray, bm.

McCadams, Eli & Margaret Bradford, 3 Aug 1841; Morgan Mebane, B. Cheek, bm.

McCadams, Hugh & Joannah Hall, 17 Dec 1816; Junia Hall, bm.

McCaddams, Hugh & Eleanor Ray, 26 Feb 1821; John Faddis, bm.

McCadams, Joseph & Mary Hancock, 18 March 1830; Robt. McKoy, Thos. D. Crain, bm.

McCadams, Levi W. & Rebecca J. Whitaker, 14 Oct 1865; Robert J. Carden, bm; m 17 Oct 1865 by Wilson Brown, J. P.

McCaddam, David & Peggy Morrow, 25 Jan 1815; James Murray, bm.

McCaddam, Hugh & Jane Teare, 24 Dec 1800; Robert Fauset, of Back Creek, bm.

McCaddam, Hugh & ____, 30 Nov 1810; Ludwick Van, bm.

McCaddam, Isaac & Peggy Whitesides, 15 Dec 1800; William McCaddam, bm.

McCaddam, Joseph & Jemima Justice, 14 Dec 1781; William McCaddam, bm.

McCaddams, Joseph & Abi Dickey, 25 March 1835; Hugh McCaddams, bm.

McCaddams, Lytle & Nancy Faddis, 28 Dec 1825; William ____, bm.

McCaddams, Samuel & Sarah Hall or Allen, 23 Dec 1819; Moses Whitsitt, bm.

McCalib, John & Catey Allison, 7 March 1810; Richard Breeze, bm.

McCallom, John & Nancy King, 3 Sept 1812.

McCallon, James & Janey Turner, 13 June 1800; Stephen Hart, bm.

McCallon, John & Margaret Dixon, 15 March 1785; Thomas Dixon, bm.

McCallum, John & Jemima King, 6 March 1834; Jery King, William Williams, bm.

McCallum, Thomas & Mary King, 14 Aug 1818; Thads. Freshwater, bm.

McCamie, James & Catharine Troxler, 26 Dec 1806; John Gibson, bm.

McCandless, Durell & Jatsy Smith, 8 Aug 1856; James Monk, bm; m 10 Aug 1856 by John L. Woods, J. P.

McCanless, John & Susanna Farmer, 14 Oct 1782.

McCanless, Samuel & Jennett Douglass, 16 Oct 1806; Robert Wilson, bm.

McCanless, William & Elizabeth Jordon, 7 Jan 1794; John McCanless, bm.

McCanless, William & Hannah Baldridge, 19 July 1798; Abner B. Bruce, bm.

McCann, Michael & Elizabeth Woody, 25 April 1801; Joseph Woody, bm.

McCauley, Absalom W. & P. Caroline Yancey, 8 May 1834; John Rich, bm.

McCauley, Andrew & Martha Walker, 9 Oct 1791.

McCauley, Benjamin & Easter Davis, colored, 29 Dec 1865; Stephen Archer, bm.

McCauley, Charles & Mary Willson, 2 Oct 1811; H. McCollumb, bm.

McCauley, Charles & Elizabeth Wilson, 11 Jan 1820; William Pritchard, bm.

McCauley, David & Mary E. Rogers, 22 Jan 1862; T. A. Long, bm; m 22 Jan 1862 by N. W. Wilson.

McCauley, George & Mary Thompson, 13 Nov 1845; Porter Thompson, bm.

McCauley, H. C. & Martha A. Hall, 21 Feb 1863; Thos. J. Freeland, bm; m 22 Feb 1863 by Nelson P. Hall, J. P.

McCauley, James & Catharine Chapman, 12 Jan 1792; Thos. Watts, Robert Ferguson, bm.

McCauley, James & Charity Williams, 13 Aug 1796; Elisha Cates, bm.

McCauley, James & Elizabeth Dilliard, 15 Jan 1828; Matthew McCauley, bm.

McCauley, James & Mary Freeland, 9 Nov 1829; A. Blackwood, bm.

McCauley, John & Polley Ellis, 15 Sept 1822; J. P. Sneed, bm.

McCauley, John & Margret Blackwood, 22 March 1830; Samuel Hunter, Jos. A. Woods, bm.

McCauley, John & Emaline Cheek, 12 Jan 1846; Alfred Cheek, James M. Palmer, bm.

McCauley, Jno. & Jennet Blackwood, 12 April 1798; Wm. Blackwood, bm.

McCauley, Mathew & Martha Johnston, 1 Feb 1783; Andrew
Patterson, bm.

McCauley, Matthew & Nancy Chapman, 7 Nov 1799; George Long, bm.

McCauley, Matthew & Lucy B. Beasley, 28 Jan 1833; James W.
Beasley, bm.

McCauley, Matthew & Silva D. Wilson, 24 Jan 1848.

McCauley, Matthew & Nancy L. Ellis, m 18 Sept 1858 by R. G.
Tinnin.

McCauley, Robert & Sarah Ann Borland, 25 Aug 1862; Presley M.
Cates, bm.

McCauley, Samuel S. & Elizabeth E. McDade, 24 Dec 1845;
Thomas E. Whyte, bm.

McCauley, William & Sally Bradford, 24 Sept 1811; Robert McCauly,
H. McCollum, bm.

McCauley, William & Cornelia Watson, 23 Jan 1833; James Long,
bm.

McCauley, William & Elizabeth King, 22 Feb 1833; Eli T. Watson,
bm.

McCauley, William & Nancy Craig, 1 March 1861; T. W. Laws, bm;
m 3 March 1861 by Ruffin R. Tapp, J. P.

McCauley, William OKelly & Sarah S. Hogan, 16 Jan 1827; John
McCauley, bm.

McCauly, Benjamin & Cynthia Nevill, 4 Jan 1830; N. J. King, bm.

McCauly, Charles & Julia A. Watson, 22 July 1856; D. McCauly,
J. A. Turrentine, bm; m 22 July 1856 by Thos. Landsdell,
minister.

McCauly, William O. & Mary Ann Gattis, 5 Jan 1847; Alex Gattis,
bm.

McCawley, William & Mary Hunter, 18 Jan 1831; Archd. Borland,
bm.

McClane, James & Rebecca Cucklereese, 8 April 1801; Vance
Lafferty, Alexander Parks, bm.

McClane, Levi & Mary C. Glass, 17 Feb 1843; J. H. Harden, Wm.
Rogers, bm.

McClellan, William & Francianah Veazey, 27 Nov 1781; William
Veazey, bm.

McClure, David H. & Levinia Jorden, 14 Aug 1835; John McCauley,
bm.

McCluskey, Thomas & Jane Hailey, 1 Nov 1821; Jacob Jackson, bm.

McCollum, Charles & Nancy E. Davis, 17 Dec 1856; Wesley
Atwater, bm; m 22 Dec 1856 by Robert G. Tinnin, minister.

McCollum, Henry & Jean McCauly, 6 Nov 1787; Wm. McCauly, bm.

McCollum, Henry & Polly Hunter, 22 Jan 1824; Aaron Tripp, bm.

McCollum, Levy & Ellen Nelson, 30 April 1818; John R. Cummins, bm.

McCollum, William & Polley Carroll, 12 Jan 1811; Edward McDade, G. Taylor, bm.

McCord, James & Susannah Breeze, 8 Dec 1819; Saml. McBrown, bm.

McCown, John & Elizabeth Arnold, 14 June 1848; James Inscore, W. A. Norwood, bm.

McCown, Moses & Rachel Cabe, 5 June 1813; Wm. McMillin, bm.

McCown, William & Louisa Laws, 31 Jan 1849; R. F. Morris, bm.

McCoy, Arthur & Sally Halstead, 11 March 1827; William Patterson, bm.

McCoy, James & Nancey Cole, 23 May 1798; John Cole, bm.

McCracken, Alexander & Rhodah Culberson, 15 Oct 1813; Stephen McCracken, bm.

McCracken, Jeremiah & Sarah Doherty, 7 Nov 1792; William Courtney, bm.

McCracken, John & Sally Hart, 20 Feb 1818; John Hartt, bm.

McCracken, John & Siney Patterson, 2 Dec 1845; Holloway McCracken, bm.

McCracken, Robert & Nelly Hart, 29 May 1810; Stephen McCracken, bm.

McCracken, Stephen & Nancy Jessup, 30 Dec 1806; John Mason, bm.

McCracken, Thomas & Susan Smith, 8 June 1833; M. Daniel, bm.

McCracken, William & Abigail Holiday, 15 Dec 1787; James Tinnen, bm.

McCracken, William & Martha Thompson, 9 Jan 1822; John Hartt, bm.

McCrackin, Alex & Jane Crawford, 19 Dec 1796; Wm. Elliott, bm.

McCrackin, Robbert H., of Alamance Co., & Lucey Durham, dau. of Aaron Durham, of Orange Co., m 9 Oct 1851 by Wiatt Cate, J. P.

McCray, Alexander & Rachel Helton, 5 Sept 1796; James Helton, bm.

McCray, George & Patience Hutchison, 16 May 1837; Jacob Dickey, bm.

McCrorey, Andrew & Elizabeth Jackson, 14 Jan 1810; James Jackson, bm.

McCrorey, Edward F. & Martha Bacon, 19 March 1864; Josiah Turner, bm; m 20 March 1864 by Benjamin J. Kinnion, J. P.

McCrorey, James & Frances McCadams, 9 Jan 1829; James Horn, bm.

McCrorey, Ludwick & Sarophine Younger, 13 March 1837; Wm. P. Griffis, bm.

McCrory, Andrew & Mary King, 10 March 1830; G. A. Mebane, bm.

McCrory, David & Mary Smith, 8 Sept 1807; Edward Faucett, bm.

McCrory, David & Peggy Cox, 27 Sept 1825; Jas. Roney, bm.

McCrory, David & Tempe Thompson, 30 Dec 1837; Anderson Thompson, bm.

McCrory, Thomas & Sarah Patton, 7 Aug 1837; Ludwick McCrory, James McLane Junr., bm.

McCuley, George & Elizabeth Gilston, 30 Sept 1807; John Walker, bm.

McCulley, John & Sarah Hurdle, 15 Sept 1797; Andrew McCulley, bm.

McCulley, Joseph & Polley Gilston, 28 Dec 1807; John Thompson, bm.

McCulley, Moore & Lidia McCulley, 25 Jan 1818; John Boon, bm.

McCulley, Thomas & Peggy Douglass, 15 Nov 1817; Wm. Hamilton, bm.

McCulley, William & Charity Garrison, 11 Nov 1828; Jacob Hurdle, bm.

McCulloch, James & Arcanna E. Fossett, 28 Nov 1840; Robert G. Tinnin, bm.

McCulloch, John & Sarah J. Taylor, 2 June 1855; William Wood, bm; m 7 June 1855 by Wm. Nelson, J. P.

McCulloch, Joseph Jr. & Mary Ann Burton, 21 Oct 1848; A. G. Gray, bm.

McCulloch, Robert & Morning Harris, 17 Nov 1829; Charles Woods, bm.

McCulloch, Robert & Peggy Lashley, 18 Feb 1830; Charles Woods, bm.

McCulloch, William & Mary Philips, 25 April 1798; Reuben Holt, bm.

McCulloch, Wm. & Charity Cates, 19 Aug 1808; James McCulloch, bm.

McCullock, Hunter & Patsy Debrular, 13 Jan 1840; Samuel P. Moore, Thomas Anderson, bm.

McCullock, Joseph & Catharine Allison, 17 Jan 1848; Jno. D. Carlton, bm.

McCullock, Peter & Caroline Whitemore, 27 Aug 1866; Peter A. Ray, bm; m 29 Aug 1866 by Wm. W. Pickett, J. P.

McCullock, William H. & Patience Jane Barlow, 21 Nov 1836; James A. Miller, bm.

McDade, Alphonso J. & Ann Hudson, 10 March 1858; Danl. C. McDade, bm.

McDade, Asahel J. & Charlot Jane Murphey, 17 Oct 1855; Haywood A. Pettigrew, bm.

McDade, Henderson & Polly Moore, 2 May 1827; John Moore, bm.

McDade, James B. & Rebecca Eaton, 2 April 1824; J. P. Sneed, bm.

McDade, James B. & Lucinda L. Freeland, 15 Sept 1845; C. J. F. McCauly, bm.

McDade, John & Livina Allison, 31 March 1798; James Gray, bm.

McDade, Josiah O. & Martha F. Maris, 6 Nov 1865; F. M. Jordan, bm; m 7 Nov 1865 by F. M. Jordan, minister.

McDade, Lewis & Sally Brooks, 27 Dec 1865; D. C. McDade, bm; m 27 Dec 1865 by James Phillips, D. D.

McDade, Samuel F., son of Henderson & Polly McDade, & Mary F. Allison, dau. of E. A. & Rebecca Allison, m 15 Oct 1867 by R. G. Tinnin, minister.

McDade, William W. & Sarah Frances Murphey, 31 Aug 1855; Haywood A. Pettigrew, bm.

McDaniel, Alexander & Edith Baker, 20 March 1816; Jno. S. Forrest, bm.

McDaniel, Daniel & Mary Horsey, 23 Oct 1786; Jacob Visage, bm.

McDaniel, Eli & Sarah Nichols, ___, 1793; John McDaniel, bm.

McDaniel, Eli & Betsey Griffin, 12 Aug 1794; James Christmas, bm.

McDaniel, Eli & Sally Pickett, 9 Sept 1808; John ODaniel, bm.

McDaniel, Eli Jr. & Fanney Warson, 2 Nov 1816; John McDaniel, bm.

McDaniel, James H. W. & Martha Ray, 17 April 1865; Willie B. Garrard, bm; m 19 April 1865 by Henry Gray, minister.

McDaniel, James R. & Hannah Holmes, 16 March 1822; J. Forrest, bm.

McDaniel, John & Margaret Russil, 23 July 1783; John Ray, bm.

McDaniel, John & Margaret McMullan, 29 Dec 1789; Henry ODaniel, bm.

McDaniel, John & Nancy Watson, 18 Sept 1817; A. Watson, bm.

McDaniel, John & Betsy Efland, 7 Aug 1821; James Pickett, bm.

McDaniel, John P. & Margarett Wilkison, 28 Sept 1831; Eli McDaniel, bm.

McDaniel, John Jr. & Peggy Coble, 14 Dec 1819; James McDaniel, bm.

McDaniel, Joseph & Eleanor Capps, 4 Sept 1816; James McDaniel, bm.

McDaniel, Lewis & Ruth Woody, 12 March 1824; Jas. McDaniel, John Stuart, bm.

McDaniel, Meleh & ____, 29 Dec 1796; Samuel ODaniel, bm.

McDaniel, William & Jane ODaniel, 19 Nov 1801; William ODaniel, bm.

McDaniel, William & Susan Smith, 13 Oct 1821; Thomas Griffin, bm.

McDaniel, William C. & Ann Stout, 30 April 1836; Robert Capps, bm.

McDannel, James & Charity Wells, 11 July 1788; John McDannel, bm.

McDole, James & Elizabeth McClure, 23 Dec 1794; George Osborn, bm.

McFarland, Allen & Lindsay McDanl, 23 Nov 1839; John O. Cole, Willis B. Dilliard, bm.

McFarland, Andrew & Caroline Cook, 1 Jan 1849; R. M. Jones, bm.

McFarland, Henry & Salley Mattison, 16 June 1800; William Tilley, bm.

McFarland, John & Elizabeth Maddison, 31 Aug 1798; Jas. Turrentine, bm.

McFarland, Larkin & Patsey Matterson, 10 May 1803; John McFarland, bm.

McFarland, Simeon & Lucretia Mangum, 20 July 1850; Henry McFarland, bm.

McFarland, William & Winefred Jones, 1 Jan 1819; Thornton McFarland, bm.

McFarlin, Thomas & Elizabeth Rose, 30 April 1796; Alex. McMullen, bm.

McFarling, Andrew & Martha Gooch, 14 April 1842; Jno. A. McFarling, bm.

McFarling, Jesse & Sally Cain, 26 Oct 1818; John Roberds, bm.

McFarling, Thornton & Leannah Madison, 26 Dec 1817; James Bailey, bm.

Mackfarling, William & Cynthia Edwards, 28 Nov 1822; Jno. Fort, bm.

McFlarnen, James & Nancy Matterson, 22 March 1809; Wm. Robards, bm.

McGee, John W. & Ann M. Satterfield, 3 July 1827; Geo. M. Johnston, bm.

McGlacklin, Joseph & Angess Dinnen, 15 Nov 1785; John Moody, bm.

McKee, David & Jinney Allison, 3 April 1817; Joseph W. Allison, bm.

McKee, James A. & Elizabeth B. Woods, 3 Sept 1856; F. G. Wilson, bm; m 11 Sept 1856 by Thos. U. Faucette, minister.

McKee, Rankin & Lydia Ray, 7 March 1807; Saml. Woods, bm.

McKee, Robert & Jane Dunn, 26 Dec 1797; John Rainey, bm.

McKee, William & Jane Jamison, 8 March 1810; Wm. Lockhart, bm.

McKee, William & Rachel P. Jorden, 9 Jan 1838; Thos. R. Jordan, bm.

McKerall, John & Viney Roberts, 16 Jan 1832; James Jackson, Whitmill Hill, bm.

McLandless, John & Elloner Smith, 26 May 1853; Anderson Tolar, bm; m 24 Feb 1854 by John L. Woods, J. P.

McLellon, Alfred & Ellen Turner, 3 Jan 1848; John Farthing, bm.

McLemore, Nathaniel & Anne Peealer Christmas, 22 Aug 1786; John Taylor, bm.

McLin, David & Fanny Scott, 26 Oct 1810; Thomas Scott, bm.

McMannen, Austin, son of Ephraim & Roan McMannen, & Lucy Jones, dau. of Sarah Jones, colored, m 1 Jan 1868 by Wm. D. Lunsford, J. P.

McMannen, Charles T. & Mary J. Turrentine, 15 June 1854; Jos. W. Latta, bm; m 27 June 1854 by James A. Dean, minister.

McMannen, Jno. A. & Elizabeth Latta, 14 Dec 1832; James F. Warren, bm.

McMannen, William E. & Mary P. Henderson, 29 June 1859; J. W. Latta, J. W. Garrard, bm; m 3 July 1859 by Nelson P. Hall, J. P.

McManus, Jno. & Elizth. Woods, 30 May 1784; William Smith, bm.

McMasters, Isaac & Irena Staley, 26 Dec 1838; Alfred McMasters, bm.

McMasters, Lewis & Nancy Patterson, 16 Oct 1797; James Bain, bm.

McMath, William & Malinde Coble, 2 Feb 1846; Stanford Way, bm.

McMennamy, Alexander & Mary Guttery, 9 May 1785; James Guthrie, bm.

McMullan, Alexander & Winnifred Parnell, 26 April 1793; Stephen Hart, bm.

McMullen, James & Jane Garrison, 27 July 1803; John Smith, John Whithed, bm.

McMullen, Thomas & Jane Woody, 12 Sept 1795; Samuel Thompson, bm.

McMullon, Samuel & Mary Woody, 9 Oct 1790; John McDaniel, bm.

McMun, William & Matty McMullan, 13 June 1793; Jno. Wilkison, bm.

McMunn, William & Peggy Miller, 6 April 1791; Robt. Smith, bm.

McMurray, John & Mary Baker, 8 Sept 1807; Joseph Baker, bm.

McMurray, Joseph & Sally Strayhorn, 3 Oct 1820; David Thompson, bm.

McMurtry, James & Jeane Brackin, 24 Nov 1788; Ned Brackin, bm.

McNeil, George & Elizabeth McNeil, 8 Sept 1812; J. S. Smith, bm.

McPherson, Colin & Elizabeth Brown, 12 Dec 1842; Alforde Brown, bm.

McPherson, Franklin & Joanna Andrews, 15 Dec 1847; J. M. Beaver, bm.

McPherson, James & Mary Ray, 11 Sept 1823; Aaron McPherson, bm.

McPherson, John & Mary Wiggs, 9 Oct 1823; Alexr. Morphis, bm.

McPherson, John & Mary Mayho, 11 Feb 1861; Meridith Hathcock, bm.

McPherson, Oliver & Deliarah Newlin, 11 Sept 1842; William McPherson, bm.

McPherson, William P. & Margeret R. McDaniel, 16 Aug 1819; Joseph McDaniel, Henry Ritch, bm.

McQuestian, Jessee & Emmaly Albright, 14 Nov 1841; William Rich, Jacob G. Rich, bm.

Macracken, John & Abigail Pyle, 10 Nov 1818; Henry G. Pyle, bm.

McRae, George & Elizabeth Hart, 8 Dec 1815; Anderson King, John Scott, bm.

McReynolds, Joseph & Rebecca Borin, 11 April 1783; Robt. McReynolds, bm.

McRory, John & Abigail Teer, 11 April 1801; Ross Hutcheson, John King, bm.

McRory, Robert & Amey Gregston, 27 March 1802; Wm. Gregson, bm.

McSwain, James & Ann Elmore, 1 May 1782; John Ellmore, bm.

McSwainey, Michael & Elizabeth Bevill, 16 Nov 1824; Elisha Bevill, Z. G. Burch, bm.

McVey, Balaam & Lydia Moon, 10 Feb 1846; Solomon Dixon, bm.

McVey, John & Letitia Robison, 18 Sept 1839; Joseph Green, bm.

McVey, Daniel & Rebecca Freeman, 30 Sept 1807; Wm. Freeman, bm.

Maben, Sidney & Polley Allen, 31 July 1858; George Allen, bm; m 31 July 1858 by Allen Edwards, J. P.

Mabene, John & Julia Pickett, 12 April 1831; John Hodge, bm.

Mabrey, John & Mary Gilliam, 10 March 1842; James Griffin, bm.

Mabrey, Willis & Patsey Jones, 13 Feb 1818; Berry Duke, bm.

Mabry, Francis & Martha Wilkey, 30 March 1819; John Hagwood, bm.

Madden, Alexander & Patsey James, 4 July 1801; Stephen Ellis, bm.

Madden, Andrew & Rebecca Rhoark, 31 Jan 1807; Richard Breeze, John Dickie, bm.

Madden, John & Jeany Gutherie, 10 Dec 1801; Alexander Madden, Henry McCollum, bm.

Madden, Staly & Martha Jane McDade, 15 March 1853; F. S. Warren, bm; m 17 March 1853 by John L. Woods, J. P.

Maddray, Jefferson & Fanny King, 17 Nov 1835; Samuel D. Strain, bm.

Madin, Samuel & Eliza Allison, 21 Feb 1799; Andw. Madin, bm.

Madin, Stephen & Eliza Hargues, 28 Dec 1791; John Elliott, bm.

Madison, John & Patsy Harris, 3 Dec 1809; Elisha Umsteed, bm.

Madrin, Robert & Susan Parish, 7 Oct 1824; Daniel Boothe, bm.

Madry, John & Nancy Potts, 7 May 1837; Thomas J. Morgan, N. H. Blackwood, bm.

Maelatt, Geo. & Elizabeth Tate, 11 May 1816; John R. Cumming, bm.

Mainder, Plesent & Tabitha Woods, 7 June 1832; Jno. Kerall Jr., bm.

Maize, Henry & Martha Hutchins, 23 Jan 1867; Simon Phipps, Gilbert Craig, bm.

Malett, Nelson & Martha Bishop, 27 April 1866; E. W. Morris, bm; m 27 April 1866 by R. F. Morris, J. P.

Mallett, George & Nancy Morton, 9 July 1839; R. M. Jones, Jno. M. Faucett, bm.

Mallett, Joseph & Nancy Craig, 21 July 1785; William Craig, bm.

Mallett, William & Nancy Miles, 2 Feb 1825; Thomas Anderson, bm.

Mallett, William P. & Caroline Deburnner Walker; 24 Oct 1841; A. F. Mallett, bm.

Malone, Harvey & Lotty Starks, 27 Feb 1837; General Roan, bm.

Malone, Isham & Elizabeth Cheatham, 30 April 1819; Robert Mace, bm.

Malone, James A. & Sarah C. Cole, 13 May 1856; Simpson Latta, bm; m 13 May 1856 by Wm. McCown, J. P.

Malone, James T. & Margaret F. Compton, 5 Dec 1856; Washington Buchanon, bm.

Malone, Sidney B. & Eliza Ann Warren, 24 Dec 1857; John H. Miles, bm.

Man, William & Essabel Raney, 19 Dec 1792; Isaac Diel, bm.

Mangom, Samuel & Jemimah Brinkly, 16 Aug 1798; Allen Parrish, bm.

Mangum, Addison & Nannie T. Speed, 30 Oct 1858; R. M. Jones, bm; m 9 Nov 1858 by Charles F. Deems, minister.

Mangum, Arthur & Dicey Carrington, 22 April 1801; James Parish(?), bm.

Mangum, Daniel & Peney Thomas, 15 March 1820; Alexander Thomas, bm.

Mangum, Dueral & Isebuler Hutchen, 3 May 1862; Presley J. Mangum, bm; m 21 June 1862 by F. C. Geer, J. P.

Mangum, Ellison G. & Elizabeth Harris, 4 Dec 1819; Saml. E. Alsobrook, bm.

Mangum, Fendal R., son of William & Elizabeth Mangum, & Martha Farthing, dau. of Thomas & Louena Farthing, m 13 Aug 1868 by Jesse Howell, minister.

Mangum, Hinton & Salley Parish, 24 Nov 1835; Oxford Moize, bm.

Mangum, James & Polly Carrington, 19 Sept 1823; Mark Parish, bm.

Mangum, Major, son of Green Parish & Jiney Parker, & Emiline Terry, dau. of Rachel Terry, colored, m 26 Dec 1867 by J. W. McKee, J. P.

Mangum, W. W. & Missouri Umsted, 29 Oct 1853; Willie J. Roberts, T. Webb, bm.

Mangum, Washington & Rianner Mingum, 10 Aug 1861; Andrew McFarthing, bm; m 11 Aug 1861 by Wm. J. Duke, J. P.

Mangum, William & Nancy Roberts, 24 Oct 1829; Mark Parrish, bm.

Mangum, William & Elizabeth A. Proctor, 16 April 1847; James F. Horn, bm.

Mangum, William G. & Elizabeth A. Harris, 15 Sept 1858; C. Wilson, bm; m 15 Sept 1858 by Charles Wilson, J. P.

Mangum, Willie & Martha Fitts, 7 April 1848; Philip Southerland, bm.

Mangum, Willie P. & Charity A. Cain, 30 Sept 1819; C. S. Hinton, bm.

Mangum, Willis & Martha Neeley, 29 Nov 1848; Hinton Mangum, bm.

Maning, Freaderick & Margret Crabtree, 17 June 1835; James Crabtree, bm.

Manir, William & Mary Ann Bledsoe, 5 Jan 1860; Giles Bledsoe, A. B. Gunter, bm; m 8 Jan 1860 by Gabril Barbee.

Mankins, Peter & Rachel Lewis, 23 Sept 1803; John Boswell, bm.

Mann, Robert & Rachel McMullin, 18 Nov 1796; Alexr. Mahan, bm.

Mannin, Charles & Sary Treble, 25 Feb 1782; Jon. Chesnhall, bm.

Manning, John & Catey Marcum, 12 June 1806; Philip Bennett, bm.

Mansfield, Charles H. & Sarah Faucett, 13 March 1849; S. Henslee, bm.

Mansfield, James L. & Emeline Henslee, 7 Jan 1852; George W. Burch, bm.

Mansfield, Thomas & Nancy Lea, 23 June 1826; Wm. Mansfield, bm.

Maras, William & Susannah Nicholson, 21 June 1811; Archd. Nicholson, John Wells, bm.

Marcom, Benjamin & Rhodah Pitchard, 29 April 1842; Jno. D. Carlton, bm.

Marcom, Henry S. & Margaret Carlton, 6 Dec 1831; Benj. A. Marcom, bm.

Marcom, John & Salley Cook, 19 Dec 1796; Thomas Cooke, bm.

Marcom, John M. & Catherine Gattis, 1 Nov 1849; James G. Watson, bm.

Marcom, John W. & Sarah Dallas, 17 Nov 1858; F. M. Proctor, T. W. Laws, bm; m 18 Nov 1858 by B. C. Hopkins, J. P.

Marcom, Joseph B. & Caroline G. Dixon, 12 Dec 1832; Levi McCollum, Asa H. Evans, bm.

Marcom, Levi & Lotia Massey, 8 Dec 1848; James M. Marcom, Jno. D. Carlton, bm.

Marcom, Levi & Sarah Vickers, 28 Aug 1866; Hardy Massey, bm; m 2 Sept 1866 by C. G. Markham, J. P.

Marcom, Thomas & Polly Bilbow, 13 Dec 1804; Thos. Bilbo, bm.

Marcom, Thomas & Salley Hutchins, 31 Dec 1839; John M. Marcom, Thomas Anderson, bm.

Marcom, Thomas A. & Candess Burgess, 23 Nov 1839; Thomas R. Shepperd, bm.

Marcom, William & Tabby Shepperd, 1 April 1820; Richd. Leigh, bm.

Marcom, Willie & Sally Calton, 12 Dec 1817; Daniel Nelson, bm.

Marcom, Willis & Melinde Barbee, 19 June 1847; John Marcom, bm.

Marcom, Willis R. & Sarah Horton, 28 Dec 1855; J. W. Markham, James Gill, bm; m 3 Jan 1856 by J. J. Allison, J. P.

Marcome, Nathan & Jane Pearson, 27 May 1819; William Pearson, bm.

Marcum, Aaron & Elezebeth Trice, 16 Dec 1830; Willis Marcom, bm.

Marcum, Charles G. & Harriett M. D. Bilbo, 7 Dec 1841; Hiram Marcom, Moses Leathers, bm.

Marcum, Dallas & Rebecca Atkins, 25 Feb 1867; B. J. Craig, bm; m 28 Feb 1867 by C. G. Markham, J. P.

Marcum, Henry & Michal Lynn, 6 Jan 1826; Willie Brasfield, bm.

Marcum, Hiram & Penny Adkins, 1 Nov 1845; William D. Carter, bm.

Marcum, Willis & Edy Barbee, 28 Dec 1812; Danl Holder, bm.

Marcum, Willis & Malinda Procter, 10 Feb 1847; M. A. Angier, bm.

Mardoch, James & Margaret Grey, 10 June 1790; Robt. Gray, bm.

Mardick, William & Elisebeth Brooks, 10 Feb 1785; William Lee, bm.

Maret, Stephen & Peggey Brown, 12 July 1782; James Carrington, bm.

Mariat, Thompson & Elizabeth Thompson, 26 Jan 1842; Jno. J. Allison, Nat. D. Bain, bm.

Maris, James S. & Ellen Jane Forrest, 13 Jan 1858; William P. Thompson, bm.

Maris, James S. & Martha Wilson, 21 June 1858; Wm. H. Faucett, bm; m 23 June 1858 by H. Terry, J. P.

Maris, John & Sarah Pickard, 17 Nov 1804; Joseph Woody, bm.

Maris, William & Delpha Riddle, 9 Dec 1816; Joseph Clark, bm.

Markam, Richard & Anne Roberts, 23 Aug 1783; John Green, bm.

Markham, Matthew & Edie Pearson, 11 May 1861; W. G. Guess, bm; m 12 May 1861 by John Mitchell.

Markom, Wesly M. & Adline Green, 8 Jan 1859; Warren W. King, bm; m 13 Jan 1859 by B. C. Hopkins, J. P.

Marlette, Joseph Jr. & Sidney Montgomery, 4 Sept 1819; Thomas Anderson, bm.

Marley, Brantley & Sarah Stone, 25 Oct 1846; Wm. P. Morley, An. J. Perry, bm.

Marley, Samuel & Nancy Merane, 20 May 1791; Alexander Robbs, bm.

Marshall, Benjm. & Ruthe Pasmore, 3 March 1789; Robert Ferguson, bm.

Marshall, Benjamin & Charity Wells, 23 April 1803; Anthony Way, bm.

Marshall, Francis & Mary Murray, 29 May 1806; William Freeman, bm.

Marshall, Joseph & Cynthia Marcu, 20 Jan 1832; Willis Marcom, bm.

Marshall, Joseph W. & Mary McCollum, 21 Jan 1828; James S. Irwon, bm.

Marshall, William & Mary Marshall, 10 May 1821; William Forgeson, William Shereden, bm.

Marshall, William & Nancy Marcum, 14 Jan 1828; Jos. Marcom, bm.

Marshell, Jacob & Prudy Ray, 9 Aug 1819; George Stafford, bm.

Marshell, William & Elizabeth Thompson, 24 Oct 1818; George Stafford, bm.

Marshill, Alfred & Elizabeth Briggs, 13 Nov 1848; William Wright, bm.

Marshill, Francis & Ruth Roberts, 18 June 1847; John Stafford, bm.

Marshill, William & Elizabeth Dixon, 9 Feb 1799; Richard Thompson, bm.

Marten, Paisley & Margaret Cope, 19 Aug 1857; Stephen B. May, Wm. McCauley, bm.

Martin, Allen & Casy Murphey, 12 July 1832; John Browning, bm.

Martin, Edward A., son of Edward F. & Francis A. Martin & Annabelle N. Thompson, dau. of William & Eliza J. Thompson, m 5 April 1868 by Charles Phillips, minister.

Martin, George & Raney Carrington, 28 May 1802; Wm. Carrington Jr., bm.

Martin, James & Susannah Johnston, 30 April 1785; John Scobey, bm.

Martin, James & Rosanah Lindsey, 28 May 1795; John Snipes, bm.

Martin, William & Salley Desern, 24 Feb 1808; Robert Murray, bm.

Martin, Zepheniah & Polley Artis, 8 Sept 1824; John Cox, Jas. Roney, bm.

Masey, James & Jane Morrison, 30 Sept 1791; Tents Massey, bm.

Masier, Peter & Barbary Lynn, 19 Nov 1840; Levi Maser, bm.

Mason, Alexander & Patience Jorden, 19 May 1810; James Hurdle, Henry Hurdle, bm.

Mason, Berry & Polley Herndon, 1 June 1829; John Horton, bm.

Mason, Jack, son of Ruffin Nunn & Rachel Mason, & Mickins Trice, dau. of Jacob & Delia Trice, colored, m 15 Sept 1867 by J. P. Mason, minister.

Mason, James M. Jr. & Eliza Hill, 11 Jan 1863; H. B. Guthrie, bm; m 12 Jan 1863 by Jno. H. Wingfield.

Mason, James P. & Mary Morgan, 30 Aug 1854; Jones Morgan, bm.

Mason, Jesse & Polly Trice, 15 Jan 1825; Alfred Boothe, bm.

Mason, John & Elizabeth Rich, 16 Aug 1811; Joseph Smith, bm.

Mason, Wesley & Ann Eliza Atkins, 7 Sept 1842; Alfred Booker, bm.

Mason, William & Rebecca Powel, 16 Oct 1805; Robert Wilson, bm.

Massey, Abijah & Jimimah Pendergrass, 13 Oct 1787; David Ray, bm.

Massey, Abner & Molsey Kelley, 29 Nov 1799; Mann Patterson, bm.

Massey, Forney D. & Martha A. Herndon, 6 March 1865; M. C. Herndon, bm.

Massey, Hardy & Lewisay Marcum, 13 Aug 1846; R. S. Leigh, bm.

Massey, Jason & Rachel A. Pearson, 6 April 1827; Joel A. Pearson, bm.

Massey, John & Elizabeth Pope, 22 Nov 1841; Eresnnas Pope, Moses Leathers, bm.

Massey, Ormond & Mary Ann Dickson, 18 April 1836; Jos. B. Marcom, John Thompson, bm.

Massey, Thomas & Susanah Sparrow, 9 May 1799; Thilman Perry, bm.

Massey, William & Jane Carlton, 20 May 1840; Thomas Macon, A. Parks, bm.

Matison, John & Elizabeth Roberts, 18 Aug 1826; Stephen Eliss, bm.

Matkins, Isaac & Sophia Lewis, 30 Dec 1818; Benjamin Busick, bm.

Matkins, Thomas & Francis Barnit, 15 April 1848; Thomas Moore, bm.

Matkins, William & Elizabeth Busick, 27 Feb 1797; Joseph Rumly, bm.

Matkins, William & Elizabeth Moor, 25 Oct 1817; William Brannock, bm.

Mattison, William & Peggy Horton, 27 Dec 1798; Moses Guess, bm.

Maulder, Jacob & Elizabeth Boreland, 24 May 1802; Henry Neal, bm.

Maurace, Isaac & Abigail Bowman, 1 Jan 1817; Holliday Hethcock, William Williams, bm.

Maxedon, Thomas & Elizabeth Woody, 3 June 1789; Samuel Hunter, bm.

Maxfield, Joseph & Elizabeth Baldridge, 12 Jan 1805; Thos Woods, bm.

Maxfield, Joseph & Elizabeth Baldridge, 15 Jan 1805; Henry Thomson Jr., bm.

May, David & Sarah A. Crabtree, 26 Oct 1854; Archa Strayhorn, bm.

May, Edmond H. & Betsy Barber, 18 July 1821; William Brannock, bm.

May, Ezekiel & Catharine Rieves, 10 March 1848; H. Boon, bm.

May, Gideon & Jane Parmer, 11 Nov 1845; Casson McDanil, bm.

May, Henderson & Orippa Southerland, 20 Oct 1832; Daniel Clemments, S. Couch, bm.

May, Hezekiah & Julia Ann Andrew, 28 Feb 1846; L. S. Boon, bm.

May, Isaac & Margaret Coble, 15 March 1848; George Albright, bm.

May, Jacob & Barbary Kimrah, 27 Aug 1792; John Liddell, bm.

May, Jacob & Sally Strader, 8 Dec 1839; David Lee, bm.

May, Jonathan & Catherine Coble, 17 Dec 1846; Mebane Coble, bm.

May, Joseph & Barbara Huffman, 25 Jan 1818; Jacob Hufman, bm.

May, Julian, son of John May, & Nancy Cheek, dau. of Henry &
Silva Cheek, m 24 Dec 1867 by James F. Mines, J. P.

May, Major Washington & Polley Forrest, 8 Oct 1799; James Cary,
bm.

May, Samuel & Hannah Himer, 2 April 1819; William Payne, bm.

May, Simmons & Polly Cates, 17 Dec 1839; James Rhoades, Wmson
Burton, bm.

May, Southerly & Sina Dorest, 30 Jan 1804; James Watson, bm.

May, Tobias & Catharine Friddle, 8 Feb 1798; Jacob Boon, bm.

May, Tobias & Delia Burrow, 21 Dec 1825; Eli Troxler, bm.

May, William & Sickey Morris, 22 Nov 1785; Bartlett Allen, bm.

May, William & Polly Shavour, 19 Nov 1831; Jacob May, bm.

May, William & Lovina Andrie, 9 Jan 1837; A. Boon, bm.

Mayho, Alfred & Sally Ray, 2 Jan 1864; Richard Mayo, bm; m 3 Jan
1864 by D. W. Jordan, J. P.

Mayho, Sam & Christinna Bass, colored, 9 Dec 1859; W. H. McDade,
bm; m 10 Dec 1859 by J. P. Mason.

Mayho, Thadedis & Patience Chavous, 18 Nov 1854; Richard Mayo,
bm; m 18 Nov 1854 by John J. Freeland, J. P.

Mayho, William & Viney Robinson, 26 Nov 1835; Jno. A. McMannen,
Henry Cruthers, bm.

Mayho, William & Nancy Boss, 18 July 1837; Samuel Thompson, bm.

Mayho, William & Martha F. Jones, 24 Sept 1861; R. M. Jones,
bm; m 24 Sept 1861 by T. C. Harps.

Mayhoe, Anderson & Jessey Tatom, 25 July 1828; Ephraim Mitchell,
bm.

Maynard, George & Polley Garrison, 21 Dec 1830; Wm. Moore, bm.

Maynard, Joshua & Nancy Dishon, 4 Nov 1802; Augustine Dishon,
bm.

Maynard, Robin & Anne Leathers, 9 June 1840; Wm. H. Brown,
C. Featherston, bm.

Maynor, William & Nancy Collins, 28 Dec 1836; John Steel,
Westley Smith, bm.

Mayo, Alfred & Annis Catharine Mitchell, 29 June 1850;
R. Nichols, bm.

Mayo, Alfred, son of A. & Betty Mayo, & Phillis Walker, colored,
m 27 May 1868 by D. N. Walker, J. P.

Mayo, Green A. & Levinia Stewart, 6 July 1849; James Valentine,
bm.

Mays, Simmons & Nelly Pritchett, 13 Dec 1827; Levi Cole, Jesse
Long, bm.

Mays, Stephen & Mary Frances Tate, 30 Dec 1852; W. C. Cheek, bm.

Mays, William & Ellen Crabtree, 4 April 1855; John Thompson,
John D. Williams, bm; m 6 April 1855 by John F. Lyon, J. P.

Meacham, James & Elizabeth Standiford, 11 Feb 1796; Samuel
Shepperd, bm.

Meacham, Jesse G. & Siney Ray, 26 Aug 1865; John A. Meacham, bm.

Meadows, David & Roame Jeffreys, 23 June 1866; Nelson Parrish,
bm; m 24 June 1866 by William D. Lunsford, J. P.

Meadows, Willie & Louisa Riggs, 20 March 1859; Joseph G.
Lunsford, bm; m 20 March 1859 by W. M. Carrington, J. P.

Meaks, Phillip & Nancy Williams, 9 Dec 1866; Thos Woods, bm;
m 9 Dec 1866 by Joseph Woods, J. P.

Mearcom, Jas. M. & Frances Davis, 19 Sept 1851; Geo. M.
Shepherd, bm; m 23 Oct 1851 by J. B. McDade, J. P.

Mebane, Alexander & Elizabeth Paul, 12 July 1835; John A.
Mebane, Alex M. Kirkland, bm.

Mebane, Elbridge G. & Susan U. Moore, 22 Sept 1825; Saml. Tate,
bm.

Mebane, George A. & Atillia Yancy, 25 April 1820; Allen Mebane,
bm.

Mebane, Isaac & Dianah Borland, 7 Sept 1865; Job Bery, Abel
Pain, bm; m 9 Sept 1865 by A. C. Murdock, J. P.

Mebane, James & Rebecca Mebane, 26 Aug 1825; Richard Wood, bm.

Mebane, James & Susan Turner, 27 June 1839; Frederick A. Nile,
bm.

Mebane, John & Elizabeth E. Woods, 29 June 1855; D. A. Mebane,
bm.

Mebane, John A. & Celia Sutton, 23 Dec 1819; J. Taylor Jr., bm.

Mebane, Thomas H. & Rachel Hurdle, 4 July 1860; Robert J. Carden,
bm; m 8 July 1860 by Freeman Walker, J. P.

Mebane, William Senr. & Elizabeth Shepperd, 22 Oct 1823; Wm. K.
Mebane, bm.

Mebane, William Senr. & Rebecca Rainey, 12 Jan 1802; James
Mebane Sr., bm.

Mebane, William B. & Frances Woods, 16 Jan 1797; Saml. Bradford, bm.

Mebane, William M. & Margerite Jane Harden, m 12 Nov 1844 by E. W. C.

Meben, William & Charity Marley, 19 Dec 1800; Samuel Meben, bm.

Medlen, Thomas & Elizzey Holder, 2 Jan 1858; Thomas Terrece, Wm(?) Pendergrass, bm.

Medlin, Samuel & Jeany Rhodes, 8 June 1831; Noah Rhodes, Alexr. Patton, bm.

Medlin, Thomas & Martha Snellings, 5 June 1841; Wm. George, bm.

Medling, Francis & Martha James, 2 Aug 1851; King Barbee, bm; m 10 Aug 1851 by King Barbee, J. P.

Megee, Scion & Polly Clark, 28 Jan 1798; Wm. Dunnagan Junr., bm.

Megee, Walter & Sarah Hunt, 29 Dec 1819; Martin Cole, bm.

Mehaffey, James & Elizabeth Denny, 22 Jan 1781; Robert Kell, bm.

Mellinton, Thomas & Nelly Crabtree, 16 June 1831; J. Taylor, bm.

Melone, John & Frances Mitchum, 27 Nov 1798.

Melton, Matthias & Betsy Shoecraft, 12 June 1821; Thomas Anderson, bm.

Melvin, George & Nancy Caroline Pugh, 10 Sept 1847; John Starling, bm.

Melvin, George & Susannah Bason, 27 Aug 1848; T. G. Miller, bm.

Melvin, Henry & Rebecca Pyles, 23 Aug 1836; Jed Raney, W. W. Patterson, bm.

Melvin, James & Catey Isley, 13 Oct 1804; John Isley, bm.

Melvin, John & Henny Rumbly, 23 April 1808; John Baldwin, bm.

Melvin, Thomas & Abigail Baldwin, 20 Feb 1802; Burrell Gilliam, bm.

Mener, John P. & Louissana Jane Stroud, 17 July 1860; m 19 July 1860 by Wilson Atwater, minister.

Meoize, Charles & Elizabeth Jones, 29 Nov 1832; Peyton C. Clements, Asa H. Man, bm.

Meridith, Henry & Milley Nelson, 28 March 1785; William Nunn, bm.

Meritt, George W. & Mary S. Forrest, 7 Dec 1861; C. C. Smith, W. P. Rhodes, bm; m 8 Dec 1861 by Ruffin R. Tapp, J. P.

Meritt, Wilie & Jane Albert, 8 July 1827; James Walker, bm.

Merret, Samuel & Sarah Newyen, 3 Feb 1792; Leonard Hays, Charles Roan, bm.

Merrett, Willie & Betsy Huske, 6 Oct 1809; William Trice, bm.

Merrit, Joseph & Nancy Stephens, 6 Jan 1800; Moses Faulkener, bm.

Merritt, Anderson & Jane Johnston, 4 Oct 1847; H. B. Rochell, bm.

Merritt, George & Alice Ledbetter, 17 Dec 1810; John Hollowell, bm.

Merritt, John & Patsy Perry, 18 Nov 1801; William Rhodes Jr., bm.

Merritt, John & Nancy Rose, 5 Feb 1834; James Fowler, bm.

Merritt, Joseph & Martha A. Smith, 11 June 1858; John W. Hart, bm; m 13 June 1858 by Wilson Brown, J. P.

Merritt, LaFayette & Lucy Purifoy, 16 May 1865; H. B. Guthrie, bm.

Merritt, Wm. Henry & Susannah Barbee, 15 Sept 1803; Francis Barbee, bm.

Mers, James & Celia Brown, 30 July 1814; James McCleur, bm.

Michael, Lenard & Catharine Staley, 12 June 1848; Joshua Whitesett, bm.

Michel, David & Elizabeth Wagoner, 2 Nov 1816; Peter Waggoner Jr., bm.

Michel, Henry & Betsey Copeland, 27 May 1828; Gabriel Barbee, bm.

Miles, Elijah & Mary Jane Thompson, 10 March 1848; George Miles, Lafayette Cheek, bm.

Miles, George & Elizabeth Tinnin, 2 Aug 1850; Addison Wilson, bm.

Miles, Westley & Nancy Squires, 21 May 1837; James Miles, James Squires, bm.

Miles, William & Hanah Killion, 20 Oct 1846; Isaac Killion, bm.

Millar, James & Polley Sutton, 19 Feb 1820; Robert Gragson, bm.

Millard, Charles & Elizab. Morris, 6 March 1783; John Kerrigan, bm.

Millen, James R. & Lydia McCullock, 24 May 1836; Wm. McCullock, Joseph Parks, bm.

Miller, Charles & Elizabeth Ragains, 21 June 1809; William Ragains, bm.

Miller, Charles & Jane Smith, 28 Feb 1854; Joseph W. McKee, bm.

Miller, Charles & Caroline Taylor, 27 Feb 1855; J. C. Turner, bm; m 9 March 1855 by H. Terry, J. P.

Miller, Charles, son of Charles & Elizabeth Miller, & Elizabeth Edwards, m 26 Dec 1867 by W. R. Gaultney.

Miller, Charles R. & Frances J. Nichols, 21 Nov 1854; Thomas Rountree, bm; m 21 Nov 1854 by Hezekiah Terry, J. P.

Miller, Edwin & Nelly Wilhoit, 26 March 1836.

Miller, James & Rachel Hall, 16 April 1796; Thomas Hall, bm.

Miller, James R. & Ruth A. Carrington, 17 March 1849; C. Wilson, bm.

Miller, James W. & Lucinda C. Murphey, 18 Jan 1864; John W. Siler, bm.

Miller, Jesse & Polley Hall, 11 Dec 1824; Thos. P. Paul, bm.

Miller, John & Isabella Ellis, 14 Dec 1820; Saml. McBrown, bm.

Miller, John & Martha M. Jackson, 21 July 1847; William Freeman, bm.

Miller, William & Polley Sutton, 3 May 1803; John Miller, bm.

Miller, William & Rebeckah Rountree, 28 April 1824; David B. Rountree, bm.

Miller, Zachariah & Caroline Smith, 22 Aug 1846; E. C. Rominger, bm.

Millican, Robert & Christean Turner, 5 May 1809; James Milliken, bm.

Milliken, James & Oney Hudson, 11 Aug 1803; Charles Milliken, bm.

Millington, John & Constant Ward, 24 June 1784; Ezekiel Chance, bm.

Millington, John & Susan Ward, 18 May 1841; Wm Ward, bm.

Millirons, Henry B. & Nancy Adams, 9 Jan 1821; Saml. S. Claytor, bm.

Millison, John & Mary Howell, 18 Nov 1797; George Maden, bm.

Milton, Alabama & Mary Ann Catharine Whiteker, m 31 Jan 1851 by J. B. McDade, J. P.

Milton, Alabama & Betsy A. Morgan, 16 Nov 1854; M. Wilkerson, bm.

Milton, Elisha & Patsey Heathcock, 26 July 1841; Alsa Chavis, bm.

Mincey, Jonathan & Sarah Carey, 5 Jan 1815; John Walters, bm.

Mincy, Deloney & Mary Bowlin, 1 May 1858; Ths. W. Laws, bm.

Miner, Franklin & Martha Syks, 17 Sept 1845; John E. Cates, J. M. Beaver, bm.

Minnis, Ashburn & Mary Ann Sykes, 22 Aug 1842; C. C. Smith, James Woods, bm.

Minnis, James & Lucy McDaniel, 14 Jan 1805; Henry O'Daniel, bm.

Minnis, James & Mary Dunegan, 13 Dec 1849; J. D. Williams, Mark C. Hall, bm.

Minnis, John & Salley Evans, 9 Sept 1858; Young Minnis, James Gill, bm; m 9 Sept 1858 by Wilson Brown, J. P.

Minnis, John R. & Nancy Hastings, 28 Jan 1832; John Wm. Smith, bm.

Minnis, John R. & Martha Jordan, 4 Aug 1846; J. M. Minnis, bm.

Minnis, William & Tempe Faulkner, 20 Dec 1818; Alfred Taylor, bm.

Minnis, Young & Polly Riley, 17 July 1855; John Minnis, bm; m 2 Aug 1855 by Wiatt Cates, J. P.

Minnis, Young & Nancy J. Pender, 3 Sept 1860; John Folkener, bm; m 5 Sept 1860 by D. W. Thompson, minister.

Minor, Joseph & Mary Brewer, 4 Feb 1815; Hugh Mulhollan, bm.

Minson, Abraham & Mary Chimnea, 28 Aug 1794; James Abbot, bm.

Mitcham, William & Emeline Williams, 25 Sept 1859; John Meerchand, John Fergeson, bm; m 25 Sept 1859 by Allen Edwards, J. P.

Mitchel, Ephraim & Sally Weaver, 15 Sept 1820; Charles Hood, Major Weaver, bm.

Mitchel, Isaiah & Sarah Vaughan, 13 Aug 1802; John King, bm.

Mitchel, James & Peggy Craig, 18 Nov 1808; Andw Baker, bm.

Mitchel, John & Elizabeth Mebane, 5 April 1813; Thos. Armstrong, bm.

Mitchel, John & Anne Walker, 20 Dec 1827; Joseph B. Pace, bm.

Mitchel, Nathaniel & Christian Levens, 2 Nov 1837; Richard Levens, bm.

Mitchel, Noah & Polley Bowles, 10 Aug 1804; Aarca Bow, bm.

Mitchel, Perry & Peggy Morrow, 27 Aug 1816; Robet. Murray, bm.

Mitchel, Randolph & Nancy Cryder, 9 Nov 1824; William Murray, bm.

Mitchel, Robert & Jeane Dickson, 16 Sept 1786; Jesse Miller, bm.

Mitchel, Robert & Kiddy Mitchel, 13 March 1811; John Boles, Joseph Mitchell, bm.

Mitchell, Adam & Elizabeth Allen, 10 July 1808; Samuel Allen, bm.

Mitchell, Archer D. & Polley Pulley, 6 Sept 1831; Britton Banks, James Clancy, bm.

Mitchell, E. G. & Julia F. Adams, 12 Dec 1855; John W. Allen, bm; m 26 Dec 1855 by R. Burwell, minister.

Mitchell, George & Jeany Craig, 7 Oct 1803; Saml. Craig, bm.

Mitchell, George & Grace Gilson, 29 Oct 1817; John Tinnan, bm.

Mitchell, James & Mary Craig, 24 Oct 1789; George Long, bm.

Mitchell, Jesse & Elizabeth Lintheycome, 28 Aug 1848; John Newlin, bm.

Mitchell, John & Nancy Lindsay, 31 July 1827; John B. C. Meacham, Sackfiele Brewer, bm.

Mitchell, John & Lucinda Carter, colored, 14 Aug 1855; Franklin Harris, bm.

Mitchell, John C. & Mary C. Palmer, 20 Nov 1834; A. M. Kirkland, bm.

Mitchell, Lemuel R. & Sarah J. Wilson, 7 April 1848; J. A. Murray, bm.

Mitchell, Perry & Mary McCadams, 23 Jan 1819; Andw. Murray, bm.

Mitchell, Ruffin P. & Margaret Tate, 14 Aug 1841; Joseph Tate, bm.

Mitchell, William & Nancy Mebane, 30 Sept 1811; Thos. Armstrong, bm.

Mitchell, Zerah & Nancy Roberts, 23 April 1819; John Young, bm.

Mize, Frederick & Anne Ragland, 31 Aug 1799; William Taylor, bm.

Moak, Willis & Ann Sheppard, 21 Oct 1818; Isaac Hailey, bm.

Moize, Allen & Rachel Roberts, 9 Sept 1808; Jonathan Mize, bm.

Moize, Durell & Cornelia Teasley, 21 Jan 1860; Westley Bowling, bm.

Moize, William H. & Elizabeth Horner, 12 Sept 1850; Jas. Latta, bm.

Molton, Jessee & Jane Croney, 9 April 1787; Henry ODaniel, James Roach, bm.

Monk, Alfred & Dicy James, 5 Oct 1849; James Monk, bm.

Monk, Charles & Martha A. Monk, 10 Sept 1861; Anderson Monk, bm; m 11 Sept 1861 by Jno. Hancock, J. P.

Monk, Harrison & Bettie Brown, 27 Dec 1866; Hugh Woods, H. B. Guthrie, bm; m 1 Jan 1867 by Thomas M. Faucett, minister.

Monk, Henderson & Frances Rhew, 29 Dec 1859; James Monk, Joseph Garrard, bm; m 29 Dec 1859 by John Hancock, J. P.

Monk, James & Mary Rhew, 14 Nov 1853; Henry T. Gatis, bm.

Monk, Larkin & Lovely Gooch, 30 Oct 1826; Reves Mangum, James P. Laws, bm.

Monk, Silas & Eliza Parish, 16 Oct 1817; Archd. Carroll, bm.

Monk, William & Ema J. Cocke, 9 March 1867; H. B. Guthrie, bm; m 10 March 1867 by F. M. Jordan, minister.

Monk, Willis & Polly Hailly, 30 Sept 1816; Andrew Hailey, bm.

Monk, Willis & Nancy McDaniel, 15 Sept 1853; J. J. Freeland, bm; m 18 Sept 1853 by J. J. Freeland, J. P.

Montague, Thomas F. & Rutha A. Umstead, 12 Sept 1858; D. C. Parrish, bm.

Montgomery, Alexander & Sophia Wilson, 28 Feb 1837; James Montgomery, bm.

Montgomery, Daniel A. & Josephine Berry, 29 April 1853; E. G. Gray, bm; m 10 May 1853 by John Witherspoon, minister.

Montgomery, Eli H. & Winney Collins, 24 Nov 1845; Porter Thompson, bm.

Montgomery, Hamiltan & Sarah Ann Wilkerson, 31 Jan 1865; Wm. H. Andrews, bm; m 1 Feb 1865 by H. Terry, J. P.

Montgomery, Hugh & Rebecca Grimes, 19 Aug 1800; Jacob Jackson, bm.

Montgomery, Hugh & Salley Davis, 10 Jan 1811; Bexter King, bm.

Montgomery, James & Mary Walker, 8 Oct 1837; A. W. Parker, bm.

Montgomery, James & Ann J. Gray, 10 Dec 1849; Minnick Miller, bm.

Montgomery, James R. & Cornely C. Trolinger, 19 Sept 1845; Daniel Montgomery, bm.

Montgomery, Jonathan & Sarah Riggs, 20 Feb 1783; John Hunter, bm.

Montgomery, Jonathan & Polly Umstead, 29 Dec 1817; Wm. Montgomery, bm.

Montgomery, John W. & Ann J. Bingham, 16 Dec 1856; Robert Burnett, bm; m 17 Dec 1856 by Thomas Lynch, minister.

Montgomery, Joseph & Mary Love, 1 April 1791; Thomas Love, bm.

Montgomery, William & Precilla Horner, 2 March 1785; George Riggs, bm.

Montgomery, William & Edy Harrell, 19 Sept 1801; Elihugh Woods, bm.

Montgomery, William Patterson & Jane Ferrell, 14 Aug 1843; J. W. Ferrill, bm.

Montgomery, William W. & Mourning Lasley, 25 June 1822; John Mickels, bm.

Moor, James & Susannah Edwards, 24 Dec 1812; George Martin, bm.

Moore, Abraham & Jane Allen, 30 Dec 1856; G. W. Roberts, Thomas Cale, bm; m 31 Dec 1856 by John L. Woods, J. P.

Moore, Alexander, son of William & Edy Moore, & Aggy Roberts, colored, m 28 Dec 1867 by William Pass.

Moore, Alfred & Elizabeth Wallace, 29 Aug 1814; Thomas Wallas, bm.

Moore, Arthur & Hannah Griffey, 18 Jan 1810; Thomas Moore, bm.

Moore, Asahel & Ibby McBroom, 24 Dec 1804; Thos. Woods, bm.

Moore, Bynum & Charity Brown, colored, m 18 Nov 1865 by Joseph W. McKee, J. P.

Moore, Chesley & Sinah Reeves, 28 Nov 1838; Green Moore, bm.

Moore, David & Elizabeth Bowles, 7 April 1804; John Moore, bm.

Moore, David & Gilley Forsythe, 3 Jan 1817; Allen N. Robeson, bm.

Moore, David & Mary Ann Bradshaw, 10 Feb 1843; James Moore, A. Thompson, bm.

Moore, David & Emley Wilson, 9 March 1861; S. H. Breeze, bm; m 12 March 1861 by Ruffin R. Tapp, J. P.

Moore, Durant K. & Sarah A. Moore, 6 Oct 1866; Wesley Atwater, bm; m 10 Oct 1866 by Jeheil Atwater, J. P.

Moore, Green & Anne Robenson, 29 Nov 1838; Chesley Moore, bm.

Moore, J. W. & Sarah A. Atwater, 20 Nov 1860; E. W. Atwater, C. M. Latimer, bm; m 20 Nov 1860 by J. A. Cunningham.

Moore, James & Ellender Moore, 13 March 1792; Henry Thompson, bm.

Moore, James & Elizabeth Lashley, 22 Oct 1796; William Grimes, bm.

Moore, James & Sarah Lett, 12 June 1797; David Dinning, bm.

Moore, James & Milley Holt, 22 March 1805; Robert Murray, bm.

Moore, James & Peggy Robinson, 6 Feb 1809; James Phillips, bm.

Moore, James A. & Annie E. Parish, 22 April 1864; Nat. D. Harris, bm.

Moore, John & Martha Torrentine, 12 Feb 1791; Henry Moore, bm.

Moore, John & Rebecca Robinson, 9 March 1808; Daniel Atkins, bm.

Moore, John & Nelly Morrow, 26 Oct 1815; James Williken, bm.

Moore, John & Betsey Ward, 8 Jan 1823; Farmer Smith, bm.

Moore, John & Mary Thompson, 22 Jan 1831; Saml. Thompson, John Thompson, bm.

Moore, John & Oreanna Anderson, 18 Dec 1841; Daniel Phillips, James Collins, bm.

Moore, John C. & Matilda Robertson, 23 May 1867; m 23 May 1867 by H. M. C. Stroud, J. P.

Moore, John I. & Tarmisia Rhodes, 10 Dec 1833; William Smith, bm.

Moore, John Lewis & Mary Pearson, 22 Jan 1821; Benja. A. Yeargin, bm.

Moore, John M. & Elizabeth H. Jordan, 14 Aug 1865; James P. Hopkins, Lambert W. Hall, bm; m 16 Aug 1865 by Thos. Wilson, J. P.

Moore, John W. & Lucy J. Leathers, 17 Sept 1863; S. D. Umsted, bm.

Moore, Joseph & Celia Stanford, 29 March 1794; Thomas Armstrong, bm.

Moore, Joseph & Eliza Shepperd, 26 July 1796; Morgan Hart, bm.

Moore, Michael W. & Sallie J. Oldham, 29 Sept 1865; John Cheek, bm; m 30 Sept 1865 by F. M. Jordan, minister.

Moore, Nathan & Nelly Robertson, 23 June 1812; Alfred Moore, bm.

Moore, Peyton P. & Maria Louisa Lea, 9 Aug 1839; L. H. Mebane, bm.

Moore, Robert & Peggy Randels, 14 Dec 1798; Frederick Smith, bm.

Moore, Robert & Jane Ezell, 20 Dec 1817; John Taylor, bm.

Moore, Robert & Rebecca Ward, 22 Dec 1829; Thomas Jones, bm.

Moore, Robert & Polley Dixon, 24 June 1836; Richard Tapp, Robert F. White, bm.

Moore, Robert & Mallie E. Riggs, 2 Nov 1866; Jas. F. Terry, W. H. Jorden, bm; m 8 Nov 1866 by J. W. McKee, J. P.

Moore, Robin & Easter Bayne, 30 April 1866; John M. Blackwood, bm; m 30 April 1866 by D. W. Jordan, J. P.

Moore, Samuel & Susan Farra, 15 June 1848; Giles J. Allison, bm.

Moore, Samuel & Elizabeth A. Stanford, 2 Jan 1866; Alexander S. Webb, bm.

Moore, Sidney & Polly P. Reed, 13 March 1813; J. B. Shaw, bm.

Moore, Thomas & Patty Barbee, 25 Jan 1805; Mason Patterson, bm.

Moore, Thomas & Elizabeth Dickey, 24 Jan 1816; William Moore, bm.

Moore, Thomas & Tabitha Berry, 21 Feb 1823; John Moore, bm.

Moore, Thomas & Jane Taylor, 21 Oct 1848; Isaac Moore, bm.

Moore, Valentine & Nancy Lashley, 22 Oct 1796; William Grimes, bm.

Moore, Valentine & Louissa Wood, 16 Feb 1839; Geo. M. Cash, bm.

Moore, William & Martha Pickard, 28 Sept 1832; John Crawford, John Jones, bm.

Moore, William & Polley Glossen, 11 Feb 1809; Abram Martin, bm.

Moore, William & Kitty Wallace, 29 Sept 1827; Elias Milliken, William Parish, bm.

Moore, William, son of Allen Mebane & Lucy Moore, & Eliza McCulloch, daughter of Peter & Caroline Whitmore, m 17 Oct 1867 by Wm. W. Pickett, J. P.

Moore, W. W. & Lucy R. Henderson, 17 July 1860; H. L. Owen, bm; m by O. J. Brent, minister, 20 July 1860.

Mordoch, David & Mary Bohannon, 12 Aug 1788; Thomas Buchannan, bm.

ORANGE COUNTY MARRIAGES, 1779-1868

Mordoch, James & Margaret Grey, 10 June 1790; Robt. Gray, bm.

Mordoch, William & Susannah Gray, 7 June 1797; Andrew Gray, bm.

More, James & Kitty Dolly, 27 Dec 1817; Wm. Murry, bm.

Moreland, Lewis & Patsey Michael, 23 Oct 1805-1807; Wm. Martin, bm.

Morgain, Allen & Charity McCauley, 25 Jan 1813; John R. Leigh, bm.

Morgan, Isaac & Mary W. Nevelle, 18 Dec 1854; Jehiel Atwater, bm; m 19 Dec 1854 by W. Atwater, J. P.

Morgan, James A. & Eliza Smith, 23 March 1821; David Strain, bm.

Morgan, James Allen & Franky Barbee, 24 Sept 1809; Mark Barbee, bm.

Morgan, John & Patsy Morgan, 13 Nov 1802; Christopher Barbee, bm.

Morgan, John & Rachel Morgan, 12 April 1828; Isaac Holden, bm.

Morgan, Jones & Amy Barbee, 4 March 1850; J. B. McDade, bm.

Morgan, Joseph & Malinda Sowell, 3 Aug 1866; George Ruffin, bm; m 4 Sept 1866 by Mager Green, J. P.

Morgan, Manly & Margarett Jane Ivy, 12 Oct 1857; James M. Ivey, bm; m 13 Oct 1857 by N. C. Cate, J. P.

Morgan, Wm. & Sarah Flintam, 12 Sept 1794; John Morgan, bm.

Morgan, Wm. D. & Elizabeth Johnson, 10 July 1850; C. J. Burnett, bm.

Morgen, Thomas & Anna Holder, 9 Jan 1796; John Morgan, bm.

Morhead, William, son of Frank & Amelia Morhead, & O'Felia Cobb, dau. of Mary Cobb, colored, m 13 June 1868 by John Cheek, J. P.

Moring, Patrick & Mary Carlton, 7 Aug 1835; Berry Mason, S. B. Taylor, bm.

Moris, John & Nancy Meachum, 6 July 1829; James Morris, bm.

Moris, Thomas & Mary Ann Crutchefield, 13 Jan 1849; Matthew Hunter, bm.

Morlow, Samuel & Nancy Pickett, 29 Oct 1858; John Leathers, bm.

Morphis, Alexander & Nancy Thompson, 7 March 1818; J. G. Bacon, bm.

Morris, Baxter & Salley Cheek, 30 Sept 1830; Stephin Poe, bm.

Morris, Isaac & Nancy Cheek, 8 Jan 1812; Henry Bailey, bm.

Morris, James & Sally Estridge, 5 Feb 1808; Thomas Lloyd, bm.

Morris, James & Susannah Fossett, 2 Jan 1832; John Moris, Tilden Morris, bm.

Morris, James & Martisha Strawn, 13 Feb 1866; Henry Brown, bm; m 14 Feb 1866 by H. McDaniel, J. P.

Morris, John & Elizabeth Beck, 24 Sept 1799; Hardey Collins, bm.

Morris, John & Nancy Caruthers, 19 Dec 1804; Ezekiel Brewer, bm.

Morris, John & Sally Moser, 25 Oct 1810; Daniel Moser, bm.

Morris, John & Hannah Riggs, 3 Dec 1818; Noah Rhodes, bm.

Morris, John R., son of Fielding & Hannah Morris, & Ann R. Blake, dau. of John & Nancy Blake, m 19 Sept 1867 by J. W. Strowd, J. P.

Morris, Richard & Sarah Lindsey, 19 Aug 1842; Wm. M. Baly, Thomas Morris, bm.

Morris, Samuel & Treny Williams, 28 Feb 1802; Burwell Handly, bm.

Morris, William & Nancy Bailey, 19 Dec 1804; John Pittman, bm.

Morris, William R. & Margaret Underwood, 13 Sept 1865; John Boggs, bm.

Morrison, Robert & Nancy Price, 10 Aug 1804; Eps Hilliard, James Crawford, bm.

Morrow, Alexander & Jennet Lassley, 17 May 1797; John Morrow, bm.

Morrow, Alexander & Cornelia M. Graves, 7 July 1834; William P. Morrow, bm.

Morrow, Andrew & Rebeckah Woody, 8 Feb 1793; Richard Thompson, bm.

Morrow, George & Sarah Jones, 20 May 1800; James Steel, bm.

Morrow, George B. & Margaret A. Jones, 17 Nov 1830; Robert Moore, Samuel Thompson, bm.

Morrow, James & Christean Ray, 31 Jan 1792; Hugh Ray, bm.

Morrow, James & Sarah Thompson, 27 Nov 1798; William Morrow, bm.

Morrow, James & Sarah Grisham, 14 Nov 1803; Richard Thompson, bm.

Morrow, James & Anne Justice, 1 July 1836; Jonathan Hobbs, J. Taylor, bm.

Morrow, James & Nancy Lloyd, 16 June 1840; Ed. Strudwick, bm.

Morrow, James M. & Martha Dixon, 4 Feb 1833; Josiah Morrow, bm.

Morrow, John & Hannah Marshal, 24 Jan 1794; Richard Thompson, bm.

Morrow, John & Peggy Criswell, 16 April 1804; Jno. Creswell, bm.

Morrow, John & Patsy McCauley, 4 Sept 1824; Jonathan Hobbs, bm.

Morrow, John & Rachel Thompson, 20 Dec 1831; Jas. Morrow, bm.

Morrow, Joseph H. & Martha Edwards, 30 Jan 1855; John Pickard, bm; m 6 Feb 1855 by Wilson Atwater, Minister.

Morrow, Josiah & Dicey Mebane, 7 May 1842; James Mebane Jr., bm.

Morrow, Robert & Sally Vincent, 29 Jan 1808; Joseph ____, bm.

Morrow, Stanford & Jennett Jones, colored, 3 Apr 1866; Franklin Morrow, bm.

Morrow, Vincent & Sally Morrow, 13 Oct 1835; James Vincent, bm.

Morrow, William & Milley Hunnicut, no date, (before 1800); William Lee, bm.

Morrow, William & Jenny Gaddes, 28 Jan 1794; John Gattis, bm.

Morrow, William & Margret Rickets, 4 Oct 1803; James Ezell, bm.

Morrow, William & Nancy Hatley, 22 Jan 1818; James Child, bm.

Morrow, William & Fanny Armstrong, 9 Feb 1839; Wm. Gattis, David D. Pace, bm.

Morton, Peter & Rachel King, 6 Feb 1810; William Morton, Benjamin Cantrill, bm.

Morton, Vincent L. & Isabella F. Oliver, 4 Dec 1848; G. M. Lea, bm.

Morton, William & Sally Simpson, 29 Jan 1812; Jacob Morton, bm.

Morton, Willey & Polley Cheek, 1 April 1822; John Cheek, bm.

Moser, Jonathan R. & Barbara Thomas, 24 July 1838; Hiram Steel, bm.

Moser, John & Margaret Kime, 23 Feb 1805; Philip Henkle, bm.

Moser, John & Jane Holt, 10 May 1849; John Moser, bm.

Moser, Levi & Molly Isley, 5 March 1835; William Steel, bm.

Moser, Martin & Polly Roberson, 5 June 1848; Daniel Thomas, bm.

Moser, William & Elizabeth Steel, 23 Oct 1832; Nimrod Moser, bm.

Moss, William Henry & Betsay Forbes, 17 Oct 1845; John Fitch, bm.

Moss, Willie & Pene Atkins, 12 May 1832; Archabald Atkin, bm.

Motheral, Joseph & Sarah Carr, 22 March 1787; Samuel Allen, bm.

Mott, Thomas S. W. & Susan A. Phillips, 29 June 1833; James Phillips, bm.

Moulder, Jacob & Elizabeth Boreland, 24 May 1802; Henry Neal, bm.

Mulhollan, Hugh & Polley McLemore, 11 May 1804; James Tate, bm.

Mulhollan, Hugh Sr. & Mary Wilanders, 22 Dec 1800; Jacob Hughans, Henry Thompson, bm.

Mumford, James & Patsy Shepperd, 5 March 1791; John Casey, bm.

Munger, Nelson H. & Mary Q. Hilliard, 25 June 1834; Carlston B. Cole, bm.

Murden, David & Judith Elizabeth Workman, 10 March 1823; Saml. Murden, Frs. B. Phillips, bm.

Murdoch, Andrew & Dicey Berry, 16 Dec 1824; J. A. Gray, bm.

Murdoch, David & Elizabeth Miller, 6 Dec 1815; Thomas Bowles, bm.

Murdoch, William J. R. & Charity C. Davis, 25 Oct 1861; J. M. Palmer, bm; m 25 Oct 1851 by Hezekiah Terry, J. P.

Murdock, Alexander & Tempy E. Pearson, 19 Dec 1860; John Murdock, Charles J. Pender, bm; m 20 Dec 1860 by Ruffin R. Tapp, J. P.

Murdock, Andrew & Polley Ray, 17 Dec 1828; A. Parks, bm.

Murdock, Catlet & Cornelia F. Pender, 12 Oct 1861; Wm. Pender, 12 Oct 1861; Wm. Pender, Thomas Webb, bm; m 15 Oct 1861 by Wilson Brown, J. P.

Murdock, Henry & Mariah M. Jackson, 2 Feb 1867; George W. Walker, bm; m 3 Feb 1867 by C. J. Freeland, J. P.

Murdock, James & Nancy Craig, 18 June 1810; A. Craig, bm.

Murdock, John & Jane Smith, 13 Nov 1856; Alexander Murdock, M. Miller, bm; m 27 Feb 1857 by Ruffin R. Tapp, J. P.

Murdock, Robert & Elizabeth Thompson, 14 Nov 1804; Alexdr. Mebane, bm.

Murdock, Thomas & Polly Wilhoit, 27 Jan 1804; Robt. Dixon, bm.

Murfey, Thomas & Nancey Graves, 8 Aug 1783; Stephen Merit, bm.

Murphey, Archibald D. & Jeany Scott, 4 Nov 1801; And. Flinn, bm.

Murphey, Archd. & Hannah Scott, 13 Sept 1830; Alexr. Allen, bm.

Murphey, Henry J. & Mary J. Farrar, 19 June 1858; William F. Anderson, bm; m 20 June 1858 by Henry Gray.

Murphey, Jonathan & ____, 15 May 1834; William Murphey, bm.

Murphey, William & Elizabeth Whitted, 22 Oct 1823; Thomas Scott, bm.

Murphy, Martin & Polly Smith, 9 Feb 1805; John McDade, bm.

Murphy, Solomon & Betsey Gun, 29 Oct 1781; John Lynch, bm.

Murphy, Thoms. C. & Hannah McIntire, 10 June 1789.

Murphy, William & Susan Hart, 13 Sept 1819; David Clark, bm.

Murray, Alfred & Anne Cryder, 26 Sept 1832; Hinton Murray, bm.

Murray, Andw. & Elizabeth Hart, 29 Jan 1823; William Anderson, bm.

Murray, Calvin & Jane Lindsey, 29 Dec 1841; Jno. J. Allison, Moses Anderson, bm.

Murray, Charles F. & Leveny McCaddam, 25 Feb 1847; Robert Morrow, bm.

Murray, David & Elizabeth Thompson, 3 Sept 1846; Weston Kimrey, bm.

Murray, Eli & Elizabeth Hutchison, 31 Oct 1821; Jas. Paul, bm.

Murray, Goodner & Anne Smith, 30 July 1832; Wm. Smith, J. S. Smith, bm.

Murray, Hinton & Sarah Catherine Ray, 9 March 1835; Chas. W. Ray, bm.

Murray, Jacob & Ann Stailey, 25 Sept 1829; Isaac Yergin, bm.

Murray, James & Margaret Baker, 1 Oct 1796; John McCaddam, bm.

Murray, James & Jeany McMinig, 29 April 1802; Jno. Taylor, bm.

Murray, James & Nancy Rogers, 5 Feb 1823; Perrey Mitchell, bm.

Murray, James & Nancy McCaddams, 7 Jan 1827; John Walker, bm.

Murray, James E. & Martha Benson, 9 Feb 1847; William B. McAdams, bm.

Murray, James J., son of James & Elizabeth M. Murray, & Cynthia A. Morgan, dau. of William & Sallie Morgan, m 24 Dec 1867 by Nelson P. Hall, J. P.

Murray, John & Elizabeth Baldridge, 17 Feb 1803; Thos. Woods, bm.

Murray, John & Jenny Tate, 9 March 1825; Andr. Murray, bm.

Murray, John G. & Elizabeth Mebane, 21 Nov 1839; Morgan Mebane, bm.

Murray, Joseph & Anne Thomas, 8 Sept 1814; Francies Marshall, bm.

Murray, Joseph & Livinia Austen, 3 Sept 1835; H. Waddle, bm.

Murray, Lambert & Elizabeth Hainey, 22 Aug 1832; Alfred Murray, bm.

Murray, Lindly & Charity Thomas, 10 Sept 1841; Jacob Murray, bm.

Murray, Robert & Polly Robertson, 20 Sept 1806; Robert Morrow, bm.

Murray, Thomas & Peggy Eccles, 19 Dec 1812; James Bauldin, bm.

Murray, Thomas & Margaret Redding, 28 March 1818; Wm. Reding, bm.

Murray, Virgil & Mary Allison, 15 Sept 1865; Devard Crawford, bm.

Murray, William & Polley Ray, 10 Nov 1807; Robert Morrow, bm.

Murray, William & Martha Pickett, 17 Jan 1818; David McCadams, bm.

Murray, William & Elizabeth Reeves, 9 Jan 1840; S. Reeves, bm.

Murray, William B. & Mariah F. Tinnen, 22 July 1863; Josiah Turner Jr., bm; m 26 July 1863 by Archibald Currie.

Murray, William C. & Sarah Jane McCaddams, 17 Dec 1844; Isaac M. McCaddams, bm.

Murray, Wm. H. & Manerva Nethery, 3 Oct 1866; James Webb Jr., bm; m 4 Oct 1866 by R. H. J. Blount, J. P.

Murray, Wm. Y & Peggie Clapp, 6 Nov 1845; Wm. Hutson, bm.

Murray, Willie & Margrit N. Forrest, 9 Jan 1833; James Mebane, bm.

Murray, Willie & Nancy N. B. Moore, 20 Nov 1862; Jas. G. McClaen, bm; m 20 Nov 1862 by Thos. H. Hughes, J. P.

Murrey, Allsee & Rachel Albert, 4 June 1807; James Gant, bm.

Murry, Green & Peggy Millington, 15 Sept 1829; A. Murry, bm.

Murry, James & Polly Ritesman, 31 Oct 1806; James Murry, William Cappins, bm.

Murry, John & Mary Scott, 24 Dec 1788; James Barton, bm.

Murry, John & Mary Picket, 3 Jan 1800; William Picket, bm.

Murry, John T. & Catherine Crawford, 27 Aug 1860; William Jen__, bm; m 27 Aug 1860 by Robert T. Tinnin.

Murry, Joseph & Celia Dannilly, 5 Sept 1842; Moses Leathers Jr., bm.

Murry, Thomas & Catharine Weaver, 23 March 1799; Frances Jones, bm.

Myers, Abram & Polley Oaky, 6 Feb 1806; Eldredg Alston, bm.

Myrack, James & Nancy Crabtree, 29 Nov 1814; Allen Crabtree, bm.

Nance, Allen & Nancy C. Terrell, 25 Aug 1860; William Watts, bm; m 27 Aug 1860 by Thomas Ferrell, J. P.

Nance, Amos & Nancy M. Pool, 26 Feb 1866; J. W. Ferrell, H. B. Guthrie, bm; m 27 Feb 1866 by R. F. Morris, J. P.

Nance, John & Frances Laws, 20 March 1826; Jno. Nance Jr., David Umstead, bm.

Nash, Henry K. & Mary Simpson, 22 Oct 1838; H. K. Nash, J. Taylor, bm.

Nash, William & Margaret Kinchen, 1 Sept 1795; S. Benton, bm.

Neal, Alvis & Agnes Herndon, 26 Oct 1858; Henry Crabtree, bm; m 28 Oct 1858 by William F. Strayhorn, J. P.

Neal, Henry & Liddia ___, 1 Sept 1798; Sandy Kinchen, bm.

Neal, Henry & Mary Redding, 25 March 1852; Riley Neal, bm; m 1 April 1852 by King Barbee, J. P.

Neal, James & Nelly Horn, 15 May 1795; Ezekeel Hinches, bm.

Neal, Wriley & Mary Horne, 19 March 1828; James Woods, bm.

Neale, John & Frances Sandy, 25 April 1825; William Horne, bm.

Nease, George Jr. & Elizabeth Neace, 13 Nov 1822; Jacob Neace, bm.

Nease, Jacob & Rebecca McAdams, 27 May 1836; Joshua Holt, bm.

Nease, John & Milly Graves, 28 Nov 1811; Martin Nease, bm.

Neeley, Jno. & Celia Carrington, 27 Feb 1818; S. Harris, bm.

Neeley, Joseph & Nancy Horton, 5 Sept 1795; Samuel Turrentine, bm.

Neeley, Thomas & Sally Oakley, 16 March 1816; Thos. Carrington, bm.

Neese, Daniel & Caty Fogleman, 11 May 1830; John Neese, bm.

Neese, Elias & Tenah Nease, 12 Sept 1818; Joseph Neese, bm.

Neese, Martin & Polly Thomas, 30 Aug 1832; William Cable, bm.

Neighbours, John & Elizabeth Inscore, 19 March 1827; Willie N. Shaw, Jeff Horner, bm.

Neighbours, Simion & Eliza Nethery, 10 Aug 1866; Nelson Neighbors, James R. Gattis, bm; m 12 Aug 1866 by Wm. J. Gray, J. P.

Neighbours, William & Tempe Ledbetter, 27 Oct 1830; Benjamin Ledbetter, bm.

Nelson, Alfred & Nancy Gill, 3 Oct 1824; David Nelson, bm.

Nelson, David & Polley Strain, 24 Sept 1811; David Tate, bm.

Nelson, James & Polly Linn, 26 Aug 1809; Joseph Gibson, bm.

Nelson, James & Barbara Phifer, 18 Jan 1823; Jonathan Phifer, bm.

Nelson, John & Jennet Tate, 1 May 1789.

Nelson, John & Nancy Burnside, 28 Oct 1824; Jos. Tate, bm.

Nelson, Paisley & Margaret Smith, 6 Sept 1837; J. N. Craig, John Smith, bm.

Nelson, Samuel & Sarah McDannel, 8 March 1790; John McDannel, bm.

Nelson, Samuel & Sarah Burnsides, 26 Dec 1831; John N. Allen, bm.

Nelson, Samul L. & Matilda Squires, 6 Nov 1866; Alex. A. Smith, bm; m 7 Nov 1866 by Wilson Brown, J. P.

Nelson, Thomas & Patty Williams, 7 May 1796; James McCauley, bm.

Nelson, William & Elizabeth Eaton, 18 April 1818; James Adams, bm.

Neves, William & Frances Allen, 20 Feb 1799; Porter Allen, bm.

Nevil, Mathew & Tabitha Bowers, 13 June 1847; Morris King, bm.

Nevill, Benjamin & Nancy Robenson, 3 Oct 1800; James Kirk, bm.

Nevill, Goodman & Jane McCauley, 15 Sept 1804; John McCauley, bm.

Nevill, James & Caroline Stroud, 15 Dec 1836; Alexander Blackwell, John Hutchins, bm.

Nevill, John S. & Margarett A. Tilly, 12 July 1861; T. A. Long, bm; m 28 July 1861 by Manly Andrews.

Nevill, Samuel & Elizabeth McCauley, 14 Jan 1810; Goodmon Neville, bm.

Neville, John & Emily Lloyd, 23 Oct 1850; Morris King, bm.

Neville, John G. & Frances S. Stanford, 23 March 1863; D. McCauley, bm; m 24 April 1863 by J. W. Stroud, J. P.

Neville, Ruffin & Nancy Blackwood, 27 Oct 1859; J. W. Carr, bm; m 27 Oct 1859 by D. Tilley, J. P.

New, John & Sally Gattley, 17 June 1815; S. Turrentine, bm.

Newcomb, William & Peggy Crabtree, 22 May 1813; H. McCollum, bm.

Newgin, Jacob & Rabeckah Wilson, 3 Sept 1796; John Pyle, bm.

Newlin, Elihu & Anna McPherson, 23 Sept 1838; Nathan Stout, bm.

Newlin, James & Eliza M. Holt, 20 Sept 1842; Jno. M. Faucett, Moses Leathers Jr., bm.

Newlin, William & Margaret Puryear, 22 July 1846; Duncan Murray, bm.

Newman, Benjamen & Ann Eliza Parten, 13 June 1860; John H. Paul, bm; m 13 June 1860 by Thos. C. Hayes, minister.

Newman, William & Elizabeth Faucette, 30 Jan 1806; Thos. Claney, bm.

Newman, Wm. & Elizabeth Scott, 12 July 1850; Porter Thompson, bm.

Newton, Isaac & Nancy Carrington, 28 May 1804; John Jamieson, bm.

Newton, James & Sarah Clark, 23 Jan 1796; Samuel Coleman, bm.

Newton, James W. & Harriet M. Gates, 26 Aug 1851; Thomas Horner, bm; m 26 Aug 1851 by Hezekiah Terry, J. P.

Newton, John & Elizabeth Harris, 28 Sept 1815; Albert Riggs, bm.

Newton, Robert & Mary Harris, 29 Dec 1808; John Riggs, bm.

Newton, W. J. & Mary C. Cooley, 3 Dec 1855; L. H. Newton, bm; m 3 Jan 1855 by H. F. Hudson, minister.

Nicholas, Jonathan & Martha Turrentine, 23 Oct 1799; William Lindsey, bm.

Nichols, Alves & Polley Dortch, 13 Feb 1830; Tho. W. Holden, bm.

Nichols, Amos & Rachel Riggs, 12 March 1801; Hugh Woods, bm.

Nichols, Duncan & Ann Kennion, 8 Nov 1833; William Moore, bm.

Nichols, George & Polley Vaughan, 23 Nov 1813; Richison Nichols, bm.

Nichols, George & Ellen D. Carrington, 2 Oct 1838; George Jackson, bm.

Nichols, James O. & Elizabeth D. Neeley, 8 Sept 1858; George W. Glenn, Alexr. Dickson, bm; m 9 Sept 1858 by Charles Wilson, J. P.

Nichols, John & Anne Riggs, 23 Sept 1797; Baldwin Nickols, bm.

Nichols, John & Dicey George, 2 April 1839; Harman Herndon, And. Borland, bm.

Nichols, Jno. & Sarah Lytle, 3 July 1788; Robt. Ferguson, bm.

Nichols, Jonathan & Mary Hall, 8 May 1789; Robert Hall, bm.

Nichols, Jonathan & Ellen R. Nichols, 14 Feb 1865; L. W. Hall, James C. Turrentine, bm; m 14 Feb 1865 by L. W. Hall, J. P.

Nichols, Leuco & Mildred Leathers, 9 July 1857; A. Nichols, bm; m 12 July 1857 by Wm. McCown, J. P.

Nichols, Nelson L. & Martha E. Nichols, 2 Sept 1865; Sampson M. Glenn, bm; m 6 Sept 1865 by Charles Wilson, J. P.

Nichols, Person R. & Nancy Wilson, 3 May 1823; J. Van Hooks, bm.

Nichols, Robert & Peggy Craig, 29 Jan 1805; Joseph Smith, bm.

Nichols, Robert A. & Mary Jackson, 29 Dec 1860; Thomas A. Williams, bm; m 31 Dec 1860 by Benjamin J. Kinnion, J. P.

Nichols, Turner & Susannah Briggs, 16 March 1822; Fielding Leathers, bm.

Nichols, William & Sarah Herndon, 24 Sept 1815; John Holloway, bm.

Nichols, William A. & Martha E. Nichols, 14 Feb 1859; Peter A. Ray, bm; m 15 Feb 1859 by H. Terry, J. P.

Nichols, Wilson & Maria Wilson, 5 April 1827; James Vincent, bm.

Nichols, Wilson A. & Louisa H. Nichols, 10 April 1861; William A. Nichols, bm; m 14 April 1861 by Benjamin J. Kinnion, J. P.

Nicholson, Archabald & Polley Fougleman, 13 Aug 1796; James Nicholson, bm.

Nicholson, Green & Polly Sharp, 1 Oct 1832; Benjamin Sharp, bm.

Nickoles, John & Sally Wilson, 13 Nov 1815; Thos. B. Patterson, bm.

Nickols, Richardson & Sally Holden, 28 March 1821; Wm. Burton, bm.

Nickols, Thomas & Hannah Jackson, 24 Dec 1819; A. Y. Jackson, bm.

Nickols, William & Sally Cloud, 11 May 1813; David S. Cloud, bm.

Night, Wile & Nancy Clinton, 12 Feb 1828; Jesse Clinton, bm.

Nixon, Isaac & Mary Bowman, 19 Nov 1828; William Porter, bm.

Noah, Austin & Milly Friddle, 2 Nov 1837; Amos Noah, bm.

Noah, Daniel & Margaret Bayley, 4 Oct 1832.

Noah, Isaiah & Nancy Mosier, 3 July 1840; Jeremiah Noah, bm.

Noblet, Abram & Margaret Upton, 22 April 1814; Joseph Holden, bm.

Noblet, William & Mary Whinnery, 18 March 1810; Jacob Friddle, bm.

Noe, Hezekiah & Elizabeth Holt, 24 Aug 1841; Levi Graves, bm.

Noe, Jacob & Elizabeth Baly, 10 June 1815; John Noe, bm.

Noe, Jeremiah & Dinah Marshal, 25 Sept 1839; Peter Moser, bm.

Noe, John & Levina Cook, 15 July 1809; Robert Dixon, bm.

Noe, Samuel & Sally Woods, 29 July 1809; John Sharpe, bm.

Norman, Joshua & Winna Berry, 19 Sept 1820; Henry Berry, bm.

Norman, Samuel & Nancy Green, 5 Nov 1804; Clement Harvey, bm.

Norman, Thomas & Catharine Green, 23 Feb 1810; James G. Norman, bm.

Norman, Thomas & Polly Luie, 11 July 1832; John Esex, bm.

Normand, Francis & Catharine Green, 23 Feb 1810; Samuel Norman, bm.

Norment, John H. & Mary Ann Spear, 9 July 1828; Geo. M. Johnston, bm.

Normon, Joshua & Mary Fowler, 27 Jan 1817; Francis Normon, bm.

Normon, Thomas & Polley McCauley, 17 Sept 1811; Burres Estridge, bm.

Northen, R. Nixon & Margaret Briggs, 15 Aug 1866; Jno. A. Owen, bm; m 15 Aug 1866 by Will C. Willson.

Norwood, Gilliam & Maria Carter, 11 May 1827; James Jones, bm.

Norwood, Hasell & Mariah L. Howerton, 3 Jan 1855; m 9 Jan 1855
    by Robert Burwell, minister.

Norwood, John W. & Annebella Giles, 23 Jan 1826; F. Nash, bm.

Norwood, Thomas & Jemima Williams, 10 July 1835; John Stout, bm.

Norwood, William & Robena Hogg, 7 Jan 1800; Ca. Campbell, bm.

Nunn, Hugh & Charlotte Yeargain, 6 Jan 1805; James Pratt, bm.

Nunn, Ilai M. & Emily Barbee, 22 Dec 1831; N. J. King, bm.

Nutt, Benj. & Ferreby Brinkley, 8 March 1817; Adam M. Douglas,
    bm.

Nutt, Erasmus D. & Jane M. Gattis, 2 Nov 1847; James K. Gattis,
    bm.

Nutt, Gilford & Leathy James, 15 Sept 1853; Harrison Ashly,
    Mermick Miller, bm.

Nutt, John & Catey Waggoner, 1 July 1814; James Jackson, bm.

Nutt, Robert & Anne Cates, 9 Sept 1820; Jesse Walker, bm.

Nutt, Robert & Mary Cate, 2 Aug 1823; William Gragson, bm.

Nutt, William & Anne H. Barton, 26 June 1857; William Crabtree,
    James Gill, bm; m 27 June 1857 by Jas. W. Craig, J. P.

Oakley, Dudley & Susanah Mary Smith, 6 March 1850; John M.
    Smith, L. Cheek, bm.

Oakley, Dudley S. & Ellen Jane Pettigrew, 10 Feb 1863; William
    Wilson, bm; m 22 Feb 1863 by R. G. Tinnin.

Oakley, Erasmus & Sarah Brown, 4 Dec 1846; John H. Breeze, bm.

Oakley, Erasmus & Mary Jane Brown, 4 Sept 1849; Evins Brown, bm.

Oakley, John & Temperance Inscore, 22 Jan 1819; Reubin Inscore,
    bm.

Oakley, Thomas C. & Bettie McCabe, m 17 April 1867 by E. M.
    Holt, J. P.

Oakley, Wm. E. & Jemima Umstead, 17 July 1838; John C. Veazey,
    bm.

O'Danel, William & Elmina Lendsey, m 22 Nov 1855 by Allen
    Edwards, J. P.

O'Daniel, Alfred & Mary Ellen Collins, 18 March 1835; Samuel
    Thompson, bm.

ODaniel, Alfred & Elizabeth Lamb, 25 April 1865; Green Cates,
    bm.

O'Daniel, Green & Nancy O'Daniel, 2 April 1825; R. C. Mabrey, bm.

ODaniel, Henry & Martha Thompson, 21 June 1824; John Morrow, bm.

O'Daniel, John & Sally Allen, 20 Feb 1800; Elisha Pickard, bm.

O'Daniel, John & Miley Minnis, 18 Dec 1848; Henry Pickard, bm.

O'Daniel, Joshua & Susanah Blackston, 21 Dec 1813; Daniel Pickard, bm.

O'Daniel, Samuel & Mary Trousdale, 13 March 1798; Wm. Trousdale, bm.

ODaniel, William & Elizabeth Brewer, 12 Jan 1822; Thomas Pickard, bm.

ODaniel, William & Mary Cheek, 19 Jan 1850; Henry ODaniel, bm.

ODaniel, William & Elmina Lindsey, 22 Nov 1855; Green Cate, James Gill, bm.

ODaniell, Henry & Dolly Cate, 31 Aug 1824; John S. Cate, bm.

Odom, Ephraim & Tempe Kimbrough, 30 Dec 1818; Willie Whiteheart, bm.

OFarrill, Barnabas & Nancy Williams, 3 Dec 1807; Wm. Rider, bm.

O'Ferrel, Thomas & Elizabeth Hencock, 2 Aug 1853; Thomas Fawcett, bm; m 2 Aug 1853 by Rich. Nichols, J. P.

O'Kelly, John & Macy Praight, 2 May 1811; Zinas O'Kelly, bm.

Oldham, Thos. B. & Elizabeth Brewer, 8 Jan 1827; Joel Parish, bm.

Oldham, Y. A. & C. C. Riggsbee, 2 June 1861; Y. A. Oldham, bm; m by B. F. Pastin.

Oldom, William & Sarah Pendergrass, 4 March 1797; Abijah Massey, bm.

Olive, Munroe C. & Aurelia C. Siler, 6 Feb 1867; John White, bm; m 7 Feb 1867 by Solomon Pool.

Omerry, John & Celia Arnold, 16 Nov 1857; Wm. J. Roberts, bm; m 16 Nov 1857 by Wm. J. Roberts, J. P.

Oneal, David & Susannah T. Miller, 8 May 1830; Isaac Ragains, bm.

O'neal, John & Salley Currethers, 3 April 1805; Wm. Lloyd, bm.

O'neal, Jonth. & Polly Swinney, 30 May 1813; Amos Swinney, bm.

Osbun, William & Susannah Snotherly, 11 April 1799; Daniel Toust, bm.

Otey, James H. & Eliza D. Pannell, 15 Oct 1821; Wm. Hillyard, bm.

Outlaw, George & Nancy Benson, 21 Nov 1825; Josiah Hunt, bm.

Overman, Benjamin & Elmina Underwood, 22 May 1841; Benjamin Overman, James Overman, bm.

Overman, Brooks H. & Eliza Ann Steel, 26 Dec 1865; Henry Ray, David Anderson, bm; m 26 Dec 1865 by Wilson Brown, J. P.

Overman, Thomas & Sally Evins, 5 Aug 1820; Daniel Coble, bm.

Overman, William & Mahala Perry, 29 July 1841; William Overman, James Simmons, bm.

Owen, Henderson & Rebecca C. Herndon, 1 March 1828; John R. Nerndon, bm.

Owen, John & Lidda Cole, 4 Sept 1784; Benja. Yeargain, bm.

Owen, John & Sally Evans, 22 Nov 1824; Reeves Riggins, bm.

Owen, Peter & Hannah Mitchel, 20 Nov 1786; Geo. Tate, bm.

Owen, Samuel & Tracia Cash, 29 Sept 1803; William Ling, bm.

Owens, Charles Harrison & Mary Cates, 30 Dec 1795; Wm. Rider, bm.

Owens, William & Rosa Scars, 7 Nov 1816; William Sparrow, bm.

Ozburn, William & Margaret Stalcup, 6 Dec 1786; Joseph Dorrin, bm.

Pace, Joseph & Elizabeth Trewitt, 8 Dec 1834; James M. Palmer, William Lipscomb, bm.

Pain, Henry & Rachel Thompson, 17 Dec 1795; James Cargin, bm.

Paisley, George & Elizabeth Freeland, 1 Feb 1810; Johnston Freeland, bm.

Paisley, Preston & Charity Anderson, 26 March 1818; Saml. Paisley, bm.

Paisley, William & Fanney Mebane, 21 Feb 1799; Jas. Mebane, bm.

Palmer, Nathaniel Jones & Lavinia Bryant, 19 July 1826; Thos. Clancy, bm.

Palmer, Thos. & Sarah Dishon, 29 Feb 1808; Lewis Dishon, bm.

Palmer, William & Elizabeth Cleacy, 6 July 1799; S. Benton, bm.

Pardue, Pleasant & Elizabeth Brooks, 12 June 1819; Anderson Brooks, bm.

Parham, Amasa & Salley Wood, 11 Feb 1814; Hubbard Blalock, bm.

Paris, Henry & Mary Johnston, 30 Nov 1806; Jno. Woods, bm.

Paris, William & Mary Millican, 1 March 1824; John Thompson, bm.

Parish, Alfred M. & Frances Pope, 23 Nov 1859; B. J. Sears, A. B. Gunter, bm; m 24 Nov 1859 by A. B. Gunter, J. P.

Parish, Dempsey & Sally Brinkley, 12 Dec 1827; Isham Brinkley, bm.

Parish, Henderson & Ruth Carrington, 13 Sept 1831; E. H. Carrington, bm.

Parish, Henry S. & Emily Jane Hester, 24 Dec 1847; S. W. Roberts, bm.

Parish, James & Polly Carrington, 25 Feb 1818; William Lunsford, bm.

Parish, John M. & Martha M. Cocke, 4 Oct 1856; John Breeze, S. H. Breeze, bm; m 5 Oct 1856 by Hezekiah Terry, J. P.

Parish, Kerson & Penny Laws, 3 Feb 1866; Doctor C. Parish, Robert H. Harris, bm; m 3 Feb 1866 by S. D. Umstead, deacon.

Parish, Nelson & Letha Mangum, 13 Dec 1819; William Duke, bm.

Parish, Sion & Sura Pettigrew, 20 Aug 1805; Hansel Pettigrew, bm.

Parish, William & Wibney Barbee, 30 Nov 1826; Alfred Boothe, bm.

Parish, William & Emeline B. Sensford, 8 Jan 1859; Robert F. Webb, bm.

Park, Emsley & Mary Hawkins, 6 Oct 1794; Simson Gevon, bm.

Parker, Abner & Polly Horner, 12 Dec 1817; James Parrish, bm.

Parker, Allen & Sarah Elmore, 4 Aug 1812; Peter Elmore, bm.

Parker, Archibald W. & Mary Woods, 8 Nov 1832; James Montgomery, bm.

Parker, David & Clary Mangrom, 29 Dec 1792; William Cozart, bm.

Parker, David & Jane R. Nelson, 5 Oct 1838; D. C. Parrish, E. Benson, bm.

Parker, David & McKinza McCawn, 11 Dec 1866; David Parker, Jno. L. Lockhart, bm; m 25 Dec 1866 by A. W. Green, Jr., minister.

Parker, George & Sarah Burton, 15 Sept 1846; J. Weelding, bm.

Parker, Harrison & Sally Parker, 22 May 1813; William Lunsford, bm.

Parker, James & Martha E. Gates, 28 Oct 1859; John Cates, bm; m 18 Nov 1859 by H. Terry, J. P.

Parker, Jesse P. & Mary Armstrong, 15 Sept 1829; Wm. Horner, bm.

Parker, Jesse W. & Mary J. Wotham, 11 Jan 1848; J. P. Parker, R. F. Morris, bm.

Parker, John & Hannah Messersmith, 6 Sept 1810; Facoe Waggner, bm.

Parker, John A. Jr. & Elizabeth J. Jordan, 30 Aug 1861; A. M. Breeze, James Hill, bm; m 13 Oct 1861 by H. Terry, J. P.

Parker, John Alvis & Susanah Gates, 21 Jan 1853; William Haunes, Wm. Y. McBroom, bm; m 30 Jan 1853 by H. Terry, J. P.

Parker, Nelson & Massey Madden, 4 April 1851; W. H. Jordan, bm; m 10 April 1851 by H. Terry, J. P.

Parker, Samuel & Lucy Shavers, 10 April 1846; T. Crawford, bm.

Parker, Samuel M., son of William & Martha Parker, & Mary J. Taylor, dau. of Henderson & Elizabeth Taylor, 28 Jan 1868; m 31 Jan 1868 by Thomas Wilson, J. P.

Parker, Thomas & Sarah Southerlan, 12 July 1847; Wm. E. Wallen, bm.

Parker, William & Patsey Madden, 20 Feb 1838; Jacob Hern, bm.

Parker, William D. & Drady Harris, 9 May 1835; Thomas Lattla, bm.

Parkes, James & Maria Clark, 7 March 1833; Michael Carroll, bm.

Parks, David & Ceney Herald, 26 Aug 1800; Wm. Groin, bm.

Parks, David & Barbary Weeks, 25 Feb 1808; Boston Isley, bm.

Parks, Randolph & Jeany Pugh, 2 May 1809; J. A. Parks, Archabel Pugh, bm.

Parks, Samuel & Levina Garner, 12 Dec 1783; Thomas Parks, bm.

Parmer, Edward & Jane Summers, 26 Sept 1846; James Melvin, bm.

Parmly, Saml. & Eliza Morgan, colored, 4 July 1866; Norris T. Loyd, bm; m 5 Jan 1866 by N. C. Cate, J. P.

Parr, Bartholomus & Caroline Lashley, 21 March 1866; Johnston Lashley, bm; m 21 March 1866 by Wiatt Cates, J. P.

Parrish, Alfred & Dicy Castleberry, 16 Aug 1852; James Watson, bm; m 19 Aug 1852 by Thos. J. Fowler.

Parrish, Calvin E. & Mary Ann Holden, 22 Nov 1828; W. A. Parish, bm.

Parrish, Charles & Christian Thompson, 25 Feb 1813; Archd. Holmes, bm.

Parrish, Charles & Elizabeth Huntington, 29 April 1819; James Child, bm.

Parrish, David & Polley Lunsford, 1 March 1843; H. Parker, bm.

Parrish, Doctor & Julia A. Carrington, 5 June 1865; W. A. Lunsford, bm; m 7 June 1865 by S. D. Unstead, L. deacon.

Parrish, Eldridge & Martha Markham, 5 May 1866; E. W. Morris, bm; m 5 May 1866 by C. G. Markham.

Parrish, Henry G. & Anges Palmer, 27 Dec 1821; N. J. King, bm.

Parrish, Henry & Caroline Roberts, colored, 10 Oct 1865; Doctor Parrish, bm; m 15 Oct 1865 by S. D. Umsted, deacon.

Parrish, Isham & Maria Carrington, 6 Nov 1833; J. Taylor, bm.

Parrish, James & Elizabeth Moring, 9 Dec 1856; James Parrish, H. Mulhollon, bm.

Parrish, James P. & Eady Parrish, m 28 May 1857 by William M. Carrington, J. P.

Parrish, John L. & Isabella E. Umsted, 29 May 1858; D. C.
Parrish, bm.

Parrish, Mark & Lotty Brinkly, 28 Nov 1823; Robt. Latta, bm.

Parrish, Nelson & Martha Tilly, 4 May 1857; Wm. K. Parrish, bm.

Parrish, William & Lucy Gwinn, 6 Dec 1793; Thomas Parish, bm.

Parrish, William K. & Bedie A. Lockhart, 12 May 1861; W. R.
Hughes, T. W. Laws, bm.

Partin, B. F. & Artelia Webster, 23 Nov 1865; B. M. Ray, bm;
m 23 Nov 1865 by A. D. Betts, minister.

Partin, Bennette & Margaret Cook, 25 Aug 1818; Charles Partin,
bm.

Partin, Charles & Frances King, 29 April 1798; William King, bm.

Partin, Green & Mary Jinkins, 3 March 1830; A. Blackwood, bm.

Partin, James & Nancy McGinnis, 12 July 1792; Benja. Yeargain,
bm.

Partin, James & Nancy Stephens, 27 Sept 1823; James Partin, John
Cheek, bm.

Partin, Lewis & Peggy King, 3 May 1809; Lewis Partin, David
Strain, bm.

Partin, Thomas G. & Artelia Cates, 29 Dec 1864; T. Watson, bm;
m 29 Dec 1864 by J. B. McDade, J. P.

Partin, William & Charlotte Underhill, 18 Nov 1810; Lewis
Partin, bm.

Parton, Charles & Ruth Cook, 21 Dec 1824; John Cook, bm.

Pascal, Ezekiel & Mary Williams, 9 Aug 1837; Moody Williams, bm.

Pascal, John & Elizabeth Hughs, 3 Oct 1839; George Hughs, bm.

Paschal, Abner & Elizabeth Ellis, 5 June 1866; Richard King,
John M. Blackwood, bm; m 5 June 1866 by Henry Gray, L. Elder
and M. G.

Pasmore, Augustine & Anne Hargess, 2 March 1795; Eli McDannel,
bm.

Pasmore, William & Dianah Elliot, 17 March 1787; William Elliott
John Elliott, bm.

Passmore, David & Catey Randels, 13 Nov 1786; Thomas Bivens, bm.

Paterson, Mann & Polly Barbee, 30 Dec 1803; Joseph Barbee, bm.

Patrun, John & Elizabeth Lankford, 30 Jan 1828; George Lankford,
bm.

Patten, Alexander & Fanny Faucett, 15 May 1826; Clem Sears, bm.

Patten, James C. & Sarah Jane Hurdle, 21 Feb 1842; Wm. M.
Rogers, bm.

Patterson, Chesley M. & Nancy Moore, 26 March 1827; Aisa Couch, bm.

Patterson, Chesley P. & Nancy Morgan, 8 June 1795; Benjamen Yeargain, bm.

Patterson, David & Polly Bain, 30 Nov 1796; Isaac Patterson, bm.

Patterson, Isaac & Barbery Coble, 29 Nov 1799; Jno. Bullock, bm.

Patterson, James N. & Mary C. Barbee, 27 Jan 1858; Levi Thomas, bm.

Patterson, John & Catey Albright, 27 Sept 1823; John Holstead, bm.

Patterson, John & Sarah Hogan, 20 July 1866; George Patterson, bm.

Patterson, John T. O. B. & Clementine H. Barbee, 31 Jan 1825; Thos Thompson, bm.

Patterson, Man & Anges Rogers, 17 Jan 1852; C. T. Boroughs, bm.

Patterson, Mann & Polley Cabe, 23 Feb 1819; Geo. Johnston, bm.

Patterson, Mark & Sally Rhodes, 9 July 1808; William Trice, bm.

Patterson, Thomas & Anne McCrackin, 16 Dec 1841; Harrison Durham, John Pugh, bm.

Patterson, Thomas B. & Betsey Walker, 28 May 1816; Saml. Woods,

Patterson, Thomas B. & Betsey Walker, 28 May 1816; Saml. Woods, Jas. Lasslie, bm.

Patterson, William & Nancy Hodge, 14 Feb 1792; John Hodge, bm.

Patterson, William A. & Polly Isley, 9 Dec 1848; Wm. Hornaday, bm.

Patterson, Willie & Ann Herndon, 4 Jan 1799; Willey Patterson, Moses Barbee, bm.

Patterson, Willis, son of Saml. McCawn & Cely Couch, & Pheby Jenkins, dau. of James Dunkin & Mima Jenkins, m 8 Aug 1867 by Samuel Couch, J. P.

Patteson, David & Anne Chambers, 3 Jan 1783; William Barnett, bm.

Patton, Alexr. & Levinia Myrack, 17 Nov 1803; Lewis Kirk, bm.

Patton, Benjamin C. & Henrietta V. Lindsey, 18 Feb 1867; James A. Faucett, W. C. Faucette, bm; m 24 Feb 1867 by Thomas U. Faucett, M. G.

Patton, Homeleus & Nancy Woods, 26 Oct 1824; David Dortch, bm.

Patton, James & Nelly Johnston, 1 April 1809; Alex Patton, bm.

Patton, Josiah & Jane Stevens, 15 July 1826; William White, bm.

Patton, Matthew & Jane Pattin, 22 Aug 1798; John Patton, bm.

Patton, Matthew & Margaret McDaniel, 29 Nov 1900; William McDaniel, bm.

Patton, Robert & Elizabeth Gutherie, 28 July 1803; Wm. Smith, bm.

Patton, Samuel & Agnes Green, 3 Nov 1810; Henry Shutt, bm.

Patton, Samuel & Nancy James, 2 April 1828; William Web, bm.

Patton, Samuel & Sarah Tyrrell, 7 June 1841; Bartholomew Tyrrell, Thos. Anderson, bm.

Patton, Samuel & Margaret Woods, 5 Jan 1846; Samuel Patton, David W. Kerr, bm.

Patton, Samuel & Una Albright, 15 Feb 1847; Jacob Boon, bm.

Patton, Samuel & Susan F. Ferrell, 17 April 1849; Samuel Patton, Jesse Gant, bm.

Patton, William & Patsy Overman, 24 March 1802; Matthew Patton, bm.

Patton, William & Margaret Johnston, 21 Oct 1823; John S. Turrentine, bm.

Patton, William & Rebeccah Albright, 3 June 1831; Paisley Patton, bm.

Paul, David D. & Mary Anne Duskins, 20 Dec 1839; H. Webb, bm.

Paul, Henry, son of George Paul & Easter Bain, & Martha E. Kelly, dau. of Atkins and Sarah Kelly, colored, m 14 Aug 1868 by Job Berry, M. G.

Paul, James & Mary Hutchison, 20 Dec 1820; W. N. Pratt, bm.

Paul, James & Martha Thompson, 27 Nov 1865; A. L. Faucett, Stephen T. Forrest, bm.

Paul, John & Margaret Pratt, 7 Jan 1795; David Ray, bm.

Paul, John B. & Martha G. Faucett, 19 Dec 1855; James P. Tate, J. Turner, bm; m 20 Dec 1855 by Gaston Farrar, M. G.

Paul, John H. & Ellen Latta, 13 Sept 1847; Robert Faucett, A. Forrest, m 16 Sept 1847 by Archibald Currie, M. G.

Paul, John H. & Isabella Faucett, 20 Feb 1866; Robert Faucett, bm; m 20 Feb 1866 by Will C. Wilson.

Paul, John M. & Mary Nelson, 15 Nov 1831; William Paul, bm.

Paul, John M. & Martha Craig, 12 May 1863; Thos. Long, bm; m 13 May 1863 by Thos. Long, J. P.

Paul, Thos. P. & Margaret Burroughs, 22 June 1827; William Paul, bm.

Paul, William & Sarah Whitted, 10 Jan 1832; L. W. Young, J. Taylor, bm.

Paxton, Thomas & Mary Ann Johnston, 30 June 1852; Thomas Paxton, B. F. Hancock, bm.

ORANGE COUNTY MARRIAGES, 1779-1868

Payne, Isaiah & Catherine Ifland, 9 March 1819; David Ephlin, bm.

Payne, James & Jane Mahan, 13 April 1785; Moses Payne, bm.

Payne, Moses & Mary Rogers, 4 Feb 1784; James Payne, bm.

Payne, William & R. Murdock, 24 July 1786; James Payne, bm.

Payne, William & Sally Nicholson, 23 May 1820; George Ephland, bm.

Peacock, Richard & Elizabeth Palmer, 23 March 1820; Martin Palmer, bm.

Peacock, Saml. & Leah Jones, 30 May 1787; Jno. Ward, bm.

Peake, William & Nancy Burton, 5 Feb 1826; Abram Fox, Ira Ellis, bm.

Pealor, Pleasant & Sophia Copley, 10 Aug 1825; Silas M. Sink, bm.

Pearce, Elijah & Elizabeth Anderson, 5 Oct 1803; Elisha Umstead, bm.

Pearse, James & Elisabeth Gomore, 7 April 1795; George Campbell, bm.

Pearson, Ellis & Peggy King, 29 Feb 1804; Richard Blackwood, bm.

Pearson, Franklin & Elmire Cheek, 13 March 1858; John M. Pearson, John Miller, bm; m 14 March 1858 by Ruffin R. Tapp, J. P.

Pearson, Green & Mehalah Bevill, 10 Nov 1829; Thomas C. Davis, bm.

Pearson, Henry & Rebecca Brewer, 2 Sept 1852; Samuel Brewer, bm; m 25 Sept 1852 by L. L. Loyd, J. P.

Pearson, Henry J. & Caroline Malone, 26 June 1848; Henry Pearson, Jno. D. Carlton, bm.

Pearson, Isaiah & Margaret Pugh, 31 Dec 1796; John Pugh, bm.

Pearson, John M. & Louisa or Susan Gilbert, 4 July 1857; John R. Hancock, bm; m 4 July 1857 by Ruffin R. Tapp, J. P.

Pearson, Osborn & Patsy Hatwood, 25 Aug 1831; Nathaniel King, William Bowers, bm.

Pearson, Presley M. & Menurvy King, 20 April 1856; Archibal Griffin, bm; m 20 April 1856 by Thos. Long.

Pearson, Richmond & Elizabeth Murley, 3 Oct 1791; Robinson Mumford, bm.

Pearson, Thomas & Sarah King, 14 Feb 1831; Stanford Pearson, Nathaniel King, bm.

Pearson, Thomas & Nancy Show, 4 Oct 1840; James Sykes, Ashburn Minnis, bm.

Pearson, William & Nanny Trice, 28 Dec 1819; Nathan Marcom, bm.

233

Peck, William & Martha Williams, 26 Dec 1809; H. Thomson, bm.

Peed, Albert & Mary Hapgood, 11 Aug 1858; Stephen Chandler, Thomas Webb, bm.

Peed, Dudley & Lucy Primrose, 25 Sept 1848; Wesley B. Mangum, bm.

Peed, Rufus R. & Rebecca J. Bowling, 9 Dec 1865; Nelson Parrish, bm; m 10 Dec 1865 by S. D. Umsted, L. Deacon.

Peeler, Benjm. & Abbe Copley, 21 June 1806; Benjm. Carroll, bm.

Peeler, Jacob & Nancy James, 3 April 1802; Thomas Scarlett, bm.

Peeler, Solomon & Salley Copley, 2 Aug 1804; Christian Peeler, bm.

Peeler, Thomas & Mary Allison, 8 Feb 1828; Archd. Borland, James N. Strayhorn, bm.

Peeler, William R. & Mary Frances Tinnin, 21 May 1849; H. J. Smith, S. N. Dunn, bm.

Peelor, Abner & Susannah Nicks, 13 July 1793; Joseph Nicks, bm.

Peelor, Marshel S. & Margret Copley, 31 Oct 1823; Hardin Couch, bm.

Pekerd, Michl. & Barbara Eafland, 1 Feb 1809; Jacob Ephland, bm.

Pelkerton, John J. & Martha Ray, 29 Dec 1836; Samuel D. Strain, bm.

Peltier, Anthony & Lucy King, 2 Dec 1845; Archibald Price, bm.

Pendar, William & Ruth Thompson, 23 Sept 1813; William Turner, Thomas Pendar, bm.

Pender, Andrew & Milly Syks, 17 May 1853; William Pender, bm; m 18 May 1853 by Wiatt Cate, J. P.

Pender, James & Beedy Squires, 23 Dec 1817; Luke Tait(?), bm.

Pender, John & Mary Pearson, 16 Jan 1860; S. F. Kirkpatrick, W. Miller, bm.

Pender, Joseph & Elizabeth Wittey, 20 Feb 1784; James Russell, bm.

Pender, Joseph & Hannah Crawford, 21 June 1816; William Turner, bm.

Pender, Joseph & Susan Qualls, 14 March 1836; D. H. Cate, bm.

Pender, Thomas & Lydia Thomason, 23 Sept 1842; G. B. Morrow, bm.

Pender, William & Catherine Sykes, 24 Oct 1853; Andrew Pender, William Rodgers, bm; m 25 Oct 1853 by Wiatt Cates, J. P.

Pendergras, William & Martha E. Lewis, 13 Feb 1861; M. J. W. McCauly, bm; m 13 Feb 1861 by W. J. Hogan, J. P.

Pendergrass, Alston & Cornelia Andrews, 20 June 1857; Robt Faucett, bm.

Pendergrass, Andrew & Mourning Montgomery, 15 Feb 1838; Barnabas Lashley, Green Fidley, bm.

Pendergrass, Auston & Rebecca Creel, 8 Feb 1848; J. Pendergrass, bm.

Pendergrass, Eduard & Polly White, 29 Aug 1806; Wm. Pendergrass, bm.

Pendergrass, George W. & Caroline Whiteker, 17 April 1847; Matthew McCaly, bm.

Pendergrass, Ilai & Betheah Clements, 20 Feb 1848; Joseph Harward, bm.

Pendergrass, J. S. & Mary or Rachel Scoggins, 10 Feb 1866; Geo. W. Purefoy, bm; m 11 Feb 1866 by Geo. W. Purefoy, M. G.

Pendergrass, John & Rebecca Fann, 3 Jan 1800; Tilmon Perry, bm.

Pendergrass, John R. & Emeline Whiteker, 19 Dec 1850; Thompson Pendergrass, bm.

Pendergrass, Levi & Nancy Brockwell, 9 Dec 1852; John Creel, bm.

Pendergrass, Monroe & Pernelia or Cornelia Cheek, 26 March 1855; James McCauley, bm; m 26 March 1855 by N. C. Cate, J. P.

Pendergrass, Nathaniel & Faney Fowler, 31 Aug 1863; John Andrews, bm.

Pendergrass, Robert & Nancy McDonnel, 7 July 1784; Alexander Anderson, John Thompson, bm.

Pendergrass, William & Tabitha Fann, 28 Sept 1805; Tilmon Perry, bm.

Pendergrass, William & Edith Fowler, 26 April 1866; Adley Andrews, bm; m 26 April 1866 by Jones Watson, J. P.

Pengegras, Peter & Jane Fowler, 27 Sept 1866; A. Mickle, W. J. Hester, bm; m 27 Sept 1866 by Jones Watson, J. P.

Pengerton, David & Margret Pengerton, 1 July 1797; Thomas Holden, bm.

Penick, P. Tinsley & Eliza J. Bingham, 4 Nov 1857; Victor C. Barringer, bm.

Pennington, Charles & Ellen Couch, 26 July 1865; M. V. Blalock, bm; m 26 July 1865 by A. C. Murdock, J. P.

Perkins, Nicholas & Elizabeth S. Perkins, 7 May 1799; Wm. Lockhartt, bm.

Perritt, Archd. & Polley Webb, 24 Nov 1824; William Webb, bm.

Perry, Barnaby & Rebecca James, 22 Nov 1792; Sterling Harris, bm.

Perry, Brinkley & Polley Hall, 3 Nov 1802; John Hall, bm.

Perry, Elijah & Sarah Crabtree, 9 July 1788; Fredrick Taylor, bm.

Perry, Isaac & Peggy Regsby, 7 April 1806; Herman Colter, bm.

Perry, James & Nancy Sharp, 10 Nov 1808; William Newcomb, bm.

Perry, James & Rosannah Lynch, 22 Dec 1829; Wm. Cole, bm.

Perry, James & Charlotte Dollar, 3 March 1840; Abner Lewis, bm.

Perry, Jesse W. & Frances Durham, 28 Oct 1859; C. M. Snipes, bm; m 28 Nov 1859 by Samuel Baldwin, M. G.

Perry, John & Ellenor Bunch, (no date, 1795-1798); Thomas Bunch, bm.

Perry, Meachum & Dicey Henderson, 7 Jan 1826; Thomas Pendergrass, bm.

Perry, Peter F. & Patsey Lindsey, 3 Aug 1829; Thomas Thompson, bm.

Perry, Samuel & Susanah Nathcock, 24 April 1823; Samuel L. Addams, bm.

Perry, Samuel & Betsey Cooper, 9 Nov 1826; James Jones, bm.

Perry, Thomas & Louisa Turner, 30 Jan 1810; William Lashley, bm.

Perry, Tilmon & Tilly Rogers, 15 Aug 1800; Jesse Peckett, bm.

Perry, Tilmon & Jemima Massey, 21 Nov 1800; Jesse Pickett, bm.

Perry, William & Jane Thompson, 7 June 1832; Aaron Williams, bm.

Person, Manly & Eliza Norwood, 14 March 1865; Samuel Williams, bm; m 14 March 1865 by J. B. McDade, J. P.

Person, Stanford & Elizabeth Henderson, 27 April 1824; John Cook, bm.

Petegrew, William & Nancy Walker, 21 Jan 1799; Riuben Baxter, bm.

Petiel, Thomas & Marion McClure, 25 Dec 1847; James Petel, Samuel Ireland, bm.

Petigrew, William & Margaret McAdams, 17 Feb 1842; Morgan Mebane, bm.

Petteford, Thomas & Jane Roland, 4 Sept 1846; William D. McClure, bm.

Pettiford, Benjamin & Anne Hammonds, 2 April 1828; John W. Shaw, Thos. M. Norfleet, bm.

Pettiford, Nelson & Clara Collins, 19 Aug 1823; David Chissenhall, bm.

Pettigrew, Abner A. & Sarah Ann Cheek, 10 April 1850; John L. Faucett, bm.

Pettigrew, Elikins & Ellen Joan Allison, 1 Aug 1838; Jos. B. Allison, Allen P. Elliss, bm.

Pettigrew, Hance & Livina Owens, 28 March 1804; John King, bm.

Pettigrew, John & Lear Owen, 24 Dec 1799; Wm. Jenkins, bm.

Pettigrew, John M. & Rowan Roberts, 16 Dec 1851; Jno. M. McDade, bm; m 18 Dec 1851 by Freeman Walker, J. P.

Pettigrew, Jon Elikins & Amanda P. Murray, 19 Oct 1864; Thomas J. Taylor, bm; m 30 Oct 1864 by J. J. Allison, J. P.

Pettigrew, Joseph & Susan A. McCadams, 20 June 1840; Thomas Faucett, Robt. Whitted, bm.

Pettigrew, Thomas & Celia Tate, 29 Nov 1825; David Lynch, bm.

Pettigrew, William & Polly Ashley, 10 Oct 1805; Elless Walker, bm.

Petty, Allen & Salley Currie, 24 Oct 1820; Thomas Morrow, bm.

Petty, Wm. S. & Emiline Strowd, 30 Oct 1857; Little John Utley, bm.

Pety, John & Delilah Thrift, 20 Jan 1809; Isham Thrift, bm.

Phifer, Emanuel & Sally Lenggard, 2 July 1828; Jonathan Phifer, bm.

Phifer, Jonathan & Elizabeth Langard, 6 Feb 1828; David Heifman, bm.

Philips, Madeson & Ellan Bradshaw, 16 Nov 1841; Joel M. Phillips, Thomas T. Turner, bm.

Philips, Nimrod & Dionora Taylor, 7 Dec 1804; Thomas Philips, bm.

Philips, Thomas & Susannah ___, __ March 1803; Nimrod Philips, bm.

Phillips, Benjamin & Dorcas Register, 11 May 1804; D. Phillips, bm.

Phillips, Benjamin & Elizabeth Brinkley, 12 Sept 1810; Moore McCulley, bm.

Phillips, Benjamin R. & Barbara Wolf, 9 Oct 1816; John Holmes, bm.

Phillips, Charles & Laura C. Battle, 7 Dec 1847; Irvin F. Phillips, bm.

Phillips, Cleverly & Betsey Cook, 27 Dec 1806; Archabald Cook, bm.

Phillips, Daniel D. & Tasmesia M. Cooley, 30 May 1843; Edwin H. Heartt, Joseph Thompson, bm.

Phillips, James & Nancy Lockhart, 20 Feb 1797; Thos. Scott, bm.

Phillips, James & Mary E. Hill, 14 Jan 1846; D. Murray, bm.

Phillips, James & Sally Williams, 11 July 1860; John S. Crawford, bm.

Phillips, John & Mary Witsman, 6 June 1819; William Paris, bm.

Phillips, John & Pegga Bass, 2 Feb 1833; Alfred Bass, bm.

Phillips, Joshua & Nancey Webb, 3 Aug 1817; Robert Web, bm.

Phillips, Samuel F. & Frances R. Lucas, 1 Dec 1849; J. B. McDade, bm.

Phillips, Thomas & Louisa Clarke, 11 June 1828; John A. McDade Jr., bm.

Phillips, Thomas & Lucinda Phillips, 10 Feb 1866; Wilson Colwell, bm; m 10 Feb 1866 by James Phillips, D. D.

Phillips, William & Peggy Weaver, 12 June 1833; W. H. Thompson, bm.

Philpot, William & Elizabeth Walker, 18 Nov 1816; Vallentine Blalock, bm.

Phipps, Ambros, son of Dudley Phipps, & Martha J. Wilson, m 4 Dec 1867 by B. C. Hopkins, bm.

Phipps, Archibald & Salley Gresham, 13 Nov 1835; Riley Vickers, bm.

Phipps, Dudley & Polly Edwards, 2 Feb 1804; Elias Turner, bm.

Phipps, James & Frances Jane Faucett, 26 Nov 1855; William Faucett, R. N. Jones, bm; m 27 Nov 1855 by N. C. Cate, J. P.

Phipps, John & Berthasaby Turner, 2 Feb 1797; Nathaniel Hix, bm.

Phipps, John & Mary Clements, 8 Dec 1809; Dudley Phipps, bm.

Phipps, Simeon & Elizabeth Hutchens, 18 Oct 1853; Green Phipps, Geo. W. Bruce, bm; m 18 Oct 1853 by John Hancock, J. P.

Phipps, Thomas C. & Martha J. Phipps, m 29 Oct 1865 by B. C. Hopkins, J. P.

Pickard, Alexander & Anne Clendening, 22 Aug 1820; Samuel Thompson, Joseph Clendenin, bm.

Pickard, Alexander & Sally Fogleman, 15 Feb 1836; Thos. C. Hayes, James Crutchfield, bm.

Pickard, Alford & Abigail R. Wadkins, 16 Dec 1848; James Taylor, bm.

Pickard, Alfred & Peggy Minnis, 14 Aug 1824; Henry ODaniel, Henry Pickard, bm.

Pickard, Asco, son of Henry & Lavina Pickard, & Sarah J. Pickard, dau. of Thomas W. & Elizabeth Pickard, m 2 April 1868 by Alvis Durham, J. P.

Pickard, Daniel & Margaret ODaniel, 13 March 1813; Archd. Holmes, bm.

Pickard, Elijah & Elizabeth Dickson, 28 Sept 1812; William McAddams, bm.

Pickard, Elisha & Susanna Daniel, 29 Nov 1796; William Crutchfield, bm.

Pickard, George & Mary E. Parris, 23 Jan 1847; Balaam Woods, bm.

Pickard, Henry & Ellenor Woods, 1 Aug 1815; Nathan Edwards, bm.

Pickard, Henry & Lavinia Minnis, 26 July 1827; Francis Ray, Robert Moore, bm.

Pickard, Isaac & Sarah Andrew, 24 Dec 1794; James Pickard, bm.

Pickard, Isaac & Polley Rickets, 16 Feb 1809; John Gilson, bm.

Pickard, James & Sarah M. Hobbs, 13 Nov 1847; Thos. C. Hayes, H. C. Cates, bm.

Pickard, Jesse & Jeany Workman, 29 July 1814; Archd. Holmes, bm.

Pickard, John & Elenor Moore, 20 March 1823; Sandy Duke, bm.

Pickard, John & Julia Ann Pickard, 6 Sept 1855; H. C. McCauley, bm.

Pickard, John H. & Anne Forrest, 10 June 1812; James Child, bm.

Pickard, John N. & Nancy Pender, 5 June 1847; Thomas W. Pickard, bm.

Pickard, John W. & Arthelia Lloyd, 1 Jan 1866; Thomas A. Williams, bm.

Pickard, Layfait & Sarah Cheek, 13 Oct 1866; Henry ODaniel, bm; m 14 Oct 1866 by Thos. Long, J. P.

Pickard, Richard & Nicey Chance, 13 July 1802; James Morrow, Elisha Pickard, bm.

Pickard, Robert B. & Mary Snipes, 24 Dec 1859; Michael Smith, T. W. Laws, bm; m 5 Jan 1860 by Wilson Atwater, minister.

Pickard, Robert P. & Julia A. Thompson, 7 April 1867; George C. Pickard, bm; m 11 April 1867 by H. M. C. Strowd, J. P.

Pickard, Thomas & Polly Workman, 16 Oct 1819; John Pickard, bm.

Pickard, Thomas & Elizabeth Cates, 13 Dec 1847; Charles Cate, bm.

Pickard, Thomas M. & Anna Jane Crutchfield, 5 Aug 1852; Michael Smith, bm; m 8 Aug 1852 by Thos. Lynch, minister.

Pickard, William & Milley Crutchfield, 19 Jan 1821; Taylor Pickard, bm.

Pickard, William & Nancy Cheek, 3 Jan 1866; Richard L. Cates, bm.

Picket, Asa & Tennesia Marcum, 8 Jan 1856; Pleasant Picett, bm; m 10 Jan 1856 by M. A. Angier, J. P.

Picket, Jesse & Cresey Fann, 21 Nov 1800; Tilmon Perry, bm.

Picket, John & Catharine Roney, 17 June 1808; Edward Picket, bm.

Picket, John & Mary Pike, 16 Sept 1830; William Steel, bm.

Picket, Mark & Mary Bryant, (no date, 1792-1795) John Rhodes, bm.

Picket, William & Elizabeth Hamilton, 16 Oct 1802; Edward Picket, bm.

Picket, William & Patsey Wright, 28 April 1847; Andrew J. Copeland, bm.

Pickett, Albert W. & Halen Rigsbee, 18 Feb 1860; C. W. Picket, Joseph J. Laws, bm; m 23 Feb 1860 by B. C. Hopkins, J. P.

Pickett, Charles & Patsy Rhodes, 3 Jan 1824; Warren Vickerson, Edward McDade, bm.

Pickett, Chesley Page & Elizabeth Frances Jane Rigsbee, 8 Jan 1861; Henry Pickett, D. D. Phillips, bm; m 13 Jan 1861 by B. C. Hopkins, J. P.

Pickett, Dempsey & Polly Whittaker, 10 Sept 1818; Thomas Pickett, bm.

Pickett, E. W. & Mary A. Vickers, 9 July 1859; Harlerson Harward, bm.

Pickett, Henry & Frances Herndon, 30 Nov 1821; Mark Pickett, bm.

Pickett, Henry & Martha C. Rigsbee, 13 March 1851; Pleasant Pickett, bm.

Pickett, Henry & Carolina Rigsbey, m 25 March 1852 by J. W. Hancock, J. P.

Pickett, Henry & Ellen J. McCauley, m 4 Jan 1866 by C. J. Freeland.

Pickett, John & Ruthy Jackson, 20 Nov 1806; John Thompson, Abel Thompson, bm.

Pickett, John & Polley Bryant, 29 July 1837; James T. Hutchins, John Bryant, bm.

Pickett, John & Laura Stafford, 13 Sept 1840; Richard Patterson, bm.

Pickett, John F. & Mary Browning, 20 Dec 1832; John Barbee, Tho. Hutchins, bm.

Pickett, Joseph & Nancy Smith, 23 April 1800; Joseph Pickett, Jos. Guin, bm.

Pickett, Lemuel & Nancy Wilkerson, 2 April 1832; James Wilkinson, bm.

Pickett, Matthew & Sarah Alston, 19 May 1806; Phillip Alston, bm.

Pickett, Plesant & Mary Marcom, 18 May 1852; Wm. P. Carlton, bm; m 20 May 1852 by John Buroughs, J. P.

Pickett, Thomas & Cassae Poe, 17 Jan 1796; Williamson Bryant, bm.

Pickett, Thomas & Lotta Cordle, 1 Feb 1864; Ruffin Rieghbee, bm.

Pickett, Walker & Jeany Bryant, 5 Nov 1815; J. Taylor, bm.

Pickett, William & Casey Langley, 2 Jan 1822; James Riggins, bm.

Pickett, William & Jeany Browning, 5 Dec 1833; Joseph Dallan, John Whititt, bm.

Pickett, William & Martha Borland, 27 Feb 1858; C. T. Pickett, bm; m 4 March 1858 by Wm. McCown, J. P.

Pickett, Willis & Patsy Chisenhall, 20 April 1825; Samuel Chisenhall, bm.

Pickett, Willis & Sarah Clark, 12 March 1862; T. W. Burs, bm; m 12 March 1862 by Jas. N. Craig, J. P.

Pickhart, Alexander & Geney Morrow, 29 Aug 1792; Suke Grimes, bm.

Pickle, Henry & Racheal Neely, 7 Feb 1804; Thomas Laws, bm.

Picot, Peter O. & Martha Potter, 4 June 1818; Nat. J. King, bm.

Pierce, Jesse & Margaret Carrigan, 24 Nov 1848; E. G. Gray, bm.

Pierson, Edward & Winney Perry, 14 Dec 1802; Henson Cotten, W. Pendergrass, bm.

Pierson, Richard & Nancy Leigh, 8 May 1823; George Bevill, bm.

Piggtt, William H. & Tempe Stout, 4 Sept 1832; Jehu W. Jackson, bm.

Pigman, Leonard & Patience Thompson, 13 June 1782; John Reeves, bm.

Pike, John & Mary Freeman, 23 Feb 1805; Zacharias Wells, bm.

Pike, John & Patsey Teague, 19 Sept 1839; Isaiah Teague, bm.

Pike, Micajah & Mary Pike, 20 Feb 1842; Micajah Pike, bm.

Pike, William & Sarah Shurdon, 13 March 1792; George Shurdon, bm.

Pike, William & Melissa Carter, 15 Aug 1834; Jonathan Zachary, J. Taylor, bm.

Pile, James & Elizabeth Rumley, 13 Nov 1800; Caleb Pyle, John Baldwin, bm.

Piper, Abraham & Rebecca Covey, 17 Jan 1797; Job Pendergrass, bm.

Piper, George & Harriett W. Green, 15 July 1832; James P. Brewer, bm.

Piper, George & Martha L. Whitaker, 25 Aug 1866; Abraham Crabtree, Thos. J. Whitaker, bm.

Piper, John & Elizabeth Herndon, 13 Jan 1796; William McCauley, bm.

Piper, Jno. & Patsy Flint, 13 June 1820; James Allison, bm.

Piper, John & Nancy Cole, 12 Feb 1829; Matthew Clinton, James P. Brown, bm.

Piper, John & Elizabeth Warren, 17 Oct 1836; Anthony Cole, Frederic Williams, bm.

Piper, Samuel & Ellenor Harris, 20 June 1831; Samuel Scarlett, James P. Brown, bm.

Piper, Samuel Junr. & Nancey King, 4 Jan 1791; William McCauley, bm.

Piper, Thomas & Mary C. Faucett, 8 Sept 1848; Jos. McCullock, bm.

Piper, William & Melinda Harris, 24 March 1830; James P. Brewer, Wm. H. Hall, bm.

Pitman, John & Elizabeth Morris, 24 Feb 1801; Burris Estridge, Aaron Boles, bm.

Pitman, Josiah & Elizabeth Eastridge, 23 Oct 1798; Boroughs Eastridge, bm.

Pittard, Samuel & Rebecca Drake, 14 April 1817; Hyner Drake, Wm. G. Clendenen, bm.

Pittiford, Reuben & Agnis Griffin, 12 June 1826; William Croker, bm.

Pitts, William & Salley Durham, 27 Nov 1807; Nathaniel Durham, bm.

Pleasant, Albert B. & Sarah A. Warren, 16 Nov 1854; Asa N. Davis, bm; m 16 Nov 1854 by William H. Brown, J. P.

Pleasant, Charles & Nancy Riggans, 17 Sept 1816; Samuel Crow, bm.

Pleasants, John & Polly Wilkins, 22 Feb 1842; John Scott, Harrison Scott, bm.

Pleasants, Robert & Anne I. Hancock, 7 Jan 1830; Robert McKay, bm.

Pleasants, Thomas & Mary Whithead, 9 Dec 1801; William Gappins, bm.

Plummer, John & Nancey Holt, 26 March 1814; Robert Fauset, bm.

Poe, Hasten & Mary Loyd, 21 July 1817; Thos. Lloyd, bm.

Poe, Matthew & Nancy Flint, 29 July 1829; Robert Pleasants, bm.

Poe, R. P. & Jane Reeves, 6 April 1859; Alexr. Hunter, bm.

Poe, William & Fanny King, 1 Aug 1838; Elijah Andrus, James Lloyd, bm.

Poe, William M. & Christen M. Hunter, 15 Jan 1840; William Loyd, A. L. Hunter, bm.

Pointer, Shadrick & Anne Meakes, 29 Nov 1866; John Pointer, bm; m 29 Nov 1866 by R. F. Morris, J. P.

Pool, Bourris & Hawkins Carden, 21 May 1856; Green Phipps, bm; m 21 May 1856 by W. W. Guess, J. P.

Pool, John & Abigail Malone, 3 March 1831; Saml. Pool, bm.

Pool, John & Catherine Riley, 1 Dec 1857; A. Browning, bm; m 3 Dec 1857 by Jno. Hancock, J. P.

Pool, Lewis & Martha Christian, 29 Nov 1855; R. M. Jones, bm; m 29 Nov 1855 by Harris Wilkerson, J. P.

Pool, Ransom & Martha Ann Etherage, 18 Nov 1861; Wm. R. Vickers, John J. Holloway, bm; m 19 Nov 1861 by Robert F. Morris, J. P.

Pool, Samuel & Sally Simmons, 2 March 1792; Wm. Pool, bm.

Pool, Samuel & Patsey House, 18 Dec 1827; John Anderson, bm.

Pool, Samuel & Sarah Markham, 1 Nov 1866; A. B. Couch, bm; m 1 Nov 1866 by C. G. Markham, J. P.

Pool, Solomon & Cornelia Kirkland, 9 June 1856; J. T. Hogan, bm; m 9 June 1856 by James Phillips, M. G.

Pope, A. C. & Arilla J. Lea, 3 Sept 1862; S. N. Dunn, bm.

Pope, Erasmus & Frances Sheppard, 26 Oct 1838; George R. Marcom, Francis Barbee, bm.

Pope, John S. & Mary J. McDade, 5 May 1859; Geo. W. Faucett, bm; m 8 May 1859 by Robert G. Tinnen, minister.

Pope, Thomas & Polly Wheely, 9 Dec 1812; Phillip Birch, bm.

Pope, Thomas Jr. & Margeret J. McBroom, 29 Jan 1849; Ezekiel Sartin, bm.

Pope, Thomas Jr. & Susan Catharine Riley, 19 July 1852; Henry P. Pope, bm; m 29 July 1852 by Hezekiah Terry, J. P.

Pope, Uriah & Susannah Robinson, 20 July 1808; D. S. Blalock, bm.

Porter, Alamon & Polly Holt, 12 June 1814; H. Wells, bm.

Porter, William & Jane Burnett, 6 March 1831; Abram Burnett, bm.

Porterfield, Andrew & Mildred Broun, 17 Nov 1847; Joshua Berry, bm.

Porterfield, David & Jane Breeze, 1 March 1847; Wm. J. Moore, bm.

Porterfield, Jackson & Lynda McCullock, 30 April 1836; Wm. Horner, bm.

Porterfield, James & Artley Jordan, 3 Jan 1850; David R. Porterfield, bm.

Porterfield, James & Moreny C. Barns, 23 Nov 1852; Erasmus Oakley, bm.

Porterfield, John & Margaret Clark, 7 Nov 1796; J. Baldridge, bm.

Porterfield, John W. & Julia Parker, 25 Jan 1861; A. M. Breeze, J. Turner, bm; m 31 Jan 1861 by H. Terry, J. P.

Posten, James & Ruth Washburn, 6 April 1795; John Barnhill, Thos. Johnston, bm.

Poteet, William & Sarah Rhodes, 22 March 1783; Aquila Roades, bm.

Potts, Jacob & Anne Blackwood, 9 Aug 1817; James Blackwood, bm.

Potts, William & Peggy Anderson, 13 Sept 1799; D. G. Mebane, bm.

Powel, A. Stanford & Mary Hatch, 19 March 1856; Alex Lashly, bm.

Powel, William & Polley White, __ Jan 1812; Richd. Street, bm.

Powell, John & Sally Elliff, 15 Aug 1794; Jeremiah Holt, bm.

Powell, John & Delia Stroud, 27 March 1817; John Powell, William Fauset, bm.

Powell, John & Mary Cooke, 14 April 1818; N. H. Horton, bm.

Powell, Jones & Sally Copeland, 1 Sept 1842; H. C. Strowd, bm.

Powell, Obid & Polley Herndon, 1 July 1805; Edward Sims Walton, bm.

Powell, Thomas & Sarah Wilhoite, 5 April 1803; John Whitsell, John Taylor, bm.

Prather, John S. & Mary Harden, 26 Nov 1812; Wm. Whitsitt, bm.

Prather, Sidney S. & Catharine Roney, 10 Sept 1835; William H. Prather, bm.

Pratt, George & Mary Campbell, 17 Feb 1796; James Pratt, bm.

Pratt, James & Polley Woody, 27 Jan 1806; Thomas Hastings, bm.

Pratt, James H. & Malvina Strayhorn, 28 Oct 1835; Wm. Cabe, bm.

Pratt, Lewis & Betsey Jeffires, 4 Oct 1866; J. B. Geer, bm; m 4 Oct 1866 by B. C. Hopkins, J. P.

Pratt, Loftin K. & Nancy Burroughs, 13 Dec 1824; W. N. Pratt, bm.

Pratt, Moses S. & Elizabeth Mitchel, 4 June 1824; Thos. D. Watts, bm.

Pratt, Thomas & Nancy Hart, 11 Oct 1838; Jno. M. Faucett, M. Gaskill, bm.

Pratt, William C. & Sarah Moore, 20 Dec 1826; James Pratt, bm.

Prewit, William & Edy Pettigrew, 28 April 1821; Taylor Duke, bm.

Price, Archibald & Biddy Brewer, 23 Aug 1820; James Crabtree, bm.

Price, Gideon & Winnifred Fanny, 22 Sept 1799; Jacob Lemmon, bm.

Price, Gideon & Dolly Alsobrook, 18 Oct 1821; J. Taylor Jr., bm.

Price, John & Rebecca King, 25 Nov 1809; John Connally, bm.

Price, John H. & Luena Duke, 4 Aug 1848; J. W. Hancock, bm.

Price, Perry & Mary Barton, 15 Nov 1846; William G. Duke, bm.

Price, Thos. W. & Polley Johns, 11 April 1798; James Phillips, bm.

Price, Washington & Susan Webb, 2 Oct 1823; Holaday R. Oldham, bm.

Price, William & Kitty Matthews, 8 Nov 1817; Barnabas Perry, bm.

Prichard, Elijah & Jane Briswell, 22 July 1835; C. M. Latimer, bm.

Primrose, John & Elizabeth Taylor, 19 Sept 1815; Jonathan Mize, bm.

Pritchard, Eason & Milia Riggsbee, 11 Jan 1859; A. S. Riggsbee, bm.

Pritchard, Errand & Sally Lynch, 3 July 1827; Jesse Cole, bm.

Pritchard, Stephen & Polly Carrolle, 5 Nov 1804; James Rainey, bm.

Pritchard, Thompson & Arena Cate, 28 Jan 1833; Exom P___, Hg. Parrish, bm.

Pritchet, Benjamin & Elvira Brown, 6 Feb 1838; Benjamin Carrole, Clemuel Crabtree, bm.

Pritchet, Nelson & Emeline Walker, 18 Jan 1831; Furrand Durham, bm.

Pritchett, John Wilson & Jeany King, 14 Dec 1839; John Kirkland, John Cheek, bm.

Pritchett, Thomas & Peggy McClure, 18 March 1804; James McClure, bm.

Prock, James & Elizabeth Weeks, 25 Nov 1807; Perry Sutton, bm.

Proctor, Anderson & Elizabeth Vaughn, 21 Oct 1848; Green Crowder, bm.

Proctor, Francis M. & Milbrey J. Pendergrass, 26 Jan 1861; Joseph Proctor, bm; m 27 Jan 1861 by S. Shepherd, J. P.

Proctor, John & Fannie Jones, 4 Dec 1866; B. L. Duke, A. A. Dixon, bm; m 5 Dec 1866 by B. C. Hopkins, J. P.

Proctor, Jonathan S. & Mary Cook, 9 Feb 1862; Moses Leathers Jr., Thomas Anderson, bm.

Proctor, Joseph & Susan Willis, 3 May 1829; Jessa Brown, bm.

Proctor, Joseph & Martha Baldwin, 14 Dec 1840; Lea C. Ray, bm.

Proctor, Joseph & Hawkins Couch, 20 April 1864; m 20 April 1864 by S. Shepherd, J. P.

Proctor, O. K. & Sarah I. Barbee, 10 Feb 1848; Malborn, A. Angier, Jno. D. Carlton, bm.

Proctor, Richard & Nancy Dollar, 25 July 1803; Abraham Whitaker, bm.

Proctor, Richard & Frances Chisenhall, 25 Jan 1854; James Willisons, Thomas Dollar, bm; m 26 Jan 1854 by John Hancock, J. P.

Proctor, Richard H. & Ruthy Jane Vickers, 4 Feb 1851; Willis
R. Markham, bm.

Proctor, Sterling & Winney Green, 29 Jan 1825; Dodson Dollar,
bm.

Proctor, Sterling Y. & Misseline E. Blalock, 7 Nov 1857; A. G.
Gainey, R. H. Proctor, bm.

Proctor, William & Susannah Cole, 8 Feb 1832; Riley Vickers,
Henry Woods, bm.

Pryor, Luke & Ellenor Rogers, 17 April 1799; Peter Waggoner, bm.

Pucket, John M. & Elizabeth Smart, 26 Sept 1817; John Smart, bm.

Pugh, Isaac & Martha A. Ashley, 20 Aug 1864; John Isard, bm;
m 30 Aug 1864 by Wilson Brown, J. P.

Pugh, James & Sarah Ricketts, 24 Nov 1801; Barney Lashley,
William Grimes, bm.

Pugh, James & Frankey Lashley, 9 Sept 1816; Hiram Lashley, bm.

Pugh, John & Elizabeth Cates, 2 April 1804; Saml. Stubbins or
Stuffins, bm.

Pugh, John & Nancy Hawkins, 10 June 1824; Moses Shaw, bm.

Pugh, John & Ann Moore, 10 Dec ___; Robert Moore, bm.

Pugh, Leander & Elizabeth Howard, 6 April 1866; Jesse Morrow,
John Crawford, bm; m 8 April 1866 by Thomas J. Cates, J. P.

Pugh, Sampson & Ellenor Mahen, 19 Nov 1791; Reuben Smith, bm.

Pulley, James & Lucy Weaver, 24 Feb 1827; Britton Banks,
C. Strayhorn, bm.

Purdeau, James & Biddy Brewer, 22 Sept 1838; Sackfield Brewer,
bm.

Purifoy, Oram, son of Thomas & Jane Purifoy, & Betsy Mason,
dau. of Mimis & Aggy Evans, m 9 June 1867 by J. P. Mason,
M. G.

Purify, George W. & Lucy C. Merrett, 30 Dec 1834; W. H. Marcom,
Jas. N. Patterson, bm.

Purify, Haywood & Frances Patterson, 13 Sept 1866; John White,
bm; m 13 Sept 1866 by J. P. Mason, M. G.

Purkinett, Henry & Susannah Farmer, 6 March 1821; Cager
Johnston, bm.

Puryear, Seymour & Polly Albright, 12 April 1822; Michl. Holt,
bm.

Puryear, Seymour & Mary Holt, 10 Jan 1826; Alfred A. Holt, bm.

Pyle, Henry & Lucy Ashford, 30 Oct 1821; Anthony Holt, bm.

Pyle, Jehu & Rutha Lindley, 8 Aug 1786; Enoch Bradley, bm.

Pyle, John & Rebecca Garrison, 16 Jan 1802; Caleb Pyle, bm.

Pyle, Thomas & Elizabeth Fonville, 10 March 1846; John McCrey, bm.

Qualls, Charles & Elsey Ray, 17 Feb 1812; Moses Cox, bm.

Qualls, James & Elizabeth Hinchey, 1 Dec 1832; Samuel Thompson, James Thompson, bm.

Qualls, John & Elizabeth Richardson, 20 Jan 1817; William Anderson, bm.

Quals, John, son of Sterling & Emily S. Quals, & Martha Sykes, dau. of James & Synthia Sykes, m 3 Aug 1867 by Thos Long, J. P.

Quals, John D. & Sarah Mollon, 31 Jan 1835; Thos. G. Phillips, bm.

Quals, Samuel & Nancy Brown, 9 Feb 1867; F. M. Jordon, Josiah Turner Jr., bm; m 9 Feb 1867 by F. M. Jordan, M. G.

Quals, Sterling & Emily Falkner, 8 Aug 1837; Wm. Chambers Jr., Henderson Fowler, bm.

Ragain, William & Amey Hargiss, 16 Feb 1811; David Ragains, bm.

Ragains, James & Margret Hammond, 29 April 1811; Allen Collins, bm.

Ragains, John & Catey Pickle, 9 Aug 1805; Jerimiah Tinnin, bm.

Ragin, Sidney M. & Martha J. Oakley, 3 Dec 1865; Martha C. Hall, bm; m 3 Dec 1865 by Nelson P. Hall, J. P.

Ragins, David & Susannah Hargiss, 11 April 1802; Thos. Barlow, bm.

Rainey (Reaney), David & Nancy Shepperd, 28 Nov 1809; Charles Christmas, bm.

Rainey, Isaac & Elizabeth H. Kirk, 7 May 1813; Lewis Holt, bm.

Rainey, James & Elizabeth Barbee, 23 Jan 1802; Mark Barbee, bm.

Rainey, Young E. & Elizabeth Guess, 1 April 1829; Wm. W. Guess, bm.

Rainy, David & Nancy Davis, 22 Sept 1798; Cligey Couch, bm.

Ramsey, John & Mary Clendening, 24 Sept 1815; James Bradford, bm.

Rand, Wm. & Elisabeth Stroud, 20 Oct 1792; And. Stroud, bm.

Raney, John & Haley Warren, 6 Oct 1827; John Cox, bm.

Rashcoe, Arthur & Mary Weedan, 27 Dec 1815; John Pleasant, bm.

Rasco, Vensen & Sarah Ray, 28 Oct 1845; Smith Rasco, bm.

Rasco, Wm. M. & Mary Ann Tate, 28 Feb 1848; William S. Tate, bm.

Ray, Asley & Ellen Leathers, 25 Nov 1865; Denard Crawford, bm.

Ray, Bogin & Betsy Ray, 23 Oct 1833; Richs. Nichols, bm.

Ray, Charles & Sarah Woods, 31 Jan 1787; A. Riston, bm.

Ray, Charles & Harriett Nipper, 14 March 1825; Thomas Cape, bm.

Ray, Chas. W. & Mary Ellen Finley, 21 March 1837; R. Sanford, bm.

Ray, Daniel & Phebe McPherson, no date (1824-1827); James McPherson, bm.

Ray, David & Rebeckah Hargues, 13 Dec 1786; Ben. Evans, bm.

Ray, David & Eliza Lashley, 24 Dec 1806; John Roach, bm.

Ray, David & Milly Qualls, 29 Feb 1812; William Ray, Robt, Mebane, bm.

Ray, David & Anne Hatch, 23 Feb 1824; Nathaniel Durham, Thos. D. Watts, bm.

Ray, David & Catharine Porterfield, 10 Sept 1825; John Woods, bm.

Ray, Francis & Elizabeth Thompson, 20 Dec 1829; Samuel Thompson, bm.

Ray, Francis & Eliza J. Rigsbee, 19 Feb 1863; Lemuel Carson, bm; m 19 Feb 1863 by D. Tilley, J. P.

Ray, George & Martha Robinson, 29 May 1792; John Robinson, bm.

Ray, George & Polley Steuart, 18 July 1795; Thos. Armstrong, bm.

Ray, George A. & Mary Jane Riggs, 20 Oct 1855; David R. McRee, bm; m 1 Nov 1855 by Hartwell Arnold.

Ray, Henry & Nicy Lashley, 4 Dec 1798; John ODaniels, bm.

Ray, Henry & Sarah Sykes, 6 Nov 1844; George Miller, James Sykes, bm.

Ray, Henry & Piety Workman, 20 Jan 1852; Shary Ray, John Crawford, bm; m 20 Jan 1852 by H. McDaniel, J. P.

Rav, Henry & Susannah Smith, 16 Feb 1854; Franklin Lasley, bm.

Ray, Henry & Nancy C. Sykes, 23 Nov 1858; Wm. Dodson, bm; m 28 Nov 1858 by Wiatt Cates, J. P.

Ray, Hugh & Rachel Lastley, 5 Nov 1795; James Morrow, bm.

Ray, Isaac & Sarah McDaniel, 27 April 1809; Wm. McDaniel, bm.

Ray, Isaac H. & Tamesia Nichols, 13 Nov 1854; G. B. Ray, John R. Kirkland, bm.

Ray, James & Hannah Lashley, 15 March 1803; Sam. Rickets, bm.

Ray, James & Mary Holmes, 20 Jan 1818; Isaiah Payne, bm.

Ray, James & Judith Wagoner, 21 Jan 1826; James Ray, bm.

Ray, James & Nancy Barlow, 5 Dec 1827; John Ray, bm.

Ray, James & Susanah Fossett, 21 July 1831; Elmore F. Forrset, bm.

Ray, James H. & Ann Latta, 28 Dec 1793; James Latta, bm.

Ray, Jesse & Rhodah Rickets, 28 June 1815; John Rickets, bm.

Ray, Joe & Sarah Walker, 25 Dec 1866; John Ray, bm; m 25 Dec 1866 by J. W. McKee, J. P.

Ray, John & Susanah Patterson, 26 Dec 1780; William Ray, bm.

Ray, John & ____, 16 Jan 1784; William Trousdel, bm.

Ray, John & Margarett Hart, 3 Dec 1795; William Parks, bm.

Ray, John & Polley Dunagan, 14 Jan 1801; A. B. Bruce, bm.

Ray, John & Nancy McDaniel, 17 Dec 1801; Wm. Williams, bm.

Ray, John & Salley Clarke, 1 July 1805; Wm. Whitted, bm.

Ray, John & Susannah Wells, 27 Sept 1806; William Wells, bm.

Ray, John & Peggy Izzard, 7 March 1809; John Johnston, bm.

Ray, John & Polly Rountree, 26 May 1821; William Cates, bm.

Ray, John & Catharine Squires, 28 Nov 1822; Thomas Ray, John Hartt, bm.

Ray, John & Jeaney Sykes, 28 Oct 1824; Richard Sykes, bm.

Ray, John & Elizabeth Cobb, 23 Jan 1826; James Ray, bm.

Ray, John & Elizabeth Redding, 30 July 1840; Nelson McKee, Geo. Laws, bm.

Ray, John B. & Telitha M. Redding, 8 Dec 1855; Louis W. Kinin, bm; m 9 Dec 1858 by H. Terry, J. P.

Ray, John M. & Jane Hanks, 3 Feb 1826; Wm. Ray, bm.

Ray, John T. & Frances A. Barton, 29 Aug 1863; Lemuel L. Carrol, bm; m 1 Sept 1863 by Henry Gray, minister.

Ray, Joseph & Susanah Wilkinson, 25 Feb 1797; James Wilkison, bm.

Ray, Joseph, son of James & Amy Ray, & Leatha A. Wilson, dau. of Emily Wilson, m 1 June 1867 by H. F. Pope, minister.

Ray, Josiah L. & Martha E. Sykes, 28 May 1865; Alson McDaniel, bm; m 1 June 1865 by W. H. Thompson.

Ray, Matthew & Jane McDaniel, 11 March 1803; Alexd. Russell, bm.

Ray, Matthew & Elizabeth White, 15 Nov 1830; Matthew Futtrell, bm.

Ray, Michael & Anne Boykin, 17 Dec 1822; Jesse Miller, bm.

Ray, Murphey & Susan Smith, 7 Feb 1856; John A. Smith, bm; m 7 Feb 1856 by Ruffin R. Tapp.

Ray, Nelson & Elmina L. Smith, 24 Feb 1862; John C. Kinrion, bm; m 27 Feb 1862 by Thos. Wilson, J. P.

Ray, Peter A. & Harriet J. Wilson, 27 Oct 1855; Joseph W. McKee, bm; m 28 Oct 1855 by Nelson P. Hall, J. P.

Ray, Peter L. & Elizabeth B. Holt, 3 April 1818; J. P. Sneed, bm.

Ray, Robert & Allendar Mardock, 2 March 1782; John Ray, bm; Robert Ray Sen., wit.

Ray, Robert & Hanna Massey, 11 July 1782; Robert Hunter, bm.

Ray, Robert & Elenor Shaw, 29 Sept 1797; Alexander Kendhen, bm.

Ray, Robert & Peggy Bradford, 3 Oct 1804; David Bradford, bm.

Ray, Ruben & Nancy Ray, 12 March 1832; Wm. M. Rogers, bm.

Ray, Sidney & Rebecca E. Sykes, 27 Jan 1859; Wm. Dodson, James Gill, bm; m 27 Jan 1859 by Ruffin R. Tapp, J. P.

Ray, Stephen & Nancy Riley, 3 Sept 1806; Joseph Hastings, bm.

Ray, Thomas & Polley Woods, 23 Sept 1800; Hugh Woods, bm.

Ray, Thomas & Salley Crutchfield, 7 June 1823; Henry ODaniel, bm.

Ray, Tyre B. & Mary McKee, 24 April 1839; David B. McKee, bm.

Ray, William & Catey Ray, 15 Jan 1783; Randolph Izzard, bm.

Ray, William & Ruthey Holloway, 23 Nov 1784; John Ray, bm.

Ray, William & Mary McGee, 10 April 1794; David Allison, bm.

Ray, William & Ellenor Roach, 10 April 1799; John Roach, bm.

Ray, William & Nancy Allison, 13 Jan 1810; Saml. Woods, bm.

Ray, William & Maria Anne Barlow, 31 Dec 1832; William Barlow, bm.

Ray, William & Emiline Wilson, 25 Feb 1867; Chs. R. Miller, Wm. C. Pickard, bm; m 2 March 1867 by J. W. McKee, J. P.

Ray, William D. & Emily Holt, 5 May 1818; Wm. McCawley, bm.

Ray, William Hamilton & Charlotte Cooper, 10 Nov 1803; Matthew Ray, bm.

Ray, William Patterson & Jeany Bradford, 28 July 1809; Joseph Bradford, bm.

Ray, William R. & Sarah Smith, 18 Dec 1849; John L. Smith, bm.

Reach, Zacariah & Rosanna Booth, 14 Dec 1801; Jacob Peeler, bm.

Read, Isaac & Susan M. Nash, 2 June 1832; Afd. W. Venable Jr., Jno. Mann, bm.

Read, John C. & Mary Ringstaff, 6 Oct 1856; John Sheeler, John Y. Adams, bm; m 6 Oct 1856 by R. Burwell, M. G.

Read, William, son of Barney & Amey Read, & Joseophine Gowen, dau. of Henry & Eliza Gowen, colored, m 29 Sept 1867 by W. S. Strayhorn, J. P.

Reaves, Archibald & Elizabeth Caldwell, 31 Jan 1809; J. McKerall, bm.

Reavis, Thos. C. & Alsey Laws, 12 Jan 1824; Samuel B. Reavis, bm.

Reavs, Micheal & Betsey Morgan, 10 Aug 1816; Jacob M. Daughety, bm.

Redding, David & Eliza Hall, 18 Dec 1833; Anderson Woods, bm.

Redding, John & Anne Roach, 19 March 1798; Henry Pickard, James Thompson, bm.

Redding, John P. & Martha McAdams, 3 Jan 1826; William McAddams, bm.

Redding, Moses N. & Martha A. Thompson, 4 May 1857; John Thompson, Isreal Turner, bm; m 7 May 1857 by John F. Lyon, J. P.

Redding, Stephen & Milley Horn, 24 Nov 1801; James Horn, bm.

Redding, Thomas Jr. & Elizabeth Grissum, 23 Jan 1820; Thos. Reeves, bm.

Redding, William & Mary J. Taylor, 13 Feb 1854; James Gill, bm; m 14 Feb 1854 by Archibald Currie, minister.

Redding, William H. & Susan Couch, 7 June 1856; R. M. Jones, bm; m 10 June 1856 by Alexander Dickson, J. P.

Redding, William W. & Lucy C. Barlow, 16 July 1860; H. Terry, J. P.

Reddins, Geo. & Fanny Tilley, 12 May 1791; John Tilley, bm.

Redin, Thomas & Margaret Carragin, 24 March 1790; John Paul, bm.

Reding, John & Nancy Redmond, 13 Feb 1797; John Riley, bm.

Reding, John & Peggy Riley, 4 April 1825; John Riley, bm.

Reding, Robert & Ellinar Woods, 13 Nov 1826; D. Dickie, bm.

Reding, William W. & Lucy C. Barlow, 3 July 1860; Stephen Dickson, bm.

Redman, John & Milly Jeans, 25 Aug 1807; James Warren, bm.

Redmon, Thaddius & Mildred E. Rhodes, 12 Oct 1865; Edward Leigh, bm.

Reed, John & Eliza Tate, 5 March 1787; James Tate, bm.

Rees, Abraham & Hannah Gott, 24 April 1790; James Railay, bm.

Rees, Joseph & Elizabeth Scarlett, 1 Feb 1855; T. J. Strayhorn, bm; m 1 Feb 1855 by Jno. Witherspoon, M. G.

Reeves, Azariah E. & Elizabeth Carroll, 7 July 1826; Deckson Carroll, Thos Clancy, bm.

Reeves, James & Elizabeth Madden, 7 Oct 1805; Frederic Reeves, bm.

Reeves, James & Mary Collins, 15 Feb 1825; George Long, bm.

Reeves, James & Mary Poe, 15 Feb 1859; T. M. Cheek, bm; m 28 Feb 1859 by Manly Andrews, minister.

Reeves, James O'Kelly & Emeline Rigsbey, 22 Nov 1824; Thomas Reeves, bm.

Reeves, John & Mary Linch, 24 Jan 1782.

Reeves, John W. & Menervy C. Williams, 26 Sept 1849; Henry J. Thompson, bm.

Reeves, Joseph & Salley Works, 13 Sept 1843; James H. Lashly, James A. Craig, bm.

Reeves, Spencer S. & Ann E. Duncan, 17 July 1839; William Christmas, bm.

Reeves, William & Sarah Rose, 9 May 1822; Jones Reavs, bm.

Reigbee, James & Mary Williams, 6 Nov 1860; Thomas Glenn, bm; m 8 Nov 1860 by William Green, J. P.

Reihbee, Ruffin & Edney Pickett, 17 March 1862; Presley J. Mangum, bm; m 18 March 1862 by S. Shepherd, J. P.

Reitsel, Christian G. & Delila Ingold, 12 Nov 1827; Adam Reitzel, bm.

Rencher, George, son of James & Margaret Rencher, & Mary A. Peeler, dau. of Carrissee Peeler, m 4 Sept 1857 by John Cheek.

Rencher, John Grant & Anne Nelson, 31 Aug 1786.

Rencher, King & Mary Cleag, colored, 9 Sept 1865; Robt Cleag, bm.

Renn, Jeremiah & Henrietta B. Glenn, 15 Dec 1821; Stephen Brown, bm.

Renn, William & Pinkey Wilbourn, 23 Oct 1823; Jno. J. Carrington, bm.

Reves, Charles & Beedy Rucker, 31 July 1792; Peter Reves, bm.

Reves, John & Nancy Baldwin, 13 June 1793; Enoch Collins, bm.

Reves, John & Elizabeth Holloway, 26 Nov 1799; Charles Reves, bm.

Revill, Kiah & Susannah Freeman, 15 Sept 1805; John Revill, bm.

Reville, Jolly & Martha Day, 15 April 1857; Jas. H. Barnes, bm.

Reyley, Washington & Sally Jones, 16 April 1823; Wilson Watson, bm.

Rhew, Irby & Artelia Browning, 29 June 1831; Benjamin Browning, bm.

Rhew, Isaac & Mary Horton, 7 March 1834; Russell James, Grief Dickson, bm.

Rhew, James & Elizabeth Carroll, 13 March 1858; J. H. Rhew, R. F. Gresham, bm; m 14 March 1858 by Samuel Couch, J. P.

Rhew, John & Peggy Dunnagan, 13 Feb 1809; Isaac Rhew, bm.

Rhew, John & Milley Crabtree, 26 Sept 1810; Andw. Crabtree, bm.

Rhew, Ruffin & Susan Roberts, 4 Oct 1836; Isaac Laws, bm.

Rhew, Silas M. & Haukins Couch, 7 Feb 1866; John A. Utley, bm; m 8 Feb 1866 by Samuel Couch, J. P.

Rhew, Thomas & Salley Hopkins, 7 April 1804; Henry ODaniel, bm.

Rhew, Walker & Lucretia Cates, 11 March 1856; John M. Cates, John Marcom, bm; m 20 March 1856 by Jno. Hancock, J. P.

Rhew, William L. & Mary S. Crabtree, 30 June 1863; Thomas Cole, bm; m 1 July 1864 by C. J. Freeland, J. P.

Rhew, William L. & Fannie Hallaway, 16 Feb 1867; John Y. Adams, bm; m 20 Feb 1867 by John F. Lyon, J. P.

Rhew, Wilson & Mahala Gates, 21 April 1830; Jefferson Rhew, James P. Brown, bm.

Rhew, Wilson & Mary Ann Cole, 14 Dec 1857; Robert Cates, Alsey Carroll, bm; m 15 Dec 1857 by John F. Lyon, J. P.

Rhoades, Richard & Salley Peteat, 28 Sept 1786; Aquila Roades, bm.

Rhoads, William & Mary Poteet, 28 Jan 1785; William Potet, bm.

Rhodes, Anderson & Jenny Rhodes, 11 Jan 1826; Noah Rhodes, bm.

Rhodes, Anderson & Dice Rhodes, 30 May 1835; Wm. T. Shields, bm.

Rhodes, Aquilla & Nancy Guess, 14 Nov 1818; Dennis Hargis, bm.

Rhodes, Aquilla & Milley White, 17 Nov 1829; William Scott, bm.

Rhodes, Benjamin & Elizabeth Cabe, 26 Oct 1805; Williamson Bryant, bm.

Rhodes, Champin & Cynthy Rhodes, 28 Jan 1804; John Rhodes, bm.

Rhodes, George & Clary Howington, 29 July 1818; John C. Geer, bm.

Rhodes, George A. & Malindia E. Vickers, 12 Oct 1861; A. J. Rhodes, bm; m 12 Oct 1861 by Solomon Shepherd, J. P.

Rhodes, George W. & Martha Turner, 11 Oct 1831; James G. Hutchens, bm.

Rhodes, Henderson & Edy Lynn, 10 Aug 1842; Spencer Hust, Thomas Sykes, bm.

Rhodes, Hezekiah & Elizabeth Moreland, 13 May 1783; Archer Graham, bm.

Rhodes, James & Patsy Edwards, 31 Oct 1805; John Edwards, bm.

Rhodes, James & Rebecca James, 6 April 1830; Riley James, bm.

Rhodes, James & Mary Riley, 3 Feb 1835; Nelson Baldwin, bm.

Rhodes, John & Hellon Barbee, 26 April 1860; Wm. G. Borland, bm; m 26 April 1860 by Solomon Shepherd, J. P.

Rhodes, John C. & Sarah Patterson, 4 Jan 1828; Jas. L. Patterson, bm.

Rhodes, Joshua & Franky Peeler, 30 Sept 1802; Benjamin Peeler, bm.

Rhodes, Noah & Anne Warren, 10 June 1815; Henry Forsett, bm.

Rhodes, Pleasant & Amy G. Trice, 11 Dec 1850; David Vickes, bm.

Rhodes, Richard & Susannah Wattes, 21 Jan 1804; Richard Procktor, bm.

Rhodes, Robert & Queen Clark, 27 Oct 1837; John M. Horn, Thos. Anderson, bm.

Rhodes, Samuel & Guellea Heflin, 14 Oct 1795; James Kannady, bm.

Rhodes, Thomas & Mary Fulton, 9 Nov 1784; James Fulton, Henry Thompson, bm.

Rhodes, Thomas & Salley James, 20 July 1815; Moses McCown, bm.

Rhodes, William & Deliah Hearndon, 19 April 1792; William Rhodes, William Pattishall, bm.

Rhodes, William & Elizabeth Moore, 24 April 1834; William Smith, bm.

Rhodes, William & Edney Brockwell, 2 Aug 1858; Jno. A. Neal, Isreal Turner, bm; m 3 Aug 1858 by Samuel Couch, bm.

Rhodes, William Jr. & Penelope Trice, 4 Nov 1815; William Trice, bm.

Rhodes, Willie & Martha McKinsey, 7 Aug 1841; James Browning, James Warren, bm.

Rhodes, Willie T. & Penisy Barbee, 20 Nov 1838; Robert Plasants, Allen Wilkins, bm.

Rhodes, Zachariah & Sarah Leathers, 20 March 1829; Moses C. Hutchins, bm.

Rhone, James & Holley Hailey, 30 Oct 1805.

Rhue, Wilson & Leweny Riley, 18 June 1847; Madison Wilkerson, bm.

Rial, William & Elizabeth Green, 7 Feb 1815; Thomas Royal, bm.

Rials, Thomas & Polley Walker, 8 Aug 1815; William Rials, bm.

Rice, John & Sally Pickett, 16 Oct 1818; William Rider, bm.

Rice, Robert K. & Martha Pettigrew, 8 July 1862; James Rice, bm; m 9 July 1862 by Wm. W. Pickett, J. P.

Rich, Jacob & Delilah Albright, 25 Feb 1834; Jeremiah Holt, bm.

Rich, John & Dililah Thompson, 12 Oct 1819; Jacob Albright, bm.

Rich, John & Jane Thompson, 15 March 1836; Michall Strader, bm.

Rich, Timothy & Nancy Bevill, 6 June 1821; Ard. Couch, bm.

Richard, Henry & Eliza J. Adams, 14 April 1842; I. A. Cox, D. D. Phillips, bm.

Richards, Jacob & Rhodey Hulgan, 23 Dec 1783; William Numan, bm.

Richardson, John & Catharine Chadwick, 10 Aug 1798; John Cate, bm.

Richardson, Robert & Polley Johnston, 8 Jan 1812; Jn. Murdoch, Thos. Whitted, bm.

Richardson, Samuel, son of Glass & Peggy Richardson, & Anny Whitted, colored, m 18 July 1867 by Zuck Horton, M. G.

Richardson, Stephen & Patsy Williams, 21 July 1827; Nathan Rippy, bm.

Richerson, William, son of Peter & Fanny Richerson & Margaret Holeman, dau. of Sally Holeman, colored, m 25 July 1867 by F. M. Gordon, minister.

Richey, William & Mary Tedford, 17 Aug 1781; George Tedford, bm.

Richmond, Adam S. & Martha Allen, 20 Sept 1839; William Paul, bm.

Richmond, Berryman G. & Sarah Anderson, 28 Jan 1834; J. Taylor, bm.

Richmond, Eligah & Ann Wilkerson, 11 July 1866; Saml. Swinell, bm.

Richmond, James B. & Annie E. Bradford, 5 May 1866; R. B. Warren, bm; m 13 May 1866 by Thos. Lynch, minister.

Richmond, James Y. & Eliza Jane King, 9 Jan 1846; Robt. W. Wiley, bm.

Richmond, William S. & Mary Jane Tinnin, 25 Dec 1843; F. A. Wiley, bm.

Rickets, Gennings & Rebecca Edwards, 12 June 1797; William Rickets, Joseph Simmons, bm.

Rickets, Jennings & Katey Pugh, 14 Nov 1811; John Pugh, bm.

Rickets, Samuel & Nelley Ray, 28 Jan 1800; William Grimes, bm.

Rickets, Wm. & Ferebee Williams, 20 Jan 1797; James Grimes, bm.

Rickets, William & Casandra Jones, 24 Dec 1811; Richard Jones, Samuel Wilson, bm.

Rickets, William & Polly Crutchfield, 22 March 1821; John Pickard, bm.

Rickman, Abraham & Rosanah Barbee, 26 March 1803; Mark Barbee, bm.

Rider, Henry H. & Susan Faucett, 9 Aug 1825; W. P. Clancy, bm.

Ridger, Wm. & Nancy Hall, 30 June 1795; Sterling Harris, bm.

Rider, William & Polly Hargiss, 6 Oct 1802; David Ray, bm.

Rider, William & Nancy Briston, 11 July 1810; Gavin Alves, bm.

Ridgen, Jossah & Susannah Johnston, 17 Nov 1816; George Coffner, bm.

Rieves, George & Margret McCollum, 8 Sept 1836; John W. Shaw, John W. Carr, bm.

Rieves, John & Mary Gwinn, 3 Dec 1793; David Allison, bm.

Riggains, Ephiam & Ruth Izzell, 11 June 1807; Robert Moore, bm.

Rigins, Powell & Ruth Trice, (no date); Gray Barbee, bm.

Riggs, Albert & Sarah Newton, 19 Dec 1812; Joseph Guess, bm.

Riggs, Alves & Petronella Ray, 10 Dec 1825; Wm. B. Camieser, bm.

Riggs, Alvin & Elizabeth E. G. Walker, 31 Dec 1858; Nelson P. Hall, bm; m 2 Jan 1859 by Nelson P. Hall, J. P.

Riggs, Augustine W. & Mary Umstead, 8 July 1835; James C. Roberts, bm.

Riggs, David & Peggy Hargiss, 5 April 1816; Wm. W. Jurdon, bm.

Riggs, George & Nancy Riggs, 11 Aug 1810; John Riggs, bm.

Riggs, George D. & Polley Hopkins, 15 Nov 1811; Jo. Hopkins, bm.

Riggs, Hugh & Elizabeth Murdock, 12 Feb 1805; S. Turrentine, bm.

Riggs, James & Hannah Nichols, 12 Feb 1784; William Hall, bm.

Riggs, James & Polley Hannah, 22 Jan 1788; Thos. Riggs, bm.

Riggs, James & Mary Woods, 17 Sept 1836; Moreland Jackson, Harrell Dorety, bm.

Riggs, James & Nancy Anderson, 4 Sept 1840; David R. Allison, James Turner, bm.

Riggs, James & Amelia Ball, 10 Nov 1846; Benton Ray, bm.

Riggs, James & Amelia Duke, 30 May 1849; Benton Ray, bm.

Riggs, James & Fanny Riggs, 20 July 1854; J. D. Lipscomb, bm; m 23 July 1854 by Wm. Lipscomb, J. P.

Riggs, Saml. & Jean Jamison, 31 Jan 1801; Saml. Woods, bm.

Riggs, Wesley & Roan Riggs, 9 Nov 1866; Charles W. Riggs, Wilas Wilson, bm; m 13 Nov 1866 by E. M. Holt, J. P.

Riggs, Willie & Margret Wilkinson, 11 Nov 1834; Sander S. Jasper, bm.

Riggsbee, Francis M. & Mary Blackwood, 3 Jan 1856; T. A. Davis, bm; m 3 Jan 1856 by John W. Carr, J. P.

Riggsbee, William & Susan Hall, 12 Oct 1848; Heirless J. Glenn, bm.

Riggsby, John & Betsey Glenn, 10 Jan 1821; William Roan, bm.

Right, John & Rachel Thompson, 1 Feb 1826; William Paris, bm.

Rightsill, John & Polly Garrett, 23 April 1842; Milton Rightsill, bm.

Rigs, William P. & Elizabeth Umsted, 26 Feb 1850; A. Y. Brown, bm.

Rigsbee, Ilai & Elizabeth Pearson, 6 Jan 1840; Norwood Crabtree, James Campbell, bm.

Rigsbee, Mark & Nancy Herndon, 2 Dec 1833; Chesley Herndon, Alexr. Dickson, bm.

Rigsby, Isaiah & Nancy Pendergrass, 4 March 1800; John Pendergrass, bm.

Rigsby, Jefferson & Louisey Copley, 9 Dec 1850; John A. Glenn, bm.

Rigsby, Jesse & Elizabeth Picket, 13 July 1801; Jesse Picket, bm.

Rigsby, Jesse & Mary Vickers, 21 July 1831; Archd. Rigsby, bm.

Rigsby, Mark & Susan Trice, 24 Nov 1837; John H. Andson, bm.

Rigsby, Mark & Winney Marcum, 10 April 1841; John H. Andson, bm.

Rigsby, Mark & Fanny Marcum, 30 April 1846; Joseph Anderson, bm.

Rigsby, Thomas & Aggy Smith, 18 Dec 1801; Absalom Smith, bm.

Rigsby, Warren & Ruth Chisenhall, 14 Sept 1815; William Roan, bm.

Rigsby, Woody & Nancy M. Glenn, 19 May 1829; Archibald Rigsby, bm.

Riks, Benjamin & Unity James, 2 Jan 1810; Adam Starr, bm.

Riks, John & Ruth Carrington, 7 July 1810; Moses Leathers, bm.

Riley, Alson G. & Polley Ray, 6 Jan 1855; Andrew A. Jones, bm; m 7 Jan 1855 by Wiatt Cates, J. P.

Riley, Anderson & Betsey Vaughan, 20 Dec 1834; Henderson Vaughan, Allen Huskey, bm.

Riley, Copeland & Milly Ward, 19 Dec 1819; Edward McDade, bm.

Riley, David & Leathy A. Crabtree, 18 Jan 1854; William McCauley, bm; m 19 Jan 1854 by John F. Lyon, J. P.

Riley, David, of A., & Mary Dollar, 3 July 1856; John Dollar of E., bm; m 3 July 1856 by C. Wilson, J. P.

Riley, Dudley & Jane Jones, 21 Dec 1860; Green Blalock, bm; m 6 Jan 1861 by Wm. J. Duke, J. P.

Riley, Durell & Ann Blackwood, 9 Oct 1861; Thos. Wilson, bm; m 10 Oct 1861 by C. J. Freeland, J. P.

Riley, Edward & Susan Ray, 18 Dec 1826; Richs. Nichols, bm.

Riley, Eli & Larcena Vaughn, m 11 June 1857 by Wm. J. Roberts, J. P.

Riley, Elza & Mary Jordan, 28 Jan 1868; C. P. Warren, bm; m 31 Jan 1858 by Charles Wilson, J. P.

Riley, Elzy & Margaret Hicks, 15 Aug 1863; Joseph Reese, bm; m 16 Aug 1863 by John F. Lyon, J. P.

Riley, Guilford & Mary Simpson, 5 March 1862; Willis P. Gates, bm.

Riley, James & Sarah Grimes, 9 Aug 1793; Wm. Belvin, bm.

Riley, James & Ellender Watson, 3 Feb 1802; Jno. Taylor, A. B. Bruce, bm.

Riley, James & Jean Dunrafer, 26 Dec 1808; William Fausette, bm.

Riley, James & Mary Donate, 8 Aug 1833; James N. Clark, bm.

Riley, James & Betsey Hall, 16 Sept 1834; Thomas Riley, bm.

Riley, James & Elizabeth Wilkinson, 2 June 1838; Wm. Wilkinson, bm.

Riley, James & Caroline Pope, 23 April 1859; Nathaniel Riley, Stephen F. Forrest, bm; m 23 April 1859 by Stephen F. Forrest, J. P.

Riley, James & Saluda Vaughn, 5 Aug 1861; C. Wilson, bm; m 6 June 1861 by L. W. Hall, J. P.

Riley, Jefferson & Eliza Pool, 14 June 1858; A. D. Umsted, T. W. Laws, bm; m 18 June 1858 by B. C. Hopkins, J. P.

Riley, John & Mary Lytle, 26 July 1785; John Whitaker, bm.

Riley, John & Polly Whitaker, 31 June 1794; Abimelech Barbee, bm.

Riley, John & Polley Collins, 11 July 1800; John Bollen, John Perry, bm.

Riley, John & Elizabeth Dollar, 1 Feb 1810; Stephen Pritchard, bm.

Riley, John & Nancy Whittaker, 7 Dec 1833; William Whitaker, N. Barton, bm.

Riley, John Jr. & Sarah Jane Sims, 9 Dec 1852; Simpson Riley, bm; m 9 Dec 1852 by Richd Nichols, J. P.

Riley, John J. & Mary E. Lindsey, 14 Oct 1860; William Wilkerson, James Gill, bm; m 15 Oct 1860 by F. M. Jordan, elder.

Riley, John R. & Margaret Thompson, 13 Feb 1867; William Rily, bm; m 14 Feb 1867 by C. E. Smith, J. P.

Riley, John W. & Tempy E. Sykes, m 23 Dec 1866 by Thomas J. Cates, J. P.

Riley, Levi R. & Jane Graves, 9 March 1846.

Riley, Nathaniel & Martha C. Merritt, 7 Aug 1858; R. M. Jones, bm.

Riley, Norwood & Elenina Taylor, 13 Aug 1839; Pleasant Riley, James Sykes, bm.

Riley, Peter & Elizabeth Woods, 21 July 1795; Robert Ray, bm.

Riley, Peter & Nancy Finley, 18 Jan 1830; J. McKerall, bm.

Riley, Plesant & Elizabeth Taylor, 2 Oct 1834; Henderson Riley, Sidney Caroll, bm.

Riley, Presley & Anna Hicks, 25 Sept 1846; Norwood Riley, bm.

Riley, Samuel & Ann Watson, 16 Oct 1840; Daniel W. Thompson, Thomas Anderson, bm.

Riley, Samuel & Mary Jane Roberts, 21 Dec 1842; D. W. Thompson, Thomas W. Holden, bm.

Riley, Sanders & Martha Thompson, 2 Feb 1828; James Thompson, bm.

Riley, Simpson & Lucenda Cates, 24 Nov 1842; John Riley, Pleasant Riley, bm.

Riley, Thomas W. & Mary Margaret Thomas, 27 April 1854; Wm. T. Cope, bm; m 14 May 1854 by Ruffin R. Tapp, J. P.

Riley, Uriah T. & Mary Bane, 17 Jan 1838; Will W. Allison, J. Taylor, bm.

Riley, Warden & Hawkin Poke, 22 May 1847; Copeland Riley, bm.

Riley, William & Elizabeth Chambers, 21 Sept 1791.

Riley, William & Sarah Dollar, 6 Feb 1792; Henry Bunch, bm.

Riley, William & Frances Hopkins, 6 July 1825; Robert Latta, bm.

Riley, William & Meada Cates, 2 April 1834; Anderson Riley, Tho. Cates, bm.

Riley, William & Susan Hall, 13 Jan 1836; James Riley, Jno. Homes, bm.

Riley, William & Judith Smith, 3 Jan 1860; Presley Riley, James Gill, bm; m 5 Jan 1860 by C. Wilson, J. P.

Riley, William H. & Catharine Miles, 20 Dec 1855; Thos. C. Hayes, bm; m 20 Dec 1855 by Tho. C. Hayes, M. G.

Riley, William L., son of Wm. & Susan Riley, & Josephen Jackson, dau. of Clemuel & Rachel Jackson, m 18 Dec 1867 by C. P. Warren, J. P.

Riley, William P. & Catherine E. Thompson, 27 Dec 1866; John R. Riley, William A. Hayes, bm; m 27 Dec 1866 by Wilson Brown, J. P.

Riley, Willie & Sarah Walker, 26 July 1848; Harwood Riley, E. G. Gray, bm.

Rimmer, John & Polley Whitfield, 21 June 1800; Wm. Whitfield, bm.

Ringstaff, Conrod N. & Lucy Tudor, 24 Aug 1808; Tho. Crabtree, bm.

Ringstaff, Henry & Sally Miller, 3 Sept 1814; William Ringstaff, Thos. D. Watt, bm.

Ringstaff, James & Rebeccah Murray, 9 Jan 1820; Joseph Murray, bm.

Ringstaff, William & Patsey Hill, 29 June 1820; Edward McDade, bm.

Ringstaff, William & Betsy Ann Griffin, 15 Nov 1845; Balaam McVay, bm.

Ripey, Joseph & Hesther Haisting, 22 Sept 1798; James Rippy, bm.

Rippey, Edward & Mary Elmore, 16 March 1782; John Elmore, bm.

Rippey, Edward & Nancy McCracken, 17 Nov 179__; James Rippy, bm.

Rippey, Jesse & Elizabeth Moody, 8 Sept 1798; James Davisson, bm.

Rippy, Benjamin & Charity Harder, 16 Feb 1822; John Rippy, bm.

Rippy, James & Sarah Dunn, 6 March 1792; James Grant, bm.

Rippy, James & Mary Ann McCaddams, 13 Nov 1833; Alfred King, bm.

Rippy, John & Nancy Pile, 30 Nov 1821; John McCracken, bm.

Rippy, Leonard & Sarah Jane Wilkins, 9 May 1846; Joseph Mcadams, bm.

Rippy, Matthew & Rosannah Williams, 29 June 1827; Wm. Coureton, bm.

Ripy, John W. & Catharine McCaddams, 7 June 1834; Robert McAddams, bm.

Ripy, Stephen & Margaret King, 20 Dec 1821; Jeremiah King, bm.

Ritch, Henry & Francis Troxlar, 31 July 1821; Daniel Hill, bm.

Ritch, Henry & Polly Albright, 4 Dec 1847; Boston Sharp, bm.

Rivers, John & Hannah Shearer, 7 Sept 1786; Jacob Moser, bm.

Rix, Abraham & Mary Rivell, 12 Aug 1840; James M. Palmer, bm.

Roach, ___ & Salley Clendening, 21 ___ 1824; James Clendenin, bm.

Roach, Absolam & Mary Middleton, 16 Dec 1794; Job Taylor, bm.

Roach, David & Patsy Cate, 6 Nov 1812; J. Taylor, bm.

Roach, David M. & Matty May, 6 March 1849; William Ray, bm.

Roach, James & Martha Ivey, 31 Dec 1819; Thomas Cate, bm.

Roach, James & Myram Garrigan, 18 Jan 1827; Robert Moore, John Moore, bm.

Roach, James & Elizabeth ODaniel, 5 Dec 1835; B. Corbett, bm.

Roach, John & Rachel Thompson, 21 Nov 1800; Wm. Roach, Joseph Green, bm.

Roach, John & Sally Pay, 24 Aug 1825; Stephen Bacon, bm.

Roach, Lewis & Anne Bartley, 27 July 1783; Henry O'Daniels, bm.

Roach, Merida & Eadie Currie, 16 May 1856; William Strain, bm; m 16 May 1856 by J. J. Freeland, J. P.

Roach, Thomas & Edith Johnston, 24 Dec 1817; Hiram Johnson, bm.

Roach, William & Milley Cates, 7 May 1796; Mosses Cate, bm.

Roach, William & Jinney Cate, 9 July 1820; Edward McDade, bm.

Roach, William & Elizabeth Ray, 29 Jan 1858; Samuel Crawford, James Gill, bm; m 29 Jan 1858 by Allen Edwards, J. P.

Roades, Robert & Frances Copley, 28 March 1810; William Allen, bm.

Roan, Daniel & Franky Daniel, 29 Aug 1810; William Leathers, William Shaw, bm.

Roan, General & Peggy James, 25 Oct 1835; Joshua Albright, bm.

Roan, James & Holley Hailey, 30 Oct 1805; Stephen Williams, bm.

Roark, James & Mary Torrentine, 22 Oct 1782; Francis Baldridge, bm.

Roark, William & Anne McMullen, 12 Sept 1800; S. Turrentine, bm.

Robards, Abel & Sally Merritt, (no date, 1832-1835); Saml Merritt, Saml. Taylor, bm.

Robards, William & Elizabeth Baynes, 28 Sept 1845; James Baynes, M. N. Workman, bm.

Robarts, Burrell & Mary Ann Sparks, 26 Nov 1849; Christopher Lynn, bm.

Robbs, William & Susanna Watson, 12 Feb 1781; Peter Walton, bm.

Robenson, Jefferson & Lytha Mayho, 3 Aug 1836; William Mayho, Tho. Anderson, bm.

Roberson, Allen J. & Julia A. Patterson, 12 Sept 1866; Cave M. Conklin, bm; m 13 Sept 1866 by W. W. Wilson.

Roberson, Daniel & Dolly Woods, 10 Aug 1866; Joseph Woods, bm; m 13 Aug 1866 by Joseph Woods, J. P.

Roberson, James S. & Martha Robertson, 19 Jan 1867; W. M. Roberson, bm.

Roberson, John & Nancy Poe, 10 Dec 1835; Jesse Poe, bm.

Roberson, John O. & Polly Tapp, 25 Dec 1866; Andy Tapp, bm; m 27 Dec 1866 by Wilson Brown, J. P.

Roberson, Merritt & Sarah Bailey, 22 Oct 1805; Merrett Roberson, Mastings Cheek, bm.

Roberson, Nathaniel & Weddy L. Lindsy, 27 Feb 1827; Stephen Roberson, bm.

Roberson, William & Elizabeth Loyd, 23 April 1839; Thomas Roberson, bm.

Roberts, Albert & Cornelia E. Paul, 1 Aug 1856; John F. Lyon, Thomas Faucett, bm; m 12 Aug 1856 by Gaston Farrar, M. G.

Roberts, Allen & Elizabeth Ellis, 7 April 1838; Sidney Ellis, bm.

Roberts, Andrew J. & Clara E. Parker, 17 Dec 1864; E. M. Holt, bm.

Roberts, Benjamin & Sally Archer, 30 June 1817; Jesse Archer, bm.

Roberts, Charles & Polly Crabtree, 29 March 1823; Watson M. Kerall, bm.

Roberts, Daniel & Ellenor Russell, 5 Nov 1834; James Johnston, bm.

Roberts, Dempsy & Viney Pettiford, 9 April 1812; Simon White, bm.

Roberts, Elisha & Mary Roberts, 31 May 1825; Jno. J. Carrington, bm.

Roberts, Ellis & Charlotte Maddison, 14 Dec 1829; Jesse Duke, Jos. A. Woods, bm.

Roberts, Ephraim & Nancy Harris, 23 Jan 1801; Claborn Parish, bm.

Roberts, Francis & Nancy Waggoner, 6 Dec 1822; Thomas Roberts, bm.

Roberts, George & Patsey Roberts, 23 Dec 1826; Watts Marcom, Silas M. Dink, bm.

Roberts, Hinton & Polly Sharp, 3 Dec 1838; Leonard Ray, bm.

Roberts, James & Sarah Parker, 14 Feb 1825; Jesse Duke, bm.

Roberts, James & Jane Carrington, 5 Jan 1833; Samuel Scarlett, bm.

Roberts, John & Nancy Durning, 1 Oct 1811; James Durning, Thos. Roberts, bm.

Roberts, John & Winnifred Umstead, 1 Nov 1820; Jesse Walker, bm.

Roberts, John & Winniford Roberts, 18 March 1826; John Jarrett, bm.

Roberts, John & Caroline Clar, 9 April 1866; D. C. Gunter, bm; m 9 April 1866 by Thomas C. Hayes.

Roberts, John J. & Louisa Cobea, 20 Sept 1842; John A. Kirkland, Moses Leathers Jun., bm.

Roberts, Joseph & Martha Weaver, 22 Aug 1835; Lewis Pettiford, bm.

Roberts, Lewis & Eliza Ann Peed, 3 Nov 1848; John Peed, bm.

Roberts, Mark & Salley Roberts, 19 Aug 1816; James Parrish, bm.

Roberts, Myatt & Eliza Hicks, 15 Dec 1856; Elbert Dossett, bm; m 16 Dec 1856 by M. A. Angier, J. P.

Roberts, Pleasant & Jenny Nelson, 23 Oct 1805; W. Cumming, bm.

Roberts, Richard & Polley Wilson, 2 Dec 1813; Peter L. Ray, bm.

Roberts, Simeon & Adaline Brinkley, 18 Dec 1857; D. McAdams, bm; m 18 Dec 1857 by W. M. Carrington, J. P.

Roberts, Thomas & Janey Beshanes, 5 May 1804; Stephens Robarts, bm.

Roberts, Thomas E. & Elizabeth Ann Miller, 14 Dec 1866; Nelson Smith, bm; m 20 Dec 1866 by Thos. Wilson, J. P.

Roberts, Vincent & Barsheba Bowles, 5 Feb 1805; John Henry Fosset, bm.

Roberts, Washington P. & Mary Jane Cate, 20 Dec 1860; John Cate, bm; m 20 Dec 1860 by Thos. Long, J. P.

Roberts, Wesley & Josephine Parker, 2 Oct 1860; Wm. R. Parrish, Thomas Webb, bm.

Roberts, Westly & Carolina Walker, 9 Feb 1837; Sidney Cates, H. L. Rountree, bm.

Roberts, William & Christiana Parish, 18 Jan 1810; Jas. Walker, bm.

Roberts, William & Charlotte Ray, 3 May 1812; James Child, bm.

Roberts, William & Elizabeth Bass, 24 Sept 1823; Simon White, Thomas Burnette, bm.

Roberts, William & Delilah Andrews, 18 Oct 1836; Henry Andres, George Andrews, bm.

Roberts, William & Nannie Garrard, 12 Jan 1867; John W. Parker, H. B. Guthrie, bm; m 15 Jan 1867 by D. C. Parrish, J. P.

Roberts, William C. & Anna J. Rountree, 5 Jan 1858; J. J. Allen, bm; m 7 Jan 1858 by M. Baldwin, M. G.

Roberts, William K., son of Green & Caroline Roberts, & Nancy Tilly, dau. of Allen & Nancy Tilly, m 15 Sept 1867 by E. M. Holt.

Roberts, Willie & Nancy Marcom, 15 Feb 1812; Willis Marcow, bm.

Roberts, Willie J. & Jane R. Holman, 2 May 1854; L. D. McMannen, bm.

Roberts, Willis & Mary Stout, 19 Jan 1838; Jacob Clapp, bm.

Roberts, Willis & Fanny Nichols, 1 Aug 1838; J. M. Roberts, bm.

Roberts, Woodson & Mahala Roberts, 26 Aug 1837; John W. York, J. Taylor, bm.

Robertson, Alvis Jackson & Eliza Ana Durham, 25 June 1842; Thomas Roberson, bm.

Robertson, Andrew & Ellienor Logen, 18 Jan 1787; William Murray, bm.

Robertson, Andrew & Ruth Robinson, 30 Jan 1816; Robert Murray, bm.

Robertson, Henry & Martha Jane Durham, 16 Aug 1858; T. H. Robeson, Ruffin Durham, bm; m 16 Aug 1858 by Allen Edwards, J. P.

Robertson, James & Catherine Masser, 22 Oct 1805; Stephen Wells, bm.

Robertson, James & Polly Thompson, 6 Feb 1827; John Graham, bm.

Robertson, James S. & Martha Robertson, 19 Jan 1867; William M. Roberson, bm; m 20 Jan 1867 by H. M. S. Stroud, J. P.

Robertson, Nathaniel & Lavica Lindey, 7 Nov 1848; James H. Lasley, bm.

Robertson, Nathaniel W. & Elizabeth Shoffner, 28 April 1847; D. S. C. H. Robertson, bm.

Robertson, Roddy & Cathrien Fogelman, 19 Sept 1821; William Fogleman, bm.

Robertson, William & Aris Nevills, 13 Sept 1804; Nathaniel Robertson, bm.

Robeson, Allen M. & Susannah Moore, 1 Jan 1822; Stephen Lindsey, bm.

Robeson, Henry & Henrettor Christmas, 27 July 1832; James A. Craig, bm.

Robetson, David A. & Salley E. Nunn, 26 Oct 1857; D. C. McDade, bm.

Robinson, Alexander & Sarah Rountree, 25 Nov 1818; John Garrott, bm.

Robinson, Daniel & Nancy Hopper, 22 Oct 1803; John Hubbard, bm.

Robinson, David M. & Sarah Ann Tapp, 11 Aug 1851; W. H.
Robinson, bm; m 14 Aug 1851 by H. Tapp, J. P.

Robinson, Jaems & Margaret Ray, 29 April 1788; David Allison,
bm.

Robinson, John & Rachael Jamison, 4 Aug 1792; Jno. Roundtree,
bm.

Robinson, Joseph & Sarah Ray, 1 April 1797; Joseph Ray, bm.

Robinson, Mark & Fanny Holmes, 14 Nov 1799; Hirum Parks, bm.

Robinson, Michal & Jennet Ray, 22 Nov 1788; David Allison, bm.

Robinson, William & Dicey Horn, 21 April 1804; William D.
Lester, James Johnson, bm.

Robinson, William & Nancy Wilson, 25 Oct 1806; Thomas Rountree,
bm.

Robinson, William & Sarah Underwood, 12 June 1809; William Scott,
bm.

Robinson, William R. & Alice Waggner, 10 June 1813; Edward
McDade, bm.

Robison, Merrit & Cathrine Fogleman, 4 Feb 1841; John Guthrie,
bm.

Robrds, Aaron & Susan Caroline Smith, 3 Nov 1845; Willis Smith,
bm.

Robson, Nathaniel & Elenor Cable, 11 Aug 1846; Isaiah May, bm.

Robson, William W. & Elizabeth Jane Russell, 12 Sept 1840;
H. J. Mann, bm.

Roch, David & Sarah Sykes, 28 April 1846; A. Mickle, bm.

Roch, John & Mahaley Ray, 9 Sept 1845; William Pickard, David
M. Roch, bm.

Rochel, Alven & Eliza H. Rone, 22 Nov 1841; William Y. Rochel,
Moses Leathers Junr., bm.

Rochel, Tapley W. & Eliza Rhodes, 15 Dec 1840; Alvin Rochell,
John Jones, bm.

Rochell, Alsey & Martha Lynn, 27 Aug 1841; J. W. Hancock, bm;
m 1 Sept 1851 by J. W. Hancock, J. P.

Rochell, Alsey H. & Mary Jane Morris, 30 Nov 1848; George W.
Rochell, bm.

Rochell, George W. & Mary Jane Hailey, 17 July 1850; Wm. B.
Vanderford, bm.

Rochell, William, son of Altine & Hawkins Rochell, & Airlee
Glenn, dau. of Duncan & Lucy Glenn, m 26 Dec 1867 by James
Stagg, J. P.

Rodgers, James & Aness Phillips, 28 April 1817; John Rogers, bm.

Rodgers, John & Elizabeth Loy, 28 Aug 1806; Jacob Loy, bm.

Rodgers, Simeon A. & Julia A. Holeman, 10 April 1861; H. R. Forbis, bm; m 11 April 1861 by F. M. Jordan, M. G.

Rodgers, William & Janey Patton, 20 Feb 1800; James Rodgers, bm.

Rogers, B. Y. & Elizabeth F. Green, 26 Sept 1859; m 5 Oct 1859 by Elijah Hester, M. G.

Rogers, Benjamin & Catharine Cabe, 21 June 1819; Wm. R. Herndon, bm.

Rogers, Idolet & Julia Outlaw, 21 Jan 1838; Russel McRay, James Mebane Jr., bm.

Rogers, James & Elener McCoy, 8 Nov 1789; Thomas Rogers, bm.

Rogers, James A. & Barbara Ann Foust, 24 Nov 1837; Wm. M. Rogers, J. H. Foust, bm.

Rogers, John & Jane Russell, 13 Sept 1813; John C. Russell, bm.

Rogers, John & Margaret L. Shepard, 27 Sept 1821; Samuel Follett, bm.

Rogers, Nathan & Nancy Teer, 10 Nov 1809; Alexr. Allen, bm.

Rogers, William M. & Mary Keck, 8 Jan 1846; Geo. W. Bruce, bm.

Roggers, Augustus & Francis Duke, 12 Jan 1867; Plummer Transil, bm; m 13 Jan 1867 by Jno. Hancock, J. P.

Rone, Ander & Salley Freeman, 10 Aug 1816; John Freeman, bm.

Roney, B. F. & Cornelia M. Hazle, 27 Feb 1849; E. G. Gray, bm.

Roney, Benjamin & Margaret Pickett, 8 Sept 1804; John Pickett, bm.

Roney, Benjamin F. & Delilah Montgomery, 27 Aug 1839; J. Gant, bm.

Roney, Henry & Elizabeth Tarpley, 27 July 1842; Jacob Hurdle, bm.

Roney, James & Polly Collins, 21 Feb 1812; Paul Kinnier, bm.

Roney, John & Mary Trolinger, 12 Dec 1815; Jacob Trolinger, bm.

Roney, John & Mary H. Thompson, 16 Jan 1849; R. F. Morris, bm.

Roney, John T. & Eliza Jane Graham, 11 Sept 1845; James Garrison, bm.

Roper, James & Mary J. Leonard, 23 Dec 1863; Lemuel L. Carell, R. M. Jones, bm.

Rose, John & Nancy Dawson, 28 May 1824; Alfred Boone, bm.

Rose, Neil B. & Polley Rainey, 17 Oct 1803; Jas. Patterson, bm.

Rose, Samuel & Mary Smith, 22 Oct 1783; Robert Baldridge, Michl. Burke, bm.

Rose, William & Betsey Beckum, 6 April 1813; John Beckum, bm.

Roseman, James T. & Marila Pleasants, 22 Nov 1866; G. W.
Pleasants, J. D. Pleasants, bm; m 22 Nov 1866 by Henry B.
Pratt.

Ross, Andr. & Alis Pratt, 29 Aug 1782; James Hunter, bm.

Ross, James & Anne Dening, 7 April 1791; Robert Ferguson, bm.

Ross, Thomas & Sarah Hall, 22 Jan 1783; Robert Hall, bm.

Ross, Thomas W. & Mahala Glenn, 7 April 1843; Thomas Anderson,
bm.

Ross, William & Polly Hobbs, 7 Sept 1829; Martin Hobbs, bm.

Rosser, James & Nancy Thrift, 20 April 1830; John Rosser,
A. Blackwood, bm.

Rosser, Joshua & Sarah Willis, 4 July 1795; Thos. Snipes, bm.

Rosser, William & Jane Williams, 23 Dec 1863; Lemuel L. Carrol,
R. M. Jones, bm.

Rosson, Asa & Ellen R. Ray, 19 July 1840; James C. Turrentine,
Thos. Hasting, bm.

Rosson, James & Mary J. Leonard, 23 Dec 1863; m 24 Dec 1863 by
Henry Gray, minister.

Rosson, William & Jane Williams, m 27 Dec 1863 by Henry Gray,
minister.

Rottenberry, Presley & Elizabeth Anne Collier, 14 Jan 1818;
John G. Collier, bm.

Roulhac, Jos. B. G. & Catherine Ruffin, 2 Nov 1856; Paul C.
Cameron, bm.

Rountre, Jno. & Raley Thompson, 23 Feb 1793; John Thompson, bm.

Rountree, Charles & Nancy Robinson, 27 March 1794; Nath Farmer,
bm.

Rountree, David R. & Salley Wilson, 19 Dec 1825; Charles Wilson,
bm.

Rountree, John W. & Anna Jane Ray, 17 April 1852; James R.
Fosshee, bm; m 21 April 1852 by Archibald Currie.

Rountree, John D., son of Henry & Jane Rountree, & Fanny
Lipscomb, dau. of Nancy Lipscomb, colored, m 17 Nov 1867
by L. W. Hall, J. P.

Rountree, Thomas & Victoria Robertson, 11 Sept 1804; Joseph
Rountree, bm.

Rountree, Thomas & Emley E. Ray, 17 Jan 1856; James R. Miller,
bm; m 17 Jan 1856 by H. Terry, J. P.

Routon, Wilson B. & Mariah L. Parks, 24 Jan 1860; L. K. Willie,
bm; m by L. K. Willie, 23 Jan 1860.

Rowan, Thomas & Eliza Holt, 20 Aug 1812; Davd. Evans, bm.

Rowark, Elisha & Ariana E. McCulloch, 20 Jan 1849; Henry P. Pope, bm; m 21 Jan 1849 by Archibald Currie, minister.

Rowland, George A. & Julia A. Horner, 22 Sept 1840; L. L. Kimball, bm.

Royall, John & Pamelia Maynard, 30 Sept 1820; Richard Maynard, bm.

Royster, James & Polley Wells, 2 June 1811(?); James Royster, Larkin Landers, bm.

Royster, William A. & Anne Glass, 12 Feb 1833; V. M. Murphey, bm.

Rue, Stanford & Hannah E. Borland, 18 Sept 1841; Alsey Ca___, Jno Horner (?), bm.

Rue (Rhew), William & Nancy Warren, 13 Nov 1833 (?); Irby Rhew, bm.

Ruffin, Thomas & Frances Revell, 29 March 1866; Susan Laws, bm.

Ruffin, Thomas Jr. & Mary C. Cain, 14 June 1858; Pride Jones, bm; m in St. Matthew's Church, Hillsborough, by M. A. Curtis, rector, 16 June 1858.

Ruffin, Wyatt, son of Wylie & Jeney Ruffin, & Milly Sutherland, dau. of Wm. & Lucy Sutherlin, m 11 Dec 1867 by Joseph Woods, J. P.

Rumbley, Ezekiel F. & Milley Heath, 30 May 1846; Enoch Rumbly, bm.

Rumbley, John & Elizabeth Boon, 7 Jan 1847; Lewis Holt, bm.

Rumbley, Nathan & Lewis Devenport, 24 Dec 1807; Henry Rumbley, Robert Baldridg, bm.

Rumbly, Edward & Chloe Kells, 13 Dec 1807; John Rumbly, bm.

Rumbly, Edward & Mary Holt, 20 July 1824; John Holt, of Israel, bm.

Rumbly, James & Nancy Ross, 17 Oct 1806; Joseph Rumally, bm.

Rumbly, Thomas & Malinda Isly, 28 Dec 1848; Edward Rumbly, bm.

Rumley, Edward & Elizabeth Murray, 12 July 1814; Aaron Rumley, bm.

Rumley, Henry & Margaret Sutton, 15 Oct 1837; Alfred Rumley, bm.

Runnals, Jethro & Kisiah Prewit, 9 Sept 1788; Reuben Chesenhall, bm.

Russel, Murphy & Cathrine Graves, 30 Dec 1847; Jacob Graves, bm.

Russel, William O. & Anne Thompson, 2 Jan 1822; James A. Craig, bm.

Russell, Alexander & Elizabeth Craig, 8 Dec 1788; John McDaniel, bm.

Russell, Alexander & Ellenor Johnston, 22 Nov 1819; James W. Russell, bm.

Russell, Jas. & Margaret Witte, 27 Dec 1781; J. L. Russel,
Samuel Baxter, bm.

Russell, James & Nancy Brewer, 12 July 1821; Levi McCollum, bm.

Russell, James W. & Nancy Johnston, 18 Nov 1816; Alex. Russell,
bm.

Russell, James W. & Frances Thompson, 11 May 1847; William H.
Thompson, bm.

Russell, John & Elizabeth Webb, 12 Sept 1804; John Galbraith,
bm.

Russell, Jno. & Sarah Johnston, 11 Sept 1841; Jno. Bingham, bm.

Russell, John C. & Rachel Thompson, 19 Oct 1816; Alexr. Russell,
bm.

Russell, Joseph N. & Polly Hawkins, 20 Sept 1822; James Jones,
bm.

Russell, Robert G. & Rebecca Lipscomb, 16 Oct 1856; J. R.
Blacknall, bm; m 16 Oct 1866 by J. L. Carroll, M. G.

Russell, William & Jane Johnston, 4 Jan 1832; William Russell,
L. W. Young, bm.

Russell, William C. & Elizabeth B. Thompson, 12 April 1827;
W. P. Clancy, bm.

Rust, Chesley & Duranna Hampton, 27 Nov 1821; Nolan Hampton, bm.

Ruth, Jeremiah & Nancy Beckham, 5 Oct 1823; John Patterson, bm.

Rutherford, John & Jenney Murdock, 19 March 1782; David Ray, bm.

Ryder, John & Margret Huskey, 28 Oct 1833; Charles S. Worren, bm.

Ryley, W. John & Tempy E. Sykes, 21 Dec 1866; G. W. P. Cates, bm.

Sabine, James & Mary Parsons, 18 April 1782; Thomas Hart, bm.

Sankston, John & Margret Armstrong, 21 March 1800; Nathl.
McLemore, bm.

Sartain, Eyekecl & Dolley Pope, 30 Sept 1837; Thomas Burch, bm.

Sartain, William & Amelia Keeling, 4 Aug 1834; William Norrace,
bm.

Sarten, George, son of Scott & Julia Sarten, & Nicy Jeffreys,
dau. of Walden Jeffreys, & Julia Curried, colored, m 1 Jan
1868 by Stephen T. Forrest.

Satterfield, Samuel & Joanna Drake, 6 Aug 1820; Saml. Pittard,
bm.

Sawyer, Joseph & Elizabeth Browning, 28 Nov 1820; Jas. Love, bm.

Saxon, William & Mary Marcom, 24 June 1782; Charles Abercrombie,
bm.

Scarlett, George & Betsey Hartsfield, 6 July 1786; Thomas Scarlett, bm.

Scarlet, James & Lidia Lewis, 21 Jan 1790; Patrick McVay, bm.

Scarlet, Moses & Jane Cater, 4 Aug 1843; Joseph Dunnagon, George Crowder, bm.

Scarlet, Stephen & Nancy Crabtree, 27 Dec 1815; William McDade, bm.

Scarlet, Thomas & Anna James, __ July 1779.

Scarlet, Thomas & Elizabeth Laycock, 2 Feb 1814; Thimothy Laycock, bm.

Scarlet, Thomas & Rebecca Ann Howard, 1 April 1840; Wm. H. Gillim, bm.

Scarlett, Allen & Polley Cain, 18 Feb 1827; Wm. Allen, bm.

Scarlett, James & Hannah Allen, 17 Nov 1819; Wm. Whitted, bm.

Scarlett, James & Mary Carson, 7 March 1820; D. B. Alsobrook, bm.

Scarlett, James & Peggy Barton, 25 Feb 1826; Thomas Pickard, bm.

Scarlett, James & Annie Day, 27 July 1864; Riley Neal, J. W. Crabtree, bm.

Scarlett, James C. & Sarah Cain, 14 Dec 1853; William R. Scarlett, bm; m 15 Dec 1853 by Alex Dickson, J. P.

Scarlett, John & Cynthia Allen, 16 Jan 1798; Stephen Scarlett, bm.

Scarlett, John & Ann Pratt, 13 Jan 1813; Thomas N. S. Hargis, bm.

Scarlett, John & Delilah Laycock, 19 Jan 1819; John Scarlett, bm.

Scarlett, John & Sally Laycock, 17 Feb 1819; Stephen Scarlett, bm.

Scarlett, Page & Salley Alston, 6 Dec 1839; Williams Harris, bm.

Scarlett, Samuel & Rebecca Lewis, 11 Aug 1794; John Lewis, bm.

Scarlett, Samuel & Ellen Warren, 19 March 1832; W. F. Allen, bm.

Scarlett, Thomas & Willie Crabtree, 28 April 1833; William Hill, bm.

Scarlett, Thomas & Rebecca Ann Howard, 1 April 1860; m by Thos. Long, J. P.

Scarlett, William & Sarah Guess, 10 Dec 1835; William F. Hollyway, James W. Guess, bm.

Scarlotte, Thomas & Martha Waitt, 25 March 1858; Edward B. Coleman, bm.

Scherer, Jacob, Rev. & Elizabeth Spoon, 8 Jan 1827; Michl. Holt, bm.

Schoolfeeld, Saml. D. & Elizabeth C. Freeland, 25 Oct 1845; Chas. J. Freeland, Thomas Faucett, bm.

Scobey, David & Esther Kenneday, 25 Sept 1783; Robert Burnsides, bm.

Scobey, Robert & Lucey Debow, 24 Jan 1786; Joseph Clendenin, bm.

Scoby, John & Polley Rice, 23 March 1792; James Christmas, bm.

Scoggin, John & Rhodah Lewellyn, 26 Feb 1816; Smith Scoggin, bm.

Scott, Harrison & Susan Faucett, 22 June 1831; Victor M. Murphey, bm.

Scott, Harrison & Elizabeth Crabtree, 17 Oct 1857; Robert Sykes, bm; m 24 Oct 1857 by Jas. N. Craig.

Scott, Henry & Sarah Workman, 11 Dec 1855; James Scott, bm; m 20 Dec 1855 by Thomas Lynch, J. P.

Scott, James & Jane Hopkins, 3 March 1857; A. Turner, bm; m 5 March 1857 by W. W. Guess.

Scott, James C. & Sally Rogers, 22 July 1863; W. M. Hall, bm; m 22 July 1863 by T. C. Hayes, minister.

Scott, John & Margaret Anderson, 18 Feb 1820; Eli Murray, bm.

Scott, John & Caroline L. Minor, 5 July 1820; J. Taylor Jr., bm.

Scott, John & Sarah Compton, 5 Aug 1851; James Scott, bm.

Scott, John & Martha Ann Crabtree, 17 Oct 1833; Wm. Scott, bm.

Scott, John M., son of John & Martha Scott, & Eliza A. Shanklin, dau. of Andrew & Ellen Shanklin, m 30 Jan 1868 by C. E. Smith, J. P.

Scott, Samuel & Nancy Bryant, 17 Feb 1794; Jas. Mebane Junr., bm.

Scott, Thomas & Mary Duffy, 12 July 1799; Duncan Cameron, bm.

Scott, Thomas & Mary E. McCullock, 1 Oct 1860; Wm. W. Pickett, Alexr. Dickson, bm; m 7 Oct 1860 by Wm. W. Pickett, J. P.

Scott, William & Elizabeth Mason, 2 Nov 1805; David Underwood, bm.

Scott, William & Rachel Perry, 19 Dec 1829; Luke Ward, bm.

Scott, William H. & Eliza Elizabeth Morris, 16 July 1859; William Pugh, bm; m 17 July 1859 by D. Churchill.

Searls, Frances & Drusilla Farmer, 12 Dec 1789; Othniel Farmer, bm.

Sears, Albirt & Mary Castlebury, 15 Jan 1790; Phillip Allin, bm.

Sears, Alburt & Delilah Jinkins, 16 Sept 1825; Young Jinkins, bm.

Sears, Clemment & Charlotte Dawson, 18 Jan 1821; Allen Stone, bm.

Sears, Henry & Elizabeth Chandler, 29 Nov 1793; Stephen Forest, bm.

Sears, John & Mary Hopson, 20 Sept 1787; Joseph Sears, bm.

Sears, Joseph & Elizabeth Searls, 27 July 1784.

Sears, Joseph & Sophronia Herndon, 7 Jan 1826; J. B. Ballard, bm.

Sears, Leonard & Salley Moore, 26 May 1820; Clem Sears, bm.

Sears, William & Naomi Atterson, 18 Oct 1793; Joseph Sears, bm.

Self, Baxter & Delilah Watson, 28 May 1796; John Hudgings, bm.

Self, Daniel & Mary Holder, 21 Dec 1826; Daniel Holder, bm.

Self, John & Phebe Dossett, 18 Nov 1821; Andrew Haley, bm.

Self, Willoughby & Hannah Blackwood, 12 May 1806; H. McCollum, bm.

Sellars, Griffin & Phebey Stanford, 3 June 1848; Joan Stanford, bm.

Sellars, Lemuel & Sarah Hufman, 24 Nov 1840; Willis Sellars, J. Gant, bm.

Sellars, Willis & Jane Crawford, 25 July 1820; Eli Murray, bm.

Sellars, Willis & Mary Ellen Ray, 1 March 1839; Wm. H. Whedbee, E. F. Watson, bm.

Sellers, Constantine & Mariah Bason, 9 Dec 1847; A. Murry Jr., bm.

Sessions, Henry & Adilade Morrow, 10 Aug 1857; J. S. Morrow, bm; m 11 Aug 1857 by Thos. Lynch, M. G.

Sewell, Christopher & Delpha Sears, 14 Nov 1866; Luke Guess, James R. Gattis, bm.

Sharp, Adam & Mary Whitsides, 15 Oct 1789; Benjamin Roney, bm.

Sharp, Alfred & Caty Sharp, 3 Dec 1838; Jacob Sharp, bm.

Sharp, Anderson & Barbara James, 23 Oct 1839; Anthony Rich, bm.

Sharp, Ashford & Elizabeth Jane Murray, 5 Jan 1858; James R. Hester, bm.

Sharp, Benjamin & Polly Coble, 24 April 1833; Thomas Peeler, bm.

Sharp, Benjamin & Tempy Loy, 21 Aug 1840; Levi Lloy, bm.

Sharp, Daniel & Malinda Kech, 19 March 1846; David Laugh, bm.

Sharp, Eli & Sally Nease, 2 Nov 1824; Jesse Boggs, bm.

Sharp, Eli & Frances Tate, 20 Dec 1848; Boston Sharp, bm.

Sharp, Frederick & Winney Levins, 10 April 1833; Abram Long, bm.

Sharp, George & Caty Kech, 16 April 1828; John Rivers, bm.

Sharp, Henry & Isabella Cook, 15 May 1805; James Cobit, bm.

Sharp, Henry & Catharine H. Finley, 7 Sept 1839; A. T. Finley, bm.

Sharp, Isaac & Elizabeth Kimbro, 10 May 1804; Malachi Hatmaker, bm.

Sharp, Isaac & Mary Ritche, 22 Nov 1822; Thos Scott, bm.

Sharp, Jacob & Phelpine Stoner, 8 April 1796; William Ray, bm.

Sharp, Jacob & Polly Andrews, 4 Nov 1840; Alfred Sharp, bm.

Sharp, Jesse & Elizabeth Slone, 12 Jan 1797; Henry Terrell, James Roberts, bm.

Sharp, Jesse & Jane Boon, 21 Dec 1823; Peter L. Ray, bm.

Sharp, Jesse & Anna Ward, 1 Jan 1864; R. G. Rinnin, T. W. Laws, bm; m 12 Jan 1864 by R. G. Tinnin.

Sharp, Joel & Elizabeth Anthony, 4 Sept 1832; L. Sharp, bm.

Sharp, John & Elizabeth Sharp, 14 July 1795; Thomas Ruh, bm.

Sharp, John & Ann Rogers, 8 May 1817; J. S. Smith, bm.

Sharp, John & Deborah Fossett, 14 Jan 1823; Wm. Fossett, bm.

Sharp, John & Sally Loy, 26 Sept 1837; Benjamin Sharp, bm.

Sharp, John & Milly Fogleman, 14 April 1829; Eli Fogleman, bm.

Sharp, John W., son of Jepe & Jane Sharp, & Sarah C. Roark, dau. of Willis & Permelia Hester, m 23 May 1867 by Thos. H. Hughes, J. P.

Sharp, Ludwick & Sally Anthony, 25 Sept 1827; L. Sharp, E. M. Holt, bm.

Sharp, Ludwick & Patsey Fogleman, __ Oct 1857; W. R. Holt, bm.

Sharp, Morris H. & Ellen Crabtree 29 Jan 1854; Wilson Crabtree, George Laws, bm.

Sharp, Peter & Eva Mosier, 31 Aug 1795; John Sharp, bm.

Sharp, Peter B. & Mary Jane Compton, 16 Dec 1856; T. F. Compton, bm.

Sharp, Soloman & Hessey Shatterby, 17 Sept 1833; John C. Troxler, bm.

Sharp, William & Elizabeth Albright, 5 Nov 1817; Joseph Albright, bm.

Sharp, William & Sally Loy, 19 March 1837; Reuben Ingle, bm.

Sharpe, Hartwell & Sally Wheeler, 7 Jan 1846; Wm. Zachary, bm.

Shanklin, James & Lidia Woods, 26 Nov 1811; Thos. Armstrong, bm.

Shannon, John & Anne Guttery, 17 Aug 1784; James Guthrie, bm.

Sharradan, John & Margaret Osborne, 7 April 1801; William Jean, bm.

Shatterley, Soloman & Polly Wrightsell, 24 Oct 1835; Isaac Essex, bm.

Shaw, Charles & Elizabeth King, 7 May 1806; James Lockhart, bm.

Shaw, Jeptha & Elizabeth Ivery, 20 Oct 1832; W. J. Hogan, Sandy Shaw, bm.

Shaw, John & Elizabeth Scott, 17 Aug 1805; Wm. Boxwell, bm.

Shaw, John & Peggy Pugh, 1 July 1813; William McAddam, bm.

Shaw, John W. & Elizabeth Walker, 29 Nov 1821; William Vincent, bm.

Shaw, John W. & Mary Clenny, 5 Oct 1832; Isa G. High, bm.

Shaw, Joseph & Sally McCadams, 2 April 1823; J. S. Shaw, James M'Caddam, bm.

Shaw, Levi & Hester Shaw, 6 May 1793; Johnston Webb, bm.

Shaw, Moses & Rebecca McCaddams, 11 Aug 1826; Robert McCaddams, bm.

Shaw, Moses & Mary Turner, 15 March 1841; D. H. Cate, bm.

Shaw, N. L. & Mary O. McDade, 18 Feb 1861; Wm. B. Harrell, bm; m 19 Feb 1861 by N. W. Wilson.

Shaw, Samuel & Jeany Gorden, 7 July 1803; Richard Woods, bm.

Shaw, William & Mary Thompson, 8 Jan 1827; A. H. Leonard, bm.

Shaw, William & Elizabeth Moore, 23 April 1837; Matthew Moore, bm.

Shaw, William & Mary Walker, ___ 1833; John C. Walker, bm.

Shearden, George & Elizabeth Pike, 15 Sept 1802; John Wells, William Wells, bm.

Shearedon, Abner & Anne Williams, 27 Oct 1784; John Murray, bm.

Shearer, Andrew & Love Holstead, (no date); ___, bm.

Shearer, Fredrick Jr. & Peggy Clap, 24 Jan 1811; Daniel Moser, bm.

Shearer, Jacob & Catey Smith, 12 Feb 1782; Andw. Smith, bm.

Shearmon, Samuel & Elizabeth Lewis, 28 May 1812; L. Bramock, bm.

Sheelor, John Jr. & Mary E. Hill, 10 Jan 1858; D. J. Jordan, bm; m 10 Jan 1858 by Thomas C. Hays, M. G.

Shelton, Freeman M. & Martha E. Kistler, 21 Nov 1859; James R. Gattis, bm.

Shelton, W. N. & Ariana Roberson, 25 Dec 1850; Tho. J. Poore, bm.

Shepard, James & Franky Trice, 1 April 1803; Sullivan Leigh, bm.

Shepherd, Geo. M. & Emeline Hutchins, 7 March 1856; J. W. Siler, bm; m 9 March 1856 by Jesse Howell, minister.

Shepherd, Soloman & Lowana J. Rhodes, 19 Nov 1856; Geo Laws, bm; m 20 Nov 1856 by W. H. Pratt, J. P.

Shepherd, Thomas & Lovina Carlton, 13 Feb 1840; Tho. Anderson, A. Parks, bm.

Shepherd, William & Polly Starr, 1 Feb 1827; Jacob Huffman, bm.

Shepherd, Wyatt & Charity W. Nutt, 3 Oct 1831; Page Shepherd, bm.

Sheppard, Henry & Polley Marcum, 28 Aug 1811; James Shepard, Sullivan Leigh, bm.

Shepperd, James & Sally Holey, 11 Sept 1833; Willis Monk, bm.

Shepperd, John & Polley Edwards, 26 June 1794; Leod Carlton, bm.

Shepperd, Samuel & Elizabeth S. Meackam, 14 Aug 1784; Francis Pickett, bm.

Shereden, William & Pricilla Ward, 21 May 1819; Josiah Lamb, bm.

Sherer, Jacob & Elizabeth Moier, 15 May 1810; Frederic Shearer, bm.

Sherreden, George & Sarah Webb, 16 Dec 1794; Job Taylor, bm.

Shew, Joseph W. & Jane Walker, 24 Oct 1845; Wm. R. Shew, bm.

Shields, John & Sarah Hardy, 31 Aug 1826; John McDade Jr., bm.

Shields, John & Susan A. Nichols, 28 Sept 1848; J. W. Strayhorn, bm.

Shoe, Phillip & Nancy Shofner, 19 Oct 1838; Peter Shoe, bm.

Shoffner, Joel & Cathron Shofner, 27 Feb 1838; Oliver Shoffner, bm.

Shoffner, Peter Jr. & Polly Albright, 26 March 1814; Fredric Shofner, bm.

Shoffner, William & Jemima Manervi Shoffner, 28 Feb 1846; H. Wartkines(?), bm.

Shofner, Danel & Barbara Clap, 19 June 1817; Soloman Albright, bm.

Shofner, Daniel & Elizabeth Warren or Beasly, 3 Nov 1811; Michl Shofner, bm.

Shofner, George & Elizabeth Bennett, 23 Dec 1816; Jacob Farmer, bm.

Shofner, Joel & Matilda Shofner, 9 April 1831; Hamblen Cook, bm.

Shofner, John & Milley Shofner, 17 Feb 1810; Christen Shofner, bm.

Shofner, Michael & Eve Moser, 26 Dec 1809; Davad Coble, bm.

Shofner, Michael & Sarah Smith, 26 Dec 1803; Henry Fogleman, bm.

Shy, Eli & Elizabeth McClary, 15 Dec 1804; Thos. Cohran, bm.

Shy, Jesse & Martha Cantern, 15 Oct 1785; John Shy, bm.

Shy, Robert & Sarah Stalcup, 11 Jan 1797; Swain Stalcup, bm.

Shy, Samuel & Sarah Cantrel, 5 Dec 1789; Samuel Everett, bm.

Silar, Andrew & Nancy McCauley, 26 Nov 1835; Thos. S. Oldham, bm.

Siler, Davis & Dilley King, 18 Nov 1840; Charles King, James Campbell, bm.

Siler, Record C. & Polley McCauly, 28 June 1836; John Kirkland, bm.

Simmon, James & Pury Warbleton, 14 March 1797; James Warbleton, David Passmore, bm.

Simmons, Gehu & Martha Moore, 4 Feb 1800; Robert Moore, bm.

Simmons, James & Anna Evans, 16 Oct 1839; Benjamin Overman, bm.

Simmons, Jo. & Elisabeth McCool, 4 May 1792; Isaac Pickard, bm.

Simons, Joseph & Sarah Edwards, 22 Feb 1810; Robert Moore, bm.

Simpson, Benjamin & Marget Garrison, 9 May 1813; Luke Simpson, bm.

Simpson, Benjamin & Caty Dickey, 28 July 1824; Moses Dickey, bm.

Simpson, Fausecett & Sarah Waynick, 20 Dec 1846; Lovick L. Lambeth, bm.

Simpson, Henry & Mary Adams, 7 Oct 1837; Jacob O. Hurdle, bm.

Simpson, John & Elizabeth Drake, 21 June 1808; Thomas Thompson, bm.

Simpson, Lemuel W. & Lucy Faucett, 17 Dec 1816; Thomas Gore, bm.

Simpson, Luke & Peggy Cook, 29 May 1809; Corsley Brinkley, Benjn. S. Simpson, bm.

Simpson, Samuel & Milley Larkey, 19 Jan 1801; Robt. Larkey, bm.

Simpson, William & Ann Riley, 31 March 1853; Chs. T. McMannen, bm; m 31 March 1853 by Jno. A. McMannen, J. P.

Simpson, William & Jane Gibbs, 11 Dec 1865; William Simpson, John Tilley, bm; m 11 Dec 1865 by Jno. Tilly, J. P.

Simpson, William F. & Nancy Foster, 13 Oct 1845; B. F. Simpson, bm.

Sims, Herbert & Nancy Carrington, 1 July 1795; Thos. Scott, bm.

Sims, Herbert & Rachel McCown, 7 April 1831; John B. Leathers, bm.

Sims, Herbert H., son of Herbert & Rachel Sims, & Maletha Patterson, dau. of James N. & Hawkins Patterson, m 31 Oct 1867 by Geo. W. Purefoy, M. G.

Singleton, William & Sally Solomon, 12 Oct 1819; Green ODaniel, bm.

Sloss, Joseph & Sarah Mebane, 1 Sept 1796; James Mebane Jr., bm.

Slown, Archebald & Polley Nelson, 6 May 1793; Kenneth Anderson, bm.

Smart, Elisha & Polley Armstrong, 7 March 1792; John Holmes, bm.

Smart, Jno. & Patty Sawyer, 10 July 1798; Charles Gross, bm.

Smith, Alexander & Sally Riley, 11 Oct 1826; Lemuel Wilkinson, bm.

Smith, Alexander A. & Margaret C. Thompson, 8 March 1860; James Gill, bm; m 15 March 1860 by R. R. Tapp, J. P.

Smith, Alfred & Mrs. M. P. Missellier, 15 July 1862; W. P. Oldham, bm; m 15 July 1826 by A. D. Cohen, minister.

Smith, Alvan & Sally Isley, 11 July 1838; Austin Isley, bm.

Smith, Anderson & Elizabeth Syke, 21 June 1831; W. A. Parish, Thos Lawyer, bm.

Smith, Anderson & Nancey Horner, 3 May 1842; Wilson Hofner, James Ray Jr., bm.

Smith, Andrew & Hannah Bracken, 16 Nov 1781; James Bracken, bm.

Smith, Andrew & Mary Johnston, 5 Jan 1813; John Johnston, bm.

Smith, Archable & Winne Robeson, 30 Dec 1819; Johns Rivers, bm.

Smith, Arnold & Lugena Patterson, 31 Jan 1863; A. J. Pickard, bm.

Smith, Bryant C. & Priscilla Johnston, 22 May 1848; N. Mangum, bm.

Smith, Buckner & Margaret Paine, 25 Feb 1786; John Hubank, bm.

Smith, C. C. & Mary Jones, 18 Feb 1842; A. Parks, bm.

Smith, C. C. & Louisa Brewer, m 9 Aug 1865 by J. Atwater, J. P.

Smith, Calvin & Tempey T. Watson, 19 Sept 1842; Thos. C. Hayes, R. H. Lee, bm.

Smith, Clavin & Susan M. McCrackin, 16 Jan 1847; Calvin E. Smith, P. Nelson, bm.

Smith, Carney C. & Louisa Brewer, 7 Aug 1865; D. C. McDade, bm.

Smith, Charles & Sally Dix, 13 April 1847; Ingram Mehheeson, bm.

Smith, Charles & Candis Hopkins, 1 Dec 1865; Lorinzo Hopkins, bm.

Smith, Charles C. & Martha Daniel, 6 June 1830; Henderson Fowler, bm.

Smith, Charles C. & Eliza C. Pickett, 21 Sept 1860; James F. McAdams, bm.

Smith, Chesley & Mary Ann Glosson, 14 May 1825; Thos. Clancy, bm.

Smith, David & Sarah Blalock, 23 March 1786; Stephen Kirk, bm.

Smith, David & Peggy Shofner, 31 Jan 1803; Adam Smith, bm.

Smith, David & Sally Roach, 10 Jan 1817; Ephraim Kates, bm.

Smith, Edward & Milly Crutchfield, 9 April 1847; William E. Bishop, bm.

Smith, Elisha & Nancy Strayhorn, 9 Feb 1809; James Whitted, bm.

Smith, Farmer & Elizabeth Griffin, 11 Dec 1821; Abel Smith, bm.

Smith, Frederick & Elizabeth Durfield, 12 March 1800; Wm. Brooks, bm.

Smith, Gabriel & Sidney Christopher, 3 Dec 1838; Phillip Burch, A. Parks, bm.

Smith, George & Nancy Weakes, 19 Dec 1795; Reuben Smith, bm.

Smith, George & Catherine Waggoner, 21 Jan 1828; Daniel Waggoner, bm.

Smith, George R. & Anne Duncan, 9 July 1841; L. D. Pickard, W. A. Norwood, bm.

Smith, H. P. & C. H. Barbee, 15 May 1862; Heziel P. Smith, Ruffin Canada, bm.

Smith, Hazell & Elizabeth Jane Freeland, m 17 Jan 1859 by Haywood Andrews.

Smith, Hosea C. & Patsey Moore, 17 Feb 1818; William Sykes, bm.

Smith, Hosea C. & Ann Rheu, 23 Aug 1855; Wm. McCauly, bm; m 23 Aug 1855 by D. D. Phillips, J. P.

Smith, Hosey & Polley Wittey, 10 June 1811; John Cate, bm.

Smith, James & Lucy Harris, 2 Jan 1813; Edward B. Harris, bm.

Smith, James A. & Mary S. Horn, 27 Dec 1855; James E. Wilkison, bm.

Smith, James H. & Louisa Horton, 29 Oct 1836; Willie Horner, Henderson Tilley, bm.

Smith, James L., son of Thomas Smith, & Delilah F. Hatch, dau. of David & Joanah Andrews, m 3 Oct 1867 by Alvis Durham.

Smith, James M. & Emily McCullock, 9 Nov 1842; James Moore, James Squires, bm.

Smith, Jesse & Anne Boone, 2 July 1796; Jacob Boon, bm.

Smith, John & Susannah Smith, 6 April 1784; Samuel Whitesides, Sutton Ward, bm.

Smith, John & Nancy Branan, 14 Aug 1786; Saml. Allen, bm.

Smith, John & Elisabeth Bradford, 22 March 1793; Thos. Smith, bm.

Smith, John & Peggy Patterson, 4 May 1803; Hugh Mulhollan, bm.

278

Smith, John & Peggy Smith, 14 Sept 1812; William Wilkinson, bm.

Smith, John & Elizabeth Mansfield, 26 May 1820; Wm. Mansfield, bm.

Smith, John & Catey Wrightsell, 27 Feb 1826; Leonard Smith, bm.

Smith, John & Catharine Ray, 28 Nov 1838; Andrew Porterfield, bm.

Smith, John & Missuriania Vestal, 21 Nov 1842; Abram Lineberry, bm.

Smith, John & Susan Stagg, 14 Dec 1863; John C. McCown, bm; m 15 Dec 1863 by W. W. Guess, J. P.

Smith, John & Bathenie Williams, 15 Oct 1865; Henry F. Ellis, bm; m 15 Oct 1865 by N. C. Cate, J. P.

Smith, John & Elizabeth Hatchell, 15 June 1866; Richard King, Jno. M. Blackwood, bm; m 17 June 1866 by R. H. J. Blount, J. P.

Smith, John H. & Elizabeth Moore, 8 Jan 1847; Wm. L. Moore, bm.

Smith, John M. & Elizabeth Currie, 22 April 1850; Wm. Woodward, bm.

Smith, Joseph & Hannah Clark, 8 Aug 1809; Carns Tinnin, bm.

Smith, Joseph & Susannah Compton, 15 Sept 1815; William Smith, bm.

Smith, Joseph & Sally McDaniel, 4 Jan 1817; Lacy Lloyd, bm.

Smith, Joseph A. & Sarah Ann Redding, 11 Dec 1847; Bedford Hurdle, bm.

Smith, Leonard & Nancy Hatchel, 6 Feb 1821; A. Hatchell, bm.

Smith, Leonard & Julia A. Pickett, 27 Jan 1849; John H. Paul, Lafayette Cheek, bm.

Smith, Leonard T. & Catherine Wilkerson, 24 July 1861; James W. Pickett, David Smith, bm; m 28 July 1861 by Archibald Currie.

Smith, Lucean C. & Julia R. Cheeck, 15 May 1861; William Watson, bm.

Smith, Murphey & Frances Cheek, 13 March 1857; Jno. N. Johnston, bm.

Smith, Peter & Dolley Johnston, 6 April 1784; Samuel Whitesides, Sutton Ward, bm.

Smith, Peter & Margaritt Powell, 13 Nov 1795; Thos. Watts, bm.

Smith, Phillip & Eva Coble, 14 Jan 1811; Nichs. Smith, bm.

Smith, Reuben & Margaret Allen, 14 April 1815; J. Taylor, bm.

Smith, Reuben & Rebecca Jones, 23 Aug 1825; Jno. Coreathers, bm.

Smith, Reuben F. & Mary Jane Smith, 9 Sept 1851; P. Nelson, bm; m 11 Sept 1851 by Presley Nelson, J. P.

Smith, Robert & Elizabeth McMunn, 5 April 1797; William McMunn, bm.

Smith, Robert & Elizabeth Kerson, 21 March 1815.

Smith, Robert & Hannah Hastings, 9 Jan 1821; James Hastings, bm.

Smith, Robert H. & Elloner Taylor, 6 Feb 1850; S. A. Smith, bm; m 8 Feb 1850 by Archibald Currie.

Smith, Samuel & Elizabeth Spier, 29 Dec 1831; Eras. D. Bullock, Thomas S. Ashe, bm.

Smith, Samon & Sally Hale, 26 Aug 1806; Major Downs, bm.

Smith, Simon & Tempy Smith, 4 Aug 1866; H. B. Guthrie, bm.

Smith, Thomas & Elizabeth Harney, 11 March 1810; James Loyd, bm.

Smith, Thomas & Elizabeth Watson, 8 Feb 1821; John Cook, bm.

Smith, Thomas & Nancy Haley, 31 May 1828; Samuel Hulet, bm.

Smith, Thomas & Francis Lashly, 12 March 1840; William Crawford, bm.

Smith, Thomas & Nancy Jones, 16 Feb 1861; M. W. Moore, bm; m 25 Feb 1861 by Alvis Durham, J. P.

Smith, Westly & Eliza Collins, 17 July 1839; Henry Cheek, bm.

Smith, William & Ruth Carter, 9 June 1783; John Pinninton, bm.

Smith, William & Lettis Holloway, 25 Nov 1788; Reuben Smith, bm.

Smith, William & Lucy Fossett, 4 June 1799; William Palmer, bm.

Smith, William & Tabitha Cates, 15 Dec 1800; Nathaniel McLemore, bm.

Smith, William & Anne Hastings, 16 April 1813; James Smith, bm.

Smith, William & Polley Coble, 4 Jan 1814; John Coble, bm.

Smith, William & Nancy Murray, 23 May 1819; William Terrayl, bm.

Smith, William & Margaret Allen, 26 May 1819; George Allen, bm.

Smith, William & Eliza Christmas, 19 Jan 1820; Rt. Glasson, bm.

Smith, William & Rachel Brown, 27 Feb 1821; Augustin Brown, bm.

Smith, William & Elizabeth Jones, 17 Oct 1826; Thomas Dodson, D. Johnston, bm.

Smith, William & Martha McDaniel, 18 Nov 1828; James Child, bm.

Smith, William & Mary Mulhollan, 16 Dec 1830; Thomas Smith, bm.

Smith, William & Temperence Hart, 9 March 1837; P. Nelson, John C. Sykes, bm.

Smith, William & Elizabeth Denson, 28 Sept 1850; W. H. Thompson, bm.

Smith, William & Martha Smith, 30 Jan 1857; James P. Hopkins,
G. T. Findly, bm; m 1 Feb 1857 by Nelson P. Shaw, J. P.

Smith, William J. & Rachel Murray, 25 Nov 1847; Co. Benson, bm.

Smith, William M. & Catharene M. Christie, 18 Sept 1852; Mimick
Mather, bm.

Smith, Willie & Nancy Robertson, 16 Oct 1804; Daniel Robertson,
bm.

Smith, Willie J. & Martha J. Ray, 1 June 1860; Anderson Tolar,
J. L. Smith, bm; m 3 June 1860 by H. Terry, J. P.

Smith, Willis & Mary Jones, 18 June 1830; W. A. Parish, bm.

Sneed, Dudly & Jacobina Parker, 13 Nov 1825; Eldredge Dunnagan,
bm.

Snipes, Alfred & Margaret Brewer, 31 March 1834; Sheffey T.
Lindsey, bm.

Snipes, Calvin P., son of Dancy & Martha Snipes, & Margaret
Odaniel, dau. of Henry ODaniel, m 7 Nov 1867 by Alvis
Durham, J. P.

Snipes, Jesse & Elizabeth Thrift, 15 May 1802; Isaac Mordecai,
bm.

Snipes, John & Cornelia A. Stanford, 13 Sept 1856; D. McCauley,
bm; m 18 Sept 1856 by Wilson Atwater.

Snipes, John W. & Sarah J. Bradshaw, 18 Oct 1848; Thos. D.
Oldham, bm.

Snipes, Marion & Tabitha Bowers, 19 Jan 1848; W. G. Bowers, bm.

Snipes, Manly & Patsy Neville, 15 Dec 1824; Wm. Durham Jr., bm.

Snipes, Mathew & Mary Laura Standford, 6 Feb 1866; T. B.
Snipes, bm; m 8 Feb 1866 by Wilson Atwater, M. G.

Snipes, Young & Celia Nevill, 12 May 1824; Manly Snipes, bm.

Snotherly, Jacob & Mary Loy, 24 Nov 1806; James Copeland, bm.

Snotherly, Josiah & Elizabeth Perdew, 20 Dec 1834; Jesse Boggs,
bm.

Scott, Tobias & Elizabeth Nease, 5 March 1836; Isom Friddle, bm.

Sorrell, William & Polley Marcum, 9 Jan 1812; Danl. Holder, bm.

Southerlan, Philip & Lucy P. Bobbitt, 11 Nov 1841; Mosses
Leathers Jr., John Hancock, bm.

Southerland, Fendal & Mary Briggs, 26 Feb 1822; John Tilley, bm.

Southerland, Mordecai & Elizabeth Manning, 28 Feb 1805; Tyree
Glenn, bm.

Southerland, Samuel & Elizabeth Gore, 11 Dec 1795; Richd.
Leigh, bm.

Southerland, William & Anna Trible, 17 Aug 1798; Tyree Glenn,
bm.

Southerland, Young & Ferabee Hargrave, 1 Feb 1866; Thomas Hogan, bm; m 23 Feb 1866 by J. P. Mason.

Southworth, John & Sophia S. Southard, 8 Oct 1807; Archible Clark, bm.

Sparrow, Browder & Elizabeth Shaw, 6 Feb 1816; James Campble, bm.

Sparrow, George & Caroline Stephens, 5 Aug 1865; Henry J. Hogan, bm.

Sparrow, Hilliary & Cornelia Crabtree, 8 April 1857; J. A. Jenkins, bm; m 9 April 1857 by J. B. McDade, J. P.

Sparrow, Houston & Caroline Heathcock, 18 May 1860; F. M. Riggsbee, bm.

Sparrow, Houston & Salina Andrews, 19 Sept 1862; A. Blackwood, bm; m 19 Sept 1862 by J. P. Mason, M. G.

Sparrow, Hudson & Louisa Walter, 21 Oct 1852; Geo. W. Purifoy, bm; m 21 Oct 1852 by Geo. W. Purifoy, M. G.

Sparrow, Hutson & Sarah Barbee, 6 Dec 1865; Geo. W. Purefoy, bm; m 6 Dec 1865 by Geo. W. Purefoy, bm.

Sparrow, J. T. & Rebecca Gootch, 2 Sept 1865; m by J. P. Mason, M. G.

Sparrow, V. B., son of John & Elizabeth Sparrow, & Nancy Bishop, dau. of Cowen & Phebe Bishop, m 18 Dec 1867 by J. P. Mason, M. G.

Sparrow, William & Dicey Booth, 2 Aug 1799; Thomas Massey, bm.

Speck, Henry & Pamelia Elizabeth Rainey, 4 March 1834; Richd. Nichols, bm.

Spencer, Jas. M. & Cornelia Ann Phillips, 19 June 1855; J. B. McDade, bm; m 20 June 1855 by Elisha Mitchell, M. G.

Spicely, Samuel & Betsey Busick (no date); William Busick, bm.

Spoon, Adam & Peggy Plunket, 1 Oct 1830-32; Allen Euliss, bm.

Spoon, Daniel & Katharine Eulis, 4 April 1826; Peter Euless, bm.

Spoon, David & Elizabeth Coble, 6 April 1804; David Coble, bm.

Sproles, Samuel & Jane McNally, 12 Jan 1795; James McCauley, bm.

Spruce, Queston & Sarah Tate, 18 April 1791; John H. Spruce, bm.

Spruill, Moses & Sarah Pearson, 21 March 1866; Moses Spruell, D. C. McDade, bm; m 22 March 1866 by Solomon Pool.

Squires, Coston & Amelia Ray, 4 Dec 1819; Samuel Hart, bm.

Squires, Frazier & Rachel Pike, 19 Dec 1814; Peleg Gifford, bm.

Squires, James & Sarah Ector, 4 April 1838; J. W. McCauly, bm.

Squires, James Jr., son of Thomas & Susan Squires, & Fanny Paul, dau. of John M. & Mary Paul, m 6 June 1857 by Wilson Brown, J. P.

Squires, John & Mary Gott, 20 Sept 1797; Richard Gott, bm.

Squires, John & Margaret Tate, 30 Jan 1828; James Nelson, James Tate, bm.

Squires, Thomas & Elizabeth Gill, 6 Jan 1802; Richard Gott, bm.

Squires, Thomas Jr. & Susannah Jones, 1 Oct 1839; Richd. M. Jones, Ruffin Cheek, bm.

Stafford, Balaam & Polly Amick, 23 Feb 1846; Wm. Hornaday, bm.

Stafford, Frederic & Sally Moffat, 24 Dec 1827; Thomas Stafford, bm.

Stafford, George & Mary Horniday, 24 Sept 1821; Michl. Holt, bm.

Stafford, George & Catharine E. McCauley, 25 Nov 1861; D. W. Thompson, J. W. Siler, bm; m 5 Dec 1861 by Robt. R. Prather.

Stagg, Francis A. & Sarrah A. C. Durham, 23 Sept 1856; Wm. McCown, bm; m 23 Sept 1856 by Wm. McCown, J. P.

Stagg, James & Polly Horner, 1 April 1818; William Sweaney, bm.

Stagg, James & Polly Duke, 16 Dec 1826; Guilford Laws, bm.

Stagg, Radford & Parthena Mangum, 7 Aug 1846; John Stagg, bm.

Stagg, William & Uley Waggoner, 22 Jan 1805; Jacob Waggoner, bm.

Stagg, William & Mary Dyson, 13 June 1840; Thomas Dixon, bm.

Stagg, William A. & Lucy H. Proctor, 12 Feb 1861; William Green, bm; m 14 Feb 1861 by William Green.

Stagg, Willey & Sally Horner, 3 Nov 1821; Hiram Laws, bm.

Stailey, Daniel & Nancy Kemrey, 23 Nov 1839; Daniel Stailey, Alfred Eulis, bm.

Stailey, Eli & Susannah Evins, 22 Sept 1833; Christian Stailey, bm.

Stalcup, George & Susa Hanley, 7 May 1793; Isaac Stalcup, bm.

Stalcup, John & Elizabeth Ray, 30 Nov 1824; J. M. Kerall, bm.

Stalcup, Solomon & Elizabeth Gillum, 10 Dec 1799; Jacob Harden, bm.

Stalcup, Swain & Barbara Miller, 13 Nov 1794; William McMun, bm.

Staley, John T. & Meliss Clendenin, 1 Feb 1848; John A. Crutchfield, bm.

Staley, Peter & Susana McDaniel, 7 Sept 1820; Leonard Smith, bm.

Staley, Solomon & Peggy Coble, 14 Dec 1824; Peter Coble, bm.

Stalkup, Peter & Polly Garrisson, 12 Dec 1785; Jacob Morten, Edward King, bm.

Stallsworth, Samuel & Martha Pickard, 20 Oct 1803; James Ezell, bm.

Standifor, Benjamin & Rachel Forrist, 14 Aug 1781; William Turner, bm.

Standiford, Isreel & Polly Rone, 4 Aug 1796; Charles Rone, bm.

Standiford, Joshua & Susannah Stowball, 5 Dec 1795; James Meacham, bm.

Stanford, Alexander & Abby Cox, 18 Dec 1822; William ___, bm.

Stanford, James & Elizabeth Handley, 6 April 1787; William King, bm.

Stanford, John & Sally Wilson, 2 Aug 1827; John Mears, bm.

Stanford, Richard & Ann Patella, 5 Nov 1846; S. Stanford, bm.

Stanford, Richard A. & Elizabeth A. Thompson, 3 July 1839; Sauvin Stanford, bm.

Stanford, W. Gaston & Caroline Oldham, 6 Feb 1863; A. C. McDaniel, bm.

Stanford, William & Anne Couch, 20 Dec 1797; James Stanford, bm.

Stanley, James & Catherine Cole, 9 Dec 1851; James Stanley, Jno. Laws, bm; m 18 Jan 1852 by H. Wilkerson, J. P.

Stanley, Richard & Polly Murray, 26 Dec 1830; John S. Fogleman, Peter Shoffner, bm.

Stanly, Herod & Betsy Ann Gooch, 11 Dec 1848; Windsor Medlin, bm.

Stanly, Richard & Dicey May, 6 Oct 1828; Wright Stanly, Henderson May, bm.

Stanly, William & Kesiah Gooch, 26 May 1849; Wm. Carroll, Marion F. Midlin, bm.

Star, Adam & Mary Kech, 4 May 1806; Anthony Thompson, bm.

Starks, Benton & Elizabeth Brister, 26 Jan 1820; R. Eaton, bm.

Starr, David & Mariah Neace, 7 Dec 1824; William Shepherd, bm.

Steel, Hiram & Margaret Spoon, 3 April 1843; Ephraim Mitchell, bm.

Steel, John & Tabitha Jones, 4 Dec 1821; Jacob Courtner, bm.

Steel, John & Nancy Webely, 3 March 1826; David Beckham, S. Hymer, bm.

Steel, John & Nancy Woody, 2 Dec 1826; John Woody, bm.

Steel, John & Milley Isley, 18 Oct 1833; Austin Isley, bm.

Steel, John & Polly Bogers, 29 July 1846; Wm. Steel, bm.

Steel, Joseph & Nancy Murdock, 17 ___ 1809; John Mebane, bm.

Steel, Joseph & Harriett Roney, 26 Sept 1834; Samuel H. Turrentine, bm.

Steel, Samuel & Rabeckah Pickart, 10 Aug 1786.

Steel, Soloman, son of Soloman Allen & Betsy Murdock, & Velia
Thompson, dau. of Hal Durham & Sina Thompson, colored, m
2 Nov 1867 by Wiatt Cates, J. P.

Steel, William & Jane Patton, 17 Oct 1798; James Steel, bm.

Steel, William & Sophia Spoon, 15 Jan 1829; John Spoon, bm.

Steel, William & Turley Moser, 26 Dec 1831; Paul Anthony, bm.

Steel, William & Asenith Underwood, 24 March 1849; Jesse Dixon,
bm.

Steele, Andrew M. & Mary Bradshaw, 5 Aug 1830; William Bowers,
bm.

Steele, William & Nancy Gappin, 26 Oct 1799; A. Benton, bm.

Stephens, John & Sally Stuart, 9 Jan 1840; Andrew Thomas, bm.

Stephens, Moore & Rebecca Moize, 3 Sept 1817; Charles Stephens,
bm.

Stephens, Thomas & Betsey Burke, 10 Sept 1833; Alfred ODaniel,
bm.

Stephens, William & Marsha Jones, 28 Jan 1838; Gray Barbee,
T. Turner, bm.

Stevens, Benjamin & Rachal Holloway, 9 June 1784; John Hastins,
bm.

Stevens, George & Anne White, 22 Jan 1822; John Cheek, bm.

Stevens, Henry & Jane Holloway, 9 Aug 1787; John Stevans, bm.

Stevens, Marshall & Elizabeth Madry, 13 Dec 1866; H. Q. Strain,
A. Maddry, bm; m 18 Dec 1866 by N. W. Wilson.

Stevens, Ned & Mary A. Henton, 11 Dec 1866; Thos. H. Hughes,
James C. Turrentine, bm.

Stevens, Thomas & Rebecca Thomas, 5 July 1804; Peter Williams,
bm.

Steward, Albert & Betheny Day, 4 Sept 1849; James Day, bm.

Steward, John & Juda Hudson, 7 April 1787; Benja Rainey, Henry
Trolanger, bm.

Steward, William R. & Sarah P. Murphey, 20 Dec 1866; A. L.
Phelps, bm; m 23 Dec 1866 by Thos. H. Hughes, J. P.

Stewart, Adison & Cornelia Ray, 31 July 1857; Evn Cate, bm;
m 2 Aug 1857 by J. W. Strowd, J. P.

Stewart, (Stward), Albert & Zelpha Chandler, 13 Dec 1841; Peter
Stewart, bm.

Stewart, Alexander & Sarah Turrentine, 14 Feb 1801; James Ray,
bm.

Stewart, Alexander & Sarah Hurst, 20 Dec 1854; Edmond Harwood, bm; m 20 Dec 1854 by J. B. McDade, J. P.

Stewart, Charles & Delilah Thomas, 6 Sept 1822; J. Taylor Jr., bm.

Stewart, James & Letis Bradshaw, 11 Nov 1819; Thomas Thompson, bm.

Stewart, John & Nancy Breedlove, 13 Oct 1824; Fisher Clindenin, bm.

Stewart, John & Nancy Thompson, 21 Nov 1838; Joseph Thompson, John Thompson, bm.

Stewart, Rapts & Anny Mason, 22 Sept 1806; Charles Whitmore, bm.

Stewart, Robert & Jane Torentine, 20 July 1795; John Turrentine, bm.

Stewart, Robert & Geales Walker, 22 March 1808; James Child, bm.

Stewart, Ruffin & Elizabeth Bibby, 30 Aug 1838; Robert Mitchel, bm.

Stewart, Samuel & Anna Woody, 30 April 1819; Thos. Bradshaw, bm.

Stewart, William & Sarah Cox, 1 March 1810; Thomas Stephens, bm.

Stiner, Daniel & Mary Wells, 22 May 1820; Isaiah Hornaday, bm.

Stith, Andrew & Polley M. Stanford, 7 Dec 1812; Abner Stith, bm.

Stockard, James L. & Mary Johnston, 17 Oct 1834; Wm. Holmes, bm.

Stockard, John & Jeany Stewart, 22 Feb 1802; William Stockard, bm.

Stockard, John & Catey Albright, 18 Aug 1810; Jacob Albright, bm.

Stockard, Robert M. & Harriett Andrews, 24 Feb 1866; William N. Cheek, A. P. Strowd, bm; m 24 Feb 1866 by W. F. Strayhorn.

Stockard, Saml. & Julia Ann Johnston, 17 Jan 1829; Alfred Whitsett, bm.

Stockard, William & Lear Mann, 28 Jan 1797; John Madin, bm.

Stoffle, William & Nancy Hinchey, 11 Aug 1825; Chesley Jenkens, bm.

Stofle, John & Hetty Collins, 2 Jan 1818; James Adams, bm.

Stofle, William & Martha Boothe, 15 Feb 1819; John Boothe, bm.

Stoner, Henry & Sally Graves, 14 June 1819; George Curtner, bm.

Stout, Aaron & Sally Davis, 8 Feb 1827; Job Stout, bm.

Stout, Charles & Judah Cain, 22 March 1809; Adam Spoon, bm.

Stout, Fadies & Mahala Gilliam, 21 Aug 1846; Anderson Wells, bm.

Stout, Francis & Cornelia A. McCauley, 30 April 1840; William Wells, bm.

Stout, Henry & Susanah Wells, 19 Feb 1824; Aaron Stout, bm.

Stout, Jacob & Judith Freeman, 26 April 1788; Elijah Beverly, bm.

Stout, Jacob & Mary Bolling, 20 Sept 1806; Robert Glenn, bm.

Stout, Jacob & Nancy Hearld, 8 Sept 1838; Simpson Boggs, bm.

Stout, Jesse & Betsey Brake, 24 April 1810; John Freeman, Brantly Coggins, bm.

Stout, John & Mildred Marshill, 3 Nov 1847; John Hunter, bm.

Stout, Lemuel & Mary Capps, 8 Feb 1825; Aaron Stout, bm.

Stout, Michal & Frances Morris, 10 May 1856; Wm. M. Baley, bm; m 11 May 1856 by A. Edwards, J. P.

Stout, Nathan & Rachel Stout, 1 Nov 1842; David Dinon, bm.

Stout, Samuel & Rachel Teal, 5 April 1790.

Stout, Thomas & Martha Ellen Ray, m 22 March 1851 by Richd. Stanford, J. P.

Stout, William & Nancy Mealer, (no date); Wm. Stagg, bm.

Stout, William & Rachel Snotterly, 17 Jan 1799; William Osbun, bm.

Stout, William & Anne Moon, 20 Dec 1800; James Steel, bm.

Stovall, Frederick & Sine Ferrill (no date); William Stovall, bm.

Stovall, Henry & Marian Wilson, 19 Sept 1821; Fred. Moris, bm.

Stowers, Adam & Polley Hinderson, 13 May 1823; A. S. Couch, bm.

Strader, Adam & Milly Topley, 15 Feb 1839; Jonathan Strader, Wm. Holt, bm.

Strader, Daniel & Elizabeth Sullenger, 13 March 1821; David Phillips, bm.

Strader, Jacob & Nancy Melvin, 8 March 1831; John Strader, bm.

Strahorn, Brian & Polly Strain, 9 Feb 1822; John Strayhorn, bm.

Strain, Alexander & Miriam Hunter, 23 Feb 1787; Jno. Strain, bm.

Strain, Alexander & Polly Burns, 6 Nov 1821; James N. Strayhorn, bm.

Strain, David & Jeany Hart, 27 July 1803; David Strayhorn, bm.

Strain, James & Elizabeth S. Gattis, 30 Oct 1827; James Gattis, Samuel Kirkland, bm.

Strain, Samuel & Aernes Brewer, 12 Sept 1833; Ransome Brewer, Wm. Beasley, bm.

Strain, Samuel D. & Julia Chambers, 20 Dec 1842; Josiah B. Davis, bm.

Strain, Thomas & Cornelia Gattis, 17 Nov 1860; William A. Gattis, bm; m 18 Nov 1860 by J. A. Cunninggim.

Strain, William & Abbey Utley, 1 Feb 1831; John Strain, Alexander Gattis, bm.

Strange, Robert & Jane Kirkland, 1 Oct 1817; Thomas C. Hooper, bm.

Strawd, John & Mary White, 14 March 1865; John Strawd, Benjamin Huddlson, bm.

Strawd, Manly D. & Martha Atwater, 5 Aug 1842; H. C. Strawd, Alfred Strowd, bm.

Strawd, Thomas J. & Sarah A. Ward, 11 Nov 1860; J. B. Snipes, bm; m 11 Nov 1860 by O. Churchill, minister.

Strawd, Thomas J. & Martha A. Pritchard, 18 July 1865; James S. Durham, bm.

Strawn, Elisha & Nancy Lindsey, 10 Nov 1833; Sheffey T. Lindsey, Claiborne Justice, bm.

Strayhorn, Archibald & Susan Borland, 15 May 1848; W. N. Strayhorn, bm.

Strayhorn, Aron & Nancy Patterson, 18 Nov 1829; Archd. Borland, bm.

Strayhorn, Charles & Mary Piper, 23 Oct 1799; John Strayhorn, bm.

Strayhorn, David & Catharine McCabe, 26 Jan 1790; Gilbert Strayhorn, bm.

Strayhorn, David & Anne Freeland, 4 May 1822; Joseph Freeland, bm.

Strayhorn, David & Martha Jane Pratt, 1 Sept 1855; Egbert H. Strayhorn, bm; m 6 Sept 1855 by B. J. Hackney.

Strayhorn, Egbert H. & Malinda Borland, 15 Dec 1856; Wm. G. Borland, bm; m 17 Dec 1856 by Alex. Dickson, J. P.

Strayhorn, George & Sarah Strayhorn, 13 Dec 1855; Thos. J. Strayhorn, bm; m 13 Dec 1855 by James Phillips, minister.

Strayhorn, George, son of Clara Strayhorn, & Clara Nunn, dau. of Jane Nunn, colored, m 28 Nov 1867 by N. C. Cate.

Strayhorn, Gilbert & Jeany Kirkland, 7 Nov 1801; John Strayhorn, bm.

Strayhorn, James & Mary Blackwood, 3 March 1829; Aaron Strayhorn, Archd. Borland, bm.

Strayhorn, James & Catherine Borland, 24 Dec 1835; H. S. Jackson, Andrew Jackson, bm.

Strayhorn, James & Rachel Cates, (no date); Wm. Strayhorn, bm.

Strayhorn, John & Anne Scoby, 24 Oct 1816; Gilbert Strayhorn, Archd. Borland, bm.

Strayhorn, John & Susannah Borland, 12 Nov 1822; Samuel C. Coble, bm.

Strayhorn, John & Eliza J. Cole, 3 Sept 1849; William T. Freeland, bm.

Strayhorn, John & Mary Hutchens, 3 Oct 1861; W. F. Strayhorn, bm.

Strayhorn, Leroy & Emeline Moore, 23 Aug 1841; Nathl. S. Groves, William Lockhart, bm.

Strayhorn, Q. G. & Caroline Strayhorn, 25 Oct 1862; m 30 Oct 1862 by C. W. Johnston, J. P.

Strayhorn, Samuel & Mary Moore, 3 Oct 1813; Gilb. Hart, bm.

Strayhorn, Samuel & Sally Hart, 16 Oct 1816; Gilbert Strayhorn, bm.

Strayhorn, V. L. & Caroline Strayhorn, 25 Oct 1862; Wm. G. Borland, bm.

Strayhorn, William & Mary Hunter, 6 Dec 1788; James Strayhorn, bm.

Strayhorn, William & Nancy Strain, 4 Oct 1806; John Hart, bm.

Strayhorn, William & Nancy Thompson, 7 April 1812; David Strayhorn, bm.

Strayhorn, William A. & Caroline E. Pratt, 12 Aug 1861; J. M. Blackwood, bm; m 15 Aug 1861 by John Buroughs, J. P.

Strayhorn, William H. & Caroline Crabtree, 12 Sept 1861; Gaston Couch, Lambert Garrard, bm; m 12 Sept 1861 by Samuel Couch, J. P.

Strayhorn, Willie N. & Margaret R. Douglas, 3 Jan 1859; S. G. Strayhorn, bm; m 6 Jan 1859 by Jno. Hancock, J. P.

Street, Jno. & Charlotte Harris, 10 Dec 1804; Henry Thomson, bm.

Street, Joseph & Peggy Carmichael, 26 Sept 1813; Andrew Hughs, bm.

Street, William & Nelly Shaw, 24 Sept 1818; James Douglass, bm.

Streyhorn, David & Penelope Berry, 9 Oct 1795; Wm. Ansley, bm.

Streyhorn, William F. & Harriett Nichols, 15 Dec 1841; Jno. M. Faucett, Moses Leathers Jr., bm.

Striett, Ritchad & Elizabeth Liner, 31 Aug 1814; William Brannock, son of Henry, bm.

Strother, John Jr. & Hannah Stroud, 12 Oct 1786; John Strother Sr., bm.

Stroud, John S. & Lois Atwater, 5 Nov 1828; Alfred Snipes, bm.

Stroud, Moses B. & Mary Oldham, 9 Feb 1855; M. F. W. McCall, bm.

Stroud, Pinkney & Julia Price, 24 Aug 1836; Charles Campbel, J. L. Smith, bm.

Stroud, Thomas & Hannah Robinson, 26 Dec 1800; Dixon Stroud, Nathaniel Robertson, bm.

Stroud, William & Francis Pettey, 28 June 1798; Jesse George, bm.

Strowd, Andrew & Susan Ann Gilliam, 1 June 1858; Manes Lloyd, bm; m 1 June 1858 by D. Tilley, J. P.

Strowd, Bryant & Martha Wilson, 9 April 1829; J. Taylor, bm.

Strowd, Charles Pinckney & Celia Atwater, 20 July 1832; John S. Strowd, bm.

Strowd, Fielden & Elizabeth Blackwood, 2 Jan 1813; Shurley W. King, bm.

Strowd, Green Murphy & Winney Winningham, 31 Oct 1837; Charles P. Strowd, bm.

Strowd, Hawken & Mary Edwards, 3 Jan 1831; D. Turner, bm.

Strowd, Henry C. & Sarah H. Holeman, 8 Oct 1845; Thos. S. Faucett, bm.

Strowd, Thomas J. & Martha A. Pritchard, 18 July 1856; m 19 July 1865 by Geo. W. Purefoy, M. G.

Strowd, Warick & Aga Strowd, 30 Nov 1866; Warick Strawd, Daniel R. Hogan, bm; m 16 Dec 1866 by Manly Andrews.

Strudwick, Dr. Edmund & Ann E. Nash, 18 Nov 1827; Wm. B. Grove, bm.

Strudwick, Frederick N. & Mary S. Burwell, 27 June 1854; Jno. D. Taylor, Daniel G. Fowle, bm.

Strudwick, William F. & Martha Sheppard, 5 Sept 1795; M. Hart, bm.

Strudwick, William F. & Elizabeth Webb, 2 June 1831; Alexr. S. J. Alston, bm.

Stuard, Jonathan J. & Emily Cane, 8 June 1857; B. J. Hackney, bm; m 8 June 1857 by B. J. Hackney.

Stubbins, James H. & Mary C. Bishop, 23 Nov 1864; William J. Workman, bm; m 23 Nov 1864 by Wm. Cheek, J. P.

Stubbins, Joseph & Patsey Blalock, 2 Jan 1798; William Hastings, bm.

Stubbins, Samuel & Deborah McCallum, 28 Dec 1801; Joseph Stubbins, bm.

Stubbins, Samuel & Nancy Crutchfield, 8 Jan 1834; James Squires, bm.

Stubbins, William H. & Emeline Smith, 11 March 1854; Daniel R. Efland, bm; m 12 March 1854 by Wiatt Cates, J. P.

Studiville, John & Hannah Everit, 14 June 1815; Luke Prendergast, bm.

Sturgis, Jno. & Elizabeth Gooden, 21 Nov 1782; Jno. Kelly, bm.

Sugg, Isaac, son of Isaac & Jane Suggs, & Martha M. Allen, dau. of Hiram & Lucy Allen, m 15 Aug 1867 by N. P. Hall, J. P.

Sugg, Maddison R. & Rebecca Watson, 11 July 1836; John Blake, W. W. Davis, bm.

Suit, Gaston & Elizabeth Anne Bowen, 14 March 1843; Samuel B. Suit, Jno. McKerall, bm.

Suit, John & Perthena Cook, 11 Oct 1819; Noland Hampton, bm.

Suite, Agustes G. & Elizabeth Ann Carden, 4 Oct 1853; G. Freemone, bm.

Suitt, Benton, son of Jordan & Elizabeth Suit, & Margaret Crabtree, dau. of Norwood & Nancy Crabtree, m 10 June 1868 by J. W. McCauley, J. P.

Suitt, John & Mary An Andrews, 29 Jan 1857; Rufus Andrews, bm; m 29 Jan 1857 by S. L. Lloyd, J. P.

Sullenger, James J. & Jane Tutterton, 18 May 1854; W. G. Burroughs, bm.

Sumbler, Abram & Jane Grayston, 1 April 1837; Abram Sumbler, Robert Pugh, bm.

Summers, Felty & Creasy Tickle, 1 Oct 1845; Simeon Tickle, bm.

Summers, John & Catherine Hobbs Jun., 4 March 1848; Wm. Zachary, bm.

Suthard, William & Bertha Thomas, 26 Dec 1848; Jonas Case, bm.

Sutton, Benjamin & Nelly Shepherd, 27 July 1848; H. A. Sutton, bm.

Sutton, Campbell & Fanny Carden, 31 Oct 1798; James Sutton, bm.

Sutton, Eli & Fanny Cook, 2 Aug 1831; Moses Cook, bm.

Sutton, James & Sally Garrett, 23 Feb 1793; Frederick Gates, bm.

Sutton, James & Grizzy Dickie, 14 Sept 1822; John White, William Hatchell, bm.

Sutton, Thomas & Winifred Warren, 30 Jan 1798; William Sutton, bm.

Sutton, Thomas & Polley McMullen, 17 July 1804; Campbell Sutton, bm.

Sutton, William & Elizabeth Hunt, 17 Dec 1792; Henry Hunt, bm.

Swan, Thomas W. & Susan A. McCadams, 14 Aug 1859; L. Sheelar, bm; m 14 Aug 1859 by Ro. Hooker, M. G.

Swann, John & Frances Waddell, 15 Sept 1841; N. Hill, Pride Jones, bm.

Sweaney, John R. & Elizabeth Carrington, 30 April 1822; John Horner, bm.

Swift, Flower & Catherine Wilhoit, 28 July 1810; Lewis Wilhite, bm.

Swift, William & Nancy Jeffers, 19 Jan 1828; Isaac Jeffrey, bm.

Swing, Daniel & Elizabeth Shavor, 6 Dec 1819; John Shavor, bm.

Swinny, Willie & Tazza Oakley, 16 May 1832; Thomas Horner, Jno. Horner, bm.

Sykes, Alleen & Winny Cate, 29 May 1792; Wm. Moore, bm.

Sykes, Allen & Lucy Kirk, 18 Feb 1817; Thomas Sykes, bm.

Sykes, Allen & Sally Hastings, 21 April 1823; Thomas Sykes, bm.

Sykes, Allen & Patsy Roach, 4 Oct 1823; Thomas Sykes, bm.

Sykes, Andrew F. & Sally Ray, 4 Dec 1860; Henry Ray, bm; m 4 Dec 1860 by Ruffin R. Tapp, J. P.

Sykes, E. & Lucy Andres, 26 April 1848; J. M. Beaver, bm.

Sykes, Henry & Elizabeth Roach, 16 Feb 1835; James Howard, Jesse Miller, bm.

Sykes, Henry & Sarah Cate, 28 March 1841; Jno. M. Faucett, bm.

Sykes, James & Cynthia Cheek, 19 Nov 1831; Robert Christian, Alvis Cheek, bm.

Sykes, James & Adeline Roach, 3 Feb 1832; Dav. Hayes, bm.

Sykes, James & Nancy Cates, 4 Jan 1855; John H. Sykes, bm; m 14 Jan 1855 by Ruffin R. Tapp, J. P.

Sykes, John & Fanny Cade, 27 Feb 1787; Allan Sykes, bm.

Sykes, John & Patsey Kirk, 16 June 1812; Allen Sykes, bm.

Sykes, John & Susannah Hastings, 26 Aug 1817; Allen Sykes, bm.

Sykes, John & Polly Kate or Cate, 27 May 1823; Henry ODaniel, bm.

Sykes, John & Sally Hastings, 24 Jan 1834; David Hayes, Thomas Sykes, bm.

Sykes, John C. & Mary Ann Turner, 23 Jan 1838; James Turner, bm.

Sykes, John W. & Susan E. Cate, 10 Oct 1866; Alfred Carr, bm; m 11 Oct 1866 by Thos. Long, J. P.

Sykes, Richard & Susannah Cheek, 2 Jan 1824; B. Cheek, bm.

Sykes, Robert & Elizabeth Burnsides, 27 Aug 1845; Robert Cheek, A. Cheek, bm.

Sykes, Samuel P., son of Pinkney & Mary Sykes, & Lucy A. Minnis, dau. of Mary A. & Ashley Minnis, m 16 Aug 1868 by D. W. Thompson.

Sykes, Sidney A., son of Henry & Elizabeth Sykes, & Nancy Moore, dau. of David & Mary A. Moore, m 27 June 1867 by John C. Sykes, J. P.

Sykes, Thomas & Rebecca Crutchfield, 2 March 1813; Paul Finnon, bm.

Sykes, Thomas & Salley Jones, 26 March 1834; J. W. Carr, bm.

Sykes, Thomas & Elizabeth Williams, 26 March 1836; David Hayes, J. Taylor, bm.

Sykes, Thomas & Mary Workman, 18 Feb 1865; Wm. Dodson, Thos. J. Freeland, bm.

Sykes, Thomas M. & Sarah Jane Dodson, 2 Jan 1866; Andrew F. Sykes, W. N. Anderson, bm; m 4 Jan 1866 by D. W. Thompson.

Sykes, Thomas R. & Rebeca J. Smith, 9 Feb 1861; Wm. G. Sykes, Alfred Carr, bm; m 14 Feb 1861 by Thos. Long, J. P.

Sykes, Wesley & Susan Jane Sykes, 30 Sept 1857; C. M. Latimer, bm; m 16 Oct 1857 by Ruffin R. Tapp, J. P.

Sykes, Wesley & Delila Lloyd, 23 Aug 1864; J. W. Siler, bm.

Sykes, William & Nancy Moore, 22 July 1815; William H. Rigsbee, bm.

Sykes, William & Mary Jones, 18 Aug 1841; Jonathan Jones, James Woods, bm.

Sykes, William & Nancy E. Bauldwin, 7 Feb 1859; Wm. Dodson, Alvis Durham, bm; m 8 Feb 1859 by Thos. Long, J. P.

Sykes, William G. & Sarah E. Smith, 26 Jan 1853; Minnick Miller, bm; m 26 Jan 1853 by Thos. Long, J. P.

Sykes, William P. & Esperan Andrews, 30 Jan 1857; Wm. Dodson, bm.

Tabern, Thomas & Matildy Holley, 20 July 1849; W. E. Oakley, D. Umsted, bm.

Taborn, Hilmon & Frances Hays, m 26 May 1854 by Nelson P. Hall, J. P.

Tabourn, Hilmon & Frances Hays, 25 May 1854; Brady Hays, W. A. Jordan, bm.

Tabown, Anderson & Mary Hayes, 20 Feb 1837; J. A. Parrish, Levi McCollum, bm.

Tabron, Henderson & Manervy Mayho, 24 April 1850; James Volintine, bm.

Taburn, Harrison & Salley Taburn, 3 Oct 1822; Vines Guy, bm.

Tade, John & Mary Nicholes, 13 Oct 1792; Alex. Tinnin, John Tidd, bm.

Talar, James & Martha Hunley, 14 July 1855; John L. Smith, William Brown, bm.

Talley, Daniel & Rebecca Robinson, 24 Oct 1820; James Lynn, bm.

Talley, James Martin & Salley Bristol, 15 Sept 1817; Sterling Talley, bm.

Talley, Sterling & Peggy Hargess, 9 Sept 1809; William Whitted, bm.

Tallow, James & Polly Futrell, 3 March 1817; Eli Tallow, bm.

Tally, Sterling & Betsey Harrell, 24 Jan 1818; James Tally, bm.

Talor, James & Lucy Barracks, 23 Sept 1864; John Jordan, bm.

Tankersley, Felix & Fannie Adel Barbee, 13 Oct 1862; Jones Watson, bm; m 17 Oct 1862 by Jno. W. Jenkins.

Tanner, Henry & Fanny Hester, 18 Oct 1820; Lewis Roberts, bm.

Tanzel, Plumer & Sarah V. Whitmore, 1 Dec 1849; Sanders Riley, bm.

Tapley, James & Polly Holt, 14 Dec 1826; Henry Tapley, bm.

Tapp, Allen, son of Harry & Amey Tapp, & Mildred Bayner, m 14 June 1868 by D. W. Jordan, J. P.

Tapp, Andrew & Julia Paul, 17 March 1866; Dennis Thompson, bm; m 17 March 1866 by David T. Clark, J. P.

Tapp, George & Peggy Forsythe, 11 Sept 1811; Pt. Gunn, bm.

Tapp, Richard & Rebecca Hopson, 3 Sept 1813; Jno. Cate, bm.

Tapp, Ruffin R. & Mary Ann Pratt, 3 Oct 1849; H. C. McCauley, bm.

Tapp, Ruffin R., son of Richard & Rebecca Tapp, & Melisse N. Dunnagan, dau. of Timothy & Nancy Dunnagan, m 19 Dec 1857 by T. N. Faucette.

Tapp, Vincent & Anne Hopson, 8 Oct 1812; Henry Womach, bm.

Tapp, William & Mary Thompson, 27 April 1842; Daniel Thompson, bm.

Tarleton, James & Susana Tolar, 31 Dec 1789; A. McBroom, bm.

Tarpley, Henry & Margeret Trolonger, 9 Nov 1833; Abram Tarpley, bm.

Tarpley, William & Tempe Holt, 23 July 1822; J. A. Whitsitt, bm.

Tart, Stephen & Polley Richard, 28 Feb 1810; William McNaman, bm.

Tate, Anderson & Mary Smith, 6 Dec 1825; J. Strayhorn, bm.

Tate, Anthony & Nancy Moore, 21 Feb 1809; Thos. Moore, bm.

Tate, George & Nancy Woods, 4 Aug 1795; George Allen, bm.

Tate, George & Nancy Strain, 4 Dec 1813; John Mulhollon, bm.

Tate, George W., son of Jack & Ann Tate, & Manerva Kelly, dau. of Atkins & Sarah Ann Kelly, m 7 Aug 1868 by Thos. C. Hayes.

Tate, George W. & Rachiel Whitaker, 22 Nov 1853; James Gill, bm.

Tate, Haywood, son of Henry Mebane & Syntha Tate, & Edy Wilson, dau. of Nelly Wilson, m 24 Aug 1867 by Wilson Brown, J. P.

Tate, James & Anne Tinnen, 6 Feb 1789; Wm. Tate, Wm. McCauley, bm.

Tate, James & Peggy Hart, 11 April 1807; Daniel Atkins, bm.

Tate, James & Fanny Gattis, 31 May 1821; William Gattis, bm.

Tate, James & Elizabeth Brown, 23 April 1842; John Williams, Leo E. Heartt, bm.

Tate, James Jr. & Charlotte Barton, 7 Oct 1830; Jo. Hartt, bm.

Tate, James F. & Elizabeth J. Paul, 11 Feb 1856; W. John Freeland, bm; m 12 Feb 1856 by C. E. Smith, J. P.
*
Tate, Jesse & Mary Jeffreys, 22 Feb 1819; Jas. Mason, bm.

Tate, John & Ruth Lynch, 5 Nov 1794; William Hughs, bm.

Tate, John & Henrietta Armstrong, 25 March 1823; Thos. Tate, bm.

Tate, John B. & Louisa Burnsides, 19 April 1823; Thos. Tate, bm.

Tate, Joseph & Margaret Curry, 11 Jan 1840; Thos. Sawyer, bm.

Tate, Robert & Kesiah Ector, 28 Oct 1817; William Tate, bm.

Tate, Robert & Eliza Morrow, 22 Dec 1845; James M. Palmer, bm.

Tate, Rowan & Hannah Dickson, 6 Feb 1841; Calvin Tate, bm.

Tate, Samuel & Salley Strayhorn, 24 Oct 1810; Samuel Strayhorn, bm.

Tate, Samuel & Polley Squires, 22 Feb 1825; Samuel Nelson, bm.

Tate, Simpson & Catherine Lewis, 22 Jan 1796; James McClure, bm.

Tate, Thomas & Polly Strayhorn, 10 Nov 1824; Aron Strayhorn, bm.

Tate, Thomas & Eliza Jane Fossett, 28 July 1838; Joseph Tate, bm.

Tate, Thomas & Jane Bowling, 22 Sept 1866; W. H. Jordan, bm.

Tate, Thomas, son of William & Mary J. Tate, & Precilla McCracken, dau. of Thomas & Catherine McCracken, m 11 Feb 1868 by Thomas Lynch.

Tate, Uriah & Hannah Street, 13 Feb 1810; Zephannah Lott, Joseph Street, bm.

Tate, William & Betsey Armstrong, 22 Aug 1816; Jno. Armstrong, bm.

Tate, William T. & Mary Jane Strayhorn, 27 Aug 1845; Pinckney Tate, bm.

Tate, William T. & Sarah R. Strayhorn, 6 Nov 1865; James M. Scott, bm; m 7 Nov 1865 by C. W. Johnston, J. P.

Tate, Zephaniah & Hannah Tate, 27 Jan 1814; William Street, bm.

Tatom, George & Betsey Brantly, 16 May 1812; David Ray, bm.

*For Tate, James & Margaret Nelson, see p. 296.

Tatom, George & Betsy Seaver, 7 May 1827; John Scott, bm.

Tatom, Stephen & Salley Owen, 24 Dec 1799; William Tatom, bm.

Tatom, Willie & Lively Weaver, 29 Aug 1822; Benjamin Hester, bm.

Tatum, George & Cynthia Mayhoe, 2 Sept 1827; John Clinton, bm.

Taylor, Alfred Moore & Jeany Minnis, 27 Nov 1809; John Com___, bm.

Taylor, David A. & Elvira B. Allison, 8 Oct 1826; John A. McDade, bm.

Taylor, Duncan & Mary Johnston, 20 Nov 1850; Skidmore Garrard, bm.

Taylor, Elisha & Polly Duke, 7 May 1813; James Hopkins, bm.

Taylor, Essin & Catharine Bowls, 13 Dec 1866; M. W. Davis, bm; m 13 Dec 1866 by Solomon Pool.

Taylor, Frederick & Katherine Spratt, ___ Dec 1784; Jacob Richards, bm.

Taylor, George & Jane Wilson, 23 March 1811; James Allison, bm.

Taylor, Green & Salley Cozart, 22 Nov 1847; H. Mangum, bm.

Taylor, Haywood, Eliza Jane (Jennett) Ray, 9 Oct 1852; John Dollar, bm; m 14 Oct 1852 by Charles Wilson, J. P.

Taylor, Henderson & Elizabeth Cates, 16 March 1840; John Waggoner, C. P. George, bm.

Taylor, J. J. & Julia F. Woods, 11 Sept 1866; Stephen Taylor, bm; m 12 Sept 1866 by Will A. Wilson.

Taylor, James & Polly Brinkley, 24 Sept 1800; Allen Parrish, bm.

Taylor, John & Polly Robard, 28 May 1811; Timothy Dunnagan, bm.

Taylor, John & Salley Manis, 24 June 1827; John S. McDade, bm.

Taylor, John & Julia Bagley, 4 April 1867; John A. Newman, bm; m 4 April 1867 by John Cheek, J. P.

Taylor, Joseph & Eletha Stafford, 5 Feb 1798; John Taylor, bm.

Taylor, Joseph & Elizabeth Tate, 24 Jan 1807; Wm. Tate, bm.

Taylor, Joseph A. & Sarah E. Hester, 29 July 1859; J. J. Allison, bm; m 3 Aug 1859 by Jno. J. Allison, J. P.

Taylor, Lewellen & Sarah F. Ashley, 11 Oct 1865; Logan G. Clayton, bm; m 15 Oct 1866 by Thos. Wilson, J. P.

Taylor, Lewis & Nancy Oakley, 3 Sept 1815; Elisha Taylor, bm.

*Tate, James & Margaret Nelson, 16 May 1785; Edward Wilson, bm.

Taylor, Robert & Jane Butler, 10 Nov 1800; James Yarbrough, bm.

Taylor, Solomon & Holley Brinkley, 25 May 1818; Mark Roberts, bm.

*See also p. 295.

Taylor, Stephen & Elizabeth Gunn, 23 June 1798; David Allison, bm.

Taylor, Thos. & Sarah Allison, 9 Sept 1801; David Allison, bm.

Taylor, Thomas & Elizabeth Woods, 8 July 1816; Moses Guin, bm.

Taylor, Thomas & Leweser Love, colored, 28 March 1867; William Maner, bm; m 31 March 1867 by J. W. Stroud, J. P.

Taylor, Thomas J. & Martha E. Reddin, 3 Sept 1855; Thomas J. Taylor, bm.

Taylor, Thomas Jefferson & Mary A. Hodge, 17 June 1860; Thomas L. Taylor, J. R. Hester, bm.

Taylor, William & Aley Dunnagan, 29 May 1810; Timothy Dunnagan, bm.

Taylor, William & Nancy Brannock, 27 June 1812; Josiah Taylor, bm.

Teague, Isiah & Elizabeth Pike, 25 Feb 1837; John Pike, bm.

Tear, Loftin & Anne Bradshaw, 23 Dec 1831; James Murray, bm.

Teasley, Elijah & Elizabeth Hunt, 27 April 1814; Jonathan Teasley, bm.

Teasley, George & Hannah Miller, 9 Oct 1799; John Miller, bm.

Teasley, John & Jeany Kell, 6 Feb 1806; David Teasley, bm.

Teasley, Jonathan & Jeany Laws, 16 June 1813; Elijah Teasley, bm.

Teasley, William & Elizabeth Nangum, 10 Jan 1801; George Teasley, bm.

Teer, Haywood & Emeline Murray, 25 July 1846; John B. Murray, bm.

Teer, John & Elizabeth Bradshaw, 22 Jan 1849; Thomas F. Turner, bm.

Teer, Luke & Jeany Clendening, 27 Jan 1801; John Johnston, bm.

Teer, Richard & Nancy Ann Bradshaw, 31 Aug 1847; Wm. P. McDaniel, bm.

Teisley, Daniel & Isabella Kell, 5 Sept 1804; Sterling Harris, bm.

Tenin, David & Jeany Mallett, 24 July 1818; William Willson, bm.

Terrel, Joseph & Sarah Brooks, 6 May 1789; And. Brooks, Andrew Cole, bm.

Terrell, Henry & Elizabeth Sharp, 2 April 1787; Benjamin Sharp, bm.

Terrell, John & Mariah Farrar, 21 Dec 1865; Saml. Terrell, John Whitted, bm; m 24 Dec 1865 by D. W. Jordan, J. P.

Terrell, Jonathan & Sarah Smith, 9 March 1803; John Smith, bm.

Terrell, Joseph Jr. & Cynthia Bradley, 12 June 1821; John Stanford, bm.

Terrell, Solomon & Rebekah Gappins, 24 Nov 1845; Moses Terul, bm.

Terrill, George W. & Eliza Rice, 30 Dec 1857; Allen Minnis, James Gill, bm; m 1 Jan 1858 by Freeman Walker, J. P.

Terrill, William & Margaret Minnis, 22 Nov 1853; Richd. M. Jones, bm.

Terry, Bedford M. & Elizabeth Riley, 18 March 1857; A. M. Breeze, R. M. Jones, bm; m 22 March 1857 by H. Terry, J. P.

Terry, Hezekiah & Jane Dunnagan, 11 Sept 1834; J. Allison, bm.

Terry, Hezekiah & Sarah F. Berry, 7 June 1860 by Benjamin J. Kinnion, J. P.

Thetford, George & Esther Piggott, 16 Sept 1782; George Thetford Sen., bm.

Thetford, Joseph & Mary Humphrey, 14 Jan 1782; Francis Bennet, bm.

Thom, David & Patsey Prather, 5 Feb 1808; J. A. Campbell, bm.

Thomas, Alexander & Nancy Foleman, 24 Aug 1829; Geo. Thomas, bm.

Thomas, Baker G. & Emily May, 13 Dec 1848; Martin Joe, bm.

Thomas, Barnet & Melessa Crompton, 23 July 1838; J. M. McMensny, bm.

Thomas, Benjamin & Margaret Costner, 22 July 1795; John Thomas, bm.

Thomas, Branon & Elizabeth Atkerson, 20 April 1823; Wm. Thompson, bm.

Thomas, Daniel & Julia Ann Andrews, 23 Feb 1846; Julus Coby, bm.

Thomas, Edward & Elizabeth Garrison, 26 Feb 1784.

Thomas, George & Susannah Perry, 3 Jan 1822; Thos. Clancy, bm.

Thomas, George & Catey McCaddams, 21 Nov 1824; James Faucet(?), bm.

Thomas, Henry & Elizabeth Anthony, 29 Feb 1808; Henry Garrett, bm.

Thomas, James & Peggy Riley, 1 Dec 1801; James Riley, bm.

Thomas, James & Mary Stevens, 24 Aug 1812; Ed. King, bm.

Thomas, James & Clara Miles, 8 Aug 1822; Robert Hastings, bm.

Thomas, Jesse & Elender Garrison, 14 April 1787; James Cook, bm.

Thomas, Jesse & Susanah Shaw, 25 Feb 1797; Jno. Wilkinson, bm.

Thomas, John & Jeane Smith, 8 Dec 1795; Hugh Shaw, bm.

ORANGE COUNTY MARRIAGES, 1779-1868

Thomas, John & Nancy Jones, 14 Jan 1826; Green Ferdley, bm.

Thomas, John F. & Zelpha Dixon, 30 Dec 1837; Joe Homor, bm.

Thomas, Josiah & Ruth Mitchel, 12 Nov 1799; Stephens Robart, bm.

Thomas, Ludwick & Barbary Albright, 24 Nov 1802; Wm. Holt Jr., bm.

Thomas, Martin & Nelly Shanklin, 31 Sept 1829; John Thomas, bm.

Thomas, Micajah & Margret Dixon, 27 July 1830; George B. Morrow, bm.

Thomas, Moses & Sally Cook, 19 Dec 1806; Benj. Burnside, bm.

Thomas, Nehemiah & Susannah Phillips, 30 July 1811; Thomas Thomas, bm.

Thomas, Nehemiah & Sarah Gilliam, 3 April 1814; William Baldwin, bm.

Thomas, Richard & Peggy King, 27 Dec 1813; Nehemiah Thomas, bm.

Thomas, Thomas & Polley Hastings, 24 May 1803; Joseph Rippy, bm.

Thomas, William & Ellen Ray, 11 Dec 1828; James Thomas, bm.

Thomason, Palmer & Lydia Wilson, 20 March 1838; Samuel Riley, J. Taylor, bm.

Thompson, Able & Peggy Wilkerson, 22 June 1803; Joshua Thompson, bm.

Thompson, Abraham & Sarah Debow, 7 May 1782; Benjn. Debow, bm.

Thompson, Alfred & Elizabeth Thompson, 21 April 1825; J. Taylor Jr., bm.

Thompson, Alson G. & Nancy A. Thompson, 22 March 1861; Thos. J. Jones, bm; m 24 March 1861 by F. S. Gladson, M. G.

Thompson, Anderson & Hannah Albright, 21 Dec 1817; Alexr. Allbright, bm.

Thompson, Anthony & Mary Holt, 29 Jan 1787; John Rice, bm.

Thompson, Anthony & Jeane Williams, 26 Dec 1787; John Umstead, bm.

Thompson, Azariah & Catharine Allison, 4 Sept 1784; David Allison, bm.

Thompson, Brittan & Nancy Robertson, colored, 6 Feb 1867; Nash Robertson, bm; m 9 Feb 1867 by H. W. C. Stroud, J. P.

Thompson, Charles & Martha Anderson, 13 Dec 1851; W. B. Cheek, bm; m 17 Dec 1851 by Wm. Nelson, J. P.

Thompson, Daniel & Hannah Riley, 14 Feb 1833; Archibald Thompson, Samuel Scarlett, bm.

Thompson, Daniel & Elizabeth Thompson, 18 Sept 1858; James Thompson, bm.

Thompson, David & Jane Strayhorn, 14 Oct 1812; Joel Cloud, bm.

Thompson, Duncan & Hannah Gappins, 11 March 1824; John B. Thompson, bm.

Thompson, Edwin G. & Eliza J. Morrow, 8 Jan 1839; James C. Turrentine, bm.

Thompson, Enoch & Patsy Lindley, 8 Sept 1808; James Thompson, bm.

Thompson, Francis M. & Nancy E. Merritt, 18 Jan 1867; Wm. T. Cape, John B. Scarlett, bm; m 19 Jan 1867 by Wm. W. Pickett, J. P.

Thompson, Franklin & Elizabeth Russall, 8 Sept 1848; Samuel Thompson, bm.

Thompson, Gabriel & Mary Ann Allen, 15 Aug 1846; William Heathcock, bm.

Thompson, George & Ann Marshal, 10 Dec 1796; Richard Thompson, bm.

Thompson, George & Susan Malred, 24 Sept 1836; G. W. Thompson, John Coble, bm.

Thompson, Henry & Pricillah Horton, 24 Sept 1788.

Thompson, Henry & Judith Jackson, 17 May 1866; Washington Day, bm; m 17 May 1866 by H. G. Hill, M. G.

Thompson, Henry Jr. & Susannah Whited, 20 Nov 1797; Bryson Dobbins, bm.

Thompson, Henry Clay & Salina Morrow, 5 June 1857; J. T. Watson, bm; m 5 June 1857 by James Phillips, M. G.

Thompson, Henry J. & Eady S. Reeves, 20 Sept 1834; William J. Hayes, bm.

Thompson, Isaac & Lucinda Mebane, 26 Dec 1865; Richard Faucett, bm.

Thompson, James & Ann Morrow, 20 March 1787; Robert Fauset, bm.

Thompson, James & Susannah Roberts, 18 Feb 1794; Henry Tyrel, William Cumming, bm.

Thompson, James & Abagail Thompson, 26 March 1803; John A. Woody, bm.

Thompson, James & Nancy Steel, 2 Nov 1809; John Taylor, bm.

Thompson, James & Mary Thompson, 10 Feb 1819; Thomas Thompson, bm.

Thompson, James & Ruth Thompson, 4 Jan 1825; Stephen Moore, bm.

Thompson, James & Nelly Hunter, 9 Nov 1830; Patterson Thompson, bm.

Thompson, James & Melinda Rosson, 23 Dec 1832; Samuel Thompson, W. H. Thompson, bm.

Thompson, James & Anne Jackson, 8 Nov 1837; D. H. Cate, bm.

Thompson, James & Louisa Carter, 18 Dec 1838; Benjamin Carter, bm.

Thompson, James & Susan A. Gooch, 18 Aug 1855; William Stanley, bm; m 30 Aug 1855 by H. Wilkerson, J. P.

Thompson, James & Cornelia Crawford, 28 June 1859; John S. Thompson, bm; m 30 June 1859 by Daniel W. Thompson, M. G.

Thompson, James M. & Nancy Carden, 31 March 1857; Thos. W. Laws, bm; m 1 April 1857 by Wm. McCown, J. P.

Thompson, John & Ann Mann, 25 Feb 1792; William Man, bm.

Thompson, John & Sarah Johnston, 14 March 1795; Richard Thompson, bm.

Thompson, John & Esther Haisting, 14 Sept 1796; William Riley, bm.

Thompson, John & Nancy Bird, 24 Dec 1802; William Bird, bm.

Thompson, John & Nelly Thompson, 9 Jan 1809; John Hunter, bm.

Thompson, John & Nancy Walker, 30 Nov 1811; William Fauset, bm.

Thompson, John & Mary Paris, 26 Jan 1819; William Paris, bm.

Thompson, Jno. & Jinnet Mebane, 29 Nov 1819; Thos. Clancy, bm.

Thompson, John & Hannah Clark, 9 July 1825; Joseph A. Woods, David Clark, bm.

Thompson, John & Betsey Wood, 19 June 1826; A. B. Leonard, bm.

Thompson, John & Catharine McCauley, 30 April 1836; A. Strayhorn, George McCauley, bm.

Thompson, John & Elizabeth White, 22 April 1847; James T. Hunter, bm.

Thompson, John & Susan Huddleston, 6 Jan 1858; Simpson Carden, Thos. W. Laws, bm; m 13 Jan 1858 by Samuel Couch, J. P.

Thompson, John F. & Mary J. Forrest, 5 Sept 1865; E. C. Thompson, bm; m 10 Sept 1865 by J. C. Deans.

Thompson, John J. & Bettie A. Williams, 17 Aug 1865; R. M. Jones, bm; m 31 Aug 1865 by James Parks, J. P.

Thompson, Jonathan & Elizabeth Holmes, 8 Jan 1798; Willis Cooper, bm.

Thompson, Jonathan & Nancey Gordan, 20 Nov 1798; R. Huntington, bm.

Thompson, Jonathan & Elizabeth Latta, 1 Oct 1838; Pomory Crafott, Thomas Anderson, bm.

Thompson, Jonathan & Zilvinah Irvin, 3 Oct 1838; George Nelson, bm.

Thompson, Joseph & Elizabeth McDannel, 15 Oct 1796; James McDannel, bm.

Thompson, Joseph & Elizabeth Holmes, 7 March 1798; John Moody, Jonathan Thompson, bm.

Thompson, Joseph & Jeany Hunter, 11 April 1800; Robert Hunter, bm.

Thompson, Joseph & Hannah Jones, 30 Sept 1835; Patterson Thompson, bm.

Thompson, Joseph & Martha Reeves, 3 March 1836; Robert McAddam, bm.

Thompson, Joseph & Sally Parris, 22 Sept 1846; William Pickard, bm.

Thompson, Joseph & Polly Albright, 9 Jan 1848; Daniel Thomas, bm.

Thompson, Joseph & Mary Jane Morrow, 25 June 1853; Samuel H. Thompson, bm.

Thompson, Joshua & Polly Jackson, 26 Sept 1799; James Thompson, bm.

Thompson, Josiah & Janie ODaniel, 20 May 1850; William Thompson, bm.

Thompson, Josiah & Cornelia F. Durhan, 14 July 1866; A. C. McDaniel, bm; m 17 July 1866 by H. McDaniel, J. P.

Thompson, Josias & Catharine Trotterly, 17 March 1802; Jonathan Thompson, bm.

Thompson, Levi & Mary Steele, 9 March 1801; James Yarbrough, bm.

Thompson, Levi & Jeany Nicholson, 19 Dec 1802; Henry Paine, bm.

Thompson, Patterson & Anne Stewart, 23 Dec 1831; Joseph Crawford, bm.

Thompson, Patterson & Rebecca Jones, 29 Nov 1836; Wm. Holmes, bm.

Thompson, Porter & Susanah Woods, 9 Sept 1846; Thomas J. Phillip, John Newmane, bm.

Thompson, Richard & Rachael Morrow, 8 Feb 1793; Andrew Morrow, bm.

Thompson, Richard & Anney Turner, 3 Feb 1794; Samuel Thompson, bm.

Thompson, Richard & Edy Nunn, 18 June 1807; Jonathan Forrest, Henry Thompson Jr., bm.

Thompson, Richard & Nancy King, 13 Feb 1819; Wm. N. Pratt, bm.

Thompson, Richard & Rachel Davis, 4 Dec 1835; Wm. W. Allison, James Forrest, bm.

Thompson, Robert & Vina Thompson, 2 March 1826; John Crutchfield, bm.

Thompson, Robert & Jane Johnston, 8 Dec 1834; Alvis Crawford, bm.

Thompson, Robert & Margret Allen, 12 Oct 1836; William Thompson, bm.

Thompson, Samuel & Jane McMullen, 10 May 1794; Alex. Mahan, bm.

Thompson, Samuel & Rebecca Woods, 6 July 1798; James Woods, bm.

Thompson, Samuel & Nancy Trice, 16 May 1807; Wm. Wall, bm.

Thompson, Samuel & Nancy Allen, 26 Oct 1810; William McDaniel, bm.

Thompson, Samuel & Peggy Chambers, 25 March 1830; Jonathan Thompson, bm.

Thompson, Samuel & Sally ODaniel, 15 July 1833; Alfred ODaniel, bm.

Thompson, Samuel & Susan ODaniel, 14 Oct 1835; Levi McCollum, bm.

Thompson, Samuel & Mary A. Chambers, 10 July 1843; N. G. Chambers, Richard Thompson, bm.

Thompson, Samuel & Levina Jones, 28 Nov 1848; S. H. Torrentine, James M. Crutchfield, bm.

Thompson, Solomon & Eliza Pickett, 30 Jan 1828; Hunter McCulloch, bm.

Thompson, Stephen & Susannah McAddams, 30 Dec 1794; James McAddams, bm.

Thompson, Theoples & Alice Boyles, 8 Oct 1818; J. A. Fausitt, bm.

Thompson, Thomas & Anne Thompson, 20 Jan 1789; John Rice, bm.

Thompson, Thomas & Eliza Cox, 28 Sept 1789; Samuel Thompson, bm.

Thompson, Thomas & Peggy L. Daniel, 8 May 1811; William Thompson, bm.

Thompson, Thomas & Sally Squires, 12 Sept 1821; James Thompson, bm.

Thompson, Thomas & Dilly Linsey, 7 Oct 1822; Thomas Thompson, bm.

Thompson, Thomas & Fanny Lashley, 4 Feb 1834; Wm. Bowers, bm.

Thompson, Thomas & Edney Morton, 23 Aug 1834; Whitmill Carter, A. C. Murdock, bm.

Thompson, Thomas & Margaret Jane Tate, 11 Jan 1847; Alexander J. Jones, C. M. Latimer, bm.

Thompson, Thomas H. & Malinday Sykes, 27 March 1866; Henry Ray, bm; m 28 March 1866 by Ruffin R. Tapp, J. P.

Thompson, Wilam & Rachel Steel, 11 Nov 1787; John Steel, bm.

Thompson, William & Martha Morrow, 31 Dec 1799; James Morrow, James Thompson, bm.

Thompson, William & Peggy Clendenin, 17 April 1820.

Thompson, William & Sally Thompson, 13 March 1826; John Thompson, bm.

Thompson, William & Elizabeth Robertson, 7 Oct 1834; Joseph Thompson, bm.

Thompson, William & Frances York, 18 July 1841; Robert W. Glenn, bm.

Thompson, William & Ausaline Hall, 8 Oct 1841; Wm. Daniels, Jary King, bm.

Thompson, William, son of Samuel Thompson, & Ellen Jane Parker, 3 Sept 1856; Wm. T. Cope, Wm. McCauley, bm; m 11 Sept 1856 by Alexr. Dickson, J. P.

Thompson, William & Melissa Holder, 30 Dec 1861; John Thompson, bm; m 2 Jan 1862 by C. J. Freeland, J. P.

Thompson, William A. & Susan Tier, 21 Nov 1848; Manliff J. Staley, bm.

Thompson, William B. & Rebecca Gattis, 25 Dec 1839; James Sneed, Sidney Smith, bm.

Thompson, William P. & Nancy A. Clendenin, 21 Dec 1841; Joseph W. Thomson, bm.

Thompson, William P. & Mary Ann Elizabeth Durham, 11 March 1854; Wm. T. Bradshaw, bm; m 14 March 1854 by John J. Roberson.

Thompson, William R. & Harriet Carrington, 20 June 1853; James Garrard, bm.

Thompson, William R. & Nancy Squires, 4 Sept 1866; William P. Riley, Jno. M. Blackwood, bm; m 6 Sept 1866 by Ruffin R. Tapp, J. P.

Thomson, Robert & Ann Holmes, 18 Nov 1795; Alexr. Mahan, bm.

Thorne, William & Patsey Bledsoe, 21 Jan 1820; Jacob Bledsoe, bm.

Thrailkill, William & Milly Ellmore, 1 April 1796; James Turner, bm.

Thrift, David & Sally Thrift, 15 Dec 1807; Isham Thrift, bm.

Thrift, Pery & Candess Lloyd, 7 Jan 1806; Wm. Lloyd, bm.

Throneberry, Ludwick & Eve Kimbro, 11 Dec 1804; Adam Smith, bm.

Thrower, John & Sephrous C. Jenkins, 29 March 1824; Aquila Herndon, bm.

Thrower, Thomas & Elizabeth Sheppard, 20 Dec 1817; Nathan Marcom, bm.

Tickle, David & Peggy McCulley, 13 Jan 1840; Jacob Clapp, bm.

Tickle, Hiram & Betsy Parks, 25 Feb 1833; Daniel Tickle, bm.

Tickle, Jacob & Catherine Berry, 20 Feb 1802; Jacob Waggoner, bm.

Tickle, Louis & Polly Wagoner, 16 Dec 1848; Josiah Manly, bm.

Tidd, John & Mary Vincen, 23 Oct 1792; Alexander McKee, bm.

Tier, Ludwick & Polly Sheppard, 11 Oct 1817; Eli Murray, bm.

Tilley, Abner J. & Nancy J. Terry, 14 Sept 1855; W. B. Tilley, Luellen Taylor, bm.

Tilley, Allen & Nancy Lunsford, 6 Dec 1839; Oxford Moye, bm.

Tilley, Allen & Mary A. Holsomback, 12 May 1866; Nelson Parrish, bm.

Tilley, Ceymore & Mary Carrington, 6 Sept 1866; Stephen Tilley, bm; m 8 Oct 1866 by Joseph Woods, J. P.

Tilley, Durell & Manerva Bullock, 20 Oct 1856; Thos. A. Long, bm; m 21 Oct 1856 by H. F. Hudson.

Tilley, George & Mary Terry, 30 July 1864; W. R. Tilley, bm.

Tilley, George W. & Ellen Morrow, 26 May 1849; Wm. H. Beach, bm.

Tilley, Henry & Betsey Maize, 23 Dec 1816; George Tilley, bm.

Tilley, Hinton & Susan A. V. Leigh, 14 Dec 1857; Jas. P. Mason, bm; m 15 Dec 1857 by Jas. P. Mason, minister.

Tilley, John & Charlotte Waggoner, 15 Dec 1817; George Tilley, bm.

Tilley, John & Mary Dunnagan, 28 Aug 1849; Jas. Riggs, bm.

Tilley, Lazarus & Elizabeth Edwards, 18 April 1825; John B. Vaughan, bm.

Tilley, Stephen & Catey Cole, 21 March 1829; Jefferson Rhew, bm.

Tilley, William & Susannah Maddison, 7 Sept 1798; George Watson, bm.

Tilley, William A., son of James & Temperance Tilly, & Carnelia E. Ball, dau. of Marcus & Edney Ball, m 19 Dec 1867 by E. M. Holt, J. P.

Tilley, Willie P. & Jane Harris, 5 July 1840; Nelson P. Hall, bm; m 18 July 1860 by C. Wilson, J. P.

Tillinghast, Samuel W. & Jane B. Norwood, 22 July 1830; Walter A. Norwood, John W. Huske, bm.

Tilly, Dewitt & Mary A. Minoey, __ Aug 1865; Elisha H. Tilley, Henderson Tilley, bm; m 10 Aug 1865 by Wm. D. Lunsford, J. P.

Tilly, Edmund & Kesiah Moize, 13 Aug 1818; John Tilly Sr., bm.

Tilly, Elisha & Edney Umsted, 27 Aug 1866; Dennis Tilley, W. W. Latta, bm; m 6 Sept 1866 by Wm. D. Lunsford, J. P.

Tilly, George & Amelia Peak, 11 June 1816; Phillip Roberts, bm.

Tilly, George W. & Susan E. McFarland, 30 April 1856; H. C. McCauly, bm; m 13 May 1856 by Jno. C. Douglas, J. P.

Tilly, Hawood & Luetta Vaughan, 28 May 1857; J. D. Umsted, bm.

Tilly, Henry T. & Rebecca F. Robinson, 28 May 1866; Robert J.
Tilley, S. W. Hall, bm; m 17 June 1866 by Joseph W. McKee,
J. P.

Tilly, James & Salley Hutchens, 13 Nov 1841; William Hutchens,
Moses Leathers Jr., bm.

Tilly, James S. & Gustine I. Leigh, 23 March 1863; H. B.
Guthrie, bm; m 26 March 1863 by J. P. Mason, Baptist minister.

Tilly, John & Avey Southerland, 3 April 1819; Thomas Tilly, bm.

Tilly, Joseph G. & Elizabeth Garrett, 26 Feb 1857; James Gill,
bm.

Tilly, Lewis & Betty Woods, 23 Jan 1866; Woodson Tilly, bm;
m 8 Feb 1866 by R. H. Harris, J. P.

Tilly, Marcas & Mary Ball, 16 Sept 1853; James N. Lunsford,
Abner Tilley, bm.

Tilly, Robert J. & Mary J. Rountree, 3 Nov 1863; James R.
Harris, bm; m 5 Nov 1863 by Charles Wilson, J. P.

Tilly, Simpson & Jane Brogden, 6 Oct 1862; Geo. Laws, bm.

Tilly, Stephen & Nancy Hall, 24 April 1806; William Davis, bm.

Tilly, Stephen & Martha Garret, 6 Oct 1847; John H. Tilly, bm.

Tilly, William, son of Stephen & Catherine Tilly, & Jan Mangum,
dau. of Martha Mangum, m 3 Aug 1867 by Joseph Woods, J. P.

Tilly, William B. & Susan Allison, 20 Oct 1855; Abner Y. Tilly,
David S. Allison, bm.

Tilly, Woodson & Nancy Harris, 11 Oct 1865; Job Berry, bm;
m 13 Oct 1865 by R. H. Harris, J. P.

Tinnen, Major & Jane Moore, 7 Oct 1865; Saml. Allison, bm;
m 19 Oct 1865 by C. W. Cheek.

Tinnen, Robert & Sarah Mason, 28 Sept 1799; Henry Mason, bm.

Tinnin, Aaron & Betsy Husbands, 25 May 1848; Saml. McPherson,
bm.

Tinnin, Alexd. & Mary Armstrong, 27 June 1787; A. James Gray, bm.

Tinnin, Catlett C. & Polley D. Hannah, 2 Feb 1824; Abraham
Bridgwater, bm.

Tinnin, David & Nancy Walker, 13 April 1823; Abram Bridgwater,
bm.

Tinnin, Gabriel & Polly Wilson, 24 Dec 1824; Tho. Horner, bm.

Tinnin, Jeremiah & Jeany Dunnagan, 25 Sept 1805; Timothy
Dunnagan, bm.

Tinnin, Kearnes & Sarah Clark, 2 Nov 1787; William Clark, bm.

Tinnin, Robert G. & Nancy A. Hall, 3 Feb 1849; Freeman Walker,
bm.

Tinnin, Thomas & Fanny Walker, 30 Sept 1816; John Armstrong, bm.

Tolar, Anderson & Victoria Cocke, m 16 May 1855; by H. Terry, J. P.

Tolar, James & Lucy Baracks, m 27 Sept 1864 by Thos. Wilson.

Toler, Anderson & Victoria R. Cocke, 5 May 1855; William Barlowe, bm.

Tool, Garrett & Elizabeth Woods, 2 Sept 1791; James Derickson, bm.

Toomer, French, son of Henry & Susan Toomer, & Harriett Turrintine, dau. of Nancy Turrintine, colored, m 22 Feb 1868 by Thomas C. Hayes.

Towel, John & Mary Madden, 11 Feb 1798; Thomas Jones, bm.

Towell, Daniel & Rebecca Dickson, 30 March 1807; Richard Thompson, bm.

Towell, John & Hannah Barnhill, 13 Oct 1811; Alexander Creswell, bm.

Townsend, Joseph & Hesther Dixon, 19 Aug 1786; Jacob Allen, bm.

Townsend, John & Beletha Oakley, 19 Aug 1826; Barton Oakley, bm.

Townsend, Joshua & Polly Reaves, 6 May 1817; Joseph A. Woods, bm.

Tracy, Micajah & Naomi Tate, 10 March 1792; Peter Writsman, bm.

Treage, Christopher & Jane Hinshaw, 13 Sept 1846; Stephen Henly, bm.

Trice, Andrew & Elizabeth Hutson, 8 Aug 1793; Edward Trice, bm.

Trice, Charles & Priscilla Hudson, 28 Aug 1797; Edward Trice, bm.

Trice, Cuff & Lizzie Pickett, 20 Dec 1866; Wm. McCauley, bm; m 23 Dec 1866 by Z. D. J. Pearson, J. P.

Trice, Edward & Nancy Mechum, 28 July 1785; Samuel Shepard, bm.

Trice, Ezekael & Marian Herendon, 11 Oct 1786; Edward Trice, bm.

Trice, Ezekiel & Elizabeth Holaway, 26 July 1803; Henry Bunch, bm.

Trice, George, son of Jane Trice, & Lucy Morgan, dau. of Zachrey Barbee & Claresia Morgan, colored, m 14 Nov 1867 by James Watson, J. P.

Trice, Henry & Carolina Holloway, 1 May 1838; Marke Rigsby, Peter, Thompson, bm.

Trice, James & Melinda Dilliard, 16 March 1824; Wm. Dilliard, bm.

Trice, James & Eliza Barber, 16 Sept 1836; A. Turner, Thomas Faucett, bm.

Trice, John & Betsy Riley, 23 March 1816; Joseph Trice, bm.

Trice, Joseph & Milley Comb, 10 Feb 1783.

Trice, Mann & Frances Davis, 11 Jan 1831; J. L. Moore, bm.

Trice, Noah & Sarah Pearson, 16 March 1822; Frederic Reeves, bm.

Trice, Noah & Milla Davis, 19 May 1851; J. B. McDade, bm; m 20 May 1857 by J. B. McDade, J. P.

Trice, Page & Susan Leigh, 9 Sept 1834; Aaron Marcom, bm.

Trice, Pleasant & Martha J. Atkins, 14 April 1842; Jno. D. Carlton, bm.

Trice, Shepard & Elizabeth House, 25 Sept 1806; Henry Trice, bm.

Trice, Thomas & Ede Daniel, 5 Aug 1794; Samuel Carlton, bm.

Trice, William & Frances Patterson, 26 May 1788; Ephraim Dickson, bm.

Trice, William & Amelia Trice, 10 Sept 1838; Ilai Davis, Absalom Harvey, bm.

Trice, Willie & Sarah Clemments, 23 Jan 1819; James Child, bm.

Trice, Zachariah & Frances Rhodes, 3 Oct 1813; Thomas Picket, bm.

Trice, Zachariah & Martha Moore, 15 May 1831; James Trice, bm.

Trip, Aaron & Elizabeth Andrews, 24 Feb 1829; Wm. Andrews, Jno. J. Carrington, bm.

Trip, John & Nancy Wilson, 23 Feb 1802; Moses Atwater, bm.

Tripp, Jerry, son of John W. & Nancy Tripp, & Louisa Suit, dau. of Jordan & Elizabeth Suit, m 4 Oct 1867 by N. C. Cate, J. P.

Tripp, Jonathan & Elizabeth Mason, 4 Dec 1823; Thos. Adams, bm.

Tripp, Jonathan W. & Elizabeth Jane Faucett, 7 Jan 1853; Enoch Sykes, bm; m 9 Jan 1853 by Wiatt Cate, J. P.

Tripp, William & Rowan Suit, 15 Aug 1844; W. F. Strowd, bm; m 18 Aug 1864 by J. W. Strowd, J. P.

Trolinger Benjamin N. & Nancy Elizabeth Montgomery, 17 April 1832; Jeremiah Bason, bm.

Trolinger, Fredrick & Absilla Anne Elizabeth Trotman, 28 Feb 1841; Joseph Trolinger, Abel Griffin, bm.

Trolinger, Jacob & Margret Bloushard, 7 April 1815; James Thomas, bm.

Trolinger, Jno. & Elizabeth Roney, 23 Jan 1810; Andrew Roney, bm.

Trollinger, Henry & Polly Blanchett, 25 April 1826; Jno. Trollinger, bm.

Trollinger, John & Polley McCullock, 6 May 1806; Allan McDougall, bm.

Trousdale, James & Sarah Faucet, 30 Nov 1787; James Stockard, bm.

Trousdale, William & Caty McCauley, 26 Dec 1801; Wm. McCauley, bm.

Troxlar, Condestan & Nelly Clap, 1 April 1835; John Calp, bm.

Troxlar, David & Betsey Graves, 5 May 1822; Barnet Troxler, bm.

Troxlar, Haywood & Catharine Geringer, 4 Feb 1840; U. W. Troxler, John Huffman, bm.

Troxler, John & Elizabeth Whitsett, 25 Jan 1817; John Keck, bm.

Troxler, John C. & Fanny Wheeler, 22 Jan 1840; John Huffman, bm.

Troxler, Powell & Mary Whitesill, 8 March 1810; Geo. Troxler, bm.

Truelove, Jesse & Elizabeth Watson, 28 Aug 1815; C. Barbee, bm.

Truette, Willis B. & Elizabeth Dixon, 14 Dec 1836; John Grayson, bm.

Truit, Levi & Polly King, 29 July 1824; Jeremiah King, bm.

Truman, Abraham, son of Winson & Lamania Truman, & Celia Ann White, dau. of David & Celia White, m 21 May 1867 by J. W. Latta, J. P.

Tudor, Henry & Miza Eubank, 3 Dec 1840; Samuel P. Moore, James H. Thompson, bm.

Tudor, Owen & Fanny McClain, 17 Sept 1816; Bradley Collins, bm.

Tufford, Peter & Mary Hill, 13 Aug 1865; William A. Hill, bm; m 13 Aug 1865 by A. C. Murdoch, J. P.

Tulloch, James & Arthrozt Martin, 13 Feb 1802; Norwood Hoskins, bm.

Turner, Andrew & Beddy Cook, 11 Aug 1837; Hugh Waddle, bm.

Turner, Charles & Katy Johnstone, 17 Jan 1815; George Johnston, bm.

Turner, David & Ellenor Tate, 11 Nov 1807; Robt. Tate, bm.

Turner, David & Rosannah Edwards, 28 Nov 1829; William Holmes, bm.

Turner, Edward & Susa Carrigan, 17 June 1794; Henry Dosett, bm.

Turner, Edward & Frances Wesson, 5 April 1825; Thos. W. Holder, bm.

Turner, Elias & Mary Umphris, 12 June 1797; Elias Turner Jr., bm.

Turner, Evans & Emme M. Nichols, 21 Jan 1866; Charles R. Wilson, bm; m 22 Jan 1866 by Thomas U. Faucette.

Turner, Ezekiel A. & Martha Jenkins, 5 April 1850; Charles Christmas, bm.

Turner, Henry & Martha Davis, 11 Nov 1847; Merrell Utley, bm.

Turner, Israel & Peggy Hutchens, 27 Nov 1807; Wm. Stovall, bm.

Turner, Israel & Nancy S. Trice, 27 July 1859; A. B. Gunter, D. C. Gunter, bm; m 28 July 1859 by A. B. Gunter, J. P.

Turner, James & Hannah McCracken, 3 June 1785; Jno. Umstead, bm.

Turner, James & Rebecah Clendening, 25 May 1790; John Johnston, bm.

Turner, James & Sarah Brinkley, 15 Nov 1798; John Agnew, bm.

Turner, James & Nancy Talley, 30 Aug 1813; Jonathan Jones, bm.

Turner, James & Martha W. Neal, 8 Aug 1818; Will Whitted, bm.

Turner, James & Betsey Gibson, 10 Feb 1840; James Quals, bm.

Turner, James Jr. & Mary H. McMannen, 15 April 1863; Geo. Laws, bm; m 16 April 1863 by A. W. Mangum.

Turner, James A. & Nancy Rosson, 16 Jan 1847; Wm. P. Willott, C. E. Smith, bm.

Turner, James A. & Martha Roach, 21 April 1854; Joseph Willett, bm.

Turner, James C. & Elizabeth M. Wilson, 15 March 1865; James S. Maris, bm; m 30 March 1865 by D. W. Jordan, J. P.

Turner, John & Ruth Morrison, 1 Jan 1803; John Milliken, bm.

Turner, John & Salley Talley, 20 Jan 1811; Sterling Talley, Richd. Rickets, bm.

Turner, John & Sally House, 6 Feb 1816; Jesse Vicars, bm.

Turner, John & Louisa Jackson, 29 Jan 1846; Porter Thompson, bm.

Turner, John J. & Elizabeth Rosser, 12 June 1847; Isaac Craig, bm.

Turner, Joseph & Nancy Ivy, 25 Aug 1846; L. L. Loyd, bm.

Turner, Joseph & Louisa A. Farthing, 20 Jan 1859; Isreal Turner, Thomas Webb, bm; m 20 Jan 1859 by John Mitchell.

Turner, Josiah & Susannah Whitted, 5 Dec 1810; S. Turrentine, bm.

Turner, Moses & Elizabeth Thomon, 1 April 1836; Andrew Turner, Jno. Horner, bm.

Turner, William & Ruthey Standifer, 14 Aug 1781; Benjamin Standifer, bm.

Turner, William & Fanny Sutherland, 2 Feb 1797; Nathaniel Hix, bm.

Turner, William & Abigail Piles, 26 July 1813; Thos. Perry, Anthony Holt, bm.

Turner, William & Catharine Clendenin, 12 Nov 1840; James Minnins, John W. Woods, bm.

Turner, William & Leania Partin, 30 May 1848; William Hunt, bm.

Turner, William & Nancy Jane Carr, 13 Dec 1859; Jno. Turner, bm;
m 15 Dec 1859 by Thos. Long, J. P.

Turner, William E. & Ellen Jane Cape, 1 April 1856; Thomas C.
Cate, bm; m 2 April 1856 by Nathl. Bain, J. P.

Turrentine, Absalom & Fanny Wilson, 14 March 1834; Samuel
Turrentine, bm.

Turrentine, Daniel & Elizabeth Steele, 13 Jan 1802; S.
Turrentine, bm.

Turrentine, James & Catherine Clower, 7 Sept 1793.

Turrentine, James & Ellena Neely, 17 Feb 1796; Jno. D. Nealey,
bm.

Turrentine, James Stewart & Elizabeth Wilson, 21 May 1801;
L. Turrentine, bm.

Turrentine, James & Hannah Wilson, 22 Jan 1806; George Wilson,
bm.

Turrentine, James C. & Margaret M. Steel, 18 Jan 1831; J. Taylor,
bm.

Turrentine, James W. & Annie B. Pearce, m 20 Jan 1863 by Wm. E.
Pell, Methodist minister.

Turrentine, Jno. & Nancy Wilson, 13 Aug 1803; James Turrentine,
bm.

Turrentine, John & Mary Barlour, 22 Feb 1791; John Barlour, bm.

Turrentine, John A. & Sallie Vaughan, 29 March 1859, m by P. A.
McMartin, M. G.

Turrentine, John S. & Elizabeth Ray, 26 Oct 1831; John C.
Turrentine, bm.

Turrentine, Meredith & Joseph Parker, 18 March 1867; Lewis
Cain, bm; m 20 March 1867 by A. M. Latta, J. P.

Turrentine, Samuel & Sarah Wilson, 7 Dec 1789; Samuel Wilson,
bm.

Turrentine, Samuel & Nancy Wilson, 2 Dec 1830; John L. Woods, bm.

Turrentine, William G. & Artealia Strowd, 16 May 1866; Henry C.
Oldham, Fred P. Clarke, bm; m 16 May 1866 by H. G. Hill,
M. G.

Turrentine, William H. & Annie Stroud, 10 Feb 1857; J. A.
Turrentine, bm; m 11 Feb 1867 by W. Atwater, Local Deacon.

Tyer, Frederick & Catherine B. Galbreath, 20 Jan 1798; John
Galbraith, bm.

Tyrrell, Edward A. & Susan D. Rice, 1 March 1858; William
Tyrrell, James Gill, bm.

Tyrrell, Joseph & Jenny Allin, 26 Jan 1824; Samuel Allen, bm.

Tyrrell, Solomon & Nancy Parks, 27 May 1824; William Anderson, bm.

Tyson, James & Martha Buroughs, 23 Sept 1857; Jas. Tyson, J. S. Hogans, bm; m 23 Sept 1857 by B. J. Hackny, M. G.

Uliss, Adam & Dorithy Shofner, 20 Aug 1803; Martin Shofner, bm.

Umstead, Daniel & Anna Chizenhall, 20 Oct 1836; J. C. Turrentine, bm.

Umstead, Dewitt & Rebecca Lunsford, 14 Nov 1857; H. McFarlin, bm; m 19 Nov 1857 by Wmson Parrish, J. P.

Umstead, Elisha & Elizabeth Laws, 16 Feb 1811; John Fergerson, bm.

Umstead, J. D. & Edney Tilly, 27 Aug 1855; Wm. McCauly, J. C. Turrentine, bm.

Umsted, Daniel & Mary Roberts, 14 Aug 1800; Wm. Hopkins, bm.

Umsted, David & Mary Laws, 20 March 1826; Jno. Nance Jr., bm.

Umsted, Dewitt C. & Sophronia Parker, 16 Jan 1865; John L. Parrish, bm; m 22 Jan 1865 by D. C. Parrish.

Umsted, Elisha & Rebecca Laws, 12 Nov 1817; Jonathan Laws, bm.

Umsted, John, son of Elisha & Eliza Umsted, & Virginia D. Holloway, dau. of Nathl. & Nancy Holloway, m 10 March 1868 by R. S. Webb, M. G.

Umsted, Smith & Elizabeth Justice, 24 Jan 1867; Jos. G. Piper, bm; m 3 Feb 1867 by Joseph Woods, J. P.

Umsted, William & Mary Furguson, 15 May 1834; Squire D. Umsted, bm.

Underwood, David & Priscilla Melton, 27 April 1804; Edmond Gilliam, bm.

Underwood, John & Sally Sawyer, 14 Nov 1813; William Daily, bm.

Underwood, Reuben & Mariam Lamb, 16 July 1813; Leonard Smith, bm.

Underwood, Thompson & Viney Patton, 22 Aug 1857; Jacob Gant, bm.

Utley, Benton & Martha Hilliard, 28 June 1836; A. K. Clements, Jas. M. Palmer, bm.

Utley, Gray & Eliza Davis, 8 Sept 1857; Wm. B. Vanderford, N. H. Blackwood, bm.

Utley, John A. & Georginna Laws, m 3 Jan 1866 by Samuel Pearce.

Valentine, James & Susan Strudwick, 21 Dec 1848; Richard Mayo, bm.

Valentine, Shadrack & Margaret Carr, 4 June 1814; Merriday Chaners, bm.

Valines, Nathaniel & Eliza Wilson, 10 March 1851; Joseph Woods, bm.

Vanderford, William B. & Sarah Williams, 27 Dec 1837; J. W. Carr, bm.

Vann, Willis J. & Teresa N. Herndon, 5 April 1835; Sam. Child, bm.

Vann, Willis J. & Martha E. Boothe, 19 Nov 1840; James M. Gilbert, C. L. Cooley, bm.

Van Dykes, Wm. Junr. & Mary Battle, 22 July 1861; James Watson, bm.

Van Wyck, William & Mary J. Battle, m 24 July 1861 by Francis W. Hilliard, M. G.

Vaughan, Afford & Ann Collins, 26 Jan 1862; Alexander Riley Wmson Parrish, bm; m 26 Jan 1862 by Wm. J. Roberts, J. P.

Vaughan, Calvin & Betsy Forrester, 20 Sept 1824; John Hopkins, bm.

Vaughan, Jesse C. & Delitha D. Nicholson, 24 Feb 1822; Seymour Puryear, bm.

Vaughan, John & Lotty Stagg, 12 March 1805; Thomas King, bm.

Vaughan, John & Susannah Dossett, 22 Sept 1812; Moses Dossete, bm.

Vaughan, John & Amelia Forrest, 21 Oct 1824; Calvin Vaughan, bm.

Vaughan, Long & Susan Ashley, 21 March 1813; Thomas King, bm.

Vaughan, Sampson & Elizabeth Jones, 28 May 1811; Taylor Duke, bm.

Vaughan, Sampson & Nancy Brown, 25 March 1831; Moses Jones, bm.

Vaughan, Samuel & Edney Ashley, 21 Sept 1859; Arthur L. Carrington, bm.

Vaughan, Sandy W. & Nancy Parker, 1 July 1807; William Wilkinson, bm.

Vaughan, Short & Elizabeth King, 22 Nov 1815; Jonathan Mize, bm.

Vaughan, Short & Nancy Mangum, 22 Nov 1830; Peyton Moser, bm.

Vaughan, Spencer C. & Bethiah Taylor, 14 May 1792; Jno. Casey, bm.

Vaughan, William & Polley Roberts, 5 July 1832; Stephen Ellis, bm.

Vaughan, Daw & Ann Tilley, 1 March 1855; Allen Tilley, M. C. Hall, bm.

Vaughan, James, son of Sampson Vaughan, & Polly Duke, dau. of Talor Duke, 23 Oct 1835; Green Crowder, bm; m 24 Oct 1835 by Andrew Jones.

Veacy, Joseph & Elizabeth Veasy, 15 Dec 1832; Elijah Veazey, bm.

313

Veazey, Abner & Delilah Rhodes, 6 March 1797; Richard Umsted, bm.

Veazey, Abner & Julian Tilley, 25 Dec 1841; Andrew J. Veazey, bm.

Veazey, Edward & Frances Roberts, 11 Nov 1837; Fielding Veazey, bm.

Veazey, Fielding & Winnie Roberts, 4 Oct 1859; A. S. Carrington, bm.

Veazey, Jesse & Salley Peak, 12 March 1783; Solomon Burford, bm.

Veazey, John & Catharine Balden, 20 Oct 1801; Gregory Wilson, bm.

Veazey, William & Annie Umstead, 26 Oct 1784; David Umsted, bm.

Veazey, William H. & Martha A. Wilkerson, 10 Jan 1859; M. Wilkerson, bm; m 11 Jan 1859 by Wm. McCown, J. P.

Vestal, John & Elizabeth Fogleman, 20 March 1816; F. P. Montgomery, bm.

Vestal, William F. & Elizabeth Piper, 19 June 1857; James Y. Whitted, bm.

Vickers, David & Elizabeth Gwinn, 6 April 1800; David Cozart, bm.

Vickers, David & Peny Rhodes, 18 May 1837; N. H. Blackwood, George W. Vickers, bm.

Vickers, Duane & OFelia Massey, 28 Nov 1860; E. W. Pickett, M. H. Turner, bm; m 9 Dec 1860 by Solomon Shepherd, J. P.

Vickers, Elmore & Caroline Gare, 5 March 1851; H. F. Pearson, bm.

Vickers, George W. & Melenda Rhodes, 27 Dec 1840; J. Allison, Daniel Vickers, bm.

Vickers, James & Frances Rhodes, 15 April 1836; Geo. W. Vickers, Jno. Cooley, bm.

Vickers, Jesse & Ruth Turner, 28 Dec 1812; Wm. Horn, bm.

Vickers, John & Nancy Rhodes, 23 Nov 1830; Wm. W. Guess, bm.

Vickers, John & Sarah H. Gooch, 30 Dec 1851; William House, bm; m 31 Dec 1851 by Harris Wilkerson, J. P.

Vickers, Moses & Sarah Menard, 5 April 1858; W. R. Vickers, bm.

Vickers, Rhyley & Mary Cozart, 12 Sept 1791; Thomas Reding, bm.

Vickers, Riley & Catharine Lynn, 22 Feb 1836; John Vickers, bm.

Vickers, Riley & Ann Mariah Ellis, 26 Feb 1846; M. A. Angier, bm.

Vickers, Rilley & Cynthia Watson, 11 April 1804; David Vickers, bm.

Vickers, Rilley & Cynthia Watson, 11 July 1804; Daniel Watson, bm.

Vickers, Washington M. & Sarah Jane Chesenhall, 4 Jan 1862;
    Presley J. Mangum, bm; m 5 Jan 1862 by S. Shepherd, J. P.

Vickers, William & Milligan Grissom, 8 Aug 1781; Moses Herrin,
    bm.

Vickers, William G. & Nancy E. Chesenhall, 17 Aug 1859; Presley
    J. Mangum, bm; m 18 Aug 1859 by M. A. Angier, J. P.

Vincent, Alexander & Frances Strut, 27 Sept 1805; John Dawley,
    bm.

Vincent, Thomas & Nancy Barnwell, 28 July 1825; John Barnwell,
    Robert Marron, bm.

Vincent, William B. & Linnah Shaw, 25 Jan 1820; Andw. Murray, bm.

Waddell, Henry M. & Elizabeth B. Brownrigg, 14 Sept 1853; Hugh
    Waddell, Geo. W. Bruce, bm; m 19 Sept 1853 by J. T. Wheate,
    M. G.

Waddell, John A. & Susan C. Davis, 27 Feb 1854; John Hutchins,
    bm; m 27 Feb 1854 by S. S. Burke.

Waggoner, George & Rebeccah Whitsell, 28 Jan 1816; Christian
    Whitsel, bm.

Waggoner, Henry & Judith Dunnegan, 27 Jan 1796; Wm. Belvin, bm.

Waggoner, Henry & Sarah Jane Waggoner, m 13 Sept 1860 by John L.
    Woods, J. P.

Waggoner, John & Boring Dunagan, 31 March 1794; James Dunagan,
    bm.

Waggoner, John & Salley Leathers, 6 April 1805; Leonard Laws,
    bm.

Waggoner, John & Sally Carey, 30 May 1812; Thomas Horner, bm.

Waggoner, John Jr. & Edney Watson, 20 May 1857; James P.
    Hopkins, bm.

Waggoner, Murphy & Mary Ray, 17 Aug 1840; Nelson McKee, bm.

Waggoner, Peter Jr. & Elizabeth Branock, 7 Jan 1824; John
    Lackney, bm.

Waggoner, Riley & Susan Rippey, 22 Sept 1840; Eli Cudle, H. J.
    Mann, bm.

Waggoner, Valentine & Hannah Tate, 5 Sept 1818; George
    Waggoner, bm.

Waggoner, William & Jane Rippey, 2 Aug 1835; Jesse Rippy, bm.

Waggoner, William & Charlotte Berry, 18 Aug 1837; William Gates,
    Henderson Taylor, bm.

Waggoner, William & Hannah Horner, 25 Jan 1849; Anderson Smith,
    bm.

Waggoner, William & Luvina Wilson, 7 7 Oct 1855 by Hezekiah Terry, J. P.

Waggoner, Wilson & Holly Davis, 13 Sept 1853; C. S. Dunnagan, bm; m 13 Sept 1853 by Hezekiah Terry, J. P.

Wagoner, George & Sarah Roberts, 13 Nov 1802; Ephraim Roberts, bm.

Wagoner, George & Turley Whitsell, 3 Aug 1817; C. Whitsell, bm.

Wagoner, Henry & Jane Dollar, 5 Feb 1862; John Gates, Jno. Lockhart, bm; m 5 Feb 1862 by Lambert W. Hall, J. P.

Wagoner, Henry & Mary C. Pettegrew, 3 Oct 1865; John Laws, bm; m 5 Oct 1865 by C. Wilson, J. P.

Wagoner, Jacob & Mary Horner, 4 Sept 1839; James Horner, bm.

Wagoner, James & Nancy E. Berry, 11 June 1849; Wm. H. Horner, bm.

Wagoner, James L. & Margaret Ray, 8 Oct 1836; J. C. Turrentine, bm.

Wagoner, James L. & Sarah Ann Terry, 19 July 1852; J. E. Wilkerson, Wm. Wilkinson, bm; m 4 Aug 1852 by Hezekiah Terry, J. P.

Wagoner, John & Susan Parker, 11 Feb 1851; J. C. Turner, bm; m 22 Jan 1852 by Hezekiah Terry, J. P.

Wagoner, John P. & Elizabeth Blalock, 12 March 1866; William Parker, bm; J. W. Cole, bm; m 22 March 1866 by H. Terry, J. P.

Wagoner, Murphey & Betsey Jane Bradford, 20 Nov 1848; William R. Ray, Wm. Nelson, bm.

Wagoner, Peter & Margaret McCracken, 7 April 1800; John Writsman, bm.

Wagoner, William & Luvenia Wilson, 4 Oct 1855; E. D. Oakley, James Gill, bm.

Wagoner, William & Sarah Jane Wagoner, 11 Sept 1860; Henry Wagoner, Anderson Toler, bm.

Wainwright, T. A. & Jane R. Carrington, 14 June 1854; Wm. K. Parrish, bm.

Wait, George N., son of Kendal B. & Emily Wait, & Mary A. Jones, dau. of Richard & Caroline Jones, m 20 May 1868 by H. B. Pratt.

Walden, Bartley & Matilda McBain, 10 Dec 1829; Abram Burnett, bm.

Walis, John & Mary Bird, 1 May 1815; Joseph Byrd, bm.

* Wallis, Doctrin & Nancy King, 28 Dec 1817; George Hurdle, bm.

* Wallis, Henry & Martha Brooks, 6 May 1861; Willies Freeman, bm; m 7 May 1861 by R. G. Tinnin.

Walker, Aaron & Sarah Bird, 29 March 1797; James Bird, bm.

*Out of alphabetical sequence.

Walker, Abner & Mary Fosset, 15 Sept 1797; Ralph Faussett, bm.

Walker, Abram & Agnis Mebane, 21 Nov 1865; Archy Harbor, bm; m 23 Nov 1865 by C. W. Chkk.

Walker, Adison & Mary Williams, 26 March 1861; Andrew Hall, Thomas D. Faucet, bm.

Walker, Anderson & Daphny Williams, 7 May 1866; Abner Banks, bm; m 7 May 1866 by R. F. Morris, J. P.

Walker, John & Phebe Picket, 19 Nov 1793; Andrew Walker, bm.

Walker, Ashford & Nancy Cantrell, 18 Aug 1804; Hugh Walker, bm.

Walker, Ashford & Phebe Bird, 13 July 1811; Jno. McCauly, bm.

Walker, Bedford & Mary F. Sellars, 2 Oct 1843; Samuel Crawford, bm.

Walker, Burk & Polley Cate, 16 May 1808; Richd. Cate, bm.

Walker, Burk & Patsey Lloyd, 26 Oct 1846; S. H. Turrentine, bm.

Walker, Connoley & Elizabeth Crawford, 15 May 1800; Samuel Crawford, bm.

Walker, Eaton & Cynthia Jones, 23 Jan 1838; John C. Sykes, bm.

Walker, Eaton & Mahala Thompson, 3 Oct 1839; B. C. Beck, bm.

Walker, Eaton & Ellen Sharp, 8 June 1864; John Laws, bm; m 9 June 1864 by A. C. Murdoch, J. P.

Walker, Fenner M. & Frances Mebane, 7 Sept 1840; G. D. Jordan, bm.

Walker, Fenner M., son of Wm. P. & Margaret Walker, & Susan Lynch, dau. of Thomas & Mary Lynch, m 31 Dec 1867 by Thos. Lynch.

Walker, Freeman & Christian Hurdle, 19 Oct 1831; James Forrest, bm.

Walker, George & Lucy Dorch, 11 Oct 1837; Jesse James, bm.

Walker, George & Mary Sellars, 13 Dec 1848; Robert G. Tinnin, bm.

Walker, George, son of George & Lucy Walker, & Frances Crabtree, dau. of Wm. & Cyntha Crabtree, m 17 Nov 1867 by C. J. Freeland, J. P.

Walker, Hinton & Milly Coulter, 2 Oct 1834; Samuel Thompson, bm.

Walker, Hugh & Fanny Grahams, 30 Aug 1806; John Grahams, bm.

Walker, Jacob & Elizabeth F. Whitecar, 26 Nov 1866; T. H. Compton, bm; m 4 Dec 1866 by Robert G. Tinnin.

Walker, James & Jeany Shaw, 1 Aug 1813; Aaron Walker, bm.

Walker, James & Jane Rider, 2 Dec 1825; Elexander Techy, bm.

Walker, James & Nancy Hurdle, 16 Feb 1837; Freeman Walker, bm.

Walker, James, son of John & Mary Walker, & Fanny Ragan, dau. of Thomas & Nancy Riggins, m 2 April 1868 by L. W. Hall, J. P.

Walker, James H. & Margaret C. Compton, 10 Aug 1855; J. W. Compton, Geo. W. Bruce, bm.

Walker, James N., son of Phillis Walker, & Harriett A. White, dau. of Jordan White & Anna Thompson, colored, m 3 Oct 1867 by Wilson Brown, J. P.

Walker, Jeremiah & Malinda Roberts, 26 July 1826; William Ashley, bm.

Walker, Jesse & Elizabeth Umstead, 29 Aug 1818; Jonathan Montgomery, bm.

Walker, Job & Sarah Garrison, 12 Aug 1810; George Walker, bm.

Walker, John & Jane Grimes, 25 Dec 1793; Philip Walker, bm.

Walker, John & Janett Morrow, 28 Jan 1812; Robert Morrow, bm.

Walker, John & Polley P. Latta, 2 Oct 1829; Jacob Wagoner, bm.

Walker, John & Jane G. Walker, 14 July 1831; A. Parks, bm.

Walker, John & Wady Workman, 11 Feb 1841; Henry Workman, bm.

Walker, John & Mary Maynard, 3 Sept 1842; George G. Walker, Moses Leathers, Jr., bm.

Walker, John A. & Eliza A. Sellers, 18 Aug 1848; William I. Murrey, bm.

Walker, Joshua & Rachel Garrison, 28 Oct 1809; Job Walker, bm.

Walker, Levi & Rachel Hurdle, 15 Dec 1830; Benj. Hurdle, bm.

Walker, Levi S. & Sarah A. Walker, 19 Oct 1863; William Faucett, bm; m 19 Oct 1863 by Benjamin J. Kinnion, J. P.

Walker, Peter & Elizabeth Hamilton, 10 March 1801; William Bradford, Thos. Whitted, bm.

Walker, Peter & Jinnett Armstrong, 18 Dec 1816; John Armstrong, bm.

Walker, Philip & Jiles Patten, 17 Dec 1790; Jno. Walker, bm.

Walker, Philip & Rebecca King, 15 Feb 1816; J. Taylor, bm.

Walker, Phillip & Harriet Wilson, 27 Aug 1837; Ezekiel Lewis, bm.

Walker, Robert & Ellenor Latta, 18 April 1791; Wm. Walker, bm.

Walker, Robert & Charlotte S. Reeves, 22 Nov 1830; Wm. Shaw, bm.

Walker, Robert S. & Letha Ann Woods, 22 Aug 1863; Willie P. Lilley, bm; m 23 Aug 1863 by C. Wilson, J. P.

Walker, Sydny W. & Mary F. Burch, 18 April 1866; Thos. S. Cates, bm; m 19 April 1866 by Alvis Durham, J. P.

Walker, William & Deborah McCulloch, 21 May 1795; Aaron Walker, bm.

Walker, William & Rachel Murrow, 27 May 1800; James Murray, bm.

Walker, William & Margret Bason, 12 March 1803; Fredrick Bason, Robert Mebane, bm.

Walker, William & Mary Wilkinson, 3 Sept 1839; John Wilkinson, C. M. Latimer, bm.

Walker, William & Hannah Andrews, 29 Jan 1840; John Williams, John Walker, bm.

Walker, William D. & Amelia Carrington, 16 Dec 1836; James Roberts, Anthony Doherty, bm.

Walker, William J. & Elizabeth W. Hester, 12 Nov 1856; Robert Faucett, bm; m 13 Nov 1856 by John Stadler.

Wall, Noah & Frances Ray, 1 April 1840; Henry Wall, bm.

Wall, William & Peggy Coonrod, 21 March 1812; Robt. Glenn, bm.

Wall, William & Peggy Raingstaff, 28 Feb 1813; Tho. Anderson, bm.

Wallace, Blount & Willie Dishon, 12 Sept 1825; J. McKerall, bm.

Wallace, Orren & Sarah Woods, 27 Nov 1807; John Jackson, bm.

Wallace, William & Mary Parks, 22 May 1825; Abel Griffis, Thos. Clancy, bm.

Wallan, William & Patsey Merrett, 28 Nov 1833; Wm. Brinkley, Even Jeffrey, bm.

Waller, Job & ____, 24 Sept 1791; William Peek, bm.

Waller, John & Jenny Laws, 4 Dec 1802; William Madeson, bm.

Waller, William & Jane Horner, 23 Sept 1850; Frederick Horner, bm.

Walles, Thomas & Priscella Huntington, 8 Nov 1814; Thos. Clancy, bm.

*
Walls, William & Lotte Thompson, 16 Oct 1799; John S. Thompson, bm.

Ward, Alfred & Chaney Ward, 5 March 1836; Stephen Ward, bm.

Ward, Archiebald & Nelly Barber, 16 Oct 1824; Shad Ward, bm.

Ward, Barzilia & Cornelia Ann Hessey, 20 Dec 1845; Wm. Ward, bm.

Ward, David & Nancy Ward, 31 March 1837; Shad Ward, D. K. Blackwood, bm.

Ward, Edward J. & Emeline B. Parker, 2 Sept 1839; James M. Palmer, Jno. M. Faucett, bm.

Ward, Eno & Elizabeth Henshaw, 12 June 1813; Isaac Henshaw, bm.

Ward, Hugh & Elizabeth Whiteheart, 10 July 1821; Archb. Ward, bm.

Ward, James M. & Harriet Blackwood, 30 Sept 1852; John Cheek, bm.

*For Wallis, see p. 316.   319

Ward, John & Jemima Walton, 8 June 1786; James Taylor, bm.

Ward, John & Linney Crompton, 15 March 1809; Sutton Ward, bm.

Ward, John & Mary F. McCaddams, 3 Jan 1846; William M'Cadams, bm.

Ward, John & Mandra Parten, 20 April 1850; J. B. McDade, bm.

Ward, Joshua & Polly Williams, 14 April 1817; Shadrick Ward, bm.

Ward, Josiah & Susannah Freshwater, 4 Feb 1826; John Moore, bm.

Ward, Lemuel & Rebecca Jane Debruler, 29 Dec 1853; James Debruler, bm.

Ward, Luke & Nancy Perry, 1 May 1823; Archb. Ward, bm.

Ward, Shadrich & Delilah Compton, 10 Sept 1818; Shadrich Ward, bm.

Ward, Stephen & Fanny Christopher, 16 Dec 1836; Wm. Ward, bm.

Ward, Stephen D. & Martha A. Ward, 6 June 1866; John H. Ward, C. E. Parrish, bm; m 8 June 1866 by F. L. Oakley, M. G.

Ward, Sutton & Nancey Crabtree, 12 March 1784; Ezekl. Chance, bm.

Ward, Sutton M. & Sarah Sharp, 6 Nov 1859; W. R. Sharp, bm.

Ward, Thomas & Nancy Crompton, 3 June 1813; J. Taylor, bm.

Ward, William & Anne Scott, 23 Nov 1811; Thomas Ward, Erasmus Crompton, bm.

Ward, William & Margaret Jackson, 5 Feb 1822; D. B. Alsobrook, bm.

Ward, William & Eliza Christopher, 17 Jan 1837; James Williams, I. C. Turrentine, bm.

Ward, William H. & Martha Tutterton, 22 Dec 1865; J. M. Scott, bm; m 24 Dec 1865 by F. L. Oakley, M. G.

Ward, Yancy G. & Nancy C. Ward, 22 Feb 1866; B. G. Ward, John Laws, bm; m 25 Feb 1866 by F. L. Oakley, M. G.

Wardrake, Willis & Elizabeth Murray, 11 June 1809; Francis Marshill, bm.

Ware, William & Lucy Burriss, 27 Dec 1796; William Ryly, bm.

Warnock, James & Peggy Bradford, 23 Sept 1798; Thomas Bradford, bm.

Warren, Biscoc & Adeline Troxler, 16 March 1824; Charles S Darren, bm.

Warren, Charles S. & Nancy Berry, 6 March 1826; John Cooley, bm.

Warren, Chesley P. & Julia A. Dunnagan, 27 Feb 1849; Sherwood H. Garrard, bm.

Warren, David & Polly Rhodes, 22 Sept 1812; Noah Rhodes, bm.

Warren, David & Polly Guess, 19 May 1828; John Guess, bm.

Warren, David C. & Susan Capley, 14 June 1860; William Warren, John Laws, bm.

Warren, James & Rhody Grisham, 11 May 1809; Robert Gresham, bm.

Warren, James & Francis Vickers, 10 Nov 1844; Thos. Warren, Thomas Hogan, bm.

Warren, James T. & Emily Harris, 2 July 1833; Thomas Latta, bm.

Warren, Jasper, son of Samuel & Emily Wells, & Jane Crumpton, dau. of Manirva Crumpton, colored, m 3 Jan 1868 by D. W. Jordan, J. P.

Warren, John & Susannah Couch, 30 April 1835; Elijah Couch, bm.

Warren, John H. & Louisa J. Lasslie, 19 Dec 1832; John W. Shaw, bm.

Warren, Josiah & Elizabeth Scoggin, 3 Jan 1822; James Warren, bm.

Warren, Ridly & Fanny Pollard, 10 Feb 1811; Woodson Daniel, Major Pollard, bm.

Warren, Thomas & Elizabeth Woods, 17 Nov 1835; James Warren, bm.

Warren, Thomas D. (Dr.) & Elizabeth A. Collins, 12 Jan 1863; Will H. Standin, bm; m 12 Jan 1863 by M. A. Curtis, minister.

Warren, William & Mary Beazle, 27 Jan 1795; Isham Hazle, bm.

Warren, William & Jane Fulton, 6 Dec 1795; James Fulton, bm.

Warren, William & Polly Vickers, 9 Jan 1836; James Brockwell, bm.

Warren, William & Ann Latta, 5 Dec 1855; Kenchen Leather, bm.

Warson, John & Salley Fogleman, 15 Jan 1826; William Loy, bm.

Washburn, Thomas & Peggy Polston, 22 Nov 1819; Thomas Reeves, bm.

Wason, Alexander & Easter Hanley, 15 Oct 1794; James Stanford, bm.

Wason, John & Nancy Murphey, 14 Jan 1799; David McCaules, bm.

Wason, Robert & Margott Foster, 12 Dec 1796; Edeson Foster, bm.

Waston, James & Nancey Nealy, 18 Oct 1842; Jno. M. Faucett, Moses Leathers Jun., bm.

Watford, Alexander & Eliza J. Anderson, 3 June 1866; A. M. Rigsbee, bm; m 3 June 1866 by R. F. Morris.

Watkins, Lewis S. & Laura L. Lyon, 16 Oct 1865; Thos. Dickson, bm; m 24 Oct 1865 by Samuel Pearce, M. G.

Watson, Andrew & Nancy Comb, 5 Feb 1800; Jos. Watson, bm.

Watson, Andrew & Teletha Williams, 8 Dec 1860; Ruffin R. Tapp, bm.

Watson, Barbee & Milley Marcum, 15 Feb 1799; Daniel Watson, bm.

Watson, Barby & Elizabeth Watson, 19 Dec 1806; Robert Faucett, bm.

Watson, Bennett & Betsy Hastings, 1 Feb 1797; Henry Hasting, bm.

Watson, Charles & Polley Ashley, 31 May 1839; Alves Nichols, Felix Wilson, bm.

Watson, Daniel & Polley Deuarm, 26 May 1785; Jno. Go. Reacher, bm.

Watson, Daniel & Elisabeth Neugee, 19 March 1792; Daniel Watson, bm.

Watson, Eli & Rachel Garrison, 2 Nov 1840; Thos. Anderson, bm.

Watson, George & Mary Allison, 29 May 1798; Hugh Montgomery, bm.

Watson, Goodwin & Holly Rigsby, 3 Feb 1802; Job Pendergrass, bm.

Watson, Green & Mildred Clinton, 12 April 1836; John Clinton, R. Stanford, bm.

Watson, Hugh & Ferabee Glenn, 28 Nov 1803; George Carrington, bm.

Watson, Isaac & Polley Hogan, 15 Sept 1801; Bennett Watson, bm.

Watson, James & Susannah Riggs, 21 Jan 1794; Jno. Watson, bm.

Watson, James & Susannah Woods, 29 Dec 1804; Solomon May, bm.

Watson, James & Margret Faucett, 11 April 1810; Mark Watson, bm.

Watson, James & Vastine Proctor, 8 March 1861; William A. Stagg, bm; m 10 March 1861 by Wm. J. Duke, J. P.

Watson, James M. & Sarah McCauley, 29 Dec 1838; Johnston McCauley, bm.

Watson, James S. & Mary Susan Holloway, 1 Dec 1852; J. S. Watson, J. Sorlette, bm; m 1 Dec 1852 by Wm. W. Albea, M. G.

Watson, James Y. & Mary L. Gattis, 5 Oct 1850; J. B. McDade, bm.

Watson, Jesulius & Emily Clifton, 10 March 1832; Jessie Wm. Smith, bm.

Watson, John & Jean Torintine, 29 Dec 1789; James Watson, bm.

Watson, John & Elizabeth Howard, 3 Feb 1808; Andrew Watson, bm.

Watson, John & Marget Williams, 29 July 1863; Thos. Garrett, bm; m 30 July 1863 by Wm. J. Duke. J. P.

Watson, Jonathan & Nelly Harris, 17 Sept 1802; John Faddis, bm.

Watson, Jones & Jane Mitchell, 9 Sept 1833; John Blake, V. M. Murphey, bm.

Watson, Mark & Patsy Breeze, 2 March 1803; David Ray, bm.

Watson, Robert & Miram Cate, 7 Nov 1816; Hosea Christmas, bm.

Watson, Thomas E. & Sarah F. Partridge, 30 June 1853; J. Thos
Wheat, bm; m 30 June 1863 by James L. Fisher, M. G.

Watson, William & Polley Brogg, 18 Sept 1807; John Young, bm.

Watson, William & Sarah Laws, 4 May 1819; Saml. Wortham, bm.

Watson, William & Polly Rhew, 30 May 1854; Edward Crabtree, bm.

Watson, William & Adilled Burton, m 6 Feb 1858 by H. Terry.

Watson, William M. & Mary A. C. Poltier, 6 April 1837; M. W.
Davis, J. C. Turrentine, bm.

Watson, Willson & Margaret Watson, 6 Jan 1828; Ja. R. Watson,
bm.

Watters, William & Mary Moore, 11 Aug 1788; J. Estes, bm.

Watts, John M. & Malinda Proctor, 30 Oct 1866; m 1 Nov 1866
by B. C. Hopkins, J. P.

Watts, Josiah & Susanna Courtney, 25 Jan 1782; John Allison, bm.

Watts, Thomas & Sarah Stubbins, 15 March 1798; S. Benton, bm.

Way, Amos & Mary McClennon, 29 July 1815; Nathan Wells, bm.

Wboen, William E. & Louisa Brewer, 13 Oct 1866; William Stream,
bm; m 14 Oct 1866 by Thos. Long, J. P.

Weatherton, Furney & Candis Rose, 30 Aug 1835; Jonathan C. Gant,
bm.

Weaver, Adkinson D. & Rutha Arnold, 7 Dec 1857; Henry Morris,
bm; m 7 Dec 1857 by Wm. M. Carrington, J. P.

Weaver, Allen & Elizabeth Clark, 27 Sept 1829; Peter S. Clark,
bm.

Weaver, Ambros & Phillis Meeks, 8 May 1866; John Amis, bm;
m 8 May 1866 by R. F. Morris.

Weaver, Arthur & Sarah Price, 30 May 1805; John Millison, bm.

Weaver, Bryant & Salley Day, 31 Dec 1828; William Weaver, bm.

Weaver, Charles & Delilah Harvey, colored, m 20 March 1866 by
D. C. McDade, J. P.

Weaver, Daniel H. & Patsy Bowden, 30 Dec 1822; Moses Harper, bm.

Weaver, David & Patsey Bird, 29 Oct 1828; John Alves, bm.

Weaver, James & Polley Johnston, 14 March 1827; Tapley P.
Pickett, bm.

Weaver, John & Betsy Wattleton, 15 March 1803; Thimothy Weaver,
bm.

Weaver, John & Nancy Faucett, 4 Sept 1839; John Lewis, Samuel
D. Strain, bm.

Weaver, John H. & Martha Jane Clayton, 31 Aug 1863; J. R. Hutchins, bm; m 1 Sept 1863 by James Phillips, D. D.

Weaver, Levin & Sally Saveyd, 4 Feb 1854; William Mayo, bm; m 5 Feb 1854 by H. Wilkerson, J. P.

Weaver, Major & Polley Scott, 20 Dec 1821; Thomas Flint, bm.

Weaver, Tian & Sally Chavis, 19 Aug 1841; Saml. Jeffreys, bm.

Weaver, Simon & Salley Pulley, 25 Feb 1827; Elijah Harris, bm.

Weaver, Simon & Susan Harris, 19 Dec 1856; Chesley Bass, bm.

Weaver, Thomas & Salley Brewer, 20 Oct 180_; Isham Brewer, bm.

Weaver, William & Polly Burnet, 17 March 1848; Silas Meredith, bm.

Weaddon, Tykee & Emily Giles, 1 Nov 1830; James Vincent, bm.

Web, Wm. & Malinda White, m 24 Feb 1856 by Allen Edwards, J. P.

Webb, James & Anne Husk, 12 Feb 1807; Richd. Henderson, bm.

Webb, James & Sarah Jane Thomas, 16 Nov 1841; Elizah Crawford, bm.

Webb, John & Elizabeth Bryan (no date); Thaddeus Freshwater, bm.

Webb, Johnston & Polley Cheek, 15 Jan 1822; David Freshwater, bm.

Webb, Jonston & Patsey Smith, 18 Nov 1822; John Moore, bm.

Webb, Richard & Louisa Horton, colored, 1 Dec 1866; John M. Blackwood, bm; m 2 Dec 1866 by C. J. Freeland, J. P.

Webb, Samuel & Mary Partin, 18 Sept 1815; James Partin, bm.

Webb, Samuel & Barbary Younger, 10 Aug 1824; John C. Younger, bm.

Webb, Thomas & Robina Norwood, 16 Nov 1854; m by R. Burwell, minister.

Webb, William & Elizabeth Grimes, 28 Feb 1786; Walter Slaughter, bm.

Webb, William M. & Malinda Wright, 22 Feb 1856; John T. Robeson, bm; m 24 Feb 1856 by Allen Edwards, J. P.

Webbs, Robert F. & Amanda F. Mangum, 6 Jan 1849; James R. Willis, bm.

Webster, Charles & Rachel Holt, 10 Sept 1807; Henry Fogleman, bm.

Webster, Robert & Margaret Merett, 23 Jan 1867; Willis Smith, bm; m 24 Jan 1867 by Geo. W. Purifoy, M. G.

Webster, William & Ann Ray, 30 March 1830; Jacob Holt, bm.

Wedding, Joseph & Louisa Burton, 11 Sept 1838; Felix Wilson, bm.

Weeden, Harrison & Sarah Fossett, 24 Dec 1824; Thomas Gorham, bm.

Weemes, John & Sarah Jones, 28 March 1791; Samuel Allen, bm.

Weemes, Wm. & Mary Eduard, 30 Oct 1791; Abraham Allen, bm.

Weever, Alexander & Esther Morgan, 18 Jan 1850; William Mangum, bm.

Welbon, John D. & Caroline Coolby, 17 Sept 1849; Elmore Woods, bm.

Welch, Jonathan & Mary Johnston, 11 Aug 1823; D. C. Johnston, bm.

Weldon, Samuel & Sady Piles, 24 March 1834; Joel Boon, bm.

Well, Alexander & Vina Woody, 1 March 1827; R. Thompson, bm.

Wells, Elisha L. & Elizabeth Smith, 10 Jan 1837; John M. Wells, bm.

Wells, James M. & Nancy J. Carroll, 12 Jan 1861; A. J. Carroll, bm; m 12 Jan 1861 by Solomon Shepherd, J. P.

Wells, John & Rebecca Herndon, 28 March 1806; George Herndon, bm.

Wells, John & Nancy Davis, 18 Jan 1830; Isaiah Hornaday, bm.

Wells, John H. & Marian Hester, 24 Jan 1838; John C. Smith, bm.

Wells, Joseph & Sarah Stoner, 13 Aug 1815; Isaiah Hornaday, bm.

Wells, Joseph & Ruth Horniday, 16 Dec 1819; John Teayrell, bm.

Wells, Joseph & Mary Johnson, 19 Jan 1833; Mebane Grahams, bm.

Wells, Miles Jr. & Mary Hardy, 9 Feb 1820; Willis Wells, bm.

Wells, Nathan & Mary Stafford, 9 Sept 1815; Pegleg Gifford, bm.

Wells, Stephen & Sarah Williams, 15 Sept 1802; John Wells, William Wells, bm.

Wells, William & Rosannah Stoner, 3 Dec 1812; Jo. Clendenin, Isaac Marshall, bm.

Wells, William & Nancy Alexander, 1 Nov 1821; Daniel Stoner, bm.

Wells, William W. & Rachel Compton, 29 Nov 1839; J. H. Wells, bm.

Wells, Willis & Elizabeth Herndon, 15 Oct 1806; Benjamin Bowles, bm.

Wells, Zachariah & Elizabeth Freeman, 17 July 1799; Henry Underwood, bm.

Welwhite, Lewis & Fanny Christmas, 19 Dec 1813.

Wesson, Littlebury & Frances Carrigan, 1 Feb 1816; M. Williams, bm.

West, Equilla & Levi Massey, 6 July 1788; James Quin, bm.

Wetson, Edward & Jane Tinning, 22 Jan 1803; M. Hart, bm.

Wever, Allen & Mary Ann Lashley, 8 Dec 1850; Joseph Crawford, bm.

Wever, William & Kiziah Izel, 1 Oct 1812; James Milliken, bm.

Whedbee, Benjamin & Sarah Holt, 5 Jan 1805; Robert Dixon, bm.

Whedbee, Joseph R. & Mary Albright, 16 April 1832; Wm. H. Whedbee, bm.

Whedbee, Samuel C. & Mary Huffman, 24 Dec 1829; Joseph R. Wheebee, bm.

Wheeler, America & Sarah Laws, 27 Nov 1826; James Laws, bm.

Wheeles, Benjamin & Amy Mansfield, 15 March 1829; Wm. Mansfield, bm.

Wheeles, Philip & Mary Compton, 13 Dec 1862; William Compton, bm.

Whitakar, Isaac & Catharine Horn, 6 Jan 1785; Edward Riley, bm.

Whitaker, Abraham & Elizabeth Copley, 6 Jan 1801; John Whitaker, bm.

Whitaker, Andrew J. & Elizabeth F. Tinnen, 21 Jan 1864; Archibald C. Hunter, bm.

Whitaker, Burton & Bedy Umstead, 19 Dec 1840; Amest Smith, Elisha Umstead, bm.

Whitaker, Chrisley & Dolly Pearson, 6 Jan 1840; James Tilley, Lamuel Carrell, bm.

Whitaker, Isaac & Sarah Clinton, 22 July 1823; William Whitaker, bm.

Whitaker, Jacob & Polley Reading, 16 May 1805; Abram Whittaker, bm.

Whitaker, James & Peggy Laycock, 25 Feb 1817; Timothy T. Laycock, bm.

Whitaker, James & Sarah Pendergrass, 11 June 1850; R. T. Wells, bm.

Whitaker, James S. & Frances C. Collins, 17 Dec 1859; James E. Wilkinson, Thomas Webb, bm; m 22 Dec 1859 by F. M. Jordon, M. G.

Whitaker, John & Elizabeth Johnston, 11 June 1830; J. G. Blackwoods, bm.

Whitaker, John & Suckey Holloway, 12 Sept 1791; Abimelech Barbee, bm.

Whitaker, John & Patsy Stephens, 19 June 1829; And. Borland, bm.

Whitaker, John & Nancy E. Whitaker, 2 Dec 1856; John H. Wilkerson, William Brown, bm.

Whitaker, Ruffin & Sarah Cheek, 31 Jan 1867; Alvis L. Daniel, bm; m 31 Jan 1867 by N. W. Wilson.

Whitaker, Thomas & Nancy Proctor, 21 Dec 1824; James Whitaker, bm.

Whitaker, Thomas & Mary McCauley, 15 Aug 1866; George Pipier, J. M. Blackwood, bm.

Whitaker, William & Lucy Holloway, 4 March 1797; William Wood, bm.

Whitaker, William & Polley Lewis, 23 Dec 1825; Andrew Browning, bm.

Whitaker, Young P. & Minerva Ann Lynch, 29 March 1849; Wilson Jackson, C. S. Warren, bm.

Whitamore, Henry & Nancy Turner, 4 Aug 1847; James Browning, Archd. Borland, bm.

White, David & Elizabeth Allen, 5 April 1799; James Clindenen, bm.

White, Edmond C. & Julia Collier, 27 April 1854; L. H. Newton, bm; m 27 April 1854 by S. S. Burkhead, minister.

White, Edwin H. & Frances E. Saunderson, 7 March 1848; Josiah Turner Jr., E. G. Gray, bm.

White, J. Thomas & Mary Ellis, 20 Dec 1833; Robt. F. White, bm.

White, J. W. & Elizabeth Moore, 24 Sept 1856; H. J. Stone, bm.

White, James & Milly Faucett, 28 Jan 1804; George Fossett, bm.

White, John & Elizabeth Show, 26 March 1802; Henry Thomson, bm.

White, John & Jeannah Hatchel, 11 Feb 1809; William Hatchett, John Harvy, bm.

White, Joseph & Hannah Bryant, 18 Aug 1799; Thomas Tate, bm.

White, Joseph & Elizabeth Couch, 7 July 1807; William White, bm.

White, Joseph & Polly Rhodes, 5 Aug 1825; William Couch, bm.

White, Joseph & Nancy Couch, 26 May 1835; John Craig, bm.

White, Ludum & Margaret Dishon, 14 July 1798; Henry Thomas Jr., bm.

White, Mark & Elizabeth Duncan, 29 Oct 1813; Willis Johnson, bm.

White, Robert F. & Mary N. Woods, 8 Dec 1846; G. W. White, bm.

White, Samuel & Nancy Mebane, 11 Feb 1808; Thos. Anderson, bm.

White, Samuel & Sarah Andrews, 14 Aug 1838; Matthew Cooper, bm.

White, Samuel C., son of W. W. & E. E. White, & Mallie G. Utley, dau. of Foster & Sallie Utley, m 19 Dec 1867 by A. S. Brent.

White, Samuel M. & Adaline V. Puryear, 23 Nov 1848; H. Scott, bm.

White, Stephen & Cynthia Bradley, 11 July 1821.

White, Stephen & Elizabeth Long, 16 Oct 1822; John Scott, bm.

White, Stephen & Issabella Johnston, 16 Dec 1832; James Johnston, bm.

White, Stephen A. & Mary J. Woods, 14 May 1856; David A. Mebane, bm.

White, Thomas V. & Mary E. Pleasant, 20 Dec 1855; Geo Laws, bm; m 20 Dec 1855 by R. Burwell.

White, William & Susannah Davis, 23 Aug 1792; William Rickets, bm.

White, William & Lucy Collier, 12 May 1824; Loften G. E. Pray, bm.

White, William & Matilda Melvin, 15 Nov 1848; Thomas Thomas, bm.

White, Willie H. & Mary A. Southerland, 28 Dec 1839; James Webb, bm.

White, Zachariah & Susanah Bets, 19 April 1821; Jos. Forshee, bm.

Whitefield, John Toler & Elizabeth Thomas, 1 Oct 1799; William Whitefield, bm.

Whitehart, Willy & Salley Barnhill, 6 May 1806; William Lasley, bm.

Whitehead, John & Susannah Watts, 7 Jan 1798.

Whitesel, David & Eliza Greeson, 11 June 1838; Jacob Cable, bm.

Whitesell, Emsley & Maria May, 26 Jan 1847; Emanuel Cole, bm.

Whitfield, John & Charlott Wilkerson, 11 Sept 1857; Benjamin S. Hunter, bm; m 13 Sept 1857 by William J. Roberts, J. P.

Whitfield, William F. & Elizabeth Wilkerson, 16 April 1855; Relam Falker, bm.

Whithead, Sidney & Salley Woody, 5 Jan 1836; Alvis Crawford, bm.

Whithed, John & Ruth Allen, 3 June 1803; William Gappins, bm.

Whithed, William & Aratha Howard, 23 Nov 1812; Thomas Pleasants, bm.

Whitiker, Presly & Emily Daniel, 13 July 1850; Wealey Couch, bm.

Whitmore, Howell & Nancy Smith, 24 March 1801; Howell Whitmore, Robert Ray, bm.

Whitmore, Jesse & Sarah Murphy, 6 Dec 1795; Qulla A. Starrberry, bm.

Whinery, Abraham & Martha Campbell, 17 Feb 1786; James Homes, bm.

328

Whitsel, Eli & Delilah Isley, 2 March 1841; Tobias May, bm.

Whitsell, Hiram & Ann Catharine May, 17 May 1837; Felix May, bm.

Whitsell, Oliver & Polly Cable, 6 Feb 1837; Jacob Huffner, bm.

Whitsell, William & Sally Clap, 1 Dec 1838; Jacob Whitsel, bm.

Whitsett, Christian & Mary Riley, 4 March 1839; James
Thompson, Porter Thompson, bm.

Whitsett, Eli & Fanny Boswell, 22 July 1848; F. A. Williams, bm.

Whitsett, James & Sarah Jackson, 22 Aug 1801; J. Collins, bm.

Whitsett, James & Polley Gant, 27 May 1824; John Harden, bm.

Whitsett, John & Milly Wilhoit, 12 Oct 1803; Adam Whitsett, bm.

Whitsett, Joseph & Delilah Coble, 21 March 1837; Henry
Whitsett, bm.

Whitsett, Moses & Nancy Bird, 8 Jan 1827; Archibo. Carmichel,
bm.

Whitsett, Samuel & Elizabeth Holt, 7 Jan 1806; James Whitsitt,
bm.

Whitsett, William & Jeany Harden, 12 Aug 1805; Samuel Whitsitt,
bm.

Whitsits, Jeremiah & Timpy Moore, 27 March 1848; Abram Sumner,
bm.

Whitsitt, John & Kezia Lowe, 13 Sept 1797; William M'Caddam, bm.

Whitsitt, John C. & Jane Wilson, 16 Jan 1832; Moses C.
Whitsitt, bm.

Whitsitt, William & Mary Thompson, 1 Aug 1785; Aseria Thompson,
bm.

Whitsitt, William Chastine & Elizabeth B. Wood, 2 March 1846;
Hardy Wood, bm.

Whittaker, Abraham & Martha Procter, 7 Jan 1797; John Riley, bm.

Whittaker, Abram & Sally Rhodes, 12 July 1832; Anderson Rhodes,
John D. Carlton, bm.

Whittaker, Robert & Viney Barrix, 18 Dec 1828; James M.
Pearson, bm.

Whitted, Alfred, son of Ed Maynor & Carolina Maynor, & Allice
Jones, dau of Barlow & Hetty Jones, colored, m 19 Oct 1867
by H. Whitted, J. P.

Whitted, Henry & Anna D. Faucett, 1 Oct 1851; John W. Shaw, bm.

Whitted, Henry & Jane Patterson, 5 Jan 1858; James Webb, bm;
m 5 Jan 1858 by Elias S. Dodson.

Whitted, Jehu & Winnifred Weaver, 28 June 1827; Benjamin Bowen,
bm.

Whitted, John R., son of Henry & Ann Whitted, & Mary P. Ray,
dau. of George C. & Martha Ray, m 17 Nov 1867 by Thomas U.
Faucette.

Whitted, Jonathan & Nancy Clark, 24 July 1821; Mason Glasson,
Jasper Glossin, bm.

Whitted, Levi & Sarah Neal, 6 Aug 1795; M. Hart, bm.

Whitted, Thomas & Peggey Lashley, 14 Dec 1807; Sterling Talley,
bm.

Whitted, William Jr. & Eliza Clinton, 3 Oct 1819; John Young, bm.

Whittington, John & Mary Pile, 15 Sept 1802; Thomas Philips,
William Pyle, bm.

Wiggins, John W. & Adeline McMannen, 9 Feb 1867; J. R. Green,
bm; m 12 Feb 1867 by N. W. Mangum, M. G.

Wilbon, John D. & Martha T. Ganes, 23 April 1856; D. C. Parks,
J. T. Hollaway, bm; m 23 April 1856 by William H. Brown,
J. P.

Wilbourn, Peter W. & Jerusia Deadman, 14 Nov 1826; John Woods,
bm.

Wilder, James & Claricy Vincent, 28 Feb 1807; Thomas Vincent,
bm.

Wilder, Joseph & Nancy Walker, 20 Sept 1832; Jones Vincent,
Josh. Wilder, bm.

Wilerford, Jas. & Jane Omerry, 26 March 1860; Pinknow Weaver,
bm.

Wilford, William & Elisabeth E. Ferrell, 9 Oct 1865; W. M.
Barton, bm; m 10 Oct 1865 by James Stagg, J. P.

Wilhoit, Jacob & Polley Powell, 2 Dec 1803; John Whitsett, bm.

Wilkens, Duncan & Malinda Cheek, 29 Oct 1841; Philip Southerland, Moses Leathers Junr., bm.

Wilkerson, Egbert S. & Julia A. Brown, 1 Sept 1852; Wm.
Wilkinson, bm.

Wilkenson, Robert & Elizabeth Walker, 29 May 1838; Charles
Wilson, William Bowls, bm.

Wilkerson, Alexander & Rosetta E. Hall, 17 Sept 1856; James P.
Hopkins, Nelson Ray, bm; m 21 Sept 1856 by D. D. Phillips,
J. P.

Wilkerson, Daniel & Elizabeth Collins, 11 Aug 1800; Wm.
Shepperd, bm.

Wilkerson, Daniel N. & Mary M. King, 29 Dec 1866; D. N.
Wilkinson, E. D. Oakley, bm; m 3 Jan 1867 by Thomas U.
Faucet, M. G.

Wilkerson, James E. & Salina Forrest, 15 Sept 1855; John P.
Forrest, James A. Forrest, bm; m 15 Sept 1855 by Gaston
Farrar, M. G.

Wilkerson, John & Elizabeth Clark, 20 April 1854; John M.
Brown, Geo. W. Bruce, bm; m 20 April 1854 by Archibald
Currie, minister.

Wilkerson, John & Nancy E. Whitaker, m 7 Dec 1856 by Richardson
Nichols, J. P.

Wilkerson, John W. & Fanna Jordan, 4 Jan 1866; Abner G. Brooks,
bm; m 7 Jan 1866 by Samuel Pearce.

Wilkerson, Madison & Sarah A. Leathers, 13 Nov 1848; W. B.
Holloway, W. T. Cole, bm.

Wilkerson, Rankin M. & Phebe Hopkins, 8 March 1864; J. W.
McKee, bm; m 9 March 1864 by Charles Wilson, J. P.

Wilkerson, Uriah M. & Sarah A. Smith, 20 Feb 1847; James R.
Wilkinson, bm.

Wilkerson, William R. & Sally Riley, 22 Dec 1860; John A.
Linch, Henry T. Gates, bm; m 23 Dec 1860 by John F. Lyon,
J. P.

Wilkey, Tobias & Elizabeth Clark, 4 July 1823; Philip Austin,
bm.

Wilkie, James & Barbary Good, 1 Nov 1805; Labon Collins, bm.

Wilkins, George Jr. & Sally Wason, 29 July 1808; George
Wilkins, bm.

Wilkins, Henry R. & Sally McFarling, 22 Sept 1847; Simon
McFarling, Thomas M. Turner, bm.

Wilkins, James & Malinda Roan, 28 Oct 1854; Thomas W. Laws,
bm; m 9 Nov 1854 by William Green, J. P.

Wilkins, James R. & Louisa B. Findley, 21 April 1847; Elmore
Faucett, bm.

Wilkins, John & Sally Cain, 28 Aug 1827; Archd. Cain, bm.

Wilkins, Jonathan & Susannah McDaniel, 2 May 1808; Wm. McDaniel,
bm.

Wilkins, Joseph & Morinda Mason, 31 Dec 1848; Henry Wilkins, bm.

Wilkins, Richard & Polly Warson, 19 March 1809; Saml. Whitsitt,
bm.

Wilkins, Richard & Levely H. Glenn, 28 Nov 1855; William Glenn,
bm; m 20 Dec 1855 by William Green, J. P.

Wilkins, William & Mary Dixon, 21 Dec 1825; John S. Rainey, bm.

Wilkins, William & Caroline A. Barbee, 20 Dec 1854; G. W.
Cheeke, bm; m 21 Dec 1854 by William Green, J. P.

Wilkins, William A., son of Alfred & Suzzy Wilkins, & Betsy
Harris, dau. of Thos. & Othy Harris, m 25 Sept 1867 by
Joseph Woods, J. P.

Wilkinson, Anthony & Dicy Tapp, m 29 June 1867 by S. M.
Wilkinson, J. P.

Wilkinson, E. A. & Julia A. Brown, m 8 Sept 1862 by
Archibald Currie, M. G.

Wilkinson, Francis & Elizabeth McDaniel, 19 Nov 1828; John
Wilkinson, bm.

Wilkinson, James & Susan Allison, 20 Dec 1806; Jacob Riley, bm.

Wilkinson, James & Nancy Bracken, 8 Jan 1825; Caleb Wilson, bm.

Wilkinson, James & Ellen Jane Thompson, 30 July 1839; J. Taylor,
bm.

Wilkinson, John & Rebecca Williams, 17 Oct 1797; James
Williams, bm.

Wilkinson, John & Polley Clark, 14 Feb 1833; A. Brown, bm.

Wilkinson, John & Margaret McKee, 27 Dec 1840; Hamilton
Montgomery, Robert Wilkison, bm.

Wilkinson, Lemuel & Betsey Wilkerson, 20 Feb 1827; Jnn. Ray,
bm.

Wilkinson, Thomas & Lucitta Ruffin Lindsey, 7 April 1825; Moses
Whitsitt, bm.

Wilkinson, William & Nancy Wilkinson, 27 May 1795; Robert
Fossett, bm.

Wilkinson, William & Polly Lindsey, 16 Sept 1819; S. Clark, bm.

Wilkinson, William F. & Moriah Ann Findly, 25 Oct 1849; Wm. R.
Ray, bm.

Wilkison, John & Anne Wilson, 19 Feb 1794; Robert Wilson, bm.

Willett, Joseph J. & Elizabeth Ann Watson, 4 Sept 1854; Wm.
Nelson, J. J. Freeland, bm; m 4 Sept 1854 by John J.
Freeland.

Willett, William & Polly Dodd, 12 Aug 1848; Thomas Cate, bm.

Willfong, John & Elizabeth Roberts, 9 Oct 1822; Thos. Thompson,
bm.

Williams, Aaron & Sarah Lindsay, 3 Nov 1832; Peter Perry, bm.

Williams, Alford Green & Rebecca Lloyd, 26 May 185; A. Y.
Williams, David Andress, bm.

Williams, Andrew & Phoeby Phillips, 14 Feb 1809; John Stockard,
bm.

Williams, Athanation N. & Barbara Long, 8 Nov 1816; George
Foust, bm.

Williams, Calep & Anne Trousdale, 25 Feb 1788; James Payne, bm.

Williams, Charles & Rebecca Harton, 29 April 1825; Stephen
Williams, bm.

Williams, David & Lydia Workman, 15 Oct 1794; Peter Williams,
bm.

Williams, Frederic & Nancy Cheek, 24 Sept 1828; Robert Cheek, bm.

Williams, Frederick & Jemimah Jones, 5 Dec 1795; Thomas Lindly, bm.

Williams, Frederick A. & Ester Bailiff, 19 March 1824; Atha N. Williams, bm.

Williams, Herbert & Elizabeth Ward, 19 Dec 1836; James Williams, J. C. Turrentine, bm.

Williams, Isaac & Betsy Thompson, 16 Aug 1806; Moses Williams, bm.

Williams, Isaac J. & Elizabeth M. Walker, 1 Jan 1828; Jno. Picket, bm.

Williams, James & Willie Crabtree, 26 Aug 1790; James Taylor, bm.

Williams, James & Elizabeth Moore, 16 Dec 1793; Isaac McCallum, bm.

Williams, James & Ruth Thompson, 18 March 1796; James Payne, bm.

Williams, James & Rebecca Guy, 22 Oct 1806; Thos. Clancy, bm.

Williams, James & Victory Wilch, 27 Nov 1823; Jesse Gant, bm.

Williams, James & Elizabeth Ward, 3 Jan 1826; John P. Reding, bm.

Williams, James & Cena Copley, 10 Jan 1833; William Hardcastle, Geo. M. Johnston, bm.

Williams, James & Fanny Pleasants, 11 Aug 1842; Bazilia Ward, James C. Turrentine, bm.

Williams, James & Nancy Curtis, 12 May 1858; Silas Mangum, bm; m 12 May 1858 by Wm. J. Roberts, J. P.

Williams, Jefferson & Mathesda Glenn, 3 June 1843; Duke Glenn, A. Waddell, bm.

Williams, Jesse & Nancy Sears, 22 Oct 1823; Albun Sears, Chesley P. Jinkins, bm.

Williams, John & Dolly Carrell, 8 Sept 1792; Peter Williams, bm.

Williams, John & Susanna Hobbs, 9 Jan 1817; Henry Crutchfield, bm.

Williams, John & Catharine Holt, 18 Dec 1835; William Wolf, bm.

Williams, John & Mary Ann Brown, 30 Sept 1842; James Williams, Moses Leathers, bm.

Williams, John & Ledya Reeves, 10 Dec 1845; Wm. Nelson, bm.

Williams, John Bryton & Karie Va. Peters, m 2 June 1864 by Francis W. Hilliard, M. G.

Williams, John G. & M. C. White, 29 Jan 1852; E. A. Heartt, bm; m 30 Jan 1852 by S. Milton Frost, M. G.

333

Williams, Kally, son of Jack Williams & Sally Miller, & Louisa Hughes, dau. of Moses & Ella Hughes, m 1 Sept 1867 by Job Bery.

Williams, Levi W. & Nancy E. Hunter, 16 Jan 1867; James C. Horton, bm; m 17 Jan 1867 by James Watson, J. P.

Williams, Mark & Penny Anderson, 27 Nov 1818; Saml. Wilson, bm.

Williams, Moses & Sarah Piles, 4 Jan 1810; James Dublin, bm.

Williams, Nash & Jane Ruffin, 1 Dec 1866; Thomas Woods, bm; m 1 Dec 1866 by Joseph Woods, J. P.

Williams, Person & Nancy McDaniels, 17 Oct 1833; Wm. Glenn, bm.

Williams, Peter & Mary Austin, 9 Dec 1788; Samuel Austin, bm.

Williams, Samuel & Izabbella Perason, 22 June 1865; Jerry Tripp, bm.

Williams, Stephen & Polley Standford, 15 Aug 1804; James Roan, bm.

Williams, Thomas A. & Lucinda E. Williams, 28 Dec 1861; P. A. Crabtree, bm; m 29 Dec 1861 by Jno. Cheek, J. P.

Williams, Vinson & Sarah Carter, 27 Oct 1806; K. Edwards, bm.

Williams, William & Salley Barbee, 19 April 1800; Thomas Burns, bm.

Williams, William & Ruth Pickard, 15 Nov 1803; James McMullin, bm.

Williams, William & ___, 18 Oct 1806; John Freeman, bm.

Williams, William & Jenny Couch, 11 Nov 1842; Page Scarlett, Wilson Jackson, bm.

Williams, William B. & Patsy Marcum, 23 Dec 1828; Benja. Marcam, bm.

Williams, William Henderson & Abigail Cureton, 25 Nov 1833; E. Adams, Richard Coureton, bm.

Williams, Yokley & Agness Smith, 9 March 1805; John Smith, bm.

Williamson, Charles & Elizabeth Wells, 5 Oct 1810; A. Compton, bm.

Williamson, James & Elizabeth Moore, 16 Dec 1793; Isaac McCallum, bm.

Willis, Austin & Edney Cook, 26 Dec 1846; Enoch W. Michael, bm.

Willis, Elisha & Uphey Pettegrew, 20 Jan 1846; J. H. McAdams, bm.

Willis, Henry & Sarah Lovins, 31 Jan 1803; James Lovins, bm.

Willis, James R. & Frances Hannah Latta, 3 May 1852; E. G. Gray, bm; m 3 May 1852 by Jno. A. McMannen, J. P.

Willis, Jetson & Carline Laseter, 22 Dec 1846; Enoch ___, bm.

Willison, Robert & Jannet Shaw, 5 Oct 1787; John Griffis, bm.

Willkey, Vincent & Polley Dockery, 13 Sept 1808; Jos. Stubbins, bm.

Willkey, Vinsen & Beady Falkner, 16 Sept 1806; Jos. Stubbins, bm.

Willoby, Edline & Elender Hinchy, 10 Jan 1804; Thomas Wynn, bm.

Willson, Hugh & Jane Tate, 5 Feb 1812; Joseph Kirkpatrick, bm.

Willson, Samuel & Mary Potter, 15 Aug 1795; Robt. Potter, bm.

Wilson, Aaron & Ruthe Carter, 9 April 1828; John Loy, bm.

Wilson, Alexander & Elizabeth Parker, 25 July 1807; Alexander McCrakin, bm.

Wilson, Anderson & Milley Fossett, 14 Feb 1829; Richard Holeman, bm.

Wilson, Archelaus & Elizabeth McMullan, 20 March 1797; Jas. Turrentine, bm.

Wilson, Caleb & Martha Fossett, 18 Aug 1831; Ar. Wilson, bm.

Wilson, Charles & Elizabeth Rountree, 10 Aug 1824; David R. Rountree, bm.

Wilson, Charles & Polly Atkinson, 28 June 1826; George Hutcheson, bm.

Wilson, Charles R. & Elizabeth Ann McKee, 4 Oct 1850; C. R. Miller, bm.

Wilson, Charles R. & Lucie M. Nichols, 3 July 1860; J. R. Miller, bm; m 11 July 1860 by C. Wilson, J. P.

Wilson, Eugene H., parents unknown, & Emma Purifoy, dau. of Geo. W. & Lucy Purifoy, m 17 Dec 1867 by Geo. W. Purifoy, minister.

Wilson, Ezekiel & Mary Harris, 25 Oct 1849; Elmore Gates, Lemual D. Lewis, bm.

Wilson, Felix & Elizabeth McCauley, 5 Dec 1836; Harvey J. Rountree, bm.

Wilson, Felix G. & Adaline Woods, 8 Nov 1851; C. Wilson, bm; m 18 Dec 1851 by H. Terry, J. P.

Wilson, George & Susannah Turrentine, 22 Sept 1806; Samuel Turrentine, bm.

Wilson, Henry & Emily Rippy, 11 Sept 1832; John C. Long, bm.

Wilson, Henry B. & Myram Massey, 28 Dec 1840; Thomas Marcom, bm.

Wilson, Hiram & Matilda Inscore, 10 Sept 1825; Eli Hastine, bm.

Wilson, Hugh & Polley Tinnen, 14 Feb 1818; William Willson, bm.

Wilson, James & Margaret Armstrong, 5 Jan 1791; Thomas Armstrong, bm.

Wilson, James & Polly Natgrass, 9 Feb 1810; James Wilson, bm.

Wilson, James & Philpena Sharp, 1 Jan 1816; Jacob Friddle, bm.

Wilson, John & Anne Smith, 17 March 1789; Reubin Smith, bm.

Wilson, John & Nancy Wortham, 2 Aug 1802; William Wortham, Chas. Wortham, bm.

Wilson, John & Anne Bowles, 2 Sept 1821; A. Y. Jackson, bm.

Wilson, John & Susan Reville, 18 Sept 1833; Henry Yarbrough, bm.

Wilson, John D. & Nancy Laws, 26 Feb 1822; Charles McCauley, bm.

Wilson, Jno. W. & Ann R. Whyte, 30 Oct 1850; J. B. McDade, bm.

Wilson, Kye & Margarett Pratt, 2 May 1866; Saml. Wilson, bm; m 2 May 1866 by John N. Kirkland, J. P.

Wilson, Plesant H. & Unicey Wayne, 3 March 1843; W. H. Thompson, Jas. Thompson, bm.

Wilson, Richard & Susannah Horton, 11 May 1785; George Hopkins, bm.

Wilson, Robert & Salley Woods, 15 Sept 1822; Caleb Wilson, James Dicky, bm.

Wilson, Samuel & Elizabeth Wortham, 7 Dec 1789; Samuel Turrentine, bm.

Wilson, Samuel & Lydia Grisham, 21 Aug 1797; Aquila Jones, bm.

Wilson, Samuel & Charlotte Chance, 24 July 1804; Charles Jones, bm.

Wilson, Samuel W. & Elizabeth M. Ray, 3 Feb 1854; Chs. P. Miller, bm; m 15 Feb 1854 by Archibald Currie, M. G.

Wilson, Silas & Letha Ann Doller, 14 Sept 1849; Robert Laws, bm.

Wilson, Soloman & Elizabeth Stephens, 7 Feb 1810; Sam. Tate, bm.

Wilson, Thomas & Jean Wood, 16 March 1789; W. Wood, bm.

Wilson, Thomas & Elizabeth Harrison, 1 Aug 1789; George Clancy, bm.

Wilson, Thomas & Elizabeth Blackwood, 24 July 1799; Andrew Watson, bm.

Wilson, Thomas & Henritta Wilson, 5 Jan 1809; Jas. Lapslie, bm.

Wilson, Thomas & Louisa Tinnen, 1 Nov 1862; Saml. P. Moore, bm; m 11 Nov 1862 by Archd. Currie, bm.

Wilson, Wesley D. & Lavinia Taylor, 19 March 1831; John Crutchfield, bm.

Wilson, William & Peggy Tinnen, 4 June 1803; Rich Hargraves, bm.

Wilson, William & Sally Qualls, 24 April 1819; Green Jones, bm.

Wilson, William & Lydia Freeland, 17 July 1849; William G. Faucett, bm.

Wilson, William & Adlet Burton, 25 Feb 1858; C. E. Parish, bm.

Winfree, James & Anne Fann, 5 Feb 1820; Henry Fosett, bm.

Winfrey, John & Franky Jane Pickett, 17 ___ 1848; James Fowler, bm.

Winick, David & Sally Martin, 4 July 1813; George Martin, bm.

Winn, Brinkley & Malida Hethpeth, 18 Jan 1865; W. B. Williams, bm.

Winnick, John & Frances Hall, 26 Jan 1818; William Hall, bm.

Winninghan, Jesse H. & Isabella C. Thompson, m 26 May 1867 by H. M. C. Stroud, J. P.

Wireck, Alfred & Sally Cable, 10 Jan 1835; John Cable, Levi May, bm.

Witaker, Abraham & Hannah Thomas, 24 Dec 1829; James M. Pearson, bm.

Witherspoon, Asgil & Sarah A. Atkins, 10 Aug 1858; Jeff Hall, R. M. Jones, bm; m 22 Aug 1858 by Hy. Whitted, J. P.

Witherspoon, Simpson, son of Robt. Witherspoon, & Mary Herndon, dau. of John & Emily J. Herndon, m 13 April 1868 by C. G. Harkham, J. P.

Witsman, Jonathan & Katharine Ray, 27 Dec 1827; Alfred Marshill, bm.

Wittie, Joshua & Ellinor Conner, 9 Feb 1787; Jas. Russell, bm.

Wolf, Jno. M. & Mary Jane Brown, 10 March 1857; Geo. Laws, T. W. Laws, bm; m 11 March 1857 by John W. F. Pearson, M. G.

Wolf, William & Rebeccah Williams, 14 April 1829; Henry McDanel, bm.

Wolf, William A. & Martha A. Cheek, 14 Feb 1857; Robert Sykes, bm; m 26 Feb 1857 by Ruffin R. Tapp, J. P.

Womack, Jacob P. & Nancy Faddis, 4 Nov 1810; C. Campbell, bm.

Womble, John J. & Lois E. Atwater, 16 April 1853; Jehiel Atwater, bm; m 19 April 1853 at the resident of Witson Atwater by R. T. Heflin, M. G.

Womble, Samuel & Mary C. Atwater, 15 Jan 1839; W. F. Strowd, bm; m 18 Jan 1859 by G. E. Brown.

Womble, William J. & Amy E. Atwater, 15 Jan 1856; J. J. Womble, bm; m by Ph. W. Archer, M. G.

Wood, David & Susannah Ward, 7 Sept 1816; Isaiah Hornaday, bm.

Wood, Dempsey & Mary Chizenhall, 11 Sept 1827; Harris Wilkerson, bm.

Wood, Dempsey & Nancy Glenn, 15 Aug 1800; Tyree Glenn, bm.

Wood, Hardy & Julia Jane Cook, 8 Jan 1824; William Ephlian, bm.

Wood, Henry & Lydia Cates, 6 Dec 1800; Salomon Cate, bm.

Wood, James & Betsy Malone, 19 May 1827; James Wood, Soloman Wood, bm.

Wood, Joseph & Sarah Reeves, 29 Nov 1828; Walter Chissenhall, bm.

Wood, Levin & Elizabeth Burn, 29 June 1797; James Byrn, bm.

Wood, Levin & Mary McBride, 1 March 1821.

Wood, Mark & Susannah Vaughan, 10 Dec 1825; Simmons May, bm.

Wood, Nelson P. & Annie Lawson, 22 Dec 1866; Wm. N. Hughes, bm; m 30 Dec 1866 by David T. Clark, J. P.

Wood, Sabret & Elanor Thompson, 8 Feb 1820; William Thompson, bm.

Wood, Sampson & Makey Chizzenhall, 22 July 1783; Alexr. Chizzenhall, bm.

Wood, Samson & Elizabeth Horner, 19 March 1815; James Jackson, bm.

Wood, Thomas & Nancy Glenn, 19 Oct 1802; Dempsey Wood, bm.

Wood, William & Jane Boggan, 7 Feb 1781; Alexander Cairns, bm.

Wood, William & Anna Burton, 29 Jan 1791; Cuttrel Burton, bm.

Wood, William & Nancy Cate, 22 March 1796; Soloman Cate, bm.

Wood, William & Ellen Davis, 11 Sept 1826; Thos. Wilson, bm.

Woodard, William & Mary Dier, 10 Oct 1840; Henry Cheek, bm.

Woodford, Evilyn S. & Mary A. McKerrall, 27 Dec 1865; J. W. Norwood, bm.

Woodle, James & Sarah Griffis, 17 March 1801; George Fossett, bm.

Woodrow, Joseph J. & Lucinda Faucett, 6 Jan 1840; William H. Carroll, bm.

Woods, Alfred & Lydia Montgomery, 9 May 1820; Willis Woods, bm.

Woods, Anderson & Eliza Allison, 12 March 1867; J. J. Allison, H. Taylor, bm; m 19 March 1867 by Thos. H. Hughes.

Woods, Charles & Beddy Lynch, 11 March 1812; James Riley, bm.

Woods, Charles & Margaret Maclain, 6 Nov 1829; Thomas Anderson, bm.

Woods, David & Harriet Hardcastle, 29 March 1826; Albert W. Glenn, bm.

Woods, David & Nancy J. Jackson, 23 Nov 1863; Samuel Couch, bm; m 23 Nov 1863 by Benjamin J. Kinnion, J. P.

Woods, David Jr. & Polly Robinson, 2 April 1821; Joseph W. Allison, bm.

Woods, Eli & Margaret Brown, 8 May 1819; William Brown, bm.

Woods, Elihu & Lucy Woods, 14 Dec 1816; William Woods, bm.

Woods, Elihugh & Eleanor Fossett, 5 Feb 1789; William Fausett, bm.

Woods, Elija & Jane Hall, 15 Sept 1825; Martin Cole, bm.

Woods, Elmore W. & Aurora F. Hatch, 29 Sept 1863; Solomon Pool, bm; m 29 Sept 1863 by Solomon Pool.

Woods, Elmore W. & Mrs. Fannie Gilaspie, 13 March 1866; Solomon Pool, bm; m 13 March 1866 by Solomon Pool.

Woods, Grandison & Jane Brown, 1 Feb 1841; Wm. H. Jurden, bm.

Woods, Hargis & Frances Laycock, 13 Jan 1849; John D. Carlton, bm.

Woods, Harris & Patsey Cardin, 23 Sept 1831; Calous Moize, bm.

Woods, Henderson & Sarah Riggs, 25 March 1826; John Walker, bm.

Woods, Henry & Elizabeth Fowler, 5 Jan 1836; Riley Vickers, Joe Craig, bm.

Woods, Henry & Nancy Carrol, 3 Feb 1853; Jacob Bledsoe, bm.

Woods, Henry L., son of Jno. W. & Margaret R. Woods, & Anzolette McKee, dau. of Jos. W. & Eliza McKee, m 9 Jan 1868 by L. W. Hall, J. P.

Woods, Hugh & Peggy Vaughan, 11 Aug 1802; Robert Hall, bm.

Woods, Hugh & Eliza Jane Ray, 20 Jan 1826; Wm. Dunagan, bm.

Woods, James & Rebecca Haily, 26 Oct 1812.

Woods, James & Polly Brown, 15 May 1818; Hugh Woods, bm.

Woods, James & Patsy Hughs, 27 Dec 1819; Wm. Criswell, bm.

Woods, James & Polley Mebane, 5 Feb 1829; Saml. Kirkpatrick, bm.

Woods, James & Mary Hall, 21 June 1850; John Hall, bm.

Woods, John & Polly Hunt, ___ 1811; Elisha Taylor, bm.

Woods, John & Levina Jones, 25 June 1822; John Rogers, bm.

Woods, John & Livily Woods, 11 Sept 1827; Henderson Woods, Eli Woods, bm.

Woods, John & Salley McKee, 19 Sept 1833; Eli Woods, bm.

Woods, John & Fanny Lockhart, m 21 July 1866 by John Cheek, J. P.

Woods, John & Nancy A. Proctor, 28 Aug 1866; Levi Marcom, Hardy Massey, bm; m 30 Aug 1866 by H. J. Pearson, J. P.

Woods, John L. & Patsey Baldridge, 30 Oct 1816; John Jurdan, bm.

Woods, John G. & Mary Wilson, 1 Jan 1846; A. W. Packer, bm.

Woods, John W. & Margarete R. Brown, 21 Jan 1842; Joseph W. McKee, bm.

Woods, Joseph & Phebee Clark, 1 Feb 1782; John Roberson, bm.

Woods, Joseph & Polley Longmire, 7 Oct 1809; Barree Chisenhall, bm.

Woods, Joseph & Nancy Ann Parker, 9 Feb 1848; Wm. Nelson, bm.

Woods, Joseph A. & Fanny E. Ray, 27 Oct 1830; J. Taylor, bm.

Woods, Joseph H. & Rebeccha W. Monk, 28 March 1864; N. P. Hall, bm; m 31 March 1864 by N. P. Hall, J. P.

Woods, Matthew & Peggy Fosset, 12 Nov 1795; George Allen, bm.

Woods, Monroe & Martha Hicks, 12 June 1852; William Woods, George Rhodes, bm; m 15 June 1852 by Harris Wilkerson, J. P.

Woods, Richard & Elizabeth Mebane, 19 Oct 1805; Alexdr. Mebane, bm.

Woods, Rufus & Elizabeth Gates, 24 July 1861; Wiley Ryley, David T. Clark, bm; m 4 Aug 1861 by Thos. Wilson, J. P.

Woods, Samuel & Jennet Allison, 2 Jan 1789; David Allison, bm.

Woods, Samuel & Elizabeth Woods, 12 Oct 1799; Hugh Woods, bm.

Woods, Samuel B. & Catharine A. Small, 3 Feb 1848; Eli Scott, bm.

Woods, Samuel K., son of John L. & Margaret Woods, & Louisa Montgomery, dau. of James & Mary Montgomery, m 18 Feb 1868 by Thomas M. Faucette.

Woods, Sanders, son of Aaron Douglas & Elender Woods, & Jane Page, dau. of Isham & Mary Page, colored, m 11 July 1868 by C. P. Warren, J. P.

Woods, Solomon & Elizabeth Haley, 4 Oct 1803; Elisha Chizenhall, bm.

Woods, Thomas & Susannah Baldridge, 24 Dec 1804; Asael Moore, bm.

Woods, Thomas & Fanny Duncan, 4 Feb 1817; John Finley, bm.

Woods, William & _____ linsey, 1 Aug 1781.

Woods, William & Elizabeth Desern, 6 Aug 1803; Wm. Carrington, bm.

Woods, William & Rachel Faucett, 0 Dec 1800; John Nealey, bm.

Woods, William & Jane Terry, 9 Oct 1852; James M. Moods, J. W. Clements, bm.

Woods, William & Anna Jane Montgomery, 5 Feb 1853; A. W. Parker, bm; m 6 Feb 1853 by J. J. Freeland, J. P.

Woods, William & Demarias Roberts, 11 Sept 1858; William
Wilson, bm; m 11 Sept 1858 by John F. Lyon, J. P.

Woods, William & Martha C. Clinton, 14 Jan 1858; A. Wilkerson,
bm.

Woods, William C. & Nancy E. Griffin, 9 March 1857; Jno. N.
Johnston, bm; m 11 March 1857 by John J. Roberson, J. P.

Woods, William D. & Emeline C. Hall, 3 Feb 1864; John Laws, bm;
m 3 Feb 1864 by Nelson P. Hall, J. P.

Woods, William H. & Jane Cabe, 9 Jan 1832; A. Parks, bm.

Woods, Willis & Polley Wilborne, 24 Nov 1823; George Scarlet,
bm.

Woods, Wilson & Princess Anne Woods, 7 April 1838; Wm. Scarlett,
Elbert Dotts, bm.

Woodward, George W., son of Andrew J. & Clara Woodward, & Delia
White, dau. of John & Temperance A. White, m 7 May 1868
by A. S. Bert.

Woodward, Gideon & Rebeccah Morton, 17 March 1833; Benjamin
Gant, bm.

Woodward, William & Sally Dur, 16 April 1837; John Lewis,
P. Stanford, bm.

Woody, Hugh & Matilda Mebane, 18 Dec 1841; Ritten Ray, bm.

Woody, James & Margret Hall, 10 July 1829; John Graham, bm.

Woody, John & Elizabeth Thomson, 22 Oct 1800; Levi Thompson,
Thos. Anderson, bm.

Woody, Joseph & Sarah Price, 20 Dec 1805; William Bradshaw, bm.

Woody, Joshua & Ruthy Jones, 27 Dec 1811; Thomas Hastings, bm.

Woody, Robert & Rachel Rickets, 18 Feb 1802; Wm. Grimes,
Barney Lashley, bm.

Woody, Samuel & Jane Holmes, 23 May 1795; Wm. Rickett, bm.

Woody, Thomas & Mary Woody, 11 Nov 1826; John Grahams, bm.

Woody, William & Biddy Loyd, 11 Jan 1812; James Stubbins, bm.

Woolcut, David & Nancy Foster, 4 July 1822; Jonn. Hailley, bm.

Workman, Berry & Fanny Workman, 30 Jan 1835; James Crabtree, bm.

Workman, Gastin & Maggie Crabtree, 9 April 1867; m by Jas. N.
Craig, J. P.

Workman, Green & Patsey Williams, 12 Oct 1820; J. F. Cate, bm.

Workman, Henry & Temperance Workman, 2 Oct 1841; James Hastings,
bm.

Workman, James & Gracey A. Lindsay, 29 April 1859; Geo. Laws,
bm.

Workman, James C. & Susannah Haley, 24 Oct 1829; John Workman, bm.

Workman, James H. & Nancy Walker, 28 July 1838; John Workman, bm.

Workman, James H. & Martha J. Wilkerson, 30 Nov 1853; James M. Cate, bm; m 1 Dec 1863 by Thos. H. Hughes, J. P.

Workman, Jess & Polley Crutchfield, 6 March 1810; John Carroll, bm.

Workman, John & Penelope Burke, 13 May 1830; Gray Grey, bm.

Workman, John & Margaret Cheek, 13 July 1831; Alvis Cheek, bm.

Workman, John & Emelea Sykes, 2 Oct 1841; James Hastings, bm.

Workman, John Jr. & Sarah Williams, 5 Nov 1808; David Cate, bm.

Workman, John B. & Mary E. Smith, 7 Oct 1865; H. P. Smith, bm.

Workman, Jonathan & Mary Stone, 29 Sept 1847; Manliff J. Staley, bm.

Workman, Maben & Lucy Powel, 14 Sept 1861; W. H. Powell, J. H. Strow, bm; m 20 Sept 1861 by J. W. Strowd.

Workman, Saven H. & Martha E. Crawford, 27 March 1865; W. N. Workman, J. E. Hobbs, bm.

Workman, William & Polly Williams, 14 Jan 1836; James Workman, bm.

Workman, William & Mary Stout, 27 Feb 1846; Henry Workman, bm.

Worrell, William B. & Mary B. Herndon, 17 Nov 1823; Wm. R. Herndon, bm.

Worth, Henry & Margaret J. Smith, 30 June 1866; John R. Smith, B. Cheek, bm; m 1 July 1866 by Wilson Brown, J. P.

Worth, Jonathan & Martisha Daniel, 20 April 1824; Edwin McHolt, bm.

Wortham, Alfred & Ruth Harris, 23 Nov 1812; Mark Harris, bm.

Wortham, Samuel & Rebecka Sims, 30 Jan 1822; Jno. J. Carrington, bm.

Wray, David & Margaret Tate, 6 Nov 1809; Saml. Tate, bm.

Wren, James W., son of Thomas & Mary Wren, & Salla Kilgrove, dau. of William & Catharine Killgrove, m 2 Jan 1868 by Mager Green, J. P.

Wright, George & Malinda Turner, 4 Sept 1847; C. E. Smith, bm.

Wright, Jordan & Delilah Evans, 27 March 1821, Reuben Evans, bm.

Wright, Thomas & Salley Adams, 25 June 1820; John King, bm.

Wright, William F. & Laura Ann Andrews, 7 Oct 1853; Enoch Sykes, bm; m 11 Oct 1853 by B. Strowd, J. P.

Wrightsel, Michael & Caty Coble, 8 Oct 1810; John Wrightsell, bm.

Wrightsell, Adam & Barbara Moser, 4 May 1805; John Wrightsell, bm.

Wrightsman, Jacob & Nancy Bevins, 9 Sept 1809; John Freeman, Jno. Woody, bm.

Wrightsman, John & Catharine Wilkerson, 12 April 1798; John Thompson, bm.

Wyatt, Fredrick & Catey King, 25 May 1801; Samuel King, bm.

Wyatt, James & Celia King, 30 April 1823; Anderson King, bm.

Wyatt, James & Celia King, 7 April 1823; Jos. Wyatt, bm.

Wyatt, Joshua & Susannah King, 28 April 1804; John King, bm.

Wyck, William Van & Mary J. Battle, m 24 July 1861 by Francis W. Hilliard, M. G.

Wyett, James & Nancy Murdock, 23 Oct 1828; Saml. Kirkpatrick, bm.

Wynne, Charles W. & Catharine Tate, 3 April 1849; R. M. Jones, bm.

Wyyot, John & Elizabeth Murdock, 31 Aug 1830; Joseph Bason, bm.

Yancy, Charles R. & Mary Merritt, 11 Feb 1827; Moses T. Pratt, bm.

Yancy, Charles R. & Martha Merritt, 7 Oct 1830; D. B. Alsobroo, bm.

Yancy, Charles R. & Charlotte Creel, 3 Oct 1851; Alfred Cheek, bm; m 3 Oct 1851 by Thos. Long, J. P.

Yarbrough, David & Nelly Doherty, 14 Sept 1805; George Anderson, bm.

Yarbrough, David, son of Ras & Jimma Yarbrough, & Ellen Henry, dau. of Lan & Sally Henry, colored, m 29 Dec 1867 by D. W. Johnson, J. P.

Yarbrough, John & Sarah A. Currie, 17 Jan 1866; George J. McCauley, bm; m by D. W. Thompson.

Yarbrough, Jordan & Kiziah Hampton, 24 March 1856; John D. Wilbon, bm; m 3 April 1856 by Andrew N. Hall.

Yates, Brantley & Fanny Marcom, 8 May 1824; Thomas Marcum, bm.

Yates, Lewis & Polley Rich, 17 Dec 1823; Joseph Boothe, bm.

Yates, William & Delilah Boothe, 23 Nov 1816; Joseph Boothe, bm.

Yearby, Leml. M. & Sarah A. Breen, 27 Nov 1865; J. W. Ferrell, J. W. Strowd, bm; m 29 Nov 1865 by Will M. Jordan.

Yeargain, Benjamin & Sarah Patterson, 14 Dec 1782; John Barbee, bm.

Yeargain, Jarratt & Amelia Patterson, 22 Jan 1795; Benja.
Yeargain, bm.

Yeargin, Benjamin A. & Susannah Moore, 11 Jan 1820; Thos. D.
Watts, bm.

Yeargin, Morgan M. & Caty Loften, 28 Feb 1806; Wil Kirkland, bm.

Yergin, Isaac & Peggy Alexander, 12 Nov 1826; John Kimble, bm.

Yockley, Mark & Catherine Parker, 11 Dec 1809; Isaiah Davis,
bm.

Young, John & Nancy Whitted, 6 Aug 1812; Saml. Webb, bm.

Young, John H. & Lucy P. Parker, 15 Jan 1841; D. C. Parrish, bm.

Young, Levi & Sarah Clancy, 15 March 1837; James W. Palmer,
Isaac B. Head, bm.

Younger, Aquilla & Leonna Jordan, 29 Sept 1812; Jonathan I.
Jordan, bm.

Younger, James & Catherine Bradford, 23 Jan 1855; James W.
Vincent, bm.

Younger, Joseph & Susanah Fitch, 15 Jan 1816; John Tounger, bm,

Younger, Richard & Nancy Ann Horn, 3 Nov 1819; Robt. A. Younger,
bm.

Younger, William & Elizabeth Webb, 8 Nov 1833; Sterling Qualls,
Jeremiah Bason, bm.

Zachary, James & Mary Quakenbush, 2 Jan 1843; William Zachary,
bm.

Zachary, William & Polly Crawford, 9 Oct 1821; Samuel Crawford,
bm.

Zachary, Wm. & Henrietta Edds, 22 Sept 1847; Wm. Compton, bm.

Armstrong, Ann 190
Betsey 295
Catharine 70
Dulceneah 81
Elizabeth 118, 157
Fanny 217
Frances 63
Henrietta 295
Jinnett 318
Jno. 160, 183, 295
John 307, 318
Joseph 21, 129
Julian 43
Margaret 336
Margret 269
Martin 188
Mary 288, 306
Mary Jane 129
Parthenia 107, 178
Parthinia 74
Polley 160, 277
Thomas 104, 214, 336
Thos. 11, 20, 59, 63,
  70, 210, 211, 248,
  273
Wm. 121
Arnold, Celia 226
Elizabeth 193
Ellis 13
H. 144
Hartwell 248
John 11
Rutha 323
Artes, John 138
Artis, Polly 203
Artz, Wm. 174
Ascue, Stephen 188
Ashe, Elizabeth 140
Thomas S. 280
Thos. S. 6
Ashford, Lucy 246
Ashley, Amanda 12
Clarance 163
Edney 313
Elizabeth 12, 67
James 12
Jarrell 107
Jarrott 163
Jeremiah 12
Martha A. 246
Mary 176
Polley 47, 322
Polly 237
Priscilla 163
Rhodah 170
Robert 93, 131, 151
Sarah 10
Sarah F. 296
Susan 313
Susannah 3
William 318
Winnifred 98
Ashly, Harrison 225
John 171
Atkerson, Elizabeth 298
Patsey 156
Atkin, Archabald 217
Atkins, Ann Eliza 203
Daniel 213, 295
Harriet 12
James 12, 54
John M. 114
Josiah 12
Leslie F..25
Louisa 17
Lucinda P. 39
Martha J. 308
Pene 217

Atkins, Rebecca 202
Sarah A. 337
Thomas 138
Wm. H. 179
Atkinson, Anne 181
Celia 119
Mary 26
Polly 335
Atkison, James 12
Atterson, Jane 75
Naomi 272
Atwater, Amy E. 337
C. C. 40
Celia 290
E. W. 213
J. 277
Jeheil 213
Jehial 40
Jehiel 40, 215, 337
Lois 289
Lois E. 337
Martha 40, 288
Mary C. 40, 337
Mary E. 62
Moses 308
Saphronia J. 40
Sarah A. 213
W. 98, 215, 311
Wesley 192, 213
Wilson 98, 207, 217,
  239, 281
Witson 337
Auldredge, Martha 174
Austen, Levinia 219
Frances 84
Mary 334
Philip 331
Samuel 334
William 13
Babb, Sarah 167
Bachelor, Thomas 13
Bacon, Ed, W. 91
J. G. 215
Joseph G. 13
Martha 90, 193
Rebecca 13
Sarah 187
Sarah B. 91
Steohen 261
Bagley, Julia 296
Bailey, Elisabeth 9
Henry 215
James 13, 196
Jones 14
Margaret 56
Mary 180
Nancy 216
Polly 14
Sarah 262
Sarah J. 41
Thos. B. 31
Will 14
William 48
Bailiff, Ester 333
John 50, 51
Nancy 50
Bain, Bettie A. 6
Easter 232
J. M. 101
James 197
James M. 67
John 186
N. D. 171
Nancy 132
Nat. D. 202
Nathaniel 91, 103,
  127, 132
Nathl. 39, 67, 311

Bain, Nathl. D. 188
Polly 231
Sally W. 98
Susan T. 173
Thomas 61
Thos. 39
Baine, Eliza 30
Baker, Andw. 210
Delilah 9
Edith 195
Elizabeth 14
Hannah 130
Harried Hill 130
James 99
Jane 79, 108
Janie 56
Joseph 56, 79, 198
Margaret 219
Mary 198
Nancy 48, 106, 123
Nelly 68
Polly 37
Robert 123
Sarah 99
Susan 42, 61, 64
Thomas 102
Balden, Catharine 314
Baldridg, Robert 268
Baldridge, Elizabeth 204,
  219
Francis 261
Hannah 191
J. 243
Jas. 167
John 167
Martha 189
Patsey 340
Robert 266
Stephen 14
Susannah 340
Baldwin, A. J. 15
Abigail 207
Alfred 42
Betsey 117
Eda 75
Elizabeth 1
J. J. 15
Jesse 15
John 207, 241
John R. 77
M. 29, 264
Martha 42, 45, 245
Mary 1
Nancy 252
Nelson 254
Patsey McDaniel 15
Samuel 31, 94, 111, 236
William 15, 299
Baley, Wm. M. 287
Baliff, Daniel 13
Ball, Amelia 256
Carnelia E. 305
Edney 305
Jas. R. 97, 110
Marcus 305
Mary 306
Nancy 165
Polley 159
Ballard, Betsey 160
Dilley 159
J. B. 272
Jane D. 12
William O. M. 20
Baly, Elizabeth 224
Wm. M. 216
Bane, Margaret 106
Mary 259
Baner, Thos. 40

349

Belvin, Wm. 93, 258, 315
Benefield, Willis 11
Benehan, Rebecca 42
Benfield, Willis 178
Bennet, Francis 298
  Hancy 31
  Jno. 59
  John 147
Bennett, Adaline 96
  Eliza A. 93
  Elizabeth 275
  John 21
  Mary E. 135
  Philip 91, 201
  Ritta 181
Benson, B. P. 21
  Co. 281
  E. 228
  Ed. 173
  Martha 219
  Nancy 226
  Stephen 21
  Wm. 21
Benton, A. 285
  Fanny 147
  J. A. 69
  Jesse 112, 123, 184
  Louisa 16
  S. 88, 138, 145, 180,
    220, 227, 323
  Sarah C. 55
Berris, Polly 134
Berry, Amanda 134
  Catherine 304
  Charlotte 315
  Delilah 139
  Dicey 218
  Elizabeth 109, 122
  Henry 22, 224
  James E. 169
  James H. 21
  Job 189, 232, 306
  Josephine 212
  Joshua 6, 243
  Mary 22
  Nancy 320
  Nancy E. 316
  Penelope 289
  Phoebe R. 35
  Robert 3
  Salley 51
  Sarah F. 298
  Tabitha 214
  Thomas 22, 51
  Thos. P. 109, 187
  Winna 224
Bert, A. S. 341
Bery, Job 71, 206, 334
Beshanes, Janey 263
Bets, Susanah 328
Betts, A. D. 13, 230
Bevans, Phebe 98
Beverly, Elijah 287
Bevil, Elisha 22
  Zachariah 99
Bevill, Elisha 22, 198
  Elizabeth 198
  George 241
  John 83, 180
  Mary 179
  Mehalah 233
  Nancy 255
  Sally 180
  Susannah 84
Bevins, Nancy 125, 343
Bibby, Elizabeth 286
Bigelow, Samuel 25
Bilbo, Harriet M. D. 201

Bilbo, Jn. 151
  Thos. 16, 88, 201
Bilbow, Polly 201
Biley, Mary 68
  Peter 7
Bingham, Ann J. 212
  Eliza 21
  Eliza J. 235
  Jno. 269
  John C. 43
  Mary S. 188
  Sally 164
  W. J. 65
Birch, Jane 166
  Phillip 243
Bird, Annis 128
  Catharine 132, 169,
    170
  Elizabeth 102, 106,
    140
  Fanny 128
  James 316
  Jane 85
  Jehu 8, 106
  John 23
  Joseph 23, 128
  Mary 316
  Nancy 30, 301, 329
  Patsey 323
  Phebe 317
  Sarah 316
  Susan 109
  Susannah 8
  William 301
Birl, William A. 82
Birnley, Mary 54
Bishop, Cowen 282
  Lydia 84
  Martha 199
  Martha J. 113
  Mary C. 290
  Nancy 282
  Phebe 282
  Salley 183
  William E. 278
Bivens, Thomas 230
Blacknal, Charity Bor-
    land 161
  Hubbard Jackson 161
  Louisa 161
Blacknall, Emma B. 143
  J. R. 269
  Sarah 24
Blackston, Susanah 226
Blackwell, Alexander 222
  Nancy Lorson 69
  Robert M. 134
  Sarah A. 34
Blackwood, A. 170, 191,
    230, 267, 282
  A. D. 24
  Ann 258
  Anne 244
  D. K. 58, 185, 319
  Edwin 170
  Elizabeth 4, 290, 336
  Fanny 185
  Frances 10
  Franklin L. 24
  Hannah 272
  Harriet 319
  J. 68
  J. M. 176, 289, 327
  James 244
  Jas. 13
  Jennet 191
  Jno. M. 138, 279, 304
  John M. 70, 77, 79,
    214, 230, 324

Blackwood, John S. 110
  Julia A. 172
  Margret 191
  Margret Jane 56
  Martha 78
  Mary 257, 288
  Mary E. 24
  N. H. 162, 199, 312,
    314
  Nancy 84, 222
  Patsey 153
  Peggy 185
  Richard 75, 153, 233
  Robert 76, 171
  Salley 115
  Wm. 191
Blackwoods, J. G. 326
Blake, Ann R. 216
  John 67, 216, 291, 322
  Nancy 160, 216
  Sarah A. 155
Blalock, D. S. 25, 243
  Elizabeth 33, 154, 316
  Green 258
  Hartwill 25
  Hubbard 227
  Jesse 33, 125
  John 25
  M. V. 235
  Misseline E. 246
  Patsey 290
  Sarah 278
  Vallentine 238
  William J. 12
  Yancey 133
Blanchet, Martha 37
Blanchett, Polly 308
Blanshard, Julia 21
  Mary 154
  Rachel 106
Blany, Pengni 70
Blealock, Mary 21
Bledsoe, Amey 127
  Giles 200
  Jacob 26, 304, 339
  John 25, 26, 128
  Mary Ann 200
  Patsey 304
  Sarah Jane 126
Bletcher, Mary 154
Blount, Alex C. 173
  R. H. J. 12, 35, 138,
    183, 220, 279
Bloushard, Margret 308
Blunt, Catherine R. 129
  R. H. J. 129
  Sarah 129
Bobbitt, Lucy P. 281
  Obedience 163
  W. H. 40
Bodine, Ester 171
Bogers, Polly 284
Boggan, Jane 338
Boggs, Allen 161
  Hannah 106
  Henry 26
  Jane 96
  Jesse 26, 272, 281
  Joel 96
  John 216
  Nancey 73
  Peter 156
  Sally 112
  Simpson 119, 287
  Stanford 26
  Tempy 119
Bohannon, Mary 214
Bolar, Susan 31

351

Browning, Andrew 327
  Artelia 253
  Benjamin 253
  Cynthia 90
  Delilah 73
  Elizabeth 269
  George 72, 73, 90, 98
  Ilai 90
  James 37, 71, 119,
    254, 327
  Jeany 240
  John 36, 37, 72, 203
  Mary 240
  Mary J. 53
  Peggy 72
  Polly 25
  Susannah 65
  Thomas 36, 106
  William 136
  Wm. 47
Brownrigg, Elizabeth B.
  315
Bruce, A. B. 14, 45, 153,
    159, 176, 249, 258
  A. Benton 105
  Abner B. 16, 191
  Chs. 86
  Frances 128
  Geo. W. 9, 20, 25, 31,
    54, 98, 103, 131,
    188, 190, 238, 266,
    315, 318, 331
  George W. 177
  Mary F. 154
Bryan, Elizabeth 324
  James 11
  Mary 70
  Peggy 95
Bryant, Cynthia 100
  Hannah 327
  Jeany 240
  John 179, 240
  Lavinia 227
  Lydia 143
  Margaret 79
  Mary 71, 239
  Nancy 156, 271
  Polley 240
  Williamson 240, 253
  Wiltha Anne 135
Buchannan, Thomas 214
Buchanon, Washington 199
Buckingham, Mary 111
Buckum, Peggy 34
Bukham, John 37
Bukinham, Jno. 111
Bukum, Hailey 37
  Joshua 34
Bull, Squire 101
Bullock, Elizabeth 45
  Eras D. 280
  James 131
  Jno. 231
  John 38, 84
  Manerva 305
Bumpass, Anderson 161
  Jinny 161
  Mary F. 161
Bunch, Ellinor 236
  Henry 259, 307
  Thomas 236
Burch, Chesley 146
  David 105
  George W. 201
  Henry 5, 17
  Mary F. 318
  Phillip 278
  Sarah 174
  Susannah 72

Burch, Thomas 269
  Z. G. 179, 198
Burchett, Catherine 68
Burford, Solomon 314
Burges, Jane 109
  Mary Ann 138
Burgess, Candess 201
  Nancy 24
Burgin, Sally 44
Burgwinn, Margret 163
Burgwinne, Carolina 71
Burk, Clary 134
Burke, Betsy 285
  Madison 38
  Michl. 266
  Penelope 342
  Polley 89
  S. S. 315
Burkhead, L. S. 55, 160
  S. S. 5, 327
Burn, Elizabeth 388
Burnes, John 19
  Zilphia 86
Burnet, Betsy 128
  Edith 160
  Polly 324
Burnett, Abigail 29
  Abram 154, 243, 316
  Alex. 39
  Aron 7
  Bettie J. 115
  C. J. 215
  Cornelia 38
  Dan 38
  Harriet Adeline 125
  Jane 243
  L. 40
  Nancy 38
  Polley 154
  Robert 212
  Sally 107
Burnette, Thomas 263
Burns, Jas. 78
  Polly 287
  Sally 78
  Thomas 334
  Winney 111, 153
Burnsid, Polly 127
Burnside, B. 177
  Benj. 299
  John 159
  Nancy 221
  Ruth 103
Burnsides, Elizabeth 292
  James 39
  Louisa 295
  Robert 271
  Sarah 221
Buroughs, John 240, 289
  Martha 312
Burres, Thomas 57
Burris, Lucy 320
Burroughs, John 7, 24,
    25, 43, 84, 138,
    179
  Margaret 232
  Nancy 244
  W. G. 291
Burrow, Delia 205
  Eliza 169
Burs, T. W. 241
Burton, Adilled 323
  Adlet 337
  Anna 38
  Cutbud 39
  Cuttrel 338
  Ermin B. 102
  Frances K. 122
  Jemima 35

Burton, Jno. 62
  John C. 40
  L. T. 107
  Louisa 324
  M. 154
  Maria 176
  Mary Ann 194
  Nancy 233
  Robert 146
  Sarah 104, 228
  Sarah Jane 149
  W. H. 152
  Wm. 224
  Wmson. 205
Burwell, Mary S. 290
  R. 210, 251, 324,
    328
  Robert 64, 73, 225
Busick, Benjamin 204
  Betsey 282
  Caleb 168
  Elizabeth 152, 204
  James 40
  John 40
  Kesiah 40
  Margaret 3
  William 282
  Wm. 102, 152
Butler, Anne 59
  Jane 296
Byars, John P. 60
Bynum, Kerney 40
  Margaret 40
  Mary 133
Byrd, Edmnd. 101
  Edmund 29
  Joseph 316
  Mary 120
Byrn, James 338
  Jas. 38
Byrns, Alfred 186
  Nancy 186
C., E. W. 129, 207
Ca(?), ALsey 268
Cabe, Catharine 103, 266
  Daniel 122
  Elizabeth 253
  Ephraim 181
  Jane 341
  Jemima 39
  John 35
  Lydia 161
  Mary 31, 132
  Nancy 108, 176
  Polley 39, 231
  Rachel 62, 193
  Salley 35
  Sarah 176
  Wm. 34, 244
Cable, Daniel 35
  Elenor 265
  Jacob 328
  John 337
  Polly 329
  Sally 152, 337
  William 221
Cade, Fanny 292
Cafe, (?) 36
Caggin, A. E. 117
Cain, Allen 41
  Anne 91
  Archd. 331
  Charity A. 200
  Dickerson 169
  Elizabeth A. 37
  James 83
  Jesse 2
  Jno. 175
  Judah 286

Cain, Lewis, 128, 311
  Mariah 157
  Martha A. 165
  Mary 68
  Mary C. 268
  Minerva 41
  Nancy 72, 91
  Parthena 46
  Polley 270
  Sally 196, 331
  Sarah 144, 270
  William 41, 160
Caine, Johanna 143
Cairns, Alexander 338
Caldwell, Elizabeth 251
  John 115
  Joseph 41
  Peggy 4
Cale, Rachael D. 115
  Thomas 212
Calep, Anne 55
Calisles, Unity 8
Calp, John 309
Calton, Sally 201
Cambell, Margaret 33
Cameron, A. R. 120
  Anne 172
  Annie R. 68
  Archd. 156
  Duncan 271
  Grace 7
  Ida 14, 20
  J. D. 155
  James S. 138
  Jno. 96, 172
  Lemuel 7
  Mary R. 96
  P. C. 120
  Paul C. 267
  Polly 7
  R. B. 8
  Rebecca B. Anderson
    120
  Rebecca T. 96
  Silvy 42
  Wm. 96
Camieser, Wm. B. 256
Camp, W. B. 60
Campbel, Charles 289
Campbell, C. 27, 337
  Ca. 225
  Catharine 18
  Daniel 86
  Elisabeth 76
  Elizabeth 19, 72
  Franky 87
  George 233
  J. A. 298
  James 19, 257, 276
  Jeany 151
  Jno. 29, 69, 81
  Martha 328
  Mary 86, 244
  Mary Ann 39
  Phebe 75
  Polley 29
  Priscilla 155
  Robt. 33
Campble, James 282
Canada, Elizabeth 22
  Ruffin 278
Canady, Margaret 49
  Mary 188
Cane, Emily 290
  Moriah 49
Caneday, R. H. 5
Canedy, Gideon 5
Caniday, Rozanah 61

Cannady, Elizabeth 43
  Wyatt 43
Canody, Liuizar 123
Canough, Ephraim 29
Canter, Joseph 43
Cantern, Martha 275
Cantol, Hannah 35
Cantrel, Jean 30
  Sarah 276
Cantrell, Nancy 317
Cantril, William 43
Cantrill, Benjamin 217
Cape, Ellen Jane 311
  Mary Ann 17
  Mary S. 101
  Patsey 106
  Redding 73
  Susan 43
  Thomas 248
Capley, Susan 321
Cappins, William 220
Capps, Eleanor 196
  James 43
  Mary 287
  Milly 43
  Robert 196
Carathers, Sarah Ann 94
Card, Annie 151
  Martha 34
  Saml. 151
  Sarah 34
Carden, Betsey 188
  Elizabeth 177
  Elizabeth Ann 291
  Elizabeth M. 188
  Emaline 72
  Fanny 291
  Giles 44
  Hawkins 242
  Ic. W. 116
  Lucindy 33
  Martha J. 189
  Nancy 35, 80, 301
  Patsy 43
  Polley 58
  Polly 178
  Robert J. 189, 190,
    206
  Silas 44.
  Simpson 301
  William 177
Cardin, Arkridge 44
  James 39
  John 44
  John 120
  John W. 44, 181
  Jones 44, 80, 178
  Patsey 177, 339
  Sally 161
  William 44
  Wm. 187
Carell, Lemuel L. 266
Carey, George 57
  Sally 315
  Sarah 209
Cargin, James 227
Carington, John 150
  Mary Ann 91
Carlisle, Peggy 103
Carll, Stephen L. 29
Carlton, A. M. 20
  Ann 179
  D. J. 20
  Daniel 59
  Harriett 168
  Jane 204
  Jno. D. 43, 44, 73,
    143, 177, 194, 201,
    233, 245, 308

Carlton, John D. 329,
    339
  Leod. 275
  Leonard 154
  Lidia A. 12
  Lovina 275
  Margaret 201
  Margaret E. 20
  Martha 7, 133
  Mary 168, 215
  Nathan 43, 137
  Reuben 168
  Sally 181
  Samuel 308
  Susannah 72
  William 44
  Wm. P. 240
Carmical, John H. 152
Carmichael, Leven 29
  Peggy 289
Carmichal, Green 133
  Laire 7
Carmichel, Archibo 329
  Levin 21
Carmichl, Loven 129
Carmickle, Levan 171
Caroll, Sidney 259
Carpenter, Isaac 176
  Sarah 176
  Susanna 41
Carr, Alfred 292, 293
  Anne 60
  J. W. 31, 84, 105,
    115, 162, 168, 256,
    257
  Margaret 312
  Mary E. 125
  Nancy Jane 311
  Sarah 217
  William 91
Carragin, Margaret 251
Carral, Benjamin 62
Carrall, James 45
Carregan, John 116
Carrel, Candis 8
  Elenor 51
  Martha 51
Carrell, Anne M. 172
  Dolly 333
  Lamuel 326
  Mary 86
  Moses 56
  Sidney 172
Carrigan, Frances 325
  John 46
  Margaret 241
  Margret 50
  Mark 153
  Susa 309
  Wm. A. 121
Carrington, A. 161
  A. S. 88, 98, 314
  Alfred 146
  Amelia 319
  Archibell 161
  Archibelle 95
  Areneah 47
  Arthur L. 313
  Benj'n. 47
  Celia 221
  Charlotte 74
  D. 25
  Delila 118
  Dicey 74, 200
  E. H. 47, 83, 227
  Elizabeth 150, 291
  Ellen D. 223
  Fanny 47

357

Clinton, Martha C. 341
  Mary C. 93
  Matthew 66, 241
  Mildred 322
  Nancy 224
  Sarah 326
  W. B. 91
  W. S. 44
Closs, Jn. 83
Cloud, David 64
  David S. 224
  Jacob 148
  Joel 64, 300
  Polly 28
  Sally 224
  Samuel 180
Clowd, Daniel 56
Clower, Catherine 311
Coasts, Burres 187
Cobb, Elizabeth 249
  George 22
  Mariah 119
  Mary 215
  O'Felia 215
  Wm. 65
Cobea, Louisa 263
Cobit, James 272
Coble, Barbara 169
  Barbery 231
  Catherine 205
  Caty 141, 343
  D. C. 65
  Daniel 3, 227
  Davad 275
  David 31, 98, 282
  Delilah 329
  Dl. 65
  Elizabeth 65, 100, 282
  Eva 279
  Jacob 21
  John 64, 108, 280, 300
  Malinde 197
  Margaret 205
  Mary 27
  Mebane 205
  Nancy 65
  Peggy 195, 283
  Peter 283
  Philip 141
  Polley 280
  Polly 272
  Sally 108, 182
  Samuel C. 288
  Sarah 21
Coby, Julus 298
Cocke, Anzolett C. 49
  Elizabeth 149
  Ema J. 211
  Martha M. 228
  Victoria 307
  Victoria R. 307
Cocklerease, Mary 6
Cocks, Betsy 99
Coe, Avery 65
  John G. 112
Coffner, George 256
Coggin, Margaret L. 43
Coggins, Brantly 287
Cohen, A. D. 277
Cohern, Hesther 83
Cohorn, Iz. 52
Cohran, Thos. 275
Cole, Allen 127
  Andrew 154, 297
  Anthony 36, 66, 241
  Betsy 162
  Carleton B. 161, 218
  Caroline 90

Cole, Catey 305
  Catherine 66, 284
  Eliza 90
  Eliza J. 289
  Elizabeth 51
  Elizabeth F. 25
  Emanuel 328
  Fanny 182
  Hannah 180
  J. W. 316
  James 65
  James A. 66
  James B. 15
  James R. 75
  Jane 112
  Jesse 245
  John 67, 148, 168, 193
  John O. 196
  John P. 119
  Levi 180, 206
  Lidda 227
  Margaret F. 75
  Martin 66, 207, 339
  Mary Ann 253
  Merriman 83
  Merrimon 65
  Nancey 193
  Nancy 241
  Nancy Jane 159
  Phebe 83
  Pheby 140
  Polley 38
  Rebecca 15, 48
  Rody 162
  S. P. 67
  Saml. 25
  Samuel 31, 47, 66
  Sarah 169
  Sarah C. 199
  Spencer 115
  Stephen 66
  Susan 66
  Susan F. 182
  Susnanah 246
  Tempe 91
  Thomas 67, 158, 180, 182, 253
  W. T. 331
  William 66
  Wm. 236
Coleman, Alley 168
  Edward B. 270
  Joseph 67
  Melena B. 67
  Meryman 157
  Saml. 67
  Samuel 222
  Sarah 53
Coling, Nancy 188
Collier, Catherine G. 137
  Elizabeth Ann 267
  Francis 133
  J. J. 143
  John G. 267
  Julia 327
  Lucretia 1
  Lucy 328
  Pattsy 162
  Rebecca T. 143
Collins, Allen 167, 247
  Andrew 50
  Andw. 134
  Ann 105, 313
  Bradley 157, 309
  Brice 14, 20, 151
  Clara 236

Collins, Derina 55
  Eliza 280
  Eliza Ann 97
  Elizabeth 140, 184, 330
  Elizabeth A. 321
  Enoch 188, 252
  Francis C. 326
  George P. 8
  Hardey 216
  Hetty 286
  Iby 77
  J. 329
  James 213
  Jean 98
  Jeany 109
  John 19, 157
  Joseph 103
  Josiah 68
  Labon 331
  Lucinda 142
  Lucy 102
  Mary 62, 252
  Mary Ellen 225
  Nancy 64, 205
  Nelly 48
  Polley 258
  Polly 266
  Saml. N. 135
  Winefred 170
  Winney 212
Colman, Thos. 126
Colter, Herman 236
  Jean 101
Colton, Caroline L. 154
Coltur, Cebe 146
Colwell, Wilson 238
Com(?), John 296
Comb, James 18
  Milly 308
  Nancy 321
Combes, David 139
Combs, Aron 167
Compton, A. 334
  Alfred 69
  Aquilla 69
  Bedord 82
  Delilah 320
  Hannah 69
  J. W. 318
  John 59, 69
  Lemuel 69
  Manerva 69
  Margaret C. 318
  Margaret F. 199
  Mary 326
  Mary Jane 273
  Norris 69
  Rachel 325
  Sarah 271
  Sarah E. 82
  Sieria G. 69
  Susannah 279
  T. F. 273
  T. H. 317
  Thos. 81
  Wesley S. 69
  William 60, 326
  Wm. 344
Conklin, Abner 50, 69
  Cave M. 262
  Jane 51
  Margaret 69
  Margarett 79
  Sally 50
Connally, John 70, 244
Connaly, Thos. 115
Connelly, Elizabeth 115

359

362

Dickey, George 103
    Harriett 87
    Jacob 87, 193
    Melisey 77
    Morgan 152
    Moses 276
    Munroe 87
    Susannah 153, 188
Dickie, D. 251
    Grizzy 291
    John 79, 199
    Polly 90
    Robt. 145
Dicks, Mary 148
Dickson, Alex. 270, 288
    Alexander 251
    Alexr. 24, 53, 62,
        66, 73, 75, 77,
        124, 159, 167, 184,
        188, 223, 257, 271,
        304
    Elizabeth 238
    Ephraim 308
    Grief 253
    Hannah 295
    James 88
    Jeane 210
    Joseph 158
    Mary 63
    Mary Ann 204
    R. W. 24
    Rebecca 307
    Stephen 251
    Susan 167
    Thomas 89
    Thos. 28, 321
    William 83
    Wm. 142, 167
Dicky, James 336
Diel, Isaac 200
Dier, Mary 338
Dilliard, Elizabeth 191
    Melinda 18, 307
    Willis B. 196
    Wm. 307
Dink, Silas M. 262
Dinnen, Angess 196
Dinning, David 287
Dinon, David 287
Dishon, Augustine 87,
    205
    Ghoston 88
    Lewis 227
    Luke 174
    Margaret 327
    Nancy 205
    Patsy 92
    Sarah 227
    Sophia 136
    Willie 319
Dishough, Geo. F. 88
Dison, Jno. 76
Dix, Sally 277
Dixon, A. A. 245
    Abner A. 88
    Adlaide M. 124
    Caroline G. 201
    Christiana 120
    Elizabeth 139, 203,
        309
    Ephraim 89
    Fanny 173
    G. W. 2
    Hannah 185
    Hesther 307
    James 61, 87
    Jane 88
    Jesse 148, 285

Dixon, Margaret 190
    Margret 299
    Martha 145, 216
    Mary 331
    Mary Ann 105
    Nancy 87
    Polley 137, 214
    Polly 110
    Reuben 52
    Robert 224, 326
    Robt. 218
    Solomon 198
    Thomas 190, 283
    Zelpha 299
Dixson, Elizabeth 45
Dobbins, Bryson 63, 300
Dobbs, Margery 46
Dockery, John 123
    Nancy 19
    Perry 4
    Polley 335
Dodd, Franky 70
    Polly 332
Dods, Wms. 154
Dodson, Edward 135
    Elias S. 329
    John 89
    Ruffin 89, 183
    Sarah Jane 293
    Thomas 30, 151, 280
    Wm. 89, 248, 250, 293
Doherty, Anthony 33, 65,
    319
    Betsy 65
    Ester 66
    Fanny 27
    Mary 97
    Nelly 343
    Polley 66
    Sarah 193
Dolar, Sarah 131
Doll, Jacob 129
Dollar, Charlotte 236
    Chesley H. 65
    Dodson 119, 246
    Dudley 45
    Elijah 89
    Elizabeth 32, 134,
        258
    Gilford 153
    Henry 64
    Jane 316
    John 52, 90, 258, 296
    John H. 45, 126
    Joseph 36
    Mary 58, 118, 180,
        258
    Milly 90
    Nancy 245
    Polley 65, 89
    Sally 10, 75, 259
    Stephen 90, 162
    Thomas 92, 245
    William 58, 67, 124
Doller, Elize 17
    Letha Ann 336
Dollerhit, Francis 138
Dolly, Kitty 215
    Rosannah 130
Donalson, Mary 62
Donate, Mary 258
Donnelly, J. B. 14, 96,
    178
Donovan, John 30
Dooly, John 45
Dorch, Lucy 317
Dorest, Sina 205
Dorety, Harrell 256

Dorman. Elizabeth 172
    John 25
Dormant, Polley 25
Dorrin, Joseph 227
Dorris, John 55, 91
Dortch, David 231
    Emmeline 184
    Polley 223
Dortherty, Anthony 91
Dosett, Ellert 41
    Henry 309
Dossete, Moses 313
Dossett, Carey 126
    Elbert 263
    Moses 21, 47
    Peggy 140
    Phebe 272
    Rachel 107
    Susannah 313
Dotts, Elbert 341
Doub, Peter 22, 83
Douglas, Adam M. 91, 225
    Celia 5
    George 142
    Jno. C. 305
    Margaret R. 289
Douglass, Demsey 8
    James 146, 289
    Jennett 191
    Peggy 194
    Rebecca 14
Dougles, Henry 91
Downs, Major 5, 107, 280
    Mary 4
Drake, Elizabeth 276
    Hyner 242
    Hynes 9, 79
    Joanna 269
    Rebecca 242
Dublin, James 334
Dudley, Molley 180
    Salley 41
    Susanna 67
Duffey, Patrick 171
Duffy, Mary 271
Duggar, Sarah 96
Dugger, Lydia 85
Duke, Amelia 256
    B. L. 245
    Berry 199
    Elizabeth 92
    Francis 266
    Henry 101
    Jesse 262
    John 93
    Kirkland 165
    Luena 244
    Martha 144
    Mary J. 143
    Nancy 144
    Nelly 32
    Peggy Cavuy 93
    Polley 178
    Polly 283, 296, 313
    Priscilla 46
    Rainy 64
    Robt. 93
    Sally 143
    Sandy 239
    Talor 313
    Taylor 244, 313
    Washington 113
    William 228
    William G. 244
    Wm. F. 44
    Wm. J. 19, 93, 113,
        139, 143, 175, 200,
        258, 322

364

Ellis, Nancy L. 192
Nathan 167
Parthena 131
Patsey 174
Polley 191
Polly 87
Sabrinah 1
Sidney 262
Stephen 199, 313
Stephen J. 98
William 176
William H. 60
Ellison, John 99
Joseph 99, 181
Margret 182
Nancy 22
Thomas 98, 182
Elliss, Allen P. 6, 236
Ellmore, John 198
Milly 304
Elmore, Ann 198
Elizabeth 61
James 71, 99
Jno. 99
John 1, 99, 260
Mary 260
Peter 228
Polley 1, 79
Sarah 228
Emerson, Adeline 78
Mariah 78
Tim 78
Emig, Nicklaus 7
Enoch, Benjamin 99
Ephland, George 233
Jacob 234
Ephlian, William 338
Ephlin, David 233
Erner, John 92
Esex, John 224
Essex, Isaac 273
John 187
Sally 187
Estes, J. 323
Jno. 57
John 142
Margaret 34
Susannah 56
Estis, Elizabeth 122
Estridge, Anne 133
Burres 48, 224
Burris 14, 242
Pattey 56
Sally 215
Susannah 133
Thomas 187
Etherage, Martha Ann 243
Franky 118
Martha Pool 66
Patsy 66
Riley 66
Ryals 118
Eubank, Dona Dorotha 18
Lydia 152
Miza 309
Euless, Alfred 100
Elizabeth 168
Marget 60
Peney 142
Peter 282
Eulis, Alfred 283
Katharine 282
Euliss, Allen 282
E. 169
Hiram 169
Milley 169
Eulys, P. 60
Evans, Agga 27

Evans, Aggy 246
Anna 276
Asa H. 201
Ben 248
Betsy Haily 131
Betsy Mason 246
Caroline 85
Dav'd. 267
Delilah 71, 342
Elizabeth 64, 100
Frances 136
Gidian 131
Henry 159
Isabella 32
Jane 159
John 180
Joseph 81
Julia 111
Mimis 246
Mins 27, 131
Moses 100
Nancy 131
Nanna 27
Patticar 141
Penelope 160
Reuben 342
Salley 209
Sally 227
Thos. 134
William 100
Evens, Mary Jane 13
Everett, Samuel 276
Everit, Hannah 290
Everydge, Betsey 119
Evins, Sally 227
Susannah 283
Ewing, David 127
Extore, Elizabeth 37
Ezell, James 217, 283
Jane 214
Faddis, And. 152
Andrew 182
Elizabeth 67, 98
Harriett 189
Jeany 69, 148, 158
John 10, 19, 139, 170,
190, 322
Martha 189
Mary 154
Nancy 190, 337
Fadis, Alexandder 59
Falker, Relam 328
Falkner, Beady 335
Emily 247
Harriett 108
Vincent 71, 126
Fann, Anne 337
Cresey 239
Elizabeth 2, 22
Rebecca 235
Tabitha 235
Fanny, Winnifred 244
Farley, Decly 170
Farmer, Coleman 161
Daniel Johnson 161
Drusilla 271
Jacob 275
Junny 161
Nath. 267
Nathan 52
Othniel 271
Rachel 167
Susanna 191
Susannah 246
Thos. 92
Farr, William 140
Farra, Martha Jane 103
Susan 214

Farrar, Gaston 232, 262,
330
Mariah 297
Mary J. 218
Farthing, John 197
Louena 200
Louisa A. 310
Martha 200
Nancy W. 143
Reuben 133
Salley 180
Thomas 200
William 143
Faucet, Anne 29
James 88, 298
Nancy 188
Samuel 95
Sarah 309
Thomas A. 119
Thomas D. 143, 317
Thomas U. 330
Faucett, A. L. 232
Albert F. 102
Allice 31
Ann 144
Anna 59, 103
Anna D. 329
Chesley F. 106
David 43, 104
Edward 194
Eleanor 186
Elizabeth 20
Elizabeth Jane 308
Elmore 331
Emma 135
Fanny 230
Frances 88
Frances Jane 238
Geo. W. 243
George A. 135
Green 102
H. 39, 88
Harriett 37
Harriett M. 103
Isabella 232
J. A. 103
J. M. 28
James A. 231
James M. 102
Jane 5, 129
Jm. M. 132
Jno. M. 6, 20, 23, 45,
57, 90, 93, 108,
117, 150, 164, 172,
184, 199, 222, 244,
289, 292, 319, 321
Jno. R. 185
John 8, 19, 25, 49,
51
John A. 114
John H. 152
John L. 23, 103, 236
John P. 132, 151
Joseph 102
Leonard 110
Levi 103
Lucinda 338
Lucy 276
Margret 322
Martha G. 232
Mary A. 43
Mary Ann 102, 142
Mary C. 242
Mary E. 9
Mary F. 167
Mary Jane 56
Milly 327
Minerva 76

370

Hall, N. P. 290, 340
 Nancy 26, 147, 256,
  306
 Nancy A. 306
 Nelson P. 10, 29, 126,
  131, 141, 146, 191,
  197, 219, 247, 250,
  256, 293, 305, 341
 Phebe 7, 104
 Polley 120, 209, 235
 Polley W. 182
 R. N. 146
 Rachel 209
 Rebaca E. 114
 Rebecca 100
 Robert 12, 171, 189,
  223, 267, 339
 Rosetta E. 330
 S. W. 306
 Salley 120
 Sarah 46, 190, 267
 Susan 257, 259
 Susanah 25
 Thomas 49, 209
 W. M. 271
 Washington 119
 William 32, 126, 256,
  337
 Wm. 127
 Wm. H. 84, 242
Hallaway, Fannie 253
Halliburton, Nancy 152
Halloway, Hawkins 62
Halsonback, Margaret J.
  75
Halstead, Sally 193
Hamhill, Stephen 165
Hamilton, A. 109, 128
 Archd. 128
 Catey 102
 Elizabeth 239, 318
 Margaret 92
 Martha 104
 Merryam 30
 Nancy 40
 Wm. 194
Hamlen, Wm. 20, 122
Hammond, John 38
 Margret 247
Hammonds, Anne 236
 Jeany 167
Hammons, John 134
Hampton, Duranna 269
 Kiziah 343
 Nolan 269
 Noland 291
 Z. 27
 Zachariah T. 129, 166
Hancock, Anne I. 242
 B. F. 232
 D. Hellen Evaline 25
 J. W. 240, 244, 265
 Jno. 44, 52, 53, 54,
  127, 159, 211, 242,
  253, 266, 289
 John 25, 86, 178, 211,
  238, 245, 281
 John R. 153, 175, 233
 Mary 80, 190
 Saml. 74
 Susan 31
 Susannah 90
 Thos. J. 135
Hancok, Thos. J. 135
Handcock, John W. 80
Handley, Elizabeth 284
Handly, Burwell 216
Hanks, Benj. F. 129
 Jane 129, 249

Hanks, Nancy 145
 Wesley 81
Hanley, Easter 321
 Susa 283
Hannah, Elizabeth 167
 Isabella 181
 Polley 256
 Polley D. 306
 William 119
Hanner, Alfred E. 100
Hansbrough, Hiram 40
Hapgood, Mary 234
Harbor, Archy 317
Hardcastle, Harriet 338
 William 333
Harden, J. H. 57, 192
 Jacob 283
 Jeany 329
 John 153, 329
 Joseph 105
 Margerite Jane 207
 Mary 105, 244
Harder, Charity 260
Hardie, Caroline 120
 Elizabeth 79
 Henretta R. 96
Hardin, Peggy 153
 Wm. H. 84
Hardy, J. B. 42
 Mary 325
 Sarah 275
Hares, Ann 144
Hargens, Elizabeth 14
Hargess, Anne 230
 Peggy 293
 Sarah 165
Hargis, Dennis 253
 Hypsiga 163
 Sally 25
 Sarah 130
 Tho. N. S. 90
 Thomas 130
 Thomas N. S. 270
Hargiss, Amey 247
 Peggy 256
 Polly 256
 Susannah 247
Hargrave, Ferabee 282
 Jesse 21
 Martha 27
 Mollie V. 168
Hargraves, Jesse 72
 Rich. 336
 Richd. 128
Hargrove, Nelson 130
 Phebe 130
Hargues, Eliza 199
 Rebeckah 248
Harguiss, Prudence 167
Hargus, Leucy 18
Haris, Charley 177
Harkham, C. G. 337
Harlow, Obadiah 181
Harmon, Leonard 39
Harney, Elizabeth 280
Harper, Ally 147
 Edmond 147
 Elizabeth 18
 Milley 160
 Moses 323
 Richard 107
 Sarah 125
 William 135
Harps, T. C. 205
Harrel, Rachel 135
Harrell, Betsey 294
 Edy 212
 Elvira E. 167
 Wm. B. 274

Harrington, George W. 60,
  107
 L. M. 130
 W. D. 130
Harris, Sir 23
 Amelia 15
 Bedy 182
 Betsey 79
 Betsy 331
 Charles 176
 Charlotte 289
 Drady 229
 Edward 85
 Edward B. 278
 Elijah 324
 Elizabeth 200, 223
 Elizabeth A. 200
 Ellender 131
 Ellenor 241
 Emily 321
 Ephraim 114, 130
 Frances 164
 Franklin 211
 Harrison 149
 Jacob F. 123
 James 130, 131
 James R. 306
 Jane 52, 305
 Jesse 131
 Louisa 10
 Lucy 278
 Mack 131
 Mark 342
 Mary 18, 85, 97, 190,
  223, 335
 Melinda 242
 Morning 194
 Nancy 262, 306
 Nat. D. 213
 Nathl. D. 178
 Nelly 322
 Othy 331
 Otly 131
 Patsy 199
 Pattey 130
 Polley 34
 R. H. 306
 Rebecca 114
 Richmond 164
 Robert 92
 Robert H. 228
 Ruth 342
 S. 23, 221
 Sarah 171, 190
 Sterling 177, 235, 256,
  297
 Susan 324
 Thos. 131, 331
 W. 124, 131
 William 270
 Wms. 131
Harrison, Elizabeth 336
 Robert 7
Harrod, Eliza 16
Harrold, Jas. A. 167
Hart, David 173
 Elizabeth 170, 198,
  218
 Ellen 40
 Gilb. 289
 James 132
 Jeany 287
 John 289
 John U. 135, 152
 John W. 208
 M. 154, 162, 290, 326,
  330
 Margarett 249
 Morgan 71, 214

377

Lloyd, Nancy Taylor 183
  Patsey 317
  Presilla 52
  Rebecca 332
  Rutha C. 15
  S. L. 291
  S. S. 10
  Salley 99
  Sarah 32, 89, 94,
    183
  Secelina 10
  Stephen 97, 187
  Stephen S. 81
  Tabitha 170
  Thomas 99, 215
  Thomas M. 183
  Thomas Morrow 146
  Thos. 32, 183, 242
  William 184
  Wm. 183, 184, 226,
    304
Lloyed, Margarett 170
Lockhart, Adline 187
  Asa 187
  Bedie A. 230
  David 143
  Eleanor 180
  Elizabeth J. 87
  Fanny 339
  James 274
  Jas. 111
  Jno. 182, 316
  Jno. L. 228
  John 184
  John P. 114
  Lucy 187
  Margarett J. 62
  Nancy 237
  Sally 61
  Temperance 184
  William 289
  Wm. 21, 197, 235
Locust, Ferabee 116
Loften, Caty 344
Logan, Elizabeth 14
  Henry 86
Logen, Ellienor 264
Loinberry, Ann 162
  Eve 108
Long, Abram 180, 272
  Adam 169
  Alexr. 135
  Barbara 332
  Charles 185
  Elizabeth 132, 185,
    328
  Elizabeth Ann 51
  Georg 14
  George 14, 192, 210,
    252
  James 68, 69, 192
  Jennet 14
  Jesse 206
  John 73
  John C. 335
  Julia 27
  Margaret E. 83
  Margarett B. 38
  Mary Jane 53
  Nelson 186
  O. F. 154
  O. T. 61
  T. 39, 81, 38, 191,
    222
  Thomas 9
  Thos. 15, 26, 42, 45,
    50, 52, 75, 113,
    117, 123, 171, 172,

(Long, Thos., cont'd)
    183, 232, 233, 239,
    247, 263, 270, 292,
    293, 311, 323, 343
  Thos.A. 305
  Willism 34
  Wm. J. 83, 168
Longmire, Polley 340
Lott, Zephannah 295
Love, A. M. 80
  Anne 39
  Delia Ann 167
  Ellenor 62
  Jas. 269
  Leweser 297
  Margret 132
  Mary 212
  Thomas 212
Lovens, Ester 112
Lovine, Delilah 168
Lovins, Polley 107
  Sarah 334
Low, Cannaday 186
  Elizabeth 32
  Jno. 32
  Joel 18, 66
  Margret 149
Lowe, Kezia 329
Lowry, Margaret 41
Loy, Elizabeth 266
  Henry 156, 186
  Jacob 266
  Jane 65
  John 335
  Mary 281
  Polly 156
  Sally 273
  Tempy 272
  William 321
  Willis 65
Loyd, Biddy 341
  Caty 32
  Delila 95
  Delilah 8
  Elizabeth 262
  Frederick 55
  H. B. 27
  James 156, 280
  John 10
  John Q. 10
  L. L. 233, 310
  Mary 242
  Nancy 32, 156
  Norris T. 229
  Owen 32
  Patsey 28
  Patty 99
  Sarah 77, 181
  Sarah C. 55
  William 183, 242
Loyed, Mary 181
Loyon, Ann B. 95
Lucas, Frances R. 238
Ludbetter, Benjamin 179
Lue, John 169
Luie, Polly 224
Lumley, Liman 3
  Mary 176
Lumly, Louisa 117
Lunch, Polley 111
Lunsford, Anguline 25
  Bob Satterfield 187
  Edy C. 93
  James N. 25, 187,
    306
  Joseph G. 206
  Nancy 305
  Polley 229

Lunsford, Rebecca 312
  Sarah 22
  W. A. 229
  William 228
  William D. 161, 206
  Winy 187
  Wm. D. 63, 87, 98,
    197, 305
Lynch, Anna J. 27
  Beddy 338
  Catharine 111
  Daniel 188
  David 237
  Elizabeth 130
  Fanny 181
  Farrabee 26
  Grief 26
  Harman 97
  James 188
  Jeany 71
  John 51, 181, 188,
    218
  L. G. 110
  M. B. 27
  Malinda 139
  Margaret J. 128
  Mary 27, 130, 317
  Minerva Ann 327
  Moses 86
  Nancy 53, 98
  Phoebe 1
  Polley 81
  Rosannah 236
  Ruth 295
  Sally 245
  Sarah 101, 160
  Susan 317
  T. M. 188
  Thomas 27, 132, 189,
    212, 271, 295, 317
  Thos. 21, 27, 43, 81,
    116, 171, 188, 239,
    255, 272, 317
Lynn, Barbary 203
  Catharine 314
  Christopher 261
  Edy 254
  James 293
  Martha 59, 265
  Michal 202
  Peter 185
  Polly 18
Lyon, C. H. 68
  J. F. 158
  John F. 37, 45 , 51,
    61, 65, 67, 75, 90,
    126, 130, 142, 153,
    157, 158, 131, 180,
    182, 188, 206, 251,
    253, 258, 262, 331,
    341
  Laura L. 321
  Loretta J. 142
  Marcom A. 165
  Tho. B. 43
  Z. J. 58
Lytle, Mary 258
  Rachel 5
  Robert 5
  Sarah 223
Lyttle, Polly 123, 160
Mabery, John 4
Mabray, R. C. 116
Mabrey, Patsey 50
  R. C. 225
Mabrie, J. A. 71
Mace, Robert 199
Mack, Jane 12

382

383

McCauley, Louisa 76
  Lucinda 110
  Mary 179, 327
  Matthew 2, 66, 171,
    191
  Nancy 183, 276
  Patsey 170
  Patsy 216
  Polley 189, 224
  Robert 131
  Sarah 322
  W. 23, 90
  William 241, 242, 258
  Wm. 39, 40, 56, 132,
    146, 203, 295, 304,
    307, 309
McCauly, Archy 172
  C. J. F. 195
  Catharine 23
  D. 192
  H. C. 305
  Henry C. 130
  J. W. 282
  Jane 185
  Jean 192
  Jno. 317
  Johnston 185
  Lucy 112
  M. J. W. 234
  Matthew 172
  Polley 276
  Robert 192
  W. 23, 160
  William 76
  Wm. 20, 65, 93, 192,
    278, 312
McCawley, John 23
  Mary 24
  Will 40
  Wm. 250
McCawn, Cely Couch 231
  McKinza 228
  Saml. 231
McClaen, Jas. G. 220
McClain, Fanny 309
McClary, Elizabeth 275
  Hetty 67
McClennon, Mary 323
McCleur, James 208
McCleure, Elizabeth 127
McClure, Anna 45
  Edith 103
  Elizabeth 196
  Henrey 125
  James 245, 295
  Marion 236
  Peggy 245
  Polley 189
  Sarah 88
  William D. 236
McClusky, Nancy 148
  Wm. 56
McColluch, Levi 24
McCollum, H. 88, 106,
    192, 222, 272
  Henry 115, 185, 199
  Levi 41, 108, 175,
    182, 201, 269, 293,
    303
  Margret 256
  Mary 177, 202
  Pevi 167
  Rosannah 108
McCollumb, H. 191
McCombs, Hannah 125
McCool, Elisabeth 276
  Mary 82
McCord, Mary 18

McCory, Susan 170
McCown, J. C. 28, 92
  John C. 129, 155,
    279
  Moses 35, 254
  Rachel 276
  W. M. 46
  William 127
  Wm. 28, 37, 44, 53,
    54, 93, 129, 142,
    155, 176, 178, 199,
    223, 241, 283, 301,
    314
  Wm. W. 44
McCoy, Elener 266
  Frances 137
  Henry 137
McCracken, Catherine
    295
  Hannah 310
  Holloway 193
  John 112, 152, 260
  John W.. 25
  Margaret 316
  Nancy 260
  Precilla 295
  Sarah 112, 135
  Stephen 193
  Thomas 295
McCrackin, Anne 231
  Salley 94
  Susan M. 277
McCraken, Joseph 158
McCrakin, Alexander 335
McCrary, Thomas 148
McCreey, George 120
McCrey, John 247
McCrorey, David 18
  George 155
McCrory, Hannah 123
  Ludwick 194
McCulley, Andrew 18, 194
  Lidia 194
  Mary 112
  Moore 237
  Peggy 304
  Sarah 128
McCulloch, Ariana E. 268
  Caroline Whitmore 214
  Catharin 26
  Deborah 318
  Eliza 214
  Elizabeth J. 170
  Hunter 7, 87, 303
  James 194
  Mary 163
  Peter 214
McCullock, Emily 278
  Emley 21
  Jos. 242
  Lydia 208
  Lynda 243
  Mary E. 271
  Molley 25
  Peggy 176
  Polley 308
  Rachel 101
  Wm. 208
McCulloh, Elizabeth 3
McCullohs, Wm. 101
McCullom, Peace 137
McCully, Josiah 106
McDade, D. C. 11, 65, 71,
    100, 151, 195, 264,
    277, 282, 323
  Daniel C. 179
  Danl. C. 195
  Edward 66, 184, 193,

(McDade, Edward, cont'd)
    240, 257, 260, 261,
    265
  Elizabeth E. 192
  H. L. 69
  Henderson 195
  J. 78
  J. B. 20, 33, 54, 103,
    110, 111, 115, 131,
    136, 150, 163, 181,
    187, 206, 209, 215,
    230, 236, 238, 282,
    286, 308, 320, 322,
    336
  J. C. 57
  J. H. 33, 98
  J. M. 90
  Jno. M. 237
  John 218, 275
  John A. 238, 296
  John H. 33
  John S. 291
  Josephine N. 110
  Martha Jane 199
  Mary J. 243
  Mary O. 274
  P. H. 17
  Polly 195
  Rosanah J. 159
  W. H. 205
  Wayne H. 33
  William 270
McDanel, Henry 337
McDaniel, A. C. 234,
    302
  Alson 249
  Alsun 163
  D. 75
  Eli 195
  Elizabeth 98, 332
  H. 22, 78, 79, 93,
    144, 163, 216, 248,
    302
  Henry 80, 186
  J. S. 97
  James 116, 195, 196
  Jane 249
  Jas. 196
  John 195, 197, 238
  Joseph 198
  Lucy 209
  Margaret 232
  Margaret R. 198
  Martha 280
  Nancy 211, 249
  Patsey 15, 133
  Sally 279
  Samuel 4
  Sarah 248
  Susannah 331
  William 112, 232, 303
  Wm. 248, 331
  Wm. P. 297
McDaniels, Nancy 334
McDanil, Casson 204
McDanl, Lindsay 196
McDannel, Eli 230
  Elizabeth 301
  James 301
  John 196, 221
  Sarah 221
McDonnel, Nancy 235
McDougall, Allan 308
McEroom, Nancy 31
McFaling, Andrew 119
McFarland, Dicey 70
  Henry 196
  John 196

385

387

Moore, Jane 160, 306
  Jennett 188
  Jo. 104, 123
  John 12, 141, 176,
    195, 213, 214, 261,
    320, 324
  John S. 45
  Joseph 141
  Julia R. 99
  Lewis 4
  Lucy 214
  M. W. 144, 280
  Margret Ellen 114
  Martha 35, 118, 165,
    276, 308
  Martha A. F. 144
  Mary 34, 114, 289,
    323
  Mary A. 292
  Matthew 274
  Nancey 144
  Nancy 132, 153, 231,
    292, 293, 294
  Nancy Jane 89
  Nancy N. B. 220
  Patsey 278
  Patsy 23, 175
  Peggy 164
  Polley 12, 44, 102,
    176
  Polly 195
  Rachael 125
  Richard 165
  Robert 54, 79, 116,
    216, 239, 246, 256,
    261, 276
  Salley 90, 272
  Saml. P. 5, 336
  Sampson 116
  Samuel P. 194, 309
  Sarah 80, 123, 153,
    244
  Sarah A. 213
  Sarah H. 175
  Sophia 124
  Step. 71
  Stephen 16, 31, 70,
    135, 300
  Susan U. 206
  Susannah 264, 344
  T. W. 20
  Thomas 188, 204, 212
  Thos. 294
  Timpy 329
  Valentine 165
  William 70, 106, 117,
    181, 212, 214, 223
  Wm. 205, 292
  Wm. J. 243
  Wm. L. 12, 177, 279
Mordach, James 37
Mordecai, Isaac 281
Morehead, Jenny 161
  Jim 161
Moreland, Elizabeth 254
  Frances 20
  Fras. 107
  Nancy 40
Morgan, Betsey 251
  Betsy A. 209
  Claresia 307
  Cynthia A. 219
  Dolley 179
  Eliza 229
  Esther 235
  Harriett 149
  John 215
  Jones 203

Morgan, Lem'l M. 148
  Lucy 307
  Mary 106, 203
  Mary Ann 187
  Nancy 231
  Patsy 215
  Rachel 180, 215
  Sallie 219
  Thomas J. 199
  William 219
  Wm. 187
  Zachrey Barbee 307
Morhead, Amelia 215
  Frank 215
Moring, Betsy 43
  Cynthia 62
  Elizabeth 229
  James 62
  Martha 16
  Patrick H. 181
Moris, Fanny E. 166
  Fred. 287
  James 158
  John 215
Morley, Wm. P. 202
Morphis, Alexr. 198
  Saml. 105
Morphus, Eliza 166
  Lizza 166
  Saml. 166
Morraw, George 80
  Jane 80
  Mary J. Thompson 80
Morray, Allsee 79
Morring, Annie E. 62
  James 62
Morris, Bettie S. 73
  Biddy 31
  E. W. 56, 59, 62,
    115, 199, 229
  Eliza Elizabeth 271
  Elizab. 208
  Elizabeth 242
  Fanny 182
  Fielding 216
  Frances 287
  Hannah 216
  Henry 323
  Isaac 66, 181
  James 175, 215
  John 14, 18, 166
  John M. 34
  Julie 50
  Mary Jane 265
  Patsey 166
  R. F. 58, 62, 66, 91,
    97, 114, 115, 120,
    122, 126, 154, 179,
    193, 199, 220, 228,
    242, 266, 317, 321,
    323
  Ralph F. 171
  Robert F. 243
  Salley 35
  Sally 106
  Sickey 205
  Thomas 216
  Tilden 215
  W. H. 26
Morrison, Dibby 161
  Jane 203
  Ruth 310
Morrow, Adilade 272
  Andrew 35, 302
  Ann 300
  Candiss 109
  Elbridge 132
  Eliza 295

Morrow, Eliza J. 300
  Elizabeth 80, 141
  Ellen 305
  Franklin 217
  G. B. 234
  Geney 241
  Geo. W. 94, 97
  George B. 299
  J. S. 272
  James 111, 239, 248,
    303
  Jane 79
  Janett 318
  Jas. 216
  Jesse 246
  John 22, 37, 216,
    225
  Josiah 216
  Levi N. 78
  Lucy Lloyd 146
  Margaret 74
  Margaret F. 110
  Margaret Justice 146
  Martha 303
  Mary Jane 302
  Nancy 190
  Nelly 213
  Peggy 190, 210
  Polley 43
  Rachael 302
  Robert 59, 219, 318
  Robt. 30
  Salina 300
  Sally 217
  Sarah 179
  Thomas 146, 237
  William 38, 216
  William P. 216
Morten, Jacob 283
Morton, Edney 303
  G. W. 16
  Harriet 128
  Jacob 217
  Nancy 199
  Nancy 199
  Rebeccah 341
  Sarah 40
  William 217
Mosely, John 5
Moser, Barbara 343
  Daniel 216, 274
  Elizabeth 109
  Eve 275
  Jacob 260
  John 217
  Molly 156
  Nelle 109
  Nimrod 217
  Peter 224
  Peyton 313
  Sally 216
  Tobias 109
  Turley 285
  William 109
Mosier, Eva 273
  Nancy 224
Moss, Clarey 18
Moulden, Jacob 148
Moulton, Elizabeth 56
Moye, Oxford 305
Mulhollan, Elizabeth 17
  Hugh 151, 210, 278
  John 88
  Mary 162, 280
  Thos. 162
Mulhollay, Thos. 3
Mulhollon, H. 229
  John 294

388

Mumford, Robinson 233
Muray, James 132
   Walter 11
Murden, Saml. 218
Murdoch, A. C. 30, 33,
   41, 78, 309, 317
   Henry 75
   Jn. 255
   Mary 37
Murdock, A. C. 77, 101,
   129, 160, 172, 206,
   235, 303
   Alexander 218
   Andw. 5
   Betsy 149, 285
   Elizabeth 86, 256,
   343
   Jane 77, 82
   Jenney 269
   John 218
   Martha E. 139
   Nancy 284, 343
   Polly 74
   R. 233
   Rebecca ALlon 130
   Solomon Allen 285
   Susan 6
Murdok, James 156
Murduk, Polley 128
Murfree, Henry J. 6
Murley, Elizabeth 233
Murphey, Casy 203
   Charlot Jane 195
   Elizabeth 69
   Jacob 39
   Lucinda C. 209
   Macons 4
   Martin 39
   Nancy 321
   Sarah Frances 195
   Sarah P. 285
   Silvey 69
   V. M. 268, 322
   Victor M. 115, 271
   William 218
Murphy, Elizabeth 118
   Sarah 328
Murray, Alfred 219
   Amanda P. 237
   Andr. 219
   Andw. 18, 211, 315
   Anne 5
   Ceelia 129
   D. 237
   Duncan 222
   E. 84
   Eli 174, 271, 272,
   305
   Elizabeth 64, 77, 268,
   320
   Elizabeth Jane 272
   Elizabeth M. 219
   Emeline 297
   Emma 215
   Fanny 155
   Hinton 218
   J. A. 211
   Jacob 219
   James 190, 219, 297,
   319
   Jane 111
   John 111, 274
   John B. 297
   Joseph 260
   Margeret 23
   Martha 7
   Mary 202
   Mary C. 105

Murray, Nancy 280
   Philpane 20
   Polley 110
   Polly 158, 186, 284
   Rachel 281
   Rebeccah 260
   Robert 203, 213, 264
   Robet 210
   Sarah 11
   W. G. 85
   William 23, 108, 210,
   264
Murrell, Henry A. 75
Murrey, James 2
   William I. 318
Murrow, Rachel 319
Murry, A. 220, 272
   James 220
   Wm. 215
Muzzale, Wm. 81
Myers, W. R. 55
Myrack, Levinia 231
Nance, Allen 26
   Jno. 220, 312
Nancy, Allen A. 178
   Charlotte 119
Nangum, Elizabeth 297
Nash, Ann E. 290
   Elizabeth S. 86
   F. 171, 180, 225
   H. K. 220
   Henry K. 22, 133
   Susan M. 250
Natgrass, Polly 336
Nathcock, Susanah 236
Neace, Betsey 152
   Elizabeth 221
   Felty 123
   Jacob 117, 221
   Mariah 284
Neal, Bitsey 74
   Edith 76
   Eliza 26
   Eliza Jane 86
   Henry 204, 217
   James 134
   Jno. A. 254
   Martha W. 310
   Mary 6
   Nancey 24
   Nancy 134
   Riley 17, 134, 221,
   270
   Sarah 330
Nealey, Jno. D. 311
   Rebecca 2
Nealy, Margaret 105
   Nancey 321
Nease, Elizabeth 281
   Martin 221
   Milly 73
   Prissey 26
   Sally 272
   Samson 185
   Simon 89
   Tenah 221
Neeley, Elizabeth D.
   223
   John 340
   Martha 200
   Wesley 161
Neely, Elizabeth 37
   Ellena 311
   Louisa 177
   Racheal 241
Nees, Jacob 26
Neese, John 221
   Joseph 221

Neighnors, Nelson 221
Neiley, Nancy 131
Nelson, Anne 252
   Betsy 164
   Daniel 201
   David 4, 5, 164, 221
   Ellen 193
   Genney 73
   George 301
   Iby 77
   Isber 5
   James 109, 283
   Jane R. 228
   Jenny 263
   Margaret 296
   Margret 132
   Mary 232
   Milley 207
   P. 132, 277, 279, 280
   Peggy 93
   Polley 277
   Presley 4, 279
   Samuel 4, 117, 295
   Wm. 1, 75, 150, 170,
   175, 194, 299, 316,
   332, 333, 340
Nerndon, John R. 227
Nese, Elias 26
Nethery, Eliza 221
   Manerva 220
Neugee, Elisabeth 322
Nevelle, Mary W. 215
Neves, John 124
Nevill, Celah 172
   Celia 281
   Charles 98
   Cynthia 192
   Elizabeth 182
   George 9
   Jesse 172, 182
   Rebecca 147
   Wm. 142
Neville, Esspran 171
   Goodmon 222
   Patsy 281
Nevills, Aris 264
   Charles 98
   Elizabeth 16
   Espram 184
   Goodwin 172
   Isperan 184
Newcomb, William 236
Newcum, Mary 76
Newland, Nelly 125
Newlin, Deliarah 198
   Duncan 97
   James 113
   Jas. 64
   John 86, 210
   Jonathan 48
Newman, Elizabeth 7
   Frances J. 74
   John 59
   John A. 296
   Sarah 39
   Susan 45
   William 105, 129
Newmane, John 302
Newton, James 15
   L. H. 83, 223, 327
   Lettice 15
   Sarah 256
Newyen, Sarah 207
Nicholes, Mary 293
   Richeson 158
Nichols, A. 126, 223
   Aletha, A. 127
   Alves 90, 322

389

Nichols, Archibald 41
Balay 93
Betsy 18
Ellen R. 223
Emme M. 309
Fanny 264
Frances 130, 178
Frances J. 208
Francis 184
Hannah 256
Harriett 289
Hy. 55
John 66, 179
Louisa H. 223
Lucie M. 335
Margret 157
Martha E. 223
Mary 108
Nancey 79
Nancy 62
Nelson 127
Polly 61
R. 206
Rich. 226
Richardson 331
Richd. 19, 25, 66,
128, 157, 167, 259,
282
Richison 35, 76, 190,
223
Richs. 52, 90, 248
258
Sarah 142, 195
Sarah E. 118
Susan A. 275
Tamesia 248
William 188
William A. 223
Wm. 26
Nicholson, Archd. 201
Delitha D. 313
James 224
Jas. 84
Jeany 302
Rebecca 166
Sally 233
Susannah 201
Nickols, Baldwin 223
Duncan 130
Nicks, Joseph 234
Susannah 234
Niece Salley 2
Niell, Riley 137
Nile, Frederick A. 206
Nipper, Harriett 248
Noah, Amos 224
Jeremiah 224
Mary 121
Noble, John 104
'lartha 92
Noe, John 224
Sam 38
Norfleet, Thos. M. 236
Norman, James G. 224
Samuel 224
Normon, Francis 224
Norner, Willis 39
Norrace, William 269
North, Ellen P. 65
Norwood, Annabella 154
Eliza 236
Eliza A. 22
J. W. 177, 338
Jane B. 305
John 154
Mary 13
Robina 324
W. A. 102, 122, 143,
193, 278

Norwood, Walter A. 40,
127, 305
Will 22
Nowlin, James 185
Nuland, Eli 116
Numan, William 112, 255
Nunn, Clara 288
David 102
Detcy 102
Edy 302
Eliz'th 81
Emily 72
Jane 288
Mary Barbee 102
Rachel 72
Ruffin 72
Salley E. 264
William 207
Nutt, Catey 93
Charity W. 275
Eliza Jane 119
Jane 50
Polley 50
Robert 93
Oakey, Samessinger 49
Oakley, Barton 307
Beletha 307
E. D. 34, 316, 330
Erasmus 243
F. L. 320
Margaret 124
Martha J. 247
Nancy 296
Sally 221
Tazza 292
W. E. 293
Oaky, Polley 220
Obrian, Louis 115
O'Dananel, Susa 19
Odanel, John 174
O'Daniel, Alfred 285,
303
Elizabeth 172, 261
Green 172, 276
Henry 80, 111, 195,
209, 211, 226, 238,
239, 250, 253, 281,
292
Jane 196
Janie 302
Jesse 151
Jinney 81
John 195
Margaret 238, 281
Martha 111
Mary 26
Mary Rlenor 39
Nancy 225
Polly 80
Sally 76, 303
Sally J. 78
Samuel 196
Susan 303
William 196
O'Daniels, Henry 261
John 248
O'Dan'l, Green 28
O'Dannel, Jane 49
O'Dear, Ester 44
O'Farhell, Thomas 68
O'Ferrell, Thomas 58
Ogburn, Wm. J. 173
Oka, Sarah 97
O'Kelly, F. 109
John 20
Margaret E. Davis
109
Martha 109
William J. 16

O'Kelly, Wm. 92
Zinas 226
Oldham, Caroline 284
George A. 20
Henry C. 311
Holaday R. 245
Mary 289
Sallie J. 214
Thos. D. 281
Thos. S. 276
Thos. T. 88
W. P. 277
Y. A. 226
Oliver, Isabella F. 217
Omerry, Jane 330
Oneal, John H. 32
Nancy 167
Rachel 47
Wm. 2
Oneil, Wm. 129
O'Neill, Thomas 102
Thos. 60, 133
Orrand, Sarah 99
Osborn, George 196
Osborne, Margaret 273
Osbun, William 287
Outlaw, Julia 266
Overbey, Hartwill S. 91
Overman, Benjamin 226,
276
James 226
Patsy 232
William 227
Owen, H. 101
H. L. 214
Jno. A. 83, 224
Lear 236
Salley 296
Owens, Livina 236
Nancy 160
P(?), Exom 245
Pace, David D. 217
Joseph B. 210
Packer, A. W. 340
Padlock, John 144
Page, Isham 340
Jane 340
Mary 340
Pain, Abel 144, 189, 206
Anne 97
Elizabeth 186
Henry 302
Paine, Margaret 277
Painey, John S. 170
Paisley, Eliza D. 183
Saml. 227
Palmer, Anges 229
Elizabeth 233
J. M. 218
James 184
James M. 45, 55, 61,
163, 181, 186, 191,
227, 261, 295, 319
James W. 344
Jas. 136
Jas. M.]3, 133, 312
Margaret W. 188
Martin 153, 233
Mary 153
Mary C. 211
Nancy 59
Nathaniel J. 70
Sarah 136
Tempe 102
William 280
Pane, Jas. M. 37
Pannell, Eliza D. 226
Jno. 29
Mary 29

Param, Rachel 160
Parck, Elender 174
Paris, Henry 146, 165
  Mary 301
  William 237, 257, 301
  Wm. 31
Parish, Alvis 53
  Annie E. 213
  Doctor C. 228
  C. E. 337
  Calven 3. 188
  Calvin E. 100, 139
  Charles 32
  Christiana 263
  Claborn 262
  Clara 105
  D. C. 131, 184
  Eliza 211
  Elizabeth 187
  Emma A. 184
  Green 200
  James 200
  Jiney Parker 200
  Joel 136, 226
  Letha 47
  Louisa M. 178
  Mark 200
  Rutha 184
  Salley 200
  Susan 199
  Thomas 230
  W. A. 125, 164, 229,
    277, 281
  William 214
  Williamson 29
Parker, A. 68
  A. W. 19, 28, 139,
    313, 340
  Anna G. 49
  Catherine 344
  Clara E. 262
  D. F. 178
  David 228
  Drady 26
  Elizabeth 149, 335
  Elizabeth E. 136
  Ellen Jane 304
  Emeline B. 319
  Ferabee 92
  Green Parish 200
  H. 12, 229
  Holly 149
  J. P. 103, 228
  Jacobina 281
  James 149
  Jiney 200
  John 43
  John A. 103
  John W. 263
  Joseph 311
  Josephine 263
  Judah 177
  Julia 243
  Louanna 131
  Lucy P. 344
  Margaret J. 188
  Mariah L. 62
  Martha 229
  Mary L. 144
  Nancy 100, 313
  Nancy Ann 340
  Nancy M. 144
  Rebecca 35, 101
  Salley 44, 149
  Sally 228
  Sarah 262
  Sophronia 312
  Susan 316
  William 229, 316

Parkes, Jonathan 87
Parks, A. 4, 66, 87, 90,
  107, 111, 179, 204,
  218, 275, 277, 278,
  318, 341
  Alexander 192
  Allen 66, 180
  Betsy 304
  Charles M. 56, 166,
    188
  D. C. 330
  H. 66
  Hirum 265
  J. A. 229
  James 1, 42, 301
  Joseph 208
  Josephine 99
  Mariah L. 267
  Mary 319
  Nancy 312
  Thomas 229
  William 72, 249
Parmer, Jane 204
  Mary 153
Parnell, Winnifred 197
Parris, Mary E. 238
  Sally 302
Parrish, (?) 74
  Dr. 229
  Allen 68, 200, 296
  C. E. 320
  D. C. 32, 74, 93, 139,
    211, 228, 230, 263,
    312, 344
  Dempsy 32
  Eady 229
  Edith 187
  H. 154
  Hg. 245
  Isham 46
  J. A. 293
  James 47, 228, 229,
    263
  Jane 20
  John L. 312
  Mark 200
  Martha A. 166
  Mary 31
  Nancy 33, 46
  Nelson 109, 206, 234,
    305
  Walter A. 80
  William 187
  Williamson 29
  Wm. K. 152, 230, 316
  Wm. R. 263
  Wm(?)son 75
  Wmson 62, 85, 100,
    187, 312, 313
Parsons, Mary 269
Parten, Ann Eliza 222
  Mandra 320
Partin, Bennett 133
  Charles 230
  Elizabeth 138
  James 56, 120, 230,
    324
  Leania 311
  Lewis 75, 230
  Mary 324
  Tabitha 68
  Tempy 70
  William 138
  Wm. 68
Partridge, Sarah F. 323
Pascal, Sarah 152
Paschael, M. 12
  Nancy 138
  Rebecca 12

Pasmore, Hannah 163
  Humpy 98
  Ruthe 202
Pass, William 212
Passmore, David 111, 276
Pastin, B. F. 226
  Ed. 112
Patella, Ann 284
Paton, James C. 79
Patram, Rebeca 100
Patrun, Elizabeth 23
  John 23
Patten, James C. 103
  Jiles 318
  Martha 136
Patterson, Amelia 344
  Amelia H. 39
  Amey 17
  Andrew 192
  Catharine 14
  Cely Couch 231
  Charity 83
  Chesley M. 49, 72
  Eliza 147
  Elizabeth 14
  Frances 246, 308
  Geo. 83
  George 231
  Hardy 17
  Hawkins 276
  Isaac 65, 231
  Isabella 17
  J. C. 144
  James N. 276
  Jane 329
  Jas. 266
  Jas. L. 254
  Jas. N. 9, 10, 12, 24,
    45, 57, 148, 246
  John 269
  Julia A. 262
  Lugena 277
  Maletha 276
  Mann 152, 204
  Mary 108
  Mary Ann 104
  Mason 214
  Milinda 72
  Nancy 30, 197, 288
  Peggy 31, 278
  Penelope 27
  R. A. 123
  Richard 240
  Saml. McCawn 231
  Sarah 16, 189, 254,
    343
  Siney 193
  Susanah 249
  Tamesia 102
  Thos. B. 224
  W. N. 187
  W. W. 207
  Willey 231
  William 193
Pattin, Jane 231
Pattishall, William 254
Patton, Alex. 162, 231
  Alexr. 207
  Ally 147
  Ellen R. 103
  Jane 3, 285
  Janey 266
  John 161, 231
  Johnston 4
  Matthew 232
  Nancy 161
  Paisley 232
  Rebecca M. 102
  Samuel 163, 232

394

Rawls, William 100
Ray, Alexander 165
  Amelia 282
  Amy 249
  Ann 324
  Anna Jane 267
  B. M. 230
  Benton 41, 49, 92,
    116, 122, 146, 178,
    256
  Betsy 248
  Burton 35
  Catey 250
  Catharine 61, 279
  Charity 42
  Charlotte 263
  Chas. W. 219
  Christean 216
  Cornelia 23, 285
  D. H. 21
  David 67, 146, 203,
    232, 256, 269, 295,
    322
  David G. 157
  Edith 30
  Edney 15
  Eleanor 190
  Eliza 114
  Eliza Jane 296, 339
  Eliza Jennett 296
  Elizabeth 169, 261,
    283, 311
  Elizabeth Ann 185
  Elizabeth M. 336
  Ellen 299
  Ellen R. 267
  Elsey 247
  Emley E. 267
  Fanney 143
  Fanny E. 340
  Frances 319
  Francis 239
  G. B. 248
  Geo. C. 149
  George C. 67, 330
  Henry 13, 226, 292,
    303
  Hugh 216
  Isaac H. 184
  Isbelle 105
  Izbel 132
  James 61, 117, 248,
    249, 277, 285
  Jane 67
  Jeany 166
  Jeney 178
  Jennet 265
  Jnn. 332
  John 6, 31, 61, 92,
    178, 195, 249, 250
  John W. 41
  Joseph 265
  Katherine 337
  Lea C. 245
  Leonard 26, 262
  Letey H. 157
  Letitia 42
  Letta 34
  Levinia 179
  Lydia 197
  Mahalah 61
  Mahaley 265
  Margaret 265, 316
  Martha 67, 108, 195,
    234, 330
  Martha E. 67
  Martha Ellen 287
  Martha J. 281
  Mary 13, 64, 198, 315

Ray, Mary Ann 177
  Mary R. W. 159
  Mary Ellen 272
  Mary Jane B. 157
  Mary P. 300
  Matthew 250
  Michael 37, 61
  Nancy 40, 69, 99, 110,
    177, 250
  Nelley 255
  Nelson 330
  Peggy D. 52
  Peter A. 194, 223
  Peter L. 145, 263,
    273
  Petronella 256
  Polley 91, 157, 218,
    219, 257
  Polly 117
  Prudy 203
  Rachel 116
  Rebecca 82
  Rhoda 52
  Ritten 341
  Robert 143, 169, 250,
    259, 328
  Robt. 105
  Salley 146
  Sally 76, 146, 205,
    292
  Sally E. 87
  Sarah 146, 247, 265
  Sarah Catherine 219
  Shary 248
  Siney 206
  Susan 258
  Thomas 249
  Will J. 30
  William 18, 38, 42,
    99, 130, 248, 249,
    261, 273
  William R. 316
  Wm. 146, 153, 249
  Wm. R. 332
Rayly, Mary 121
Reacher, Jno. Go. 322
Read, Amey 251
  Barney 251
  Wm. 116
Reading, Polley 326
Reaney, David 247
Reaves, Archibald 151
  Polly 307
  Susannah 9
Reavis, John 80
  Samuel B. 251
  Thos. 150
Reavs, Jones 252
Redden, Elizabeth 77
Reddick, Jean 60
Reddin, Martha E. 297
Redding, Elizabeth 147,
    249
  Fanny V. C. 171
  Margaret 219
  Mary 221
  Moses 77, 157
  Nancy 13
  Sarah Ann 279
  Telitha M. 249
  Willi H. 126
  William H. 77
Reding, Eliza 172
  John 98
  John P. 333
  Stephen 147
  Thomas 314
  Thos. 40, 149
  Wm. 219

Redman, Elizabeth 36
Redmon, Leah 36
Redmond, Nancy 251
Reed, John C. 89, 130
  Polly P. 214
Reeder, Francis H. 36
Reese, Joseph 33, 157,
    258
Reeves, Ann W. D. 112
  Azariah 84
  Betsey 84
  Charlotte S. 318
  Eady S. 300
  Eliza Jennet 52
  Elizabeth 82, 189,
    220
  Frederic 252, 308
  George 15, 122
  Hugh L. 75
  J. M. 62
  James 68
  Jane 242
  Jenny C. 84
  John 128, 241
  Ledya 333
  Lydia 28
  Martha 172, 302
  Mary A. 7
  Nancy 15
  Polley 9
  S. 220
  Sarah 338
  Sarah F. 95
  Sinah 213
  Tabitha 172
  Thomas 252, 321
  Thos. 251
  Wm. H. 123
Register, Dorcas 237
Regsby, Peggy 236
Reitzel, Adam 252
Rencher, James 252
  John G. 141
  Margaret 252
Renn, Joseph 158
Renny, David 72
Revell, Frances 268
Revels, Betsey 85
Reves, Charles 252
  Fanny 85
  Peter 252
Revill, Faithy 153
  John 252
  Susan 336
Reynolds, J. 19
Rheu, Ann 278
  John W. 53
  Thomas 2
Rhew, Anne 92, 175
  Elizabeth 93, 158
  Ellinder 76
  Frances 211
  Irby 268
  Isaac 46, 47, 253
  J. H. 253
  Jefferson 253, 305
  Louisa 36
  Lucy Anna 68
  Luena 158
  Margaret 47, 71
  Martha 76
  Mary 211
  Mary S. 158
  Milley 125
  Nelson 48
  Polly 323
  Thos. 92
  Wm. L. 75
Rhoades, James 205

395

Riley, Tempe 25
  Thomas 258
  William 301
  William H. 69
  William P. 304
  William W. 46
  Willie 90
  Wm. 260
Rily, Copeland 146
  James 141
  Nancy 176
  William 259
Ringstaff, Conrod 91
  Mary 251
  Sally 40
  William 260
Ringstep, Henry 67
Rinnin, R. G. 273
Rinnon, Robt. G. 10
Rippey, Anne 99
  Edward 99
  Jane 315
  Jesse 80
  John 1
  Julia 2
  Mary 99, 163
  Polly 155
  Susan 315
Rippy, Alford T. 155
  Emily 335
  James 67, 260
  Jesse 315
  John 260
  Joseph 299
  Nancy 70
  Nathan 255
  Sally 112
  Stephen 70
  Thomas 70
Ristell, Adam 106
Riston, A. 248
Ritch, Henry 198
  Polley 79
  William 12
Ritche, Mary 273
Ritesman, Polly 220
Rivell, Mary 261
Rivers, Elizabeth 168
  John 272
  Johns 277
Roach, Adeline 292
  Anne 251
  Elizabeth 50, 292
  Ellenor 250
  James 211
  John 40, 248, 250
  Margret 109
  Martha 310
  Mary 94
  Nancy 162
  Patsy 292
  Rebecca 123
  Sally 278
  William 52
  Wm. 261
Roades, Aquila 243, 253
Roan, Gen. 199
  Charles 207
  James 334
  Malinda 331
  Mary 71
  Milly 126
  William 257
Roark, Permelia Hester
    273
  Sarah C. 273
  Willis 273
Robard, Polly 296

Robards, Wm. 196
Robart, Stephens 299
Robarts, Stephens 31, 263
Robbards, Tempe 26
Robberson, Allen 14
Robbs, Alexander 202
  Sophiah 43
Robenson, Anne 213
  Mary 11
  Nancy 222
Roberds, John 196
Roberson, Ariana 274
  David 97, 181
  Jefferson 19
  John 340
  John J. 97, 180, 304,
    341
  Keziah Elizabeth 4
  Louisa 182
  Marriot 101
  Merrett 262
  Nathaniel 10
  Permelia A. 95
  Polly 217
  Sally 97
  Stephen 262
  Susan C. 180
  Thomas 262, 264
  W. M. 262
  William M. 264
Roberts, Aggy 212
  America 138
  Aminda 158
  Anne 202
  Caroline 229, 264
  Delila 49
  Demarias 341
  Dempsey 79
  Elizabeth 12, 204,
    332
  Ephraim 316
  Frances 50, 117, 314
  Francis 70
  G. W. 212
  Green 264
  Haley 89
  J. M. 264
  James 65, 112, 149,
    273, 319
  James C. 256
  John 172
  Judah 12, 118
  Keate E. 83
  Lewis 294
  Mahala 264
  Malinda 318
  Margaret 146
  Mark 296
  Martha C. 125
  Mary 262, 312
  Mary Jane 259
  Minerva 109
  Nancy 5, 92, 176, 200,
    211
  Patsey 262
  Phillip 84, 305
  Polley 10, 313
  Polly 61
  Rachel 211
  Richard 134, 174
  Roland 12
  Rowan 237
  Ruth 203
  S. W. 228
  Salley 31, 263
  Sally 17, 139
  Sarah 316
  Shadrach 92

Roberts, Susan 102, 253
  Susan D. 34
  Susannah 300
  Susannah Hawkins 117
  Thomas 32, 262
  Thos. 263
  Viney 197
  Vinson 29
  William J. 328
  Willie J. 200
  Winnie 314
  Winniford 263
  Wm. J. 1, 32, 88, 98,
    144, 176, 226, 258,
    313, 333
Robertson, D. S. C. H.
    264
  Daniel 281
  Elizabeth 304
  M. N. 59
  M. S. 60
  Martha 262, 264
  Mary A. 28
  Matilda 213
  Milly 60
  Nancy 281, 299
  Nash 299
  Nathaniel 264, 289
  Nelly 214
  Polly 219
  Robert 28
  Syllah 94
  T. H. 44
  Victoria 267
Robeson, Allen N. 213
  Jno. 106
  John T. 324
  T. H. 264
  Winne 277
Robinson, Alex 11
  Catharine 37
  Hannah 289
  Jenny 72
  John 248
  Martha 248
  Mary 94
  Michael 37
  Nancy 267
  Nancy Jane 124
  Peggy 213
  Polly 339
  Rebecca 213, 293
  Rebecca F. 306
  Ruth 264
  Salley 87
  Susannah 243
  Viney 205
  W. H. 265
  William R. 87
Robison, Letitia 198
  Susan 23
Robson, John 161
  Margaret 161
  Matilda 141
  Wm. 54
Roch, David M. 265
Rochel, William Y. 265
Rochell, Altine 265
  Alvin 63, 265
  George W. 265
  H. B. 208
  Hawkins 265
  Henderson B. 85
Rodgers, James 26C
  Jean 145
  William 234
Rogers, Anges 231
  Ann 273

397

399

400

405

411